Contemporary Debates in Political Philosophy

Contemporary Debates in Philosophy

In teaching and research, philosophy makes progress through argumentation and debate. Contemporary Debates in Philosophy provides a forum for students and their teachers to follow and participate in the debates that animate philosophy today in the western world. Each volume presents pairs of opposing viewpoints on contested themes and topics in the central subfields of philosophy. Each volume is edited and introduced by an expert in the field, and also includes an index, bibliography, and suggestions for further reading. The opposing essays, commissioned especially for the volumes in the series, are thorough but accessible presentations of opposing points of view.

1. Contemporary Debates in Philosophy of Religion *edited by Michael L. Peterson and Raymond J. Vanarragon*
2. Contemporary Debates in Philosophy of Science *edited by Christopher Hitchcock*
3. Contemporary Debates in Epistemology *edited by Matthias Steup and Ernest Sosa*
4. Contemporary Debates in Applied Ethics *edited by Andrew I. Cohen and Christopher Heath Wellman*
5. Contemporary Debates in Aesthetics and the Philosophy of Art *edited by Matthew Kieran*
6. Contemporary Debates in Moral Theory *edited by James Dreier*
7. Contemporary Debates in Cognitive Science *edited by Robert Stainton*
8. Contemporary Debates in Philosophy of Mind *edited by Brian McLaughlin and Jonathan Cohen*
9. Contemporary Debates in Social Philosophy *edited by Laurence Thomas*
10. Contemporary Debates in Metaphysics *edited by Theodore Sider, John Hawthorne, and Dean W. Zimmerman*
11. Contemporary Debates in Political Philosophy *edited by Thomas Christiano and John Christman*

Forthcoming Contemporary Debates are in:

Philosophy of Biology *edited by Francisco J. Ayala and Robert Arp*
Philosophy of Language *edited by Ernie Lepore*

Contemporary Debates in Political Philosophy

Edited by

Thomas Christiano and John Christman

A John Wiley & Sons, Ltd., Publication

This edition first published 2009
© 2009 Blackwell Publishing Ltd

Blackwell Publishing was acquired by John Wiley & Sons in February 2007. Blackwell's publishing program has been merged with Wiley's global Scientific, Technical, and Medical business to form Wiley-Blackwell.

Registered Office
John Wiley & Sons Ltd, The Atrium, Southern Gate, Chichester, West Sussex, PO19 8SQ, United Kingdom

Editorial Offices
350 Main Street, Malden, MA 02148-5020, USA
9600 Garsington Road, Oxford, OX4 2DQ, UK
The Atrium, Southern Gate, Chichester, West Sussex, PO19 8SQ, UK

For details of our global editorial offices, for customer services, and for information about how to apply for permission to reuse the copyright material in this book please see our website at www.wiley.com/wiley-blackwell.

The right of Thomas Christiano and John Christman to be identified as the author of the editorial material in this work has been asserted in accordance with the Copyright, Designs and Patents Act 1988.

Wiley also publishes its books in a variety of electronic formats. Some content that appears in print may not be available in electronic books.

Designations used by companies to distinguish their products are often claimed as trademarks. All brand names and product names used in this book are trade names, service marks, trademarks or registered trademarks of their respective owners. The publisher is not associated with any product or vendor mentioned in this book. This publication is designed to provide accurate and authoritative information in regard to the subject matter covered. It is sold on the understanding that the publisher is not engaged in rendering professional services. If professional advice or other expert assistance is required, the services of a competent professional should be sought.

Library of Congress Cataloging-in-Publication Data

Contemporary debates in political philosophy / edited by Thomas Christiano and John Christman.
    p.cm. – (Contemporary debates in philosophy)
  Includes bibliographical references and index.
  ISBN 978-1-4051-3321-0 (hardback : alk. paper) – ISBN 978-1-4051-3322-7 (pbk. : alk. paper)
1. Political science–Philosophy. I. Christiano, Thomas. II. Christman, John Philip.
  JA71.C5773 2009
  320.01–dc22

                                                      2008044641

A catalogue record for this book is available from the British Library.
Set in 10 on 12.5 pt Rotis Serif by Graphicraft Limited, Hong Kong
Printed and bound in Malaysia by Vivar Printing Sdn Bhd

1 2009

Contents

Acknowledgments   vii
Notes on Contributors   viii

1 Introduction   *Thomas Christiano and John Christman*   1

QUESTIONS OF METHOD   **21**

2 Facts and Principles   *G.A. Cohen*   23

3 Constructivism, Facts, and Moral Justification   *Samuel Freeman*   41

4 Reason and the Ethos of a Late-Modern Citizen   *Stephen White*   61

LIBERALISM   **79**

Political Neutrality   79

5 The Moral Foundations of Liberal Neutrality   *Gerald F. Gaus*   81

6 Perfectionism in Politics: A Defense   *Steven Wall*   99

Liberty and Distributive Justice   *119*

7 Individualism and Libertarian Rights   *Eric Mack*   121

8 Left-Libertarianism and Liberty   *Peter Vallentyne*   137

Equality   *153*

9 Illuminating Egalitarianism   *Larry S. Temkin*   155

10 A Reasonable Alternative to Egalitarianism   *John Kekes*   179

DEMOCRACY AND ITS LIMITS   195

The Value of Democracy   195

11 The Supposed Right to a Democratic Say   *Richard J. Arneson*   197

12 Democracy: Instrumental vs. Non-Instrumental Value
    Elizabeth Anderson   213

Deliberative Democracy   229

13 Deliberative Democracy   *Russell Hardin*   231

14 Reflections on Deliberative Democracy   *Joshua Cohen*   247

Constitutionalism   265

15 Constitutionalism – A Skeptical View   *Jeremy Waldron*   267

16 Constitutionalism   *Larry Alexander*   283

PERSONS, IDENTITY AND DIFFERENCE   301

Individualism and Community   301

17 Individualism and the Claims of Community   *Richard Dagger*   303

18 Liberalism, Communitarianism, and the Politics of Identity
    Margaret Moore   322

Identity and the Politics of Difference   343

19 Relational Liberalism and Demands for Equality, Recognition,
    and Group Rights   *Anthony Simon Laden*   345

20 Structural Injustice and the Politics of Difference   *Iris M. Young*   362

GLOBAL JUSTICE   385

Cosmopolitanism   385

21 Cosmopolitanism and Justice   *Simon Caney*   387

22 Distributive Justice at Home and Abroad   *Jon Mandle*   408

Human Rights   423

23 The Dark Side of Human Rights   *Onora O'Neill*   425

24 A Defense of Welfare Rights as Human Rights   *James W. Nickel*   437

Index   457

Acknowledgments

A longer version of Chapter 2 appeared as an article by Prof. Cohen, "Facts and Principles," in *Philosophy and Public Affairs* 31(3) (Summer 2003): 211–45. Chapter 20 is a revised version of a paper by Prof. Young which appeared in *Multiculturalism and Political Theory*, ed. Anthony Laden and David Owen (Cambridge: Cambridge University Press, 2007). Chapter 24 is a revised and expanded version of Prof. Nickel's "Poverty and Rights," *The Philosophical Quarterly* 55 (2005). Chapter 23 is reprinted with permission from *International Affairs* 81 (2) (2005): 427–39. All previously published material used by permission with the gratitude of the editors. We would also like to thank our indexers, Daniel M. Silvermint and Justin Tosi.

Notes on Contributors

Larry Alexander is a Warren Distinguished Professor of Law at the University of San Diego School of Law. He is the author of *Is There a Right of Freedom of Expression?* (Cambridge: Cambridge University Press, 2005); (with Emily Sherwin) *The Rule of Rules: Morality, Rules and the Dilemmas of Law* (Durham, NC: Duke University Press, 2001); *Constitutionalism: Philosophical Foundations* (Cambridge: Cambridge University Press, 1998); (with Paul Horton) *Whom Does the Constitution Command?* (New York: Greenwood Press, 1988); several anthologies; and more than 160 articles, book chapters and review essays in jurisprudence, constitutional law, criminal law, and normative ethics. He has been a member of the faculty at the University of San Diego School of Law since 1970. He is the co-editor of the journal *Legal Theory*, and he serves on the editorial boards of *Ethics*, *Law and Philosophy* and *Criminal Law and Philosophy*. He is co-executive director of the Institute for Law and Philosophy at the University of San Diego and he is past president of AMINTAPHIL.

Elizabeth Anderson is John Rawls Collegiate Professor of Philosophy and Women's Studies at the University of Michigan, Ann Arbor. Her research has focused on democratic theory, egalitarianism, the ethical limits of markets, theories of value and rational choice, the philosophies of John Stuart Mill and John Dewey, and feminist epistemology and philosophy of science. She is the author of *Value in Ethics and Economics* (Cambridge, MA: Harvard University Press, 1993). She is currently writing a book on the ideal of ethno-racial integration in democratic theory.

Richard J. Arneson is professor of philosophy at the University of California, San Diego, where he has been employed since 1973. His current rank there is Professor, Above Scale (Distinguished Professor). In winter, 2006 he held a visiting appointment at the Centre for Public Philosophy and Applied Ethics at Australian National University. His works mainly concern political and moral philosophy. Several of his recent essays explore one of two topics: (1) how best to integrate sensible accounts of individual responsibility and human well-being into an egalitarian theory of social justice; and (2) how best to defend act consequentialism in the light of the most serious recent criticisms this doctrine has attracted.

Simon Caney is Professor in Political Theory and Tutorial Fellow in Politics at Magdalen College, Oxford. He has published articles on justice, rights, perfectionism, and global justice, in philosophy, politics and law journals. He is the author of *Justice Beyond Borders* (New York: Oxford University Press, 2005). He is working on a book entitled *On Cosmopolitanism* (for Oxford University Press) and a book entitled *Global Justice and Climate Change* (co-authored with Dr Derek Bell and also for Oxford University Press). He currently holds a three-year ESRC Leadership Fellowship on Climate Change.

Thomas Christiano is Professor of Philosophy and Law at the University of Arizona. He is also the co-director of the Rogers Program in Law and Society in the College of Law. He has been a fellow at the National Humanities Center, a visiting fellow of All Souls College, Oxford, and a visiting fellow in the Research School of the Social Sciences at the Australian National University. He has published widely in the areas of moral and political philosophy and is the author of *The Constitution of Equality: Democratic Authority and Its Limits* (Oxford: Oxford University Press, 2008), The *Rule of the Many: Fundamental Issues in Democratic Theory* (Boulder, CO: Westview Press, 1996). He is currently finishing a book on the foundations of equality.

John Christman is Associate Professor of Philosophy, Political Science and Women's Studies at Pennsylvania State University, where he specializes in contemporary social and political philosophy. He is the author of *The Myth of Property* (New York: Oxford University Press, 1994), *Social and Political Philosophy: A Contemporary Introduction* (London: Routledge, 2002), and *The Politics of Persons: Individual Autonomy and Socio-historical Selves* (Cambridge: Cambridge University Press, 2009).

G. A. Cohen was educated at McGill and Oxford Universities where he obtained, respectively, the degrees of B. A. in Philosophy and Politics in 1961 and B. Phil. in Philosophy in 1963. For twenty-two years he was a Lecturer and then a Reader in Philosophy at University College, London. In 1985 he became Chichele Professor of Social and Political Theory and a Fellow of All Souls College, Oxford. Professor Cohen is the author of *Karl Marx's Theory of History: A Defence* (1978; expanded edn, New York: Oxford University Press, 2000), *History, Labour, and Freedom* (New York: Oxford University Press, 1988), *Self-Ownership, Freedom, and Equality* (New York: Cambridge University Press, 1995), *If You're an Egalitarian, How Come You're So Rich?* (Cambridge, MA: Harvard University Press, 2000) and Rescuing Justice and Equality (Harvard University Press, 2008). Cohen has given lectures all over the world, including the Tanner Lectures at Stanford University in 1991 and the Gifford Lectures at Edinburgh University in 1996. He was made a Fellow of the British Academy in 1985.

Joshua Cohen is professor of political science, philosophy, and law at Stanford University, where he directs the Program on Global Justice. He has been editor of the *Boston Review* since 1991. A collection of his papers on issues of democratic theory will be published by Harvard University Press in 2009.

Richard Dagger is Professor of Political Science at Rhodes College, where he also directs the Search for Values Program. He is the author of *Civic Virtues: Rights, Citizenship, and Republican Liberalism* (New York: Oxford University Press, 1997) and co-author, with Terence Ball, of *Political Ideologies and the Democratic Ideal* (7th edn, New York: Longman, 2008). His recent essays in political and legal philosophy include: "Republican Punishment: Consequentialist or Retributivist?" in C. LaBorde and J. Maynor, eds., *Republicanism and Political Theory* (Malden, MA: Blackwell, 2008); "Punishment as Fair Play," *Res Publica* (2009); and "Republicanism and Crime," in S. Besson and J.-L. Marti, eds., *Legal Republicanism* (New York: Oxford University Press, 2009).

Samuel Freeman is Professor of Philosophy and Law at the University of Pennsylvania. He is the author of *Justice and the Social Contract* (New York: Oxford University Press, 2006) and *Rawls* (New York: Routledge, 2007), and has edited *The Cambridge Companion to Rawls* (New York: Cambridge University Press, 2002), as well as John Rawls's *Collected Papers* (Cambridge, MA: Harvard University Press, 2001) and his *Lectures on the History of Political Philosophy* (Cambridge, MA: Harvard University Press, 2007).

Gerald F. Gaus is James E. Rogers Professor of Philosophy at the University of Arizona. Among his books are *On Philosophy, Politics, and Economics* (Belmont, CA: Wadsworth, 2008), *Contemporary Theories of Liberalism: Public Reason as a Post-Enlightenment Project* (New York: Sage, 2003), *Justificatory Liberalism* (New York: Oxford University Press, 1996), and *Value and Justification* (New York: Cambridge University Press, 1990). He and Chandran Kukathas edited the *Handbook of Political Theory* (New York: Sage, 2004). Along with Jonathan Riley, he is a founding editor of *Politics, Philosophy and Economics*. He is currently completing a book on *The Order of Public Reason* (New York: Cambridge University Press) and, with Julian Lamont, is writing a book on *Economic Justice* (Malden, MA: Blackwell).

Russell Hardin is professor of Politics at New York University. He is the author of many books, including *How Do You Know?* (Princeton, NJ: Princeton University Press, forthcoming), *Indeterminacy and Society* (Princeton, NJ: Princeton University Press, 2003), *Trust* (Cambridge: Polity Press, 2006), and *Liberalism, Constitutionalism, and Democracy* (New York: Oxford University Press, 1999).

John Kekes has retired after many years, first as Professor of Philosophy, and then as Research Professor, and now works as an independent author. His many books include *Against Liberalism* (Ithaca, NY: Cornell University Press, 1997), *A Case for Conservatism* (Ithaca, NY: Cornell University Press, 1998), and most recently *Enjoyment* (New York: Oxford University Press, 2008). He is at work on *The Human Condition: A Secular View*. His email address is jonkekes@nycap.rr.com.

Anthony Simon Laden is Professor of Philosophy at the University of Illinois at Chicago, where he has taught since 1996. He is the author of *Reasonably Radical* (Ithaca, NY: Cornell University Press, 2001) and co-editor, with David Owen, of *Multiculturalism and Political Theory* (New York: Cambridge University Press, 2007). His research focuses

Notes on Contributors

on liberalism, democratic theory, feminism and the politics of identity, and the nature of practical reason and reasoning.

Eric Mack is Professor of Philosophy and a faculty member of the Murphy Institute of Political Economy at Tulane University. He specializes in moral, political, and legal philosophy. He has been a Visiting Fellow in Political Philosophy at Harvard University, a Visiting Research Scholar at the Social Philosophy and Policy Center at Bowling Green State University and a Resident Scholar at Liberty Fund, Inc. He has edited two books, Auberon Herbert's *The Right and Wrong of Compulsion by the State and Other Essays* (Indianapolis, IN: Liberty Fund, 1978) and Herbert Spencer's *Man versus the State and Other Essays* (Indianapolis, IN: Liberty Fund, 1982). He has published many articles in scholarly journals and anthologies – primarily on such topics as the agent relativity of value, the nature and foundation of moral rights, property rights, economic justice, Lockean provisos, rights and public goods, liberalism and pluralism, justified killing, anarchism, and bad samaritanism. His book, *John Locke*, is forthcoming.

Jon Mandle is chair of the Philosophy Department at the University at Albany (SUNY). He is the author of *What's Left of Liberalism?* (Lanham, MD: Lexington Books, 2000), *Global Justice* (Cambridge: Polity Press, 2006), and a forthcoming book on John Rawls's *A Theory of Justice.*

Margaret Moore is Professor in the Political Studies department at Queen's University (Kingston, Canada). Since receiving her Ph.D. from the London School of Economics in 1989, she has published a number of books and articles on issues of distributive justice, nationalism and multiculturalism. Most notable are: *Foundations of Liberalism* (Oxford: Oxford University Press, 1993) and *Ethics of Nationalism* (Oxford: Oxford University Press, 2001).

James Nickel is Professor of Law at Arizona State University. He is an affiliate professor in the Department of Philosophy and in the School of Global Studies. During 2008–9 Nickel is a Visiting Professor at Georgetown University Law Center. Nickel teaches and writes in jurisprudence, constitutional law, political philosophy, and human rights law and theory. From 1982–2003 Nickel was Professor of Philosophy at the University of Colorado where he served as Director of the Center for Values and Social Policy (1982–8) and as Chair of the Philosophy Department (1992–6). Nickel is the author of *Making Sense of Human Rights* (2nd edn., Malden, MA: Blackwell, 2006). Other recent writings include: "Who Needs Freedom of Religion?"; "Are Human Rights Mainly Implemented by Intervention?"; and "Rethinking Indivisibility: Towards a Theory of Supporting Relations between Human Rights."

Onora O'Neill is Principal of Newnham College, Cambridge. Her books include *Faces of Hunger: An Essay on Poverty, Development and Justice* (George Allen and Unwin, 1986), *Constructions of Reason: Exploration of Kant's Practical Philosophy* (Cambridge: Cambridge University Press, 1989), *Towards Justice and Virtue* (Cambridge: Cambridge University Press, 1996), *Bounds of Justice* (Cambridge: Cambridge University Press, 2000), and *Autonomy and Trust in Bioethics* (Cambridge: Cambridge University Press, 2002). She is a former member and chair of the Nuffield Council on Bioethics and the

Human Genetics Advisory Commission, and chairs the Nuffield Foundation. Dr. O'Neill is a Member of the House of Lords (Baroness O'Neill of Bengarve), sits as a crossbencher and was a member of the Select Committee on Stem Cell Research.

Larry S. Temkin is Professor II of Philosophy at Rutgers University. He is the author of *Inequality* (New York: Oxford University Press, 1993), as well as many articles in ethics and political philosophy. A former Danforth Fellow, he has been a Visiting Professor/Fellow at the National Humanities Center, Pittsburgh University, Harvard's Safra Foundation Center for Ethics, All Souls College Oxford University, the National Institutes of Health, and the Australian National University. He is also the recipient of eight major teaching awards. Temkin is currently working on a book, tentatively titled "Rethinking the Good, Moral Ideals, and the Nature of Practical Reasoning."

Peter Vallentyne is Florence G. Kline Professor of Philosophy at the University of Missouri-Columbia. He writes on issues of liberty and equality – and left-libertarianism in particular. He is co-editor of *Economics and Philosophy*. He edited *Equality and Justice* (New York: Routledge, 2003, 6 vols) and *Contractarianism and Rational Choice: Essays on David Gauthier's* Morals by Agreement (New York: Cambridge University Press, 1991), and he co-edited, with Hillel Steiner, *The Origins of Left Libertarianism: An Anthology of Historical Writings* and *Left Libertarianism and Its Critics: The Contemporary Debate* (Basingstoke, Hants: Palgrave Publishers Ltd., 2000). He has held an American Council of Learned Societies fellowship and directed a National Endowments for the Humanities project on ethics across the curriculum. He can be contacted at Vallentynep@missouri.edu.

Jeremy Waldron is University Professor in the School of Law at New York University. He has also held appointments at Oxford, Edinburgh, Berkeley, Princeton, and Columbia. He has delivered the Seeley Lectures at Cambridge, the Carlyle Lectures at Oxford, and the Storrs Lectures at Yale Law School. Professor Waldron's books include *The Dignity of Legislation* (New York: Cambridge University Press, 1999); *Law and Disagreement* (New York: Oxford University Press, 1999); and *God, Locke, and Equality* (New York: Cambridge University Press, 2002). He is the author of more than 100 published articles in legal and political philosophy. Particularly well known is his work on cosmopolitanism, homelessness, judicial review, the rule of law, and torture and security issues. He was elected to the American Academy of Arts and Sciences in 1998.

Steven Wall is associate professor of philosophy at the University of Connecticut. He is the author of *Liberalism, Perfectionism and Restraint* (New York: Cambridge University Press, 1998) and the editor (with George Klosko) of *Perfectionism and Neutrality: Essays in Liberal Theory* (Lanham, MD: Rowman & Littlefield, 2003).

Stephen K. White is James Hart Professor of Politics, University of Virginia. Former editor of the journal, *Political Theory*. Recent books include *Sustaining Affirmation: The Strengths of Weak Ontology in Political Theory* (Princeton, NJ: Princeton University Press, 2000); *Edmund Burke: Modernity, Politics and Aesthetics* (Rowman & Littlefield, 2nd edn., 2002); *What Is Political Theory?* (New York: Sage, 2004), co-edited with

Notes on Contributors

J. Donald Moon; and *The Ethos of a Late-Modern Citizen* (Cambridge, MA: Harvard University Press, 2009).

Iris Marion Young (before her death in 2006) was Professor in Political Science at the University of Chicago. She was the author of numerous works in political philosophy, feminism, social justice and other areas, including: *Intersecting Voices: Dilemmas of Gender, Political Philosophy and Policy* (Princeton, NJ: Princeton University Press, 1997); *Justice and the Politics of Difference* (Princeton, NJ: Princeton University Press 1990); *Inclusion and Democracy* (New York: Oxford University Press, 2000); *Female Body Experience* (New York: Oxford University Press, 2005); and *Global Challenges: War, Self-Determination, and Responsibility for Justice* (Cambridge: Polity Press, 2007).

Introduction

Thomas Christiano and John Christman

"Man was born free and he is everywhere in chains.... How can this be made legitimate?" Jean-Jacques Rousseau's profound observation and question express the fundamental concerns of political philosophy. Accordingly, political philosophy is primarily a normative project, one whose main focus is on the principles that guide the evaluation and reform of political and economic institutions that have pervasive effects on our lives. Government, bureaucracy, law, police, property, markets, the welfare state and courts have profound effects on all our lives. And while these institutions enhance our freedom and benefit almost all of us in a great variety of ways, they also impose costs and restrict our freedom in many ways as well. The protection of the property of a person guarantees the freedom of the property holder, for example, but it also restricts the freedom of those who do not hold this property. The efforts to ensure a reasonable distribution of wealth require that taxes be imposed on some to benefit others. Indeed, the whole scheme of institutions guaranteeing security is costly and so requires each to make a contribution to its maintenance.

The question for us as members of societies is which of these types of institutions are ethically defensible? And how should we reform institutions if they are ethically defective? This is a significant part of the stuff of political debates in democratic societies. But this raises the question about what the appropriate normative standards are by which we make these assessments. The assessments we make are at least partly based in more general principles, but we disagree often about the basic principles as much as about the policy questions. One does political philosophy when one articulates and rationally defends some of these principles and criticizes others.

There is much disagreement concerning the legitimacy of each one of the activities modern states engage in, raising the suspicion in each case that they are merely the misguided efforts of some or the thievery of others. Many argue, for example, that there is not enough redistribution of wealth in society or there is too much inequality and that as a consequence the protection of private property is in effect the protection of a privileged class of persons. Others argue that there is *too much* redistribution and that the government that carries out these activities is engaged in simple thievery no matter how fine sounding its rhetoric may be. A theory of distributive justice attempts to elaborate and defend principles by which we can adjudicate these issues by determining the correct answers to the general question of what justice requires regarding the distribution of wealth.

Furthermore, when there is such pervasive disagreement about how society should be organized, we must then ask who ought to decide such contentious issues? Traditionally many argued that the wisest ought to decide, but in the modern world it is generally assumed that people ought to decide together as equals in a democracy. Still others argue that there ought to be severe limits on what democracies can decide, leaving the leftover areas of social life to be determined by individuals themselves. But how extensive should these limits be? Who ought to decide this matter? Theories of democracy and constitutionalism attempt to answer these questions in rationally defensible ways.

Moreover, one of the profound questions of political philosophy concerns how to deal with the centuries-long *injustices* done to minorities, women and others, especially since the injustices of the past have had a tremendous impact on the present (if indeed they have ended at all). These injustices and their current effects often remain unacknowledged or at least ignored by the larger society and thus create fresh new injustices in the present. The experiences of minorities are belittled and their plights blamed on them. What is the just response to the overhang of great injustice of this sort? Again, the activity of political philosophy expresses the hope that these questions can be given generally defensible answers.

Finally, the focus of political philosophy has expanded in the last thirty years beyond its initial focus on the assessment of the nation-state to include questions about the nature of global justice and the place of the nation-state in the larger global order. Some have argued that the principles that were thought to apply to individual political societies in fact apply to the world as a whole. Why, these thinkers ask, should we focus on issues of poverty only in our own societies? Why shouldn't we be even more concerned with global poverty, which is often much more serious? These cosmopolitan views are criticized by those who think that there is still an important place for the modern state in our moral appraisals of political power. They argue that citizens have special obligations to their compatriots that they do not have towards others and that these obligations include those of distributive justice. But all theorists agree that the assessment of the modern state and its policies must now be carried out with an eye to its position in the larger global order. Many theorists, then, are interested in developing conceptions of human rights that take into account the interests of all human beings and that set minimal standards for the assessment of the activities of states towards people in other countries. Still there is much disagreement about the nature and basis of human rights among contemporary theorists.

For most philosophers, political theory involves a commitment to the idea that the questions above have objectively valid answers and that the issues can be understood and progress can be made on them by means of rational argument and good judgment. Many of the papers in this volume display the efforts at rational discussion central to the project of political philosophy. They approach the issues with an eye towards clarifying the central concepts and problems. They advance alternative

Thomas Christiano and John Christman

systematic theories of the principles of justice and the common good. And they defend theories by means of rational arguments in favor of the theory and against alternatives. To be sure, even this commitment should be brought under scrutiny when we think as philosophers, as the fourth essay does. The book as a whole can be thought of as an invitation to participate in rational debates on the basic standards by which we evaluate modern political societies and their place in the world.

~~

In this volume we attempt to capture the main currents of contemporary political philosophy as practiced, for the most part, in the so-called analytic style but with due attention to alternative approaches. This is perforce a selective enterprise, where many themes are left in the background despite their importance and relevance. Surveying the present landscape, though, suggests certain dominant preoccupations as well as trajectories in new directions. In this Introduction, then, we will discuss some of the main trends and topic areas that have preoccupied political philosophers in the current landscape and, in so doing, provide a brief overview of the excellent papers contained in the volume.

Questions of Method

How should political philosophy proceed? What mode of thought should predominate in theoretical exchanges about such complex and tortuous controversies as are the subject matter of politics? The legacy of the European Enlightenment, and the modernist philosophical framework it helped spawn, has long suggested that "reason" in some form provide the fundamental basis for moral principle and thus, by extension, the justification of political principles. However, much nineteenth- and twentieth-century political and philosophical thought insisted that we reappraise the role of reason in the justification of political positions especially given the pervasive human tendency to be irrational, moved by subconscious motives, given to rationalizations and subterfuge, and so on, not to mention the fact that various injustices that were supported by "reason" in those Enlightenment (and later) thinkers themselves.

Stephen White, in Chapter 4, takes as a starting point the radical challenges to the modernist approach to political justification, challenges which pointed out these patterns of subterfuge and domination under the banner of reason. In his examination of the aftermath of these challenges, he surveys ways that being "reasonable" might now substitute for a traditional foundational understanding of the grounding of principles in untethered "reason." He proceeds to examine the way "reasonableness" functions in four areas of political discussion: the justification of basic social and political structures; the foundations of ethical-political judgments; and the struggle for recognition of identity. He considers the ways that seeing ideal rationality as a personal and social (and philosophical) ideal has, in the past, led to all manners of exclusion and domination (specifically of those "others" who were by implication labeled "non-rational"). He traces the idea of "reasonableness" as a substitute for the traditional idea of reason as the foundation of political power in ways that is more sensitive to our many and deep differences as well as our mortality and finitude.

White's essay differs from most of the others here both in style and perspective; this is due to his focus on ways that paradigm methodologies in political philosophy have been questioned.

One of the key issues in political philosophy is the relationship between ethical theorizing and social science. This issue pervades many of the discussions in political philosophy. But it is nowhere more in evidence than in John Rawls's political philosophy. On Rawls's view many of the fundamental principles of justice depend for their validity on facts about human nature and society. For instance, Rawls asserts that the virtue of justice only arises in the context of the circumstances of justice in which humans are only moderately altruistic and there is moderate scarcity of the things that people want. Furthermore, Rawls argues that the principles of justice are those that would be chosen by individuals in a suitable set of circumstances and assuming knowledge of the general facts about human nature and society. More generally, many have argued that principles of justice must be feasible in order for them to be valid. Thus, facts about feasibility constrain the choice of principles. So the complete carrying out of the project of elaborating and justifying fundamental principles of justice requires a good deal of social science and psychology.

G. A. Cohen has questioned this frequently cited methodological constraint. In his contribution in Chapter 2, he argues that the fundamental principles of political philosophy must be fact insensitive. By this he means that the truth or validity of fundamental principles of political philosophy must hold regardless of the facts. To the extent that facts play a role in these principles, it is a conditional one. That is, facts affect the conditions under which principles are to be applied, they may also be present in principles as conditions for requirements. But any fact that appears to play a fundamental role does this only because there is a deeper grounding principle that explains this role. Ultimately, Cohen argues that this grounding relation must terminate in fact insensitive principles.

Samuel Freeman responds in Chapter 3 to Cohen's challenge by defending the Rawlsian account of the relation of facts to principles of justice. His reply depends on making a distinction between fundamental principles of conduct such as principles of justice and fundamental justificatory principles such as the principle of impartiality, and the freedom and equality of persons, which determine for Rawls the need for and the nature of the initial position in which persons are to agree on principles of justice but are not themselves fundamental principles of conduct. The idea is that principles of conduct can be fundamental in the sense that they are not grounded in any other principles of conduct even though they are grounded in facts and fundamental justificatory principles, which are not principles of conduct though they are normative principles.

This exchange raises the broader question of what *kinds* of facts might be relevant to the shape and legitimacy of normative political principles. Facts about the historical and sociological conditions of democratic societies, to which such normative principles are to apply, might include, for example, a record of poverty, social hierarchies, violence, and division. Actual constitutional democracies that even pretend to be fully inclusive and egalitarian, after all, are very recent phenomena. This speaks to a broader issue of whether political philosophy should proceed in an *ideal* fashion, where past and ongoing patterns of *in*justice, domination, and violence are ignored or bracketed in order to specify the precise nature of normative principles. Are the

Thomas Christiano and John Christman

principles that would be justified under relatively ideal conditions the same as would be required in real world settings where centuries of inequality and oppression have left their marks (and continue unabated in many settings)?

However, when one does turn to the specification and justification of normative principles for a society, one paradigm has dominated the landscape in many ways, at least since the seventeenth century in Europe and continuing to the present day, and that is the paradigm of *liberalism*. There are many forms of liberalism and several fundamental components to it, but the domination of this framework for normative political principles in recent decades is notable and indeed is even taken for granted by liberalism's several critics. It is fitting, then, that this paradigm be represented in full force, including many of the central issues raised about and within it in recent work in political philosophy.

The Troubled Dominance of the Liberal Paradigm

"Liberalism" refers generally to the broad approach to the justification of social and political power that sees such power as legitimate only if it is based on popular sovereignty, the rule of law, and the protection of basic rights and liberties of individuals, whether these basic rights are seen as derivative from universal (moral) principles or simply the required postulates of a political compromise based on the freedom and equality of citizens. Several issues in political philosophy arise concerning the core elements of this paradigm. One such element is the idea that insofar as just political institutions must meet with the popular approval of those living under them, they must remain *neutral* toward all of the various value frameworks and moral views those citizens follow. This is supposedly in opposition to the more ancient view that the purpose of state institutions is to advance the virtue or good of the citizenry, where those concepts are defined objectively and apart from citizen consent. But the question of whether state neutrality is feasible and what its implications are is a prominent one in recent philosophical work.

State Neutrality

In Chapter 5, Gerald Gaus defends a strong version of liberal neutrality, which he traces from a view of morality generally and concepts of freedom and equality in particular. He argues that all coercion of one person by another person (or state) without sufficient justification is prima facie morally wrong, and that to justify coercion to another moral (free and equal) person we must provide sufficient justification from her (rational and reflective) point of view. Such a position, then, implies what he labels "Liberal Moral Neutrality." This principle states that in treating all others (in ways that may involve coercing them) we must be neutral between our own and their evaluative standards, their moral point of view. Then, if we assume that *states* must follow moral dictates that apply to persons (and he claims we should), then a principle of Liberal *Political* Neutrality follows, namely that state policies must be neutral between (justifiable from the point of view of) all citizens. His arguments for these claims are painstaking, and the conclusions he draws are dramatic, namely that very few state policies are in fact justifiable by these standards, since very few of them could plausibly be justified from all reasonable and reflective evaluative standards given people's deep differences in moral outlook and ranking of values.

Neutrality is typically pitted against *perfectionism*, which is generally the view that state policies, rather than claiming some kind of neutral position vis-à-vis moral value, should actually promote the most worthwhile values and ideals for their citizens. Stephen Wall defends such a view in Chapter 6. He claims that liberal neutralists such as Gaus (as well as political liberals like Rawls and others) cannot consistently justify their view that disagreement about conceptions of the good can give way to consensus about (supposedly neutral) procedures for determining the *right*. Wall questions whether there we can ever devise procedures that are justifiable from a broad spectrum of citizen points of view and that have specific content without relying on perfectionist values in the end.

Wall and Gaus may not be as far apart as they first appear, as both agree that a purified conception of liberal neutrality leads to very little in the way of justified state policy. But Wall favors the alternative to liberal neutrality, namely that the state should promote lives of its citizens that are in fact "worthwhile." Some values, Wall claims, are justified on objective grounds, even if some people do not grasp those grounds.

Distributive Justice

Principles of distributive justice have been at the heart of debates in political philosophy in the second half of the twentieth century and the early twenty-first century. The basic questions of distributive justice concern how the good things of social life such as wealth, power, or honors ought to be distributed. In the modern era many have asked a somewhat more abstract question of distributive justice: how ought happiness or opportunity or other intrinsically good things in human life be distributed? And in modern political debates, many have argued that the great inequalities of wealth or opportunities we see are morally indefensible.

The classical tradition of political philosophy in Plato and Aristotle articulated and defended principles concerning the just distribution of goods in society. Aristotle argued that wealth and political honors should be distributed in accordance with merit. The more virtuous persons in political society deserved to have more political power than the less virtuous. The scholastic natural law tradition carried on Aristotle's tradition of distribution according to merit but theoretical discussions of distributive justice waned in the seventeenth century. Hobbes thought that considerations of distributive justice were not of fundamental importance, and Locke makes no mention of distributive justice, though the satisfaction of needs plays a central role in his thought. The idea begins to make a reappearance in theoretical discussions with John Stuart Mill and Karl Marx, who is responsible for articulating the deeply egalitarian principle: "To each according to his needs and from each according to his ability."

The person most responsible for the revival of interest in the theoretical grounding and elaboration of principles of distributive justice in the second half of the twentieth century is John Rawls in his *A Theory of Justice*. Rawls thinks of the whole of social justice as being concerned with questions of distribution. He articulates two central principles of distributive justice. The first principle is that each person is to have the

Thomas Christiano and John Christman

maximal amount of basic liberty consistent with an equal basic liberty for all. The second asserts that each is to have fair equality of opportunity and that inequalities of wealth and power are justified only if they work to the advantage of the worst off. Rawls's arguments and principles have been taken by many as reasons for reducing the levels of inequality of wealth and power in society subject to the restriction that we must not intrude in the basic liberties of persons.

Contemporary debates about distributive justice focus on two sorts of questions. The first is whether distributive justice is a genuine part of justice at all. Libertarians have famously argued that there really is no such thing as distributive justice as a distinct moral set of principles. Robert Nozick (*Anarchy, State, and Utopia*), for example, argues that the distribution of goods is just to the extent that it comes about through a process of voluntary exchange among persons who have property rights to the things they exchange. Any concern to redistribute goods so that the distribution accords more with some principle of distributive justice, he claimed, would involve a deep interference in human freedom to which each has a fundamental natural right. Eric Mack's contribution in Chapter 7 attempts to give a philosophical grounding to an account of distributive justice that continues in the Nozickian line of analysis. Mack follows Nozick in seeing rights to self-ownership and companion rights to private property as the cornerstone of distributive justice. Seeing people as "separate," on his view, means taking seriously the independent importance that any person's well being has *for her* as compared to the importance it typically has for others (though of course this can vary). The natural and, for Mack, least controversial starting point for theorizing about morality is an assumption of the basic rationality of prudence, that a person has a particular interest in how her own life goes. Mack argues that taking seriously this special importance will be meaningful only if we correspondingly recognize, at the social level, special rights-based *protections* against others interfering with one's pursuit of one's good. Without these second sorts of protections, the first sort of regard (for the importance of people's pursuing their own good in their own way) has no real weight. This, for him, establishes the fundamental right of self-ownership that justice must always respect.

But Mack proceeds from these basic ethical considerations to specifically libertarian conclusions, namely that protecting people's rights to non-interference and by extension their right to full private property rights (as an extension of this basic self-ownership) is the central tenet of distributive justice. No further attempt to equalize people's chances at achieving well-being or in any other way promoting the "public good" should proceed unless these basic rights are respected. This means that the extension of these personal rights to non-interference support property rights to "extra-personal" objects and material. The "practice of private property," as he puts it will protect individuals from the intrusions by others that basic self-ownership forbids.

This attention to basic self-ownership – that we all have fundamental moral rights against all others to move and use our bodies, develop our talents, and otherwise pursue our goods, within the bounds of others' rights of the same sort – also grounds Peter Vallentyne approach to justice (Chapter 8). But Vallentyne takes a turn from here, in that he suggests that the protection of self-ownership rights of the sort Mack lays out is consistent with a number of different positions on the principles governing the overall distribution of goods. The "right-libertarian" stance of the sort Mack aligns himself with, combines individual self-ownership with individual capitalist property rights in the basic principles of distributive justice, resulting in a prominent role of free markets and minimal state interference in capitalist economic activity in the society. But Vallentyne rejects this position, and pursues instead the "left-libertarian" strategy of claiming that justice requires the protection of individual rights to self-ownership along with "equal opportunity left-libertarianism," which insists any individual claim of property ownership must be consistent with others having an opportunity for well-being that is at least as good as the opportunity for well being that the first person has in acquiring the property. This is a strict egalitarian approach to the distribution of resources built upon the kind of moral individualism that theorists such as Mack emphasize.

Vallentyne's position illustrates the way that in many accounts of distributive justice, *equality* plays the central role in conceptions of justice in modern political philosophy. Historically, the principle of equal distribution is associated with demo-cracy. Citizens in Athens and other Greek city-states claimed rights to an equal amount of political power on the basis of equal citizenship. And Aristotle cites this principle of equality as the foundation of democracy. He criticized the idea of equality on the grounds that the more virtuous deserved greater power than the less virtuous. To be sure, no one in ancient Greece argued for universal equality, women and slaves were to be excluded from political power by both the democrats and by Aristotle. On Aristotle's view, distributive justice was to be understood as proportionate equality. That is, each person was to receive in proportion to his merit so that the proportion of benefit to merit is the same. And this conception of distributive justice was to be the dominant conception through the scholastic period.

Though Rawls did not defend an egalitarian principle, the principles he does defend are close to egalitarian ones. The first principle is a principle of equal liberty and the second principle includes a principle of equal opportunity and a principle that takes equality of wealth and power to be the baseline from which departures must be justified. And Rawls is the main source for one of the principal contemporary arguments for equality. Rawls argues that differences in people's meritorious qualities should not serve as the basis for differences in the distribution of social goods. The reason for this is that differential meritorious qualities are primarily the result of factors for which the persons who have them are not responsible. To think that I can deserve greater rewards for qualities for which I cannot be held responsible is to think that I can deserve more good things than another merely as a result of my greater good luck, which seems quite arbitrary. Indeed, a large part of a person's ability to navigate successfully in the modern world is due to good family background and education and other environmental factors available to some and not to others. These are factors for which the person in question is not responsible. Rawls takes this argument one step further when he says that the natural talents I am born with that make a great difference in how well my life goes are also features that I am not responsible for. I am born with them. The final step in this argument is to deny that even differential efforts ought to be the basis of differential rewards. Rawls argues that the amount of effort I am willing to put forth is itself in significant part a function of environmental factors and natural talent. So even differences in effort could often be attributed to differences in background conditions for which persons do not have responsibility.

Larry Temkin's contribution (Chapter 9) defending the principle of equality as a comparative principle of distribution takes this kind of Rawlsian argument as given.

Thomas Christiano and John Christman

He tentatively endorses the formulation that one person's life should not go worse than another's life through no fault of his own. Only qualities or actions for which people can be held responsible are legitimate bases for differential rewards. Temkin generalizes the basic idea by saying that departures from equality must be fair and that no one ought to suffer unfair disadvantage relative to others. This is in order to capture the idea that it is not unfair that a criminal who has not been caught by the police suffers disadvantage through no fault of his own.

Temkin then discusses the question of what equality should be equality *of.* The traditional account of equality has been of equality of wealth or income. But most have rejected this kind of metric of equality on the grounds that some people are much needier than others because of health problems or disabilities (for which they are not responsible). The natural conclusion seems to be that each should have equality of well-being. But the worry here is that some persons may exploit a concern for equality of well-being and develop highly expensive tastes, which require the redistribution of resources to them. So this has led some to prefer equality of opportunity for well-being or equality of resources so that people have the opportunities to achieve the same level of well-being but they also have the opportunities to pursue more expensive projects without being able to impose the costs on others. Temkin's position is to endorse a pluralism with respect to these different kinds of equality, a pluralism that accords with a more general moral pluralism that he also endorses. One of the main, indeed perhaps the main objection to the principle of equality is what is called the leveling down objection. Some have thought that a commitment to a principle of equal distribution implies that one must always prefer an equal distribution of good to an unequal distribution even if everyone is better off in the unequal distribution. Not all egalitarians accept that the principle of equality has this implication. Temkin does accept it, though. he argues that it is not an objection, it only shows that the principle of equality is not the only principle of morality. He claims that our aversion to leveling down is not explained by a rejection of the principle of equality, it is explained by the fact that in addition to a principle of equality we also think it is morally important to advance well-being. And he says the principle that enjoins advancing well-being overrides the principle of equality in this instance.

John Kekes argues *against* the principle of equality in Chapter 10. His principal objection is to the idea that persons are owed equal concern and respect, sometimes taken as a key ground of the principle of equality. On his account the idea that persons are moral equals is highly implausible. He complains first that no one has offered any justification for this principle of equal moral status and most seem to think that none is needed. This complaint is sharpened by the observation that we do not think of people as equals in many important circumstances. Parents do not treat their children as the equals of other children; citizens do not treat foreigners as the equals of fellow citizens; and criminals are not treated as equals with ordinary law-abiding citizens. Kekes considers a number of possible ways of blunting the force of this kind of objection and finds them all wanting. He also objects to egalitarianism on the ground that it seems to criticize what is a necessity for the social organization of the vast majority of developed societies: the existence of inequalities in prospects among persons in those societies. Moreover, he argues that the only genuine source of appeal for equality is not a concern for equality *per se* but a compassion for those who are badly off.

Kekes defends what he calls a reasonable alternative to egalitarianism. It starts from the observation that certain conventional rules are necessary for the maintenance and flourishing of societies. He enumerates three central kinds of rules (without claiming that this is an exhaustive list): those pertaining to family and special relationships, those pertaining to compliance with promises and contracts and those protecting the security of persons. These conventional rules are such that those who abide by them deserve praise and those who violate them deserve punishment. Furthermore these rules also subvert equality by creating special obligations towards family members and persons to whom one has promised things or made contractual relations with. And these inequalities are essential to the maintenance of society, so Kekes argues that egalitarianism subverts societies and is therefore dangerous.

Democracy

The ideal of democracy was first explicitly articulated, as far as we know, in ancient Greek city-states around the sixth century before the Christian era. In these societies all free males were equal citizens, and women, slaves and laborers were excluded. Even this modest form of democracy was undermined in the ancient world by the development of large empires and by the work of philosophers who argued that power ought to be in the hands of the most virtuous or the most knowledgeable. The arguments of Plato and Aristotle were for the most part unanswered for over 2,000 years. This answer came, though, with the idea that those governed by the power of a sovereign ought to be the ultimate source of that sovereign's legitimacy. The idea of popular sovereignty was developed by a few medieval thinkers but the rise of democratic thinking must wait until John Locke, Jean-Jacques Rousseau and John Stuart Mill to reach its fruition.

One of the major issues to be dealt with in the theoretical development of democracy is how to accommodate the demands of equal citizenship with a large nation-state. Rousseau thought that equal citizenship was only possible in a small city-state. James Madison agreed with him but thought that some kind of citizen participation was possible in large nation-states and indeed he argued that in some respects it could be more successful than city-state republics. John Stuart Mill is however the most important thinker to try to show how the demands of active citizenship could be made compatible with and indeed enhanced by the large nation-state.

In contemporary theorizing there are two main sources of debate concerning the normative underpinnings of democracy. The first is whether democracy is merely instrumentally justified or whether there is some intrinsic merit to democratic ways of making decisions. Some have thought that if democracy and indeed any political institutions are justified they must be justified by reference to the consequences such political institutions have for the society in which they rule. Hobbes, for example, thought that political institutions were to be evaluated solely according to their propensity to establish social peace in the society and argued that monarchy was superior to democracy in this respect. But one could evaluate democracy or political institutions more generally in terms of the quality of legislation that is produced, the quality of the relationships that arise in such societies and the quality of character traits that are generated in such a society.

Thomas Christiano and John Christman

Richard Arneson and Russell Hardin both argue forcefully for an exclusively instrumentalist approach to the evaluation of democracy. Arneson's master argument in Chapter 11 is that whenever a person exercises power over others the legitimacy of that exercise of power must be evaluated in terms of the consequences it has for the rights and interests of the persons over whom power is exercised. Arneson also argues against the idea that democracy has intrinsic value by defending the idea that inequality of power is a necessary feature of any political society in which a division of labor is necessary and in which the input of any particular citizen is extremely small. This is important because the usual reasons given for thinking that democracy is intrinsically valuable is that it realizes a kind of equality among citizens in the making of collective decisions. Arneson also thinks that we do not require democratic decision-making in voluntary associations in societies and seem perfectly happy with the hierarchies we live with in corporations, universities and churches. He argues that if we really thought equality in the process of collective decision-making were required, we would require it in these associations.

In Chapter 12 Elizabeth Anderson argues, to the contrary, that democracy has intrinsic value. That is, it is important not only that we have our interests advanced in our political societies but that we advance them *ourselves* and don't have them handed on a platter to us. Our participation is essential. Anderson makes an analogy with shopping. She thinks most of us don't merely want to have our interests in having consumer goods satisfied, we want to go about getting the things for ourselves, with all the deliberation and experimentation that this involves. Anderson's argument is not primarily based on equality but rather on a deep interest in participation. She places the democratic process narrowly conceived within the context of a larger democratic society in which people treat each other as equals in ongoing processes of cooperation and experimentation.

Deliberative Democracy

The other issue that has been particularly prominent in modern debates about democracy has been the question of deliberative democracy. By deliberation we mean the participation in discussion and debate of citizens in society with an eye to giving reasons for their positions and being open to the reasons that others give for their own positions. The ideal of deliberative democracy is that collective decisions are made as much as possible on the basis of this good faith exchange of reasons and ideas among citizens. Contemporary debates focus on the feasibility of deliberation in democracy as well as its desirability. The first question concerns whether deliberation on a large scale is feasible. In Chapter 13 Russell Hardin argues that deliberation on a society wide scale is neither feasible nor desirable. His fundamental concern is grounded in the minimal influence ordinary citizens can have on the political process of any modern state. The idea is that since citizens have so little impact on the outcome of elections, they have virtually no incentive to acquire an even modest ability to engage in the kind of sophisticated deliberation envisaged by deliberative democrats. Hardin thinks that most people are for the most part self-interested so they are simply not going to do what is necessary for participating in deliberation. So large-scale deliberation is not likely to come about. But such deliberation is not desirable either since he thinks that given its large scale and low levels of citizens' information the deliberation would be of quite low quality. Furthermore, Hardin argues, it is better for citizens to spend the limited time they have devoting themselves to the productive jobs they have and to their private lives where their knowledge can make a significant difference. Joshua Cohen worries about the feasibility of deliberation in large-scale democracies as well (Chapter 14). He argues that deliberation is an ideal because he thinks that it is most likely to produce justice understood as the terms of association free and equal persons would agree on if they were reasonable and rational. Deliberation also has beneficial effects on the understanding and characters of citizens. And finally deliberation among equal citizens embodies an ideal of mutual respect. However, Cohen is concerned with whether deliberation in actual societies can live up to the ideals of deliberative democracy. He discusses the worry that deliberation might in fact empower those who are well to do and well educated over others and thus increase the inequality of power in modern political societies, but he marshals empirical evidence that the poor in various closely studied cases were, through deliberative participation, able to enhance their political power. He is also concerned with some recent arguments that deliberation may not produce reasoned discussion but rather group-think and narrow-mindedness. In his view, this possibility calls for good institutional design as a remedy. Cohen is also concerned with the problem of scale. The studies he cites in favor of deliberation tend to be studies of small groups. The big question is whether this can be scaled up. Cohen is cautiously more sanguine than Hardin on this question, based on the observations that people can learn how to participate as equals in more local contexts and use these skills in larger settings and that civic institutions such as interest groups, political parties, and the media can enhance deliberative capacities.

Constitutionalism

An issue mentioned earlier was whether liberal democracies must have in place legal structures that define and protect basic rights and liberties prior to and independent of the workings of democracies. This is what constitutions do. A constitution is a set of laws that enables and structures the process of collective decision-making and sets limits to what collective decisions may be made. It subjects the process of making law to the rule of law. The big questions concerning constitutionalism have been whether a written constitution is necessary, whether constitutions must include both laws enabling the making of legislation and limiting the power of the legislature, and whether constitutions should be legally enforced by an independent judiciary.

In Chapters 15 and 16 Jeremy Waldron and Larry Alexander articulate the different purposes for constitutional arrangements and focus on the issue of the limits constitutions can impose on democracy. Waldron argues that aside from the work that constitutions do in enabling collective decision-making, their capacities to limit subsequent democratic decision-making are problematic particularly when supplemented with an independent judiciary with powers to legally enforce limits on the decision-making of democratic assemblies. Waldron worries that this allows earlier decision-makers to constrain latter decision-makers even though there may be good faith disagreement between them. He also sees that it allows an independent and unelected judiciary to constrain a democratic legislature on issues on which there is also good faith and reasonable disagreement. Here Waldron proceeds from a conception of the

Thomas Christiano and John Christman

intrinsic value of democratic decision-making in circumstances where there is serious good faith disagreement among equals and argues that it is unclear how it can be legitimate in these circumstances to give decision-making power to unelected judges.

Alexander's chapter gives an account of the different dimensions of constitutions. He gives an account of the different steps in the construction of constitutions and attempts an account of their basic nature and functions. Alexander takes issue with Waldron's thesis that constitutional limitations on democratic legislatures coupled with judicial review is illegitimate. Ultimately his argument proceeds from a largely instrumentalist account of the value of democracy. Since democracy and all political institutions are to be evaluated solely in terms of the results of democratic institutions, Alexander sees no fundamental reason why constitutional limitations and judicial review ought not to be imposed on democratic legislatures. The relation between constitutions and democratic activity strike at the center of the philosophical examination of the promise and limitations of the liberal project, for it raises the issue of whether principles of justice can be justified on philosophical grounds prior to, and independent of, contextual factors about societies, citizens, and institutions. This continues the question of the viability of the liberal project particularly in raising the issue of whether normative political principles can apply universally across populations and independent of specific facts about people and societies.

The Political Person

All normative political theorizing presupposes what Michael Sandel has called a "political anthropology" in that they rest upon a model of the person or self or citizen that is understood as those who are subject to those principles. How one models these subjects will affect the content of those normative principles in at least two ways. First, such models reflect the basic interests that human beings, as members of societies, share and to which political structures should respond.

Second, the model of the person represents the perspective from which the legitimacy of political institutions is established. That is, if one follows in the wake of the social contract tradition in seeing that the basic institutions of political power are justified only if the persons living under them, in some sense, agree to, accept, or endorse them, then the way in which we model those persons will affect whether we think this kind of endorsement is possible or likely.

Traditionally, the liberal approach to these questions is to put forward what was taken to be a generic, neutral conception of the person (and her interests) as the linchpin of conceptions of justice. However, from a number of directions this assumption has been challenged, for example over whether such a "generic" conception of the person is really a disguised form of privileging some kinds of people over others. For instance, the charge is made in different ways that the liberal conception of the person is overly *individualistic* in that it assumes that persons' fundamental interests are concerned only with the pursuit of their own individually formulated ends. Such a model of the person renders less significant the needs and interests (as well as the self-conceptions) of those people who define themselves with fundamental reference to groups, cultures, and communities. Such people and groups, it is claimed, are not adequately represented by the model of the person/citizen in standard liberal conceptions of justice.

Beginning in the 1980s, this challenge arose from the so-called "communitarian" critique of liberalism, exemplified most forcefully by writers such as Charles Taylor, Michael Sandel, Michael Walzer, and Alasdair MacIntyre. Richard Dagger and Margaret Moore engage with this debate in their chapters here, taking us from the original formulations of the communitarian challenge and bringing things up to date. Dagger in Chapter 17 helpfully lays out the main prongs of this challenge to liberalism as well as some now standard liberal rejoinders. For example, to the claim that liberalism assumes a problematic conception of the person as somehow "prior to" all her ends and values, liberals reply that this is a misunderstanding. Conceptions of the person in liberal principles of justice require only that no *particular* end or purpose is immune from re-examination, not that all ends and commitments could be set apart from my self-understanding and accepted or rejected *in toto*.

This is a debate that, on the terms in which it was staged, liberalism largely won: to the extent to which the value of communal ties to groups and traditions was meant to trump the protection of basic (liberal) rights afforded to individuals, no plausible view would insist that protection of the community is more crucial. But the debate did, Dagger explains, force liberals and other theorists to look more carefully at the relation between self and community that principles of justice assume. For example, Dagger looks closely at the ideas of "individualism" and "community" to suggest that some conceptions of these two political ideals may well face challenges from the other direction. For example, he favors a conception of community which is narrow enough to capture the uniqueness and importance of communal relations for many people but leaves open the ultimate value of communities – some are good and worth protecting politically, others not so much. The upshot, however, is that insofar as communal connections do or should take on a political dimension, the resulting political view amounts to civic *republicanism* – the view that one's freedom and well being is defined, protected and promoted by one's status as an equal citizen in a self-governing democracy. This view has now gained prominence among various theorists, some of them latter-day "communitarians."

Margaret Moore, in Chapter 18, picks up this discussion but suggests that, contrary to the way this debate was fashioned in its earlier form, the challenge to liberalism waged by both communitarian and multicultural theorists (about which more below) cannot be resolved *abstractly* but will depend on and vary according to the contexts in which they play out. Moore sees the communitarian challenge to have morphed not into republicanism of the sort just mentioned but into identity-based critiques of the assumption of the generic individual citizen central to liberalism. This challenge, she argues, has more bite in that it raises serious questions about whether the liberal conception of the citizen can accommodate the demands of "difference" – the variable and culturally grounded modes of identity that are increasingly found in modern societies.

Moore discusses how identity-based claims should have an importance to which (liberal) theories of justice must respond for a number of reasons, for example that social identities and the interests connected to them are often central to the person's sense of self, and that it is therefore inconsistent with respect for people's integrity to ask them to pursue social goals that deviate significantly from this self-conception. However, some claims of this sort can be accommodated under neutral political

Thomas Christiano and John Christman

principles by allowing exemptions from general rules, such as allowing Sikhs to wear turbans instead of motorcycle helmets. Such exceptions can be derived from the more abstract liberal commitment to equality: treating people fairly involves affording different treatment to people who are different in significant ways, in the same way that conscientious objection exemptions are allowed for military service.

But a more trenchant challenge to liberal neutrality, Moore points out, comes from cases in which members of identity groups require policy responses that afford positive recognition of needs rather than simple toleration, such as calls to reform marriage laws to allow gay and lesbian marriage. Classical liberal versions of toleration simply respond to such claims by allowing activities (without criminal penalty) as simply a private matter. But in these cases, group members call for positive affirmation of a way of life, an affirmation that requires restructuring public policies in a zero-sum manner relative to the traditional practice. The particular resolution to these problems, she argues, cannot be determined in the abstract but only in a context-dependent manner that looks carefully at realistic options for treating all interests equally.

This attention to historical context echoes considerations mentioned earlier about the relations between abstract normative political principles and facts about the people and society to which those principles are to apply. Political critique and evaluation relates to particular kinds of societies such as the constitutional democracies of the late modern age. Such social settings are (assumed to be) characterized by sub-populations with differing identities and contrasting commitments to values, religious affiliations, and so on. This is all part of what Rawls calls the fact of (reasonable) pluralism. But in addition to these differences in value frameworks and moral commitment, there are differences in relation to historical experience. Sub-populations in modern democracies have in fact experienced what any plausible theory would call injustice and oppression, as in the experience of racial minorities, women, and indigenous peoples. All of these historical (and ongoing) patterns of oppression are said by some to be relevant to the normative principles that are intended to apply to these geo-political locales.

In Chapter 19 Anthony Laden begins with the observation that political philosophy generally develops in reaction to social events and movements. In particular, the rise of social movements characterized by a politics of identity – feminism, the civil rights and gay rights movements, calls for cultural recognition and group rights – put pressure on the standard liberal doctrines of difference-blind equality, where the assumption was that abstract principles of liberty and equality would apply to all regardless of particulars of identity or social situation (except insofar as that was relevant to whether individuals were equal or unequal). The perceived failure of liberal *policies*, for example of enforcing anti-discrimination law and guarantees of equality of opportunity – to achieve meaningful equality for traditionally oppressed groups caused a re-thinking of liberal *theory*. As Moore suggests, there is a complex dynamic between policy conflicts in particular contexts, such as calls for particular rights or exemptions by specific social groups, and revisions of abstract principle. Laden agrees, as he traces the debates between critics who claim that liberalism is insufficient for accounting for the special injustices suffered by identity groups and liberal theorists attempting a response.

The particular forms of injustice contested in the demands for full equality by women and minority groups, calls for recognition by cultural groups, and in arguments for self-determination rights by national minorities, are not easily accounted for in the standard liberal paradigm. That paradigm remains hamstrung in classifying these kinds of injustice as either violations of basic individual rights, types of discrimination (denying equality of opportunity), or a mal-distributions of resources. But these social movements call for an end to kinds of oppression and marginalization that are not easily classified in these ways. Laden helpfully traces the give and take between identity-based critiques of liberal justice and various attempts by liberal philosophers to respond. In the end, however, he argues that a more fundamental revision of liberal justice must be pressed to take account of these challenges. In particular, he claims that justice should be seen not in terms of individual rights and conditions but rather in the kinds of social *relations* that should be enjoyed in a legitimate democracy.

Iris Young confronts these issues in Chapter 20 with reference to the "politics of difference," a phrase that she prefers strongly to the "politics of identity." Identities are, she thinks, always contestable in that the particular contours of our gender, ethnic, or racial identities, and the particular interests that attach to them, are not fixed quantities or settled matters. In her essay, she contrasts two ways of responding to struggles by social groups of the sort we are discussing, which she calls the "structural inequality approach" and the "societal culture approach." The latter is most associated with those liberal philosophers such as Will Kymlicka, Joseph Raz, and several others, who have attempted to explain the injustice of group oppression without forsaking the fundamentals of the liberal commitment to individual rights based on autonomy and equality. The crucial step in this type of argument, though, is the claim that the groups in question (upon whose behalf the critiques of liberal justice are made) form a homogeneous cultural unit that its members see as giving meaning to their life pursuits. But Young argues that such an approach, while valuable in some ways, cannot give a plausible account of the injustice experienced, for example, by women, racial minorities, and the disabled. This last group, for instance, is victimized not simply by a lack of a resource, such as a skill, but a lack of accommodation or *fit* between their abilities and the physical environment that is considered normal for the rest of the population. In addition, women suffer inequality because of a gender-specific division of labor that does more than deny opportunities but defines acceptable social *roles* that relegate women into constraining and stereotypical social categories.

The structural inequality approach, on the other hand, documents how groups interact along social axes that can be characterized by hierarchy and differential privilege in areas of the division of labor, social decision-making power, and the establishment and maintenance of dominant norms of behavior, appearance, dress, and so on. This way of analyzing the injustice of group-based social experience need not rest on problematic assumptions of homogeneity or essentialism about identity groups, something the societal cultures view trips over. Young argues further that calls for a revised conception of justice to take full account of the politics of difference have been often misunderstood because it has been assumed that such conceptions share the traditional liberal view that questions of justice only apply to the formal, coercive institutions of the *state*. She claims that many aspects of civil society that underlay oppressive social conditions enforce dominant norms less formally (though sometimes quite coercively), and these patterns of behavior and relations must

Thomas Christiano and John Christman

also be the subject matter of political critique and philosophy. This marks a profound departure from traditional (liberal) political philosophy that began with the question of what justified legitimate state power and rarely looked beyond the operations of what Rawls calls the institutions of the basic structure.

International Issues

Cosmopolitanism

Contemporary political philosophy until recently has focused largely on individual political societies and their evaluation. John Rawls explicitly limited his theory of justice to consideration of the justice of an individual political society understood as a closed system which people enter into by birth and exit by death alone. This focus on the individual state as the unit of concern for ideas of justice is common to political philosophy since Plato and Aristotle. In part it has been supported by the two main traditions of thought on international relations: realism and natural law theory. Realism, first articulated (though not necessarily endorsed) by Thucydides in ancient Greece asserts that the world of states constitutes a kind of violent anarchy in which moral norms do not hold between states even while they do hold within states. The principles of justice obtain only among relations between persons within states. The second view articulated most clearly in the scholastic and Protestant natural law theories of Francisco de Vitoria and Hugo Grotius asserts that the international system is a society of societies. On this view there are independent political societies that owe each other duties of non-interference, duties flowing from voluntary agreements and duties of aid in times of profound crisis such as attack by other states. The principles of just war and of global justice more generally are modeled on the principles that apply to domestic political societies. This view gives pride of place to domestic political societies in the development of international norms and theorizes about international society on the basis of analogies with domestic political societies.

Still, cosmopolitanism is not an entirely new doctrine in political philosophy. The stoic philosophers invoked the idea of a citizen of the world. But political reflection in defense of the idea of world government was given an early articulation by Dante Alighieri. Another more modest defense of global political institutions was given by Immanuel Kant, though he defended not world government but a federation of the states of the world. And much socialist and Marxist thought conceives of workers as part of an international movement for the establishment socialism.

The modern era has called the prominence of the state in political theory into question because of the myriad relations that citizens of one society hold with those of other societies. The massive expansion of international trade, finance, communications, transportation and migration of peoples and the increasing awareness of public evils such as pollution and global warming coupled with the rise of international institutions that have significant political power tie persons in all parts of the globe with each other. These facts make salient questions of distributive justice on a global scale and questions about the legitimacy of global political institutions as well as about moral norms of a global reach more generally.

One question of particular interest to contemporary political theorists is the question of the proper scope of principles of distributive justice. Cosmopolitans with respect to distributive justice such as Simon Caney (Chapter 21) have argued that the proper scope of principles of distributive justice is a global one. The principles of equality of opportunity ought to apply to everyone in the world so that a child born in Malawi ought to have the same valuable opportunities as a child born in Sweden. This is a striking and ambitious claim that seems to imply more or less immediately that the world is profoundly unjust. The fundamental argument for this thesis is that the political society one is born into is something for which one cannot be held responsible. So one person's life should not go worse than another's on the basis of the fact that one was born in one political society and another in a different political society. The reader will see the similarity of structure in this argument to the basic arguments for egalitarianism. Caney defends this argument against a number of recent objections from a number of quarters.

One such recent argument is proposed by Jon Mandle in Chapter 22. Mandle argues for the conclusion that principles of distributive justice apply particularly within the context of a political community and not to the world as a whole, at least as long as it is not a unified political community. The basic argument Mandle gives proceeds from a conception of justice that ties it to freedom in a distinctive way. Mandle argues that the foundation of justice is the principle that one may not subordinate the wills of others to one's own. He argues that in the case of individuals in the world, not related through political institutions, this requirement of non-subordination implies that one may not violate their basic human rights. If I enslave or kill another person or fail to help in providing them for their basic human needs in order to advance some arbitrary aim of my own, I am subordinating that person's will to my own. But beyond this, there is no requirement of distributive justice for people generally For Mandle, the picture changes when we live under common political institutions that are coercive and expect compliance. In this case, he says, we do subordinate another's will to our own if we impose laws or institutions on him that cannot be justified to him. Only if the laws and institutions that expect him to comply can be justified to him can he be said not to be subordinated. Mandle thinks that it is in the context of this requirement of mutual justification of law and institutions that the requirements of democracy and then of distributive justice arise and not otherwise. So it is only within domestic political institutions that considerations of distributive justice have application. And so the international realm ought to be regulated by institutions that respect human rights but not distributive justice.

Human Rights

The great majority of contemporary political philosophers, cosmopolitan and non-cosmopolitan alike, agree on the central importance of human rights in the evaluation of the international order. Everyone owes respect for the human rights of every other person. There have been many disagreements, however, about how such rights ought to be defined and how they are grounded. Are they merely institutional protections of basic human interests conferred by international institutions, or do they have a basis in the natures of human beings? The latter answer is most clearly asserted by the tradition of natural law theory. But many modern theorists have chosen the

Thomas Christiano and John Christman

former reply. In addition, one of the most hotly debated questions among contemporary political thinkers concerns the content of these human rights. Some have argued that there are only negative human rights, which implies that human rights imply only negative duties of non-interference on others' parts. Others think that in addition to negative human rights there are also positive human rights, or rights to the positive provision of goods to persons by others. These rights imply positive duties to aid others or to provide them with basic needs. This kind of approach finds some of its most formidable support in the fact that all the central human rights treaties and declarations include both positive and negative rights.

The idea that there are only negative human rights is partly supported by the contribution of Onora O'Neill in Chapter 23. She argues that rights must be correlated with duties. And she argues that negative rights are correlated with negative duties that are easily assignable to all human beings. So each person can make a claim against every other person in the world that that person not interfere or harm them. But, she argues the situation of positive rights, such as a right to education, is not so easy to understand. Who must provide the education to the person in Malawi? Do we (citizens of the U.S.) have a duty to do this? O'Neill appears to think that this is implausible. Perhaps the state of Malawi has this duty. But in this case, the thought is, we are assigning a duty to an entity that is a contingent product of institutional arrangements. In the case of negative rights we have them against all persons and no institutional setting is required for determining what duties people have, but it appears that in the case of positive rights, the duties must be assigned by institutions and this will depend on a myriad contingencies making them special rights and not human rights. Hence it is not clear how there can be positive human rights.

James Nickel offers an account of human rights that is meant to support the thesis that there are positive human rights to economic and social goods (Chapter 24). His account of human rights is grounded in the idea that respect for human dignity implies the need to protect the fundamental interests of persons. These fundamental interests are in life, agency, and in avoiding cruel and degrading as well as severely unfair treatment. These ground certain fundamental moral claims on others. Nickel argues, then, that the provision of goods, education and health care are necessary to the satisfaction of these fundamental claims. Since human rights are grounded in the fundamental interests associated with human dignity, they can be thought of as universal human rights without the supposition that they entail universal and clear duties on the part of all persons. Indeed, Nickel claims that the primary addressee of human rights is the state in which a person lives and failing that the other states in the international community.

This concludes our overview of the dominant themes of the volume and, we think, of "mainstream" political philosophy as it is currently practiced in academic settings. Much has been omitted, of course, which would be of great interest to the student of political theory. Examples include the nature of political authority, the nature and value of political freedom, the justification of revolution, and other such topics. In addition, there are some of the most powerful challenges to mainstream (especially liberal) political philosophy from theorists outside of the analytic tradition, including critical theory (and the work of Jürgen Habermas), pragmatism (especially John Dewey), and post-modern theory. We might also mention that feminism, critical race theory, and post-colonial studies are not specifically included, though we hope that the issues raised by attention to identity, democracy, and international justice discussed in the chapters here will permeate these specific trajectories of thought. Though we don't pretend, of course, to have captured the several and multifaceted aspects of those approaches.

One final note: although this series is called "Debates in ... ," we have not held strictly to a debate format here. We think that the topics covered, which are themselves a selective sample of a broad field, do not admit easily of a "for" and "against" format of the sort the word "debate" connotes. We think of these pieces as overviews with distinct point of view, and we have paired the essays so that the points of view tend to be in tension. But all of these issues admit of far more than two sides, and arguments laid out here show common ground as well as disagreement. The purpose here is to provide a cross-section of some of the best thinking about particular topics and to suggest where some of the most trenchant fault lines between contrasting approaches to those topics can be found.

Thomas Christiano and John Christman

QUESTIONS OF METHOD

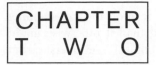

Facts and Principles[1]

Gerald A. Cohen

a.   In this paper, I argue for a thesis, which I state in section d. below, about the relationship between facts and normative principles (or, as I shall call them, for short, "principles"). A normative principle, here, is a general directive that tells agents what (they ought, or ought not) to do, and a fact is, or corresponds to, any truth, *other than (if any principles are truths) a principle*, of a kind that someone might reasonably think supports a principle. Note that, under the foregoing stipulations, it is not excluded that normative principles might themselves be facts in a different sense of "fact" from that which is here stipulated. Principles might, that is, be facts in the broader sense of "fact" in which *all* truths, including, therefore, true principles (if there are any), represent facts. I myself believe that there exist true normative principles, but the thesis about principles and facts to be defended here is, as I shall explain at q. below, neutral with respect to whether any normative principles are truths.

b.   The very little (almost nothing) that I just said about what constitutes a *fact* suffices for my demonstrative purposes. I am happy for facts to be whatever my opponents in this debate, whose position I shall describe in c., (*reasonably*) understand them to be: my argument, so I believe, is robust across permissible variations in the meaning of "fact," and it is also neutral across contrasting conceptions of the relationship of fact and value. Nor does my view about facts and principles, or so I argue at l. below, require me to take a position on the famous question of whether an "ought" can follow from an "is." It bears emphasis that the question that my thesis answers is neutral with respect to controversies about the objectivity of principles, the relationship between facts and values, and the "is-ought" question, and, let me add, for good measure, the realism/anti-realism/quasi-realism/a-little-bit-of-realism-here-not-so-much-realism-there controversy. The question pursued here is distinct from those that dominate the meta-ethical literature, and, so far as I know, it is hardly discussed in that literature. You will inevitably misunderstand me if you assimilate the thesis I shall state to one within those familiar controversies.

The independent status of the issue canvassed here in relation to long-standing controversies makes the present discussion less interesting than it otherwise might be, in that it has a limited effect on those popular philosophical controversies, but also in one way more interesting than it otherwise might be, in that it addresses a relatively novel and, I think, consequential issue, an issue which philosophers don't argue about much, but about which most of them spontaneously, or, when appropriately provoked, display strongly opposed and unargued views, which each side finds *obviously true*: that circumstance suggests that there's something of a philosophical problem here, about which most philosophers are at least in part mistaken (because a view is unlikely to be *obviously* true if a goodly number of reflective thinkers believe it to be *obviously* false).

c.   The thesis to be defended here contradicts what many people (and, I believe, most moral and political philosophers) are disposed to think, to wit, that our beliefs about matters of normative principle, including our beliefs about the deepest and most general matters of principle, should reflect, or respond to, truths about matters of fact: they should, that is, – *this is how I am using "reflect" and "respond to"* – include matters of fact among the grounds for affirming them. So, for example, many find it obvious that our beliefs about principles should reflect facts about human nature, such as the fact that human beings are liable to pain, or the fact that they are capable of sympathy for each other, and they also think that our beliefs about principles should reflect facts about human social organization, such as the tendency for people to encounter collective action problems, or for societies to be composed of individuals who have diverse interests, and conflicting opinions. These people believe that *all* sound principles are, as I shall say, *fact-sensitive*, by which, once again, I mean neither more nor less than that facts form at least part of the grounds for affirming them. Constructivists about justice believe that,[2] and it was my interest in that constructivism that led me to think about, and to address, the issue under discussion here. I explore, here, in general terms, the relationship between principles that are grounded in facts and the facts that ground them. I apply what results to constructivism in the study mentioned in the opening footnote of this article. (A brief sketch of some of that application will be found in sections s. and t. below.)

d.   The view that all principles for governing human life are sensitive to facts about human life sounds reasonable, and it seems, indeed, to many people to be obviously correct, but I believe it to be demonstrably mistaken. I believe that it cannot be true of *all* principles that they are sensitive to fact, and that it is true of *some* principles only because it is false of other, fact-*in*sensitive, principles, which explain why given facts ground fact-*sensitive* principles. In my view – and this is my thesis – *a principle can reflect or respond to a fact only because it is also a response to a principle that is not a response to a fact*. To put the same point differently, principles that reflect facts must, in order to reflect facts, reflect principles that don't reflect facts.

My thesis depends on what it is for a principle to be a principle and, more particularly, on what it is for a fact to ground a principle. The thesis is not restricted in scope to principles that are in some or other sense correct. The thesis applies to anyone's principles, be they correct or not, *so long as she has a clear grasp both of what her principles are and of why she holds them*[3] (where "grasping why she holds

Gerald A. Cohen

them" is short for "knowing what grounds she believes she has for holding them" rather than for "what causes her to hold them"). It also characterizes (under an appropriate reformulation) whatever (if anything) constitutes the *correct* set of principles.

e. Let me now develop the advertised thesis. First, I proceed abstractly, but what I hope is a helpful illustration follows shortly.

Suppose that proposition *F* states a factual claim, and that, in the light of, on the basis of, her belief that *F*, a person affirms principle *P*. We may then ask her *why* she treats *F* as a reason for affirming *P*. And, if she is able to answer that question, then her answer, so I believe, will feature, or imply, an affirmation of a more ultimate principle (call it *P1*), a principle that would survive denial of *P* itself, a principle, moreover, which holds whether or not *F* is true, and which explains *why F* is a reason for affirming *P*: it is always a further principle that confers on a fact its principle-grounding power. The said principle, *P1*, is insensitive to whether or not *F* holds, although *P1* may be, as we shall see, sensitive to other facts: I have not yet argued that the original principle, *P*, presupposes a principle that is insensitive to *all* facts, a principle, that is, which is insensitive not only to *F*, but which is *altogether* fact-insensitive.

Let me illustrate what I am in course of claiming. If I am right, what I say about the forthcoming example provides an argument for my thesis, since what I say about it is, I believe, both patently true and patently generalizable.

Suppose someone affirms the principle that *we should keep our promises* (call that *P*) because *only when promises are kept can promisees successfully pursue their projects* (call that *F*). (I am not saying that that is the *only* basis on which *P* might be affirmed: that it is *one* plausible basis suffices for my purposes). Then she will surely agree that she believes that *F* supports *P* because she affirms *P1*, which says, to put it roughly, that *we should help people to pursue their projects*. It is *P1*, here, which makes *F* matter, which makes it support *P*, but the subject's affirmation of *P1*, as opposed to whether or not that affirmation induces her to affirm *P* itself, has nothing to do, essentially, with whether or not she believes that *F*. She would affirm *P1* whether or not she believed the factual statement *F*: *P1* is not, in her belief system, sensitive to whether or not *F* is true. If she came to think that facing broken promises builds character, and that *F* is therefore false, she would have reason to abandon *P* but no reason to abandon *P1*.

f. Although a principle that makes a fact matter, in the indicated fashion, is insensitive to whether or not *that* fact obtains, it may yet be sensitive to (other) facts. To see this, return to the promising example, in which *P1* says that we should help people to pursue their projects. What, we may now ask, supports *P1*? A possible answer is a fresh factual claim (call it *F1*), which says that people can achieve happiness only if they are able to pursue their own projects. But, manifestly, *F1* then supports *P1* only in the light of a yet more ultimate principle, *P2*, which says that, absent other considerations,[4] people's happiness should be promoted, and it is possible that there will be no fact on which *that* principle, *P2*, is grounded.

Merely "possible," though, if only because some might base *P2* on the (supposed) fact that promoting people's happiness expresses our respect for them. But then they must hold principle *P3*, namely, that we ought to express our respect for people, which, if itself based on fact, is based on the fact that people possess what are thought to be respect-meriting characteristics. The relevant basic fact-free principle *P4*, will then be: one ought to respect beings, human or otherwise, who have the relevant characteristics. Note that *P4* is immune to denials that human beings, or any beings, have the relevant characteristics. To be sure, *P4* is inapplicable if no beings have such characteristics, but that certain beings *do* have such characteristics is nevertheless no ground for affirming *P4*.

Many will think that the consideration (F) that *only when promises are kept can promisees successfully pursue their projects* is not the right, or at any rate not the *only*, ground for the principle that we should keep our promises. For many (for example, I) think that breaking promises is wrong because doing so constitutes a violation of trust. Now that ground for the promising principle might be regarded as other than a *fact*, in which case I need make no comment on it here: non-factual grounding of principles falls outside the scope of my thesis. But if anyone *does* want to present the claim that promising violates a trust as a fact, then I would point out that what makes that (putative) fact a ground for the promising principle is the more ultimate principle that one should not violate a trust. And that more ultimate principle is either itself fact-insensitive, or, if it is indeed fact-sensitive, you will know by now how I would press beyond it to a fact-insensitive one.

g. My argument has three premisses. The first premiss says that whenever a fact *F* confers support on a principle *P*, there is an explanation *why F* supports *P*, an explanation of how, that is, *F* represents a reason to endorse *P*. That first premiss rests upon the more general claim that there is always an explanation why any ground grounds what it grounds. I have no argument for that more general claim – it strikes me as self-evidently true, under a properly unrestricted understanding of what would qualify as such an explanation.

Note that this first premiss places no restriction on the form that the answer to a question about why a ground grounds what it grounds must take. So, for example, it is allowed here to be an explanation of why *p* (if it indeed does) supports *p* that they are the same proposition. A restriction of the form that the answer to the relevant why-question takes in our specific case, that of facts supporting principles, is affirmed not by the first but by the second premiss of my argument.

For the second premiss says that the explanation whose existence is affirmed by the first premiss invokes or implies a more ultimate principle, commitment to which would survive denial of *F*, a more ultimate principle that explains *why F* supports *P*, in the fashion illustrated above. For this second premiss my defence is simply to challenge anyone who disagrees to provide an example in which a credible explanation of why some *F* supports some *P* invokes or implies no such more ultimate principle.

(Note that the second premiss doesn't say that the pertinent *more* ultimate principle is either ultimate (*tout court*) or fact-insensitive – as opposed to insensitive to the particular fact F. That stronger claim is the forthcoming conclusion of the argument. Note, further, that as I stated the second premiss, it presupposes the truth of the first. But, for those who like the premisses of an argument to be independent of one another, the presupposition can be dropped, through restatement of the second premiss in conditional form. It then says that *if* there is an explanation why fact F supports principle P, then it invokes a more ultimate principle that is insensitive to F).

Gerald A. Cohen

Armed with these premises, we may ask anyone who affirms a principle on the basis of a fact what further and more ultimate principle explains why that fact grounds that principle and, once that more ultimate principle has been stated, whether *it*, in turn, is based on any fact, and so on, reiteratively, as many times as may be required, until she comes to rest with a principle which reflects no fact, unless the sequence of interrogation proceeds indefinitely. But the third premiss of my argument is, simply, a denial that it will so proceed. The case for that premiss is threefold. First, it is just implausible that a credible interrogation of that form might go on indefinitely: if you disagree, try to construct one, one that goes beyond citation of, say, five principles. Second, such an indefinitely continuing sequence would require something like an infinite nesting of principles, and few will think that there exist a relevantly infinite number of principles. Finally, an unending sequence of justifications would run against the requirement (laid down in **d.** above) that she who affirms *P* has a clear grasp of what her principles are and of why she holds them: for we can surely say that a person who cannot complete the indicated sequence, because she has to go on forever, does not know why she holds the principles she does. To sum up the case for the third premiss: the sequence cannot proceed without end because our resources of conviction are finite, and, even if they were not, proceeding without end would violate the self-understanding stipulation.

It follows from the stated premises that, as I claimed, every fact-sensitive principle reflects a fact-insensitive principle: that is true *both* within the structure of the principled beliefs of a given person, as long as she is clear about what she believes and why she believes it, *and*, by a certain parity of reasoning that I shall not lay out here, within the structure of the objective truth about principles, *if* there is an objective truth about principles.[5] But, as I indicated at **b.** above, my thesis about principled beliefs, or "beliefs," holds even if there is no objective truth about principles, and even if what we call "beliefs" about principles are really expressions of endorsement, or universal commands, or non-truth-bearing items of some other kind: see, further, **t.** below.

[Three subsections follow in the original article, in each of which one of the three premisses of the argument is defended against objections. There is room to reproduce only the challenge to the first premiss here].

g (i). The first premiss does not say that everything, or every principle, has to have a justification: I am neutral on that claim. The premiss rather insists that there is always an explanation that explains why a ground grounds what it grounds. What initiates the sequence of principles is not a need for justification – that, we may suppose, has already been fulfilled, by the cited fact – but a need for explanation (of why a stated justification justifies).

Nor is it a valid objection to, or a truth about, my thesis that it implies that (beliefs about) ultimate principles cannot themselves be justified: my view lacks the stated implication. What rather follows from it is that ultimate principles cannot be justified *by facts*. My view is neutral on whether they can be justified in some other way. For my argumentative purposes, fact-free principles might be self-evidently true,[6] or they might for some other reason require no grounds or they might need grounds and have grounds of some non-factual sort (they might, for example, be justified by some methodological principle which is not itself a normative principle but a principle that says how to generate normative principles[7]), or they might need grounds but lack them, or, as we shall see at q., they might be judged to be outside the space of grounds because, as some non-cognitivists think, they might not be objects of *belief* at all.

Let me amplify the foregoing clarification of my first premiss by explaining why that premiss does not say anything like what Lewis Carroll's tortoise said to Achilles.[7] That misguided tortoise said that an inference is valid only if the principle that validates it is stated as a further premiss of the inference. An unmanageable infinite regress ensues, and the take-home lesson is that principles of inferential validity do not function as premisses in the arguments that they validate.

Lewis Carroll's lesson is no challenge to my first premiss because that premiss concerns not inferences and what makes them valid but justifying grounds and what makes them justify. What the tortoise says to Achilles is that "q" doesn't follow from the conjunction of "if p then q" and "p" alone: he says the inference fails unless you add "If 'if p then q' and 'p', then 'q'" as a further premiss. But in my proceedings no inference is ever said to be invalid, and therefore needful of a further premiss. When someone claims that a fact *grounds* a principle, she affirms a *grounding* relation, not one of deductive inference. And I do not say: no, that fact doesn't ground that principle, unless we add . . . I simply ask, non-rhetorically, *why* the fact supports the principle, and I *claim* that a satisfactory answer will always feature a further principle, P1: that is, precisely, a (correct!) claim, not a move demanded by logic. And, unlike the sequence generated by the tortoise, the sequence that my claim generates is finite: it comes to an end with the statement of a principle that is fact-insensitive, and, therefore one to which my sequence-generating question ("Why does this fact support this principle?") doesn't apply.

i.   I should observe that the clarity of mind requirement (see p. 6 above) is by no means universally satisfied by affirmers of principles: people display contrasting degrees of certainty with respect to why they affirm the principles they affirm. So, for example, a person might say with assurance that the reason why she affirms that, if a being is vulnerable to suffering, then, absent other considerations, it should be protected against suffering, is (quite simply) that beings should be protected against suffering: protection against suffering is, for her, the relevant ultimate norm. But another person who affirms the stated principle may just not know whether that principle is, for her, as it is for the first person, (entirely) fact-insensitive, or whether she affirms it (at least also), for example, on the basis of the fact that suffering interferes with projects (including, *inter* very many *alia*, the project of avoiding suffering itself) together with the principle that, absent other considerations, people's projects should be facilitated. And, if she affirms the original anti-suffering principle for that further, projects-centered, reason, then she may not know whether she means thereby to endorse human freedom to pursue projects as such, or whether she affirms the project-respecting principle for the reason that not freedom as such but welfare as such is to be promoted, and a person is (usually) better than other people are at discerning the path that leads to her welfare.

Another example. As a matter of fact, zygote/foetuses become progressively more babylike as they proceed towards birth. But suppose things were different. Suppose, for example, that they were initially more babylike, and regressed to a less and less

Gerald A. Cohen

babylike condition until one day before birth, when they undergo a spectacular humanization. Then it would not be a reason for not aborting a day or two before birth that the foetus was already babylike. I think that might throw us into normative turmoil. Our norms are formed under the factual constraint that foetus-age goes with foetus-level-of-development, but, being so formed, we don't know what we should think the ultimate warrant of our norms is.

It is true that we don't need to know what that warrant is, for practical purposes, but (in my view) philosophy's role is not to tell us what we *need* to know (in that sense), but what we want or ought (for non-practical reasons) to know. Not all will agree. Some might attack my philosophical presuppositions as "philosophist." In that spirit, they might accept the three premises of my argument but deny the propriety of the clarity of mind requirement.

j.   I have argued that affirmations of fact-insensitive principle are logically prior to affirmations of principle that are made when factual information is brought to bear. But the priority enjoyed by fact-insensitive principles is purely logical, and not temporal or epistemic, or, at any rate, not epistemic in at least one sense of that term. The priority of fact-insensitive principles is a matter of what utterances of principle *commit* one to, not of how one comes to believe or know what one says in uttering them. That is why I do not deny (in fact, I would assert) that asking what we think we should do, given these or those factual circumstances, is a fruitful way of determining what our principles are; and sometimes, moreover, responses to actual facts reveal our principles better than our responses to hypothesized facts do, because the actual facts present themselves more vividly to us, and, too, they concentrate the mind better, since they call for actual and not merely hypothetical decisions. But none of those considerations bear on whether commitment to fact-sensitive principles carries with it commitment to fact-insensitive principles.

k.   My thesis is conditional: it is that *if* any facts support any principles, then there are fact-insensitive principles which account for that relationship of support (and, by the same token, if we have any principles at all, then we have fact-insensitive principles). I also believe the consequents of those conditionals, if only because I believe their antecedents, and I therefore believe that *there exist fact-insensitive principles*, but I have not argued for the italicized unconditional thesis as such.

The conditional character of my thesis renders it consistent with the view (with which, independently of the claims of the present paper, I disagree) that there exist cases in which no general principle is required for a fact to justify an action. The thesis is also consistent with the stronger view, defended by different thinkers on various grounds, that reasons for action quite generally do not presuppose principles.[9] The stated consistencies obtain because my thesis concerns what happens if and when facts ground principles, not whether actions can be justified by facts only through principles. Most people think, as I indeed do, that facts do ground principles, and my thesis claims that they are thereby committed to acknowledging the existence of fact-insensitive principles. But my thesis doesn't depend on people being right when they claim that there are principles that respond to facts, or that facts justify actions only through principles. To be sure, my thesis is less interesting if those claims are false, but it is not for that reason less true.

l. Some people think that one can, as the idea is often expressed, "'go' from an 'is' to an 'ought'," that, for example, the statement that Harry is in pain *entails* that Harry ought to be assisted, or that the statement that Harry is innocent *entails* that it would be an injustice to punish Harry (where "*p* entails *q*" says that it would be a contradiction to affirm *p* and deny *q*, because of what "*p*" and "*q*" mean). David Hume (is widely thought to have) rejected that view, and, on first acquaintance with my thesis about facts and principles, many understand it to be a reissue of Hume's (when Hume is so understood: henceforth I drop that qualification).[10] But that understanding is mistaken. I do not say, Hume-like, that, *since* one cannot go from an "is" to an "ought," a person who affirms *P* on the basis of *F* must also affirm the truth of some fact-independent normative statement. No such Humean premiss was part of my argument. Nor does my conclusion support Hume's view.[11] I believe that I have demonstrated my conclusion, but I cannot claim the remarkable achievement of having *proved* that one cannot go from an "is" to an "ought."

To see that my argument presupposes no denial that one can go from an "is" to an "ought," observe that, far from rejecting my thesis, someone who thinks that one *can* go from an "is" to an "ought" need not deny my thesis, and she must, indeed, affirm it, *if*, that is, and as I shall now suppose, she believes that facts support principles at all. [12] Suppose, then, that someone who does believe that facts support principles also thinks that you *can* go, by semantically based entailment, from an "is" to an "ought." Like many other people, she affirms the principle that injured people should be assisted, and, when asked why, she defends that, as other people do, by reference to the fact that injured people suffer pain and/or other disability: for simplicity, I'll stick to pain. But then she must believe the further principle that *people in pain should be assisted*, and, if asked why she believes *that* principle, she will say something like this, which distinguishes her view from that of other people, including David Hume's: that it is a conceptual truth that people in pain should be assisted, that a person doesn't understand what the words "pain" and/or "assist" and/or "should be" (and so on) *mean* if she doesn't think so. But, if this anti-Humean is right, then her principle, *if X is in pain, then X ought to be assisted*, *is* insensitive to fact, since it is an entailment, and entailments, being *a priori*, are insensitive to fact. No change in her beliefs about facts would cause her to doubt the italicized principle.

My view that all fact-sensitive principles presuppose fact-insensitive principles, doesn't, then, require that an "ought" can't follow from an "is." My position is neutral with respect to *that* dispute, and, as far as its disputants are concerned, it is not the Humeans but the anti-Humeans (that is, the "'is' to 'ought'" brigade) who must agree with me.[13]

m. Whatever anybody may think about "is" and "ought," most people think that "ought" implies "can," and that is no doubt true under *some* interpretations of those words. So let me reply to the following would-be objection to my thesis: facts often make a mooted ultimate principle impossible to follow, and, since "ought" implies "can," facts thereby disqualify the mooted principle. But, whether or not that is all true, it is no objection to my thesis, which is that facts ground principles only in virtue of further principles that are not grounded in facts and that explain why the given facts ground the given principles. The objection lacks application because excluding a principle (because it can't be complied with) isn't grounding any principle.

Gerald A. Cohen

Someone might say that, while the foregoing reply to the "'ought' implies 'can'" objection saves the letter of my thesis, it also reveals a restriction on its scope that was not initially made explicit: the thesis appears to allow that facts can *refute* (supposed) ultimate principles. And it is true that I have defended no stronger thesis here that forbids what that weaker one allows: but I now proceed to do so.

When a fact of the kind here in question, that is, a fact about human incapacity, excludes a principle because it can't be obeyed, then we may ask what we should say about the excluded principle on the counterfactual hypothesis that it *could* be obeyed. And it is only when we thus clear the decks of facts about capacity, and get the answer to that counterfactual question, that, so I claim, we reach the normative ultimate.[14] Anyone who rejects "one ought to do *A*" on the sole ground that it is impossible to do *A*, anyone, that is, who would otherwise affirm that principle, is committed to this fact-insensitive principle: "One ought to do *A* if it is possible to do *A*."

If I am right, the dictum that "'ought' implies 'can'" is misused when it is used, as it often is, in an attempt to show that *feasibility* constrains the content of ultimate normative judgment. The following argument, or something like it, should be familiar to readers:

1. Normative judgments are "ought"-statements.
2. "Ought" implies "can."
∴ 3. If "One ought to do Λ" cannot be complied with, "One ought to do A" is not a normative judgment.

Consider, the statement-form that I introduced a couple of paragraphs back, that is, "One ought to do *A* if it is possible to do *A*." Call it 4. Now either 4 is an "ought"-statement or it is not one. Suppose that 4 is an "ought"-statement. Then premiss 2 is false, because 4 entails no relevant "can"-statement. But suppose, instead, and perhaps more naturally, that 4 is not an "ought"-statement. Then premiss 1 fails, because conditional statements of form of 4 say something essential about the normative.

The foregoing point applies to the virtue of justice, with respect to which two inquiries must be distinguished. If we are interested in obeying injunctions that carry the authority of justice, and we have a number of injunctions before us, then, in course of satisfying the stated practical interest, we may cross out any injunction that fails the "ought"-implies-"can" test. But the result of that procedure does not provide us with a complete picture of the nature of justice itself. Our picture is incomplete unless we can say of rejected injunctions whether they are rejected *solely because of their infeasibility*. And where that is indeed the only reason for rejecting them, then, once again, we find fundamental justice within claims of the form: if it is possible to do A, then you ought to do A. If I am right, *all* fundamental principles of justice, whether or not we call them "ought"-statements, are of that conditional form. We derive unconditional ought-statements from them when reality is plugged in. But reality, as it were, affects the "possible" part, not the "ought" part, of the statement.

What goes for justice goes for all values that generate injunctions, and even for the "ought" of practical rationality, if there is such a thing, and whatever relationship rationality may bear to justice and to other values. For I would claim that the ultimate deliverances of rationality take the form "If it is possible to do A, then you ought (that is, rationality requires you) to do A." We readily say things like, "Even if that course were possible, it would be irrational." This means that we make judgments, however merely implicitly, of the form "If that course were possible, it would be rational." And I claim that, when our evaluation is fundamental, we evaluate practical rationality, as we evaluate justice, and the normative in general, independently of factual possibility, and we therefore at least implicitly affirm principles of the indicated "conditional-possible" form.

q.   Although my thesis is undoubtedly meta-ethical, it is neutral with respect to what may reasonably be regarded as the central question of meta-ethics. My thesis *is* meta-ethical, because it is a thesis about principles that is silent about which principles should be accepted and which rejected: it is not a contribution to what is sometimes called substantive, as opposed to meta-ethical, ethics. But my thesis is neutral on that central question of meta-ethics which concerns the objectivity or subjectivity of normative principles, and which asks "What is the status of normative principles?" in the sense of "status" in which objectivists, realists, cognitivists, subjectivists, imperativists, emotivists, expressivists, error theorists, and so on, provide variously contrasting and overlapping answers to that question. My claim is that anyone who is entirely clear about what her principles are and why she holds them has principles that are independent of her beliefs about facts, whether or not her affirmations (or "affirmations") of fact-insensitive principles are to be understood as claims about a timeless normative reality, or as expressions of taste, or as emotional commitments, or as universally prescribed imperatives.[15]

To be sure, my thesis would have to be rephrased to suit certain answers to the central question of meta-ethics. Under emotivism, for example, it would have to be stated with eschewal of such phrases as "believes principle *P* to be true." Under an emotivist construal of the "affirmation" of the principle that one ought to keep one's promises, the speaker is really saying (or uttering, or emitting): "Boo to breaking promises!" Now that "Boo!" no doubt reflects her factual beliefs, perhaps, for example, the belief that breaking promises prejudices people's projects. But then, clearly, she is disposed to say (or shout) "Boo to prejudicing people's projects!," and, if I am right, she is committed to an ultimate "Boo!," perhaps a rather long "Boooooooo!," that depends on no factual beliefs. (Some would say that emotivists must deny that people have what are, strictly speaking, *principles*, and/or that the facts that people adduce to explain their "affirmations of principle" constitute *grounds* for them. If they are right, that is no threat to my thesis, for that thesis, I remind you (see section k. above), is the *conditional* one that, *if* facts support principles, then there are principles that are not supported by any facts. If, on the other hand, emotivism *does* countenance principles and grounds, then the reading of my thesis within the emotivist position is as given in the pre-parenthetical part of the present paragraph).

r.   I remarked in section b. that the meta-ethical literature says very little about the question pursued in the present paper. But a notable exception is the work of John Rawls, who argued that fundamental principles of justice, and, indeed, "first principles" in general, are a response to the facts of the human condition. (That is why the principle-choosing denizens of the original position are provided with extensive factual information.) Rawls calls the alternative to that view "rational intuitionism," and he disparages that alternative.[16]

Gerald A. Cohen

"There is," according to Rawls, "no objection to resting the choice of first principles upon the general facts of economics and psychology." He adds, in illustration of his claim, that the difference principle "*relies* on the idea that in a competitive economy (with or without private ownership) with an open class system *excessive* inequalities will not be the rule."[17]

But the illustration that is here supposed to show the innocence of the dependence of first principles on fact is unequal to its task. For it follows from what Rawls says (note "*relies*") that, if he appraised the facts differently, he would reject the difference principle, *because it permitted too much inequality*. But it then further follows, in line with the second premiss of my argument (see the second paragraph of g. above), that there *is* an unarticulated background principle of equality (something like: "One ought not to cause too much inequality") that explains why the stated fact about a competitive economy supports the difference principle, and, for all that Rawls shows, *that* further principle *either* itself does not depend on any facts, *or* points to a still more ultimate principle behind it that does not do so. [18] Rawls needs to deny what I regard as the evident truth, affirmed in the second and pivotal premiss of my argument, that a fact supports a principle only in the light of a further principle, yet the very phrase, "excessive inequalities," that he uses in the example at hand confirms that premiss, since it fuses reference to a fact with reference to a principle that renders that fact relevant: excess qualifies as *excess* only in the light of a principle which says how much is *too* much.[19]

But I want to make a further point that cries out to be made here even though it is less relevant to the immediate dispute. And that is that the official two principles of justice do not really exhaust what Rawls thinks justice is. For, alongside them, and of equal status to them, there is, his illustration shows, an independent principle which forbids more than a certain amount of inequality and against which the claims of (at any rate) the difference principle must be traded off. In a more perspicuous presentation of the Rawlsian position both "promote equality" and "promote the condition of the worst off" would be fact-free injunctions whose claims are to be balanced against one another.

Despite the curiously mishandled illustration of his position, Rawls says that those, like me, who affirm the rival position that ultimate principles are fact-independent, make

> moral philosophy the study of the ethics of creation: an examination of the reflections an omnipotent deity might entertain in determining which is the best of all possible worlds. Even the general facts of nature are to be chosen.[20]

But it is flatly untrue that the view that ultimate principles are independent of fact commits those who hold it to legislating not only principles but also facts. That would follow only on an assumption *opposite* to what we affirm: that, contrary to what we affirm, all principles must be chosen in the light of facts (so that, having decided to ignore the actual facts, we should have to make up for that by *legislating* facts). The second sentence of the above passage can best be regarded as a slip that should be ignored.[21]

A more apt application of the fact-free-principles-are-only-for-deities motif appears in Rawls's argument that, in the absence of factual input, the parties to the original position will have no idea what to choose:

How . . . can they possibly make a decision? A problem of choice is well defined only if the alternatives are suitably restricted by natural laws and other constraints, and those deciding already have certain inclinations to choose among them. Without a definite structure of this kind the question posed is indeterminate. For this reason we need have no hesitation in making the choice of the principles of justice presuppose a certain theory of social institutions. Indeed, one cannot avoid assumptions about general facts. . . . If these assumptions are true and suitably general, everything is in order, for without these elements the whole scheme would be pointless and empty.[22]

This argument falls before the distinction between logical and epistemic priority that was made at section j. above. However difficult it may be to decide on principles, to *know* what *all* your normative beliefs are, in the absence of facts, decisions of principle that *indeed* reflect facts carry a commitment to foundational fact-independent principles, and that is the point at issue between those who affirm and those who reject what Rawls *calls* "rational intuitionism."[23] Because of a perfectly ordinary poverty of imagination, the denizens of the original position, and we ourselves,[24] may need factual information to provoke appropriate reflection, but the result of that reflection does not repose upon that information.

In the full version of this paper I have occasion to remark (in the final paragraph of section g(ii), which is omitted in the present abridged version) that Rawls's thesis that first principles rest on fact sits ill with the circumstance that seemingly non-fact-based principles justify the use of the original position machine: it is justified by the "free and equal" standing of members of society, but that standing reflects fact-free principles about the proper treatment of beings of the sort that they are. So, it might be asked, "How much difference would it make if Rawls did not call his two principles 'first principles' but reserved that designation for the principles that justify the original position machine?" The answer depends on the particular intellectual concern that is in play. To our assessment of the desirability of the principles that *A Theory of Justice* tells us to follow it might make no difference at all. But it would manifestly make a massive difference to the thesis of fact-sensitivity and the arguments for it scouted in this section, since it would represent the abandonment of both, and it is that thesis, and not its importance within the Rawlsian enterprise, that is immediately at stake here. If the arguments scouted in the present section were sound, then the principles that help to explicate "free and equal" standing *could* not be fact-free, because the stated arguments deny that there are *any* fact-free principles.

s.   Many object to utilitarianism that it recommends slavery for conditions in which slavery would promote aggregate happiness. Many utilitarians reply that such conditions do not, in fact, obtain. I close my criticism of Rawls's defence of his thesis that first principles are grounded in fact by examining his endorsement of that utilitarian recourse to fact:

It is often objected . . . that utilitarianism may allow for slavery and serfdom, and for other infractions of liberty. Whether these institutions are justified is made to *depend upon* whether actuarial calculations show that they yield a higher balance of happiness. To this the utilitarian replies that the nature of society is such that these calculations are normally[25] against such denials of liberty.

Gerald A. Cohen

> Contract theory [and, therefore, Rawls] agrees . . . with utilitarianism in holding that the fundamental principles of justice quite properly depend upon the natural facts about men and society.[26]

Rawls here endorses neither utilitarianism nor its defenders' factual claim about slavery. But he endorses the procedure of invoking "natural facts about men and society" to defend a fundamental principle, such as the supposed natural fact that slavery is not a happiness-maximizing arrangement for human beings.

I hope that the ensuing discussion of the quoted passage will reinforce the case for my view about facts and principles, show that Rawls's contrary view is ill-considered, explain why he makes the mistake that he does, and expose the importance of the present dispute.

The beginning of wisdom in this matter is to mark an ambiguity which Rawls misses in the slavery objection to utilitarianism. The words of the first two sentences of the exhibited passage formulate what are in fact two independent slavery objections to utilitarianism, but Rawls treats the two as variant expressions of a single objection. Objector A and objector B below are differently animated, but what A says is in line with the first sentence of the Rawls passage and what B says is in line with its second:

> A: I oppose utilitarianism because if we adopt utilitarianism then we might face circumstances in which (because it maximizes happiness) we should have to institute slavery, and I am against *ever* instituting slavery.
> B: I oppose utilitarianism because it says that if circumstances were such that we could maximize utility only by instituting slavery, then we should do so.

To see that objectors A and B are differently animated, observe that the stated single reply to their two objections (to wit, "slavery will never in fact be happiness-maximizing") should silence A but should leave B unsatisfied. A was worried that slavery might have to be imposed, in obedience to the utilitarian command. She learns that there is no such danger, so her reason for objecting to utilitarianism is overcome. But that slavery is not in fact optimific should cut no ice with B. B's objection was that whether slavery is justified should not be made to "*depend upon*" an "actuarial calculation." Saying that the result of such a calculation will always be reassuring is no reply to the objection that whether or not we institute slavery *shouldn't depend upon* such a calculation. (Note that, while B may, like A, oppose slavery under any circumstances, her objection commits her to no such stance. She might think slavery a just punishment for terrible misdeeds yet remain outraged at the thought that it would be right to impose it if it produced enormous happiness, at whatever cost in unhappiness to innocent slaves).

Observe that I used the word "adopt" in the statement of A's objection but not in the statement of B's. And that is because of the difference of status that the utilitarian principle enjoys in the different optics of the two objections. B attacks utilitarianism not as a rule for regulating our affairs that we might consider *adopting*, but as a principle that formulates the moral truth or, to speak with more meta-ethical neutrality (see section q. above), as a principle that formulates an ultimate conviction or commitment. But A attacks utilitarianism as a rule of regulation, that is, as a certain type of social instrument, to be legislated and implemented, whether by government itself or within social consciousness and practice. A principle of regulation is "a device for having certain effects,"[27] which we adopt or not, in the light of an evaluation, precisely, of its likely effects, and, therefore, in the light of an understanding of the facts. And we evaluate those effects, and thereby decide which fact-bound principles to adopt, by reference to principles that are *not* devices for achieving effects but statements of our more ultimate and fact-free convictions.

Rawls fails to distinguish between rules of regulation that we decide whether or not to adopt and (his expression) "first principles" that are not in that way optional. That is why he is able to endorse the utilitarian reply-procedure without qualification and that is why he is correspondingly able to believe that even first principles are rooted in fact. It is a fundamental error of *A Theory of Justice* that it identifies the first principles of justice with the principles that we should adopt to regulate society. Rawls rightly says that "the correct regulative principle for anything depends on the nature of that thing"[28]: facts are of course indispensable to the justification of rules of regulation. But rules of regulation necessarily lack ultimacy: *they* cannot tell us how to evaluate the effects by reference to which they themselves are to be evaluated. Sociology[29] tells us what the effects of various candidate rules would be, but a normative philosophy that lacks sociological input is needed to evaluate those effects and thereby to determine, jointly with sociology, what rules we should adopt.

If *A*'s objection were the only objection to *adopting* utilitarianism, *and* the factual reply to it were correct, then, for all practical purposes, the utilitarian principle would be fine. But only for all practical purposes, not otherwise, and not, in particular, for the purpose of formulating our ultimate convictions. Such convictions include a hostility to slavery that is not utilitarianly based, a hostility, be it noted, that is shared by any soi-disant utilitarian who thinks it necessary to cite the facts to silence objector *A*. And that hostility to slavery expresses the fact-free conviction that no beings characterized as human beings happen to be characterized should be in a relationship of slavery to each other (or some more qualified fact-free convictions that allows slavery under special circumstances: see note 25).

The question, What principles should we adopt? is not the question, What principles formulate our fundamental convictions? And an answer to the first question presupposes an answer to the second: in the sense of "adopt" that governs here, we adopt the principles that we adopt in the light of principles that we don't adopt. The distinction is transparently important, but it is not only not recognized but expressly rejected by Rawls, since he *identifies* the fundamental principles of justice with the principles that specially designed choosers would adopt for the sake of regulating society. Whatever the merits may be of that design, and whether or not it ensures a sound answer to the question as to what principles should be adopted, that the denizens of the original position ask and answer *that* question ensures that the output of the original position is not a set of first principles of justice.

The defender of Rawls's view might respond thus: "Fine. I accept your distinction between basic principles and principles of regulation. But why should I care about basic principles? I care about what we should *do*, and the principles of regulation that we adopt in the light of the facts determine that." The response is unsustainable because we necessarily have recourse to basic principles to justify the rules of regulation that we adopt: facts cast normative light only by reflecting the light that fact-free first principles shine on them.

The facts determine what questions will arise from (but *only* from) a practical point of view. Joshua Cohen infers that "we do not need to have principles of justice that address" circumstances that will not in fact obtain. So, for example, he continues, "we need not have anything definite to say about what we *would* do if [contrary to fact-based expectation] the satisfaction of the difference principle led to" great inequality.[30] Now, it is indeed true that in order to decide what to do we need say nothing definite, and, in fact, nothing at all, about that. But suppose that, like me, you think that political philosophy is a branch of philosophy, whose output is consequential for practice, but not limited in significance to its consequences for practice. Then you may, like me, protest that the question for political philosophy is not what we should do but what we should think, even when what we should think makes no practical difference.

t. My thesis, that principles which reflect facts reflect principles that don't reflect facts, is, if correct, of interest for several reasons.

First, it is of interest in itself, simply as a piece of neglected, and routinely denied, meta-ethical truth, one, moreover, which answers a meta-ethical question that is surprisingly distinct from the "is"/"ought" question.

But my thesis is also of interest, so I believe, because the fact-free principles that lie behind our fact-bound principles are not always identified in contexts where they should be identified, partly because neglect of the meta-ethical truth that I believe I have established has meant that there has been insufficient effort to identify them. And identifying our (one's, their) fact-free principles has value both for self-clarification and for clarification of what is at stake in controversy. Sometimes, to be sure, when we expose the unstated fact-insensitive principle that undergirds a fact-sensitive one, it will provoke no surprise. Sometimes, however, it will be unexpected. And it will always be worthwhile to expose it to view.

The thesis also has the merit that, as we saw in section s., it generates a distinction between ultimate fact-free principles and adopted rules of regulation, a distinction which, we also saw, refutes Rawlsian constructivism as a meta-theory of justice. For Rawlsian constructivism, fundamental principles of justice, for all that they are fundamental, which is to say, not derived from still *more* fundamental *principles*, reflect facts. Rawls believes that because he misidentifies the question "What is justice?" with the question "What principles should we adopt to regulate our affairs?" For facts undoubtedly help to decide what rules of regulation should be adopted, that is, legislated and implemented, if only because facts constrain possibilities of implementation *and* determine defensible trade-offs (*at the level of implementation*[31]) among competing principles. But the principles which explain, with the facts, why a given set of principles *is* the right one to adopt, don't reflect facts, and non-exposure of those more ultimate principles means failure to explain *why* we should adopt the principles that we should adopt.

The distinction between rules of regulation and the principles that justify them helps to illuminate what is at stake in normative controversy. Such controversy is better conducted when the status of the norm under examination – basic or regulative – is clearly specified. For example: Certain recent critiques of the "luck egalitarian" view of justice, while undoubtedly containing some good challenges, are disfigured by failure to distinguish between rejection of the luck egalitarian view as a proposed rule of regulation and rejection of it at the fact-insensitive fundamental level at which the view is properly pitched. Thus much (not all) of Elizabeth Anderson's broadside against the "luck-egalitarian" view of justice[32] highlights the effect of striving to implement the luck-egalitarian principle without compromise, but difficulties of implementation, just as such, do not defeat luck egalitarianism as a conception of justice, since it is not a constraint on a sound conception of justice that it should always be sensible to strive to implement it, whatever the factual circumstances may be.[33] Justice is not the *only* value that calls for (appropriately balanced) implementation: other principles, sometimes competing with justice, must also be variously pursued and honoured. And the facts help to decide the balance of due deference to competing principles: the facts constitute the feasible set that determines the optimal point(s) on a set of fact-independent indifference curves whose axes display packages of different extents to which competing principles are implemented. (That is why I emphasized "at the level of implementation" in the preceding paragraph. The trade-off values, the rates at which we are willing to allow reduced implementation of one principle for the sake of increased implementation of another, are *a priori*: the facts determine only which implementation packages are feasible).

Notes

1 The present paper is an abridged version of the original, which appeared in *Philosophy and Public Affairs* in 2003. Whole sections have been deleted: hence the gaps in the lettering of the sections. There are also other unrecorded deletions, and a few paragraphs have been added to section m. (A somewhat expanded version of the original article appears as Chapter 6 of my *Rescuing Justice and Equality*, Harvard University Press, 2008).

2 Thus Rawls writes: "Conceptions of justice must be justified by the conditions of our life as we know it or not at all," and he does not thereby mean to leave room for the affirmation of principles more ultimate than those of justice which do not depend on such conditions for their justification (*A Theory of Justice*, p. 454/p. 398: here and throughout Rawls references in that style cite pages from, respectively, the 1971 and 1999 editions of *A Theory of Justice* (Cambridge, MA: Harvard University Press)).

3 The italicized requirement constrains what is here said about an individual's principles, but it also serves as a heuristic device for highlighting truths about how normative principles justify and are justified, within a structure of normative principles, and independently of anybody's belief. In speaking of the structure of the principles held by someone who is fully clear about her principled commitment, I am speaking not only, precisely, of that, but also of the structure of a coherent set of principles as such, and, therefore, more particularly, of the structure of the principles that constitute the objective normative truth, *if* there is such a thing.

4 "Absent other considerations" is required because other principles might override the stated principle when it is stated without that rider. To reduce the danger of irritating the reader, I won't in what follows always insert this phrase where it is plainly required.

5 Cf. the heuristic role assigned to the "clarity of mind" stipulation at note 2 above.

6 As some anti-Humeans think: see section l. below.

7 Note that the possibility acknowledged within these parentheses does not imply that such a methodological principle might explain, in the absence of any further normative principle, why a certain fact supports a certain principle. That further supposed possibility contradicts my second premiss: see section g(ii) of the unabridged version of this article.

Gerald A. Cohen

8 See "What the Tortoise Said to Achilles," in Lewis Carroll, *Symbolic Logic*, William Warren Bartley, III (ed.) (Hassocks, West Sussex: Harvester, 1977), pp. 431–4.

9 See, e.g., Jonathan Dancy, *Moral Reasons* (Oxford: Blackwell, 1993), Chapters 4–6, and John McDowell, "Virtue and Reason," in *Mind, Value, and Reality* (Cambridge: Harvard University Press, 1998), pp. 57ff.

10 No thesis about what Hume himself thought is material to my purpose. If he is thought to have said something different, and more problematic for my purposes, then it would be that different thing that matters (and I would welcome its being aired), but not that Hume said it.

11 How could it, there being nothing about "is-to-ought" in the premises used to reach it? One might say: if you don't include a prohibition on going from "is" to "ought" in the premises, you won't find one in the conclusion.

12 That "if"-clause is enforced by the point about the conditionality of my thesis that was made in section *k*.

13 I of course think that Humeans, too, should adopt my position, but only because it is the correct position, not because it follows distinctively from the Humean position. My position follows distinctively *only* from the anti-Humean position.

14 Compare the distinction between ultimate principles and fact-bound principles of regulation that is laid out in section s. below: facts about agent incapacity are the end of the matter with respect to the latter principles but not with respect to the former.

15 I personally believe in moral objectivity with respect to these matters. But note that it is only if (≠ if and only if) one *adds* something like a thesis of moral objectivity to my denial that facts control morals that one can suppose that my argument has been a rationalist one, one that says that moral norms come *a priori* from *reason*. *A priori* (that is, non-*a-posteriori*) they come, but, as far as the present paper's claims are concerned, not necessarily from reason.

16 See *A Theory of Justice*, pp. 158–61/pp. 137–9; "Kantian Constructivism in Moral Theory," in *Collected Papers* (Cambridge, MA: Harvard University Press, 1999), pp. 343–6; and "Themes in Kant's Moral Philosophy," in *ibid.*, pp. 510ff.

17 *A Theory of Justice*, p. 158/p. 137, my emphases.

18 "For all that Rawls shows" puts the case mildly: I believe that not much reflection is required to see that "Don't cause too much inequality" is either itself fact-insensitive or immediately dependent on a closely related fact-insensitive principle. Accordingly, Rawls's illustration of the supposed unobjectionability of fact-dependent "first principles" not only fails to illustrate the latter but also illustrates the very opposite of what Rawls seeks to illustrate.

19 See, further, *A Theory of Justice*, p. 536/p. 470; *Justice as Fairness: A Restatement* (Cambridge, MA: Harvard University Press 2001), p. 67.

20 *A Theory of Justice*, p. 159/p. 137.

21 In his *Lectures on the History of Moral Philosophy* (Cambridge, MA: Harvard Universtiy Press, 2000) Rawls characterizes Leibniz's "ethics of creation" as one that "specifies principles that lie in God's reason and guide God in selecting the best of all possible worlds" (p. 108, and cf. p. 107). So Rawls perhaps means, in the exhibited curious *Theory* passage, that the *function* of fact-independent principles is to determine what the general facts of nature are to be. The right reply to which, here, is: they might have that function for God, but they need not therefore have that function for us.

22 *A Theory of Justice*, pp. 159–60/p. 138. There is, in my opinion, a tension between the quoted methodological statement and an element in Rawls's account of reflective equilibrium – see the reference to "all possible descriptions" at *ibid.*, p. 49/p. 43 – but I shall not pursue that claim here.

23 I emphasize "calls" because "rational intuitionism" is too specific a name for the wide family of positions about principles each member of which, so I have argued (see section q.) is consistent with denial that facts affect ultimate principles.
24 See the penultimate paragraph of section g(ii) above on the relationship between them and us.
25 In my forthcoming discussion of this passage I shall prescind from the occurrence of this (as I believe it to be) infelicitous modifier.
26 *A Theory of Justice*, pp. 158–9/p. 137, emphasis added.
27 Robert Nozick, *The Nature of Rationality* (Princeton, NJ: Princeton University Press, 1993), p. 38.
28 *A Theory of Justice*, p. 29/p. 25.
29 Including armchair sociology, which is sometimes enough, or nearly enough, for the purpose stated here.
30 "Taking People as They Are?", *Philosophy and Public Affairs* 30 (4) (2001), p. 385. Cf. the discussion of the difference principle and "excessive inequality" at p. 33.
31 For a comment on this phrase, see p. 38.
32 Elizabeth S. Anderson "What Is the Point of Equality?," *Ethics* 109 (1999); Cf. Samuel Scheffler, "What Is Egalitarianism", *Philosophy and Public Affairs*, Winter (2003).
33 Richard Arneson makes a related point in his reply to Anderson when he contrasts "a set of principles of justice" with "a specification of just institutions or just practices": see his "Luck Egalitarianism and Prioritarianism," *Ethics* 110 (2000): 345.

Constructivism, Facts, and Moral Justification

Samuel Freeman

In justice as fairness the first principles of justice depend upon those general beliefs about human nature and how society works.... First principles are not, in a constructivist view, independent of such beliefs, nor ... true of all possible worlds. In particular, they depend on the rather specific features and limitations of human life that give rise to the circumstances of justice. – (John Rawls)[1]

Kant famously advocates an ethics of "pure reason" which says that the fundamental principles of moral conduct and their justification are not to contain any empirical concepts. No major twentieth-century moral philosopher was influenced by Kant more than Rawls. Yet Rawls rejects Kant's idea that first moral principles are to be formulated and justified independent of contingent assumptions. Rawls's position might be explained on general philosophical grounds: along with many contemporaries, he rejected the dualisms underlying Kant's and other traditional philosophical positions, including distinctions between analytic and synthetic, pure vs. empirical reason, necessary vs. contingent truths, and a priori vs. a posteriori propositions.[2] But general philosophical reasons of the kind that Quine, Wittgenstein, Dewey and others relied upon are not the reasons Rawls gives for invoking general facts to justify his principles of justice. His reasons are specific to moral theory, as befits his claim of "the independence of moral theory" from metaphysics and epistemology. And these reasons relate to the one notable exception among Kant's dualisms that Rawls retains: Kant's sharp distinction between the theoretical vs. the practical uses of reason.

My aim here is to discuss some reasons why general facts should be relevant to a justification of fundamental principles of justice. G. A. Cohen argues the opposing position. He advocates

the a priori thesis that, if facts ground principles, then fact-free principles are at the foundation of the structure of the belief of anyone who is clear about what they believe and why they believe it, just as it is a priori that anyone who is rational maximizes, or satisfices, or whatever.[3]

Cohen's criticism is directed against constructivism in moral philosophy.[4] He says, "Constructivists about justice . . . believe that all sound principles are, as I shall say, fact-sensitive, by which I mean neither more nor less than that *facts form at least part of the grounds for affirming them.*" Now strictly speaking, this is not true of Kant's constructivism, for whom the reasons for the Moral Law are a priori and based in "pure reason" alone.[5] Nor does Rawls regard "all sound principles" as "fact-sensitive" (for example, the veil of ignorance and formal constraints of right are not). But Rawls does contend that his "fundamental principles of justice" are based in certain general facts about the human condition. Since Cohen's account of constructivism is closely tied to features of Rawls's constructivism, I will focus on that. I leave aside Rawls's later political constructivism, since it can take no position on the meta-ethical issues Cohen raises. Only justice as fairness regarded as a (partially) comprehensive constructivist position set forth in *A Theory of Justice* and "Kantian Constructivism in Moral Theory" is at issue here.

I discuss three reasons why the first principles of a moral conception of justice should be "fact-sensitive" or presuppose general facts in their justification:

(1) First, a conception of justice should be *compatible with our moral and psychological capacities.* It should respond to basic human needs; moreover, given their natural tendencies, conscientious moral agents who affirm the conception should be capable of developing appropriate attitudes enabling them to normally act upon its demands.

(2) Second, a conception of justice should provide *principles for practical reasoning* and fulfill a *social role in supplying a public basis for justification* among persons with different conceptions of their good.

(3) Third, *a moral conception should not frustrate, but should affirm the pursuit of the human good.*

In order to meet each of these reasonable conditions, a conception of justice must take into account facts about human nature and social cooperation in justifying first principles of justice. I argue for this thesis in sections II–IV. Before that, I clarify what Cohen and I mean by "fundamental principles of justice" and what is at stake in this dispute.

I: What Are Fundamental Principles of Justice?

Suppose we were constructed by nature so that we had equal concern for everyone and cared no more for our own well-being than the next person's. We might then, as Hume says, have no need for property and other norms of distributive justice, for then we would be willing to produce and share goods and services without self-concern. Similarly, suppose nature were so bountiful that all our desires could be satisfied without anyone's labor or forbearance – the objects of our wants appear "like manna from heaven." Again we would have no need for property or distributive justice. But circumstances are different. We are characterized by "limited altruism" – we have attachments to particular persons or groups and care more for our own projects and commitments than for others'. Also there is "moderate scarcity" of goods – enough

Samuel Freeman

to meet everyone's needs, but never enough to satisfy all their desires; thus humans must produce, save, and invest their product to satisfy present aims and future ambitions. These "circumstances of justice" give rise, Hume says, to the "cautious, jealous virtue of justice." Were general facts about humankind entirely different we might have no need for rules of property and principles of distributive justice that determine who should receive and control income and wealth in exchange for specified contributions. Rawls follows Hume in regarding justice as a particularly human virtue.

It might be replied that none of this shows that the *content* of principles of justice, or what they *require of us*, is either conditioned upon and or justifiable by appeal to facts about human nature. Whether justice requires that we maximize aggregate goodness, or distribute goods equally, or according to need, or effort, or contribution, or to maximally benefit the least advantaged, or to redress the effects of brute luck, or whatever the criterion – it's *this* question that is not dependent upon facts about human nature but rather upon moral considerations that ultimately are "fact-insensitive." Cohen says "Ultimate principles cannot be *justified* by facts"[6] (FP 212, emphasis added), not that they cannot contain any allusions to facts. Yet Rawls explicitly appeals to general facts about human nature (our limited altruism and psychological tendencies of reciprocity) and social phenomena (the chain-connection and close-knitness of economic distributions) to argue that the difference principle is preferable to the principle of utility or a stricter egalitarian principle. As I understand Cohen, this is the problem, namely conditioning the *justification* of principles of justice upon general facts about human propensities, economic tendencies, and social institutions. The problem is that when facts are invoked to justify principles of justice, these principles then cannot be *fundamental* principles but rather must be the application or extension or "implementation" of fundamental principles to particular factual circumstances. For this reason, Rawls's difference principle cannot be the "fundamental," "ultimate," or "first principle" of distributive justice (all being terms Rawls's uses).[7]

In support of Rawls's position, the following four levels of normative principles can be distinguished. They are to be found not only in Rawls, but also Sidgwick, Mill, Kant, and other major moral philosophers:

(1) *Substantive moral principles*, which are among the *basic principles of conduct (for individuals or institutions)*; examples include Rawls's two principles of justice, the principle of utility, Kant's Moral Law, W. D. Ross's seven prima facie principles of Right, Nozick's entitlement principles. I contend that these principles of conduct are *fundamental* in that they are the ultimate standards that determine if and when actions, laws, and institutions are right or just.

(2) *Principles of justification*, which are among the ultimate reasons and considerations which are used to justify the substantive principles of justice mentioned in (1). These justifying reasons have a different function than providing ultimate standards for right conduct or just distributions; they have primarily an epistemic role. Examples would be Rawls's ideal of free and equal moral persons, the formal constraints of right (universality, generality, publicity, etc.), and the veil of ignorance, all of which are part of the original position; or Kant's assumption of practical freedom in his "transcendental deduction" of the Moral Law; or Sidgwick's principles of impartial benevolence and of equity (treat similar cases similarly), used to justify the principle of utility; or Harsanyi's

impartiality condition and assumptions regarding rational choice and equiprobability of outcomes, used to justify a principle of average utility; and perhaps (as he regards it) Cohen's luck egalitarian principle. Some account of practical rationality and moral reasoning and justification normally accompany principles of justification and is utilized in the justification of fundamental principles of conduct for individuals and institutions.

(3) *Principles of application*, which are used to determine what (1) substantive principles of justice require; examples include "equal consideration is to be given to equal interests" in applying the principle of utility; or the final three stages of Rawls's "Four-stage sequence" for applying the principles of justice; or Kant's categorical imperative procedure for applying the Moral Law.

(4) *Secondary principles and rules of conduct*, which result from the application of first principles of justice in (1); examples are rights of freedom of speech and expression that liberals contend are justifiable by a principle of liberty; the rules of a constitutional, property-owning democracy that Rawls contends are justified by applying the principles of justice; or the rules of a capitalist welfare state that welfare economists justify on grounds of the principle of utility; or duties of fidelity, veracity, and charity justified by many moral conceptions.

Within this four-part schema, epistemic principles of justification (at level 2) do not themselves determine when actions, laws and institutions are right or just. For example, there is nothing about Rawls's ideal of free and equal moral persons, the five formal constraints of right, the veil of ignorance, and the account of rational plans of life, taken by themselves, that would determine whether one distribution is more just than another, or whether socialism, property-owning democracy, welfare-state capitalism, or laissez-faire capitalism are required by justice. Instead, these justificatory principles are among the relevant reasons that must be taken into account in arguing for and justifying substantive principles of distributive justice by way of the original position. It is not the role of these principles of justification to provide the ultimate standard for just distributions. To know the standards to use to decide which economic institutions or distributions are more or less just, we have to look at the fundamental substantive principles of justice themselves (the difference principle, the principle of utility, libertarian entitlement principles, or some other account of distributive justice).

Cohen holds that so long as a principle has a justification via other "normative principles," it cannot be a fundamental principle.[8] This implies that nothing can be a *fundamental* substantive principle of conduct unless it is itself self-evident, or follows from non-factual methodological principles. But the fact that normative justificatory principles (e.g. an impartiality condition implicit in the veil of ignorance) are needed to argue for ultimate substantive principles of justice should not deprive the latter of their status as fundamental moral principles. What *makes* a substantive principle of conduct fundamental is not that it is self-evident or otherwise without normative justification, but that *it is the ultimate standard for determining conduct and there are no more basic principles of which it is an application*. Thus, for Rawls distributions of income, wealth, and powers and positions of office are just when they result from an economy designed to implement fair equality of opportunity and the difference principle. There is no more fundamental principle to which we can appeal to determine just distributions; the second principle is the limit.

Cohen himself distinguishes between "justifying principles" and "regulative principles." He contends that Rawls's principles of justice are regulative principles, and that *as such* they are non-fundamental: only justifying principles, like the principles informing Rawls's ideal of free and equal moral persons, can be fundamental principles.[9] But the regulative nature of the principles of justice should not make them any less "fundamental" than the principles used to justify them. For justificatory principles and regulative principles of conduct work at different levels. The former are the argumentative ingredients that combine to provide epistemic support for regulative principles. But importantly, they are *not adequate by themselves to tell us what we ought to do* or how we ought to structure social institutions and relations. Instead, justificatory principles provide *fundamental reasons* that enable us to decide what are the *equally fundamental substantive principles* of conduct that regulate what we are to do. This justifying role is taken on in Rawls by the conception of free and equal persons, the veil of ignorance and other assumptions that go into Rawls's original position; they are among the "restrictions that it seems reasonable to impose on arguments for principles of justice, and therefore on these principles themselves" (TJ 18/16 rev.) Utilitarians such as R. M. Hare and John Harsanyi would argue the same is true of the impartiality assumptions and accounts of rational choice as utility-maximization that underlie their impartial choice arguments for a principle of utility. These fact-free principles are fundamental reasons for accepting fundamental substantive principles of conduct. Hence, the fact that substantive principles of justice have a justification should not undermine the claim that *substantive principles are the fundamental principles of justice to which we ultimately are to appeal in social and political relations in deciding how to structure institutions and make laws and other rules of conduct*. There are *no more basic principles*, including fundamental principles of justification, which taken by themselves can answer *that* question for us.

But this diverts us from the main issue; which is whether *factual* considerations can play any role in establishing what I am calling first principles of conduct. Cohen says, "Ultimate principles cannot be justified by facts" (FP 219). Rawls denies this and goes against a long tradition in philosophy which says that the justification of fundamental moral principles must depend only on a priori truths. Rawls says, to the contrary, that fundamental principles of justice must invoke and rely upon general facts about human tendencies and social cooperation. His opponents, including Cohen and Habermas,[10] reply that once empirical considerations are invoked to support principles we have no longer a fundamental principle, but rather something less: an "application" (Habermas) or "implementation" (Cohen) of some fact-free fundamental principle(s). In the following three sections I address and take issue with Cohen's and Habermas's claims that only fact-insensitive principles can be fundamental principles of justice.

Why is this issue important? What's the point behind Cohen's "meta-ethical truth" that "Ultimate principles cannot be justified by facts" (FP 219)? It might be purely philosophical, akin to Kant's ambition to discover the principles regulative of "pure practical reason" whatever its empirical conditions. Another reason is the fear that appeals to facts make moral principles contingent on circumstances, thereby raising the specter of relativism.[11] But if the facts Rawls appeals to are permanent and apply generally to human beings as such, then there should be no threat of the cultural relativism of moral principles of justice (which is the kind of relativism that matters practically speaking). Finally, a third factor that might be motivating Cohen's critique is that, if his argument regarding facts and principles is true, then it might insulate his luck egalitarian thesis from recent criticisms. I return to this issue in the concluding section.

II. Justice, Human Needs and Moral Capacities

The first reason cited earlier for the relevance of facts to first principles of justice is:

(1) *A conception of justice (like any moral conception) should be compatible with our moral and psychological capacities.* It should be responsive to basic human needs and interests, at least in so far as conscientious moral agents who affirm the conception should be capable of developing appropriate attitudes enabling them to normally and regularly act upon its demands given the constraints of human nature.

A primary example of a fact about human beings that is relevant to fundamental moral principles is the value that we put upon self respect. By "self respect" I mean a psychological attitude that includes a sense that our individual lives matter and are worth living, that our primary pursuits are also worthwhile, and that we are capable of realizing these pursuits. In traditional societies a shared religion often provided a principal basis for self-respect, but in a modern democratic society, self-respect generally depends upon others' recognition of a person as an equal citizen. If we were strongly disconnected selves, with little sense of our own good or even of our past or future, we would not be so concerned about either self-respect or others respect for us as persons; nor would we likely be so concerned about individuals' rights. As Derek Parfit argues, this might strengthen the case for the principle of utility. It is safe to assume that our sense of our personal identity is not based in our having a soul or being an immutable substance. It is a contingent fact whether we are psychologically dissociated, disconnected selves, or are "strongly connected" with a sense of our selves and our good. This suggests that self-respect is a contingent belief and attitude too.

Rawls says that self-respect is perhaps the "most important primary good" (TJ 440/386 rev.). The parties in Rawls's original position consider the effects of principles and institutions on their sense of self-respect in comparing and deciding on principles of justice. Among the bases of self-respect, Rawls contends, are principles and institutions that maintain persons' status as equal citizens, including equal political liberties, equality of fair opportunities, and other equal basic rights and liberties. Why should we be concerned about having *equal* liberties and equal fair opportunities, rather than *just enough* to do what we need or seek to do? Here the bases of self-respect and our desire to be regarded as equals play a central role in Rawls's argument for egalitarian principles and institutions. Principles of justice are responsive to the "basic needs" of persons who conceive of themselves as we do. Other primary goods Rawls recognizes (liberties, powers and opportunities, and income and wealth) also have an empirical basis in psychological and social tendencies.

It might be replied that the goodness or desirability of these primary goods is not contingent upon facts. Even if our desire for self-respect depends upon the psychological fact that we conceive of ourselves as strongly individuated selves with a past and a future, still it is *good*, independent of any such facts about ourselves, that we have such a strong sense of individual self and a concomitant desire for self-respect. If we met with a tribe whose members had no long-term aims or life-plans and little or no sense of individual self, but who lived like drones always selflessly serving some dominant communal end (maximizing the King's pleasures and offspring, for example), we rightfully would think this is a bad way for people to live since it results in their exploitation and violation of human rights. Even if they do not think of themselves as worthy individuals with their own purposes and separate lives to live, still they *should* since maintaining individual dignity, or free self-development and individuality (for example) are fundamental human goods. So, the objection continues, even if Rawls were to rely only upon psychological and social facts to justify the primary goods, they nonetheless have an independent philosophical grounding in moral values he does not invoke.

Rawls himself might be interpreted as providing (on the Kantian interpretation, TJ §40) a non-empirical grounding for the primary social goods. The Kantian interpretation suggests that our conception of ourselves as unified selves extending over time with ends and a life-plan of our own is not simply a contingent fact, but is rooted in the conditions of rational moral agency, the moral powers, which constitute our "nature as free and equal rational beings." For a person to act and have reasons at all requires having a coherent plan of life and developed moral powers. Otherwise, like drones, one is a being to whom things just happen and whose behavior is aimless and without reason, or at most a being without self-awareness who does not act but rather engages in activities (like dogs digging bones – there is aim-directed activity but not action).[12] On the Kantian justification of the primary social goods, they are no longer contingent needs of persons who happen to conceive of themselves as we do. They are rather necessary conditions for fully realizing rational and moral agency.

Perhaps then the contingent grounding of primary social goods (and therewith principles of justice) might be replaced in some way by this or some other argument from their necessity. Still, it is not so clear that the relevance of other factual grounds to principles of justice are expendable. Suppose that principles of justice demand more of us than we are humanly capable of doing. It is often argued that the principle of utility makes extraordinary demands on people. A sincere and conscientious utilitarian is a person who should have no special concern for himself or herself and who impartially promotes everyone's interests. But it is beyond our capacities to forgo whatever aims and interests we have and develop a settled disposition *always* to take everyone else's interests *equally* into account and act to maximize overall utility. To contend that we nonetheless *ought* to do so when we by nature *cannot* is to make an unreasonable demand. How can a reasonable morality demand something realistically impossible for people?

One way to mitigate or neutralize the effects of the "ought implies can" requirement is via the indirect application of moral principles. Thus, the principle of utility might avoid the problem of imposing unreasonable demands by "effacing" itself (Parfit) and becoming "esoteric" (Sidgwick). Given the limitations of human nature perhaps the best way to maximize utility may be to inculcate in people a non-utilitarian morality whose rules, when generally observed, in fact create greater utility than any other rules humans are capable of regularly observing. On this indirect and esoteric application of the principle of utility, it can be argued that we indeed are capable of complying with the demands of the principle of utility, by directly observing other moral rules designed to take our limitations into account.

The indirect and "esoteric" application of a moral principle is one way to reconcile "ought implies can" with an overly demanding principle that is beyond human capacities for regular compliance. Sincere conscientious moral agents then are those who are committed to acting on and from the secondary moral rules that best implement the overly demanding principle (e.g., of utility) in light of human nature. This may be one way to defend Cohen's claim that "regulative" principles of justice are not ever fundamental but rather "implement" fundamental principles. Regulative principles might be regarded in the same manner as indirect utilitarians conceive of secondary moral principles; they are applications of more fundamental normative principles which are beyond our capacities regularly to comply with if directly applied. I do not think that Cohen himself would accept the "esoteric" approach to fundamental principles, largely for reasons I discuss momentarily. Next I will discuss features of a contractarian conception of justice that prevent the esoteric approach, and show why facts must be taken into account in the justification of ultimate principles of justice.

III: The Social Role of a Conception of Justice

(2) *A conception of justice should provide moral agents with principles for practical reasoning and fulfill a social role in providing a public basis for justification among persons with different conceptions of their good.*

To orient discussion of this second methodological condition, consider Cohen's and Rawls's different conceptions of political philosophy:

(i) "The question for political philosophy is *not what we should do but what we should think*, even when what we should think makes *no practical difference*" (G. A. Cohen, "Facts and Principles," p. 243, emphases added).

(ii) "A conception of justice is framed to meet the *practical requirements of social life* and to yield a public basis in the light of which citizens can *justify to one another* their common institutions" ("Kantian Constructivism in Moral Theory," Rawls's *Collected Papers*, p. 347, emphases added).

These statements reveal a significant difference between Rawls's and Cohen's conceptions of the role of a moral conception of justice. For Cohen its role is mainly theoretical; in the first instance a moral conception seeks the truth regardless of its practical consequences for social relations and cooperation. Of course, any moral theory seeks truth in the ordinary sense that it is an inquiry into, and justification of the *correct principles*. But if one thinks of moral truth and the role of a moral conception as making potentially "no practical difference" (Cohen, FP, p. 243), then it is hard to avoid the idea that principles of justice are prior to and independent of

Samuel Freeman

our practical reasoning about them as moral agents who are situated and engaged in social life. Rawls suggests that philosophers who regard moral philosophy as a search to discover the truth of antecedent normative principles are not going to be in a position to see the possibility of constructivism as a distinct method in ethics.[13] For the unmediated quest for true moral principles, pursued as if they are to be discovered by theoretical reason like any other basic theoretical laws or principles, leads to neglect of the arguably equally important conception of the person and its relationship to principles of justice, and neglect therewith the *social role* of moral principles.

The primary role of a conception of justice for Rawls is a *practical* (as opposed to theoretical) and *social* one. This means: (1) A moral conception is geared to provide, not all possible rational and reasonable beings, but rational and reasonable persons like us, who conceive of ourselves as free and equal moral agents and who are subject to the constraints of human nature, with *practical guidance* regarding what *we* ought to do. To fulfill this practical role, fundamental moral principles should provide us with *principles of practical reasoning* that we can reasonably accept and knowingly apply in our capacity as free and equal moral agents. (2) A moral conception has a *social role*, to provide beings like us with a *public basis for justification* regarding our moral, social, political relations. These two conditions on a conception of justice suggest that fundamental moral principles of justice ought to be *publicly knowable and generally acceptable* to those to whom these principles apply, so that principles can fulfill their practical and social roles as *principles of practical reasoning for free and equal moral agents, providing us with practical guidance and a basis for public justification suitable to our status as free and equal persons.*

Assigning priority to the practical and social roles of a moral conception rules out formulating a moral conception true of all possible worlds.

> Some philosophers have thought that ethical first principles should be independent of all contingent assumptions, that they should take for granted no truths except those of logic and others that follow from these by an analysis of concepts. Moral conceptions should hold for all possible worlds. Now this view makes moral philosophy the study of the ethics of creation: an examination of the reflections an omnipotent deity might entertain in determining which is the best of all possible worlds. Even the general facts of nature are to be chosen. Certainly we have a natural religious interest in the ethics of creation. But it would appear to *outrun human comprehension*. (TJ 137 rev., emphases added)

Rawls's point is that there is something misguided in conjecturing a morality for all possible worlds. Moral philosophy should take up the *practical perspective of moral agents* engaged in deliberation about what he or she (or groups of which they are members) ought to do. This contrasts with an epistemological point of view of the detached observer who seeks moral truth by inquiring into the way the world (or all possible worlds) really is or ought to be. Constructivism situates the inquiry into moral principles practically by asking not (simply) "What moral principles should I believe correct or true?" but "What principles of justice ought I endorse and act upon in my capacity as a free rational moral agent with human propensities and situated in the social world?"

So conceived constructivism puts center stage a conception of the person as moral agent and seeks to discover principles of justice that are most appropriate for expressing/realizing this conception. A conception of the person as free and equal, reasonable and rational moral agent is then interwoven into the content of principles of justice. By contrast, rational intuitionism and related views, due to their direct inquiry into true moral principles unmediated by their social or practical roles, are led to eschew any conception of the person as a central feature of a moral conception. The *social role* of morality and the related *publicity* condition on first principles are relevant to this conception of persons. Rawls endorses the following: (A) *respect for persons as free and equal moral persons* requires that we *justify our conduct to them* on terms that they can *reasonably accept* in their capacity *as* rational moral agents; (B) the *freedom and equality* of moral persons requires that they be in a position to *know and accept* the fundamental moral bases of their social relations.[14] I discuss the implications of (A) in this section, and of (B) in section IV.

Reasonable acceptability: How do general facts enter into the justification of moral principles, *given* the contractarian assumption of reasonable acceptability of principles to persons in their capacity as free and equal persons? What does attending to general facts have to do with respect for people as free and equal moral persons? Contractarians inspired by Kant (Rawls and Scanlon are the primary examples) contend that to respect persons as rational moral agents requires that the basic moral principles structuring and regulating their relations be *justifiable to* them. Rawls understands this idea (justification to a person) to mean that *principles are to be shown to be reasonably acceptable to persons in their capacity as free and equal moral agents with moral and rational capacities and a conception of their good, and in view of general facts about humans and their social relations.*[15]

There are a number of ways to work out the contractarian idea of "justification to a person," suggesting potentially several different kinds of contract views. (For example, what kind of knowledge are people presumed to have to whom justifications are made? What are their desires and interests? Are people presumed to be situated in the status quo, a state of nature, or behind a veil of ignorance?) I will focus on but one issue, namely, whether we are to assume that the hypothetical moral agents to whom contractarian justifications are directed are subject to general facts of human nature and social life, and take these facts into account in comparing and deciding on the acceptability of alternative principles? Or are they to leave aside considerations regarding human capacities and social cooperation in deciding whether principles are more or less reasonable? On the one hand it might be argued that moral persons, who are by definition reasonable and hence morally motivated, should not take into account these facts, and instead should agree on principles that apply whatever the facts about their nature and circumstances turn out to be. Then they would be choosing principles true of all (or many) possible worlds. The principles that these hypothetical people could or would agree to would then be designated the most reasonable principles of justice for us. On the other hand, it might be argued that since all moral persons known to us are subject to human tendencies, in justifying principles *to* them we should take into account general facts about human nature such as our tendency to disagreement in philosophical, religious, and moral convictions, our different commitments and conceptions of the good, and the fact that our capacity to act on and from moral principles is constrained by natural psychological

Samuel Freeman

tendencies (such as limited altruism). The principles of justice that free and equal moral persons would or could agree to, in light of their distinctly human tendencies and general social conditions, are likely to be quite different than if they did not take into account the human condition at all.

Rawls and Scanlon opt for this second position. Principles of justice are to be justifiable *to* reasonable and rational persons with natural human tendencies and who are subject to normal conditions of social life among beings with different conceptions of their good. It would be *unreasonable* to impose demands on people that did not take their natural propensities and limitations into account. One consequence of our human nature under free conditions is that we do have different interests and final aims as well as conflicting philosophical, religious and moral beliefs. For this and other reasons humans have different conceptions of the good and of what gives their lives meaning. Rawls seeks principles of justice which take these "subjective circumstances of justice" into account, and which can gain general acceptance within a *feasible social world* among reasonable and rational persons constrained by human propensities. The aim is to find the conception of justice that respects us, not simply as reasonable and rational beings, but as distinctly *human* persons who regard themselves as free and equal.

Assume it is a condition of the (philosophical) justification of a moral conception that it be able to fulfill the social role Rawls assigns to it – namely, it should be capable of providing a *public basis for justification* of social and political relations among persons who are reasonable and rational, who regard themselves as free and equal, and who have different conceptions of the good. To fulfill this role, reasonable people must find a moral conception "reasonably acceptable," meaning (in part) (1) that their human capacities enable them to regularly comply with its demands, and (2) they can accept it for moral reasons and not simply because it is the best compromise they can reach in pursuit of their non-moral interests. A conception of justice must then engage our "moral nature," including our capacities for a sense of justice. The crucial point here is that, to fulfill a social role of public justification, a moral conception cannot place such great demands upon people's natural capacities or permissible conceptions of their good that it exceeds their capacities for compliance or consistently frustrates their pursuit of their reasonable aims and commitments. Any moral conception which exceeds these factual limitations is *unreasonable*.

This responds to the problem raised at the end of the preceding section, where I discussed how two-level moral conceptions might satisfy the "ought implies can" requirement by applying fundamental moral principles indirectly to conduct. The problem with this is that, given their *social role, moral* principles of justice have to serve free and equal persons with a human nature as *public principles of practical reasoning* that *agents themselves can apply as citizens* to determine and justify their institutions and actions. It is because of this *social role of fundamental principles of justice* that the "self-effacing," "esoteric" approach to first principles of justice will not suffice. Sincere, conscientious moral agents have to be capable of understanding, accepting, applying, voluntarily acting upon and sincerely committing themselves to first moral principles. Their acceptance and commitment to principles assumes that principles are publicly known and fulfill a social role in providing a basis for public justification of laws and basic social institutions. Otherwise principles are unreasonable for free and equal persons; they fail to respect persons as free and equal with the capacities to reason about justice and do what justice requires for its own sake. The idea that basic principles of justice should be publicly knowable and serve a social role by providing a public basis for justification among conscientious moral agents with different conceptions of their good is then implicit in recognition and respect for others as free and equal persons.[16]

To decide on the reasonableness of moral principles means that we need to know a good deal about human psychology, economics, and biology – including knowing the normal stages of development of people's moral sensibilities – in order to determine what people's moral and other capabilities are and the limits of their tolerance of restrictions upon reasonable conceptions of their good. For example, if a moral conception places such great demands on some people well beyond their capacities for willing compliance (the less advantaged, for example, are required to give up achieving their primary aims so that those more advantaged may enjoy still greater rewards), then this is a compelling, perhaps sufficient reason for disqualifying that moral conception. (Rawls rejects utilitarianism for this and other reasons.)

IV. Justice and the Human Good

(3) *A moral conception should not frustrate, but should affirm achievement of essential human goods.*

There are different ways to construe this third condition, depending upon how the human good is conceived. I will elaborate the claim by reference to Rawls's "full theory of the good" in *A Theory of Justice*. Accordingly, (3) becomes the thesis (3"): A conception of justice should enable us to realize (a) the *values of community*, and (b) our nature as rational moral agents, making possible the good of *individual and moral autonomy*. Non-Kantians may find these claims [(3") (a) and/or (b)] unacceptable but might still accept the more general claim (3) on grounds of some other conception of the human good.

Rawls's non-consequentialism presupposes that the concepts of "the Right" and "the Good" require different principles. He characterizes the good in terms of rational choice, or according to certain principles of rationality. Generally, a person's good is the rational plan of life that person would choose under hypothetical conditions of deliberative rationality (with full knowledge of relevant facts, fully understanding the consequences of choice, etc.). Rawls contends other principles formally characterize morality and the concept of right. These "reasonable principles" occupy a different position within our practical reasoning than do the "rational principles" providing shape to rational life plans and individuals' good. The role of reasonable principles is to regulate individuals' and groups' pursuit of their rational good and constrain their choice of ends. But if the Right regulates and subordinates the Good, how can acting right and justly according to reasonable principles be a good or rational activity for a person? The problem of "congruence" of the Right and the Good is to show that justice and reasonableness can themselves be rational and integral to a person's good. Within Rawls's framework, congruence requires a showing that it is rational for each person in a well-ordered society of justice as fairness to cultivate a willingness to do justice *for its own sake*.

52 | **Samuel Freeman**

A critic might reply that the congruence problem is not essential to deciding the content of first principles of justice.[17] For what justice requires must be independent of the question whether it is good for us to do what justice requires. Some philosophers have argued that whether or not it is good for any person to do their duty is irrelevant to the question of what duty should be.[18] This conception of morality, as detachable from the human good, led Nietzsche to regard "morality" as a calamity for us. For, being entirely independent of the human good, the constraints morality imposes must stunt the development and exercise of higher human capacities, thus undermining the realization of human flourishing. Why then should we not regard the promptings of our moral sense of justice as neurotic compulsions, resulting from a sense of weakness and inferiority, or a fear of authority? The requirement that a conception of justice be "congruent" with the good is responsive to these and similar criticisms. A reasonable constraint on a conception of justice is that its principles and ideals not undermine the human good, but be compatible with, and ideally even affirm it. If so, then the crucial point for my purposes is that general facts about human nature are integrally related to most any reasonable conception of the human good. For whether some activity or state of affairs is a good for a person depends upon that person's capacities to engage in or enjoy it.

Now assume that the good for any person consists (at least in part) in their exercising and realizing their distinctively *human* capacities. This resembles a psychological claim that Rawls calls the "Aristotelian principle." This "deep psychological fact" (TJ 379 rev.) suggests (roughly) that human beings generally enjoy activities that engage the exercise of their realized capacities, and their enjoyment increases the more the capacity is realized and the greater an activity's complexity (TJ 374 rev.). (Thus (Rawls's example) assuming a person is equally proficient at chess and checkers, he or she will normally prefer playing chess to playing checkers.) Absent special circumstances, to leave one's mature capacities undeveloped normally results in a life that will be found boring and unsatisfactory. Rawls contends that "accepting the Aristotelian principle as a natural fact" (TJ 376 rev.), it is rational for individuals to realize and train mature capacities, and to choose plans of life that in significant measure call upon the exercise and development of their complex human capacities (id.).

Now, relying on the Aristotelian Principle, there are two *intrinsic human goods* Rawls appeals to in *A Theory of Justice* to confirm and thus justify the principles of justice:

(A) *The Good of Community*: The Aristotelian principle enables Rawls to argue that development and exercise its *own sake* of our social capacities for a sense of justice are integral to a person's good since they enable a person to participate in a social union of social unions.

It follows from the Aristotelian Principle (and its companion effect) that participating in the life of a well-ordered society is a *great good* (§79). . . . Because such a society is *a social union of social unions*, it realizes to a preeminent degree the various forms of human activity; and given the social nature of mankind, the *fact* that our potentialities and inclinations far surpass what can be expressed in any one life, we depend upon the cooperative endeavors of others not only for the means of well-being but to bring to fruition our latent powers. . . . Yet to *share fully* in this life we must acknowledge the

Constructivism, Facts, and Moral Justification   53

principles of its regulative conception, and this means that we must affirm our sentiment of justice. . . . What binds a society's efforts into one social union is the *mutual recognition and acceptance of the principles of justice*; it is this general affirmation which extends the ties of identification over the whole community and permits the Aristotelian Principle to have its wider effect. (TJ 500 rev., emphasis added)

The details and soundness of Rawls's argument for the good of a social union of justice are beyond the scope of my discussion. But the general point can be made without the details. Rawls is trying to show how "the values of community" (which would include "solidarity" and "fraternity") are part of the human good. This is a central feature of many moral conceptions of justice, including G. A. Cohen's. Rawls contends that in order to realize the good of community, individuals must act on and from the correct principles of justice. Whether or not one accepts Rawls's justice as fairness, the general point is: Assuming that the values of community are partially realized by people *complying with correct principles of justice for their own sake*, then a moral conception that affirms that community is essential to the human good must in turn rely upon general facts about human nature and peoples' capacities to act on and from the appropriate principles of justice. Thus, when Cohen himself maintains that community, solidarity, or having an "ethos of justice" are human goods (as he suggests elsewhere)[19] then it seems that his principles of distributive justice also must be responsive to human social capacities for justice and to pursue and achieve their good. Otherwise, the purported good of community and the ethos of justice would not be achievable and perhaps would be beyond human reach.

(B) *Moral Personality and Moral Autonomy*: Rawls's second argument for congruence of the Right and the Good is more controversial, for it stems from Rawls's "Kantian interpretation of justice as fairness" (TJ §40). In general, Rawls's Kantian interpretation rests upon an account of human agency and practical reasoning: By virtue of the moral powers to be reasonable and rational (our capacities for justice and for a rational conception of the good), we are capable of engaging in practical reason and acting on the reasons that the Right (morality) and the Good (rationality) provide. These capacities also enable us to form and rationally pursue a conception of our good, and therewith they enable us to unify our lives and provide "unity to the self" (TJ §85). In *Theory* Rawls says the moral powers constitute our "nature as free and equal rational beings." The aim of Kantian Interpretation and of Kantian Constructivism is to depict the principles of justice as derivable from a "procedure of construction" (the original position), which itself "models," "represents," or "expresses" these capacities for moral and rational agency. Kant defines autonomy as acting from principles that reason legislates for itself. One point of Rawls's Kantian constructivism is to provide content to this troublesome idea. Since the principles of justice are "constructed," via the original position, upon the basis of the capacities that constitute our "nature and free and equal rational beings," Rawls can say that the principles of justice are among the principles that reason "gives to" or "legislates for itself" out of our nature as free and equal reasonable and rational beings.

The general point for my purposes is that, the justification and content of principles of justice are conditioned by the moral powers, these *"natural attributes"* (TJ 444 rev.). To be a morally autonomous agent who freely designs and acts upon a conception of the good in compliance with principles that are the product of our

Samuel Freeman

moral powers for practical reasoning, we have to take into account the contingencies of human nature and the optimal conditions for the development and exercise of these same capacities. Again, suppose we were empirically constructed so that we did not expect reciprocity from others with whom we cooperate; instead, we have no more concern for our own well-being than that of complete strangers, and our sense of justice is more responsive to (Sidgwick's) principle of impartial benevolence than to Rawls's reciprocity principles. Then it may well be that the principle of utility would be the most suitable principle for the development and exercise of our capacity for a sense of justice, and therewith realizing this essential good. But given human nature, the principle of utility does not express or realize our capacities for justice and the good. It is beyond the capacities of even the most sincere and conscientious utilitarian to regularly act upon the demands of the principle of utility. As Rawls's psychological principles of reciprocity state, we tend to form attachments to principles and institutions that do not undermine, but rather support our pursuit of our good. This is good reason for preferring Rawls's principles of justice to the principle of utility, assuming that a conception of justice should be compatible with the human good. And the argument depends upon natural facts about our capacity for a sense of justice, including the fact that it is more likely to be developed and realized by the principles of justice than the principle of utility.

V. Methodological Remarks

Returning now to Cohen, first I will consider very briefly a potential defense of his thesis, and then will conclude with some remarks on the practical significance of this issue. Cohen's thesis is that fundamental principles are a priori and "fact-free" and that once facts are stated in support of any principles, they must be secondary principles that are implementations of fact-free fundamental principles. Consider the following defense of Cohen's thesis, suggested by Gideon Rosen.[20] Any allegedly "fundamental" fact-sensitive principle, such as Rawls's difference principle, can be incorporated as the consequent of a complicated conditional statement which has as its antecedent a priori justifying principles (Pn) conjoined with a (conditional) statement of all the facts (F_n) which together justify that fact-sensitive principle (D). (Grossly simplifying: $[(P_n \text{ & } F_n) \rightarrow D]$.) This complicated conditional statement does not itself assert the truth of any facts, and thus is itself "fact-free." Now given the added premisses F_n stating the facts in the antecedent of this complicated conditional, the fact-sensitive principle D follows (by modus ponens). But if so, then Cohen is correct: any fact sensitive principle D can be shown to presuppose a fact-free principle in the form of our complicated conditional statement.

I am not sure whether Cohen would accept Rosen's claim as a friendly amendment to his argument. It raises several questions and issues which I can only mention, but am not in a position to adequately address here. First, how are we to individuate principles? Is the complicated conditional $[(P_n \text{ & } F_n) \rightarrow D]$ a principle, or is it a concatenation of numerous fundamental and subordinate moral principles, methodological conditions, conditional facts, and logical connectives and operators? Second, how can this complicated conditional serve as a "fundamental principle" in Cohen's sense (see note 6)? (Could it really be, on anyone's account, self-evident, or follow from any reasonable methodological principle?) Third, is the complicated conditional capable of serving a public social role as a principle of practical reasoning that individuals and deliberative groups apply (see Part III), or is it simply too long, complicated, and beyond normal comprehension for those purposes? Fourth, does Rosen's claim assume that Rawls's argument for the principles of justice is a deductive argument? If so wouldn't this mischaracterize the nature of the argument from the original position, which surely is not so linear and tightly drawn?[21] Instead, the original position argument is a number of distinct reasons and arguments whose conjunction establishes a preponderance of reasons in favor of choosing the principles of justice over all the other alternatives principles considered. Finally, does Rosen's claim presuppose that logical connectives and operators and rules of inference that are part of the complicated fact-free conditional statement are themselves propositional? If so then this raises the question whether the logical form of sentences and rules of inference such as modus ponens can serve as premises of arguments or objects of cognition from which we reason? Are they rather not the conditions of judgment and inference that make reasoning possible?[22] Again, these and other questions would need be addressed to respond adequately to Rosen's claim. It would be interesting to see whether Cohen himself would welcome Rosen's suggestion, or regard it as contrary to his purposes.

Finally, what of practical significance is at stake in Cohen's "meta-ethical" argument? Again, Cohen says:

> Certain recent critiques of the "luck egalitarian" view of justice . . . are disfigured by failure to distinguish between rejection of the luck egalitarian view as a proposed principle of regulation and rejection of it at the fact-insensitive fundamental level at which the view is properly pitched. . . . [D]ifficulties of implementation, just as such, do not defeat luck egalitarianism as a conception of justice, since it is not a constraint on a sound conception of justice that it should always be sensible to strive to implement it, whatever the factual circumstances may be. (FP 244)

Oddly, this argument parallels Rawls's own remarks regarding luck egalitarianism, or what he calls "the principle of redress" – "to redress the bias of contingencies in the direction of equality" (TJ 86 rev.). Rawls like Cohen says this principle cannot be used by itself to decide distributions, but only in conjunction with other considerations. But rather than contending that the principle of redress is a "fundamental principle" as Cohen does, Rawls says, "It is plausible as most such principles are only as a *prima facie principle*, one that is to be weighed in the balance with others" (TJ 86). Rawls regards the luck egalitarian principle as a component of moral intuitionism (in his sense), the view that there are a plurality of prima facie principles that are to be taken into account and weighed against one another to decide what is right or just to do. This seems to be Cohen's contention too; in deciding on the regulative principles of distributive justice for structuring economic institutions and distributing income and wealth, we are to assign appropriate weight to undeserved contingencies, along with other principles, and then redress peoples' situations as much as circumstances allow. But why call these luck egalitarian considerations, "fundamental principles"? What if the luck egalitarian intuition is grounded in some more fundamental principle; perhaps, as Rawls conjectures, the difference principle?[23]

Here Sidgwick's account of first ethical principles is relevant. Sidgwick says first principles (i) must be at least as *certain* as any other moral principles, (ii) of *superior*

Samuel Freeman

validity to other principles; and (iii) *really self-evident*, deriving their validity, or evidence, from *no other principles*. This closely resembles Cohen's criteria for fundamental principles. Like Cohen's argument against Rawls, Sidgwick's account of justice (*Methods*, Bk. III: Ch. 5) is designed to show that none of the principles of justice found in common sense morality meet his criteria for first principles, and hence must be "middle axioms," or subordinate principles.[24] Suppose Cohen's luck egalitarian principle, suitably elaborated, meets Sidgwick's conditions listed above. Still, there are further requirements Sidgwick imposes that Cohen's principle cannot meet: (iv) First principles must contain *no limitations, or exceptions, or restrictions*, unless these are self-imposed; that is, follow from the principle itself, and are not simply appended as unexplained provisos; (v) First principles *cannot be prima facie principles* but must yield judgments of "actual rightness," all things considered; (vi) First principles must *systematize* subordinate principles to organize them into *a complete and harmonious scheme*; (vii) They must serve for rational agents as *an actual guide to practice*, and *cannot be vague, imprecise, or ambiguous*; (viii) a first principle must be one that *corrects our pre-reflective judgment*.[25] Rawls's principles of justice meet these further conditions much better than Cohen's luck egalitarian principle. (For example, note the parallel between (vii) and the publicity requirement, which requires that first principles serve reasonable and rational agents as principles of practical reason. Sidgwick's requirement in (vii) that first principles be actual guides to practice is one that Cohen's luck egalitarian principle, regarded as a justificatory principle, cannot meet.) Sidgwick argues of course that the principle of utility satisfies all conditions better than any other alternative he considers. But Rawls rejects (iii) the requirement of self-evidence because of his constructivism and reflective equilibrium (and rejects perhaps (i), (ii), and (iv) depending on how they are construed), and argues that the principles of justice are superior to the principle of utility when measured by conditions resembling (v)–(viii), *plus* other appropriate conditions discussed above in sections II–IV.

This is not an argument against Cohen. But it raises the questions, (1) what other methodological conditions, in addition to those he mentions, he imposes on a conception of justice; (2) whether and if so why he rejects the four further conditions, (v)–(viii), which are accepted by both Rawls and Sidgwick as conditions on first principles; and more generally (3) what conception of practical reasoning underlies Cohen's conception of justice and moral justification?

Finally, Cohen's claim that the luck egalitarian principle is a fundamental justifying principle leaves open the possibility that Rawls's account of distributive justice may be true when regarded as principle of regulation in Cohen's sense. This is not far off from Rawls's claim:

> Although the difference principle is not the same as that of redress, it does achieve some of the intent of the latter principle . . . The difference principle represents, in effect, an agreement to regard the distribution of natural talents as in some respects a common asset and to share in the greater social and economic benefits made possible, by the complementarities of this distribution. Those who have been favored by nature, whoever they are, may gain from their good fortune only on terms that improve the situation of those who have lost out. (TJ 87 rev.)

Unlike intuitionists, for whom the luck egalitarian principle is to be weighed against other relevant principles to decide a just distribution, for Rawls the principle of redress is regarded as a "common sense precept of justice" (TJ §47) which, along with other precepts (to reward people according to their needs, their efforts, and their contributions, among other considerations) is to be accounted for by the difference principle when all relevant considerations are taken into account in reflective equilibrium.

The likelihood that some version of the difference principle is consonant with Cohen's luck egalitarian principle is also suggested by Rawls's political liberalism.[26] According to it justice as fairness can be regarded as a "political conception of justice" that fits as a "module" within reasonable comprehensive moral doctrines, which are in an "overlapping consensus" about justice in the ideal conditions of a well-ordered society. So regarded justice as fairness would be, within these doctrines, clearly derivative and non-fundamental. But political liberalism is not a concession to Cohen's argument. Rather, it avoids such meta-ethical issues and provides another way to regard justice as fairness as the correct conception of justice without disturbing Cohen's anti-constructivist position. I on the other hand have tried to make the philosophical case for rejecting Cohen's argument against constructivism, based in an alternative account of moral justification than the one he endorses.[27]

Notes

1   "Kantian Constructivism in Moral Theory," The Dewey Lectures 1980, in John Rawls, *Collected Papers*, Samuel Freeman, ed. (Cambridge, MA: Harvard University Press, 1999), p. 351 (cited as *CP* in text).

2   Rawls specifically notes at the beginning of the Dewey Lectures that there "There are a number of affinities between justice as fairness and Dewey's moral theory which are explained by the common aim of overcoming the dualisms in Kant's doctrine" (Id., *CP* 304).

3   G. A. Cohen, "Facts and Principles," *Philosophy and Public Affairs* 31 (3) (2003): 211–45, at 233 (cited as FP in text).

4   Cohen indicates that "Facts and Principles" is part of a larger project he calls "Rescuing Justice from Constructivism." This manuscript has been published as *Rescuing Justice and Equality* by Harvard University Press, where he restates the argument in "Facts and Principles." All my remarks here are based on that earlier paper and do not take into account any changes or additions Cohen makes in the subsequent manuscript.

5   Here I assume the "Moral Law" is Kant's fundamental principle. It's true that the categorical imperative, an instance of the Moral Law, applies to "beings with needs." Similarly, the principle of utility applies to beings like us who are capable of experiencing pleasure and pain. But as I understand Cohen, this factual limitation in the range of application of these principles does not mean that they presuppose empirical facts in their justification. Cohen's position is that *if* there are sensuous beings who have these experiences, their pleasures are to be maximized in the aggregate. This does not require that any such beings actually exist.

6   "Ultimate principles cannot be justified by facts. . . . [These] fact-free principles might be self-evidently true, or they might for some other reason require no grounds, or they might need grounds and have grounds of some non-factual sort (they might, for example, be justified by some methodological principle that is not itself a normative principle but a principle that says how to generate normative principles), or they might need grounds but lack them, or . . . they might be judged to be outside the space of grounds." (FP 219)

7   To support his claim that Rawls's principles of justice are not "fundamental principles," Cohen points to the assumption of free and equal persons behind the original position

Samuel Freeman

(FP 238) and other fact-free justifying principles implicit in Rawls's argument for the difference principle, such as "one ought not cause too much inequality" (FP 236). This suggests (to Cohen) that Rawls himself relies on more fundamental fact-free principles to justify his principles of justice (that moral persons ought to be treated equally, etc.). Other "fact-free" fundamental justifying principles Rawls invokes that Cohen might have mentioned are the formal requirements of right (including generality, universality, ordering of claims, finality and publicity), as well as the strong impartiality condition implicit in the veil of ignorance.

8   See the quotation from FP 219 in note 6 above. Cohen says that what makes principles (or reasons) "ultimate" or alternatively "foundational" is that they are at the "summit" (a term he uses) in the chain of reasons that justify substantive (or regulative) moral principles. Seemingly for Cohen only (some) justifying principles can be "ultimate" or "foundational" principles. Also, Cohen says that "constructivists about justice" hold that "*all* sound principles are . . . fact sensitive [and that] facts form at least part of the grounds for affirming them" (FP 213). But in the quote from Rawls that Cohen uses to support this claim (FP 213n), Rawls says that "*Conceptions* of justice must be justified by the conditions of our life as we know it or not at all." Conceptions of justice for Rawls consist of both substantive and justificatory principles regarding morality and practical reason. For Rawls's it is *substantive principles of justice* that must be fact-sensitive, and not all justificatory principles. As Cohen himself notes (see note 7 above), many of the assumptions in the original position (the conception of free and equal moral persons, the veil of ignorance, etc.) are not fact sensitive in Cohen's sense. On the other hand, *if* Cohen's claim that "[for constructivists] *all* sound principles are . . . fact-sensitive" is meant to be a point about Rawls's *reflective equilibrium*, then it may be true. For Rawls there are no fact-free foundational principles that are taken as self-evident, necessary, or dogmatically unrevisable whatever new information we might encounter. This is in the nature of establishing a reflective equilibrium of moral principles with considered moral convictions, including fact-sensitive moral convictions, at all levels of generality. Cohen rejects such "holism" but says "even if true, holism (and quasi-holism) do not threaten my proceedings" (FP 223).

9   Cohen says that his argument "refutes Rawlsian constructivism as a meta-theory of justice" (FP 243). One reason he gives is that Rawls fails to distinguish between "principles of regulation and the principles that justify them" (FP 244). Consequently, "he misidentifies the question 'What is justice?' with the question 'What principles should we adopt to regulate our affairs?'" (Id.) Rawls's principles of justice cannot be fundamental principles of justice, for these must be principles of justification on Cohen's account.

10 Habermas rejects Rawls's stability argument as part of the justification of the principles of justice, since it appeals to a number of facts about human nature and social cooperation. See Jürgen Habermas, "Reconciliation Through the Public Use of Reason," *Journal of Philosophy* 92 (March 1995). Rawls replies in Lecture IX of *Political Liberalism*, "Reply to Habermas."

11 Thanks to Sebastiano Maffetone for pointing this out.

12 David Velleman draws a distinction between action and activity in his *The Possibility of Practical Reason* (Oxford: University Press, 2000), Ch. 1, and Christine Korsgaard similarly distinguishes between actions and acts in her Locke Lectures.

13 "A consequence of starting with methods of ethics defined as methods that seek truth is not only that it interprets justification as an epistemological problem, but also that it is likely to restrict attention to the first principles of moral conceptions and how they can be known. First principles are however only one element of a moral conception; of equal importance are its conception of the person and its view of *the social role of morality*. Until these other elements are clearly recognized, the ingredients of a constructivist

doctrine are not at hand" ("Kantian Constructivism in Moral Theory," Rawls's *Collected Papers*, p. 342).

14 Here freedom is to be taken, among other ways, in the sense of persons' rational autonomy as authors of their life plans and their moral autonomy as authors of moral laws. Knowing and accepting moral principles of course is a precondition for acting for the sake of moral laws, which is required by moral autonomy.

15 Scanlon has a somewhat different conception of justification to a person, that is tailored to his more general project of providing an account of moral duties we owe to each other.

16 The social role of principles is closely related to T. M. Scanlon's idea that correct moral principles are those that could not be reasonably rejected as a basis for general agreement and justification among people who are conscientious and morally motivated.

17 Brian Barry makes this criticism in his review of Rawls's Political Liberalism, in "John Rawls and the Search for Stability," *Ethics* 105 (4) (July 1995): 874–915.

18 H. A. Prichard, "Does Moral Philosophy Rest on a Mistake?" (1912) in his *Moral Obligation* (Oxford: Clarendon Press, 1949), Ch. 1.

19 See *If You're an Egalitarian How Come You're So Rich?* (Cambridge, MA: Harvard University Press).

20 This reconstructs my understanding of Rosen's argument, which he suggested at the 2006 UNC Philosophy Colloquium. No doubt he could make the argument more persuasively than I do here.

21 I am grateful to Michael Williams for this suggestion. Rawls concurs in *Justice as Fairness*, pp. 133–4.

22 I am grateful to R. Jay Wallace and to Mark LeBar for discussion of this point.

23 See Rawls, TJ, 318/280 rev. There's nothing on its face that makes the difference principle "fact-sensitive." One might contend that it should be intuitively obvious or "self-evident" that, since the social product is jointly produced and the most advantaged rarely work as hard or experience the gravity of risk that the least advantaged do, then fairness requires that the economy be designed to maximize the share going to the least advantaged over their lifetimes. Whether this is an appropriate way to regard the difference principle – as an intuitively obvious fundamental principle (in Cohen's sense) that accounts for our luck egalitarian intuitions – Cohen's account does not seem to rule it out.

24 Among the subordinate principles Sidgwick discusses are a principle of equal freedom, *Methods*, pp. 274ff.; and principles of distribution according to conscientious effort, actual contribution, "fair price," and free market value, *Methods*, pp. 283ff., etc.

25 For an account of these conditions see the "Lectures on Sidgwick," Lecture I, in Rawls's *Lectures on the History of Political Philosophy* (Cambridge, MA: Harvard University Press, 2007).

26 Cohen has other arguments against the difference principle elsewhere. But his arguments do not appear to invalidate the difference principle itself but only Rawls's interpretation of it as applying directly to the basic structure, and only indirectly to individual actions. "Why not apply it directly to both?" (Cohen asks in effect).

27 I am grateful to: Andrews Reath for his extensive comments, and to Tom Hill, Gideon Rosen, Philip Kitcher, and other participants at the 2006 University of North Carolina, Chapel Hill Philosophy Colloquium; to Michael Williams, Steven Gross, and other members of the Johns Hopkins Philosophy Department; to Bruce Brower and others at Tulane University, to Mark LeBar, Alyssa Bernstein, and other members of the Philosophy Department at Ohio University; to Sebastiano Maffetone and Ingrid Salvatore and others at LUISS in Rome; and to Kok Chor Tan, Samuel Scheffler, and R. Jay Wallace, all for their helpful remarks and criticisms.

Samuel Freeman

Reason and the Ethos of a Late-Modern Citizen

Stephen K. White

Through much of the tradition of Western political thought, an appeal to reason occupies a central role. In that appeal, there resides a conviction that an orientation to reason carries with it at least some sort of initial traction for our engagement with the most significant problems of political life. By "traction," I do not mean merely an instrumental grip on problems in the sense of a rational strategy that promises to efficiently enhance my self-interest.[1] Rather, I also mean at least a minimal cognitive and dispositional grip in the sense of some orientation toward justice and general well-being. When one appeals to reason in this fuller sense, one has what I will call an "emphatic" conception of practical reason.[2]

In the history of Western political thought, this emphatic character was often represented by images of intense light and penetrating vision. Think of Plato's description of emerging from the cave into the light. Or think of the representations of Enlightenment ideals in the eighteenth century that show the sun penetrating through the rain clouds and bringing renewed warmth, clarity, and well-being to the town below.[3] Translated into moral-political terms, reason in this sense promises to reveal a clear foundation of universal, just principles that can slacken the propensity to social conflict and rise above the discordant particular claims of different traditions, classes, religions, and nationalities. Such an emphatic conception of practical reason came in for increasingly intense criticism in the twentieth century. The most important line of critique for present purposes is the one usually seen as stretching from Max Horkeimer and Theodor Adorno's *Dialectic of Enlightenment* in 1947, as well as Martin Heidegger's essays of that period, to the work of Michel Foucault and other post-structuralists beginning in the 1970s and continuing today.[4] At the most general level, these philosophers argue that those who have operated within the dominant spirit of the Enlightenment have failed to understand adequately a danger underlying the determined pursuit of freedom and reason. The confident pursuit of these ideals in the form of universalizing ideologies and techniques of human organization betrays an unacknowledged will to dominate. This will knows itself only as a benign desire to subdue nature and to reform the recalcitrant qualities of self and society, all in the name of an increasingly just and progressive society. A wholehearted adherence to this range of projects became all the more pressing as religion was increasingly pushed toward the margins of modern life. The loss of Christianity's promise of immortal life had to be compensated for by the promise of an unending expansion of human capacities and well-being. The anxiety of finitude was thus displaced by a will to dominate that increasingly brought with it what one might call a sense of immanent infinitude. Edmund Burke was perhaps the first to perceive this phenomenon. He saw it taking shape in the French Revolution. Even before the period of the Terror, when rooting out enemies of the revolution became an unending task for true patriots like Robespierre, Burke saw in the great revolutionary festivals a new sense of the infinitude of human will and reason.[5]

Curiously enough, then, it is a conservative who first develops the key insight out of which radical critics of the twentieth century launch their arguments. The claim is that entangled with the admirable ideals of enlightened Western life is a more disturbing and unacknowledged willfulness. Divine Providence has been replaced by a mode of reason that embodies "an attentive 'malevolence' that turns everything to account."[6] It is only after we have fully embraced the world as standing completely open to our projects that we can – with the best of intentions – find ourselves simultaneously pursuing emphatic notions of reason and freedom, while at the same time persistently expanding the reach of what Foucault famously calls "disciplinary power" and "normalization."[7]

Thus, for Foucault and the other twentieth-century critics of modernity, attempts to reason toward justice and common good that style themselves as anything like the beneficent spreading of light into darkness are deeply deficient. Although Foucault, as well as Horkheimer and Adorno, often spoke as if this deficiency extended to every possible variant of emphatic practical reason, they should not be taken at their most hyperbolic word. There is evidence in each case that they did not so much condemn emphatic reason per se, as they counseled far more caution and self-reflection in our appeals to reason.[8] We always retain at least some capacity to develop dispositions and practices that persistently chasten reason's grand promise to reconcile the different voices of humankind.

The overall aim of this paper is to offer a sketch of what such an appeal to a *chastened, but still emphatic* notion of practical reason might look like, and what sort of core normative disposition or ethos we might affirm as appropriate to a reason that bears this late-modern burden. I want to refer to such a chastened appeal and minimal orientation as expressing the qualities of "reasonableness." When I call upon you to be reasonable in this sense, I have an expectation that, first, is oriented by the acceptance of certain *late-modern insights* that can be gathered under the umbrella concern of an insufficiently acknowledged will to dominate; and, second, takes the form of a kind of *moral attentiveness* and *restraint* displayed in relation to the clashing voices that engage one another within the spaces of reason-giving that together constitute the characteristic infrastructure of late-modern ethical-political life. I will refer to one who manifests such a disposition as having embraced an ethos of late-modern citizenship. In sum, I will be trying to bring to life this idea of a spirit or disposition that we can draw upon as a resource for engaging the institutions, practices, and competing faiths of contemporary political life.

Stephen K. White

I understand "reasonable" to be an essentially contested concept.[9] This means that the criteria for applying the concept will always, at least potentially, be a matter of dispute. There may be, however, clear consensus on some minimal criteria for the use of the concept; specifically, I would argue that the ones just noted – attentiveness and restraint – constitute such criteria. While there might be relatively strong agreement here, things get more contentious when one tries to specify exactly how one is supposed to satisfy these criteria in different contexts.

My intention is to delineate how this might be done within four analytically distinguishable, but overlapping, spaces of reason-giving: where agreement is sought involving the justice of basic social and political structures; where reasons are articulated for affirming the "foundations" or "sources" of our ethical-political judgments and actions; where reason is appealed to in the struggle for recognition of identity; and where we argue about and pursue the progressive realization of democracy. Within each of these four interrelated spaces, we can delineate a corresponding core ethical disposition that, in turn, is animated by a particular set of ontological figures. The constellation of disposition and supporting figures will provide a minimal content in relation to which the expectations of attentiveness and restraint will be oriented within the respective spaces. A late-modern ethos of citizenship will accordingly display its full character in the judgments and actions of individuals who sustain this fourfold set of expectations.

I will take up only the first three of these spaces of reason-giving. I have elsewhere dealt with the fourth.[10] Accordingly, the paper is divided into three sections that correspond to those first three sites. **Section I** considers the site upon which one seeks possible grounds for cooperation involving the basic fairness of social and political structures. A major reason for starting here is that Rawls's efforts on this terrain can function both as an aid and as a foil for my own. In *Political Liberalism*, he proposes an exemplary way of construing what it means to be reasonable in this space, and how that orientation constitutes a central component of a late-modern account of justice.[11] Rawls calls his principles "political" in the sense that they can be agreed to in a fashion that is "freestanding" in relation to foundational philosophical or religious views.[12] This strategy of argument makes good sense generally, but I will draw attention to one way in which his account is in fact dependent on foundational commitments. By this I mean that his criteria for what it means for a person to be reasonable are quite strong; and, as Charles Larmore has persuasively argued, the only way he can justify so strong a definition is through a tacit affirmation of the foundational moral idea of equal respect and a corresponding ontology that constitutes persons as entities having dignity and thus being worthy of respect.

My intention in calling attention to this foundational element in Rawls is not to contest directly the validity of his theory of justice. Rather, it is to help isolate one of the central moral-ontological constellations within which a persuasive notion of a late-modern reasonableness can take shape. Another way of saying this is that Rawls may not be obliged to worry about implicit foundational issues, given his specific goal of constructing a political conception of justice, but I am, given my task of providing a sense to the idea of an ethos that reflects more broadly on the relation of reason and politics today.

In **Sections II and III**, I pursue this task further by teasing out what it might mean to be reasonable in relation to the other two sites. In **Section II**, I consider more directly the site where we articulate the central ontological figures that provide the foundations or sources of our core normative claims in ethics and politics. In **Section III**, I turn to what is often called the struggle for recognition of identity. This third site is somewhat different from the first two. These two have traditionally been at the center of political reflection in the Western tradition. What is different today is exactly how we orient ourselves on two sites. But the very existence of the third site is to a significant extent an artifact of late-modern times.[13]

My overall intention is to elucidate how the claim to reasonableness would draw us to be attentive and exercise restraint at each of these three sites. The criteria of attentiveness and restraint operate differently at each site; but the claim to reasonableness at one site is constitutively entangled with the corresponding claim to reasonableness on the other two. One whose action embodies such a full, threefold claim can be said to manifest what an emphatic but chastened reason might mean for a late-modern citizen.

I. Site One: The Terms of Cooperation

Rawls's *Political Liberalism* is a justly famous effort to sketch out what the implications are of appealing to "reasonable" individuals for the purpose of constructing a theory of justice. He understands this appeal to reason as one that (in my terms) is chastened but still emphatic. It is chastened by a primary insight or lesson to be learned from the history of modern Western political life: that the clashes between different conceptions of the good show no signs of being definitively resolved in favor of any one of them; and, accordingly, we must take account of this underlying "fact of reasonable pluralism" when we reflect upon political life today.[14] A failure to accept this fact leaves a society open to political domination by one group or another claiming the right to enforce its view of the good. A theory of justice that rejects this kind of claim must configure itself in such a way that it remains, as I noted a moment ago, freestanding in relation to any particular foundational, or, in Rawls's words, "comprehensive" moral or political view. Rawls's theory is thus chastened in the sense that it disallows appeals to reason that claim to be capable of peering through and fully resolving differences between alternative foundational claims. A theory of justice such as his finds its basis of agreement at the level of an "overlapping consensus" between adherents to different, but reasonable, comprehensive views of the good.[15]

If this is the way Rawls interprets reason's being chastened, how does he interpret its being emphatic? This is apparent in the normative and dispositional content he assigns to being "reasonable." Being "reasonable" means that one is willing "to propose fair terms of cooperation and to abide by them provided others do." One is to be attentive to a standard of fairness between competing claims; and to restrain oneself so as to affirm and seek agreement on only those political arrangements that embody such a standard. In the same spirit, one restrains any propensity for intolerance of comprehensive doctrines one might dislike, as long as they can plausibly be seen as within the bounds of reasonable pluralism.[16]

For the most part, Rawls's interpretation here of attentiveness and restraint in relation to the matter of the justice of basic structures seems to me to make good sense. It also makes good sense for him to seek to make his account of justice as freestanding as he can. But, as I indicated earlier, it is not entirely freestanding. Larmore

Stephen K. White

has made this point quite clearly.[17] He contends that Rawls's notion of reasonable agents who are willing to seek and abide by fair terms of cooperation tacitly builds into his account an "underlying view of human dignity and of the respect we thereby owe each other and every human being."[18] In other words, it is only individuals already embracing this disposition of equal respect who will be motivated to orient themselves toward agreement on fair principles of cooperation. If Rawls did not presuppose this core normative disposition of respect and some ontological figure of dignity that orients it, then the notion of "reasonable" would have to contract to something weaker – and thus less useful – like "exercising the basic capacities of reason and conversing in good faith."[19]

What exactly is the status in Rawls's theory of this implicit affirmation of dignity and equal respect? Larmore thinks Rawls is not as clear as he should be about this issue.[20] Rawls does not claim that his theory of justice is totally freestanding in relation to all moral-ontological foundations. He admits that it may require the affirmation of some minimal content; but such affirmation is justified only if it is "necessary to the political aim of consensus."[21] Presumably, Rawls would find this to be the case with regard to dignity and respect, although he does not explicitly say so. If he did clearly affirm dignity and equal respect, would that mean he owes us some sort of further justification of its foundational character? Probably not; rather he would argue that his affirmation merely reflects what is already a widely shared assumption in "modern democratic society." It is simply the cultural presence of this affirmation that is the key issue for getting his conception of justice started.[22] As long as dignity and respect are affirmed, he need not look further into issues of how such an affirmation is justified.

This stance is perfectly plausible from the point of view of Rawls's intention to construct a political conception of the justice of the "basic structure" of a society.[23] But from the broader perspective I am taking in this paper – an ethos of late-modern citizenship – such a stance of non-engagement with the foundational issues above cannot be justified. The reason for this is that such an ethos inquires not only about the justness of basic structures, but also about how we go about "living . . . the structures" (in Charles Taylor's words).[24] This means we must be as concerned with everyday dispositions and motivations, as we are with fundamental structures. Rawls does, of course, imagine that citizens who live in a fully just state would adequately internalize his basic principles and thus spontaneously support such an order. But perhaps the matter of individual obligation and motivation in the midst of political contest would never be so simple. If so, then even in a relatively just polity one would need to think further about how a given ethos might, here and now, bias the reproduction of social structures in directions that are more rather than less hospitable to justice.

A useful way of understanding what is at issue here might be to consider the range of concerns expressed by J. S. Mill in "On Liberty." Mill certainly wants to have a political system with just constitutional and other legal structures. But he is also concerned with a broader ethos of citizenship that will help motivate individuals to go beyond the minimum obligation to obey just laws. This broader ethos emerges in relation to what is, in essence, a basic insight about social life in modern democratic societies; namely, the emergence of the threat of a "tyranny of . . . prevailing opinion and feeling."[25] This is the danger presented by the pressure to conform to majority opinion that operates not just inside of the constitutional and legal structure, but also outside of it. In this context, one can see Mill as appealing to an ethos of reasonableness that reaches beyond legal obligation. It draws its cognitive and motivational force from the foundation to which he appeals; that is, his basic sense of what a morally progressive individual and society look like.

In order for this sort of ethos to be robustly sustained in everyday life, one would expect that the foundation animating judgment and action would be more consistently scrutinized, refined and drawn upon as I confront new situations to which it must be applied. As long as we stay with Rawls's structural portrait, we are not expected to have to draw upon foundations in such situation-inflected ways. But at the level of ethos, where we are pressed by this expectation of congruence between a specific situation requiring judgment and my foundational commitment, it seems plausible to think that we will begin to discover ways in which the implications of my foundations will run counter to those of yours.

In sum, one can say that an ethos of late-modern citizenship will motivate us to affirm a "political conception of justice" (for example, either Rawls's or some roughly comparable, procedural one) to a substantial degree, but it will not insulate us entirely from mutual engagement and contestation regarding how our moral-ontological foundations draw us toward some courses of action versus others. Given that such an ethos thus cannot avoid some entanglement with foundational issues, what guidance might it provide at this more basic level of reflection?

II. Site Two: Ontological "Sources" and Their Resistance to Full Articulacy

An adequate answer to the foregoing question will require, first, some general account of the activity of reflecting on one's most basic beliefs and commitments. I will argue that the two most familiar ways of envisioning such reflection – uncovering foundations and choosing frameworks – are insufficiently sensitive to the insights of late modernity. More adequate would be a variant of the account Charles Taylor offers with his notion of "sources of the self".[26] I want to elucidate this model, showing how and why it is superior for present purposes to the two more familiar ones (A). Then I turn to fleshing out the way such a portrait of our ontological-ethical background helps specify the sort of attentiveness and restraint that would have to be displayed at this site by a reasonable individual (B).

A. In its most general sense, reflection upon what is basic to human beings is a search for meaning in light of human finitude. I mean by the latter, first, that we have foreknowledge of our mortality; and, second, that this knowledge tinges the important aspects of our lives, whether we want it to or not.[27] When we think of reflecting upon what gives our lives meaning, we tend, as I suggested above, to gravitate toward one of two models for comprehending such a search. We tend to envision ourselves, on the one hand, as uncovering or *discovering* a foundation that possesses authority because of its transcendent character; or, on the other hand, as *choosing* the most basic immanent framework of values that will then have priority over all of our other values. I will briefly delineate these two models and then suggest that they are too one-sided to fully capture the insights that press upon us as

Stephen K. White

late-modern individuals. In this regard, we do better to affirm a model that captures the basic qualities of *both* discovery and choice.

In the foundations model, we envision ourselves digging down to discover what animates and lends certainty to our lives and the commitments that guide them. The figure of depth is intended to signal the existence of what is transcendent or beyond the everyday, something permanent and infinite that awaits fuller illumination. The truth or rightness thus discovered gains its peculiar affective and cognitive force precisely because it resides beyond the everyday. The figure of God represents the most familiar such foundation.

Alternatively, we might see the activity of reflection on basics as a kind of periodic cognitive check-up of the relation between our judgments and beliefs in every-day life, on the one hand, and our considered support for then, on the other. This supporting structure or framework of belief is one we have chosen or freely affirmed; its greater authority for us rests in a crucial way on the condition that we have willed it. Things could have been otherwise; I could have willed completely differently and I may in the future. Utilitarianism is an example of a philosophical perspective that would have us see authority in this fashion.[28] One simply has full sovereign authority over oneself and exercises it by making choices and arranging preferences related to one's values and principles.

Taylor construes the character of reflection on basic matters quite differently. Let me first contrast his alternative with the foundations model. In place of the excavation of foundations, he substitutes the "articulation" of "sources."[29] Although both imply a gesture of working toward the illumination of something crucial to one's practical investments, Taylor's picture embodies key differences. Part of this difference follows from everyday connotations. The achievement of clarifying foundations has a strong connotation of enhancing my knowledge, of *making my beliefs more solid* by illuminating the ground of their truth. Having recourse to "sources" can certainly have something of this sense. But it can also carry the implication of *being sustained or animated* by the cleaner water one finds by journeying up a stream in search of its source.

Taylor affirms the latter, ordinary meaning, and adds two other dimensions that give his account of attending to "sources of the self" its peculiar shape. The first of these is that the process of seeking one's sources involves not only discovering but also creating and choosing. Within the foundations model, exploration is typically construed as a clearing away of the earth that obscures a fuller view of one's sources. In short, something already there but not in sight is progressively brought to light. But the light metaphor is misleading. According to Taylor, the process of bringing a source into language is itself unavoidably creative; no meanings stand fully present to themselves outside of language, awaiting only a moment of photographic illumination. This characteristic is related to another, namely that one never attains full articulacy in regard to sources. As the world throws up new experiences, I must progressively bring them to bear on the sources that animate me. There is no point of completion or full articulacy, both because my life is open-ended and because articulacy is always achieved in the medium of ordinary language, in relation to which I can never find sovereign transparency.[30] Our mortality means, of course, that there will be an end to this interpretation; but cessation does not equate to fullness of articulation.

Such characteristics make the activity of articulation take on the qualities of a quest or a process of continually working on a puzzle.[31] One always seeks greater insight; but since full articulacy always remains up ahead, the dispositional qualities I manifest within the activity of searching itself become as important as the intimations I might have of the ultimate goal of my journey or of the character of the completed puzzle.

One further contrast between the two models must also be highlighted. Within the picture of excavating foundations, hard work is supposed to discover or draw out something of essentially fixed shape and solidity whose significance is then rendered fully evident. In effect, I know where I stand and I know the ground is solid. This image of clarity, solidity, and epistemological certainty stands in sharp contrast with Taylor's, where there is no fixed endpoint, no certainty about the truth of one's beliefs. In a world where it is a source that I articulate, I may justifiably come to feel the deepest and strongest commitment to that source, but I should not mistakenly equate that with increasing certainty of knowledge. In short, a deepening of commitment that sustains me more robustly does not equate to a growing cognitive certainty that my commitments will promptly trump others that they encounter.

Here one can see that the one-sidedness of the foundations model lies in its commitment to the notion that reflecting on basics is a matter of enhancing my conviction of truth. When I operate with this portrait, I have located the other who contests my views between the truth and me. This creates a persistent tendency to script the other as an obstacle to my further elaboration and implementation of the truth. The danger this might involve for ethical-political life is readily apparent.

At this point, a glance back at Rawls is helpful. He emphasizes a late-modern insight whose affirmation helps keep us from succumbing to the preceding, dangerous train of thought. A reasonable person, he tells us, will admit to the persistence of "burdens of judgment." This means that one will recognize that the attempt to insert comprehensive foundational truths into the basic arrangements of a polity is an exercise that is almost certain to go wrong.[32] The admission that there are such burdens that affect the reliability of one's judgments is clearly one of the primary lessons learned by modern Western societies from the Reformation to the present.

A proponent of the articulation model would certainly affirm Rawls's way of trying to operationalize this lesson in the form of recognizing the burdens of judgment; she would, however, also argue that a late-modern ethos applying to the site of basic matters requires more of us. For Rawls, we can clearly distinquish those "reasonable comprehensive doctrines" that have taken to heart the fact of pluralism from the unreasonable ones that have not.[33] For a late-modern ethos, however, things are not so clear-cut. Such an ethos certainly affirms the idea of a distinction like this one, but it also has to be more attentive to the fact that lessons are sometimes less-than-fully learned or susceptible to degrees of qualification that deplete their power to guide action. This kind of worry is hardly hypothetical in the post-9/11 era, especially in the United States. President George W. Bush referred to the ensuing war on terror as a "crusade;" and he made it clear that he consulted God on the decision to invade Iraq.[34] Such statements, as well as the 2004 prisoner-abuse scandal at Abu Ghraib and the pressure to curb civil liberties within the U.S., should make us entertain seriously the possibility that a significant sector of the American population may increasingly envision the U.S. as something like a "Christian security state."

Stephen K. White

If this heady mix of ideas gains ground, it will do so at the cost of a depletion of the restraint promised by the notion of acceptance of the burdens of judgment.

It is in the context of such worries that one can see more clearly why imagining our most fundamental commitments in terms of the articulation model would appear to be more reasonable than imagining them in terms of the foundations model. The latter typically envisions human dignity as warranted by our status as agents of God's truth. The difficulty with this ontological figure, however, is that despite all the historical lessons learned, it still draws truth and absoluteness together in ways that can drift in politically dangerous directions.

In what way might an affirmation of the articulation model render us potentially less susceptible to such a drift? The answer to this question rests on the elucidation of a different figuration of dignity that is as congruent with that model as the figure of the agent of God's truth is with the foundations model. I am going to let the shape of this alternative figure emerge slowly through the remainder of the paper. For the moment, let me just say that the figure is that of a traveler with a distinctive sort of disposition and consciousness. At this point, the only crucial thing to understand about such a figure of dignity is that its character would be such as to make it unreasonable for this being to imagine itself in possession of the fullness of truth about its sources and thus encouraged to divide its world into those fateful and self-righteous categories of believers of truth, on the one hand, and their opponents, on the other. The implication of this is that the expectation of reasonableness has to find some foothold already at the site of sources and not just when we arrive at the site of fair terms of cooperation, as within Rawls's project.

The articulation model makes it possible to imagine the soft collar of reasonableness being brought to bear at the site of basic matters, because it puts the linguistically mediated character of human being at the center of the process of articulation. Sources cannot be directly revealed in any fashion not mediated by language and thus involving all the difficulties inherent to any process of interpretation. Taylor takes this to be another central, late modern insight, one that emerged with the linguistic turn in philosophy, especially in Wittgenstein, Heidegger, and Gadamer in the mid-twentieth century. When we consider reflection upon basic matters in light of this insight, it helps us to comprehend the shortcomings of the foundations model and the kind of subtle gravitational force certainty of belief exerts on it.

This issue opens onto a related sense in which the articulation model honors what I called earlier the anxiety of finitude rather than seeking to repress or transcend it. The problem with the foundations model in this regard is that it posits human being's finitude in such a way that the gravitational force toward what is certain, transcendent, and infinite feeds a perfectly understandable wish to jump the gap between finitude and infinitude. The former becomes merely a temporary, inessential condition, away from which my attention ought to be directed.[35]

It might be objected at this point that the foregoing criticisms of the foundations model all tend in the same direction; namely, toward disqualifying from the start any variant of theism. But that is not the case. Here it is useful to remember that Taylor develops his articulation model in the context of a broad case for a kind of theism that is responsive to the central insights of modernity. His is a theism able to engage quietly and persistently with finitude, especially as it is manifest in our character as linguistically mediated beings. What is most important to emphasize at this point is simply that the embrace of this model does not stack the deck for or against theism.

I want to turn now from what has been shown to be the one-sidedness of the foundations model to the claim that the chosen-framework model is similarly guilty. Its problem of one-sidedness, however, is just the opposite of the sort foundationalism displays; that is, the problem now is an overemphasis on creating and choosing as opposed to an overemphasis on the discovery of that which has essential solidity, authority, and truth prior to the activity of trying to comprehend it.

The chosen-framework model is oriented to gaining clarity in the name of getting greater potential control over all aspects of our lives. The increase in control promises, in turn, to increase human happiness. The idea of fulfilling this promise is one of our core Enlightenment legacies. The problem in the present context is: what effect is there when we figure reflection upon the most basic matters of our lives along these lines? One might describe this change as one of willing all that is the background of our lives into the foreground where it can be more manageably entered into rational calculations about our happiness. But when we have committed ourselves to such a task, we have also thereby implicitly embraced an ontological figure of humans as sovereign entities. As Burke, Adorno, and Foucault all realized in different ways, once this occurs, we have fashioned ourselves as figures whose wills are in principle unlimited and whose reason is in no need of chastening. Here there emerges that will to infinitude about which such critics of modernity wish to warn us. It is crucial in thinking about this danger not to limit our concern to the most visible and grandly egregious variants, such as Burke observed in the French revolution, or recent generations have observed in twentieth-century fascism and state socialism. We need to worry as well about the more unobtrusive variants such as Foucault highlights with his notion of disciplines that seem to spread almost without specific human intention.

B. So far I have attempted to sketch out a picture of the general terrain upon which we can reflect on basic matters in a fashion that is sensitive to the conditions and insights of late modernity. Now I turn to the question of what it would mean to conform to the call to be reasonable as we articulate our sources in relation to one another. More specifically, how do we construe the attentiveness and restraint that largely constitute the fulfillment of the expectation of reasonableness?

Attentiveness would be displayed by an affirmation of the twofold character of the articulation of sources: the sense in which such reflection involves both discovery and creation. In being so attentive, I continually remind myself of the ways in which some accounts of basic matters require us to repress too many of the insights that we late modern citizens have. The criterion of restraint is displayed in the acceptance of the insight that in pursuing basic matters we are always left with something less than full articulacy; and thus the next "other" I meet may hold something crucial to a fuller understanding of my sources. When restraint is comprehended in this way as oriented around the articulation model, it is not difficult to see how virtues of carefulness and humility toward the other are prefigured more clearly here than is the case in either the foundations model or the framework model, where the other is more susceptible to being quickly scripted as either an obstacle or an entity of possible instrumental use.

Stephen K. White

Attentiveness and restraint gain their content in relation to that figure of a journey that I have suggested is implied in the notion of articulating sources. Reasonableness accordingly refers us to the orientation of a traveler who has a rough sense of the direction in which she must head but is also crucially dependent on the insights of those she meets along the way for clues as to her ultimate destination. Additionally, she knows that although she may gain an increasingly fuller sense of that destination, she will nevertheless remain a traveler who is always still on her way to that destination.

The construal of dignity around the portrait of the anxious, but quietly committed traveler is certainly not uncontroversial in its figuration of human being or in its affinity for some ethical virtues rather than others. But then no portrait can guarantee that it will meet with universal agreement. The real issue is not whether it is uncontroversial, but whether it coheres with central, late-modern insights, and whether it might be more inclusive than, say, the traditional, theistically based figurations. And, on this point, the figure of the perpetual traveler whose encounter with life quietly and persistently honors its subjection to mortality seems better able to include at least some theists as well as some non-theists.[36]

I want to turn now to the final aspect of my account of late-modern reasonableness. Just as I showed earlier that reasonableness in relation to fair terms of cooperation implies an engagement with reasonableness in relation to the articulation of sources, so I now want to suggest that reasonableness in the latter sense is also similarly entangled with reasonableness in relation to the demand for the recognition of identity. What is the nature of this entanglement, and what exactly does reasonableness amount to on this third site?

III. Site Three: Recognizing Identity

If we think in terms of agents and their articulation of sources, it seems to follow pretty clearly that what agents take to be their identity is constitutively involved with that process. The horizon provided by that articulation allows me to know where I stand in moral space; and, as Taylor nicely puts it: "To know who I am is a species of knowing where I stand."[37] Now part of what is involved in this interconnection is my identity in a universalizable sense. As we saw in Sections I and II, one thing that an ethos of reasonableness expects of us is a recognition of your and my status as persons who possess dignity and who are thus deserving of respect. Obviously such recognition is significant, but just as obviously this dimension does not incorporate all of what, over the last few decades, has been referred to with the phrases "identity politics" and "the politics of recognition."[38] These phrases draw our attention not to respect for persons in the universalistic sense, but rather to the acknowledgement of people's diversity, their distinctiveness of language, religion, nationality, and traditional practices. This demand that my/our identity be acknowledged in its distinctiveness or difference is one of the most controversial subjects in contemporary political theory. So it is important to emphasize that my analysis of this site of reflection has a limited aim. I am only trying to elucidate a certain spirit or disposition that can be brought to the reflection on, and contestation of, such issues under the banner of a certain sort of claim to reason. Such a spirit or disposition will constitute part of a threefold, reasonable, late-modern ethos.

As a way of initially engaging this topic, let me return to the beginning of this essay, where I discussed some twentieth-century critics of the Enlightenment's understanding of reason. For such critics, Enlightenment reason carries an unacknowledged will to dominate inside of its more admirable manifestations. Thus the will to know, to construct, to control, to resolve, and to reconcile are all more ambivalent in their effects than was originally thought in the eighteenth century, when the "party of reason" arrayed itself categorically against the party of ignorance, superstition, and domination. One key site where reason and domination evolve as co-conspirators rather than simple opponents is in the construction and reproduction of the identity of the self. The process of constructing myself as an epitome of enlightenment – that is, as a free, rational, and responsible being – can only proceed by means of contrasts. In other words, the construction of my identity necessarily involves the simultaneous construction of others, even if only implicitly, who are unfree, irrational, and irresponsible – in short, non-sovereign and potentially threatening. Prominent examples of this dynamic at work in the history of the United States include the way Native Americans were positioned in relation to the expansion westward of white civilization, especially in the nineteenth century, and the way the identity of the "Un-American" was engendered in the mid-twentieth century during the Cold War. In the last couple decades, the exposure of this dark side of Enlightenment reason has sometimes seemed so thoroughgoing as to vitiate entirely any ideal of constructing an admirable, late-modern self within the spirit of modern, enlightened reason. But that conclusion betrays a perfectly resistible desire to over-simplify what is in fact a complicated issue.[39]

I intend rather to unpack some of the philosophical complexity that resides upon this problematic site, and then see if some other conclusion might be warranted; more specifically, one that allows us to see how a sense of reasonableness might infuse the discourse of identity recognition. Toward this end, it is useful to begin by separating out two insights about identity and difference that are at the core of the critique of our Enlightenment legacy. The first informs us that identity and difference stand in a mutually constitutive relationship at the ontological level. A process of identity formation is always simultaneously a process of difference formation. And this means that identity will always be ontologically indebted to difference. The second insight builds upon the first and shows how modern ideas of the self as free, rational and responsible have given rise to particular historical formations of difference within whose scope all manner of groups have fallen.

The combined weight of these two insights would seem to constitute a solid battering ram against any comforting talk about enlightenment. This is because it seems necessarily to implicate reason as a central co-conspirator in perpetuating some of the great injustices that have accompanied Western colonization and enlightenment. We can, however, resist such an implication if we focus attention upon exactly how we understand the relationship between these two insights. Consider the way in which I initially introduced them. They appear to be constitutively joined. For example, the identity of nineteenth-century white Americans as the active subjects of the geographic extension of reason and freedom necessarily and simultaneously constituted Native Americans in such a way as to ensure that their distinctiveness would be denied

Stephen K. White

recognition. And, of course, that would make it more justifiable (and thus perhaps easier on the conscience) to treat them in barbaric ways. The upshot of grasping the relation of the two insights in this fashion has rather stark consequences for how we understand identity and recognition. By this I mean that once the relationship is understood in this way, then the very process of identity formation itself is always already implicated in the *mis*recognition of the other.

Accordingly, if I ask what I can do to alleviate the harms arising from such misrecognition, an adequate answer will require me to go back to the most basic level of my identity constitution; more specifically, I must somehow de-construct my identity from the ground up. That is the only way to relieve the pressure of misrecognition.

Perhaps the most visible recent example of this logic of identity is contained in Judith Butler's *Gender Trouble*.[40] There she seems to be saying that the only way to interrupt the fateful relation between identity formation and misrecognition is to engage in a process of continual, "insistent rifting" of my identity.[41] In short, in order to extend recognition to the other, I must renounce the idea of an identity that has coherence and continuity. As critics pointed out, this makes it seem as though the very idea of a stable identity is "inherently oppressive."[42]

Clearly, such an extreme remedy for the ills of misrecognition could not qualify as something one should feel compelled to administer to oneself as a result only of the soft collar of reasonableness. It may be that one cannot even coherently imagine what it would be like to be "perpetually undoing the identities one is nevertheless bound to construct."[43] Is there, however, an alternative way of conceiving the problem of identity and recognition within which we can identify a remedy, the recourse to which might qualify as reasonable?

There is, in fact, a place on this problematic terrain at which an appeal to the reasonable might plausibly be seen as getting a foothold. This place becomes increasingly evident the more we think in terms of teasing apart the two insights about identity, recognition, and misrecognition. The most cogent effort in this regard comes from William Connolly.[44] He fully accepts the insight about identity and difference being constitutively implicated ontologically with one another. But he differentiates between the construction of difference intrinsically entailed by the constitution of my identity, on the one hand, and an at least partially separable, resilient "temptation that readily insinuates itself" into that onto-logic, on the other.[45]

An identity is established in relation to a series of differences that have become socially recognized. These differences are essential to its being. If they did not coexist as differences, it would not exist in its distinctness and solidity. Entrenched in this indispensable relation is a second set of tendencies, themselves in need of exploration, to congeal established identities into fixed forms, thought and lived as if their structure expressed the true order of things. When these pressures prevail, the maintenance of one identity (or field of identities) involves the conversion of some differences into otherness, into evil, or one of its numerous surrogates. Identity requires difference in order to be, and it converts difference into otherness in order to secure its own self-certainty[46]

It is the latter phenomenon, the conversion of difference into otherness, that can be seen as varying historically and can be resisted by various means. In modern Western culture, there has been a distinctive emphasis on control or mastery of the world around us. It is this persistent orientation – as well as the underlying anxiety of finitude that persistently activates it – that makes us especially vulnerable to the temptation that Connolly identifies.[47] In short, whatever cannot be mastered or comprehended within familiar categories draws upon itself the status of something that, or someone who, is a potential threat to the security and sovereignty of my identity.

It is in relation to *this* propensity that we can reasonably be expected to show some restraint. Such a disposition does not require a wholesale de-constructing of my own identity. But it does require more work on the self than the sort of commitment to tolerance that received its classical expression in Mill's work. In saying this, I don't mean to denigrate Mill. He certainly realized that intolerance is deeply ingrained in human life; and, as I suggested earlier, he tried to combat this by looking not just to legal structures, but also to an ethos that might suffuse all of public life and slacken the insistent pressure of majority opinion.[48] Nevertheless, Mill does not give us an adequate understanding of the roots of intolerance and other associated modes of denigrating those who are constituted as the others of our modern projects and identities. One value of putting things in these terms is that it provides us with a plausible way of comprehending how Mill can be so eloquent about liberty while simultaneously making his infamous remarks about non-Western peoples as "barbarians" who must be constrained by colonial powers to accept the forms of Western civilization.[49]

In order to draw ourselves away from similar mistakes, we need to locate the roots of this whole complex of issues concerning otherness in the temptations associated with the highly charged process of identity consolidation. Only after this shift of attention will we be capable of sketching out what a reasonable, late-modern ethos might ask of us on this site. The processes of pluralization and globalization today exert enormous pressure on the self as it tries to adhere to the elusive ideal of the sovereign, rational, and responsible human being. These pressures can evoke a continual low-grade fear of, or hostility to, diversity, as well as frustration with a political world that so often seems to disappoint those excessive, normalizing expectations about what the world owes us.[50] A late-modern ethos would ask us to develop strategies of the self that work toward dampening that hostility and moderating those expectations. Strategies of this sort have been elaborated by a number of contemporary philosophers who are wrestling with questions of late-modern life. These efforts might usefully be comprehended as different ways of portraying the idea of an ethos of "presumptive generosity" toward the other. Examples would include "critical responsiveness" (Connolly); "fundamentally more capacious, generous and 'unthreatened' bearings of the self" (Butler); "hospitality" (Derrida); "receptive generosity" (Romand Coles); and "opening ourselves to the surprises" of engagement with the other (Patchen Markell).[51] Crucial in all of these perspectives is a sense of the cognitive and affective need to dampen the initial wariness and certainty that we are likely to carry into our engagement with those whom we all too easily size up as radically other to us.

Gathering together the threads of the preceding discussion, I can now specify more directly what it would mean to respond to the call to be reasonable in regard to the recognition of identity. The sense of attentiveness is to be attached to a willingness to continually be receptive to the distinction between the onto-logic of the mutual constitution of identity and difference, on the one hand, and the psychosocial temptation to transform difference into otherness, on the other hand.[52] And the sense

Stephen K. White

of restraint to which the expectation of reasonableness would bind us is shown in the willingness to resist this temptation. One of the primary means of doing this effectively lies in the cultivation of a kind of initial generosity – a willful, temporary suspension of the engagement of my full, critical apparatus of practical judgment.

When we construe the call to reasonableness in this way, we are subtly repositioning it as a virtue appropriate to the self as host, as the one who stands on familiar ground and crafts the affective and cognitive terms upon which he will respond to the approach of another to his door. The figure of the host is as central here to an enlarged sense of reasonableness as is the figure of the traveler in the domain of articulating sources.

As we imagine this central role of the host in identity recognition, it is also crucial to acknowledge that it cannot be construed in isolation from the first site of reason-giving; namely, where the underlying fairness of the terms of interaction is at issue. By itself, the ethos of the admirable host forms a sphere of reasonable engagement; but when it is so construed, it can mask structures of privilege that can in turn inconspicuously corrupt the scene of hospitality. To say this is merely to emphasize that the dynamic of identity recognition always operates against a background of social relations and structures that embodies claims about justice and injustice. In short, the third sphere of reasonableness must always be understood as constitutively entangled with the first.

IV. Conclusion

The idea that practical reason in its emphatic sense should guide political life has come in for some hard knocks over the last century or so. To my mind, one cannot ignore these blows. But neither is one obliged to abandon the idea of emphatic reason as thoroughly trounced. Accordingly, I have tried to tease out a remaining, minimal, or chastened, account of reason that one might plausibly feel obliged to sustain. My sketch of this account is composed of a threefold set of expectations about the attentiveness and restraint that should be met by citizens who understand their obligations to arise not just from a given polity in which they reside, but also from the time in which they live. Reasonable citizens will thus affirm a broadly conceived ethos that embodies the central insights regarding what we have learned, often a great cost, in the course of Western modernity.

Acknowledgements: I would like to thank my colleagues at the University of Virginia, George Klosko and Lawrie Balfour, as well as Mort Schoolmon, for their very helpful comments on an earlier draft.

Notes

1 For a classic attempt to reduce the problem of the social contract to a collective action problem resolvable purely through strategic rationality, see James Buchanan and Gordon Tullock, eds., *The Calculus of Consent: Logical Foundations of Constitutional Democracy* (Ann Arbor, MI: University of Michigan Press, 1962).

2   Theodor Adorno uses the term "emphatic" ("nachdrucklich") in a somewhat similar, but not identical way in *Negative Dialectics,* trans. E. B. Ashton (New York: Continuum Publishing Company, 1966), pp. 24, 150–51.

3   See the cover illustration of James Schmidt, ed., *What Is Enlightenment? Eighteenth Century Answers and Twentieth Century Questions* (Berkeley, CA: University of California Press, 1996).

4   Max Horkheimer and Theodor Adorno, *Dialectic of Enlightenment: Philosophical Fragments.* ed. Gunzelin Schmid Noerr, trans. Edmund Jephcott (Stanford, CA: Stanford University Press, 2002); originally pubd 1947. For Heidegger, see Martin Heidegger, "Letter on Humanism" and "The Question Concerning Technology," in David Farrell Krell, ed. and trans., *Martin Heidegger: Basic Writings* (New York: Harper and Row, 1977). The first essay was originally published in 1947; the latter was first given as a lecture in 1949, and published in a revised form in 1954. For Foucault, see especially Michel Foucault, *Discipline and Punish: The Birth of the Prison*, trans. Alan Sheridan (New York: Vintage Books, 1979). Also insightful is William Connolly, "The Politics of Discourse," in *The Terms of Political Discourse* (Princeton, NJ: Princeton University Press, 1993, 3rd edn), pp. 213–43; and *Identity\Difference: Democratic Negotiations of Political Paradox* (Minneapolis, MN: University of Minnesota Press, 2003, 2nd edn).

5   See my *Edmund Burke: Modernity, Politics, and Aesthetics* (Lanham, MD: Rowman and Littlefield, 2002, 2nd edn), Ch. 4.

6   Foucault, *Discipline and Punish*, p. 139.

7   Foucault, *Discipline and Punish*, Part III.

8   See, for example, Foucault, "What Is Enlightenment?," trans. C. Porter; and "Politics and Ethics: An Interview," in Paul Rabinow, ed., *The Foucault Reader* (New York: Pantheon Books, 1984), pp. 32–50, 373–80; and Horkheimer and Adorno, *Dialectic of Enlightenment*, p. xviii.

9   For a good account of the character of essentially contested concepts in political philosophy, see Connolly, *The Terms of Political Discourse*, Ch. 1. W. B. Gallie introduced the notion in "Essentially Contested Concepts," *Proceedings of the Aristotelian Society*, Vol. 56 (London, 1955–6), cited in Connolly, p. 10.

10 Issues related to the domain in which we argue about and pursue the progressive realization of democracy are taken up in my *The Ethos of a Late-Modern Citizen* (Cambridge, MA: Harvard University Press, 2009).

11 John Rawls, *Political Liberalism* (New York: Columbia University Press, 1993), pp. 48–81.

12 Rawls, *Political Liberalism*, pp. 9–10.

13 An important account of the problem of identity recognition is Charles Taylor's "The Politics of Recognition," in Amy Gutmann, ed, *Multiculturalism: Examining the Politics of Recognition*, intro. Amy Gutmann. (Princeton, NJ: Princeton University Press, 1994), pp. 25–73.

14 Rawls, *Political Liberalism*, pp. 17–18, 36ff.

15 Rawls, *Political Liberalism*, pp. 10–11, 54–60.

16 Rawls, *Political Liberalism*, pp. 54–8, 81.

17 Larmore, "The Moral Basis of Liberalism," *Journal of Philosophy* 12 (Dec. 1999): 599–625; and "Respect for Persons," *The Hedgehog Review*. Special Issue on *Commitments in a Post-Foundationalist World: Exploring the Possibilities of "Weak Ontology."* 7 (2) (Summer 2005): 66–76.

18 Charles Larmore, "Respect for Persons," p. 71; and "The Moral Basis of Liberalism," pp. 601–2, 607–8.

19 Larmore, "Respect for Persons," p. 75.

20 Larmore, "The Moral Basis of Liberalism," p. 606–9; and "Respect for Persons," p. 75.

21 Rawls, "Overlapping Consensus," *Oxford Journal of Legal Studies* 7 (Feb. 1987): 14.

22 Rawls, *Political Liberalism*, pp. xvi, 8.

23 Rawls, *Political Liberalism*, pp. 11–12, and Lecture VII.

24 Charles Taylor, *Philosophical Arguments* (Cambridge, MA: Harvard University Press, 1995), p. xii.

25 J. S. Mill, *"On Liberty" and Other Writings*, ed. S. Collini (Cambridge: Cambridge University Press, 1989), pp. 8–9.

26 Charles Taylor, *Sources of the Self: The Making of Modern Identity* (Cambridge, MA: Harvard University Press, 1989), p. 505.

27 The second, broader sense of finitude is meant to include insights such as not having the time or capacity to satisfy all of my desires and knowing that when I take a major decision in life, I cannot later revisit that decision point in exactly the same way as the first time, only this time choosing differently.

28 Here I am following Taylor, *Sources of the Self*, pp. 30–2, 331–2.

29 Taylor, *Sources of the Self*, pp. 8–9, 91–6.

30 Taylor, *Sources of the Self*, pp. 18, 22, 34, 334, 419.

31 Taylor draws some of his sense of human being figured as a quest from Alasdair MacIntyre in *After Virtue: A Study of Moral Theory* (Notre Dame, IN: University of Notre Dame Press, 1981), pp. 203–6. This is true to a degree, but the sense of a quest that emerges in the articulation model is not set against MacIntyre's stark master narrative of late modernity as "the new dark ages which is already upon us" (ibid., p. 245). Such a division of the world into light and dark threatens to swallow up the more engaging implications of the idea of life as a deeply uncertain sort of journey.

32 Rawls, *Political Liberalism*, pp. 54–61.

33 Rawls, *Political Liberalism*, pp. 58–64.

34 Quoted in Peter Ford, "Europe Cringes at Bush's 'Crusade' against Terrorists," *Christian Science Monitor* Sep. 19, 2001; *http://www.csmonitor.com/2001/0919/p12s2-woeu.html*. Accessed on Feb. 14, 2006.

35 Consider here the way the idea of the "Rapture" seems to function today among some Protestant fundamentalists in the United States.

36 Obviously, huge questions remain for the expanded sense of reasonableness delineated in this section, as well as for the alternate figure of dignity that I contend is implied in such an expansion. For example, one might object that a perfectly plausible alternative figure of dignity could be easily erected out of the qualities like reason, freedom, or agency. For reasons of space, I cannot take up such options here. But I have tried elsewhere to show that these alternatives are not nearly as easy to construct as one might think. See "Uncertain Constellations: Dignity, Equality, Respect and . . . ?" in M. Schoolmon and D. Campbell, eds., *The New Pluralism: William Connolly and the Contemporary Global Condition* (Durham, NC: Duke University Press, 2008). Very insightful as to how difficult it is to articulate the notion of equality that is necessary to any account of dignity is Jeremy Waldron's analysis of Locke in *God, Locke and Equality: Christian Foundations in Locke's Political Thought* (Cambridge: Cambridge University Press, 2003), Chs. 3 and 8.

37 Taylor, *Sources of the Self*, p. 27.

38 For some general sense of the debates, see Taylor, "The Politics of Recognition"; Patchen Markell, *Bound by Recognition* (Chicago: University of Chicago Press, 2003); and A.-G. Gagnon and J. Tully, eds., *Multinational Democracies* (Cambridge: Cambridge University Press, 2001).

39 See Sankar Muthu, *Enlightenment Against Empire* (Princeton, NJ: Princeton University Press, 2003), for an excellent treatment of the diversity of views among Enlightenment thinkers in regard to how they did or did not associate reason and freedom with the legitimacy of empire.

40 Judith Butler, *Gender Trouble* (New York: Routledge, 1990).

41 Butler, "The Force of Fantasy: Feminism, Maplethorpe, and Discursive Excess," *Differences* 2 (2) (1990): 121.

42 Nancy Fraser, "False Antitheses: A Response to Seyla Benhabib and Judith Butler," in S. Benhabib et al., eds., *Feminist Contentions: A Philosophical Exchange* (New York: Routledge, 1995), p. 71. For a discussion of how Butler has overcome this problem in later work, see my *Sustaining Affirmation: The Strengths of Weak Ontology in Political Theory* (Princeton, NJ: Princeton University Press, 2000), Ch. 4.

43 Markell, *Bound by Recognition*, p. 23. He calls this "the Penelope problem."

44 Connolly, *Identity\Difference: Democratic Negotiations of Political Paradox*, especially the Introduction.

45 Connolly, *Identity\Difference*, pp. 8–9.

46 Connolly, *Identity\Difference*, p. 64.

47 Connolly, *Identity\Difference*, pp. 9, 16–20, 29–32; and *The Ethos of Pluralization* (Minneapolis, MN: University of Minnesota Press, 1995), pp. 16–20. He finds that the temptation also grows in the context of religious attitudes of attunement.

48 Mill, *"On Liberty" and Other Writings*; at one point, Mill calls intolerance more natural than tolerance; p. 11.

49 Mill, *"On Liberty" and Other Writings*, p. 13.

50 The force of this portrait is supported by empirical social science; see John R. Hibbing and Elizabeth Theiss-Morse, *Stealth Democracy: Americans' Beliefs about How Government Should Work* (Cambridge: Cambridge University Press, 2002), pp. 105–6, 134–5, 149–50, 156–7, 221–3. Americans tend to be "conflict averse" and deeply suspicious of amorphous "others" who seem to foment disagreement that disturbs the deep consensus they believe (incorrectly) characterizes the American population.

51 Connolly, *The Ethos of Pluralization*, pp. 178–88; Butler, "For a Careful Reading," in *Feminist Contentions: A Philosophical Exchange*, p. 140; Jacques Derrida and Anne Dufourmantelle, *Of Hospitality* (Stanford, CA: Stanford University Press, 2000); Romand Coles, *Rethinking Generosity: Critical Theory and the Politics of Caritas* (Ithaca, NY: Cornell University Press, 1997), p. 23; and Patchen Markell, *Bound by Recognition*, pp. 14–15, 32–6.

52 Connolly, *Identity\Difference*, pp. 8–9.

LIBERALISM

POLITICAL NEUTRALITY

CHAPTER FIVE

The Moral Foundations of Liberal Neutrality

Gerald F. Gaus

Section 1 of this essay explicates the concept of neutrality. Section 2 provides two arguments supporting a conception of *Liberal Moral Neutrality*. Given a certain understanding of moral and rational persons, I argue, moral neutrality is a fundamental and inescapable commitment. Section 3 shows how liberal moral neutrality leads to *Liberal Political Neutrality*. Fully grasping the nature of this liberal political neutrality, I argue in section 4, has radical implications for our understanding of the proper limits of government.

1. The Concept of Neutrality

For the last few decades political theorists have vigorously debated whether liberalism is committed to some doctrine of "neutrality," and whether neutrality provides a plausible constraint on legitimate laws and policies. In my view, this long-running controversy has been disappointing: theorists tend to stake their claim as advocates or critics of neutrality, yet the precise contours of the concept and its justification remain vague. To be sure, we have witnessed some important advances. Discussions of neutrality are now careful to distinguish: (i) the idea that a *justification* (say, of a policy) should be neutral; (ii) the claim that the *aims* of policymakers should be neutral; (iii) the claim that the *effects* of policy should be neutral.[1] Yet interpretations of neutrality are far more diverse than most analyses recognize.[2] Neutrality is sometimes understood as a doctrine about: constraints on legislation or legislators,[3] the proper functions of the state,[4] the prohibition of the state "taking a stand" on some issues,[5] the prohibition of the state enforcing moral character,[6] or the requirement that the state take a stance of impartiality.[7] Alternatively, neutrality can be understood as a requirement of a theory justice rather than state action.[8] There are also differences about whether neutral states (or theories of justice, or legislators) are supposed to be neutral between conceptions of the good,[9] controversial conceptions of the good,[10] conceptions of the good that citizens may rightfully adopt,[11] comprehensive doctrines and conceptions of the good,[12] particular sets of ends,[13] particular or substantive conceptions of the good,[14] ways of life,[15] or final ends.[16] And it is unclear whether every principle of neutrality is inherently one of liberal neutrality, or whether liberal neutrality is a specific sort of neutral principle.[17]

To make a start at clarifying just what the debate is about, I propose the following general definition-schema:

> A's ϕ-ing is neutral between X and Y concerning X's and Y's difference D iff ϕ does not treat X and Y differently on the basis of D.

The definition-schema is, I think, fully general about claims concerning neutrality. It must be stressed that the definition-schema is not intended to resolve substantive disputes about the proper interpretation of neutrality; the aim is to get clearer about the variables around which controversy centers. Each conception of neutrality provides a different interpretation of the variables. The most familiar controversy, which I mentioned above, concerns the proper interpretation of "treatment." Varying conceptions proffer different explications: those who think that neutrality requires *neutrality of effect* hold that unless A's ϕ-ing has the same effect on X and Y with respect to D, A's ϕ-ing treats them differently; those who uphold *neutrality of justification* maintain that A treats X and Y the same when A has a justification for ϕ that does not appeal to D.

To better see how the definition-schema is to be applied, consider the classical case of a government that is neutral between two combatants. The government (A) is neutral between the combatants (X and Y) concerning the differences in their war aims (D) when A's decision, say, about shipments of arms or war-related matters (ϕ) does not treat X and Y differently on the basis of their war aims, alliances, etc. Note a few points. (*i*) The range of ϕ – what sorts of actions must be neutral – is in dispute between different notions of state neutrality in war (just as it is in liberal neutrality). In 1914 President Wilson insisted that

> The United States must be neutral in fact, as well as in name. . . . We must be impartial in thought, as well as action, must put a curb upon our sentiments, as well as upon every transaction that might be construed as a preference of one party to the struggle before another.[18]

But that is an extreme interpretation of ϕ (and was not lived up to). The Swedish Government in 1941 declared that

> Neutrality does not demand that nations not participating in an armed conflict should be indifferent to the issues of the belligerents. The sympathies of neutrals may well lie entirely with one side, and a neutral does not violate his duties as long as he does not commit any unneutral acts that might aid the side he favors.[19]

Adopting this, let us call ϕ such acts by the state. (*ii*) Notice that the Swedish doctrine explicitly allows that A (the neutral government) need not always refrain from different treatment of X and Y on the basis of their war aims (D): A's public schools might still favor X's aims, and treat X and Y differently in its curriculum, but this would not impair A's neutrality regarding ϕ – e.g., arms shipments or war materials. (*iii*) Note also that the definition-schema does not require a neutral A to always treat X and Y the same when ϕ-ing. Suppose A sells arms to both X and Y, but X has paid and Y has not (international law allows neutrals to sell arms). Then A may treat X differently than Y even regarding ϕ, because the difference in treatment is not grounded on D (their war aims), but on whether payment has been made.

Moving a little closer to our concern, think about a neutral umpire. The neutral umpire (A) does not treat the players (X and Y) differently with regard to what team they are on or whether she personally likes them (D), when making calls in the game (ϕ). But, of course, A does treat them differently in making calls in the game (ϕ) depending on whether one has violated the rules. And A can still be a neutral umpire if, when buying Christmas presents, she selects her hometown team's jersey, so does sometimes base her differential treatment on D (but not when ϕ-ing).[20]

Philosophy differs from mystery writing: in philosophy we can give the ending away without ruining the story. It may help to give a general description of the conceptions of neutrality that I defend here.

Liberal Moral Neutrality: A [a free and equal reasonable moral person] making ϕ [a moral demand] addressed to Y [a free and equal reasonable moral person] must be neutral between X and Y [where A is also person X; that is where A is one of the relevant parties]: the justification of A's moral demand must not treat Y and A differentially based on the differences (D) in their evaluative standards.

Liberal Political Neutrality: A [an agent of the state] when ϕ-ing [exercising coercion on citizen X who is also a free and equal reasonable moral person, or participating in the authorization of such coercion] must be neutral between X and Y [where Y = any other rational citizen/moral person]: the justification of A's coercion must not appeal to X's and Y's differences (D) in their evaluative standards.

Liberal Moral and Political Neutrality, as I explicate them, are not concerned with neutrality between conceptions of the good (or, more broadly, what I will call "evaluative standards"). Liberalism, I shall argue, is neutral between *persons*, and this neutrality requires not treating them differentially on the basis of their differing evaluative standards (or, loosely, conceptions of the good). Liberalism is not concerned with neutrality between conceptions of the good, as if conceptions of the good themselves had claims to neutral treatment. It is only because citizens hold such conceptions that neutrality between citizens has consequences for the way conceptions of the good can enter into moral and political justification. This might seem to be a distressingly pedantic point, but, I think, it helps us avoid confusion. Suppose at time t_1 there are two conceptions of the good in society, C_1 and C_2 but at time t_2, everyone has come to embrace C_1. It would seem that, if liberalism is really committed to neutrality between conceptions of the good *per se*, then even at t_2, it must be neutral between C_1 and C_2. But this seems implausible. As I understand liberal neutrality, since it is a requirement to be neutral between persons, appealing at t_2 to C_1 does not run afoul of neutrality, since there are no differences between citizens on this matter. So it is not in itself non-neutral to appeal to conceptions of the good; it all depends on the differences that obtain among moral persons and citizens.

2. Liberal Moral Neutrality

2.1 Free and equal moral persons

I take as my starting point the supposition that we conceive of ourselves and others as (*i*) moral persons who are (*ii*) free and equal. Although these features are assumed in this essay, we should not suppose that these assumptions cannot themselves be defended. John Rawls rightly argues that this general conception of moral persons is implicit in our public culture.[21] In much the same vein, I have argued that our commitment to the public justification of our moral demands on each other follows from our present conception of ourselves and others.[22] Let me briefly explain each of these two fundamental characteristics.

A moral person is one who makes, and can act upon, moral demands. Moral persons thus conceive of themselves as advancing moral claims on others. Alternatively, we can say that moral persons understand themselves to be owed certain restraints and acts.[23] Not all humans – not even all functioning adult humans – are moral persons: psychopaths do not appear to understand themselves as pressing moral claims on others that demand respect, nor do they see others as moral persons.[24] As well as advancing moral claims, moral persons have the capability to act on justified moral claims made on them. In this sense moral persons are not solely devoted to their own ends; they have a capacity to put aside their personal ends and goals to act on justified moral claims. Moral persons, then, are not simply instrumentally rational agents;[25] they possess a capacity for moral autonomy. Insofar as moral autonomy presupposes the ability to distinguish one's own ends from the moral claims of others, the idea of a moral person presupposes some cognitive skills.[26]

In the *Second Treatise* John Locke held that "The natural liberty of man is to be free from any superior power on earth, and not to be under the will or legislative authority of man, but to have only the law of Nature for his rule."[27] To conceive of oneself as morally free is to understand oneself as free from any natural moral authority that would accord others status to dictate one's moral obligations. This is not at all to say that one sees oneself as unbound by any morality; as Locke suggests, we may have the law of nature as our rule. Although we are by no means committed to a natural law conception of morality, the crucial point, again one in the spirit of Locke, is that free moral persons call on their own reason when deciding the dictates of moral law. A free person employs her own standards of evaluation when presented with claims about her moral liberties and obligations. A free person, we can say, has an interest in living in ways that accord with her own standards of rightness, value and goodness. At a minimum, to conceive of oneself as a morally free person is to see oneself as bound only by moral requirements that can be validated from one's own point of view.[28] This conception of freedom has much in common with Rawls's notion of the rational autonomy of parties to the original position, according to which "there are no given antecedent principles external to their point of view to which they are bound."[29]

Now to say that moral persons are equal is to claim, firstly, that qua moral persons they possess the minimum requisite moral personality so that they are equal participants in the moral enterprise and, secondly, that each is morally free insofar as no one is subjected to the moral authority of others. The equality of moral persons

Gerald F. Gaus

is their equality qua free moral persons: it is not a substantive principle of moral equality but is a presupposition of the practice of moral justification insofar as it defines the status of the participants in moral justification. While a modest conception of moral equality, it rules out some conceptions of moral justification. Rawls not only conceives of moral persons as advancing claims on each other, but stresses that they view themselves as "self-authenticating sources of valid claims."[30] It would seem, and apparently Rawls agrees, that those who understand themselves as authenticating their own claims would not see themselves as bound to justify their claims on others – they would not suppose that only claims justified to others are valid.[31] But to advance a self-authenticating claim on others is not to respect their moral freedom, for others are bound only by moral claims that they can validate through their own reason: "there are no given antecedent principles external to their point of view to which they are bound." The supposition of equal moral freedom thus requires that one's moral claims can be validated by those to whom they are addressed.

Many have advanced stronger conceptions of moral equality. Some have claimed, for example, that the very practice of morality presupposes an "equal right of each to be treated only with justification."[32] In a similar vein S. I. Benn and R. S. Peters defended the principle that "The onus of justification rests on whoever would make distinctions. . . . Presume equality until there is a reason to presume otherwise."[33] Such a principle of moral equality does not simply require us to justify our moral claims to others: it requires us to justify all our actions that disadvantage some. Now, leaving aside whether some such presumptive egalitarian principle could be morally justified,[34] this conception of moral equality is not presupposed by the very idea of a justified morality among free and equal moral persons. If I accept this principle, I claim that others act wrongly if they disadvantage me without good justification. But unless this non-discriminatory principle itself can be validated by others, I disrespect their moral freedom, as I am making a moral claim on them to non-discriminatory action that is not validated by their own reason.

Validation from the rational and reflective perspective of another, however, is not the same as her actual consent. To treat another as a free and equal moral person is to accept that moral claims must be validated from her perspective when she employs her rational faculties in a competent manner and reflects upon them. Now, although as John Stuart Mill noted, there is a strong presumption that each knows her own perspective best, this is not necessarily so.[35] Just as others can make sound judgments about a person's beliefs and principles, and be correct even when the person disagrees, so can others be correct, and the moral agent wrong, about what is validated from her perspective when she reflects on it. Knowledge of oneself is generally superior to others' knowledge of one, but it is not indefeasible. People may withhold assent for a variety of reasons, including strategic objectives, pigheadedness, confusion, manifestly false beliefs, neurosis, and so on. Nevertheless, respect for the equal moral freedom of another requires that the presumption in favor of self-knowledge only be overridden given strong reasons for concluding that she has misunderstood what is validated from her own point of view. Suppose that Alf and Betty reasonably disagree about whether some moral principle P is validated from Betty's rational and reflective perspective. Say that Alf has good reasons to conclude that Betty has misunderstood what is validated from her point of view: P, he says, really is validated from her point of view. Betty has reason to insist it isn't. For Alf to insist that his merely reasonable view of Betty's commitments override her own reasonable understanding of her moral perspective constitutes a violation of her moral freedom, for Alf is claiming authority to override her own reasonable understanding of her moral commitments with his merely reasonable view.[36] Crucial to moral freedom is that, over a wide range of deliberative competency, that one's moral deliberations lead you to conclude α authorizes you to believe α.[37]

2.2 Morality as giving others reasons

We can reach much the same conclusion by a different route. Rather than relying directly on respecting the equal moral freedom of others, we can appeal to a theory of *moral reasons*. Morality is inherently a rational and practical enterprise insofar as addressing moral claims to others is to give them reasons to comply. To say that I have valid moral claims but these give others – even rational others – no reason to comply with them seems to undermine the point of advancing moral claims. If we are not simply concerned with calling others names – criticizing them for "doing wrong," "being guilty," "violating the rights of others," and so on – what is the point of advancing moral claims that do not appeal to their rational nature? To be sure, views of morality that attenuate its practical or rational nature in this way are often defended. Some see moral judgments as essentially descriptive and so not essentially practical ("ϕ is best described as a right action"). And some understand moral statements as a way express disapproval at what others are doing, and so are not essentially rational ("Boo to ϕ!", "I disapprove of ϕ and you should too!"). Such views do not capture the crux of moral practice: it is a way for us to relate to each other as rational agents, who can give each other reasons to perform, or refrain, from actions of certain types.

If we accept that morality is necessarily about giving reasons to others, then our understanding of moral justification will be deeply influenced by our understanding of what constitutes a reason. We cannot enter here into the complexities of different accounts of reasons; consider, however, a plausible view. To give someone a reason is to give her a consideration to ϕ that, if she employs her rational faculties in an informed, careful, competent, and reflective way, she can see as counting in favor of ϕ. Suppose Alf claims that R is a reason for Betty to ϕ, but Alf admits that even were she to be fully informed about information that is relevant, and she carefully and competently reflects on R, she still could not see how R is a consideration in favor of ϕ-ing. It is hard to see in what way Alf can say that R is a reason for Betty to ϕ; he has admitted that it really cannot be grasped by her reflective deliberation, and given that, it cannot be a reason *for her* to do anything. The idea of a reason that is unable to play a role in deliberation is surely odd. Perhaps it would be good for Betty to ϕ, but it seems implausible to say that *she* has *any* considerations that count in favor of ϕ.

If we accept this plausible view of what it is to give another a reason, combined with our practical and rational conception of the moral enterprise, we are again led to the view that, for Alf to make a valid moral claim on Betty that she ϕs, this claim must be validated from Betty's perspective: there must be a reason *for her*.

Gerald F. Gaus

2.3 Liberal Moral Neutrality

Given the requirements for treating others as free and equal moral persons and the requirements of moral justification, the task of publicly justifying a moral principle P requires that P be validated from the perspective of each rational and reflective free and equal moral person. To publicly justify a moral principle is to justify it to all rational and reflective free and equal moral persons within some public, who confront each other as strangers.[38] I shall assume that the relevant public here is something like a society; we could also define the public in terms of all persons (a universalistic cosmopolitan morality) or a smaller community. As our main concern is with morality insofar as it relates to political justice, focus on the notion of a society's morality is appropriate.

Abstracting from the notions of goods, values, moral "intuitions" and so on, let us provisionally say that Σ is an evaluative standard for moral person Alf if and only if holding Σ, along with various sound beliefs about the world, is a reason for or against a purported moral principle, etc. from Alf's rational and reflective point of view.[39] So a person's evaluative standards are to be distinguished from justified moral requirements. Suppose, then, that Alf attempts to justify some moral principle P on the basis of his evaluative standard Σ_a, which is not shared by Betty. He clearly has not justified P. For P to be justified it must be validated from Betty's viewpoint. Thus, appealing to an evaluative standard about which Alf and Betty rationally and reflectively disagree cannot be justificatory: if Betty's careful and rational reflection cannot endorse Σ_a as a consideration in favor of P, then P has not yet been justified as a moral principle at all. Even if a careful, rational and reflective Betty can see Σ_a as a consideration in favor of P, this is still not enough to show that P is validated from her view. She might also have reason to embrace Σ_b and that may be a consideration against P; the matter then turns on which consideration defeats the other in her overall ranking of evaluative standards.

It is crucial to appreciate that this argument does not show that Alf has a moral obligation to justify his claims on Betty.[40] On such a view, although Alf may have a moral obligation not to insist on P without justification, he might have an overriding moral obligation to act on P even if it cannot be justified to her. On the account I have articulated here, unless P is validated from Betty's perspective, it is not a moral principle at all, and so cannot ground *any* moral reasons. Its status as a reason-giving moral principle applying to society depends on its validation from the public perspective. Morality supposes impartiality, and impartiality requires that the principle by validated by all members of the moral public.

If Alf is to respect others as free and equal moral persons and provide them with genuine moral claims, he is committed to:

> *Liberal Moral Neutrality:* Alf's moral demands addressed to Betty must be neutral between his and Betty's evaluative standards: the justification of Alf's moral demands must not rely on relevant differences between his and Betty's evaluative standards.

Let us consider more carefully why Alf is committed to Liberal Moral Neutrality.

(*i*) We are supposing that Alf is committed to treating others as free and equal moral persons, and is he is a moral person committed to making moral demands on others. If this is so, he must advance moral demands on others, and for these to be valid moral demands (i.e., to actually be moral demands) they must be justified to those others.

(*ii*) Liberal Moral Neutrality does not require that Alf present, or even be aware of, the justifications for his moral demands – he may be unable to articulate arguments about what others have reason to accept. But for his moral demands to be genuine, they must provide considerations for all reflective and rational others. Now given this, it cannot be the case that their justification either favors his evaluative standards or theirs on a relevant difference between them. If there is a relevant difference (a difference that affects the justification of *P*), then if Alf is biased towards his own evaluative standards he will not be providing Betty with adequate reasons; should for some reason he favor Betty's, then the moral demand would not be validated from his view: it would not provide him with a sufficient reason. Note that if their evaluative standards converge on *P*, then the justification of the demand may be based in their different evaluative standards because it would not then be exploiting a difference between them, but appealing to their commonality. This is important. Public justifications may be based either on consensus or convergence of evaluative standards.[41] A consensus justification maintains that *P* is justified because everyone has grounds to endorse it on the basis of the same evaluative standard; a convergence justification maintains that *P* is justified because Alf has grounds to endorse it on the basis Σ_a, Betty on the basis of Σ_b, etc. Now a consensus justification is perfectly neutral: the justification does not rely on our disagreements about evaluative standards but, instead, on our agreement about the implications of our standards. Thus we must reject the plausible idea that liberal neutrality prohibits appeal to "controversial conceptions of the good"; we see here that in some cases such appeals treat all as free and equal moral persons to whom we owe reasons.

(*iii*) It should be clear why "treatment" is to be understood in terms of justification. The reason we are led to Liberal Moral Neutrality is a conception of free and equal moral persons who are committed to making moral demands on others that provide reasons from everyone's perspective. The grounding of morality is impartial treatment qua moral justification. Any more robust requirement of non-differential treatment – say, that every state policy should equally impact each conception of the good life – would have to be justified *within* the moral or political enterprises. Such robust conceptions of non-differential treatment are surely not presuppositions of the moral enterprise itself.

3. Liberal Political Neutrality

3.1 The Non-coercion Principle

I deem this conception of moral neutrality "liberal" because it starts from the quintessentially liberal conception of moral persons as free and equal, rational and reflective, agents. It is not, however, liberal in any more substantive sense. In order to move toward Liberal Political Neutrality we must first make a basic, and I think fairly uncontroversial, claim *within* morality. If any claim can be justified within the constraints of Liberal Moral Neutrality, it is surely:

The Non-coercion Principle: (*i*) It is *prima facie* morally wrong for Alf to coerce Betty, or to employ force against her. (*ii*) With sufficient justification, Alf may have a moral right to use of coercion or force against Betty.

Almost every liberal political philosopher has understood the Non-coercion Principle as a basic moral commitment of liberal political philosophy. The principle's core claim is that, other things equal, the use of force or coercion against another is wrong. To show that other things are not equal, and so that the use of force and coercion is morally permissible, a moral justification is required.[42]

It is hard to see a plausible case against the Non-coercion Principle.[43] Whatever one's evaluative standards, so long as one has any reason to act on them, and so be an agent, one must have strong reason to object when others exercise force or coercion to thwart one's agency. Someone who seeks to coerce you (without justification) to make you do as he wishes is attacking your fundamental interest in acting on your own evaluative standards. The wrongful coercer supplants your evaluative standards with his own as the grounds for your action. Jeffrey Reiman aptly describes this as a case of "subjugation": i.e., "the judgment of one person prevails over the contrary judgment of another simply because it can and without adequate justification for believing it should."[44] As Reiman suggests, the "suspicion of subjugation" can be dispelled – we can distinguish "might from right" – if there is adequate justification:[45] to say that coercion is "prima facie" wrong is to say that reasons can be provided to vindicate some instances of coercion. Suppose someone denies this: she says that coercion can never be justified: she accepts part (*i*) of the principle but denies (*ii*). Such an objector must, then, see self-defense as always wrong: in response to the wrongful force by another, it would still be wrong for her to employ force to resist. Though some have advanced such extreme pacifist views, the claim that one is never justified in employing any degree of coercion to repel any wrongful aggression against oneself is highly counterintuitive; I will not pause to consider it further. If our agency is of fundamental importance to us, then we must accept that, at least in some cases, we have reason to endorse a principle that allows coercion – at the very least, to counter coercion against us.

3.2 The moral claims of, and constraint on, liberal governors

Government officials participate in the authorization of coercion; unjustified coercion is wrong, so if officials are not to act wrongly their coercion must be justified. Consider first the two-person case: official Alf is coercing citizen Betty, say, by imposing a law. So, at a minimum, Alf must have a justified moral liberty to coerce Betty: it must be, morally, not wrong for him to coerce her.[46] And, of course, this justification must meet the demands of Liberal Moral Neutrality: he cannot favor his own evaluative standards. But for the same reason, the justification cannot favor the evaluative standards of some third party, Charlie, when coercing Betty. Now take any law that applies to both Betty and Charlie: the justification of the law Alf cannot exploit differences in Betty and Charlie's evaluative standards, since then one of them will have inadequate reason to accept that Alf has a moral right to impose the law. So Alf's act of imposing the law is only morally permissible if there is a justification for the imposition that meets Liberal Political Neutrality.[47]

This all supposes that the Non-coercion Principle applies to governments and its agents (qua agents). This is not entirely uncontroversial; a recurring view in the history of political philosophy insists that the "normal" moral restraints that apply to individual actors do not apply to the state; "the State, as such, certainly cannot be guilty of personal immorality, and it is hard to see how it can commit theft or murder in the sense in which these are moral offenses."[48] More generally, what has been called "political realism" insists that the constraints of "ordinary" morality are not applicable to politics. As Machiavelli famously observed, "A man who wishes to make a profession of goodness in everything must necessarily come to grief among so many who are not good."[49] If governors have a duty to protect the interests of their citizens, it has seemed to many that in the unpredictable and morally lax environment in which politicians often operate, they must ignore the normal precepts of everyday morality and look to promote the good of their people. As the realist sees it, to insist that the Non-coercion Principle applies to those in government fails to appreciate the distinctive character of the political.

We need to distinguish three different conceptions of the special nature of politics.[50] (i) The "realist" insists that there is an "ineluctable tension between the moral command and the requirements of successful political action."[51] On this conception successful politics requires immorality: one must often have morally "dirty hands" to be a successful politician. The liberal tradition in politics rejects such realism: politics is neither above nor outside the claims of morality. (ii) The first view is puzzling: why should the fact (if it be a fact) that political success requires immorality be a reason to ignore morality rather than to forgo political success? If a trade union official told us that success for the union requires immorality, we would hardly think that this excuses her immorality. A moral plausible view is that while morality applies to the government, it is an entirely different morality: the state, we are told by some, cannot be guilty of personal immorality – it is held accountable to a higher morality: "successful political action" is "itself inspired by the moral principle of national survival," and so politicians have no "moral right" to sacrifice their state in the pursuit of fidelity to the principles of individual morality.[52] This special "morality of the state" is also rejected by the liberal tradition: there is not one morality for persons and a different one for states, as if states were not composed of individuals with commitments to respect the moral personality of others. (iii) However, to deny that there is a special morality of the state is not to deny that that the special circumstances of politics may allow for justifying acts that otherwise would be wrong. Liberals (although not perhaps libertarians) accept that the conditions under which the agents of the state can justifiably employ coercion differ from the conditions under which private individuals may. This, of course, is the fundamental concern of political philosophy: how does the state come to be authorized to employ coercion (such as to punish) while private individuals are not so authorized? To accept that the agents of the state are justified in employing coercion when non-state agents are not does not mean that the Non-coercion Principle fails to apply to governors: the liberal claims that there are arguments that meet the test of Liberal Moral Neutrality that, in some cases, allow only agents of the state to justifiably coerce.

The upshot is that unless we wish to join the realist in withdrawing politics from the purview of morality, or allow that the state is subject to its own special morality of national interest, the actions of those who are agents of the state must conform

Gerald F. Gaus

to requirements of morality, specifically the Non-coercion Principle, and the only way to overcome the presumption against coercion is though a justification that conforms to the demands of Liberal Moral Neutrality. We thus have:

> *Liberal Political Neutrality*: An agent of the state when coercing a citizen, or participating in the authorization of such coercion, must be neutral between that citizen and any other citizen: the justification of the state official's coercion must not treat differentially reasonable and reflective citizen's differences in their evaluative standards.

Notice that we have switched our focus from *moral persons* to *citizens*. For the most part, I shall leave open the relation between these two classes. We do need to suppose that all members of the class of citizens are also free and equal moral persons, since the moral foundations of Liberal Political Neutrality lie in Liberal Moral Neutrality. Perhaps *all* moral persons residing within a jurisdiction should be considered as citizens (I am certainly sympathetic to this proposal); however, I shall leave open the possibility that that some moral persons within a jurisdiction (i.e., resident aliens) might be excluded from the class of citizens. This is an important issue in political theory, but we cannot pause to discuss it here. Nothing I say in what follows turns on this point.

3.3 The coercive nature of the state

Does Liberal Political Neutrality apply to all, or only some, action by state officials? John Stuart Mill distinguished authoritative from non-authoritative interventions by government; while the former take the form of a command backed by enforcement, the latter gives advice and information, or establishes an agency to deal with a problem while allowing others to compete.[53] Although the government threatening drug users with prison sentences is indeed an act of coercion, drug education programs, on Mill's view, would not be coercive. George Sher makes much of this point. In order to promote certain aims, governments might offer rewards, engage in economic policies that favor the aim, fund educational programs, and so on.[54] If these policies are not coercive, then they do not fall under the Non-coercion Principle.

What is sometimes called the "libertarian" response must be right here: each of the supposedly non-coercive measures is only possible because of a prior act of coercion, be it threats associated with the tax code, threats that back up banking regulations (relevant, say, to setting interest rates), and so on. The action "conduct an educational program" presupposes the action "raise via taxation the revenues to conduct the program." Assuming the former is impossible without the latter, it is inappropriate to separately evaluate them. An act that depends on having certain resources or powers cannot be evaluated without consideration of the legitimacy of obtaining those resources or powers. Here at least is a case where the dictum that "He who wills the end must also will the means" is appropriate: to insist that there is nothing coercive about the end, when the only way to achieve the end is through a coercive means, is disingenuous. To say that it is not coercive to spend your money, even though I must use coercion to get my hands on it, hardly seems convincing. The object of evaluation should be the complex act {raise revenues through taxation & spend them on an educational program}. That the complex should be the focus of evaluation is by no means simply a libertarian view: the American Civil Liberties Union sues public authorities that use tax money to advertise religion (say, by using public workers to erect signs saying "Jesus is Lord").[55] The idea is that this is not a mere educational measure that does not impose burdens on some; it does impose burdens that must be born by dissenting citizens because of threats of punishment by the taxation department.

It can, though, plausibly be maintained that some state actions are less coercive than others. Just as a threat of a short prison sentence is less coercive than threat of a long one, and threat of a small fine is less coercive than threat of a moderate jail term, so too the coercion involved in an extra one percent marginal tax rate is typically less coercive than the threat of jail.[56] Thus, if we concern ourselves with the strength of the justifications required to legitimate the coercion, then a distinction between stronger and milder forms of coercion will be relevant.[57] But that distinction is not relevant to the Non-coercion Principle, which concerns the set of actions that require justification.

4. The Implications of Liberal Political Neutrality

4.1 The demanding nature of Liberal Political Neutrality

To paraphrase Robert Nozick, so strong and far-reaching is Liberal Political Neutrality that it raises the question of what, if anything, the officials of the state may do.[58] It is unclear whether much in the way of public policy survives the neutrality test. Since we have seen that whenever state officials act they participate in a coercion-authorizing process, to implement any such policy would require a justification that does not exploit differences in the evaluative standards of reasonable and reflective citizens – i.e., is neutral between them. Some may think that this is not terribly demanding. It is reasonable to suppose that, after all, citizens do share many evaluative standards. Although we may not have consensus on a full-fledged conception of the good, we might still identify "a public conception of the good": there might be substantive shared values that are a matter of overlapping consensus of everyone's conceptions of the good – say, health, security and happiness.[59] Suppose, for example, that some evaluative standard Σ is shared by all. Then it would seem that an appeal to Σ in a justification for policy P would not run afoul of Liberal Political Neutrality: implementing policy P treats all citizens neutrally since the justification for it does not appeal to their reasonable differences in evaluative standards. But this moves too quickly, for we need to take account of different citizens' rankings of their evaluative standards. Reason R does not justify a policy consistent with neutrality unless it would be accepted by all fully rational and reflective citizens. Now although a rational Betty might reject R as a reason because it appeals to an evaluative standard that she does not share, she will also reasonably reject it as a good reason in favor of P when it appeals to a ranking of evaluative standards that she does not share; R may be *a* reason in favor of P, but it is overridden in her ranking by R^*, which is a reason against P. According to Milton Rokeach, a psychologist, Americans agree in affirming a set of thirty-six values; what they differ on is "the way they organize them to form value hierarchies or priorities."[60] If so, our main disagreements are not about what is of value (what is an evaluative stand-ard), but the relative importance of our evaluative standards. Even if everyone agrees, say, that smoking causes cancer and that this is *a* reason for a policy discouraging smoking, rational people clearly do disagree about whether the pleasures are worth the risk of death. Given that rational people weigh the relative values of pleasure and safety differently, coercive acts that can only be justified on the grounds that the pleasure does not outweigh the risk to health fail to provide a neutral case. Thus, although the badness of ill health caused by smoking can be invoked in a neutral justification, that its badness outweighs the goodness of the pleasure of smoking cannot; and without that, no state policies discouraging smoking will be justified. This has direct relevance to United States drug policy, which is based on certain middle class value rankings, and which results in policies that place inordinate costs on the poor.[61]

This fundamental point deserves emphasis. Political philosophers are usually insensitive to what economists call "opportunity costs": the cost of getting one thing you value is that you must forgo something else you value.[62] It is often assumed that once we recognize a shared value, we have the basis for a neutral policy; but everything depends on whether achieving this shared value requires that some give up something of greater value. If it does, then for those citizens pursuing this shared value is irrational: they are giving up something more important for something they prize less. So it does no good to simply point to shared value: we must point to a shared ranking of values, so that all rational and reflective citizens will agree that achieving this value is more important than any other values that might be achieved. But this is a daunting task: rational and reflective, free and equal persons appear to disagree deeply on the rankings of their evaluative standards (what is a "conception of the good" but a scheme in which values are weighted?). It looks as if almost any collective pursuit of values will involve some citizens being coerced into pursuing a value than is less important to them than a value they had to give up (say, because they were taxed for the collectively pursued value).

Some try to blunt the radical implications of Liberal Political Neutrality by restricting the range of the neutrality principle (the class of cases covered by ϕ) to a small set of basic political matters.[63] Rawls, for example, appears to restrict ϕ to constitutional issues or matters of basic justice: unless an issue concerns a "consti-tutional essential" neutrality does not apply – apparently non-neutral justifications can be employed in everyday (non-constitutional) politics. Can they? Suppose that we have a neutral justification of a constitution, and now are advocating policy *P*, which is not itself about a constitutional matter. There are two possibilities. It might be that the constitution which is, *ex hypothesi* neutrally justified, authorizes *P*. In this case *P does* have a neutral justification insofar as it is justified through the con-stitution which is neutrally justified. The issue, though, is whether a constitution with extensive authorizations of this sort *could* be neutrally justified. It seems doubtful indeed that, for example, a constitution that allows the government to use taxation to discourage smoking, encourage a healthy life-style, regulate drugs, fund the arts, go to war to spread democracy, seek to advance human flourishing, protect the family, or promote community, is capable of neutral public justification. Given what has been said above, there is a strong presumption that all coerced citizens could not be given impartial reasons of the requisite sort for granting the state authority over these matters. The other alternative is that the constitution is neutrally justified, but only the constitution; there is no indirect neutral justification via the constitution for policy P. The case for P is another matter entirely, outside of the scope of Liberal Political Neutrality. But this implies that P is a coercive act without adequate justification and, so wrong. Neutrality cannot be restricted to a certain "level" because the Non-coercion Principle is a fully general principle, applying to all coercive acts.

4.2 The specter of anarchism?

If Liberal Political Neutrality is *that* demanding, is any law justified? Do we end up with anarchism? Everything I have thus far said about public policies that seek to advance values such as health would seem to apply to matters of basic political justice, such as a regime of property rights. While every rational and reflective citizen may agree that some system of property rights is better than none (for then we avoid the state of nature, where there is no "mine and thine"), no argument for a specific system of property can function as a neutral justification of the requisite sort, as it will be rationally rejected by some. Some will, say, rank a libertarian system of property higher than a welfare state system, while others will have evaluative standards that lead them to the reverse ranking. The difference between the smoking case and the property rights case lies in where the option "no policy at all in this matter" is on each rational citizen's rankings. Suppose that all rational citizens endorse or prefer systems of property $\{Pr_1, Pr_2, Pr_3\}$ over no system of property rights, but some prefer no system of property rights over $\{Pr_4, Pr_5\}$. If so, there is a Liberal Political Neutralist justification for selecting from the set of $\{Pr_1, Pr_2, Pr_3\}$; our evaluative standards converge on the conclusion that any member of that set is better than no property regime at all. What is required next – and this is where democracy enters in – is a justified procedure to select from that set.[64] If we have such a procedure, then we will have a fully justified system of property rights despite the disagreements about what is the best system – disagreements on the relative merits of $\{Pr_1, Pr_2, Pr_3\}$. In contrast, in the typical public policy case, at least over a very wide range of issues, for *each and every* policy P in the set of options, a number of citizens rank P as inferior to "no policy at all on this matter." No policy whatsoever will be preferred, first, by those who prefer no policy to every policy, and so rank P and all other policies behind no policy at all (e.g., classical liberals regarding pornography regulation). Second, P will also be ranked worse than no policy at all by those who prefer some other policy P^* to no policy at all, but prefer no policy at all to P.[65] Thus on issues where some rational citizens fall into one of these two groups no public justification of P can be advanced. Of course, if there is a public justification for *some policy* on this matter (for example, regarding a public good such as pollution control), and P is in the set of admissible policies, then we move to a case like that of property rights. It is very likely, though, that once we take account of comparative judgments, Liberal Political Neutrality precludes a great deal of contemporary legislation.

4.3 Liberal Political Neutrality: critical or apologetic?

Liberal Political Neutrality is a radical principle: it expresses a suspicion that coercion threatens subjugation and, based on our understanding of others as free

Gerald F. Gaus

and equal moral persons, advances a demanding test to overcome this suspicion. *Pace* almost all contemporary advocates of Liberal Neutrality, I have argued that Liberal Political Neutrality is genuinely liberal in the sense that it is suspicious of all coercion and drastically limits the scope of government. Many of the things that contemporary states do fail the test of Liberal Political Neutrality – which is to say that contemporary states are not genuinely liberal. Some advocates of "liberal neutrality" see this conclusion as a *reductio ad absurdum*.[66] To these liberals, any adequate conception of liberal neutrality *must* show that most of what contemporary governments do is justified. Thus some tell us that if a conception of liberal neutrality excludes, say, public school classes in drama and music, it is shown to be an absurd conception.[67] This common view presupposes what liberals must question: that state coercion is justified. I see no good reason to accept what amounts to a conception of political philosophy as an apology for the current state. To appropriate a contemporary if not pellucid term, in the eyes of liberals the state is problematic. That is why the classic social contract theories begin with the state of nature – a condition without any government – and seek to show that construction of a limited government is consistent with moral principles. Current advocates of neutrality work the other way around: they start with government as we know it and test moral principles by showing that they justify it.

Even supposing it is true that "daily politics is irretrievably perfectionist" – that the aim of politics is to make people more autonomous, or healthier, or wiser, or more family-oriented, or more God-fearing – this would by no means show that anti-perfectionism is absurd or misguided.[68] If compelling moral claims show that most state coercion is unjust, then the loser is state coercion, not these fundamental moral convictions. Liberal moral principles are indeed "self-stultifying"[69] when what is being stultified is unjustified coercion of some by others. Morality stultifies a host of things that we may wish to do, including making others more perfect in our own eyes.

Notes

1. See Charles Larmore, *Patterns of Moral Complexity* (Cambridge: Cambridge University Press, 1987), pp. 43ff.; Will Kymlicka, "Liberal Individualism and Liberal Neutrality," *Ethics* 99 (Jul. 1989): 833–905; Simon Caney, "Consequentialist Defenses of Liberal Neutrality," *The Philosophical Quarterly* 41 (Jan. 1991): 457–77.

2. The most careful discussion is George Sher, *Beyond Neutrality: Perfectionism and Politics* (Cambridge: Cambridge University Press, 1997), Ch. 2.

3. See Jeremy Waldron, "Legislation and Moral Neutrality" in his *Liberal Rights* (Cambridge: Cambridge University Press, 1993), pp. 149ff.

4. Peter Jones, "The Ideal of the Neutral State" in Robert E. Goodin and Andrew Reeve, eds., *Liberal Neutrality* (London: Routledge, 1989), p. 9; Govert Den Hartogh, "The Limits of Liberal Neutrality," *Philosophica* 56 (1995): 59–89 at p. 61.

5. Colin M. MacLeod, "Liberal Neutrality or Liberal Tolerance?" *Law and Philosophy* 16 (Sep. 1997): 529–59 at p. 532; Paul Rosenberg, "Liberal Neutralism and the Social-Democratic Project," *Critical Review* 8 (1994): 217–34 at p. 218.

6. Wojciech Sadurski, "Theory of Punishment, Social Justice and Liberal Neutrality," *Law and Philosophy* 7 (1988/89): 351–74 at p. 371.

7. See Jones, "The Ideal of the Neutral State," p. 9.

8. See Philippe van Parijs, *Real Freedom for All* (Oxford: Oxford University Press, 1995), p. 28.
9. Bruce A. Ackerman, *Social Justice in the Liberal State* (New Haven, CT: Yale University Press, 1980), p. 11.
10. Larmore, *Patterns of Moral Complexity*, pp. 53ff.
11. Robert Talisse, *Democracy After Liberalism* (London: Routledge, 2005), p. 33.
12. See John Rawls, *Justice as Fairness: A Restatement*, ed. Erwin Kelly (Cambridge, MA: Belknap Press of Harvard University Press, 2001), p. 152.
13. Jones, "The Ideal of the Neutral State," p. 9.
14. See Brian Barry, *Justice as Impartiality* (Oxford: Clarendon Press, 1995), pp. 139–45; Ronald Dworkin, "Liberalism" in his *A Matter of Principle* (Cambridge, MA: Harvard University Press, 1985), p. 191; Roger Paden, "Democracy and Liberal Neutrality," *Contemporary Philosophy* 14 (1): 17–20.
15. Kymlicka, "Liberal Individualism and Liberal Neutrality," p. 886.
16. J. Donald Moon, *Constructing Community: Moral Pluralism and Tragic Conflicts* (Princeton, NJ: Princeton University Press, 1993), p. 55.
17. See Barry, *Justice as Impartiality*, pp. 125ff. Robert E. Goodin and Andrew Reeve, "Liberalism and Neutrality" in their edited collection, *Liberal Neutrality*, pp. 1–8.
18. Woodrow Wilson, *Message to Congress, 63rd Cong.*, 2d Session, Senate Doc. No. 566 (Washington, DC, 1914), pp. 3–4.
19. http://lawofwar.org/Neutrality.htm
20. This assumes that expressive stances are a form of treatment. On this see Christi Dawn Favor, "Expressive Desert and Deserving Compensation," in Julian Lamont, Christi Dawn Favor and Gerald Gaus, eds., *Essays on Philosophy, Politics and Economics* (Stanford, CA: Stanford University Press, 2009).
21. See John Rawls, "Kantian Constructivism in Moral Theory," in Samuel Freeman, ed., *John Rawls: Collected Papers* (Cambridge, MA: Harvard University Press, 1999), pp. 303–58, esp. 305ff. This is not to say that Rawls and I advance precisely the same conception of free and equal moral persons, as shall become clear in what follows.
22. See my *Value and Justification* (Cambridge: Cambridge University Press, 1990), pp. 278ff.
23. See here J. R. Lucas, *On Justice* (Oxford: Clarendon Press, 1980), p. 7. For a development of this conception of morality, see Thomas Scanlon, *What We Owe Each Other* (Cambridge, MA: Belknap Press of Harvard University Press, 1998), esp. pp. 177ff.
24. I argue this in *Value and Justification*, pp. 281ff.
25. See John Rawls, *Political Liberalism*, paperback edition (New York: Columbia University Press, 1996), p. 51.
26. I argue for this claim in "The Place of Autonomy in Liberalism," in John Christman and Joel Anderson, eds., *Autonomy and the Challenges to Liberalism* (Cambridge: Cambridge University Press, 2005), pp. 272–306.
27. John Locke, *Second Treatise of Government* in *Two Treatises of Government*, ed. Peter Laslett (Cambridge: Cambridge University Press, 1960), §22.
28. It also provides the basis for understanding morality as self-legislated. I develop this idea further in "The Place of Autonomy in Liberalism."
29. Rawls, "Kantian Constructivism," p. 334.
30. Rawls, *Justice as Fairness*, p. 23. The importance of the idea of self-authentication is easily overlooked in Rawls's thinking. It first appeared in his 1951 paper on an "Outline of a Decision Procedure for Ethics," which conceived of ethics as adjudicating the claims of individuals, which he clearly saw as self-authenticating. See section 5 of that paper in Rawls's *Collected Papers*, Ch. 1.
31. Hence, because of this, parties to Rawls's original position are not required to advance justifications for their claims. Rawls argues this in "Kantian Constructivism," p. 334.

32. Hadley Arkes, *First Things: An Inquiry into the First Principles of Moral and Justice* (Princeton, NJ: Princeton University Press, 1986), p. 70. Italics omitted.

33. S. I. Benn and R. S. Peters, *Social Principles and the Democratic State* (London: George Allen and Unwin, 1959), p. 110.

34. I argue that it cannot in *Justificatory Liberalism* (New York: Oxford University Press, 1996), pp. 162ff.

35. J. S. Mill, *On Liberty*, in *On Liberty and Other Essays*, ed. John Gray (New York: Oxford University Press, 1991), pp. 84–5 (ch. IV, para. 4). Mill also was aware that this assumption does not always hold true. See his *Principles of Political Economy*, in J. M. Robson, ed., *The Collected Works of John Stuart Mill* (Toronto: University of Toronto Press, 1963), vols. II and III, Book V, Ch. xi, § 9.

36. I deal with this complex question more formally in *Justificatory Liberalism*, Parts I and II.

37. Again, I recognize the complexities of this matter. I try to shed a little more light on it in "Liberal Neutrality: A Radical and Compelling Principle," in Steven Wall and George Klosko, eds., *Perfectionism and Neutrality: Essays in Liberal Theory* (Lanham, MD: Rowman & Littlefield, 2003), pp. 136–65, at pp. 150ff, and *Value and Justification*, pp. 399–404.

38. On the concept of the public, see S. I. Benn and G. F. Gaus, "The Liberal Conception of the Public and Private," in S. I. Benn and G. F. Gaus, eds., *Public and Private in Social Life* (New York: St. Martin's, 1983), pp. 31–66.

39. I leave aside here whether Σ is itself a belief about the world, as ethical naturalists would have it. It is important to stress that nothing in my account precludes moral realism as a meta-ethical or metaphysical thesis; the epistemic constraint on moral reasons is the crucial principle on which the analysis rests.

40. This interpretation is advanced by Christopher Eberle, *Religious Convictions in Liberal Politics* (Cambridge: Cambridge University Press, 2002), Ch. 3.

41. On convergence as a mode of justification, see Fred D'Agostino, *Free Public Reason: Making It Up As We Go* (New York: Oxford University Press, 1996), pp. 30–1.

42. In order to simplify, I will henceforth refer to "coercion" rather than the more cumbersome "force and coercion."

43. I have considered some possible objections in "Liberal Neutrality: A Radical and Compelling Principle."

44. Jeffrey Reiman, *Justice and Modern Moral Philosophy* (New Haven, CT: Yale University Press, 1990), p. 2.

45. Reiman, *Justice and Modern Moral Philosophy*, p. 2.

46. According to Wesley Hohfeld, Alf has a liberty to ϕ, if and only if Betty has no claim against Alf that he not ϕ. For Hohfeld's classic analysis, see his "Some Fundamental Legal Conceptions as Applied in Judicial Reasoning," *Yale Law Review* 23 (1913): 16–59.

47. Note that should the law not apply to some other party, the law would not have to be justified to him: a law might apply to only a "section of the public." Think, for example, of a law that regulates motorcycle use: it may not require justification to some class of citizens (say, those who do not drive). Stanley Benn and I explore the idea of a "section of the public" in "The Liberal Conception of the Public and Private."

48. Bernard Bosanquet, *The Philosophical Theory of the State* in *The Philosophical Theory of the State and Related Essays*, ed. Gerald F. Gaus and William Sweet (Indianapolis, IN: St. Augustine Press, 2001), p. 285. Even Bosanquet, however, insisted that, while the state as such could not be guilty of immorality, "if an agent, even under the order of his executive superior, commits a breach of morality, *bona fide* in order to do what he conceives to be a public end desired by the State, he and his superior are certainly blamable . . ." (p. 284).

49. Niccolò Machiavelli, *The Prince* in *The Prince and the Discourses* (New York: Modern Library, 1950 [1515]), p. 56.
50. I consider these issues in more detail in "Dirty Hands" in R. G. Frey and Kit Wellman, eds., *The Blackwell Companion to Applied Ethics* (Oxford: Basil Blackwell, 2003), pp. 169–79.
51. Hans J. Morganthau, *Politics Among Nations*, 5th edn (New York: Alfred A. Knopf, 1973), p. 10. See also Reinhold Neibuhr, *Moral Man and Immoral Society* (London: Student Christian Movement Press, 1963).
52. Morganthau, *Politics Among Nations*, p. 10. Note that Morganthau seems to advocate both positions (i) and (ii). It is often difficult to know whether "realists" are arguing against applying moral considerations to politics, or are arguing for a special political morality.
53. Mill, *Principles of Political Economy*, Book V, Ch. XI.
54. Sher, *Beyond Neutrality*, pp. 34–7.
55. *The Times-Picayune* (New Orleans), Sunday Feb. 24, 2002, Metro Section, p. 1.
56. See Daniel M. Weinstock, "Neutralizing Perfection: Hurka on Liberal Neutrality," *Dialogue* 38 (1999): 45–62.
57. I explore the problems of degrees of coercion and strength of justification in "Coercion, Ownership, and the Redistributive State," *Social Philosophy & Policy* (forthcoming 2010).
58. Nozick, *Anarchy, State and Utopia*, p. ix.
59. Weinstock, "Neutralizing Perfection," p. 55.
60. See Milton Rokeach, *The Nature of Human Values* (New York: The Free Press, 1973), p. 110; Milton Rokeach, "From Individual to Institutional Values," in his *Understanding Values* (London: Collier Macmillan, 1979), p. 208.
61. See J. Donald Moon, "Drugs and Democracy" in Pablo De Greiff, ed., *Drugs and the Limits of Liberalism* (Ithaca, NY: Cornell University Press, 1999), pp. 133–55.
62. George Klosko is something of an exception. He acknowledges that people disagree in their rankings, but he insists that somehow this is not a problem for justification. Thus he tells us that it is not "forbidden that government policy priorities reflect some conceptions more than others. Neutrality requires only that public policies be intended to realize nonsectarian values and that the relevant means be similarly defensible." ["Reasonable Rejection and Neutrality of Justification" in Steven Wall and George Klosko, ed., *Perfectionism and Neutrality: Essays in Liberal Theory* (Lanham, MD: Rowman & Littlefield, 2003), pp. 167–89 at p. 178.] Klosko's position seems to be that so long as policy is justified on "non-sectarian" grounds, it is neutrally justified, even if the policy "reflects" some citizens' ranking over others. I cannot see the motivation for restricting justification to the kinds of reasons advanced but not their importance; unless a more complicated account is offered, a person has no reason to accept a policy that is based on a ranking of evaluative criteria that she reasonable rejects. Klosko thus defends motorcycle helmet laws as "neutral" even though he admits that they presuppose rankings of values that are rationally rejected by some citizens. Klosko's main motivation, I think, is simply to ensure that liberal neutrality does not have radical implications; see §4.3 below.
63. Weinstock, "Neutralizing Perfection," p. 54.
64. I have argued that constitutional democracy is such a procedure in *Justificatory Liberalism*, Part III.
65. I explore this problem in much more depth in "The Legal Coordination Game," *American Philosophical Association's Newsletter on Philosophy and Law* 1 (Spring 2002): 122–8.
66. See, e.g., Klosko, "Reasonable Rejection and Neutrality of Justification," pp. 175ff.; Weinstock, "Neutralizing Perfection," p. 47.
67. See Klosko, "Reasonable Rejection and Neutrality of Justification," p. 175. Klosko is reporting, but apparently concurring with, the views of Richard Kraut.
68. Den Hartogh, "The Limits of Liberal Neutrality," p. 59.
69. This term is Weinstock's.

Perfectionism in Politics:
A Defense

Steven Wall

Many contemporary writers on politics hold that the state cannot legitimately promote the good – at least when the good that is to be promoted is subject to reasonable disagreement. Perfectionist political theories reject this claim.[1] According to these theories, the fact that some proposed political arrangement[2] that aims to promote the good is subject to disagreement, reasonable or otherwise, may provide a reason not to establish the arrangement in this or that circumstance, but it does not show that doing so is in principle illegitimate.

This paper defends perfectionism in politics. It does so in part by clarifying the core claims of perfectionist political theory. A variety of claims have been associated with the general notion of perfectionism in moral and political philosophy.[3] Distinguishing the core from the inessential claims allows perfectionist political theory to sidestep some of the common objections that have been pressed against it. The paper also defends perfectionism by rebutting some influential arguments that correctly identify its core claims. Finally, the paper defends perfectionism by advancing one modest argument in its favor. This argument holds that perfectionist political theory, unlike its chief anti-perfectionist rival, is compatible with the holism of political and moral justification – a holism of justification that is independently compelling.

I. The Perfectionist Idea

In speaking of the core claims of perfectionist political theory, I mean to identify a set of claims that are both plausible and general. They should be plausible in the sense that they express ideas that contemporary and historical writers associated with perfectionist politics seek to defend. They should be general in the sense that they are compatible with a wide range of competing perfectionist views. The idea is to present perfectionism as a general theoretical approach to politics that is both attractive and historically distinctive.

We can begin with a widely cited, but unsatisfactory, characterization of perfectionism. According to John Rawls, perfectionism is "a teleological theory directing society to arrange institutions and to define the duties and obligations of individuals so as to maximize the achievement of human excellence in art, science and culture."[4] To be fair, Rawls is not attempting to offer an account of perfectionist politics. He presents perfectionism as a general moral theory. But since his characterization has been influential in political theory, it is worth pausing to consider it.

Rawls's characterization is insufficiently general because it identifies a particular set of goods – achievement in art, science and culture – as the goods that that ought to be promoted by the perfectionist society. A general characterization of perfectionism should not be tied to particular accounts of the good that is to be promoted. Rawls's characterization is also not very plausible. I am aware of no contemporary perfectionist writer who holds that the state should *maximally* promote the goods of art, science and culture.[5] Most perfectionist writers hold that if these particular goods should be promoted they should be promoted to some non-maximal extent along with other goods that have a claim to support. A more promising idea is that the perfectionist state should maximally promote not particular goods, but the good, however this is conceived.[6] But, while more promising, this idea too should not be included within a general characterization of perfectionism. For, depending on how the good is characterized, a maximizing approach, as opposed to say a satisficing approach, will look more or less attractive.

A general characterization of perfectionist political theory, then, should not be tied to particular goods that warrant state support and should not include the maximizing injunction. What positive claims should be included in the characterization? I claimed above that all perfectionists hold that the state can legitimately promote the good, even when what is good is subject to reasonable disagreement. This claim requires unpacking. How, more specifically, do perfectionists understand the good that is to be promoted? Here it is helpful to distinguish an account of perfectionist goods from a perfectionist account of the good life.[7] The good to be promoted by the perfectionist state might refer to either or both of these. Perfectionist goods may contribute to the goodness of a human life, but they need not. It is possible that the preservation of the rain forests in South America is a perfectionist good, even if it does not contribute to the goodness of any human life. By contrast, a perfectionist account of the good life identifies activities, states, events, character traits, etc. that are valuable because and to the extent that they contribute to good human lives.

A general characterization of perfectionist political theory should not take sides on whether the state should promote good human lives only or whether it should also promote perfectionist goods that do not contribute to good human lives. Still, most perfectionists put the accent on the first of these. The state, they believe, should take an active role in creating and maintaining social conditions that best enable their subjects to lead good lives.[8] I shall assume, accordingly, that this is the primary function of the perfectionist state; and I shall not say anything more about the possible legitimacy of promoting perfectionist goods unrelated to good human lives.

A good human life can be understood in at least two importantly different ways. On the one hand, it can be understood in terms of well-being. On this understanding, a good human life is a life that goes well for the person who leads it. On the

Steven Wall

other hand, it can be understood in terms of value. A maximally valuable life need not be one that is best in terms of well-being, for it is possible that the most valuable life that a person could live requires him to make sacrifices in his own well-being for the sake of other persons or goods.[9] Since the notion of a valuable life is broader and more inclusive than the notion of well-being, there is reason to hold that the perfectionist state should promote it rather than well-being.

The point can be developed as follows. The perfectionist state should protect and promote valuable human lives. It may turn out that the best way for it to do so is to protect and promote the well-being of those subject to its authority. Thus, it may be true that the "promotion of well-being is the pivotal ethical precept of public action,"[10] but this fact might be explained ultimately by appeal to the good of promoting valuable lives.

The difference between these two goals – promoting valuable lives and promoting well-being – depends in part on the account of well-being that is being assumed. If it is thought, for example, that a person's well-being is largely a function of his success in pursuing worthwhile goals, and if worthwhile goals are objectively valuable and must be pursued in ways that are appropriately responsive to the good of others, then the difference will be small. In this case, it may be appropriate to characterize the primary function of the perfectionist state in terms of the protection and promotion of well-being. Still, in presenting a general characterization of perfectionist political theory, we should not insist on a particular account of well-being. We should hold that the primary function of the perfectionist state is to promote valuable human lives.

This claim, at this level of abstraction, does little to distinguish perfectionist from anti-perfectionist political theory. For surely any plausible political theory will hold that the state should play a role in protecting and promoting valuable human lives. We need, accordingly, to add some concreteness to the characterization. Perfectionism is not tied to any particular account of the good, but it does require the rejection of subjective theories of the good. Writers who have identified themselves, and who have been characterized by others, as perfectionist, whatever their differences, have tended to accept what I shall call the *objective good component* of perfectionist political theory.[11]

Subjective theories of the good explain the value of things to persons by reference to their mental states – desires, attitudes, experiences, sensations, emotions, etc. In its crudest formulation, subjectivism holds that something is good for someone if, and only if, he actually desires it. Less crude, and more philosophically respectable, versions of subjectivism explain the value of things by reference to pleasurable experience or informed desire. Perfectionists reject all such views. According to the objective good component of perfectionist political theory, at least some things that are good are not made so because of any connection to the mental states of persons. An example illustrates the idea. Knowledge of the physical world is valuable not because people desire it or would desire it if they were fully informed, but because it is a good. The fact that it is a good (if it is a fact) provides people with reasons to seek it.

Perfectionists often relate objective goods to the development of human nature. The development of rationality, for example, is often considered to be an objective good because it is a capacity essential to and distinctive of human nature. Following Aristotle, a number of contemporary writers have sought to develop accounts of the human good along these lines.[12] We can use the term *human nature perfectionism* to refer generally to accounts of the human good that relate objective goods to the development of human nature. Recently, however, a number of writers have characterized perfectionism without any reference to human nature. Derek Parfit, for example, characterizes perfectionism in terms of the achievement or realization of "the best things in life."[13] Here it is the existence of the objective goods, and not their relation to the development of human nature, that is highlighted. We can use the term *objective list perfectionism* to refer generally to accounts of the human good that identify perfectionist goods without relating them to the development of human nature.[14]

Proponents of human nature perfectionism must defend an account of human nature. More precisely, they must give an account of the properties or capacities that are central to human nature and the development of which have value. By contrast, proponents of objective list perfectionism must explain why some goods, and not others, are included. Objective list perfectionists need not formulate an exhaustive list of objective goods. They may believe such an undertaking to be misguided. But they should have something to say about what makes an alleged good an objective good, one worthy of pursuit.

As these remarks bring out, the objective good component of perfectionist political theory presents a host of questions and puzzles. It is natural to wonder how features or states of the world generate reasons for action for persons, and how persons can come to appreciate and respond to these reasons. But perfectionism as such does not rest on any particular set of answers to these questions. What is crucial is the commitment to an objective understanding of the good, however this might be explained.

The objective good component is neutral with respect to the issue of pluralism. Whether there is one or many ways of life that are objectively good for persons is left open. Further, the objective good component does not exclude the possibility that some goods for persons have subjective conditions. With respect to many objectively valuable activities, it may be that in order for them to contribute to the value of the lives of those who engage in them the activities must be pursued willingly or in the right spirit.[15] The presence of certain attitudes is here understood to be a necessary condition of successful engagement with these objectively valuable activities.[16] Recognition of these points blunts the common criticism of objective accounts of the good that they are insensitive to differences between individual persons.

The objective good component distinguishes perfectionist political theory from a range of influential political theories that openly or tacitly rest on subjectivism about the good.[17] But some who reject perfectionism, including some of the most influential contemporary critics of the view, also reject subjectivism about the good. These writers hold that perfectionism in politics, even when it is based on a sound understanding of the good, is unjustified. This brings us to a second component of perfectionist political theory, one that we can call the *rejection of state neutrality*.

The doctrine of state neutrality has been much discussed in recent years. The doctrine holds that the state must be neutral between rival conceptions of the good.[18] The doctrine articulates a principled (i.e. non-contingent)[19] constraint on permissible or legitimate state action. The constraint can, and has been, formulated in different ways.[20] Three formulations of the constraint have attracted support of late, and can be mentioned briefly here.[21]

Steven Wall

(a) The state should not promote the good, either coercively or non-coercively, unless those who are subject to the state's authority consent to its doing so.

(b) The state should not aim to promote the good unless there is a societal consensus in support of its doing so.

(c) The state should not justify what it does by appealing to conceptions of the good that are subject to reasonable disagreement.

As these formulations bring out, the idea of state neutrality has been understood very broadly in recent political theory.[22] A natural interpretation of the doctrine of state neutrality would allow the state to promote the good, so long as it did so in an even-handed manner. But most proponents of the doctrine wish to keep the state out of the business of promoting the good altogether, at least if the good to be promoted is controversial or subject to reasonable disagreement.

Perfectionism rejects the doctrine of state neutrality on all these formulations. According to the rejection of state neutrality component, there is no general theoretically grounded constraint in political morality that forbids the state from directly promoting the good, even when the good is subject to reasonable dispute. It will be helpful to spell out in a little more detail the implications of this component.

The first formulation presented above follows from a consent-based account of political legitimacy. Perfectionist political theory rejects consent theory and so rejects this formulation of the neutrality constraint. The second formulation appeals to societal consensus, rather than actual consent. It holds that in large pluralistic societies, the state should not aim to promote the good, since often what is good will be subject to controversy. This formulation of the constraint is not extensionally equivalent to the first one, since there can be a societal consensus that something is a good and ought to be promoted by the state even when there is not universal agreement on the matter.

The second formulation also targets the aims of state officials. These aims are not always open to view, and state officials may have a variety of different motivations in mind when they make political decisions. For this reason, some have thought that it is more promising to apply the neutrality constraint not to the aims of state officials, but rather to the justifications they give in public for the decisions they make. This yields the third formulation of the neutrality constraint. Defenders of state neutrality often defend the doctrine by appealing to the ideal of public reason. Public reasons, they argue, must be shareable in a way that excludes appeal to controversial ideals of the good. State neutrality and public justification in politics thus emerge as different sides of the same coin.

The second and third formulations of the neutrality constraint figure in recent influential versions of social contract theory, most notably that of Rawls and his followers.[23] These views represent the chief contemporary rival to perfectionist political theory. In developing an account of political morality, these modern day contractualists[24] instruct us to bracket our full understanding of the human good. Only by so doing, is it possible to present an account of political morality that has a hope of securing the allegiance of citizens who hold very different conceptions of the good. This bracketing strategy marks a sharp break with the mainstream tradition of political philosophy. As we shall see below, this is a break that perfectionists believe to be seriously misguided.

Consent theorists and contractualists reject perfectionism because they believe that, at least in large and pluralistic societies, it is illegitimate for the state to promote objectively valuable human lives. The doctrine of state neutrality, on these views, has a principled rationale. Even if the state can effectively promote the good, it should not do so. But other critics of perfectionism have sought to show not that perfectionist politics are in principle illegitimate, but rather that they are or would be self-defeating. A few writers even have suggested that the best way for the state to promote the good is for it to adhere strictly to the doctrine of state neutrality.[25]

Do these views represent a genuine departure from perfectionism? On the characterization of perfectionism I have provided, the answer is not straightforward. True, some writers have proposed an objective account of the good life and then derived a commitment to state neutrality from it.[26] Their proposed account of the good life explains why direct efforts by the state to promote the good are ruled out in principle. This kind of view is not perfectionist. But others, while conceding that the primary function of the state is to promote valuable lives, have argued that, for a variety of contingent reasons, direct efforts by the state to promote the good are unlikely to be successful. Whether this kind of view counts as perfectionist is less clear-cut.

We can distinguish local from global versions of the self-defeating worry. A person might think that a particular state should not directly favor some conceptions of the good over others. He might think this because he believes that those currently in power are incompetent. Alternatively, he might think that states in general should not directly promote particular types of goods. He might think, for example, that friendship is a good that contributes to the objective value of human lives, but that if states try to promote it directly they will do more harm than good. These are both instances of the local self-defeating charge. The global version generalizes from either or both of these worries. It holds either that all states lack the competence to promote the good or that all (or perhaps most) goods are such that it would be counterproductive for the state directly to promote them.

Local worries about the effectiveness of perfectionist politics present no problem for perfectionist political theory. No serious writer on politics does not share them to some extent. There are good reasons, however, to reject the global version.[27] Global distrust of perfectionist politics rests on implausible claims about the good or exaggerations of valid worries about the potential for states to abuse their power. Still, it is important not to confuse means with ends. The end of perfectionist politics is the protection and promotion of objectively valuable human lives. The question of where and how often the state should rely on indirect, rather than direct, measures to promote the good is a question within perfectionist political theory.[28] Though nothing of much importance turns on it, I propose to categorize a view that holds that perfectionist political ends are, for contingent reasons, always best pursued indirectly as a genuine instance of perfectionism. It is not a plausible view, but it remains perfectionist nonetheless.

Having distinguished the two components of perfectionist political theory, it is natural to wonder how they are related. As we have seen, the rejection of state neutrality does not follow directly from the objective good component. It is possible to reject the former and affirm the latter and *vice versa*. But while not logically connected, the two components complement each other. Perfectionists hold that the state should take an active role in creating and maintaining social conditions that best

Steven Wall

enable their subjects to lead good lives. Good lives are understood in objective terms, thus making it plausible to believe that the state (or state officials) have a duty to encourage some pursuits and discourage others. The satisfaction of this duty, in turn, requires the rejection of the constraint of state neutrality. Furthermore, the two components taken together, mark perfectionism as a distinctive approach to politics, one that contrasts with Kantian social contractualism, Hobbesian/Humean subjectivism, and Lockean consent theory.

II. Pluralism and Skepticism

The core claims of perfectionist political theory do not settle the issue of pluralism. But since this issue is of great importance for contemporary politics, we need to say something about it. Is the best version of perfectionism one that holds that there is but one way of life that is best for human beings, or one that holds that there are a plurality of equally – or perhaps incommensurably – valuable ways of life for human beings?

The question is much too large to answer here. But it will be helpful, for present purposes, to come to a better understanding of the issues it raises. Several dimensions of pluralism are worth marking. Pluralism can refer to the *beliefs* of people. The term "reasonable pluralism" has come to refer to the purported fact that reasonable people, under free conditions, will affirm incompatible comprehensive doctrines about how to live.

Pluralism is more commonly associated with "value pluralism" – the view that there exists a range of irreducibly distinct objective values. On this view, two or more ways of life may be equally valuable if (a) they realize the same objective goods, but order them differently or (b) they realize different objective goods. Further, the plurality of objective values might be traceable to a single source or might not be unified in this way. Some recent defenses of perfectionism take the former more moderate view[29], while others advance a radical form of pluralism, asserting the existence of a plurality of goods without seeking to tie them to a common source.[30]

Value pluralism, of the moderate or radical variety, can help to explain the pluralism of reasonable beliefs. For if value pluralism were true, then we would have an explanation for how reasonable people can affirm different and incompatible evaluative doctrines. Still, what Rawls terms "reasonable pluralism" is compatible with the claim that there is only one ultimate value. Reasonable pluralists can be value monists.[31]

I shall have more to say about reasonable disagreement in politics shortly. For now I want to explore the implications of taking pluralistic perfectionism seriously. Pluralistic perfectionism refers to any version of perfectionist political theory that affirms either the radical or moderate doctrine of value pluralism distinguished above. Critics of perfectionism often overlook the possibility of pluralistic perfectionism. This has led to some bad arguments for state neutrality. Rawls, for example, lumps contemporary pluralistic perfectionists together with those who hold that "there is but one reasonable and rational conception of the good."[32] He then argues that a conception of justice informed by such views could be stable only if it were backed up by the oppressive use of state force.[33] To achieve a stable non-oppressive political order, he concludes, we must avoid perfectionist politics and seek a conception of justice that can be accepted by people who affirm different conceptions of the good.

Since pluralistic perfectionism rejects the claim that there is but one reasonable and rational conception of the good, this argument has no force against it. If it were true that reasonable people can affirm different conceptions of the good life, then a concern for non-oppressive political stability would provide a reason to reject monistic versions of perfectionism. However, it would provide no reason to favor state neutrality over pluralistic perfectionism.

The lesson to draw from this is simple: to accommodate pluralism we need not embrace anti-perfectionism. Still, despite its acceptance of value pluralism, pluralistic perfectionism purports to distinguish sound from unsound accounts of the good. For some critics of perfectionism this is the problem. These critics argue that perfectionist politics rests on indefensible epistemological claims.[34] On this skeptical view, it is thought that when two people, for example, disagree over the importance of religious practice to the good life, then – while there may be a fact of the matter as to who is right – neither party can know that the other side is mistaken.

Skepticism with respect to questions of the good life is often fueled by the adoption of implausibly high standards for knowledge in this domain. If knowledge of what contributes to a good human life requires certainty[35], then we may have little or no knowledge of such matters. But surely this sets the bar too high. In other areas of inquiry, we do not (and should not) demand certainty as a condition of knowledge. Further, although I have not argued for this here, the best versions of perfectionism are fallibilist and open to revision.

A better skeptical move is to argue that questions of the good life raise special epistemological difficulties not present in other evaluative domains. One common strategy is to draw a sharp distinction, for instance, between the right and the good and then argue that knowledge of the latter is problematic in a way that knowledge of the former is not. Doctrines of justice, including the principle of state neutrality, can be known. Doctrines of the good cannot. Call this the *asymmetry claim*. A defense of the asymmetry claim can proceed in one of two ways. A general defense seeks to identify features of the good life that are especially problematic from an epistemological standpoint, without taking a stand on what is the best account of a good life. By contrast, a particular defense of the asymmetry claim assumes particular accounts of justice and the good life. To take an example, consider a theory that affirms a Kantian view of justice and a Sidgwickean view of the human good.[36] On such a theory, knowledge of the good may raise special epistemological difficulties (e.g. how exactly are we to know which life we would choose if we had full information of all the possibilities?) not present with knowledge of justice. The difficulties here follow from the particular account of the good that is affirmed.

General defenses of the asymmetry claim have proven to be unpromising. No one has identified a general reason to think that the good is harder to know than, say, the right or the beautiful.[37] Those who wish to defend the asymmetry claim must first defend an account of the good and then show that knowledge of the good is hard to come by, given this account. The issues raised by the asymmetry claim are therefore issues that really concern the objective good component of perfectionist political theory. If it could be shown that the best account of objective good generates special epistemological difficulties, then the asymmetry claim would have force.

Steven Wall

It would provide an independent reason to reject perfectionist politics. Lacking any good reason to think that the best account of objective good has this consequence, we can leave the asymmetry claim behind.

Skepticism is, in all likelihood, an exaggerated response to a genuine problem. This is the problem presented by seemingly intractable disagreement. It is easy to slide from the thought that two people reasonably disagree about some matter to the conclusion that neither side could have a good reason for thinking that his own view was correct.[38] The slide, of course, is unwarranted; but the serious objection to perfectionist political theory has nothing to do with skepticism. It concerns disagreement in politics and how best to respond to it. The worry is that perfectionist political theory fails to appreciate the political challenge posed by intractable disagreement about morality and the good. This is a worry I shall attempt to allay in the next two sections.

III. The Challenge of Justificatory Liberalism

Thus far I have rebutted a number of objections to perfectionist political theory that misfire because they misidentify its core claims. But some objections to perfectionism do not rest on misunderstanding. An important strand of contemporary political philosophy holds that, at least under modern conditions, the central political task is to find principles of political association that, to as great an extent as possible, people can agree on despite their differences. Since perfectionist political theory has tended to reject this characterization of the political task, it is open to the objection that it fails to respond adequately to political controversy under modern conditions.

The objection is often formulated in terms of political legitimacy. A legitimate political order, it is said, is one that has a publicly justified constitution and set of laws. Public justification is the proper response to intractable political disagreement under modern conditions. Public justification, in turn, demands that each member of the political order be given a justification for the political arrangements that bind him that he can accept, given his background beliefs.[39] The problem with perfectionism, on this view, is that it does not take the project of shared public justification seriously enough. Perfectionist political theory must be rejected because it yields a flawed account of political legitimacy.

Let us use the term *justificatory liberalism* to refer to any political theory that accepts the public justification condition on political legitimacy.[40] If any version of justificatory liberalism is correct, then perfectionism in politics is misguided; for the public justification condition on political legitimacy rules out perfectionist political action that is subject to reasonable disagreement.[41] Justificatory liberals embrace the bracketing strategy I mentioned earlier. Controversial perfectionist political action is ruled illegitimate in principle, irrespective of whether it is based on defensible claims about the human good.

Justificatory liberals have developed an impressive challenge to perfectionist political theory. Nevertheless, I shall argue that the challenge can be met. I shall argue that there is no good case for accepting the public justification condition on political legitimacy. Defenses of public justification either (i) overstate the values served by public justification or (ii) ground the condition of public justification on an implausible account of moral reasons.

We can begin by looking at the values that the public justification condition is alleged to serve. According to Rawls, the requirement of public justification serves two important, and interrelated, values: stability and reciprocity. A publicly justified political order will be more stable than one that lacks public justification. The stability in question is what Rawls terms "stability for the right reasons;" namely that each citizen can view the political order as justified from within his own more comprehensive set of evaluative beliefs. Stability for the right reasons also ensures that each citizen is treated with reciprocal concern. Reciprocity characterizes the relations between citizens in a well-ordered political society. It establishes that relationship as one of "civic friendship."[42]

Stability and reciprocity are values that come into their own given the expectation of intractable disagreement on morality and the good. If citizens were inclined to agree on these fundamental matters, then stability and reciprocity would lose much of their normative significance. With this in mind, we can distinguish the *content* of a conception of justice from its *justificatory reach*. Think of the content of a conception of justice as consisting of the substantive principles it proposes for determining the assignment of rights and entitlements to persons.[43] And assume that the content of a conception of justice is determined by drawing on "the full resources of philosophical reason." By contrast, the justificatory reach of a conception of justice refers to the range and number of persons to whom it can be justified. The values of stability and reciprocity give us reason to favor a conception of justice with greater justificatory reach over one with less. With this distinction in hand, we can ask, should a concern for stability and reciprocity also lead us to modify the content of what we take to be a sound conception of justice?

It is hard to know what Rawls himself thought on this matter. He believed that justice as fairness identifies the correct content of justice. But he also believed that justice as fairness could be presented in a way that ensures that it has wide justificatory appeal. If Rawls is right, then we can have it both ways. We can keep sound content while increasing justificatory reach. But if Rawls is wrong, then we will need to decide how much weight the values of stability and reciprocity have with respect to other values served by justice.

These points cast some light on the public justification condition. Suppose we view public justification as an ideal in the sense that it serves the values of stability and reciprocity. And suppose we think that this ideal, while important, nonetheless can be overridden. That is, suppose we think that sometimes we must choose between expanding the justificatory reach of our conception of justice by modifying its content or retaining its content but making no advance on its justificatory reach. This understanding of public justification is one that perfectionists can take on board. But it is not an understanding that fits well with the idea that public justification is a necessary condition of political legitimacy.

An alternative understanding of public justification views it as a constraint on legitimate political action. On this understanding, the values of stability and reciprocity either never come into conflict with other values relevant to justice or, when they do come into conflict with them, they always override them. This understanding of

Steven Wall

public justification supports the claim that public justification conditions political legitimacy, but it is hard to accept. Why should we think that stability and reciprocity always take precedence over other values, or even that they do so most of the time?[44]

My suspicion is that Rawls avoids this problem by assuming optimistically that the content of justice as fairness need not be altered when it is presented as "a political conception of justice." Perfectionists do not have the luxury of this conceit. They know that, at least under modern conditions, the pursuit of justice brings them into conflict with those who hold different views about morality and the good. In the face of this conflict, it may be necessary to alter the content of the principles of justice that one proposes in order to increase their justificatory appeal. This may be necessary both for low-level pragmatic reasons and because the values of stability and reciprocity that Rawls calls attention to have some weight.

None of this requires a commitment to public justification as a necessary condition of political legitimacy. Perfectionist political theory can accommodate the values that underlie public justification by including them within a more comprehensive account of political morality, one that centers on establishing and maintaining social conditions that enable people to live objectively valuable lives. Indeed, this more comprehensive account of political morality, will provide guidance as to the weight that should be assigned to values like stability and reciprocity when they come into conflict with other values relevant to justice. Absent, then, some convincing argument that the values underlying public justification should always take precedence over other values, the appeal to public justification provides no reason to reject perfectionist political theory and pursue a less sound, but possibly more widely justifiable, conception of justice.

I have been assuming that the soundness of a conception of justice can be assessed independently of an assessment of its justificatory reach. But this assumption can be challenged. In effect, I have been arguing that if there are sound values that underlie the ideal of public justification, then these values can be accommodated within a perfectionist account of political morality. But it may be thought that public justification is not so much an ideal to be accommodated, but rather an essential feature of moral justification in politics.

Gerald Gaus has recently presented an interesting argument along these lines.[45] Gaus argues that the public justification condition derives from a deeper account of moral reasons, one that we should accept. Moral reasons, he contends, are impartial reasons; and impartial reasons are reasons that all fully rational persons would acknowledge. Reconstructed, Gaus's argument unfolds as follows.

(i)   All interferences with the actions of persons stand in need of justification.
(ii) When the state interferes with the actions of persons its interference stands in need of justification.
(iii) To justify an interference with a person's action one must present the person with a reason for the interference.
(iv) A consideration R is a reason for a person, if and only if, the person, if he were fully rational, would accept that it was a reason.
(v)   Therefore, for state interference to be fully justified, it must be the case that each person interfered with is presented with a consideration that, if he were fully rational, he would accept as a reason.

Perfectionism in Politics: A Defense

Assuming that "justified" and "legitimate" political action are synonymous, then it follows, on the argument, that legitimate instances of state interference require the state to justify its actions to each person interfered with in terms that each person can rationally accept. This is a modest version of the public justification condition.

The first premiss of Gaus's argument articulates a principle that establishes a general presumption in favor of non-interference. Versions of this principle have been subject to vigorous critique.[46] For argumentative purposes, however, I shall grant it. The key premiss, in the present context, is premiss (iv). As Gaus recognizes, his argument succeeds in grounding the public justification condition only if we accept a particular account of what it means to give a person a reason.[47] This requires a specification of the crucial phrase "if he were fully rational" that appears in premiss (iv). Gaus provides the following procedural specification.

> A rational person takes into account all the relevant available evidence, makes no errors when evaluating it, makes all the correct inferences, and so is not subject to various distortions of deliberation or action (for example, he is not under the influence of drugs or compulsions), and so on.[48]

When this procedural specification is plugged into premiss (iv), Gaus's argument establishes that the justification of state interference must be directed to each person given his epistemic situation. This delivers the conclusion that legitimate state interferences must be publicly justified.

So construed, Gaus's argument holds that reasons relevant to the justification of state interference must be impartial reasons in the sense that all persons subject to the interference must be able to rationally accept them. In effect, his argument holds that all reasons relevant to the justification of state interference are a special kind of internal reason. To be a justifying reason a consideration must be one that a person would acknowledge to be a reason, irrespective of his initial set of values, beliefs, motivations, etc, if he deliberated rationally in the specified procedural sense.

I shall now argue that this account of reasons is not plausible on independent grounds. It therefore cannot provide independent support for the public justification condition. To bring this out, consider the following two reason statements:

(R1) David has a reason to do A in circumstances C.
(R2) Sally has a reason to do A in circumstances C.

And now consider the following two possible states of affairs:

(S1) David does not accept that consideration R is a reason for him to do A in circumstances C, but he would accept this if he had access to information I.
(S2) Sally does not accept that consideration R is a reason for her to do A in circumstances C, but she would accept this if she did not suffer from deficiency D.

On the account of reasons that we are now considering, (R1) will be false in (S1) if information I is not rationally available to David. This has counterintuitive implications. Suppose the information is not rationally available to David because no one knows it or suppose the information is available to David in some sense, but it is not rationally available to him because it would be irrationally costly for him to

Steven Wall

acquire it. In both of these cases, it is plausible to hold that while the consideration that makes it true that David has a reason to do A is not rationally available to him he nonetheless has a reason to do A in circumstances C. Likewise, (R2) will be false in (S2) if Sarah's deficiency D is not one associated with the mechanisms of cognitive processing mentioned in the procedural specification of rationality. The deficiency in question, for example, might involve a character defect that prevents Sarah from recognizing that a relevant evaluative consideration applies to her.[49] Once again, it is plausible to hold that Sarah nonetheless has a reason to do A in circumstances C.

These examples illustrate a fundamental point about reasons for action, including moral reasons. The failure to acknowledge that one has a reason do something may, but need not, involve irrationality. Note that this point can be accepted by both proponents and critics of the claim that all reasons for action are internal reasons. (Call this claim internalism and its denial externalism.) Many proponents of internalism will say that (R1) is true, given (S1), if the information that David lacks is information relevant to some goal or concern that he has. The fact that the information is not rationally available to him does not change the fact that it provides him with a reason. Externalists will concur, but add that (R2), given (S2), is true as well.

This is not the place to consider the relative merits of these two views about reasons. Most perfectionists, I suspect, accept an externalist account. Other things being equal, the fact that some action would further a person's objective good is a reason for him to undertake it, whether or not he would rationally accept that it is a reason. Deficiencies of various kinds can prevent people from recognizing the reasons that apply to them.[50] So, at the very least, Gaus's argument begs the question against the externalist perfectionist. Still, even if externalism is put to one side, Gaus's argument for the public justification condition can be rejected since it rests on an account of reasons that implausibly conflates considerations of rationality with reasons for action. The conflation is crucial for deriving the conclusion that public justification is a necessary condition of political legitimacy from the general presumption in favor of non-interference and relatively modest claims about the nature of moral reasons.

Now it might be said, in reply, that reasons for the justification of interference are different in kind from other reasons. One might advance, as a substantive claim, the following: *R* is a reason to interfere with the actions of another person if and only if *R* would be accepted by that person, if he were fully procedurally rational. This claim does not follow from a deeper account of moral reasons, but it might be correct nonetheless.[51] The importance of values like reciprocity and mutual respect might explain why justifying reasons for interference must be such that they can be recognized by all rational agents subject to the interference. But this line of argument brings us right back to the Rawlsian strategy of grounding the public justification condition on political legitimacy by appeal to the values that underlie public justification – a strategy that we have already considered and found wanting.

IV. Justification, Power, and Restraint

The challenge to perfectionism posed by justificatory liberalism can be answered. Yet the worry that perfectionist political theory does not take political disagreement seriously enough may persist. If legitimate state action does not need to meet a public justification test, then it may seem that perfectionists lack any principled ground for restraint in the pursuit of political ends. As one critic has put it, "[T]he application and enforcement of [perfectionist] principles is a function merely of power – the force of those who happen to have superior ability to enforce their view of the good."[52] There is an element of truth in this charge; but to bring it into sharp focus it is necessary to say more about the relation between justification and power.

Proponents of public justification insist that justification in politics is relational. Unlike a proof or a demonstration, a justification is directed toward those with whom one disagrees. To be successful, a justification, so understood, must proceed "from what all parties to the discussion hold in common."[53] If this is the notion of justification in play, then perfectionists reject it. It does not follow that perfectionists cannot be concerned with the justifiability of their principles or that they must view the application and enforcement of these principles as raising merely issues of power.

To mark this point, it will be helpful to distinguish *justification simpliciter* (justification$_s$) from the *relational justification* (justification$_r$) just mentioned. To justify$_s$ a political arrangement one must present valid reasons for accepting it and these reasons must be of sufficient weight to override competing reasons for rejecting the arrangement. Valid reasons need not be reasons that one's political opponents accept or even are in a position to appreciate fully. This notion of justification is rooted firmly in the first-person standpoint. Still, successful justification$_s$ of a political arrangement requires that the reasons one offers in support of the arrangement not only are believed by one to be valid and sufficiently weighty, but also in reality are.

Nothing in the idea of justification$_s$, however, excludes the possibility that a concern for the character of relations between citizens in a political society can provide reason to show restraint in the pursuit of sound political objectives. What Rawls terms "civility" or "civic friendship" may provide a reason to show restraint, even if this reason does not always, or even often, override other considerations. It also may be true that these considerations – call them *civility considerations* – can be grounded in a perfectionist account of the good. I shall not explore this possibility here. The present point is merely that the rejection of justification$_r$ in favor of justification$_s$ does not exclude principled reasons for restraint.

I now want to argue that justification$_s$ is prior to justification$_r$ as an account of justification in politics. The case for its priority rests on the holistic nature of political and moral justification. This argument, if sound, supports perfectionist political theory over its chief anti-perfectionist rival.[54] We have seen that a prominent strand of anti-perfectionist political theory holds that citizens should bracket their controversial ethical beliefs when formulating principles of political morality. The recommendation, in effect, is for citizens to "wall off" some of their ethical beliefs from others when thinking about principles of justice for their political society. This recommendation, on its face, runs counter to a basic requirement of practical rationality; namely, that when deciding what to do in a given context one should consider all the reasons that is one aware of that apply to the decision. Someone who brackets some of his ethical beliefs in thinking about the requirements of justice will run afoul of this requirement, at least if those beliefs bear on the matter of justice. This basic requirement of practical rationality reveals, or perhaps expresses, the holism of political and moral justification.

Steven Wall

The basic requirement of practical rationality is not as simple as my crisp formulation of it suggests. Properly understood, it does not exclude indirect strategies for complying with the demands of reason. Rule-based decision-making, for example, satisfies the requirement to the extent that it enables one to comply better with the demands of reason, even if the rules direct one to ignore certain considerations that are relevant to the decisions the rules address. To adopt some familiar terminology, some valid reasons for action are second order "exclusionary reasons."[55] Compliance with the basic requirement of practical rationality does not require one to act only on first-order reasons. But this complexity in the structure of practical rationality, while important, does not affect my present argument.

This argument holds that if one accepts the basic requirement of practical rationality, then one should favor justification$_s$ over justification$_r$ for purposes of political justification. But here it is important to tread slowly. It is true that, in some contexts, we have a good justification$_s$ for bracketing reasons that apply to a given decision. Think, for instance, of a criminal proceeding in which jurors are instructed to disregard information that is plainly relevant to forming a belief on the accused's innocence or guilt. Still, this practice of "walling off" relevant information must be justified$_s$, if it is justified at all. Or so I claim. Perhaps the anti-perfectionist proponent of the bracketing strategy has a similar idea in mind. He might believe that there is a sound case from within his own comprehensive set of ethical beliefs for recommending that citizens bracket their controversial ethical views when formulating principles of justice for a pluralistic society.[56] That is, he might think that the justifying reasons for advancing a political conception of justice are reasons that should not be openly presented. But taking this line makes it plain that for purposes of political justification justification$_s$ ultimately is prior to justification$_r$.

I mentioned above that one might support an anti-perfectionist conception of justice because one believes that the values of stability and reciprocity always take precedence over all competing considerations. That view, I suggested, is not very plausible; but now we can see that, if it were sound, it would justify$_s$ the practice of "walling off" controversial considerations from deliberations about the requirements of justice. If, however, this view is rejected, then the basic requirement of practical rationality that I have been discussing favors perfectionist theories over anti-perfectionist theories, like that of Rawls, that give primacy to relational justification in politics.

Return now to the charge that perfectionism makes the enforcement of political principles turn on considerations of power. Plainly, if there is no political support for a perfectionist proposal, then, irrespective of its merits, it will not be undertaken. Likewise, if political support increases for a particular proposal, then it will become easier to enforce it successfully. To this extent, perfectionism in politics is sensitive to balance of power considerations.

The charge that perfectionism makes the enforcement of political principles turn on considerations of power now looks pretty innocuous. Every conception of political morality makes the enforcement of its principles sensitive to balance of power considerations to some extent or degree. Even the achievement of a Rawlsian overlapping consensus turns on the presence of sufficient political support for such a consensus. Yet it remains true that, unlike some influential versions of contemporary liberalism, perfectionist political theory does not tie political legitimacy to the consent of the governed, whether actual or hypothetical. This clean break with the consent tradition in politics is, in my judgment, a strength of perfectionism. Efforts to depict principles of justice as expressing or resting on shared commitments have become increasingly strained as the pluralism of modern societies has been fully recognized. Still, the longing for a consensual politics, however misplaced it may be for our times, continues to motivate work in political philosophy. This longing does much to explain why some conclude that even a sound perfectionist political program would require for its implementation an unacceptable measure of subjugation.

V. Conclusion

Perfectionist political theory has two basic components: the objective good component and the rejection of state neutrality component. I have been defending the second component in some detail. I have said very little in defense of the first. The main reason for this is that the most influential arguments against perfectionism in politics have sought to vindicate some version of state neutrality. But a full defense of perfectionist political theory must defend the first component against subjectivist and skeptical challenges. In not discussing these challenges in detail here, I certainly do not mean to downplay their importance.

For a variety of reasons, many have lost confidence of late in the capacity of human reason to resolve evaluative questions. This loss of confidence – sometimes dramatically referred to as the "failure of the Enlightenment project" – has provoked some to embrace relativism and/or skepticism about values generally. In others, it has prompted the more moderate response of restricting the scope of reason to fewer and fewer evaluative domains. Thus, it is now fashionable to think that reason can settle questions of fair dealing and justice, but that it is silent on questions concerning the human good. To respond to these anti-rationalist tendencies, perfectionist political theory needs an account of objective value that can abate the puzzles that nourish them. The successful completion of such an account is eagerly awaited.[57]

Notes

1 Perfectionist political theory includes a broad range of historical views including those of Plato, Aristotle, Aquinas, Mill (at least on some interpretations) Marx and T. H. Green as well as a large number of less influential thinkers. Among contemporary writers perfectionism in politics has been defended by, among others, Richard Arneson, John Finnis, Thomas Hurka, Jospeh Raz, and George Sher.

2 I use the term "political arrangement" to refer indiscriminately to political institutions, constitutions, laws, policies, directives, etc.

3 Perfectionism can refer to a moral theory, an account of well-being or an account of politics. In this chapter I use the term to refer to an account of politics.

4 John Rawls, *A Theory of Justice* (Cambridge, MA: Harvard University Press, 1971), p. 325.

5 Rawls's characterization appears to be based on his reading of Nietzsche's elitist version of perfectionism. He cites Nietzsche's statement that "Mankind must work continually to produce individual great human beings – this and nothing else is the task ..." (*A Theory*

Steven Wall

of Justice, p. 325, n. 51). But this elitism is incidental to perfectionist political theory, and the best versions of perfectionism reject it.

6 See Hurka's claim that "the best perfectionism is a maximizing consequentialism that is time- and agent-neutral, telling us to care equally about the perfection of all humans at all times." Thomas Hurka, *Perfectionism* (New York: Oxford University Press, 1993), p.55.

7 George Sher, *Beyond Neutrality* (New York: Cambridge University Press, 1997), p. 154.

8 See my characterization in Steven Wall, *Liberalism, Perfectionism and Restraint* (Cambridge: Cambridge University Press, 1998), p. 8.

9 The distinction is drawn by T. M. Scanlon. See *What We Owe to Each Other* (Cambridge, MA: Harvard University Press, 1999), p. 112.

10 Joseph Raz, *Ethics in the Public Domain* (Oxford: Clarendon Press, 1994), p. vi.

11 See, for example, Vinit Haksar, *Equality, Liberty and Perfectionism* (Oxford: Oxford University Press, 1979), Joseph Raz, *The Morality of Freedom* (Oxford: Clarendon Press, 1986), John Finnis, *Natural Law and Natural Rights* (Oxford: Clarendon Press, 1979), Thomas Hurka, *Perfectionism*, and George Sher, *Beyond Neutrality*.

12 See Thomas Hurka, *Perfectionism* and Phillipa Foot, *Natural Goodness* (New York: Oxford University Press, 2001).

13 Derek Parfit, "Overpopulation and the Quality of Life" in Peter Singer, ed., *Applied Ethics* (New York: Oxford University Press, 1986).

14 The distinction drawn here between human nature and objective list perfectionism is similar to Hurka's distinction between narrow and broad perfectionism. See Thomas Hurka, *Perfectionism*, p. 4.

15 See the discussion of "whole-hearted" engagement in Joseph Raz, *Ethics in the Public Domain*, pp. 5–6.

16 An extreme version of this view holds that all objective goods have subjective conditions. While not very plausible, such a view is consistent with the objective good component. By contrast, subjectivists about the good hold that the presence of appropriate mental states is not only necessary, but also sufficient, for something to contribute to the value of a person's life.

17 It distinguishes perfectionism from classical utilitarian accounts of political morality, like that defended by Bentham and Sidgwick and from writers in the social contract tradition who follow Hobbes. It also distinguishes perfectionism from Hume's sentimentalist political ethics.

18 For a clear defense, see Charles Larmore, *Patterns of Moral Complexity* (Cambridge: Cambridge University Press, 1987), pp. 40–68.

19 The importance of the qualifier "principled" will become apparent shortly.

20 Defenders of state neutrality differ as to which political decisions the constraint applies to: to all political decisions, to constitutional issues only, to coercive laws and policies, etc. I ignore this complication here.

21 It is common to mention the view that the consequences of state action should be neutral between conceptions of the good. Here the constraint is formulated in terms of neutrality of effect. But proponents of state neutrality generally mention this view to put it to one side. Whether they are entitled to do so is discussed in my "Neutrality and Responsibility," *Journal of Philosophy* (2001).

22 Raz distinguishes the doctrine that the state should not take sides between different conceptions of the good from a doctrine that enjoins the exclusion of ideals from political justification. See Joseph Raz, *The Morality of Freedom* (Oxford: Clarendon Press, 1986), pp. 108–9. I am using the doctrine of state neutrality to include both of these doctrines.

23 See John Rawls, *Political Liberalism* (New York: Columbia University Press, 1993), Thomas Nagel, *Equality and Partiality* (New York: Oxford University Press, 1991), Charles Larmore, *Patterns of Moral Complexity* and Brian Barry, *Justice as Impartiality* (Oxford: Clarendon Press, 1995).

24 There may be versions of contractualism that are compatible with perfectionist politics. I use the label to refer to the views of Rawls and his followers.

25 See, for example, Will Kymlicka, *Contemporary Political Philosophy* (New York: Oxford University Press, 1990), pp. 199–205.

26 See Ronald Dworkin, "The Foundations of Liberal Equality," *The Tanner Lectures on Human Values: Volume XI* (1990).

27 See George Sher, *Beyond Neutrality*, pp. 106–39, Thomas Hurka, "Indirect Perfectionism: Kymlicka on State Neutrality," *Journal of Political Philosophy* 3 (1995): 36–57, and Simon Caney, "Consequentialist Defences of State Neutrality," *The Philosophical Quarterly* 41 (1991): 457–77.

28 On this point see the distinction between state-centered and multi-centered perfectionism in Joseph Chan, "Legitimacy, Unanimity, and Perfectionism," *Philosophy and Public Affairs* 29 (1) (Winter 2000): 5–42.

29 See George Sher, *Beyond Neutrality*, pp. 199–244.

30 See Joseph Raz, *The Morality of Freedom*.

31 This point is well developed by Charles Larmore, "Pluralism and Reasonable Disagreement," *Social Philosophy and Policy* 11 (1) (1994): 61–79.

32 John Rawls, *Political Liberalism*, p. 135.

33 John Rawls, *Political Liberalism*, p. 37.

34 Brian Barry, *Justice as Impartiality*, pp. 168–73.

35 As Barry among others, holds.

36 Not an idle possibility, for such a position is found in Rawls's *A Theory of Justice*.

37 Rawls's appeal to the "burdens of judgment" is a case in point. If these factors explain reasonable disagreement concerning matters of the good, then they also explain reasonable disagreement in other evaluative domains.

38 For a good instance of the slide see Joshua Cohen, "Moral Pluralism and Political Consensus" in David Copp, Jean Hampton, and John E. Roemer, eds., *The Idea of Democracy* (New York: Cambridge University Press, 1993), p. 284.

39 A weaker version of the demand holds that there must exist a public justification for the political arrangements that bind each member, such that each member of the political order could accept it, given his background beliefs. Since nothing I say here turns on whether the public justification must be actually presented or merely one that could be presented, I shall ignore this complication in what follows. I shall also ignore the very difficult issue of how to specify the background beliefs to which public justification is relativized.

40 The term is taken from the title of Gerald F. Gaus's book *Justificatory Liberalism* (New York: Oxford University Press, 1996). He uses it to refer to his own favored political theory; and not, as I do, to theories in general that make public justification a necessary condition of political legitimacy. For a helpful summary of different versions of justificatory liberalism see Fred D'Agostino, *Free Public Reason* (New York: Oxford University Press, 1996).

41 Perfectionism is compatible with some relatively weak formulations of the public justification condition. Here I understand public justification in the strong sense that it has come to have in contemporary political philosophy, one that demands that political justifications not only be presented openly, but also they be acceptable to all reasonable or rational persons.

42 John Rawls, *Political Liberalism*, p. li.

43 So, on this distinction, the content of justice as fairness is given by the two principles of justice and the lexical ordering relations that hold between them.

44 Rawls claims that political values "normally have sufficient weight to override all other values that may come into conflict with them" (*Political Liberalism*, p. 138). But note that

Steven Wall

political values for Rawls includes justice. Since perfectionists also value justice, the relevant contrast is between the values of reciprocity and stability, which are distinctive of a political conception of justice, and other values, which may or may not include justice.

45 See Gerald F. Gaus, "Liberal Neutrality: A Radical and Compelling Principle" in Steven Wall and George Klosko, eds., *Perfectionism and Neutrality: Essays in Liberal Theory* (Lanham, MD: Rowman & Littlefield, 2003), and Gerald F. Gaus, "The Place of Autonomy within Liberalism" in John Christman and Joel Anderson, eds., *Autonomy and the Challenges to Liberalism: New Essays* (Cambridge: Cambridge University Press, 2005).

46 See Douglas Husak, "The Presumption of Freedom," *Noûs* 17 (3) (1983): 345–62.

47 Suppose we construe "if he were fully rational" to mean "if he were to see matters rightly." This would make premiss (iv) a trivial claim. It would also disable Gaus's argument from justifying any recognizable public justification condition.

48 Gerald F. Gaus, "The Place of Autonomy," p. 290. See also "Liberal Neutrality," pp. 143–4.

49 In failing to appreciate the evaluative consideration, Sarah may make no rational mistake. On this point see Scanlon's discussion of internal and external reasons in *What We Owe to Each Other*, pp. 363–73.

50 Talk of deficiencies in capacities to appreciate reasons might suggest to some an elitist picture of moral reasons, whereby some have unimpaired access to moral truths while others do not. But such elitism is not integral to an externalist account. Each of us, in varying ways and to varying degrees, may suffer from such deficiencies. Certainly no one is immune from them.

51 See, for example, Gaus's interesting discussion of the claim that each person's reasoning merits some respect: "Liberal Neutrality," pp. 149–55. This claim is a substantive addition to the argument about the nature of moral reasons that we have been discussing.

52 John Christman, "Procedural Autonomy and Liberal Legitimacy," in James Stacey Taylor, ed., *Personal Autonomy: New Essays on Personal Autonomy and Its Role in Contemporary Moral Philosophy* (Cambridge: Cambridge University Press, 2005), p. 291.

53 John Rawls, *Theory of Justice*, p. 580.

54 Obviously, it does not support perfectionism over all anti-perfectionist views.

55 For the seminal discussion of this idea, see Joseph Raz, *Practical Reason and Norms* (London: Hutchinson, 1975).

56 Rawls does claim that citizens need to find a way to embed the political conception within their more comprehensive views. But when it comes to political justification citizens "are to conduct their fundamental discussions within the framework of what each regards as a political conception of justice based on values that [other citizens] can reasonably be expected to endorse." *Political Liberalism*, p. 226.

57 Thanks to David Sobel for helpful comments on an earlier draft of this chapter.

LIBERALISM

LIBERTY AND DISTRIBUTIVE JUSTICE

Individualism and Libertarian Rights

Eric Mack

I. Introduction

This essay is a partial defense of the rights that are at the core of libertarian political theory. It provides some lines of reasoning in defense of rights-based political theory that arrives at libertarian conclusions.[1] To say that the theory is rights-based is to say that its most fundamental interpersonal norms are expressions of rights that individuals possess against others – rights that restrict the permissible actions of those other agents. To say that the theory is rights-based is not, however, to say that it takes those fundamental rights to be philosophical primitives or self-evident truths. Thus, the need for the defense that this essay partially provides. Even the provision of a partial defense of these rights is, to say the least, a formidable philosophical task. My hope is that this excuses the bold and highly programmatic presentation of this essay's substantive normative argument – and its neglect of meta-ethical niceties. The two fundamental rights that will come to the fore as we proceed are the right of each individual over her own person (the right of self-ownership) and the right of each individual to the practice of private property. Sometimes two versions of libertarianism are identified – "right" libertarianism which combines self-ownership and (at least almost) unrestricted private ownership of extra-personal material – and "left" libertarianism – which combines self-ownership and some form of egalitarian ownership of (at least natural) extra-personal material. This essay supports the core rights of the first version of libertarianism.

The general strategy that I employ here for the defense of such rights is to situate the affirmation of such rights within a more encompassing moral individualism. So I need to begin with a brief description of this moral individualism and of the non-question-begging bases on which its affirmation is reasonable. I take the central – and independently plausible – root idea of this individualism to be the separate, freestanding importance of each individual's life and well-being. Moral individualism is an articulation of this root idea. The more the articulation captures and clarifies what makes it attractive in its more inchoate form, and the more the articulation yields a moral structure composed of mutually reinforcing elements, the more the plausibility of that root idea is enhanced.

If we take seriously the separate importance of persons, we should expect that individual A's own separate importance will have a different sort of directive impact on her than the separate importance of others has for A. Thus, the key working hypothesis associated with the root idea is that, for each individual, the separate, freestanding, irreducible importance of each individual's life and well-being has two distinct kinds of directive import. For each individual, the directive import of her own separate importance is that her life and well-being – her life going well – stands as the final rational end of her actions; her goal-oriented rationality consists in her choosing and acting in ways that result in or constitute her living as well as possible. In affirming the separate, freestanding, and irreducible importance of each individual's life and well-being, each individual A affirms that the rational final end for each other individual B is the advancement of B's own life and well-being. But the separateness of the importance of B blocks any inference from B's life going well standing as a final rational end (for B) to its being a final rational end for A.[2]

If the separate importance of B's life and well-being as such has any directive import for A, it must be different in kind than providing A with an end she is rational to promote. Intuitively, there does seem to be this second, different in kind, directive import. The most intuitively objectionable treatments of B by A are treatments in which A disposes of B as though B is a resource available for A's use and exploitation. These actions are naturally described as A's treating B as though B is not a being whose life and well-being are of separate, freestanding importance – as A's treating B as though B is not a being with rational ends of his own. If the sense that it is unreasonable for A to engage in such actions *because of the separate importance of B's life and well-being* is correct, it must be because B's separate importance has directive import for A – where that import is a requirement in reason that A not treat B as though he is not a being whose life and well-being are of separate importance. Such a requirement imposes constraints on the means by which A may transact with B in the course of promoting her valued ends.

So, the root idea of the separate, freestanding importance of each individual's life and well-being seems to have both goal-oriented (teleological) import and means-eschewing (deontic) import. The first import provides individuals with the ends that they respectively have reason to promote; the second import provides individuals with restrictions on their treatment of others which they have reason to respect. The first (teleological) import supplies the key distinctive feature of moral individualism's theory of the good, viz., the individualization or agent-relativization of the good; each individual's life and well-being is an ultimate good – relative to the agent whose life and well-being it is. The second (deontic) import supplies the core interpersonal norms of moral individualism's theory of the right, viz., rights-correlative restrictions on the means that agents may employ in the pursuit of their respective ends. Moral individualism's root idea gains plausibility as that which provides through its articulation a unifying explanation for the independently plausible view that to be rational in the pursuit of ends is to be genuinely prudent and for the independently plausible view that it is reasonable for individuals to constrain their conduct towards other persons independent of that constraint being conducive to their rational pursuit of

Eric Mack

ends. It seeks to provide a unifying picture of the rationality of the promotion of goals and the reasonableness of constraint in the course of that promotion – a reasonableness of constraint that does not reduce to the expediency of that constraint.

Since the rationality of prudence is the most minimal and uncontroversial claim about practical rationality, it is the natural starting-point for moral theory. Normative theorizing naturally begins with the principle of choice for the individual according to which "A person quite properly acts, at least when others are not affected, to achieve his own greatest good, to advance his rational ends as far as possible."[3] Much theorizing then proceeds by arguing that the rationality of prudential action is merely a special case of the rationality of promoting the general social good. The rationality of an individual imposing some sacrifice upon herself for the sake of a greater gain for herself is, according to such theorizing, merely a special case of the rationality of an individual imposing such a sacrifice upon herself for the sake of a greater gain for members of society at large. The goal of rational action is the common social good; and this common social good provides the standard for adjudicating disputes among individuals who champion conflicting actions. If individual A favors scratching her nose with her right index finger and B favors seasoning a stew with that finger, the interpersonally sound resolution of their dispute will be supplied by a determination of which action (or set of rules for picking among conflicting actions) will directly (or indirectly) more enhance the common social good.

Moral individualism, however, fully joins John Rawls and Robert Nozick in their contention that the attempt to construe the rationality of prudence as a special case of the rationality of social optimization fails to take seriously the separateness of persons.[4] Yet this reaffirmation of the rationality of prudence may be thought to leave us without any principles capable of providing interpersonally sound resolutions of disputes among the champions of conflicting actions. Or, at best, such principles will be ungrounded and unconnected with the salient starting-point for normative theorizing, the rationality of prudence. The defense of rights and rights-correlative restrictions that will be offered here traverses a different route from the rationality of prudence to the affirmation of interpersonally forceful norms – a route that does not abandon its own starting-point. The first leg of the route is from the rationality of prudence and the associated prerogative of each individual to eschew imposing sacrifices upon herself for the sake of advancing the ends of others to the separate, freestanding importance of each individual; in the language we shall soon employ, this leg takes us to the *rationale* for the affirmation of this prudence and this prerogative. The second leg is from this root idea – or rationale – to the affirmation of rights-correlative restrictions. The route begins with a move from prudence and the prerogative of eschewing sacrifice to the root idea or rationale that has prudence and this prerogative as its first directive import; it then proceeds to the rights and constraints that are the second – and different in kind – directive import of that root idea or rationale.

I traverse this route by responding to a challenge that Samuel Scheffler issues in *The Rejection of Consequentialism*.[5] Scheffler agrees that the separateness of persons – which he casts as the natural independence of the personal point of view – has the first kind of directive import. The natural independence of each individual's viewpoint allows her to give at least some special weight to her own interests in her decisions about whether she will sacrifice her interests in service to the external impersonal standpoint. But, Scheffler, in effect, denies that the separateness of persons has the second kind of directive import; the natural independence of the personal point of view is not a rationale for affirming rights-correlative restrictions. Scheffler challenges those who think that the separate importance of individuals has both kinds of directive import to show that a morality that incorporates the first kind of directive import – a prerogative of giving at least some special weight to one's own interests – is unacceptable if it does not also incorporate the second kind of directive import – constraints on the means that individuals may use in their pursuit of valued ends.

In the sections that follow, I further explain and meet this challenge.[6] I show how meeting it supports individualism's linkage of the goal-oriented rationality of prudence with the means-eschewing reasonableness of compliance with rights. Indeed, the conjunction of (i) the recognition that a morality that incorporates a prerogative to eschew imposing costs on oneself must also incorporate rights-correlative restrictions against interferences with the exercise of that prerogative and (ii) the affirmation of an appropriate robust prerogative yields the core libertarian rights to self-ownership and the practice of private property. Further, the fact that the argument offered here for the right of self-ownership also supports the right to the practice of private property undermines the left libertarian contention that one can coherently endorse the first of these rights without endorsing the second.

II. Prerogatives, Rationales, and Restrictions

While the natural independence of the personal point of view is manifested in each individual's tendency to be moved by her own core desires or commitments "out of proportion" to their significance from any impersonal perspective, what is crucial is that, for each individual, "[h]is own projects and commitments have a distinctive *claim* on his attention.[7] Thus, the natural independence of the personal point of view provides a rationale for the inclusion within morality of a personal prerogative according to which it is at least morally permissible for each individual to give special weight to her own separate system of ends in her determination of how she shall act. The inclusion of such a prerogative in morality amounts to the recognition that the attainment of an individual's good has agent-relative value and that agent's prospective good provides her with reason to go for that good quite aside from any agent-neutral reason that agent may have to go for or to forego that good.

On Scheffler's view, the recognition of the independence of the personal viewpoint and the associated recognition of agent-relative values and reasons for action provide a rationale for a modest prerogative; one that merely allows each individual to give *some* special weight to her own good in the determination of how she shall act. Each agent must still first identify which action available to her would be socially optimal, i.e., would most advance the overall agent-neutrally valuable social good. Only then may an individual determine whether her prerogative allows her to forego this socially optimal action. A Scheffler-style prerogative will specify some M such that, if the personal cost to A of the socially optimal action multiplied by M is equal to or greater than the impersonal gain to the world if A were to perform the socially optimal action, then it is permissible for A to eschew that socially optimal act. So, e.g., if all lives have equal weight in this calculus and M = 4, then A may decline

Eric Mack

to donate her vital organs to save three otherwise doomed strangers; for the personal cost to A (1) multiplied by M (4) exceeds the net loss to the world (2) of her eschewing the socially optimal act. If, instead, six strangers could be saved by A's donation, then A would remain obligated to perform that socially optimal act. In effect, a Scheffler-style prerogative provides individuals with a limited dispensation from compliance with the demands for personal sacrifice that are issued from the impersonal standpoint.

Scheffler recognizes that theorists who favor the incorporation of a prerogative into morality are also likely to favor the incorporation of deontic restrictions that protect individuals against interference with their chosen actions even if those actions are not optimal from some standpoint external to their own. Indeed, such theorists – among whom moral individualists are the most ardent – tend to think that the basis for the incorporation of a prerogative into morality is also the basis for the introduction into morality of deontic restrictions and the rights that are correlative to those restrictions. They tend to think that the separate, freestanding importance of each individual or the separateness of persons or the natural independence of the personal point of view underwrites both a personal prerogative and rights-correlative deontic restrictions. Scheffler issues a general challenge to theorists to show that a morality with a prerogative but without rights-correlative restrictions is unacceptable. And he issues the more specific challenge to those who tend to think that the basis for the incorporation of a prerogative into morality is also the basis for the introduction into morality of deontic restrictions to show that the rationale for the former is also a rationale for the latter. Meeting this more specific challenge would, of course, also nicely meets the more general challenge. To meet Scheffler's specific challenge, I shall defend the following *central claim*:

> "The rationale for the incorporation of a personal prerogative into morality will not be satisfied unless that prerogative is accompanied by rights-correlative restrictions that protect individuals against interference with the exercise of that prerogative."

The introduction of a naked prerogative will not satisfy the rationale for its introduction; the rationale will be satisfied only if the prerogative is protectively clothed in rights-correlative restrictions. That is why a prerogative without accompanying restrictions is unacceptable. And that is why, if it is reasonable to incorporate a prerogative into morality, it is also reasonable to incorporate rights-correlative restrictions against interference with the exercise of that prerogative.

A modest Scheffler-style prerogative reflects the view that there are some agent-relative values and value-oriented reasons for action and that these provide a bit of counter-weight for each individual against the requirement that she devote herself as much as is possible to the service of agent-neutrally best outcomes. Accordingly, the rationale that Scheffler locates for this prerogative is comparably modest. That rationale is the partial (perhaps quite marginal) liberation of the individual qua agent of her own system of ends from the authoritative external demands of the impersonal point of view – the impersonal standpoint being, for Scheffler, the salient external standpoint. In contrast, what we might label the "individualist prerogative" reflects the view that all values and all value-oriented reasons for action are agent-relative; the idea that the agent-neutral value of (purportedly) optimal social outcomes summon the individual to their promotion so that, at least sometimes, the individual has all-things-considered reason to sacrifice her good for the sake of the social good, is entirely repudiated. The much more robust rationale for this much more robust prerogative is the total liberation of the individual qua agent of her own system of ends from the demands of standpoints external to the agent. This includes liberation from the supposed, but specious, demands of the impersonal standpoint *and* liberation from the now emancipated standpoints of other individuals. The more robust a prerogative is, the greater the range of actions that will be at least morally permissible for individuals. For this reason, if the central claim is correct, the more robust the prerogative is, the more extensive will be the range of moral immunity that individuals enjoy in virtue of the rights-correlative restrictions to which others are subject.

So what is the argument for the central claim and, *a fortiori*, for the instance of it that concerns the individualist prerogative and its robust rationale? The argument is that there are two distinct crucial dimensions along which the rationale of liberation from external viewpoints can be satisfied or left unsatisfied and that a prerogative can only provide satisfaction of this rationale along one of those dimensions. A prerogative without accompanying rights-correlative restrictions against interference with exercises of that prerogative will, therefore, leave the rationale for the prerogative entirely unsatisfied along a crucial second dimension and, thus, will fail to satisfy the rationale for that prerogative. Those two dimensions can be designated as the "self imposed subjugation" dimension and the "other imposed subjugation" dimension.

Consider individual A who is faced with the choice between action E that most serves an external viewpoint – either the impersonal standpoint insofar as that standpoint is still in play or the personal standpoint of another individual insofar as this has come into play – and action P that better serves A's interests. Suppose also that A possesses a prerogative that allows A to choose P rather than E. This is to say that, given the costs from that external viewpoint of A choosing P and the personal costs to A of her choosing E, A's prerogative protects A from the requirement that she herself subjugate herself to the external viewpoint that E best serves. Any prerogative will, in this way, provide A with some degree of liberation from self-imposed sacrifice in service to some external viewpoint. Nevertheless, however robust A's prerogative is, however extensive is A's liberation along this self-imposed subjugation dimension, A's bare prerogative leaves A entirely subject to other-imposed subjugation in the service of the relevant external standpoint.

Suppose that A, in the exercise of her prerogative, chooses action P over action E; but suppose, further, that B, an agent for the relevant external standpoint, can intervene without significant cost from that external standpoint to override A's choice and get A to perform E. Nothing about A's prerogative protects her against such intervention by B; and everything about the external standpoint that agent B serves calls upon B to subjugate A to that external standpoint. Although it is within A's prerogative to do P rather than E – if A can get away with doing P under the watchful eye of the relevant external viewpoint – nothing precludes agents of that external viewpoint from suppressing A's choice and subjugating A to the demand that she optimally serve that external viewpoint. Although A's prerogative liberates A to some degree from the requirement that she impose sacrifices on herself for the sake of the relevant external viewpoint, it does nothing to limit the sacrifices that others may impose upon her in the name of the external viewpoint.

126   **Eric Mack**

Of course, if the intervention to override A's choice itself has significant costs from the external standpoint that is in play, it may be that the agent of that standpoint ought not to intervene. But, in such cases, the reason for non-interference with A's exercise of her prerogative is simply that interference is not optimal from that external viewpoint. The fact that sometimes, from some external viewpoint, it will not pay to suppress A's exercise of her prerogative does not indicate any degree of liberation of A from other-imposed subordination to that external viewpoint. The absence of restrictions against interference with the exercise of that prerogative leaves A totally unliberated from the relevant external standpoint along the other-imposed subjugation dimension. Given that the rationale for the prerogative is the liberation of the individual from external stand-points, a prerogative without accompanying restrictions fails to satisfy that rationale. A morality provides A with little liberation from the demands of an external standpoint if, as agents of that standpoint drag her off to the sacrificial altar, it at most requires those agents to assure A that she was not morally required to volunteer for this fate.

These points can be made more concretely and vividly by considering for a moment Scheffler's modest prerogative and the sort of liberation it would provide or fail to provide for individual A from the impersonal standpoint (which remains the relevant external standpoint within Scheffler's moral scheme). Suppose that the socially optimal action E is A's surrender of four of her vital bodily organs the transplantation of which into four dying strangers will save those four persons, and that the personally less costly action P is A's retention of those organs. Suppose further that through its specifica-tion of M a Scheffler-style prerogative makes it morally permissible for A to chose P over E. The crucial point is that the permissibility of A's declining to sacrifice herself for the four strangers is entirely consistent with its being permissible or even obligatory for an agent of social optimization (e.g., the government) to impose that sacrifice upon A. Indeed, it will be permissible and obligatory for this agent to impose that sacrifice upon A unless there are very substantial peripheral social costs – costs from the impersonal standpoint – associated with the imposed organ transfer.[8]

So A's Scheffler-style prerogative does not at all liberate her from other-imposed subjugation to the external viewpoint that remains salient within Scheffler's scheme. And being subject to other-imposed subjugation to this external viewpoint pretty much makes a mockery of A's modest liberation from the requirement that she herself choose that subjugation. This should be no surprise, as Scheffler repeatedly emphasizes that, within a code that includes a prerogative but no restrictions, it always remains permissible to engage in socially optimal action.[9]

My sense is that, when Scheffler says this, he is thinking of individual A remain-ing morally free, despite her prerogative, to choose to engage in the personally sacrificial and socially optimal action. Yet the more striking implication of everyone remain-ing morally free to engage in socially optimal action is that B, the agent of the imper-sonal standpoint, remains morally free (and usually obligated) to engage in socially optimal action by imposing socially optimizing sacrifices upon A. It is because of this absence of restrictions against interference with A's exercise of her prerogative that the liberationist rationale for a Scheffler-style prerogative is unsatisfied along the other-imposed subjugation dimension.

The moral individualist is, of course, particularly interested in the instance of the central claim that concerns the individualist prerogative and its rationale. This is the more specific claim that:

"The rationale for the incorporation of the individualist prerogative into morality will not be satisfied unless that prerogative is accompanied by rights-correlative restrictions that protect individuals against interference with the exercise of this prerogative."

To affirm this instance of the central claim is to affirm that, if it is reasonable to endorse the individualist prerogative, it is also reasonable to endorse individual rights against interference with the exercise of that prerogative. Given the moral individualist's endorsement of the antecedent in this conditional proposition, the individualist arrives at the reasonableness of endorsing those rights. Furthermore, to affirm this more specific claim is to affirm individualism's contention that what underwrites the teleological directive import of the separate importance of individuals – an import that appears within the present argument as the individualist prerogative – also underwrites the deontic directive import of the separate importance of individuals – an import that appears within the present argument as those rights-correlative restrictions against interference with the exercise of that prerogative.

As I have just said, the conjunction of the reasonableness of the individualist prerogative and the claim that the rationale for the prerogative will be satisfied only if that prerogative is accompanied by rights-correlative restrictions yields the reasonableness of affirming those restrictions and the rights that are correlative to them. Yet we can seek and should be pleased to find further explanation for the reasonableness of this affirmation. The further explanation proposed by moral individualism is that the root phenomenon of the separate, freestanding importance of each individual's life does have both kinds of directive import. While the directive import for individual A of the separate importance of her life is the rationality of her promotion of her good, the directive import for others of the separate importance of A's life and well-being is the reasonableness of their being circumspect in their treatment of A in the course of their respective pursuit of valued ends.

III. The Individualist Prerogative and Self-Ownership

What is included within the individualist prerogative and *a fortiori* protected by rights-correlative restrictions against interference with the exercise of that prerogative? Personal prerogatives are incorporated into morality to liberate individuals at least to some degree from the requirement that they impose sacrifices on themselves to make the world better from some external standpoint. This is why a prerogative is always cast as making it at least morally allowable for the individual to decline to surrender her good for the sake of advancing the ends of others. There is no reason to understand any such prerogative as including the permissibility of the individual imposing sacrifices upon others in order to achieve gains for herself. (To say that such prerogative does not include the permissibility of imposing sacrifices on others is not to say that it includes the impermissibility of imposing such sacrifices.) Indeed, a prerogative's non-inclusion of the permissibility of the imposition of losses on others is an *implicit* condition of our taking its incorporation into morality to be reasonable.

Shelly Kagan nicely points out that Scheffler's explicit formulation of his prerogative has symmetrical implications for the permissibility of A's declining to impose sacrifices upon herself and the permissibility of A's attaining gains through imposing

Eric Mack

sacrifices on others.[10] As far as the explicit formulation goes, a Scheffler-style prerogative in which M = 4 allows healthy A to decline to surrender three of her vital organs even if this would save the lives of three strangers; but it equally allows sick A to extract organs from three healthy strangers in order to save herself. My point is that Kagan's point is nicely *surprising* precisely because, given the liberationist role of a prerogative, we implicitly take a reasonable prerogative to allow individuals to eschew sacrifice and *not* symmetrically to allow their imposition of sacrifices.

Here is another way of making this point about the role of personal prerogatives. Prerogatives are incorporated into morality to allow each individual to devote *herself* to their own valued ends and not the valued ends of others; they are not incorporated into morality to make it permissible for each individual to devote *others* to her valued ends. If we think in terms of *who*, according to a specific prerogative, each individual may especially devote to the service of her separate system of ends, we presume that this prerogative says that each individual may especially devote herself (not others) to that end. Upon inspection, this implicit presumption is evident even in Scheffler's own discussion of his proposed prerogative. Scheffler repeatedly casts his prerogative in terms of the permissibility of A devoting "attention and energy" to her own favored ends out of proportion to the impersonal importance of those ends. Scheffler never explicitly says *whose* attention and energy A may especially devote to her own ends. However, anyone who reads these passages in Scheffler with the question in mind, "*Whose* attention and energy may A especially devote to her own ends?" will take Scheffler to be saying that it is *A's* attention and energy that A may especially devote to advancing her ends. Had Scheffler meant that A's prerogative also operates over others' attention and energy, he would have seen immediately that *ceteris paribus* his proposed prerogative just as much allows A to extract vital organs from each of three healthy strangers to save her life as it allows her to decline to surrender three of her vital organs to save the lives of three (otherwise) fatally ill strangers.

We should note a further argument for why a prerogative – in particular, the individualist prerogative – should not be understood as encompassing the permissibility of the individual's imposition of sacrifices upon others to achieve gains for herself. If the individualist prerogative did include the permissibility of the individual imposing such sacrifices, then given the unacceptability of a prerogative without accompanying rights-correlative restrictions against interference with the exercise of that prerogative, we would arrive at rights against interference with the eschewing of such sacrifices *and* rights against interference with the imposition of such sacrifices. B would have a right against interference with his exercise of his prerogative to decline to be subject to sacrifices imposed by A and A would have a right against interference with her exercise of her prerogative to impose sacrifices upon B to advance A's good. We would, then, arrive at a set of deeply incompossible rights. To avoid this theoretically unattractive conclusion, we need to avoid the misstep that consists in taking the individualist prerogative to include the permissibility of imposing sacrifices on others.

Let us continue to think of the individualist prerogative as a specification, for each individual, of whom that individual may devote to the attainment of her own good. Unlike less robust prerogatives, the individualist prerogative says that each individual may *always* devote her own person to the attainment of her greater advantage. If we cast matters this way, we arrive at an alternative statement of the rights that are correlative to the restrictions that must accompany the individual prerogative if the rationale for that prerogative is to be satisfied. The rights that are correlative to the restrictions against interference with individuals' respective exercise of this prerogative are their respective rights over their own person. If one (i) incorporates the individualist prerogative into morality; (ii) specifies the range of actions that are rendered permissible by that prerogative in terms of whom each individual may always deploy as she sees fit in service of her ends; (iii) recognizes that it is unacceptable to incorporate this prerogative without also incorporating restrictions against interference with its exercise, one will arrive at each individual's rights over her own person, i.e., over personal resources that constitute her person. That is, one arrives at the familiar libertarian right of self-ownership.

IV. The Individualist Prerogative and the Right to the Practice of Private Property

Rights-oriented libertarian theorists commonly first go for self-ownership and then employ the premiss of self-ownership within a further and discrete argument for individual rights over extra-personal objects. Locke, qua proto-libertarian theorist, first establishes each individual's property in his own person, infers from this that each has a property in his own labor, and affirms property in extra-personal objects on the basis of each individual retaining his rights over the labor that he has invested in extra-personal objects. Nozick, while seeking to avoid Locke's mixing of labor metaphor, grounds his Lockean entitlement doctrine of property rights in the claim that all alternatives to entitlement doctrine require the violation of individuals' rights of self-ownership. In contrast, I want to explore the possibility that the argument that I have presented as yielding a right of self-ownership will, if more broadly construed, also yield rights with respect to extra-personal objects. I say "rights with respect to extra-personal objects" because the rights I have in mind are not particular rights to actual holdings but rather the abstract right possessed by each individual that others abide by norms under which that individual is protected in her acquisition, transformation, deployment, and consumption of extra-personal objects. I refer to this abstract right as *the right to the practice of private property*.[11] Particular rights to actual holdings will obtain in virtue of individuals acquiring those actual extra-personal objects in accordance with the norms compliance with which fulfills individuals' rights to the practice of private property.[12]

As I have presented it, the argument from the individualist prerogative to rights takes that which the individual may devote to her valued ends to be the mental and physical components and capacities that constitute her person. But, on reflection, we should see that this construes too narrowly and too statically the ambit of what, under that prerogative, each individual may dedicate to the service of her system of ends. Few actions and no extended course of action involve only the agent's deployment of components or capacities of her person. Almost all actions and all extended courses of action involve also the deployment of extra-personal resources. Action rarely is performed entirely within the space defined by the outer surface of the agent's skin; and even when such action is performed, it is almost always made possible by other performances of the agent that require the deployment of extra-personal resources and is almost always in service of yet further action that involves the

Eric Mack

deployment of extra-personal resources. It would be much closer to the mark to say that, under the individualist prerogative, each individual may devote her *life* – as it develops through her ongoing purposive engagement of her person with diverse extra-personal material – to her valued ends.

So, rather than explicating the individualist prerogative merely in terms of *who* each individual may devote to the attainment of her good, we should explicate it more broadly in terms of *what* each individual may devote to the attainment of her good – where, for each individual, the specified resources for permissible action will *include* her person. What is also within the ambit of any given individual's prerogative are the extra-personal materials that she has purposively incorporated into her life or that she can purposively incorporate into her life without thereby interfering with any other individuals' disposition of extra-personal materials that they have incorporated into their own lives. What is not within the ambit of a given individual's prerogative are other persons *and* the extra-personal materials they have respectively incorporated into their own lives. The individualist prerogative permits her to direct her life – not merely to direct her person – to her own ends. She need not diminish that life in order to enhance the lives of others. But, since the prerogative does not encompass the permissibility of any individual diminishing the lives of others in order to enhance her own, the ambit of the prerogative does not include other persons and the extra-personal material that they have integrated into their respective lives. Intuitively, the picture is simply that of the permissibility of individuals out there in the world, living their lives as they see fit in large measure through the acquisition, use, transformation, retention, exchange, consumption, and disposal of extra-personal material. It should, on reflection, be no surprise that a personal prerogative – especially a robust personal prerogative – will affirm not just the moral liberty of each to dispose of her person as she sees fit but will, more broadly, affirm the moral liberty of each to live her world-interactive life as she sees fit.

Although each actual person is within the ambit of her prerogative to live her life as she sees fit, what particular extra-personal material will come under the ambit of her prerogative will depend upon what extra-personal material that agent actually permissibly incorporates within her developing life. The prerogative is a prerogative to acquire, use, transform, retain, exchange, consume, and otherwise dispose of extra-personal material that is not already – or not until the point of some voluntary exchange – within the ambit of any other's like prerogative. There is no pre-ordained share of extra-personal material – not even any preordained share of *natural* extra-personal material – that defines the scope of each individual's permissible endeavors. There is no more some antecedent rule about the proper or fair or rightful distribution of extra-personal material – even natural extra-personal material – than there is an antecedent rule about the proper or fair distribution of personal resources.[13]

Recall, however, that even as we construe the individualist prerogative as liberating not merely persons but persons' world-interactive lives, that liberation is only from the moral requirement that they themselves forego gains in their lives in order to promote gains in the lives of others. As we have seen, by itself this liberation from *self-imposed* losses, leaves each individual entirely subject to the same or similar *other-imposed* losses. The bare prerogative leaves each individual entirely subject to interferences with the exercise of her prerogative. So, the prerogative by itself fails to satisfy its rationale of thoroughly liberating the individual from subordination to external viewpoints. What is also needed for that rationale to be satisfied are rights-correlative restrictions against interference with the exercise of that prerogative. What is needed is a structure of rights that immunizes the individual in her chosen life-constituting world-interactive endeavors. Such a structure of rights will include both the right of self-ownership and the right to the practice of private property. The former protects the person – from the outer surface of her skin inward – in the course of her endeavors. The latter protects her life endeavors by morally securing for her the results of her prerogative-sanctioned acquisitions, transformations, retentions, exchanges, and dispositions. So, e.g., A need not keep that gathered acorn within her sweaty grasp in order for others to be required not to seize it, and B need not introduce his body between the object he has traded for and those who covet it in order for them to be required to respect his dominion over it. This moral protection of agents' world-interactive endeavors is accomplished through a system of rules that specify just what processes of acquisition, transformation, exchange, and so on confer ownership on the part of the agent to the resulting holdings. The right that individuals have which accomplishes their moral liberation as world-interactive agents from subordination to external viewpoints is the right to others' respect for the entitlements that the rules comprising such a practice of private property confer.

The argument heretofore has focused on the need to include such a right to the practice of private property for morality to accomplish the liberation of individuals from other-imposed subordination to external viewpoints. In addition to this moral liberation, there are the excellent *consequences* of general recognition and compliance with the rules constitutive of such a practice. That general recognition and compliance provides individuals with actual, predictable liberation from other-imposed subordination. It thereby provides individuals with the incentive to engage in the protected endeavors of acquisition, transformation, exchange, and so on. Further, this structure of private rights extends the liberty to determine how any particular resource will be used to the agent who has the most specific information about the useful properties of that resource – or enables the agent with that information to become the party with the protected liberty of choosing its disposition. This is good for the individual whose world-interactive endeavors are protected; and it is good for those comparably shielded individuals who interact directly or indirectly with the protected individual. To put it as contentiously as possible, it is good for the agents to have their capitalist acts protected; and it is also good for those similarly shielded individuals who interact with those capitalists as, e.g., employees or customers or suppliers or imitators. The contention is that the protection of capitalist acts releases a rising tide that at least strongly tends to elevate all (who are willing to swim with it or whom swimmers are willing to tow along).

It is worth mentioning one additional connection between the teleological and deontic facets of moral individualism. The teleological facet with its focus on the agent-relativity of value and its endorsement of the individualist prerogative involves the rejection of any agent-neutralist measure of alternative social states. It thereby undercuts any attempt to adjudicate disputes about which of two or more incompatible actions – e.g., A scratching her nose with her right index finger and B using that finger to season a stew – by determining which of those actions yields (or is expected to yield) the agent-neutrally better overall outcome. In the absence of such a teleological adjudication of such disputes, how can there be any public,

Eric Mack

interpersonally sound adjudication? The answer is, by determining who has the right over and, hence, the right to dispose as she or he sees fit of the resource at the root of the dispute – e.g., who as the right over A's right index finger. A comprehensive structure of individual rights provides a comprehensive alternative approach to the adjudication of such disputes by disaggregating the decision-making authority over the resources over which there is contention. Under this disaggregation of decision-making authority, one particular deployment of a given resource can be said to be favored by morality – but only in the sense that it is the deployment chosen by the agent who has title over that resource. A dispute between A and B about which of them *should* have authority over some currently unowned object will, of course, not be resolvable by appeal to existing titles. Such a dispute can only be resolved by one of the parties acquiring (through initial acquisition or exchange) the sought after object in accordance with the rules of the applicable practice – which will include rules against acquisition through conduct that violates the already existing rights of others.

Circumventing of the need for a shared social evaluation of contentious action by this disaggregation of decision-making authority defuses social conflict by allowing each to dispose of himself and his own without the presumption that all endorse the chosen dispositions. B can concede that A has the right to determine by her choice how A's finger will be used without at all betraying his belief that it would be far better for the finger to be used in seasoning that stew than in scratching A's nose. B can concede that A has the right to determine by her choice how any of her bodily parts are employed without at all traducing his conviction that A's chosen employment is wicked. B can concede that A has the right to sacrifice *her* calves – the bovine sort – in the course of her religious rites without at all betraying his belief that God abhors such sacrificial rites.[14] An abiding feature of liberal individualism – and more specifically of moral individualism – is the deep-seated rejection of the idea of a shared substantive social end or hierarchy of ends to which all members of society are to be devoted. The more serious this rejection of a shared social end that is supposed to order and coordinate our lives, the more serious must be the turn to a structure of rights that protects individuals in the pursuit of their own valued ends, of their own conceptions of the good, and – not accidentally – that provides a framework within which individuals can non-sacrificially coordinate their own chosen endeavors.[15]

V. A Self-Ownership Proviso

Locke and Nozick following Locke attach a *Lockean Provsio* to their doctrines of self-ownership and private entitlements. Such a proviso renders impermissible some actions that would otherwise count as legitimate exercises of rights, e.g., certain instances of owner A excluding individual B from drinking from A's waterhole. Such a proviso takes some of the sharp edge off of libertarian doctrine. I believe that Locke and Nozick are correct to adopt such a proviso, but that they do not properly tie their provisos to the claims of self-ownership. The adoption of a proviso with a specific grounding and character is an important issue for libertarian theory – and for the relationship between "right" and "left" libertarianism. For this reason, I pause before my concluding section to indicate briefly how a proviso may be founded upon the same recognition of individuals as world-interactive agents that grounds the right to the practice of private property.[16] Here I will consider only the most obvious and simple application of a proviso, viz., its application to the exercise of property rights that have arisen through the initial acquisition of natural material.

The crucial intuitive idea is that, because individuals are world-interactive agents, their self-ownership rights can be contravened not only by trespasses upon their persons but also by some actions that block them from purposively bringing their self-owned powers to bear on the extra-personal world. If A gently encases sleeping B within a capsule composed of A's moldable plastic and refuses to release B, A nullifies B's self-owned world-interactive powers and contravenes B's self-ownership. The question is, what other dispositions of rightful holdings by some individuals *similarly* contravene the self-ownership rights of other individuals? I think the roughshod, but correct, libertarian answer is, dispositions that on net leave individuals with an environment less open to their bringing their powers to bear in pursuit of their ends than those individuals would face were individuals unable to establish private property rights. Solely as a rough illustration, consider the case of first arrivers to a previously unowned region and their subsequent disposition of the property they obtain through initial acquisition.

The first arrivers' establishment of property rights blocks later arrivers from bringing their powers to bear *by way of initial acquisition.* However, that initial establishment of property may well, *in other ways*, increase the later arrivers' opportunities to bring their powers to bear in the service of their ends over what those opportunities would have been had first arrivers and later arrivers not been morally empowered to establish property rights over those natural materials. Without their intending their actions to have this result, the pioneers and their establishment of initial entitlements may well create a world that is on net more hospitable to the endeavors of the individuals in the subsequent wave than those individuals would encounter were individuals in all waves pecluded from establishing private titles. It is very misleading to think that those who arrive first and engage in initial acquisition do well in their pioneering endeavors at the expense of those who get to follow in the paths they have blazed. Surely all (or almost all) of we path-followers are better off than we would have been had we – not others – had to be the first acquiring pioneers.[17] (Think of how much more hospitable Hong Kong was in the last decades of the twentieth century to innumerable waves of later arrivers than it would have been had earlier arrivers not been able to establish private property rights.)

Nevertheless, still focusing on the easy cases of first versus subsequent arrivers, the first arrivers *might* so act as to render the world they have entered less hospitable on net to later arrivers bringing their powers to bear in the service of their ends. The first arrivers *might*, e.g., devote much of their time and energy to building barriers to prevent the landing of second and third waves. If they do so, they would act in violation of the self-ownership proviso; the blocked immigrants would have a case on the basis of their libertarian rights against such blocking actions. A well-developed rights-oriented libertarian theory would spell out how such a proviso would apply to the historically complex world in which we live – as it would address all those questions about what sort of political and legal institutions that worked out theory would legitimate.[18]

134　**Eric Mack**

VI. Conclusion

I have maintained that the rationality and moral permissibility of individuals pursuing their own distinct ends in their own chosen ways and the possession by individuals of the rights of self-ownership and private property that characteristically protect individuals in their chosen pursuits are two distinct directive imports of the root idea of the separate, freestanding importance of each individual's life and well-being. The linkage between the first (teleological) import and the second (deontic) import has been supported by showing why a normative code that includes a robust prerogative that allows the individual to eschew imposing sacrifices on herself must be also include broad restrictions on others that forbid them from interfering with the individual's exercise of that prerogative. The rights that are correlative to those restrictions are the libertarian rights of self-ownership and private property. Moreover, the linkage between that robust prerogative and those rights is their shared rationale – which is nothing but the separate importance of each individual's life and well-being. Finally, I have gestured toward a complication within libertarian rights doctrine – the self-ownership proviso – which allows the libertarian theorist to explain the impermissibility of certain dispositions of holdings that otherwise appear to be permissible on libertarian grounds.

Notes

1   I gratefully acknowledge support for portions of the work on this essay that I have received through grants from the Earhart Foundation and the Murphy Institute of Political Economy at Tulane University.
2   Of course, for *some* As and *some* Bs, enhancements of B's good are instrumentally or even constitutively conducive to A's good. The good of particular individuals does not obtain in atomic isolation.
3   John Rawls, *A Theory of Justice*, 1st edn (Cambridge, MA: Harvard University Press, 1971), p. 23.
4   See *A Theory of Justice*, 22–7 and Robert Nozick, *Anarchy, State and Utopia* (New York: Basic Books, 1974), pp. 32–3.
5.   Samuel Scheffler, *The Rejection of Consequentialism* (Oxford: Clarendon Press, 1982).
6.   My response to Scheffler appears in more lengthy form in Eric Mack, "Prerogatives, Restrictions, and Rights," *Social Philosophy and Policy* 22 (1) (Winter 2005): 357–93. For an earlier and similar criticism of Scheffler, see Lawrence Alexander, "Scheffler on the Independence Agent Centered Prerogatives from Agent-Centered Restrictions," *Journal of Philosophy* 84 (1987): 277–83.
7.   *The Rejection of Consequentialism*, p. 57, emphasis added.
8.   If there are significant personal costs for agent B who would be imposing the sacrifice upon A, then *B's prerogative* will render it permissible for B to eschew imposing the sacrifice upon A. However, it still could easily be the case that agent C, the back-up agent for social optimization, should step in and impose upon B the costly (to B) act of imposing costs upon A.
9.   Aside from his denial that the rationale for any prerogative would also be a rationale for accompanying restrictions, Scheffler offers a number of grounds for disbelief in rights-correlative restrictions. One is his unshakeable conviction that it is *always* at least permissible to engage in socially optimal action. From this it follows that there can be

no right against being subject to such action. Another ground for Scheffler is his belief that deontic rights are paradoxical because – as every friend of deontic rights insists – they forbid acts that violate those rights even if those acts would minimize the overall violation of rights.

10. Shelly Kagan, "Does Consequentialism Demand Too Much?," *Philosophy and Public Affairs* 13 (1984): 239–54.

11. See Eric Mack, "Self-Ownership and the Right of Property," *The Monist* 73 (4) (October 1990): 519–43.

12. When I say that individuals have a right to the practice of private property I do not mean that individuals have a right that such a practice be invented and delivered to them. Rather, I mean that, should such a practice have come to exist within an individual's social order, that (lucky) individual will have a right to others' compliance with its constitutive norms. Furthermore, had a somewhat different set of norms evolved in that social order – but still a set that qualifies as a practice of private property – the individuals inhabiting that order would have rights to others' compliance with the norms constituting that practice.

13. Here I mark my opposition to the "left-libertarian" attempt to combine a doctrine of self-ownership with a doctrine of original rights to equal shares – or equal joint ownership of – natural extra-personal objects. For advocacy of this view see Peter Vallentyne's contribution to this volume. For some criticism of it, as it has been advanced by Hillel Steiner, see the section "Against Left-Wing Liberalism" (pp. 12–20) in Eric Mack, "Right-Wing Liberalism, Left-Wing Liberalism, and the Self-Ownership Proviso" in Karl-Heinz Ladeur, ed., *Liberal Institutions, Economic Constitutional Rights, and the Role of Organizations* (Baden-Baden: Nomos Verlagsgesellschaft, 1997), pp. 9–29.

14. John Locke, *A Letter Concerning Toleration* (Indianapolis, IN: Hackett Publishing, 1983), p. 42.

15. On how a system of "rules of just conduct" that largely operates to specify what is mine and what is thine is the culturally evolved solution to the problem of how individuals who radically differ from one another in their values, preferences, beliefs, skills, and circumstances can live together to mutual advantage, see the first two volumes of F. A. Hayek's *Law, Legislation, and Liberty* – "Rules and Order" (Chicago: University of Chicago Press, 1973) and "The Mirage of Social Justice" (Chicago: University of Chicago Press, 1976), esp. pp. 107–13 of the latter.

16. A case for this self-ownership proviso is developed in Eric Mack, "The Self-Ownership Proviso: A New and Improved Lockean Proviso," *Social Philosophy and Policy* 12 (1) (Winter 1995), 186–218 and further developed in Eric Mack, "Self-Ownership, Marxism, and Egalitarianism: Part II" *Politics, Philosophy, and Economics* 1 (2) (June 2002): 237–76, esp pp. 243–51.

17. See David Schmidtz, *The Limits of Government* (Boulder, CO:Westview Press, 1991), Ch. 2.

18. Rights-based libertarian theory must also address the issue of the absoluteness of rights. For one preliminary discussion, see Eric Mack, "Non-Absolute Rights and Libertarian Taxation," *Social Philosophy and Policy* 23 (2) (Jul. 2006): 109–41.

 Eric Mack

Left-Libertarianism and Liberty

Peter Vallentyne

I shall formulate and motivate a left-libertarian theory of justice. Like the more familiar right-libertarianism, it holds that agents initially fully own themselves. Unlike right-libertarianism, it holds that natural resources belong to everyone in some egalitarian manner. Left-libertarianism is, I claim, a plausible version of liberal egalitarianism because it is suitably sensitive to considerations of liberty, security, and equality.

1. Justice

I shall be formulating a left-libertarianism theory of justice, but the term "justice" is used in several different ways. Here I shall understand duties of justice to be *duties that we morally owe someone*. Justice in this sense is concerned with avoiding *interpersonal wrongs* (i.e., actions that violate someone's rights), but not with *impersonal wrongs* (i.e., actions that are wrong whether or not they wrong anyone; e.g., perhaps, destroying cultural relics when no one is harmed and everyone consents). As long as rights are understood broadly as perhaps pro tanto and highly conditional constraints protecting the holder's interest or her will, justice in this sense is a broad topic. It is sensitive to all moral issues affecting the moral permissibility of actions, except those issues that are relevant only to impersonal duties (which, by definition, are not sensitive to the interests or wills of individuals).

In what follows, references to what is permitted should be understood as references to what is permitted *by justice*. An action is so permitted if and only if it violates no one's rights.

2. Libertarianism

Libertarianism is sometimes advocated as a derivative set of rules (e.g., on the basis of rule utilitarianism or contractarianism). Here, however, I reserve the term for the natural rights doctrine that agents initially *fully own themselves* in a sense that I shall clarify below. All forms of libertarianism endorse full self-ownership. They differ with respect to the moral powers that individuals have to acquire ownership of external things. The best-known versions of libertarianism are *right-libertarian* theories (e.g., that of Nozick 1974), which hold that agents have a robust moral power to acquire full private property in natural resources (e.g., space, land, minerals, air, and water) without the consent of, or any significant payment to, other members of society. *Left-libertarianism*, by contrast, holds that natural resources belong to everyone in some egalitarian manner and thus cannot be appropriated without the consent of, or significant payment to, other members of society.

Below, I shall first examine the content and defend the plausibility of full self-ownership. Following that, I shall discuss the role of liberty and security in libertarian theory. Finally, I shall discuss the moral powers that agents have to appropriate unowned resources. I shall suggest – but without elaborate defense – that a version of left-libertarianism offers the most plausible account of these moral powers.[1]

3. Full Self-Ownership

Libertarianism is committed to the thesis of full self-ownership (for agents), according to which each agent, at least initially (e.g., prior to any wrongdoings or contractual agreements), morally fully owns herself. The rough idea of full self-ownership is that of having all the moral rights over oneself that an owner of an inanimate thing (e.g., a car) has over it under the strongest form of private ownership of inanimate things. The rough idea is also that a full self-owner *morally* has all the rights over herself that a slave-owner *legally* has over a slave under the strongest possible legal form of private slave-ownership.[2]

Throughout, we are concerned with *moral* self-ownership as opposed to legal self-ownership. We are concerned, that is, with a particular set of moral rights independently of whether these are recognized by any legal system. The slaves of the antebellum U.S.A. were legal slaves, but morally speaking, on the libertarian view, they fully owned themselves. Indeed, it is because they morally fully owned themselves that legal involuntary slavery was such a great injustice.

Ownership of a thing is a set of rights over that thing, and the core right is the right to control *use* of that thing. For these purposes, use is understood broadly to include all the ways that agents can physically impact upon an object. Possession, occupation, incursion, intrusion, disposition, alteration, and destruction are forms of use in this stipulative sense.

An agent has full self-ownership just in case she fully owns herself. This is simply the special case of full ownership, where the owner and the entity owned are the same. Assuming that one's body is part of oneself, this entails that one owns one's body. Full ownership of an entity consists of a full set of the following ownership rights:

(1) *control rights* over the use of the entity (both a liberty-right to use it and a claim-right that others not use it),

(2) *rights to compensation* (when someone uses the entity without one's permission),

(3) *enforcement rights* (of prior restraint if someone is about to violate these rights),

Peter Vallentyne

(4) *rights to transfer* these rights to others (by sale, rental, gift, or loan), and

(5) *immunities to the non-consensual loss* of these rights.

Full ownership, like ownership generally, is a bundle of particular rights. It is simply the *logically strongest* set of ownership rights over a thing.[3] Ownership can come in various degrees and forms and few, if any, legal systems recognize full ownership in this sense. One can, for example, have full control rights over a thing without having rights to transfer those rights. The thesis of *full self-ownership* does not claim that ownership is either all or nothing. It claims that, as a matter of normative fact, agents *fully* own themselves as opposed to something weaker or not at all.[4]

There are, of course, different conceptions of rights. Some argue that rights protect choices whereas others argue that rights protect interests. For brevity of expression, in what follows, I shall assume a choice-protecting conception of rights. This is how ownership rights are normally understood and how rights are normally understood by libertarians. My own view is that rights protect both choices and interests with the former being lexically prior. Introducing this view, would, however, introduce needless complexities for the purposes of this paper.[5]

So far, we have considered the *content* of the concept of full self-ownership. Let us now consider its *plausibility*. I should emphasize that my goal is very modest: to provide a reasonably plausible rationale for endorsing full self-ownership. As with all fundamental moral principles, it is impossible to provide a *compelling* justification. My goal is simply to provide enough defense of full self-ownership to establish that it needs to be taken seriously as a moral principle.

Full self-ownership is the thesis that one has, in a fullest (or strongest) manner possible, control rights, compensation rights, enforcement rights, transfer rights, and immunity rights over oneself (e.g., one's body). Most people accept some form of partial self-ownership. It can be partial in the sense that only some of the above types of rights are present or it can be partial in the sense that the *force* of the rights, for a given element, is less than full. Moreover, the force of a right can be less than full in two distinct ways. One is that the right may not be *conclusive* (or absolute) in the sense that its infringement is *always* wrong. The rights could be merely *pro tanto* moral considerations, or (more strongly) pro tanto considerations that are lexically prior to impersonal considerations (i.e., that are weighed against other conflicting rights but trump impersonal considerations). The second way that the force of a right can be less than full is by being *conditional* (holding only under certain conditions). For example, the right not to be killed might be conclusive (absolute) but apply only where no social catastrophe is at issue.

Below, I shall attempt to defend *full* self-ownership (conclusive and unconditional rights for each of the four elements). A fallback position is to defend some form of partial self-ownership (e.g., control self-ownership in some pro tanto and/or conditional form). This, however, would be a departure from libertarianism in the strict sense.

We shall consider the security rights, liberty rights, transfer rights, and immunities to loss that are part of full self-ownership. (Here we leave aside the compensation and enforcement rights, since there is indeterminacy with respect to these in the concept of full ownership.) Consider first, the *security rights* that are part of the control rights of ownership. These are claim rights against interference with one's person.

The security rights of self-ownership are, I claim, a plausible constraint on how agents may be treated by others. Agents are not merely objects in the world. They have moral standing and are capable of autonomous choices. As a result, they have a kind of moral protection against interference that limits how they may be used. For example, it is unjust to kill or torture innocent people against their will – no matter how much it promotes other important moral goals (equality, total utility, or whatever). The security rights of full self-ownership reflect this special status that agents have.

Of course, some deny – as act consequentialists do – that there are any non-goal-based constraints on how individuals may be treated. Even if one agrees that there are some such constraints, however, one might still deny that individuals have any *rights* against being so treated. Instead, one might hold that there is simply an *impersonal duty* (owed to no one) not to treat people in certain ways. Suicide and gay sex, for example, may be wrong even when consensual, in the interests of the individuals, and done by adults in private.

It is certainly possible (indeed held by some) to hold that all constraints are impersonal constraints, but it is a very illiberal view. First, it fails to recognize that certain forms of treatment (such as killing or assault) are not merely wrong – they wrong the individuals so treated. Second (and closely related), it fails to recognize that the valid consent (or alternatively non-set-back of the interests) of an individual to be treated in various ways (e.g., be killed or touched) is sufficient to remove the moral force of that constraint. The purpose of constraints is to protect individuals from certain kinds of interference in their lives. If a person has validly (e.g., informedly and freely) consented to a certain treatment (e.g., being punched as part of a boxing match), then there is nothing morally wrong with such treatment if others are not adversely affected. The constraints protecting individuals, that is, are rights-based, rather than impersonal constraints.

Even if one agrees that individuals have all the rights of self-ownership, one might still insist that the rights have only a pro tanto (all else being equal) force and/or are only conditional (e.g., when no social catastrophe is involved). Libertarianism (of the standard sort here considered), however, holds that rights are conclusive (absolute) and unconditional.[6] So understood, the thesis of full self-ownership is subject to the powerful objection that it entails that it is wrong to slightly injure a person in order to save millions of lives. This is indeed an implication of the view and it is admittedly very difficult to swallow. Clearly, reasonable and decent people would typically infringe the security rights of self-ownership in such cases. This does not, however, establish that it is just to do so. It may simply be that it is reasonable to behave unjustly in such extreme circumstances. Indeed, this is what I claim. For in such cases, all the usual concomitants of injustice are still present. Guilt is appropriate for what one did to the sacrificed individuals. Compensation is owed to the individual. And so on. As long as we recognize, as I think we should, that reasonable and decent people sometimes act unjustly when the stakes are sufficiently great, the admitted counterintuitiveness of recognizing conclusive and unconditional security rights of self-ownership need not be a conclusive objection. Of course, it remains a significant counterintuitive implication, but all theories have some such counterintuitive implications. The real test of a theory is its overall plausibility – both in the abstract and in application over a broad range of cases. Sometimes intuitive judgments about concrete cases must be rejected in light of plausible abstract principled considerations.

Peter Vallentyne

My claim is that those intuitions that conflict with the thesis of full self-ownership should be rejected.

So far, we have considered the *security rights* that are part of the control rights of full self-ownership. Let us now consider the *liberty rights* that are the other part of these control rights. A full self-owner has a full liberty right to use her person. This does not mean that she is permitted to do anything that she wants with her person. Clearly, using her fist to punch you in the nose is not permitted. Having a liberty right to use one's person only means that no one else has any claim-right on one's use of one's person *as such*. Thus, although I need your permission for it to be permissible to *use the car* that you own, I don't need to get anyone's permission to *use my person* to drive the car (as a full slave would, and a partial slave might). The full ownership liberty rights over oneself, that is, give one a full liberty to use one's person, but, since every action involves the use of other resources (land, air, etc.), it leaves open (depending on the ownership of the other resources) what actions are just.

The liberty rights of initial full self-ownership reflect the view that others initially have no claim against us concerning the use of our person. Initially, we do not require their permission, nor are their interests relevant, in order for us to permissibly use our person as such – although, of course, we need their permission to use resources that they own. Of course, we can lose some of our liberty rights over ourselves through our actions – for example, when we contract to provide personal services or violate someone's rights.

Having full liberty rights to use one's person has the counterintuitive implication that we have no (initial) duty to provide personal assistance to others. The most problematic case is where we could avert a *social catastrophe* (e.g., the death of millions of people) at only a small personal cost (e.g., push a button so that a terrorist bomb does not go off). (Unlike the security rights issue above, the issue here concerns the duties of agents to provide personal services, whereas the security rights issue concerned the permissibility of others using one's person.) A very significant, but somewhat less dramatic case is one where one could provide a great benefit to a single person (e.g., save her life) at only a small personal sacrifice. Less significant, but still troublesome, are cases where one could provide a small benefit to others at a smaller cost to oneself as part of a cooperative enterprise that generally benefits all. Again, in the extreme cases these are indeed powerful objections. Nonetheless, I believe that their force can be weakened enough to make them palatable – given the general plausibility of the view that we are initially at liberty to use our person as we please. Let me explain.

There are several well-known ways of softening this objection. One is to agree that it is highly morally desirable that one helps in these cases, but to insist that one has no obligation to do so. We all agree that there is something morally flawed about not providing personal services when this would greatly benefit others and impose only a small cost on oneself. Not all moral flaws, however, involve wrongdoing. Failing to help an elderly neighbor carry her groceries when she is having difficulty and we could do so easily is not morally ideal, but it is not typically morally wrong.

A second way of softening the objection is to grant that it may be wrong to fail to provide personal services to others in need (etc.), but deny that they have any *right* to such help. If they have no right – and no one else does either – then there is no injustice in failing to provide the services in question. It is an impersonal duty, but not a duty owed to anyone. Given that we are here concerned only with the theory of justice – the duties we owe each other – failure to recognize impersonal duties is not a defect. The topic of impersonal duties is simply a topic that is not being addressed. Because I believe (but shall not here argue) that there are no impersonal duties, this reply does not seem promising to me. Nonetheless, it is open to those who believe that there are impersonal duties.

Yet another way to soften the objection against full liberties to use one's person is to point out the radical implications of recognizing an obligation to others to help even in the special cases where the benefit to them is great and the cost to one is small. For there are typically a great number of people (poor people, severely disabled people, orphans, etc.) that would greatly benefit from an hour's personal service per week. Most of us deny that we have a duty to provide such service.

A final and important way to soften the objection against having full liberties to use one's person is to note that the claim is only that individuals have this full liberty *initially* (e.g., at the start of adult life). It can be weakened or lost by our choices over time. For example, if, as I shall suggest below, the use or appropriation of more than one's share of natural resources generates a limited duty to promote equality of effective opportunity, then some of the full liberty rights of self-ownership will be lost when one uses or appropriates more than one's share. The more general point here is that the implications of full self-ownership cannot be determined without knowing how other things are owned.

In sum, I fully acknowledge that the security rights and the liberty rights of full self-ownership have some significant counterintuitive implications. On the other hand, all theories have some such implications, and the normative separateness of persons reflected in full security rights and full liberty rights has great theoretical appeal. Although it is highly controversial, I claim, that on balance the thesis of full *control* self-ownership is sufficiently plausible to be taken seriously.

Even if agents have full control self-ownership (full liberty rights and full security rights) over themselves, it does not follow that agents fully own themselves. The determinate core of full self-ownership includes two additional rights that must be defended: the full power to transfer those rights to others and the immunity to non-consensual loss except, perhaps, under certain conditions.

Consider first the immunity to non-consensual loss of rights. It holds that individuals lose their rights of ownership only up to the extent that they owe compensation for the use of other resources or to the extent they lose some security rights so as to make it permissible to stop them from violating the rights of others. This leaves open a wide range of views between no loss and maximum loss within these constraints. Moreover, the constraints on loss of rights are also fairly plausible. One does not, for example, become someone else's slave simply for taking an apple from his property. One merely owes compensation (trivial in most cases) and one loses only those security rights that interfere with effective ways of stopping one from violating the other's rights (one does not, for example, lose one's right to life when one can be stopped from the violation simply by being yelled at). One may lose one's right to life when being killed is the only (or perhaps the only cost effective) way of stopping one from violating rights, but one does not lose rights that do not interfere with such prevention.

More controversial is the full power to transfer the rights of self-ownership. This means that one has the moral power to sell, rent, loan, or give away one's rights over oneself. This includes, as an extreme case, the right to sell (or gift) oneself into slavery. *Involuntary* enslavement, of course, is a gross violation of full self-ownership, but *voluntary* enslavement is something that full self-ownership allows. Intuitively, of course, this seems problematic.

One objection to the right of self-enslavement is that there is no such right, since it is *impossible* to transfer one's agency (control of one's person) to another.[7] The core idea is that it is impossible to alienate one's will. This is true but irrelevant. Only you can exercise your agency, but that leaves open whether someone else has *moral authority* over your agency (i.e., whether you have a moral duty to obey someone else's commands). You cannot transfer agency, but you can transfer rights over that agency and thereby transfer the authorizing power of consent concerning the use of the person. When I sign a contract to mow your lawn, I give you some moral authority over the exercise of my agency. It becomes wrong for me to fail to mow your lawn as contracted without your consent. The issue concerns transfers of rights – not of agency. So a different argument is needed if the rights of self-ownership are to be non-transferable.

Another objection to voluntary enslavement is that it makes one "a mere tool of someone else's will."[8] The idea here is that a slave has no moral agency, but no agent (no being that has the psychological capacity for agency) can be without moral agency (moral responsibility). Hence, morally legitimate enslavement is not possible. The first premiss of this argument, however, is false. Slaves are still moral agents. First, slaves may own external property. A slave is someone who is owned by someone else. This is compatible with the slave owning some things (although admittedly his use of those things will be subject to his owner's will). Second, slaves still have moral duties. For example, they have moral obligations to their owners. Moreover, slaves have all the normal duties to other people (e.g., not to kill them). A person can transfer some of her *rights* to someone else, but she can't transfer her *interpersonal duties to others* unless the person to whom the duty is owed consents. In typical cases, the people to whom the duties are owed do not consent to any transfer of duties and, hence, typically slaves have all the normal duties to others. Slaves have fewer rights, but they do not automatically have fewer duties.

A deeper point to note is that full self-ownership on its own does not entail that voluntary enslavement is permitted by justice. Full self-ownership includes the moral power to transfer one's rights over oneself, but it does not ensure that others have the moral power to *acquire* those rights. Transfer of rights from one person to another (by exchange or by gift) requires that both that the transferor have the power to transfer the rights and consents to do so and that the transferee have the moral power to acquire the rights and consents to do so. Full self-ownership is thus compatible with no one having the power to acquire by transfer rights over another person. Full self-ownership ensures that one has the power to renounce (i.e., abandon) one's rights over oneself (which does not require a recipient), and that one has the power to consensually transfer one's rights to anyone who has the power to receive them. It does not, however, require that anyone have the power to receive them. That issue concerns the powers that *others* have with respect to one's person (viz. the power to acquire rights over one under certain conditions). Of course, most libertarians hold that all agents initially have these powers to acquire rights over others (as well as over natural resources and artifacts), and so the objection is indeed applicable to most versions of libertarianism. The point here is that the legitimacy of voluntary enslavement does not follow from self-ownership alone. It requires certain moral powers to acquire rights over other persons.[9]

Finally, it is not clear that the moral possibility of voluntary enslavement is so implausible. If one thinks that a main concern of justice is to protect the *having* of effective autonomy, or to *promote* the having, or exercising, of effective autonomy, then voluntary enslavement will indeed seem problematic. On the other hand, if one thinks that a main concern of justice is to protect the *exercise* of autonomy, it is not. A well-informed decision to sell oneself into slavery (e.g., for a large sum of money to help one's needy family) is an exercise of autonomy. Indeed, under desperate conditions it may even represent an extremely important way of exercising one's autonomy. The parallel with suicide is relevant here. In both cases an agent makes a decision that has the result that she ceases to have any moral autonomy and thus ceases to exercise any. In both cases it will typically be one of the most important choices in the agent's life. Surely, assuming no conflicting commitments, protecting the agent's *exercise* of her autonomy in such a case overrides any concern for protecting or promoting her *continued possession* of moral autonomy. One has the right to choose to cease to be autonomous (by dying or by losing rights of control). Thus, genuine voluntary enslavement is not problematic. It is simply the limiting case of the sorts of partial voluntary enslavement that occurs when we make binding commitments and agreements (e.g., to join the military).[10]

I conclude, then, that the thesis that agents initially fully own themselves is sufficiently plausible to be taken seriously. All forms of libertarianism are committed to full self-ownership. They differ with respect to the moral powers that agents have to use and appropriate natural resources. Below, I shall defend a form of left-libertarianism, which holds that natural resources are to be used to promote effective equality of opportunity for a good life. First, however, it will be useful to comment on the role of liberty and security in libertarian theory.

4. Freedom: Liberty and Security

Libertarianism is concerned with freedom. It is sometimes claimed that libertarianism is the theory that maximizes individual freedom. Shelly Kagan (1994), however, has insightfully shown that at most a highly qualified version of this claim is true. In this section – which draws heavily on Kagan's work, but does not purport to represent his views – I clarify how libertarianism is concerned with freedom.

The first point to note is that libertarianism is not concerned with maximizing the total (or average) freedom that individuals have. At best, it is concerned with maximizing (initial) freedom subject to the constraint that all have *equal* (initial) freedom. It is concerned with maximum equal freedom.

Second, libertarianism is concerned with *moral* freedom as opposed to *empirical* freedom. It is concerned with the range of actions that individuals are morally permitted to perform and the range of interfering actions that others are morally prohibited from performing – as opposed to the range of actions that individuals can

Peter Vallentyne

actually (empirically) perform and the empirical absence of interference by others. Libertarianism condemns, for example, imprisoning an innocent person even where this is an effective means to promoting maximum equal empirical freedom. Such imprisonment is a morally prohibited use of force against the person. Libertarianism is concerned with giving everyone maximum equal *moral* freedom and not with maximum equal *empirical* freedom.

Third, libertarianism is concerned with freedom in the broad sense that includes both *negative freedom* (freedom from interference from others) and *positive freedom* (freedom of action). This is reflected in its endorsement of the two kinds of control rights of full self-ownership: *Security rights* of full self-ownership ensure that others are not permitted to use your person against your will as long as you have not violated the rights of others (negative moral freedom). *Liberty rights* of full self-ownership ensure that you are permitted to use your person as you choose as long as doing so does not violate the rights others (positive moral freedom). Individuals can have moral security rights without having any significant moral liberty rights. For example, everyone might have a duty to maximize happiness in the world subject to the constraint against violating anyone's security rights against forcible interference. One can also have liberty rights without any moral security rights. For example, everything might be morally permitted for everyone. Libertarianism rejects both of these views (as well as the view that one has neither kind of right). It holds that individuals have strong moral security rights *and* strong moral liberty rights and that full self-ownership is the core of the basis for these rights.

Finally, even where no one has violated any rights, there is an indeterminacy in libertarian theory concerning security rights and liberty rights (in addition to the one, noted above, involving compensation rights, enforcement rights, and immunity to loss). So far, we have considered full self-ownership as the only source of liberty and security rights. Full self-ownership, however, is compatible with the rest of the world (the non-agent part of the world) being owned by one person. If this is so, then others have effectively no freedom of action, since – although they have full liberty rights over their person – they have no liberty rights to use other things in the world. Since all action requires the use of things in addition to one's person (e.g., land to stand on, air to breathe), other agents have no freedom of action (since any action requires the permission of the owner). All libertarians, however, want to guarantee a more robust initial freedom of action. Thus, all libertarians impose some conditions on the initial liberty and security rights that individuals have to use natural resources. Libertarians also impose conditions under which these initial rights can be modified and individuals can appropriate natural resources. Full self-ownership is compatible with many different positions on what moral property rights individuals have, or can acquire, in external things. A full libertarian theory needs to specify what liberty rights and security rights individuals have beyond those of full self-ownership.

5. Natural Resources: Liberty Rights to Use and Moral Powers to Appropriate

Full self-ownership gives agents certain rights over themselves. This leaves open, however, what rights agents have to *use* non-agent resources (natural resources and artifacts). It also leaves open what moral powers agents have to *acquire additional rights* (over other agents, natural resources, and artifacts): powers to acquire by consensual transfer (e.g., by sale or gift) and powers to acquire rights without the consent of others (e.g., unilateral appropriation of unowned resources). The plausibility of any given version of libertarianism depends crucially on its position on these issues. For simplicity, I shall focus solely on *natural resources* in their initial state – that is, all the non-agent resources in the world prior to modification by agents. Moreover, I shall focus on the rights to *use* them and moral powers to acquire non-consensually rights over them (appropriation).

As will become apparent, I favor a highly egalitarian view of rights over natural resources. This view is highly controversial and in need of a defense. My aim here, however, is modest. I merely hope to articulate and motivate the egalitarian stance as a way of setting the stage for the debate.

One (crazy) possible view holds that initially no one has any liberty right to use, or any moral power to appropriate, natural resources. A radical version of *joint-ownership left-libertarianism*, for example, holds that individuals may use natural resources only with the collective consent (e.g., majority or unanimous) of the members of society. Given that all action requires the use of some natural resources (land, air, etc.), this leaves agents no freedom of action (except with the permission of others), and this is clearly implausible. A less radical version of joint-ownership left-libertarianism allows that agents may use natural resources but holds that they have no moral power to appropriate natural resources without the collective consent of the members of society (e.g., Grunebaum 1987). Although this leaves agents a significant range of freedom of action, it leaves them inadequate security in their plans of action. They have the security that others are not permitted to use their person (e.g., assault them) without their consent, but they have only limited security in their possessions of external things (except with the consent of others). Agents are permitted to cultivate and gather apples, but others are permitted to take them when this violates no rights of self-ownership (e.g., when they can simply take them from the collected pile).

Given the central importance of security of some external resources, it is implausible that agents have no power to appropriate without the consent of others. More specifically, it is most implausible to hold that the consent of others is required for appropriation when communication with others is impossible, extremely difficult, or expensive (as it almost always is). And even when communication is relatively easy and costless, there is no need for the consent of others as long as one appropriates no more than one's fair share.[11] Joint-ownership left-libertarianism is thus implausible.

A plausible account of liberty rights and powers of appropriation over natural resources must, I claim, be *unilateralist* in the sense that, under a broad range of circumstances (although perhaps subject to various conditions), (1) agents are initially permitted to *use* natural resources without anyone's consent, and (2) agent initially have the power to *appropriate* (acquire rights over) natural resources without anyone's consent. This is just to say that initially natural resources are not protected by a property rule (requiring consent for permissible use or appropriation).

According to a unilateralist conception of the power to appropriate, agents who first claim rights over a natural resource acquire those rights – perhaps provided that certain other conditions are met. These additional conditions may include some kind

Peter Vallentyne

of an interaction constraint (such as that the agent "mixed her labor" with the resource or that she was the first to discover the resource) and some kind of "fair share" constraint. In what follows, for simplicity, I shall ignore the interaction constraint and focus on the fair share constraint.[12]

Let us, then, consider some unilateralist versions of libertarianism. *Radical right-libertarianism* – such as that of Rothbard (1978, 1982), Narveson (1988: Ch. 7; 1999), and Feser (2005) – holds that that there are no fair share constraints on use or appropriation.[13] Agents may destroy whatever natural resources they want (as long as they violate no one's self-ownership) and they have the power to appropriate whatever natural resources they first claim. On this view, natural resources are initially not merely unprotected by a property rule; they are also unprotected by a compensation liability rule. This view, however, is implausible. No human agent created natural resources, and there is no reason that the lucky person who first claims rights over a natural resource should reap all the benefit that the resource provides. Nor is there any reason to think the individuals are morally permitted to ruin or monopolize natural resources as they please. Some sort of fair share condition restricts use and appropriation.

The standard fair share condition on appropriation is the *Lockean proviso*, which requires that "enough and as good be left for others."[14] Indeed, as long as this clause is allowed to be interpreted loosely (as we shall), the Lockean proviso simply is the requirement that some kind of fair share condition be satisfied. Throughout, we'll interpret the Lockean proviso (following Nozick) to allow that individuals may appropriate more than their fair share of natural resources as long as they compensate others for their loss from the excess appropriation. The Lockean proviso, that is, is a requirement that a fair share of the *value* of natural resources be left for others.[15]

The Lockean proviso is often interpreted as applying only to acts of appropriation (and not to mere use) and as imposing a condition that only needs to be met at the time of appropriation. I, however, shall interpret it more broadly. A fair share requirement is just as plausible when applied to mere use. One is not at liberty to use natural resources any way that one wants. Others have some claims to enough and as good being left for them. One is not permitted, for example, to destroy, ruin, or monopolize more than her fair share of natural resources – even if one makes no claims of ownership. Moreover, with respect to appropriation, it is not sufficient to satisfy the fair share condition merely at the time of appropriation. The fair share condition is an ongoing requirement for continued ownership. Suppose, for example, that there are just two people in the world and they divide natural resources between themselves in a fair way. Ten years later, two more people pop into existence (but not as a result of any choices the first two people made). It is implausible to think that the division of rights over natural resources remains fair just because it was initially fair. Instead, the Lockean proviso (or fair share test) should be understood as an ongoing requirement that can be initially satisfied but then fail to be satisfied due to later brute luck changes in the total value of natural resources or the number agents in the world.[16]

Let us now consider *Lockean libertarianism*, which allows unilateral use and appropriation but requires that some version of the Lockean proviso be satisfied. It views natural resources as initially unprotected by any property rule (no consent is needed for use or appropriation) but as protected by a compensation liability rule. Those who use natural resources, or claim rights over them, owe compensation to others for any costs imposed but such use or appropriation.

Nozickean right-libertarianism interprets the Lockean proviso as requiring that no individual be made worse off by the appropriation compared with non-appropriation.[17] This, I would argue, sets the compensation payment too low. It bases compensation on each person's *reservation price*, which is the *lowest* payment that would leave the individual indifferent with non-use or non-appropriation. Use or appropriation of natural resources typically brings significant benefits even after providing such compensation. There is little reason to hold that those who first use or claim rights over a natural resource should reap all the excess benefits that those resources provide.

Sufficientarian (centrist) libertarianism interprets the Lockean proviso as requiring that others be left an adequate share of natural resources (on some conception of adequacy).[18] There are different criteria that might be invoked for adequacy, but the most plausible ones are based on the quality of one's life prospects: for example, enough for life prospects worth living, enough for basic subsistence life prospects, or enough for "minimally decent" life prospects. Depending on the nature of the world and the conception of adequacy, the sufficientarian proviso may be more, or less, demanding than the Nozickean proviso. If natural resources are sufficiently abundant relative to the individuals, then Nozickean proviso will be more demanding (since many individuals would get more than an adequate share without the use or appropriation), but if natural resources are sufficiently scarce, then the sufficientarian proviso will be more demanding than the Nozickian one.

Although sufficientarian libertarianism is an improvement over Nozickean libertarianism by being sensitive to the quality of life prospects left to others by the use or appropriation, it nevertheless fails, I would argue, to recognize the extent to which natural resources belong to all of us in some egalitarian manner. Suppose that there are enough natural resources to give everyone fabulous life prospects, and someone appropriates (or uses) natural resources leaving others only minimally adequate life prospects and generating ultra-fabulous life prospects for herself. It is implausible to hold that those who use or first claim a natural resource are entitled to reap all the benefits in excess of what is needed to leave others adequate life prospects. Natural resources were not created by any human agent and their value belongs to all of us in some egalitarian manner.

Let us now consider *left-libertarianism*.[19] It holds that natural resources initially belong to everyone in some egalitarian manner. We have already rejected one version – joint-ownership left-libertarianism – for failing to be unilateralist (i.e., because it requires the permission of others for use or appropriation of unowned natural resources). We shall now focus on Lockean (and hence unilateralist) versions of left-libertarianism.

Equal share left-libertarianism – such as that of Henry George (1879) and Hillel Steiner (1994) – interprets the Lockean proviso as requiring that one leave an equally valuable per capita share of the value of natural resources for others. Individuals are morally free to use or appropriate natural resources, but those who use or appropriate more their per capita share – based on the *competitive value* (based on demand and supply; e.g., market clearing price or auction price) under morally relevant conditions – owe others compensation for their excess share.

Peter Vallentyne

Equal share libertarianism is, I would argue, not sufficiently egalitarian. Although it requires that the competitive value of natural resources be distributed equally, it does nothing to offset disadvantages in unchosen internal endowments (e.g., the effects of genes or childhood environment). Equal share libertarianism is thus compatible with radically unequal life prospects.[20]

Consider, then, *equal opportunity left-libertarianism* such as that of Otsuka (2003).[21] It interprets the Lockean proviso as requiring that one leave enough for others to have an opportunity for well-being that is at least as good as the opportunity for well-being that one obtained in using or appropriating natural resources. Individuals who leave less than this are required to pay the full competitive value of their excess share to those deprived of their fair share. Unlike the equal share view, those whose initial internal endowments provide less favorable effective opportunities for well-being are entitled to larger shares of natural resources.

I claim that equal opportunity left-libertarian is the most plausible version of libertarianism. All versions of libertarianism give agents a significant amount of liberty and security. The main issue at hand concerns requirements for some kind of material equality of agents (equality of life prospects). According to equal opportunity left-libertarianism, one has the power to use or appropriate natural resources as long as one pays for the competitive value of the use or rights in excess of one's equality of opportunity for well-being share. The payment is owed to those who have been left with less than equal opportunity for well-being. Thus, equal opportunity left-libertarianism holds that there is a *limited* duty to promote equality. One does not need to do everything possible to promote equality. One has no duty at all to promote equality if one has not used up or appropriated more than one's equality of opportunity share of natural resources. If one uses up or appropriates more, then one acquires a duty to promote equality of effective opportunity for well-being, but that duty is limited to what can be efficiently achieved with the payment that one owes.

In sum, given the importance of liberty and security, a plausible version of libertarianism must be unilateralist and permit the use and appropriation of natural resources without the consent of others. If one also grants the importance of equality of life prospects, then equal opportunity left-libertarianism is, I claim, the most plausible version of libertarianism. Obviously, the importance of equality in general, and equality of life prospects (effective opportunity for well-being) in particular, are highly controversial, but I shall not attempt a defense here. My goal here has been simply to lay out the main issues that separate different versions of libertarianism and to suggest – without defense – that equal opportunity left-libertarianism is at least a plausible version.[22]

Notes

1   I shall not here address libertarian positions on the justice of the state. For the development of a left-libertarian position defending the possibility of a just state, see Vallentyne (2007).
2   For insightful analysis of the notion of ownership, see Christman (1994). For a superb analysis of the concept of self-ownership, upon which I build, see Cohen (1995), especially Ch. 9.
3   Here, for simplicity, I treat the notion of full ownership as fully determinate. In fact, although it has a determinate core, it has some significant indeterminacy concern rights to

compensation, enforcement rights, and immunity to loss. See Fried (2004, 2005) and Vallentyne et al. (2005).

4 It's worth noting that, because we are focused solely on the duties that we owe each others, we are concerned with the notion of full *interpersonal* ownership – which is compatible with the existence of impersonal constraints on liberty rights and impersonal limitations on powers (e.g., transfer or acquisition).

5 For more on the choice-prioritizing conception of rights that I favor, see Vallentyne (2007).

6 An important possible exception is Nozick (1974), who, in the note on p. 30, leaves open the possibility that it may be permissible to infringe rights in order to avoid moral catastrophe.

7 This objection is made by Rothbard (1982: 40, 134), Barnett (1998: 77–82).

8 In an otherwise excellent article, Kuflik (1984: 286) makes this mistaken claim.

9 Of course, many will still object to the power to renounce one's rights over oneself, and so there is still a debatable issue about the alienability of one's rights over one's person.

10 For further defense for the right of voluntary enslavement see: Steiner (1994: 232–4); Feinberg (1986: Ch. 19); Nozick (1974: 331)).

11 For elaborations of this criticism, see, for example, Fressola (1981) and Cohen (1995).

12 Given greater space, I would argue that no interaction constraint is needed. All the agent needs to do is to *claim* rights over unowned resources and satisfy the fair share constraint.

13 Kirzner (1978) also argues against any fair share condition. He does so, however, on the ground that those who discover a resource are actually creating it and that creators are entitled to their creations. I believe that this argument fails but cannot here argue the point.

14 Locke (1980 [1690]) was not a Lockean libertarian. He disallowed appropriation that would lead to spoilage, he rejected the right of voluntary self-enslavement, and he held that one had a duty to provide the means of subsistence to those unable to provide for themselves.

15 The Lockean proviso could be understood more weakly as requiring that enough and as good be left for others, *if this is compatible with one obtaining life prospects worth living.* In a world in which there are not enough natural resources to give everyone life prospects worth living, this weakened proviso would allow individuals to use or appropriate whatever is necessary for them to obtain life prospects worth living. Although I believe this weakening to be plausible, for simplicity, I shall here ignore it.

16 The need for an ongoing proviso that also applies to mere use is forcefully and insightfully defended by Mack (1995) – although he defends a very weak proviso. Roark (2006) defends the need for a proviso on use and not merely on appropriation.

17 Nozick (1974) sometimes interprets the proviso as requiring only that the *system* of private property make no one worse off than a *system* of common use (where everyone is free to use what they want). This appeal to systems, however, is inappropriate for libertarian theory. The focus must be on the specific act in question.

18 Simmons (1992, 1993) defends a position roughly of this sort – although his position is not strictly libertarian in a few respects.

19 Left-libertarian theories have been propounded for over three centuries. For selections of the writings of historical and contemporary writings, see Vallentyne and Steiner (2000a, 2000b).

20 Steiner (1994) argues that germ-line genetic information is a natural resource and appeals to this as a way of compensating for unequal internal endowments. I am not, however, convinced by his arguments.

21 Van Parijs (1995) is in the same spirit as equal opportunity left-libertarianism – although with significant twists on gifts and job rents.

22 For helpful comments, I thank Jason Glahn, Axel Gosseries, Eric Heidenreich, Justin McBrayer, Eric Roark, Alan Tomhave, and Jon Trerise.

References

Barnett, Randy. 1998. *The Structure of Liberty: Justice and the Rule of Law* (Oxford: Clarendon Press).

Christman, John. 1994. *The Myth of Property* (New York: Oxford University Press).

Cohen, G. A. 1995. *Self-Ownership, Freedom, and Equality* (Cambridge: Cambridge University Press).

Feinberg, Joel. 1986. *Harm to Self* (New York: Oxford University Press).

Feser, Edward. 2005. "There Is No Such Thing as an Unjust Initial Acquisition," *Social Philosophy and Policy* 22: 56–80, esp. 58–9.

Fressola, Anthony. 1981. "Liberty and Property," *American Philosophical Quarterly* 18: 315–22.

Fried, Barbara. 2004. "Left-Libertarianism: A Review Essay", *Philosophy and Public Affairs* 32: 66–92.

Fried, Barbara. 2005. "Left-Libertarianism, Once More: A Rejoinder to Vallentyne, Steiner, and Otsuka," *Philosophy and Public Affairs* 33: 216–22.

George, Henry. 1879. *Progress and Poverty* (New York: Robert Schalkenbach Foundation).

Grunebaum, James. 1987. *Private Ownership* (New York: Routledge & Kegan Paul).

Kagan, Shelly. 1994. "The Argument from Liberty", in Jules Coleman and Allen Buchanan, eds., *In Harm's Way: Essays in Honor of Joel Feinberg* (Cambridge: Cambridge University Press), pp. 16–41.

Kirzner, Israel. 1978. *Competition and Entrepreneurship* (Chicago: University of Chicago Press).

Kuflik, Arthur. 1984. "The Inalienability of Autonomy," *Philosophy & Public Affairs* 13: 271–98.

Locke, John. 1980 [1690]. *Second Treatise of Government*, ed. C. B. Macpherson (Indianapolis, IN: Hackett Publishing).

Mack, Eric. 1995. "The Self-Ownership Proviso: A New and Improved Lockean Proviso," *Social Philosophy and Policy* 12: 186–218.

Narveson, Jan. 1999. "Original Appropriation and Lockean Provisos," *Public Affairs Quarterly* 13: 205–27, esp. 218. (Reprinted in *Respecting Persons in Theory and Practice*, Lanham, MD: Rowman & Littlefield Publishers, 2002, pp. 111–31).

Narveson, Jan. 1988. *The Libertarian Idea* (Philadelphia, PA: Temple University Press).

Nozick, Robert. 1974. *Anarchy, State, and Utopia* (New York: Basic Books).

Otsuka, Michael. 2003. *Libertarianism without Inequality* (Oxford: Clarendon Press).

Roark, Eric. 2006. "Using and Coming to Own: A Left-Libertarian Treatment of the Just Use and Appropriation of Natural Resources" (U. Missouri-Columbia, dissertation, 2008).

Rothbard, Murray. 1978. *For a New Liberty* (New York: Macmillan Publishing).

Rothbard, Murray. 1982. *The Ethics of Liberty* (Atlantic Highlands, NJ: Humanities Press).

Simmons, A. John. 1992. *The Lockean Theory of Rights* (Princeton, NJ: Princeton University Press).

Simmons, A. John. 1993. *On the Edge of Anarchy* (Princeton, NJ: Princeton University Press).

Steiner, Hillel. 1994. *An Essay on Rights* (Cambridge, MA: Blackwell Publishing).

Vallentyne, Peter. 2007. "Libertarianism and the State", *Social Philosophy and Policy* 24 (1) (Jan.): 187–205.

Vallentyne, Peter and Hillel Steiner, eds. 2000a. *The Origins of Left Libertarianism: An Anthology of Historical Writings* (New York: Palgrave Publishers Ltd.).

Vallentyne, Peter and Hillel Steiner, eds. 2000b. *Left Libertarianism and Its Critics: The Contemporary Debate* (New York: Palgrave Publishers Ltd.).

Vallentyne, Peter, Hillel Steiner, and Michael Otsuka. 2005. "Why Left-Libertarianism Isn't Incoherent, Indeterminate, or Irrelevant: A Reply to Fried", *Philosophy and Public Affairs* 33: 201–15.

Van Parijs, Philippe. 1995. *Real Freedom for All* (New York: Oxford University Press).

LIBERALISM

EQUALITY

Illuminating Egalitarianism*

Larry S. Temkin

The goal of this article is modest. It is simply to help illuminate the nature of egalitarianism. More particularly, I aim to show what certain egalitarians are committed to, and to suggest, though certainly not *prove*, that equality, as these egalitarians understand it, *is* an important normative ideal that cannot simply be ignored in moral deliberations.

The article is divided into six main sections. In section I, I distinguish between different kinds of egalitarian positions, and indicate the type of egalitarianism with which I am concerned. In section II, I discuss the relations between equality, fairness, luck, and responsibility. In section III, I make several methodological points regarding the equality of what debate. In section IV, I defend egalitarianism against rival views that focus on subsistence, sufficiency, or compassion. In section V, I introduce prioritarianism, and defend egalitarianism against the leveling down objection. In section VI, I illustrate egalitarianism's distinct appeal, in contrast to prioritarianism's. I end with a brief conclusion.

I. Distinguishing Different Kinds of Egalitarianism

Numerous quite distinct positions – ranging from utilitarianism, to libertarianism, to Rawls's maximin principle – have been described as, or perhaps conflated with, versions of egalitarianism. But, of course, most of these positions have little in common. Correspondingly, in discussing equality it is extremely important that one be clear about the sense one is using the term. In this section, I distinguish several egalitarian positions, and clarify the sense in which I shall be using the notion of egalitarianism.

Philosophers have long distinguished between purely *formal* and *substantive* principles of equality. Unfortunately, this distinction is not especially clean or helpful. More usefully, one might distinguish between equality as *universality*, as *impartiality*, or as *comparability*.

A basic principle of rationality, *equality as universality* reflects the view that all reasons and principles must be universal in their application. This is the view embodied in Aristotle's famous dictum that equality requires that likes be treated alike. Notice, since it applies universally, even the view that all tall people should be well off, and all short people badly off, meets this "egalitarian" principle.

Equality as impartiality reflects the view that all people must be treated impartially. Of course, positions vary dramatically regarding what *constitutes* treating people impartially. For example, for Kantians impartiality requires treating people as ends and never merely as means, while for Utilitarians it requires neutrality between different people's interests when maximizing the good. Arguably, it is the conception of equality as impartiality that Amartya Sen has in mind in contending that *all* plausible moral views are egalitarian, they merely differ in the answers they give to the "equality of what?" question.[1]

While all plausible moral theories are committed to equality as universality and impartiality, *equality as comparability* reflects a different, and I believe deeper, commitment to equality. Equality as comparability is fundamentally concerned with how people fare *relative to others*. This is a distinctive substantive view that rivals "non-egalitarian" positions like utilitarianism and libertarianism.

Another important distinction is between *instrumental* egalitarianism, where equality is valuable only insofar as it promotes some *other* valuable ideal; and *non-instrumental* egalitarianism, where equality is sometimes valuable *itself*, beyond the extent to which it promotes other ideals. On non-instrumental egalitarianism, any complete account of the moral realm must allow for equality's value.

I believe that many who think of themselves as egalitarians are, in fact, merely instrumental egalitarians; or, more accurately, instrumental egalitarians combined with equality as universality and impartiality egalitarians. This is true, for example, of many humanitarians, Rawlsians, communitarians, and so-called democratic egalitarians, who only favor redistribution from better to worse off *as a means to* reducing suffering, aiding the worst off, fostering solidarity, or strengthening democratic institutions. Such reasons are morally significant, and compatible with equality as universality and impartiality. But each is also compatible with the rejection of non-instrumental egalitarianism and equality as comparability.

We might further distinguish between *person-affecting* versions of egalitarianism, according to which inequality only matters insofar as it adversely affects people; and *impersonal* versions, according to which inequality can matter even when it doesn't adversely affect people. Similarly, we can distinguish between *deontic*-egalitarianism, which focuses on duties to address the legitimate complaints of victims of inequality by improving their situations; and *telic*-egalitarianism, which focuses on removing objectionable inequalities as a means of improving the goodness of outcomes. Deontic-egalitarianism focuses on assessing agents or actions, so unavoidable inequalities for which no one was responsible do not matter; whereas telic-egalitarianism focuses on the goodness of outcomes, so such inequalities may matter.[2]

With these distinctions in mind, I want to stress that my concern in this article is with equality as comparability, understood as a substantive version of non-instrumental egalitarianism. As I present and develop this position, it is an impersonal, telic version of egalitarianism.

Larry S. Temkin

Finally, let me emphasize that egalitarians are pluralists. No reasonable egalitarian believes that equality is *all* that matters. But they believe that it matters *some*. Thus, for the egalitarian, equality is only one important ideal, among others, including, perhaps, freedom, utility, perfection, and justice.[3]

II. Equality, Fairness, Luck, and Responsibility

If I give one piece of candy to Andrea, and two to Rebecca, Andrea will immediately assert "unfair!" This natural reaction suggests an intimate connection between equality and fairness. Arguably, concern about equality is that portion of our concern about comparative fairness that focuses on how people fare relative to others. Specifically, concern about equality reflects the view that inequality is bad when, and because, it is unfair, where the unfairness consists in one person being worse off than another no more deserving.

Thus, I claim that people who are egalitarians in my sense are *not* motivated by *envy*, but by a sense of *fairness*. So, on my view, concern for equality is not separable from our concern for a certain aspect of fairness; they are part and parcel of a single concern. We say that certain inequalities are objectionable *because they are unfair*; but by the same token, we say that there is a certain kind of unfairness in certain kinds of undeserved inequalities.

Many contemporary egalitarians, including Cohen, Dworkin, and Arneson, have been identified as so-called *luck egalitarians*.[4] Acknowledging the importance of autonomy and personal responsibility, *luck egalitarianism* supposedly aims to rectify the influence of luck in people's lives. Correspondingly, a canonical formulation of luck egalitarianism, invoked by both Gerry Cohen and myself, is that it is bad when one person is worse off than another through no fault or choice of her own.[5] So, luck egalitarians object when equally deserving people are unequally well off, but not when one person is worse off than another due to her own responsible choices, say to pursue a life of leisure, or crime.

In fact, I think luck egalitarianism has been misunderstood by most of its proponents, as well as most of its opponents. The egalitarian's *fundamental* concern isn't with luck *per se*, or even with whether or not someone is worse off than another through no fault or choice of her own, it is with *comparative fairness*. But people have been confused about this because, as it happens, in most paradigmatic cases where inequality involves comparative unfairness it *also* involves luck, or someone being worse off than another through no fault or choice of her own.

Thus, on close examination, the intimate connection between equality and fairness illuminates the ultimate role that luck plays in the egalitarian's thinking, as well as the relevance and limitations of the well-known "through no fault or choice of their own" clause. Among *equally* deserving people, it *is* bad, because *unfair*, for some to be worse off than others through no fault or choice of their own. But among *unequally* deserving people it isn't bad, because not unfair, for someone less deserving to be worse off than someone more deserving, even if the former is worse off through no fault or choice of his own. For example, egalitarians needn't object if a fully responsible criminal is worse off than a law-abiding citizen, even if the criminal craftily avoided capture, and so is only worse off because, through no fault or choice of his own, a falling limb injured him.

Additionally, in some cases inequality is bad, because unfair, even though the worse off *are* responsible for their plight; as when the worse off are so because they chose to do their duty, or perhaps acted supererogotorily, in adverse circumstances not of their making. So, for example, if I'm unlucky enough to walk by a drowning child, and I injure myself saving her, the egalitarian might think it *unfair* that I end up worse off than others, even though I am so as a result of my own responsible free choice to do my duty to help someone in need.[6]

Correspondingly, on reflection, luck *itself* is neither good nor bad from the egalitarian standpoint. Egalitarians object to luck that leaves equally deserving people unequally well off. But they can accept luck that makes equally deserving people equally well off, or unequally deserving people unequally well off proportional to their deserts. Thus, luck will be approved or opposed *only to the extent* that it promotes or undermines comparative fairness.

Some luck egalitarians distinguish between *option luck*, luck to which we responsibly open ourselves, and *brute luck*, luck that simply "befalls" us, unbidden.[7] This distinction's advocates believe that any option luck inequalities that result from people autonomously choosing to gamble, or invest in the stock market, are unobjectionable. By contrast, brute luck inequalities that result from some being born with less intelligence, or to poorer parents, or some being struck down by lightning, or an accident, are objectionable.

I reject the way the option/brute luck distinction is typically invoked. In part, this is because drawing the line between them is difficult. But more importantly, I believe that it *is* objectionable if Mary takes a prudent risk, and John an imprudent one, yet Mary fares much worse than John, because she is the victim of bad, and he the beneficiary of good, option luck. Likewise, if Mary and John are equally deserving, and choose similar options, but John ends up much better off than Mary, because he enjoys vastly greater option luck, I believe there *is* an egalitarian objection to the situation. As with paradigmatic cases involving brute luck, in such a case Mary ends up much worse off than John, though she is in no way less deserving than he. This seems to me patently unfair. It is a case of *comparative* unfairness to which my kind of egalitarian should, I think, object.

This discussion is relevant to many practical issues of public policy. *If* it is true that people can have personal responsibility for their actions in a way that is compatible with a meaningful conception of desert – and I should stress that this is a big "if", but one that many accept, and that I shall assume in the rest of this discussion – then for the reasons suggested above not *all* substantive inequalities will involve comparative unfairness, and hence be objectionable from an egalitarian standpoint. This position has deep and important implications for the nature and extent of our obligations towards the less fortunate whose predicaments resulted from their own fully responsible choices. This might include conditions resulting from individually responsible choices involving job selection, lifestyle, risky behavior, and so on.

Clearly, the scope of this issue is too large to deal adequately with it here, but let me just make five relevant points. First, the starting point of our discussion is that the mere fact that some are much worse off than others, does *not* mean that there is an *egalitarian* reason to aid them. There is an egalitarian reason to aid someone

Larry S. Temkin

if her situation is *unfair* relative to others, and whether this is so or not will surely depend on facts of individual responsibility pertinent to the case.

Second, even if there is no *egalitarian* reason to aid someone who is needy, there are many powerful normative considerations that may dictate our doing so. These may include maximin or prioritarian considerations that speak in favor of giving special weight to those who are poorly off, humanitarian considerations to ease pain and suffering, utilitarian reasons to promote the general welfare, virtue-related reasons of compassion, mercy, beneficence, and forgiveness, and so on. As noted above, egalitarians are rightly committed to pluralism, and we have to be sensitive to the full range of reasons for aiding the needy that having nothing to do with considerations of comparative fairness.

But third, where the other morally relevant factors are equal, or even sufficiently close, egalitarian reasons of comparative fairness may well help determine who among the needy has the strongest moral claim on scarce resources. So, for example, if one *has* to choose between who gets the last available bed in the ICU unit, perhaps it ought to go to the innocent pedestrian who was struck by a drunk driver, rather than the person who was driving drunk.

Fourth, from the standpoint of comparative fairness, it is crucial that one determine appropriate comparison classes, so that one is comparing all relevant types of behavior in the same way. For example, it would be objectionable to downgrade the medical claims of AIDS patients who engaged in unprotected sex, if one wasn't similarly prepared to downgrade the medical claims of pregnant women who engaged in unprotected sex, or perhaps obese stroke victims who did nothing to curb their indulgence of food.

Finally, in accordance with the point about option luck noted above, it is important from the standpoint of comparative fairness, that one not merely compare the "losers" of those who make poor choices with the "winners" of those who make good choices, but that, in addition, one compare the winners and losers of *both* categories with each other. Most smokers don't develop lung cancer, most people who overeat don't have a stroke, and most helmetless motorcyclists don't end up in the emergency room. Thus, from the standpoint of comparative fairness, it is important to bear in mind that full responsibility for one's choices doesn't automatically translate into full responsibility for one's predicament. Indeed, as Kant rightly saw, the two are only loosely, and coincidentally, connected. Correspondingly, consideration of equality as comparative fairness requires that we pay attention not only to *actual* outcomes, but to considerations of expected utility. More particularly, considerations of comparative fairness will require that we pay attention to the extent to which different people end up better and worse off than the expected value of their choices. Unfortunately, I cannot pursue these issues here.

III. Equality of What?

Many egalitarians have debated the following question: insofar as we are egalitarians, what *kind* of equality should we seek. A host of candidates have been championed, including, among others: income, resources, primary goods, wealth, power, welfare, opportunity, needs satisfaction, capabilities, functionings, rights, and liberties. It is difficult to exaggerate the importance of this topic, since equality of one kind will often *require* inequality of another. For example, equality of income may correlate with *inequality* of need satisfaction between the handicapped and the healthy, and vice versa.

I shall not try to offer a particular substantive answer to the "equality of what?" question. However, I shall make several observations pertinent to this topic.

I begin with a methodological remark. Philosophers favoring different conceptions of what kind of equality matters have gone to great lengths illustrating cases where rival conceptions have implausible implications. These philosophers seem to assume that such considerations provide good reason for rejecting the rival conceptions. Moreover, many seem to implicitly assume that concern for one kind of equality rules out concern for others. Unfortunately, on a pluralistic view of morality, to which *all* reasonable egalitarians are committed, such assumptions are dubious.

Elsewhere, I have pointed out that the fact that ideals like equality, utility, or freedom sometimes have implausible, or even terrible, implications, does *not* show that those ideals do not matter. It merely shows that each ideal, alone, is not *all* that matters.[8] Likewise, the fact that different conceptions of what kind of equality matters sometimes have implausible implications does not necessarily show that those conceptions do not matter. Equality, like morality itself, is complex. And more than one conception may be relevant to our "all things considered" egalitarian judgments. Perhaps different kinds of equality matter in different contexts. Or perhaps even in the same context there are strong reasons for promoting different kinds of equality. Thus, the "equality of what?" question may have several plausible answers.

My own view is that a large component of the egalitarian's concern should be with equality of *welfare*; but as I use it "welfare" is a technical term that needs to be interpreted broadly, and with great care. It must appropriately include, among other things, most of the elements that Amartya Sen carefully distinguishes in his sophisticated account of functionings, capability sets, freedom, agency, and well-being.[9] However, I also think the egalitarian should give weight to equality of opportunity.

Suppose, for example, that we lived in a world not too unlike the actual one, in which a relatively small percentage of people were very well off, while the vast majority were much worse off. Concern for equality of welfare would impel us to raise everyone to the level of the best-off. But suppose, given limited resources, this were not possible. Concern for equality of welfare might then impel us to redistribute from the better-off to the worse-off. But if the percentage of better-off were small, this might do little to improve the worse-off, its main effect might be to reduce the better-off to the level of the worse-off. Even if we think this *would* be an improvement regarding equality of welfare, we *might* agree it would *not* be an improvement all things considered, and in any event it might not be politically feasible. Thus, we might conclude that in such a case we must accept, even if not happily, a significantly unequal situation regarding welfare.

Still, we might distinguish two versions of this scenario. In one version, the better-off group are members of a hereditary aristocracy. They, and their descendants, have been guaranteed a place in the better-off group. Likewise, the members of the worse-off group, and their descendants, are destined to remain in the worse-off group regardless of their abilities or efforts. In a second version, there is genuine equality of opportunity. At birth, each person, and his or her descendants, has an equal chance of ending up in the better-off group.

By hypothesis, the two versions of the scenario are equivalent regarding equality of welfare. Yet, I think most would agree that the second is better than the first all things considered, and better largely, if not wholly, because it is better regarding equality of opportunity. I think, then, that qua egalitarian, one should care about equality of opportunity. But this concern should be *in addition to*, rather than *in place of*, a concern for equality of welfare. The second situation may be *perfect* regarding equality of opportunity – but it still involves many people who are worse off than others through no fault or choice of their own, in a way that involves comparative unfairness. The egalitarian, *qua* egalitarian, will regard this as objectionable. It would be better, regarding equality, if, in addition to everyone having equal *opportunities*, those equally deserving actually fared equally well.

Equality of opportunity plays a crucial role in debates about rationing. In the face of scarce resources, where not all needs can be met, what system will ensure that among those who are equally needy and deserving, everyone at least has an equal opportunity to have their needs met? Note, there may be different ways of fully or partially satisfying the ideal of equality of opportunity. And of course, here, as elsewhere, there will be other moral ideals that compete with the ideal of equality of opportunity, or provide reasons for fully or partially satisfying it one way rather than another.

The preceding considerations are relevant to several related topics, such as whether we should be concerned about *ex ante* equality – equality in people's *prospects* concerning the lives they might lead – or *ex post* equality – equality in *outcomes* concerning the actual lives that people end up leading; and similarly, whether the egalitarian's concern should be mainly with *procedural* fairness, or with some more robust outcome-related conception of *substantive* fairness, according to which an outcome that resulted from a perfectly fair procedure, might nonetheless be substantively unfair, and require amelioration. These topics raise a host of complex issues, that cannot be adequately dealt with here; but let me give a sense for my view of these topics, and offer a few examples that help illustrate my reasoning.

First, just as I think one should care about both equality of opportunity and equality of welfare (broadly construed), so I think that for similar reasons one should care about both ex ante and ex post equality, and also about both procedural fairness and a more robust outcome-related conception of substantive fairness. In some cases, perhaps, ex ante equality, or procedural fairness, will be all that is realizable, and in others our main concern might be with ex post, or substantive fairness. But in fact, in certain circumstances the two will be intimately related. So, for example, it is arguable that under certain circumstances, whatever outcome results from a situation that meets sufficiently demanding criteria for ex ante equality, or procedural fairness, will, in fact, also be guaranteed to meet the most plausible conception of ex post equality, or substantive fairness. Moreover, it is also arguable that under certain circumstances, no coherent account can be given of what ex post equality, or substantive fairness demands, independently of certain favorable conditions initially obtaining that would at least partially satisfy the criteria for ex ante equality or procedural fairness.

I cannot fully defend these claims here, but let me offer some observations to help illuminate them.

Egalitarians recognize that in the game of life, each of us, to some extent, must play the cards we are dealt. But they also recognize that sometimes our cards are both dealt to us, and played for us. On this analogy, the concern for ex ante equality, and procedural fairness, reflects the concern that the deck should not be stacked against certain players, and that there should be no cheating in the play of the hand. So, minimally, the egalitarian wants each person's hand to be determined by a fair deal and fairly played. If, for example, the deck is stacked in favor of whites or men, so that they are always dealt aces and kings, while blacks or women are always dealt deuces and treys, that situation will be patently unfair, and it can be rightly criticized from the standpoint of ex ante equality, or procedural fairness. Likewise, it will be unfair if the cards are dealt fairly, but unfairly played; if, for example, whites or males are allowed to look at the hands of blacks or women, before deciding what cards to play.

Ensuring that each person's hand will be determined by a fair deal and played fairly ensures that, in advance of the deal, the *expected value* of each hand is the same, and we can say that that meets an important criterion for ex ante equality, or procedural fairness. But surely, the egalitarian wants more than just a fair deal and a fair play, since, by itself, this would do nothing to preclude the result that some people will be dealt aces and kings, while others, no less deserving, will be dealt deuces and treys. That is, in the game of life, the cards don't have to be *stacked* against particular groups or individuals for it to still *turn out* that some are born with extraordinary advantages, and hence extraordinary life prospects, relative to others. For the egalitarian, this is deeply unfair, even if, in an important sense, it is not *as* unfair as such a situation would have been had it resulted from a stacked deck of bias or discrimination.

The preceding suggests that the egalitarian not only wants the *deal* to be fair, he wants, as it were, each *hand* to be fair. That is, he does not merely want the expected value of each hand to be the same in *advance* of each deal, he wants the expected value of each hand to be the same *after* the deal. Thus, it should not only be that *in advance* of bringing a child into the world, one can reasonably expect the expected value of its life to be as good as anyone else's, but rather that any child that is actually brought into the world should face a constellation of natural and social circumstances that give its life prospects an expected value as good as anyone else's. Notice, this view reflects a concern that in one way resembles an ex post view – since it seeks equality in people's life prospects after the deal, as it were. But in another way it resembles an ex ante view – since it focuses on the expected value of people's life *prospects*, rather than the outcome that will result when the hand is actually played, which is to say the value of the lives that the people actually end up *leading*. For my purposes, I shall count such a view as setting further requirements on the criteria that must be met for ex ante equality, or procedural fairness, to be fully satisfied.

But these criteria need further strengthening. To see this, let us develop our card analogy a bit. Suppose that each person is to be dealt four cards, each of which represents a possible life that someone might lead. Suppose further that one of these cards will be selected at random. If an ace is selected, someone will lead a very high quality life with a value of 20,000, if an eight is selected someone will lead a moderately high quality life of value 10,000, and if a deuce is selected someone will lead a very poor quality life of value 0. Now suppose that in outcome A each member of a large population has been dealt four cards. And suppose that as a result of a completely fair deal, involving many decks, half the population has been dealt two aces

Larry S. Temkin

and two deuces, while the other half has been dealt four eights. Here, we meet the initial criteria that prior to the deal the expected value of each life is the same, and we further meet the additional criteria that after the deal the expected value of each life is the same, namely 10,000. Still, although the *expected values* of their lives are the same, it is clear that some people in A face significantly different life prospects. Those who have been dealt four eights face the certainty of a life of value 10,000, and the statistically near certain outcome of ending up in their society's middle-off group.[10] Those who have been dealt aces and twos, face the equal probability that they will end up with a life of value 20,000 or a life of value 0, and it is certain that they will either end up in their society's best-off group, or its worst-off group. Hence, whatever happens, it is *certain* that those who were dealt different kinds of cards will lead significantly different kinds of lives of significantly different value.

Contrast outcome A with outcome B, where, *everyone* is dealt four eights, and hence faces the certain prospect of living a life of value 10,000, or outcome C, where, *everyone* is dealt two aces and two deuces, and hence faces an equal probability of living a life of value 20,000 or a life of value 0. Clearly, there is a respect in which each person's overall life prospects are the same in B, and similarly in C, but not in A. I believe that the respect in which this is so reflects an important element of what one should care about insofar as one cares about ex ante equality, or procedural fairness. Arguably, from the standpoint of ex ante equality, or procedural fairness, B and C are both perfect. One should be indifferent between them, and, each should be preferred to A.

If right, the preceding suggests that insofar as one cares about ex ante equality, or procedural fairness, one should not merely be concerned with the *expected value* of different lives, either in advance of their coming to be, or even at birth. Rather, for each kind of life, L, with value V, that someone faces at birth with probability p, it will be desirable if everyone else, at birth, also faces a kind of life, L', with probability p, that also has value V. Note, this position does *not* commit one to the kind of radical egalitarian position that Kurt Vonnegut Jr. skewered in his notoriously anti-egalitarian diatribe "Harrison Bergeron," which would require that everyone face the exact same set of circumstances, and that everyone be exactly the same in all of their characteristics.[11] On the view in question, each kind of life, L and L' may differ substantially in all sorts of respects, as long as their *overall* value is the same.

Suppose we fully achieved ex ante equality, or procedural fairness, along the lines suggested above. So, for every two people there would be a one-to-one correspondence of equivalent alternatives involving the different life prospects they faced, the value of those prospects, and their probabilities. In this case, we would have met the egalitarian goal that no one should be disadvantaged relative to another merely by the circumstances surrounding their birth. Still, the egalitarian would want more than this, as such ex ante equality, or procedural fairness, would be compatible with undeserved *ex post* inequality of any size. And egalitarians will object to such inequality precisely when, and because, it involves the substantive, comparative unfairness of some people being worse off than others, though they are no less deserving.

Consider an outcome like C, above. Suppose, at birth, everyone faces one of two prospects with equal probability. Either they will live a very high quality life of value 20,000, or a very low quality life of value 0. Let us assume that this reflects a fair situation, equivalent to each being dealt a fair hand, from a fair deck that has been fairly shuffled. And suppose that it will be pure chance which kind of life they end up leading, so that no charge of bias or unfairness can be made regarding the "play of the hand" that ultimately determined what kind of life they would lead. Even so, if one assumes that no one is less deserving than anyone else, the egalitarian will regard it as comparatively unfair if half the people end up with lives of value 20,000 and half with lives of value 0. Ex ante equality and procedural fairness may be desirable, but in such circumstances, they are no substitute for ex post equality, or substantive fairness. In such a case, at least, the egalitarian would not be satisfied with the resulting outcome. Instead, she would much prefer the fairer substantive outcome where each person lived a life of value 10,000.

Next, suppose that the game of life was "stacked" so that at birth certain groups had a much greater chance of ending up well off than others. On the analogy we have been using, we can imagine that some people have been unfairly dealt three aces and a deuce, while others have been unfairly dealt three deuces and an ace, but that, as before, what life each person will actually lead will be determined by a random selection of one of her cards. Clearly this would be objectionable from the standpoint of ex ante equality and procedural fairness, and there would be egalitarian reason to try to prevent such unfairness in people's initial starting points if one could. Still, assuming that neither the advantaged nor disadvantaged were less deserving than the others, if, in fact, both groups of people had aces drawn, so that both ended up living very high quality lives of value 20,000, the egalitarian would see no reason to change the outcome. And similarly, if both groups of people had deuces drawn. If, on the other hand, one of the groups of people had an ace drawn, and the other a deuce, the egalitarian would favor redistribution between the better and worse off *whichever group* was better off. Here, it seems clear that the concern for ex post equality, and substantive fairness, would dictate how the egalitarian would respond to the actual lives people ended up leading, and any concerns she might have about ex ante equality or procedural justice would play no role in that response.

Might the egalitarian simply focus on achieving ex post equality, and not worry about whether or not ex ante equality, or procedural fairness obtains? I think not. Let me make several points regarding this.

First, the concern for ex ante equality and procedural fairness, reflect the view that it not only matters how people *end up*, it matters how they have been *treated*; for example, that they are treated *as equals* so that no one is discriminated against, or otherwise dealt an unfair hand to play. Importantly, it also matters that each person be given a fair start from which to autonomously plan and lead a life of their own choosing, so that each person is significantly responsible for their own lot in life. Moreover, such factors are relevant to telic considerations regarding the goodness of outcomes, and not merely deontic considerations of how people ought to act. Thus, for example, it is not only true that people *ought* to treat people as equals, it is true that treating people as equals is *itself* a good-making feature of outcomes; so that, other things equal, an outcome in which people have been treated as equals is better than one where they have not.

Second, as noted above in discussing equality of opportunity, there may be some cases where ex post equality is unobtainable, or undesirable all things considered, where it would be better, precisely because fairer, if the outcome resulted from an initial situation of ex ante equality, or procedural fairness, than if it didn't.

Larry S. Temkin

Third, ex post equality is itself desirable only when it reflects a situation of comparative fairness. So, as indicated earlier, other things equal, the egalitarian should not prefer an equal outcome in which a fully responsible criminal ended up as well off as a law abiding citizen. Likewise, suppose that John is dealt an initial hand that enables him to live a life ranging in value from 10,000 to 20,000, while Mary is dealt a hand that only enables her to live a life of value from 0 to 10,000. Even if John and Mary end up equally well off, so there is perfect ex post equality, the egalitarian would have good reason to worry that the outcome was comparatively *unfair*. It might well be that Mary, having done her best to take full advantage of every opportunity available to her, ought to end up much better off than John, who may have willingly and knowingly frittered away the abundant opportunities available to him. So, the comparative fairness egalitarian can't just ignore questions of ex ante equality, and procedural fairness, and focus on bringing about outcomes of ex post equality.

But this raises a fourth important issue. One can't simply assume that Mary deserves to be better off than John, based on the extent to which they differed in maximizing their potential. Perhaps if John had been given Mary's initial starting point, he would have acted as Mary in fact did, and similarly for Mary. In that case, perhaps Mary and John deserve to be equally well off after all, despite their completely different, and seemingly unfair, initial starting points. This shows that it may be important to promote ex ante equality and procedural fairness, to ensure that people have sufficiently comparable starting points, in order to make meaningful judgments of comparative fairness.[12] Furthermore, if, contrary to fact, one could ensure that people's initial starting points fully met the robust criteria for ex ante equality and procedural fairness – so, in particular, people had been dealt similar hands in terms of talents, temperament, individual responsibility, and life prospects – and if, in addition, one could later remove or rectify the influence of luck on people's choices – so, ultimately, each person was responsible for how they ended up relative to others; then, of course, the comparative fairness egalitarian *would* be fully satisfied with the outcome, regardless of whether it involved ex post equality, in the sense of people actually ending up equally well off.

Finally, let me conclude this section with another methodological point. There is, I believe, much truth to the maxim that "to a person with a hammer, everything looks like a nail." So, for example, someone with a bad back is likely to receive a very different treatment depending on whether he goes to a chiropractor, a psychologist, or a back surgeon. Understandably, each of us confronts problems in terms of the models and theories that we have mastered, and which have served us well in other contexts, especially if the problems seem both amenable to analysis, and tractable, in terms of our familiar models and theories.

The point is obvious, but it is important to bear in mind in thinking about the "equality of what" debate. The world is filled with inequalities, and among the starkest of these, of normative significance, are the vast economic inequalities of income and wealth. Correspondingly, many of the brightest minds who have taken up the topic of equality have been economists. Naturally, they have used the powerful tools of economics to assess inequality, and, in fact the problem of inequality seems particularly amenable to analysis, and potentially tractable, when the focus is on economic equality. After all, we have highly developed economic theories that provide precise ways of identifying and measuring economic inequalities, and that yield solid guidance as to how social and economic policies might be changed to ameliorate such inequalities.

Given all this, it is, perhaps, unsurprising, that while philosophers have defended a wide range of answers to the "equality of what?" question, in the "real world" the battleground of egalitarianism is largely an economic one. Policy makers rely heavily on economists to meaningfully measure disparities in income and wealth, and social policies are devised with the goal of reducing economic disparities. But, as we shall see next, this may be problematic.

Consider the old bromide that if you don't have your health you don't have anything. On this view, while it may be better to be rich than poor, it is even more important to be healthy than ill. This view may well express a deep and important truth. Suppose, on reflection, we think it does. This, of course, would have important egalitarian implications. Instead of focusing on improving the lot of the poor, there would be strong reason to focus on improving the lot of the ill. To be sure, there would be reason to focus on the ill poor, before the ill rich, but there would also be reason to focus on the ill rich, before the healthy poor. After all, increasing the income or wealth of the healthy poor would reduce the gap between the healthy poor and the healthy rich, but in doing this it would *increase* the gap between the healthy poor and the ill rich. On the view in question, this would be akin to improving the lot of some who were, in fact, *already* among the world's better off in terms of what matters *most*, and this might, in fact, *worsen* the situation's overall inequality.

Similar remarks might hold for other components that play a central role in our lives. So, to note but one other example, if, as some believe, most love-filled lives are better than most loveless lives, and if, as seems plausible, being rich is neither necessary nor sufficient for having a love-filled life, then it may well be that efforts to increase the income or wealth of the poor would often involve reducing the gap between the love-filled poor and the love-filled rich, but *increasing* the gap between the love-filled poor and the loveless rich. As before, this might amount to improving the lot of some who were *already* among the world's better off in terms of what matters *most*, and might actually *worsen* the situation's overall inequality.

Let me be clear. I am not arguing that we have reason to be complacent about our world's extraordinary economic inequalities. Indeed, as has been amply demonstrated, there are important correlations between economic status and many other central components of well-being.[13] Still, the preceding discussion may have important implications regarding the aims and focus of egalitarianism. If the inequalities that matter *most* are actually inequalities of food, health, safety, and the like, or inequalities in rights, freedom, stable homes, or love, then there may need to be a profound shift in the tools, approach, and policies of real world egalitarianism.

Perhaps egalitarians need to consult doctors, nutritionists, agronomists, political scientists, psychologists, sociologists, social workers, and others. Perhaps they require meaningful measures of serious illness, nutritional deprivation, human rights realization, political stability, functional family life, or meaningful love, at least as much as measures of economic inequality. Similarly, perhaps the focus of egalitarianism needs to change from efforts to shift the wage scale, alter people's savings habits, or redistribute wealth, to altering the focus and distribution of medical care, increasing

Larry S. Temkin

crop yields, changing patterns of nutritional consumption, promoting political stability or human rights, developing stable families, fostering loving relationships, and so on.

Even to suggest that egalitarians should take on such tasks may sound ludicrous. After all, it is by no means clear what might even count as a fully satisfactory situation in some of these respects, much less how one might go about quantifying, or measuring, some of these factors. Moreover, it may seem utterly beyond our reach to think we could develop effective social policies to reduce the inequalities in some of these areas, even if we agreed that doing so might be desirable. And no doubt the messiness and complexities associated with the tasks envisioned, help to partly explain the propensity to focus on economic inequalities; which, as noted above, are readily identifiable, measurable, and, in principle, rectifiable via discernible economic policies. Moreover, it may seem clear that economic inequalities *are* bad, and *should* be addressed, even if they are not the only inequalities that matter.

However, the preceding remarks suggest that the contemporary preoccupation with economic inequalities may be problematic. Focusing on economic inequality may direct our attention away from the inequalities that actually matter most, and so involve a waste of effort and resources in the fight for meaningful equality. Worse, in some cases reducing economic inequality might not merely be inefficient, it might be counterproductive, exacerbating overall inequality in terms of what matters most.

I conclude that we must be wary of regarding the problem of inequality as a kind economic "nail," because we are in possession of, and fairly adept at using, the powerful "hammer" of economic analysis. We must take seriously the full range of complex answers that might be given to the "equality of what" question, thinking hard about what factors are most central and valuable for human flourishing, and how the various components of well-being are related and distributed. Correspondingly, in identifying, measuring, and addressing inequality, we may need to use, and perhaps even forge, a host of other, non-economic, "tools" for social, cultural, and psychological analysis.

IV. The Subsistence Level, Sufficiency, and Compassion

Some believe that the subsistence level has a special role to play in our understanding of inequality's importance – or lack thereof. They imagine conditions of scarcity, where there are insufficient resources to support everyone. They then note that if the resources are distributed equally, so that everyone is at the same welfare level, or has equal access to advantages, everyone will be below the subsistence level, and hence everyone will die. If, on the other hand, resources are distributed unequally, at least some, though not all, will live.

Consideration of such examples has led some people to conclude that inequality doesn't matter, since the unequal outcome in which some people live is clearly preferable to the equal outcome in which everyone dies.[14] Others have used such examples to support the conclusion that inequality matters less in poor societies than rich ones, as only rich societies can "afford the luxury" of equality.[15]

Such arguments are popular. This is unfortunate. Undoubtedly, the unequal situation in which some people live is better than the equal situation where everyone dies *all things considered*. But this does not mean that inequality in a poor situation doesn't matter, much less that inequality doesn't matter at all. Rather, such arguments merely serve to remind us that inequality is not *all* that matters. But who would have thought differently?

Surely, the egalitarian would say, the worse-off people in the unequal situation have a significant complaint regarding inequality. They are much worse-off than the others, though no less deserving (we are supposing). Moreover, the difference between the quality of their lives is most significant. It is a difference measured in terms of life's basic necessities; a difference, quite literally, between who lives and dies. To suggest that such undeserved inequality doesn't *matter* is ludicrous. And to respond to such situations, as non-egalitarians are wont to, that "nobody said that life was fair," is to admit, even in one's cynicism, the perspective of the comparative egalitarian. To the egalitarian, the inequality in the situation where some live, and others die, is *very* bad and it matters a *great* deal. Still, as bad as the situation's inequality is, *if* the cost of removing it were a situation where *none* survived, even the egalitarian could admit, qua pluralist, that the cost was too high.

Let us next consider the claim that instead of caring about equality, we should care about *sufficiency* – that people have "enough," and the related claim that it is important to show *compassion* for people who are poorly off, but not to promote equality, *per se*. Harry Frankfort has argued that "It is . . . reasonable to assign a higher priority to improving the condition of those . . . in need than to improving the condition of those . . . not in need," but he asserts that this is only because we have reason to give priority to the *needy*, not because there is any general obligation to give priority to those who are worse off.[16] Thus, he contends that "We tend to be quite unmoved, after all, by inequalities between the well-to-do and the rich. . . . The fact that some people have much less than others is morally undisturbing when it is clear that they have plenty."[17] Roger Crisp echoes Frankfort's position. He believes that when circumstances warrant our compassion we have reason to give priority to one person over another, but when people are "sufficiently" well off, compassion is no longer warranted and there is *no* reason to give priority to one person over another *merely* because the one is worse off.[18]

Frankfort and Crisp's positions challenge egalitarianism. But I believe we should reject their views. To see why, consider the following example.

I have two daughters. My daughters aren't super-rich, but by the criteria that *truly* matter most, they are they are incredibly well off. Suppose the following is true. Both are extremely attractive and intelligent, have deep friendships, a stable home, a family that nurtures them, excellent schools, high self-esteem, financial security, rewarding projects, good health, fantastic careers and a long life ahead of them. In short, imagine that my two daughters are destined to flourish in all the ways that matter most. By any reasonable criteria, we must assume that my daughters will have "sufficiently" good lives.

Suppose I know this about my daughters. Suppose I also know that in fact Andrea is a little better off than Becky in most of the relevant categories, and as well off in all of the others. So, Andrea is smarter, has more rewarding friendships, will live longer, and so on. And suppose that the difference between Andrea and Becky is just a matter of blind luck. Neither Andrea nor Becky has done anything to deserve their different fortunes.

Larry S. Temkin

Finally, to make the example simple and clean, imagine that Andrea's incredibly good fortune even extends to the most trivial of matters. She is, in a word, just plain lucky in everything she does. Here is one way in which she is lucky. Every time she goes for her weekly walk, she finds a twenty-dollar bill. She doesn't look for money as she walks, or take particular routes where she thinks rich people with holes in their pockets tread, she just always comes across money when out walking. Blind luck. Of course, for someone as well off as she is in terms of what truly matters in life, finding twenty dollars once a week doesn't make much of a real difference to her life, but she never loses the thrill of finding money on her path, and it invariably brightens her day, and briefly brings a warm smile to her face and a glow in her heart.

Becky, on the other hand, doesn't share her sister's incredible luck. She walks even more regularly than Andrea, and takes similar paths at similar times. But for some reason she never finds any money. Of course, in a life as rich and fulfilling as hers, this hardly matters; it simply means that she misses the excitement Andrea feels when she comes across money, together with its attendant outward smile and inward glow.

Finally, let us suppose that Andrea never mentions the money that she finds, not because she is hiding it from anyone, but because it never comes up. So, Becky isn't the least bit envious of her sister's good fortune. Indeed, we may add, if we like, that Becky is such a precious child, she wouldn't be envious of Andrea's good fortune even if she knew about it – she would just be happy for her.

Now suppose I knew all of this to be the case. And I was out walking with my two daughters. If I was walking down the path, and saw twenty dollars floating towards Andrea (yes, like manna from heaven!), I have no doubt that I would regard it as a good turn of events if a gust of wind arose to redirect it towards Becky. My immediate wish would be for Becky to discover that wonderful pleasure of "finding" money on a walk. But more generally, I would regard it as better if Becky found the money rather than Andrea, to make up for the fact that Andrea was already destined to be better off than Becky over the course of her life.

On Crisp's view, since Andrea and Becky both lead "sufficiently" good lives, compassion won't be warranted, and hence there would be *no* reason for me to give Becky priority over Andrea in this way. I think Crisp is half right. I agree that in this case I wouldn't feel *compassion* for Becky. Hers is not a life of misery or suffering, nor is it a life lacking in any of the ways that matter most. Still, I would give Becky priority in the manner suggested.

My reason for this is egalitarian in nature. It is pure luck that Andrea continually finds money and Becky doesn't. Pure luck that Andrea is better off in many ways that matter. Hence, Becky is not merely worse off than Andrea, she is worse off through no fault, or choice, of her own. Egalitarians believe this crucial fact about the relation between Becky and Andrea provides them with reason to give Becky priority over Andrea. Not the reason provided by compassion, but the reason of equality, or comparative *fairness*.

Note, as above, if someone were to claim, on Becky's behalf, that it wasn't *fair* that she never found money, while her sister always did, it would be no *answer* to that charge for someone to retort that "life isn't fair." To the contrary, such a cynical retort vindicates the egalitarian's view of the situation, even when it is offered in support of the view that we needn't *do* anything about Becky's situation. The egalitarian is acutely aware that "life isn't fair." That is the starting point of her view. What separates the egalitarian from the anti-egalitarian is the way she reacts to life's unfairness. The essence of the egalitarian's view is that comparative unfairness is bad, and that if we *could* do something about life's unfairness, we have *some* reason to. Such reasons may be outweighed by other reasons, but they are not, as anti-egalitarians suppose, entirely without force.

V. Prioritarianism and the Leveling Down Objection[19]

For many years, non-egalitarians have argued that we should reject substantive non-instrumental egalitarianism. Instead, some believe, we should be *prioritarians*, and in fact, I believe that many who think of themselves as egalitarians actually *are* prioritarians. Roughly, prioritarians want everyone to fare as well as possible, but the worse off someone is in absolute terms, the greater weight they give to her claims in their moral deliberations. This view tends to favor redistribution between the better- and worse-off, but the key point to note is that while on this view one has a special concern for the worse-off, one's ultimate goal is for each to fare as well as possible.

Prioritarianism may seem to capture some of the strengths of utilitarianism and maximin, while avoiding their shortcomings. Like utilitarianism, it gives weight to the concerns of *all*, and hence is able to avoid maximin's *exclusive* – and implausible – focus on the worst-off. But like maximin, prioritarianism expresses a special concern for those worse-off, and hence is able to avoid utilitarianism's exclusive – and implausible – focus on maximization.

Still, prioritarianism has mainly been offered as an alternative to substantive non-instrumental egalitarianism. In particular, many think that prioritarianism is the closest thing to a plausible egalitarian position. The gist of this view is *not* that prioritarianism is a plausible version of non-instrumental egalitarianism, but rather that non-instrumental egalitarianism is implausible. Hence, if one generally favors transfers from better- to worse-off – as many do – one should be a prioritarian *instead* of a non-instrumental egalitarian.

Many are attracted to the foregoing by the *Raising Up* and *Leveling Down Objections*. Roughly, the Leveling Down Objection claims that there is *no* respect in which a situation is normatively improved *merely* by leveling down a better-off person to the level of someone worse-off. Likewise, the Raising Up Objection claims that there is *no* respect in which a situation is normatively worsened *merely* by improving some people's lives, even if those people are already better off than everyone else. But, it is claimed, since leveling down may undeniably decrease inequality, and raising up may undeniably increase inequality, this shows that there is *nothing* valuable about equality *itself*, and hence that substantive non-instrumental egalitarianism must be rejected.

Elsewhere,[20] I have argued that the Leveling Down and Raising Up Objections have great intuitive appeal, but that they derive much of their force from a position I call the *Slogan*, according to which one situation *cannot* be worse (or better) than another *in any respect*, if there is *no one* for whom it *is* worse (or better) in any respect. I have shown that the Slogan must be rejected, and contended that this deprives the Leveling Down and Raising Up Objections of much of their rhetorical force.

Larry S. Temkin

Many people accept my claims about the Slogan, but still find the Raising Up and Leveling Down Objections compelling against non-instrumental egalitarianism. Most such responses turn on rejecting the Slogan, as a *narrow* person-affecting principle, in favor of a *wide* person-affecting principle[21] that assesses the goodness of alternative outcomes not in terms of how the particular people who would be in each outcome would be affected for better or worse, but rather in terms of how people are affected, for better or worse, in each outcome.[22] Tim Scanlon once wrote that "rights . . . need to be justified somehow, and how other than by appeal to the human interests their recognition promotes and protects? This seems to be the uncontrovertible insight of the classical utilitarians."[23] Followers of the view in question extend the "uncontrovertible insight" beyond rights to all of morality. As Roger Crisp puts the point, "the worry arises from the idea that what matters morally could be something that was independent of the well-being of individuals."[24]

I accept my critics' claim that one could reject the Slogan and still endorse the Leveling Down and Raising Up Objections, by moving to a wide person-affecting principle. And I readily grant that the wide person-affecting principle also has great initial appeal. But while a wide person-affecting principle can handle *one* of the problems I leveled at the Slogan, namely the Non-Identity Problem,[25] it can't handle any of the other problems I raised for the Slogan. For example, I noted that most people firmly judge that there is at least *one* respect in which an outcome where vicious sinners fare better than benign saints, is worse than an outcome where the sinners and saints both get what they deserve, even if the saints fare just as well in the two outcomes. But neither the Slogan *nor* the wide person-affecting principle can capture this judgment. Thus, like the Slogan, the wide person-affecting principle is unable to capture the non-instrumental value of proportional justice, a value to which many are committed. More generally, the wide person-affecting principle has the same fundamental shortcoming as the narrow principle, namely, that it allows *no* scope for *any im*personal moral values.

I have argued against basing the Leveling Down and Raising Up Objections on a wide-person affecting view at length elsewhere,[26] and shall not repeat those arguments here. Still, let me observe the following. Wide person-affecting views combine the following two claims: claim 1, only sentient individuals are the proper objects of moral concern; and claim 2, for purposes of evaluating outcomes, individual well-being is *all* that matters. Although both claims can be questioned, for the sake of argument I am willing to accept claim 1. But claim 1 must be carefully interpreted if it is not to be deeply misleading. For example, claim 1 is most plausible – though still questionable – insofar as it asserts the moral primacy of sentient individuals, as opposed to groups or societies. But, importantly, sentient individuals are not merely the *objects* of moral concern, they are also the *source* of moral concerns, and of both moral and non-moral values. Thus, for example, rational agents can give rise to moral concerns and values that non-rational beings cannot.

Once one recognizes that sentient individuals are not merely the *objects* of moral concern, but also the *source* of moral concerns and values, claim 2 loses its appeal. For purposes of evaluating outcomes, why should we *only* care about the *well-being* of individuals? Why shouldn't we *also* care about whether moral agents get what they deserve (justice), or how individuals fare relative to others (equality), or whether rational agents have acted freely, autonomously, or morally? Most humans have extraordinary capacities beyond their capacity for *well-being*. These capacities serve as a source of value in the world; for example, the value that can be found in friendship, love, altruism, knowledge, perfection, beauty, and truth. None of these values arise in a world devoid of sentient beings, and that truth may underlie claim 1's appeal. But, importantly, such values *do* arise when rational or moral agents stand in certain relations to each other or the world. Moreover, I submit that the value of such relations is *not* best understood instrumentally; and in particular, that it does *not* lie *solely* in the extent to which such relations promote individual well-being. Individual well-being *is* valuable; but it is a grotesque distortion of the conception of value to think that it is the *only* thing that matters for the goodness of outcomes.

If one situation *couldn't* be worse than another in *any* respect, if it wasn't worse for people, then the Raising Up and Leveling Down Objections would be compelling against egalitarianism. But if one situation *could* be worse than another in *one* respect, even if it wasn't worse for people, then the Raising Up and Leveling Down Objections do little more than point out an obvious implication of non-instrumental egalitarianism. The non-instrumental egalitarian claims that there is one respect in which an equal situation is better than an unequal one, even when it is not better *for* people. Proponents of the Raising Up and Leveling Down Objections insistently deny this; but, however heartfelt, an insistent denial hardly constitutes an argument, much less a crushing one.

Isn't it unfair for some to be worse off than others through no fault of their own? Isn't it unfair for some to be born blind, while others are not? And isn't unfairness bad? These questions, posed rhetorically, express the fundamental claims of non-instrumental egalitarians. Once one rejects person-affecting principles as capturing the *whole* of morality relevant to assessing outcomes, as I believe one should, there is little reason to forsake such claims in the face of the Raising Up and Leveling Down Objections.

But, the anti-egalitarian will incredulously ask, do I *really* think there is some respect in which a world where only some are blind is worse than one where all are? Yes. Does this mean I think it would be better if we blinded everyone? No. Equality is *not* all that matters. But it matters *some*.

Consider the following example. Many children are afraid of death. Parents who don't believe in an afterlife are often at a loss as to what they can honestly say to assuage their concerns. And in truth, there is not much one *can* say that will genuinely answer their children's worries. So, instead, grasping, parents often make a lot of orthogonal points – about how the old must make way for the young, about how much of what makes life so *valuable* is related to death, and so on. And one point parents often emphasize is how death is a part of life, that in fact *everyone* dies, and indeed, that *all* living things die.

It is striking that one should hope the *universality* of death would provide comfort to one worried about her *own* death. After all, the fact that everyone else will *also* die, doesn't lessen the terror of one's *own* death. Yet somehow, it seems worth noting that we are *all* in the same predicament. *Each* of us who lives, inevitably dies.

But suppose it weren't that way. Suppose some people had accidentally stumbled across, and eaten, some rare berries that miraculously made them immortal. So that in fact, while some people died, others lived forever. What should one then say if one's child lamented that she didn't want to die, and then added the plaintive complaint

Larry S. Temkin

that it wasn't *fair*! Why, as one's child might put it, should *she* have to die, when Katie doesn't? It seems to me that in such a situation the charge of unfairness strikes deep and true. The situation *would* be unfair, *terribly* unfair, and this would be so even if the immortality berries weren't actually worse for those who remained mortal, but merely better for those on whom they bestowed eternal life.

Does this mean I think it would actually be worse, all things considered, if there were a limited supply of such berries? Not necessarily. But on the other hand, I'm glad I don't actually have to make such a decision. For as great as the gains of immortality might be for the fortunate ones, the resulting unfairness would be of cosmic proportions. It would be, to my mind, *terribly* unfair, and to that extent bad. So I contend that here, as before, something can be bad in an important respect even if it is not bad *for* people.

Advocates of the Raising Up and Leveling Down Objections are among the many anti-egalitarians mesmerized by "pure" equality's terrible implications. But, of course, as observed earlier, equality is not the only ideal that would, if exclusively pursued, have implausible or even terrible implications. The same is true of justice, utility, freedom, and probably every other ideal. Recall Kant's view that "justice be done though the heavens should fall." Do we *really* think, with Kant, that it would be wrong to falsely imprison an innocent man for even five minutes, if that were necessary to save a million innocent lives? Or consider the principle of utility, which would require us to torture an innocent person if only *enough* people had their lives improved by the tiniest of amounts because of our action. Or finally, consider the implications of unfettered freedom to act as one wants without government interference, as long one doesn't interfere with the rights or liberties of others. Such a principle might allow *complete* neglect of the least fortunate, even regarding *basic* necessities such as food, clothing, shelter, and healthcare. Such considerations do *not* show that justice, utility, and freedom should be rejected as moral ideals, only that morality is complex.

The main lesson of the Raising Up and Leveling Down Objections is that we should be pluralists about morality. Egalitarians have long recognized, and accepted, this lesson. Unfortunately, the same cannot be said for their opponents.

VI. Equality or Priority? Illustrating Egalitarianism's Distinct Appeal

Egalitarians and prioritarians will often agree on the same course of action. This is especially so given that egalitarians are pluralists. But it is important to emphasize that equality and priority express separate concerns, and represent distinct positions. To see this, consider the following example. Though far-fetched, it clearly illuminates what is at stake between egalitarianism and prioritarianism.

Imagine that you are in a spaceship, heading towards a distant galaxy. You learn that there is a mineral-rich asteroid that will soon arrive where you currently are. If you delay your travels, you can use your phasers to safely divert it to a planet below. Doing so will benefit the planet, because it will then be able to use the asteroid's rich minerals. If you don't linger, the asteroid will carry its minerals into deep space, where they will be of use to no one.

Here, most agree that I have *some* reason to linger and divert the asteroid, though the force of that reason will depend, among other things, on how much I'd be giving up by doing so, and how much the planet would actually benefit from my action. For example, if waiting for the asteroid would cost my child her life, and hardly benefit those below, then surely I could permissibly fly on. On the other hand, if diverting the asteroid merely meant missing the opening act of an intergalactic opera, and the planet would use the minerals to save thousands, it would be heinous to fly on.

Next, consider two scenarios. On the first, it turns out that the planet below is *loaded* with valuable resources, and in addition has already received *many* mineral-rich asteroids. It is, in fact, smack in the middle of a mineral-rich asteroid path. Moreover, *no* other planets have benefited from such good fortune. To the contrary, the people on other planets have only been able to eke out a decent living by dint of incredibly hard work. Thus, on the first scenario, it turns out that the people on the planet below are, though no more deserving, *much better* off than everyone else in the universe.

On the second scenario, the people below are, in absolute terms, as well off as they were in the first scenario. But their planet has few natural resources, and they have had to work incredibly hard to achieve their current level of well-being. Moreover, they have been terribly *unlucky*. While they are in the middle of a mineral-rich asteroid path, they have yet to have a *single* mineral-rich asteroid land on their planet. There have been near misses, indeed *lots* of them. But nothing more. Moreover, every other populated planet is *loaded* with natural resources, and each has benefited from the arrival of *countless* mineral-rich asteroids. Thus, on the second scenario, it turns out that the people on the planet below are, though no less deserving, *much worse* off than everyone else in the universe.

Now the simple question is this. Does it make *any* difference at all, to the strength of one's reasons to divert the asteroid, whether scenario one or two obtains? On a prioritarian view the answer to this question is "no." All that matters on a prioritarian view is the *absolute* level of the people I might aid. Since, by hypothesis, the people are at the same absolute level in scenarios one and two, the sacrifice I should be willing to make to aid the people should be the same in both cases. On an egalitarian view matters are different. What matters is not merely the absolute level people are at, but comparative fairness. In scenario one, the people below are already better off than *everyone* else in the universe, due to pure good luck. In scenario two, the people below are already worse off than *everyone* else, due to pure bad luck. In the second case the people are the victims of natural unfairness. In the first, they are the beneficiaries of it. To my mind, however much I should sacrifice for the people below in the first scenario, I should sacrifice more, if necessary, in the second scenario, where the situation exerts a greater claim on me. The greater force of reasons in the second scenario has an egalitarian explanation. It is the difference in comparative unfairness that accounts for my reaction to the two scenarios.

This kind of an example is not an *argument* for egalitarianism. But it clearly illuminates the difference between egalitarianism and prioritarianism. And I am pleased to report that many share my judgment that the reasons for helping are more compelling in the second scenario than the first.

Still, some people are unmoved by such examples. They insist that *all* that matters to them is the absolute level of the people, so that the extent to which they

Larry S. Temkin

should go out of their way to divert the mineral-rich asteroid would be the same in both scenarios.[27] I can't *prove* that such a position is mistaken, but I have a hard time believing that most people who espouse such a view are really governed by it in their thinking. To see why, let me consider one final example.

This example concerns a fairly "typical" poor person in the United States, whom I shall call "Ruth." Ruth isn't desperately ill or wretched, but she is the mother of four, works two jobs, drives an old car, frequently worries how she'll meet the payments on her two-bedroom house, and has *no* idea how she'll be able to send her children to college on the family's annual income of $20,000.

Many are deeply moved by the plight of people like Ruth in a land where *so* many others live in half-million-dollar homes, own two or three fancy new cars, send their kids to private schools, take expensive vacations, and have annual household incomes well over $100,000.

Isn't it clear that the extent to which people are moved to help people like Ruth is heavily influenced not merely by how she fares in *absolute* terms, but by how she fares *relative to the other members of her incredibly well-off society*? After all, we may suppose, at least Ruth has a roof over her head, indoor plumbing, a telephone, a TV, and a car. Moreover, she isn't living in a war-torn country, or ruled by a dictator, and she needn't fear smallpox, tuberculosis, malaria, or diphtheria. She drinks safe water, eats three meals daily, and has a reasonably long life-expectancy. In short, without romanticizing the plight of America's poor, it seems that for most of human history, someone as well off as Ruth would be among the very best off. Moreover, importantly, I think Ruth must probably be counted among the world's fortunate even taking full account of the genuinely bad effects of being poor in a rich society. To put the point bluntly, as bad as it may typically be to be relatively poor in a rich society, it is much worse to watch one's child dying of starvation or disease!

I suspect, then, that if the world didn't include others who were even better off, so that Ruth was actually better off than *everyone* else, we wouldn't be *nearly* as concerned to improve her situation as we now are, and that this is so even if we assume, contrary to fact, that her absolute level in that situation would be *exactly* the same as it is now. Surely, our attitude towards America's poor is deeply shaped by the presence of so many others who are *so* much better off. Assuming I'm right, is this just a mistake on our part? Prioritarians must contend that it is. I, respectfully, disagree. Although there are powerful reasons to care greatly about absolute levels, relative levels *also* matter. It seems unfair, and hence bad, for someone like Ruth to be much worse off than others who she is no less deserving than. This view is captured by egalitarianism, but not by prioritarianism.

I submit, then, that however much we may care about other ideals, including, perhaps, prioritarianism, we should *also* care about equality as comparative fairness. I have certainly not *proven* that we should, but I believe that the considerations I have provided support such a view.

VII. Conclusion

This article has tried to illuminate the nature and appeal of egalitarianism, understood as a position whose fundamental concern is with comparative fairness. Though it has addressed many issues, it has, perforce, had to ignore many other important issues. For example, it has not broached any of the complicated issues associated with inequality's enormous complexity, with inequality's mattering more at low levels than high levels, with how variations in population size affect inequality, or with whether egalitarians should be concerned about comparing people's lives taken as complete wholes, or different segments of their lives.[28] Nor has it broached the issues of the extents, if any, to which egalitarians should be concerned about inequalities across time, space, societies, or species.[29] But if this article is right, we cannot simply ignore such issues; for equality as comparative fairness is one important ideal, among others, that must be taken seriously.

Notes

* Over the years I have been influenced by many people on the topics discussed here. While my poor memory prevents me from properly acknowledging them all, I'd like to thank John Broome, G. A. Cohen, Roger Crisp, Nils Holtug, Susan Hurley, Thomas Nagel, Derek Parfit, Ingmar Persson, and Andrew Williams. I'd also like to thank the editors of this volume, Thomas Christiano and John Christman. Finally, I need to acknowledge that this article draws on a number of my previously published works, especially, "Equality, Priority, and the Levelling Down Objection" (in Matthew Clayton and Andrew Williams, eds., *The Ideal of Equality*, Macmillan Press Ltd. and St. Martin's Press, Inc., 2000, pp. 81–125); "Inequality: A Complex, Individualistic, and Comparative Notion" (in Ernie Sosa and Enriquea Villanueva, eds., *Philosophical Issues* 11, Blackwell Publishers, 2001, pp. 327–52), and "Egalitarianism Defended" (in *Ethics* 113, 2003: 764–82).

1 See Amartya Sen, *Inequality Reexamined* (Cambridge, MA: Harvard University Press, 1992).

2 Derek Parfit introduces the terminology of *telic* and *deontic egalitarianism* in "Equality or Priority?" (The Lindley Lecture, University of Kansas, 1991, copyright 1995 by Department of Philosophy, University of Kansas; reprinted in *The Ideal of Equality*. Corresponding notions are also introduced in Chapter 1 of my book *Inequality*, New York: Oxford University Press, 1993, p. 11).

3 There can be pluralism at many levels. So, for example, I believe that different versions of equality may all be plausible to varying degrees; that within any given version of egalitarianism different kinds of equality may be plausible (see section III); that different aspects of equality may be relevant for measuring any particular kind of equality that matters (see *Inequality*); and so on. Moreover, I believe that some conceptions of equality, and in particular equality as comparability, can themselves be regarded as but one component of a conception of justice, which itself is but one component of a still wider conception of justice, that can include such diverse elements as a Rawlsian conception of justice that focuses on the plight of the worst off group, and a Kantian conception of absolute justice, according to which the good deserve to fare well, and the evil deserve to fare poorly. Likewise, there may be more than one plausible conception, kind, or aspect of freedom, utility, perfection, or any other ideal that matters.

4 For classic statements of their views, see Richard Arneson, "Equality and Equal Opportunity for Welfare," *Philosophical Studies* 56 (1989): 77–93; Ronald Dworkin, "What is Equality? Part 1: Equality of Welfare," and "Part 2: Equality of Resources," *Philosophy and Public Affairs* 10 (1981): 185–246, 283–345, and G. A. Cohen, "On the Currency of Egalitarian Justice," *Ethics* 99 (1989): 906–44.

5 See Cohen's "On the Currency of Egalitarian Justice" and my *Inequality*.

6   Here I'm assuming that one might have a duty to save the drowning child. But one might feel the same way about the case if we thought the person acted supererogatorily in helping the child. However, not all instances of someone's ending up worse off than others as a result of supererogatory action might warrant egalitarian rectification. Perhaps some cases would involve comparative unfairness, but others not.

7   The distinction between option luck and brute luck is introduced by Dworkin in his "What Is Equality?" articles; see also Chapters 1 and 2 of Dworkin's *Sovereign Virtue* (Cambridge, MA: Harvard University Press, 2002). For an important critique of the distinction, see Kasper Lippert-Rasmussen's "Egalitarianism, Option Luck, and Responsibility" (*Ethics* 111, 2001: 548–79).

8   I have made this point in numerous publications, including *Inequality*, "Equality, Priority, and the Levelling Down Objection," and "Inequality: A Complex, Individualistic, and Comparative Notion."

9   See *Inequality Reexamined*, and also Amartya Sen's "Well-being, Agency, and Freedom: The Dewey Lectures 1984," *Journal of Philosophy* 82 (1985): 169–220.

10 In a large group, approximately half of the other group's members should end up better off than they, and half worse off. Still, I have to say "virtually certain" to acknowledge the extraordinarily remote statistical possibility that, by cosmic coincidence, *every* member of the other group would end up at the same level.

11 Vonnegut's "Harrison Bergeron" appears in his collection *Welcome to the Monkey House* (Dell Publishing, 1998); it is reprinted in Louis Pojman and Robert Westmoreland's collection *Equality* (Oxford: Oxford University Press, 1997, pp. 315–18). Interestingly, Bernard Williams raises a worry similar to Vonnegut's regarding the ultimate implications of the demand for equality, at the end of his classic article "The Idea of Equality" (in Peter Laslett and W. G. Runciman, eds., *Philosophy, Politics, and Society*, Second Series, Oxford: Basil Blackwell, 1962, pp. 110–31). The view that everyone should be exactly the same was dubbed "radical egalitarianism" by Hugo Bedau in his article "Radical Egalitarianism" (in R. Pennock and J. Chapman, eds., *Nomos IX: Equality*, Palo Alto, CA: Atherton Press, 1967, pp. 3–27).

12 Susan Hurley stressed the importance of this point in an important article challenging the coherence of egalitarian views that try to recognize the significance of individual responsibility. See her "Luck and Equality," *Supplement to the Proceedings of The Aristotelian Society* 75 (2001): 51–72. See also her *Justice, Luck and Knowledge* (Cambridge, MA: Harvard University Press, 2003).

13 See, for example, the classic work by Sir Michael Marmot on one aspect of this issue, the social determinants of disease. A representative publication is his "Economic and Social Determinants of Disease," *Bulletin of the World Health Organization* 79 (2001): 906–1004.

14 See, for example, Nicholas Rescher's *Distributive Justice* (Indianapolis, IN: Bobbs-Merrill, 1967).

15 Amartya Sen seems to imply that various economists have held this position in *On Economic Inequality* (Oxford: Clarendon Press, 1973).

16 "Equality as a Moral Ideal," *Ethics* 98 (1987): 267.

17 Ibid., p. 268.

18 See Crisp's "Equality, Priority, and Compassion," *Ethics* 113 (2003): 745–63.

19 I first introduced the term *prioritarianism* in my article "Equality, Priority, and the Levelling Down Objection" to replace Derek Parfit's term "the Priority View" (suggested in Parfit's "Equality or Priority?" delivered as the Lindley Lecture at the University of Kansas, November 21, 1991. Copyright 1995 by Department of Philosophy, University of Kansas. Reprinted in *The Ideal of Equality*). But I first discussed prioritarianism, which I then called "extended humanitarianism," in early drafts of my 1983 Princeton Ph.D. dissertation, "Inequality." Many of the points noted below, and that Parfit notes in "Equality or Priority?"

can be traced to my early dissertation drafts, including the fact that prioritarianism was often conflated with egalitarianism, can avoid the leveling down objection and, hence, might appear to many as the most defensible version of, or plausible alternative to, egalitarianism.

20 See for example, Chapter 9 of *Inequality*; "Harmful Goods, Harmless Bads" (in R. G. Frey and Christopher Morris, eds., *Value, Welfare and Morality*, New York: Cambridge University Press, 1993, pp. 290–324); and "Equality, Priority, and the Levelling Down Objection."

21 Derek Parfit introduces the distinction between narrow and wide person-affecting principles in Part Four of *Reasons and Persons* (Oxford: Clarendon Press, 1984), see esp. sections 134–6.

22 Advocates of this kind of view include Nils Holtug, in "Good for Whom?" (*Theoria* LXIX, Part 1–2, 2003: 4–20); Brett Doran in "Reconsidering the Levelling-down Objection against Egalitarianism" (*Utilitas* 13, 1, 2001: 65–85); Campbell Brown in his typescript "How to Have the Levelling Down Intuition and Reject the Slogan Too"; and Roger Crisp in his "Equality, Priority, and Compassion."

23 "Rights, Goals, and Fairness," reprinted in Stuart Hampshire, ed., *Public and Private Morality* (Cambridge: Cambridge University Press, 1978), p. 93. Scanlon's article originally appeared in *Erkenntnis* 11 (1977): 81–95.

24 "Equality, Priority, and Compassion," p. 3.

25 Here I followed Derek Parfit, who identifies the Non-Identity Problem and demonstrates its devastating implications for narrow person-affecting principles in Part Four of *Reasons and Persons*.

26 See, for example, "Personal versus Impersonal Principles: Reconsidering the Slogan," *Theoria* LXIX, Part 1–2 (2003): 21–31. This is a response to Nils Holtug's "Good for Whom?"

27 Dan Brock once claimed to hold such a view in a seminar I gave on "The Meaning of Equality" in the Department of Clinical Bioethics at the National Institutes of Health (Bethesda, Maryland, Spring 2002). However, Brock recently informed me that he has since come around more to my view.

28 I address these issues, among others, in *Inequality*. But there is much more to be said on each of these topics.

29 I address questions about inequalities across space, time, and societies in "Justice and Equality: Some Questions about Scope" (in E. F. Paul, F. D. Miller, and J. Paul, eds., *Social Philosophy and Policy* 12, New York: Cambridge University Press, 1995, pp. 72–104). Peter Vallentyne discusses the question of interspecies inequality in "Of Mice and Men: Equality and Animals," *Journal of Ethics* 9 (2005): 403–33. However, as above, much work remains to be done on these topics.

A Reasonable Alternative to Egalitarianism

John Kekes

I

This paper has a critical and a constructive part. The first shows that egalitarianism is unreasonable; the second provides a reasonable alternative to it. This is a large topic, I must keep it within the allotted space, consequently some of what I have to say will be sketchy.[1] The basic idea of egalitarianism has been expressed in different ways: human beings ought to be treated with equal concern; everyone's interests matter equally; or everyone ought to have an equal share of material resources.[2] Egalitarians regard this idea as a truism that ought to be accepted by all reasonable and morally committed people in contemporary Western democracies.[3]

A little thought, however, is sufficient to cast doubt on this supposed truism. Human beings differ in character, personality, circumstances, talents and weaknesses, capacities and incapacities, virtues and vices; in moral standing, political views, religious convictions, aesthetic preferences, and personal projects; in how reasonable or unreasonable they are, how well or badly they develop native endowments, how much they benefit or harm others, how hard-working or disciplined they were in the past and are likely to be in the future; and so forth. Why should they, then, be shown equal, rather than unequal, concern?

The questions mount when it is asked, as it must be, who owes whom equal concern? Clearly, parents should not treat their own and other people's children with equal concern; we do not owe equal concern to those we love and to strangers; governments betray their elementary duty if they treat citizens and foreigners with equal concern; and a society would be self-destructive if it showed equal concern for its friends and enemies. The questions grow in number and urgency when it is asked, as it must again be, what differences would warrant unequal concern? If differences in morality, reasonability, law-abidingness, and citizenship count, then very little remains of equal concern, since there are great differences among people in these respects. And if such differences are not allowed to count, then how could it be justified to ignore them in how people are treated? These questions show at the very least that the basic idea of egalitarianism is not a truism and that it needs a reasoned defense that answers these questions. Yet when critics ask them, their questions are deplored as signs of immorality and irrationality.[4] Egalitarians simply assume that equal concern is a basic requirement of reason and morality, and to question it is to violate reason and morality. What justification do egalitarians offer for this assumption?

The plain truth is that they offer none. Moreover, they claim with various degrees of self-righteousness that none is needed. Richard Arneson concedes that "non-utilitarian moralities with robust substantive equality ideals cannot be made coherent."[5] He nevertheless regards disagreement with them as beyond the pale of civilized dialogue.

Brian Barry says: "The justification of the claim of fundamental equality has been held to be impossible because it is a rock-bottom ethical premiss and so cannot be derived from anything else."[6] This is a mealy-mouthed admission that egalitarianism rests on an unjustifiable assumption.

Isaiah Berlin tells us:

> Equality is one of the oldest and deepest elements in liberal thought and it is neither more nor less 'natural' or 'rational' than any other constituent in them [sic]. Like all human ends it cannot be defended or justified, for it is itself which justifies other acts.[7]

So egalitarianism is based on a rationally indefensible article of faith.

Ronald Dworkin writes:

> I have tried to show the appeal of equality of resources, as interpreted here, only by making plain its motivation and defending its coherence and practical force. I have not tried to defend in what might be considered a more direct way, by deducing it from more general and abstract political principles. So the question arises whether the sort of defense could be provided. . . . I hope it is clear that I have not presented any such argument here.[8]

And a little further on we have:

> My arguments are constructed against the background of assumptions about what equality requires in principle. . . . My arguments enforce rather than construct a basic design of justice, and that design must find support, if at all, elsewhere than in these arguments.[9]

Dworkin thus admits that the assumptions on which his view rests, and on the basis of which he regards disagreement with it as immoral and shameful, have not been justified.

Joel Feinberg declares that egalitarianism "is not grounded on anything more ultimate than itself, and it is not demonstrably justifiable. It can be argued further against skeptics that a world with equal human rights is *more just* world . . . a less *dangerous* world . . . and one with a *more elevated and civilized* tone. If none of this convinces the skeptic, we should turn our back on him and examine more important problems."[10] I wonder whether egalitarians would be satisfied with such a response when they question conservative or religious attitudes.

Will Kymlicka claims that

John Kekes

every plausible political theory has the same ultimate source, which is equality. . . . A theory is egalitarian . . . if it accepts that the interests of each member of the community matter, and matter equally. . . . [I]f a theory claimed that some people were not entitled to equal consideration from the government, if it claimed that certain kinds of people just do not matter as much as others, then most people in the modern world would reject that theory immediately.[11]

This invites us to accept as an obvious truth that most people would immediately reject the view that torturers and their victims, or the scourges and benefactors of humanity do not matter equally. Kymlicka gives no reason for this breathtaking claim: it is the assumption from which he proceeds.

Nagel says that he is going to explore a "type of argument that I think is likely to succeed. It would provide a moral basis for the kind of liberal egalitarianism that seems to me plausible. I do not have such an argument."[12] This does not stop him, however, from claiming that "moral equality, [the] attempt to give equal weight, in essential respects, to each persons' point of view . . . might even be described as the mark of an enlightened ethic."[13] Years later he says: "My claim is that the problem of designing institutions that do justice to the equal importance of all persons, without unacceptable demands on individuals, has not been solved," but he nevertheless "present[s] a case for wishing to extend the reach of equality beyond what is customary in modern welfare states."[14] Although Nagel explicitly acknowledges the lack of justification, he holds that the mark of an enlightened ethic is to accept his unjustified view. Imagine the howl of indignation if conservatives claimed that although they can offer no justification for it, they nevertheless holds that the mark of enlightened ethic is to accept conservatism.

John Rawls concludes his discussion of "The Basis of Equality" by saying that "essential equality is . . . equality of consideration," and goes on: "of course none of this is literally an argument. I have not set out the premises from which this conclusion follows."[15]

Thus the assumption that reason and morality require equal concern for moral and immoral, reasonable and unreasonable, law-abiding and criminal people is put forward with the explicit acknowledgment that the premises from which it is supposed to follow have not been justified. In reading through much of the writings of contemporary egalitarians, I have not found even an attempt to provide a reasoned case for this basic egalitarian assumption.

II

Let us now consider how egalitarianism may nevertheless be defended. It might be said that the requirement of equal concern is simply the formal requirement of treating like cases alike. It is perhaps this that explains why egalitarians regard it unnecessary to justify their position. If equal concern were a formal requirement, then it would be one that everyone must either meet or forfeit the claim to being reasonable. But claiming that equal concern is a formal requirement involves an elementary confusion between consistency and equal concern. Consistency is indeed a formal requirement: treating like cases alike and different cases differently is a condition of the application of all rules. It makes no difference what the rule is about, or what makes cases alike or different. Rules of arithmetic, tennis, beauty contests, and legal proceedings must all be applied consistently. Equal concern, by contrast, specifies what similarities and differences are relevant to how people should be treated. It is not a formal requirement, but a substantive rule. Of course people who are alike should have like good or bad things, but unless it is specified what makes people alike, equal concern says nothing about how in particular they should be treated. The egalitarian requirement of equal concern, therefore, must go beyond formal consistency and specify in substantive terms what makes people alike, or, if it remains formal, it will be useless as a guide to how people should be treated.

Now egalitarians do provide a substantive specification: they say that in all relevant respects people are alike and that is why they should be treated with equal concern. But this, of course, requires justification that goes far beyond the justification needed for consistency. Egalitarians need to justify their claim that differences in how reasonable, moral, or law-abiding people are should be regarded as irrelevant to how they are treated. And, as we have seen, this is precisely what they disdain of doing. In the absence of the needed justification, critics can agree that people who are alike in all relevant respects should be treated with equal concern and point out that very few people indeed are alike, since there are relevant differences between most people in respect to how reasonable, moral, and law-abiding they are. That is why, according to critics, they should not be treated with equal concern.

A second thing that may be said in defense of egalitarianism is that the requirement of equal concern is prima facie, not absolute. Reason and morality normally require equal concern for everyone, but there may be reasons for unequal concern in exceptional cases. This prima facie requirement may be further qualified by saying that it is governments (not individuals) who should treat with equal concern their citizens (not everyone). These qualifications make the supposed truism appear more plausible, but the appearance is deceptive for egalitarianism thus qualified faces a dilemma it can neither avoid nor resolve. The dilemma is posed by the question: do differences among citizens in how reasonable, moral, and law-abiding they are count as reasons for the government's having unequal concern for them?

If the answer is yes, then very little remains of the prima facie requirement of equal concern since there are great differences among people in these respects. It makes sense to talk about a prima facie requirement only if it holds as a rule, normally and usually, and rare exceptions to it need justification. The prima facie requirement to tell the truth, keep promises, pay debts means that people are normally expected to do that, unless exceptional circumstances intervene. Or, saying that there is a prima facie reason for supposing that people want to stay alive and be healthy means that most of us normally want both, but there may be rare exceptions in unusual situations. But the differences among citizens in how reasonable, moral, and law-abiding they are do not occur in exceptional cases or unusual situations, these differences exist as a rule; they are normal, usual, and predictable. If there is a prima facie requirement, it is for the government to have unequal concern for the vast majority of their citizens who differ in these respects.

Suppose, then, that the answer is that differences among citizens in how reasonable, moral, or law-abiding they are have no effect on the government's obligation to show equal concern for them. This would require the government to treat citizens

John Kekes

who are terrorists and hostages, murderers and intended victims, homeowners and burglars, taxpayers and tax-cheats with equal concern. The result of conformity to this supposed obligation would be to ignore the predictable consequences of immoral, unreasonable, and illegal actions, and thus endanger the essential conditions of civilized life that reason, morality, and the law are supposed to protect. Any government that did this would betray its most elementary obligation to protect the security of its citizens. I conclude that the attempt to defend egalitarianism by interpreting it as imposing a prima facie (not an absolute) requirement on the government (not on individuals) does not help to make the falsely supposed truism of equal concern any the less plausible.

Egalitarians may attempt to defend their position by claiming that they would have to face this dilemma only if the prima facie requirement of equal concern were based on people's actions, which admittedly differ in respect to morality, reason, and legality, but the obligation of equal concern is not based on actions. It is based the capacity for autonomy that all normal human beings are assumed to possess it equally.[16] If this were true, the dilemma would not arise and egalitarians could consistently acknowledge the obvious differences among people in what they do with their autonomy. Reason and morality could then be said to require equal concern for all who possess the capacity for autonomy because they possess it equally.

The capacity for autonomy includes the capacity for choice, but goes beyond it. For choices can be arbitrary, uninformed, forced, or irrational. Autonomy involves the capacity to choose among alternatives that one has understood and reasonably evaluated.[17] If autonomy is understood in this sense, then this egalitarian attempt to avoid the dilemma cannot succeed. For people possess the capacity for autonomy unequally; even if they possessed it equally, it would not warrant equal concern; and if it warranted equal concern, it would be unjustified to restrict the governments obligation of equal concern to citizens.

It is obvious, however, that people possess the capacity for autonomy unequally since autonomy is a complex capacity that depends on numerous other capacities. The reasonable understanding and evaluation of available alternatives depends on a considerable degree of intelligence, education, emotional stability, attention span, self-knowledge, self-control, objectivity, and so on. There are enormous differences among people in the degree to which they possess these capacities. Since the capacity for autonomy depends on the possession of these other capacities and these capacities are possessed unequally, it follows that people possess the capacity for autonomy unequally. If concern for people depends on their capacity for autonomy, then the government's concern for people ought to be unequal, not equal as egalitarians claim.

Let us grant, however, for the sake of argument and contrary to fact, that people have an equal capacity for autonomy. Why should reason and morality require that the government's concern for citizens should be based on a capacity they have, rather than on what they do with the capacity they have? The conditions of security and civilized life that reason, morality, and the law are intended to protect are not violated by people's possession of a capacity, but by actions that the capacity makes possible. It is true that without the capacity there would be no action. But it is also true that the capacity need not result in any action; if it results in action, the action may be moral or immoral, reasonable or unreasonable, legal or criminal; or it may be an action that has no significant bearing on such weighty issues as reason, morality, or the law. Surely, the government's concern must be with what people do, not with what they can do. And since what people do differs greatly in morality, reasonability, and legality, the government's concern must take these differences into account, and hence be unequal. This remains true regardless of whether people's capacity for autonomy is equal or unequal. Consequently the dilemma stands: if the government recognizes these differences, reason and morality require it to show unequal concern for citizens who differ in these ways; if the government fails to recognize these differences, it fails in its elementary obligation to protect the conditions of security and civilized life for its citizens.

Suppose, however, again for the sake of argument and contrary to fact, that the capacity for autonomy is equal and its possession warrants the government's equal concern. Clearly, the possession of an equal capacity for autonomy would not be the exclusive possession of the citizens of a state, but the universal possession of all normal human beings. If the government's obligation of equal concern were based on the possession of an equal capacity for autonomy, then the government ought to show equal concern for all human beings, not just for its citizens. Any government that acted on this supposed obligation, however, would betray its most elementary obligation to those who elected it to represent their interests, not the interests of foreigners. It would impose on a government the absurd obligation to be equally concerned with the health, education, security, living standard, happiness, and so forth of its own citizens and the citizens of other states; to use tax moneys collected from its citizens to promote the welfare of all human beings, not just its citizens'; to wage war, when it must, by showing equal concern for its own and for the enemy's troops; and to be as concerned with the infrastructure of other states as with its own. No reasonable person can take such absurdities seriously, but the absurdities would follow if egalitarianism were true.

One further attempt to defend egalitarianism rests on an emotional appeal that is likely to be shared by many people. One expression of it is the rhetorical question: "how could it not be an evil that some people's prospects at birth are radically inferior to others?"[18] There are two things to be said about this. First, given any population and any basis of ranking prospects, some will rank much lower than others. Lowest-ranked prospects will be radically inferior to the highest-ranked ones. Inveighing against this statistical necessity is like lamenting differences in intelligence or manual dexterity. To call it an evil is a sentimental cheapening of the most serious condemnation morality affords. It misdirects the obligation people feel. If egalitarians would merely say that it is bad if people undeservedly suffer and those who can should help them, then many people would agree with them. But this agreement has to do with decency, pity, or fellow-feeling, not with equal concern. We respond to the emotional appeal because we are moved by undeserved suffering, not because we are committed to the psychological absurdity of being equally concerned with everyone's well-being.

Second, the emotional appeal of this question invites the thought that contemporary Western democracies are guilty of the evil of dooming many of their citizens to a life of poverty. What this often-repeated charge overlooks is the historically unprecedented success of Western democracies in having only a small minority of poor citizens (about 10–15 percent) and a large at least modestly affluent majority (about

John Kekes

85–90 percent). The typical ratio in past societies was closer to the reverse. It calls for celebration, not condemnation, that for the first time in history we have a political system in which a large part of the population has escaped poverty. If egalitarians had a historical perspective, they would be in favor of protecting this system, rather than advocating radical changes to it with incalculable consequences.

I conclude that egalitarianism is not only unreasonable, but also dangerous, because conformity to its requirements endangers security and civilized life. Instead of abusing their critics by calling them "white supremacists," "Nazis," "shameful," "immoral," or "lacking in moral decency,"[19] egalitarians should heed the words of their ally: "The worst offense...which can be committed by a polemic is to stigmatize those who hold contrary opinions as bad and immoral."[20] And instead of self-righteously spurning the badly needed justification of their position, egalitarians should provide it – if they can.

III

The constructive part of the argument is to propose a reasonable alternative to egalitarianism. I want to stress, however, that its constructive and the critical parts are independent. The preceding criticisms of egalitarianism would not be affected by the failure of the constructive alternative I will now propose.

Suppose you have to choose to live in one of two societies that are identical in all but one respect: in the first, good and bad things are enjoyed or suffered randomly across the population; in the second, there are exactly the same good and bad things, but good people have the good ones and bad people the bad ones. I will call the first society haphazard, and the second commensurate. In which society would you choose to live? I have asked many people and I have yet to meet one who would not choose to live in a commensurate society. This choice is reasonable because those who live in the haphazard society have no reason to believe that their actions will lead to their goals. Discipline and self-indulgence, considered and thoughtless choice, intelligent and stupid action have exactly the same chance of success. In the commensurate society, by contrast, people have much more control over the goodness or badness of their lives, and that is why it is preferable to the haphazard society.

In order to understand better the nature of this control, consider a simple situation leading to an action. It is a beautiful day, I enjoy being outside, and I decide to go for a walk on a nearby country lane. This involves a set of beliefs (e.g., the weather is unlikely to change, there are no teenagers with loud radios, the country lane has not been paved over) and possession of the required capacities (e.g., I can walk, trust my memory to find the lane, take pleasure in being alone in nature). The constitutive elements of the situation, then, are motive, belief, capacity, goal, and decision.

Each of these elements may be defective. My real motive may be to escape from boring work. My belief may be false because a storm is closing in. I may misjudge my capacity because I am coming down with an illness. My goal may be unattainable because the lane is closed. And my decision may be ill-advised because I will miss an important deadline. Suppose, however, that none of the constitutive elements is defective and I act as prompted by their conjunction. I expect, then, that my action will be successful. In simple situations we normally have good reason to think that the elements are free of defects and our expectation will be met.

Control over our actions, however, is made much harder by difficulties that transform simple situations into complex ones. We often have several motives prompting incompatible actions. We must frequently judge the reliability of our beliefs on the basis of imperfect knowledge and insufficient evidence. We can rarely be certain whether we have adequate capacities, energies, and time to achieve our various goals. And we routinely have to decide about the relative importance of our conflicting goals. Coping with such complexities requires good judgment, which is difficult to have.

Suppose, however, that our judgment is good, we use it to decide what we should do in a complex situation, and we do it. This is not sufficient for control because the success of many of our actions depends on the cooperation, or at least the non-interference, of others, and they may have good reasons not to cooperate or to interfere with us. They may have more important concerns; they may want for themselves what we want for ourselves; or what we want may run counter to the interest of the institution, cause, or collectivity they wish to protect. Having control over our actions, therefore, requires us to cooperate with one another. The rules of cooperation will have to be set and be known by those who live together in a society, and they must be adequate for maintaining the conditions in which as many of us as possible can go about getting what we want. I will shortly discuss what makes such rules reasonable, but assume for the moment that whatever it is, they have it.

It is now possible to say more clearly why life in the commensurate society is preferable to life in the haphazard one. It is because if people living in it have achieved some control over their actions through good judgment and conformity to reasonable rules of cooperation (simply "rules," from now on), then they have a reasonable expectation that their actions will be successful. This reasonable expectation is of having the good things they deserve and not having the bad things they do not deserve. The likelihood that their expectation will be met is a benefit practical reason is meant to provide.

I am proposing, therefore, the following constructive alternative to egalitarianism. The unreasonable belief that the government has an obligation to treat citizens with equal concern should be replaced with the reasonable belief that the prevailing rules should make it more likely than it would otherwise be that people who control their actions will have the good things they deserve and will not have the bad things they do not deserve. The reasonability of rules depends on the extent to which they succeed in making this possible. I now turn to the question of how they can do that.

IV

These rules are conventions regarding the good and bad things that people living in a particular society at a particular time deserve or do not deserve. There are very many such rules in every society. I doubt that they can be enumerated, and I do not propose to try. I will consider instead three general types that no enduring society can dispense with. Being conventional, these rules reflect the practices that have emerged

John Kekes

in the course of the history of a particular society. They change, but usually slowly. At any given time, however, they provide a continuum of possible evaluations that range between the termini of good and bad, with many intermediate judgments in between them. The resulting evaluations imply obligations that people in that society have; praise when the obligations are honored; blame when they are not; and conditions under which failure may be excused or blame extenuated. Many of people's reasonable expectations regarding their own and others' conduct are based on these rules.

One type of rule concerns relationships between lovers, friends, parents and children, teachers and students, judges and defendants, physicians and patients, and so on. Rules of this type specify the obligations people in such relationships have toward one another and they create reasonable expectations that the obligations will be honored. A second type of rule governs agreements, such as promises, contracts, employment, commercial transactions, political or legal representation, memberships in private or public organizations, and the like. Some of these agreements are formal, written down, and legally binding. Others are informal, derived from the spoken or tacit understanding of the parties, and the force behind them is mutual trust and reciprocal good will. A third type of rule regulates actions that affect the security of others. A society cannot endure unless it protects those living in it from murder, mayhem, theft, and like injuries. Take, for instance, homicide. All societies must have rules specifying when it constitutes murder, when it is justified or excusable, and what the status is of capital punishment, infanticide, euthanasia, suicide, abortion, dueling, and other forms of killing.

These three types of rule are general. Societies cannot do without them, but there are many ways in which a general type may be instantiated in a particular context. Rules may be written or unwritten; enforced by law, priests, elders, or public opinion; violations may be punished severely, mildly, physically, or psychologically; they may specify acceptable justifications and excuses very differently; and ways and means of changing or registering changes of them may vary greatly. Enduring societies are alike, therefore, in having such rules, but they differ in the specific forms the prevailing rules have. To say that these rules are conventional is to recognize that they may vary with contexts, but it is to recognize also that human well-being requires the specification of the possibilities and limits, as well as the obligations and expectations, that regulate relationships, agreements, and security in a particular society at a particular time.

The importance of these rules for the reasonable alternative to egalitarianism that I am proposing is that they go some way toward establishing what people in a particular context deserve and do not deserve.[21] They deserve what the rules specify and they do not deserve what would violate the rules. The rules thus provide reasons for some of the obligations and expectations people have, as well as standards with reference to which obligations and expectations can be justified or criticized, and claims regarding what is or is not deserved evaluated. Children deserve a decent upbringing from their parents because that is how we understand their relationship; sellers deserve to be paid by buyers because that is part of what we regard as their commercial agreement; and murderers deserve to be jailed because that is how we protect security. Human well-being requires that children be brought up, the transfer of property be regulated, and lives be protected, but we in this society are who we are partly because we have our way of meeting these requirements and our own views about who deserves what good or bad things. How we do all this is conventional, but it is not conventional that we must either do it in some way or another or risk the disintegration of our society.

One obvious implication of this way of thinking about what people deserve is that different people deserve different good and bad things because their relationships, agreements, and actions affecting the security of others differ. And that means that the egalitarian belief that the government should treat all citizens with equal concern is contrary to human well-being because it is contrary to the requirements of the rules on which human well-being depends. It is important to realize that this, to my mind fatal, objection to egalitarianism is not based on the particular rules we happen to have in our society. All such rules have anti-egalitarian consequences because, regardless of their particular forms, they impose the obligation to treat differently people who unavoidably stand in different relationships, make different agreements, and perform different actions affecting the security of others. Since the equal concern egalitarians mistakenly favor violates the rules, egalitarianism is not merely unreasonable, but also dangerous.

V

Claims about what people deserve may be mistaken, of course. I will consider two ways in which this may happen: first, the rules on which the claims are based may be reasonable, but their application is mistaken; second, the rules themselves may be faulty. Any claim about what someone deserves may be invalidated if it involves a mistake about the relevant facts. A person mistaken for a criminal does not deserve to be punished; an incompetent physician does not deserve accreditation; and an abusive parent does not deserve respect. Even if the facts are what they are taken to be, mistakes in proportion may occur. A thief deserves punishment, but not to have an arm cut off; a good performance deserves applause, but not adulation; a lawyer deserves a fee for services rendered, but not the deed to a client's house. Mistakes about fact or proportion are relatively simple mistakes about what people do or do not deserve. Such mistakes occur, but they can be corrected, and, in any case, do not count against the misapplied rule. What is at fault is the application, not the rule applied. Claims about what people deserve are fallible, as other claims are, but just as occasional mistakes do not make all perception, calculation, or memory unreliable, so they do not cast doubt on all claims about what is deserved.

Another, far more serious, mistake about what is deserved is to rely on an unreasonable rule. This brings us back to the question of what makes rules reasonable. A rule is reasonable if it meets the following conditions. First, for many years people have generally acted in conformity to the rule in appropriate circumstances and those who did not were blamed for their failure. There may be many reasons, of course, why people generally act in conformity to a rule. If the rule is reasonable, however, then they follow it voluntarily, not because of coercion or the absence of alternatives. A reasonable rule, therefore, meets the second condition that people conform to it voluntarily even in circumstances when they have the option of not conforming. But, once again, people may conform to a rule voluntarily for many reasons. They may be stupid, deceived, indoctrinated, bribed, or lazy and habit-ridden. A rule is reasonable if people generally conform to it for a particular reason: namely, they believe that the rule helps them have a better life than they would have without the rule. And that is the third condition that a reasonable rule meets. Beliefs of this kind need not be conscious or verbalized. The reason for ascribing them to people may be that they act as if they held the beliefs and it would be mysterious without ascribing the belief to them why they act as they do when they have other options. Such beliefs, of course, may themselves be reasonable or unreasonable. The fourth condition of a reasonable rule, therefore, is that the tacitly or explicitly held belief – that conformity to the rule makes the believer's life better – is reasonable.

What makes such beliefs reasonable is that, as a consequence of general conformity to the rules, people are more likely than otherwise to have the good things they deserve and need for a better life and not have the bad things they do not deserve and which would make life worse. As I have noted, there is a great variety of these good and bad things, but the benefits derivable from human relationships, reliable agreements, and physical security are prominent among them. Or, to put the same point slightly differently, such beliefs are reasonable if by following the rules people achieve better control over their actions and thus make their success more likely. Of course this requires that the rule be followed generally so that people can rely on the cooperation or at least the non-interference of others.

In sum, a rule is reasonable if people conform to it generally, voluntarily even when they have other options, because they believe that conformity will make their lives better, and their belief is reasonable. In a commensurate society there are many reasonable rules, they enable people to control their actions better, make it more likely that people will have the good things they deserve and not the bad things they do not deserve, and, as a result, their lives will in fact be better than they would be otherwise. This is, then, why it is reasonable to prefer to live in a commensurate society rather than in a haphazard one.

It may be thought that this account of what makes a rule reasonable is unsatisfactory. The supposedly reasonable alternative to egalitarianism is that different people should be treated differently, not with equal concern, because they deserve different good and bad things depending on how reasonable, moral, and law-abiding they are. What particular things they deserve is said to depend on the prevailing rules, and these rules govern the obligations and expectations people have in relationships, agreements, and actions affecting security. But, it may be thought, this account is silent about the possibility that people may follow a rule they regard as reasonable and yet be mistaken because the rule is, in fact, unreasonable. On what grounds could it be decided, it may be asked, whether a rule that is thought to be reasonable is indeed reasonable? This is a legitimate question, but the answer to it readily follows from what has already been said.

That a rule has been followed generally, voluntarily, and a for long time, that people who follow it believe that it is a reasonable rule because it makes their life better are reasons for thinking that the rule is reasonable, but not conclusive reasons. If critics doubt the reasonability of the rule, then they must have some reasons for their doubt. What might these reasons be? Well, it might be that the application of the rule involves mistakes of fact or proportion, or that people have been bamboozled and that is why they follow the rule voluntarily, or that the rule is detrimental to relationships, leads to unfair agreements, or fails to protect some people's security. Such mistakes, of course, may happen and have happened with many rules in many societies. Master–slave relationships are prejudice-ridden because they falsely suppose that slaves are inferior to masters. Marriage contracts in which the husband acquires control of the wife's property are unfair because they wrongly deny the wife's capacity to make reasonable decisions. The punishment of theft by mutilation is deplorable because of its disproportionality. But what underlies all these reasons is the claim that rules are unreasonable because following them prevents people from having what they deserve or not having what they do not deserve. The reasons for doubting the reasonability of particular rules, therefore, appeal to the basic idea that motivates the alternative to egalitarianism, namely, that people should have what they deserve and not have what they do not deserve.

It must be acknowledged, of course, that there may be serious disagreements about whether or not a particular rule is reasonable. Such disagreements, however, concern questions of detail about what particular good or bad things are deserved, not whether people should have whatever that is. These disagreements about the rules occur only because the parties to them already accept that people should have what they deserve. The very existence of such disagreements, therefore, counts in favor of the alternative to egalitarianism I am proposing and against the supposed obligation of equal concern. It is compatible with this alternative view that many rules in our society, or in any society, are in fact unreasonable, regardless of what people believe about them.

The alternative to egalitarianism is thus not that people should have what the prevailing rules say they deserve. The alternative is that people should have what they deserve according to reasonable rules. And what makes rules reasonable is that they have been generally and voluntarily followed, that they are believed to be reasonable by those who follow them, and they are free of mistakes in fact and proportion, and help rather than hinder people's relationships, agreements, and security.

VI

An often-voiced objection made by both egalitarians and some of their opponents to the sort of view I have been proposing is that it is unrealistic to aim at a society in which people have what they deserve and do not have what they do not deserve.[22] In contemporary Western societies, it is said, there is no agreement about what things are good and bad. People's beliefs about good and bad things derive from their conceptions of a good life, but there are very many different conceptions held by people who differ in their religious, moral, political, and aesthetic views. Consequently they will disagree about what people deserve. Furthermore, what people deserve can be ascertained only by taking into account their beliefs and efforts, as well as the beliefs they might have held and efforts they might have made, but did not. Such actual and possible beliefs and efforts are not open to observation. It is unrealistic to suppose, runs the objection, that rules governing what people should or should not have could take into account such subjective psychological states.

190   **John Kekes**

This objection assumes, first, that what people deserve depends on their psychological states and, second, that it is the government's obligation to assure that people have what they deserve. Both assumptions are mistaken, but each contains part of the truth, so neither is totally mistaken. Reasons for saying that people do or do not deserve something may be based on their psychological states, but they may also be based on their relationships, agreements, and actions, which are readily observable and not subjective. The government does have the obligation to assure that people have some of what they deserve, but there are numerous non-governmental civic institutions that have the same obligation.

The good and bad things that people deserve, I have argued, are based on the rules that govern relationships, agreements, and actions that affect the security of others. Rules about psychological states, such as virtues and vices, may be reasonably added to these other rules, but this would not make the first assumption on which the objection rests more plausible. Even if psychological states were subjective and unobservable, they would not be the sole basis for saying what people deserve because the other bases – relationships, agreements, and actions – would remain, and be neither subjective nor unobservable. But, of course, often there is no great difficulty in ascertaining what people's psychological states are because they can be inferred from what they say and do or what they do not say or do. Families, lovers, friends, teachers, employers, coaches, and judges, among others, often draw such inferences. Such inferences may be more or less reliable, but reliable ones establish conclusively that what this assumption claims to be impossible is, in fact, possible. And when the inferences are bad, it is often insufficient information or personal bias that stands in their way, not any impossibility.

The second mistaken assumption on which this objection rests is that the government has the obligation to assure that people have what they deserve. Its mistake is twofold. Although the government has that obligation, it is not alone in having it. Civic institutions, such as schools, universities, corporations, athletic competitions, small businesses, orchestras, museums, foundations, parole boards, and many other more or less formal associations also have the obligation to assure people have the good things they deserve and not the bad things they do not deserve. Such civic institutions award good things, like money, honors, prestige, prizes, promotion, and so forth. Even if the government could not discharge the obligation to award the appropriate good things on the basis of what people deserve, there are other ways by other institutions in which it may be done. Moreover, it is obvious that the government can discharge that obligation because it often does it. The government has no great difficulty in identifying some requirements of relationships (e.g., of parenthood or citizenship); of agreements (e.g., of taking out a mortgage or enlisting in the army), or of actions affecting the security of others (e.g., driving a car or practicing medicine).

I conclude, therefore, that this objection is groundless because the assumptions on which it rests are mistaken. But the sense may nevertheless persist that it is unrealistic to hold that the good and bad things people have should be based on what they deserve to have. In closing, I want to say something about this lingering doubt.

Nothing I have said is meant to imply that people having what they deserve and not having what they do not deserve depends only on reasonable rules. Such rules are necessary but not sufficient for the achievement of this immensely desirable end. In fact, however, no matter how desirable it is, it will not be achieved. We can only come closer to approximating it because the contingency of life and the scarcity of resources stand in the way.

Not even the most reasonable rules can prevent the misfortune of undeserving victims. Lightning will strike, buildings will collapse, volcanoes will erupt, cancer will attack, viruses will mutate and invade the immune system. Human life cannot be freed from such contingencies and from the undeserved bad effects they cause. The same is true of scarcity, if we take a broad and realistic view of how we understand resources. It is not just a question of money or food, but also of talent and training. Good teachers, physicians, plumbers, and politicians are always in shorter supply than needed; the means for the distribution of urgently needed food, medicine, sanitation, or clothing are often lacking; ignorance, prejudice, corruption, and misunderstanding frequently stand in the way making use of available goods.

If the lingering sense that it is unrealistic to expect that reasonable rules will assure that people have what they deserve is based on the obstacles presented by the contingency of life and the scarcity of resources, then I share it. Reasonable rules do not guarantee that good people will have good things and bad people bad things. But if the lingering sense of unrealism is based on doubting that reasonable rules are possible, then I think it is misguided. There is no reason why we could not make existing rules more reasonable, and there are good reasons why we should try to do so. Reasonable rules are the bulwark that protects civilized life from barbarism. They are indispensable means to making life better.

Notes

1   For a fuller statement, see *Against Liberalism* (Ithaca, NY: Cornell University Press, 1997), *A Case for Conservatism* (Ithaca, NY: Cornell University Press, 1998), and *The Illusions of Egalitarianism* (Ithaca, NY: Cornell University Press, 2003).
2   "Every nation of the world is divided into haves and have-nots. . . . The gap . . . is enormous. Confronting these disparities, the egalitarian holds that it would be a morally better state of affairs if everyone enjoyed the same level of social and economic benefits." Richard J. Arneson, "Equality," in Robert Goodin and Phillip Pettit, eds., *A Companion to Contemporary Political Philosophy* (Oxford: Blackwell, 1993), p. 489. "From the standpoint of politics, the interests of the members of the community matter, and matter equally." Ronald Dworkin, "In Defense of Equality," *Social Philosophy and Policy* 1 (1983): 24–40/24. "Everyone matters just as much as everyone else. [I]t is appalling that the most effective social systems we have been able to devise permit . . . material inequalities." Thomas Nagel, *Equality and Partiality* (New York: Oxford University Press, 1991), p. 64. "Being egalitarian in some significant way relates to the need to have equal concern, at some level, for all persons involved." Amartya Sen, *Inequality Reexamined* (Cambridge, MA: Harvard University Press, 1992), p. ix. "A basic principle of equality [is] the principle of equal consideration of interests. The essence of the principle of equal consideration of interests is that we give equal weight in our moral deliberations to the like interests of all those affected by our actions." Peter Singer, *Practical Ethics*, 2nd edn. (Cambridge: Cambridge University Press, 1993), p. 21. "We want equalization of benefits . . . [because] in all cases where human beings are capable of enjoying the same goods, we feel that the intrinsic value of the enjoyment is the same. . . . We hold that . . . *one man's well-being is as valuable as any other's.*" Gregory Vlastos, "Justice and Equality," in Richard B. Brandt, ed., *Social Justice* (Englewood Cliffs, NJ: Prentice-Hall, 1962), pp. 50–1.

3   "No government is legitimate that does not show equal concern for the fate of all those citizens over whom it claims dominion and from whom it claims allegiance." Ronald Dworkin, *Sovereign Virtue: The Theory and Practice of Equality* (Cambridge, MA: Harvard University Press, 2000), p. 1; "The fundamental argument is not whether to accept equality, but how best to interpret it." Will Kymlicka, *Contemporary Political Philosophy* (Oxford: Clarendon Press, 1900), p. 5; "The principle that all humans are equal is now part of the prevailing political and ethical orthodoxy." Singer, *Practical Ethics*, p. 21; "We want equalization of benefits . . . [because] in all cases where human beings are capable of enjoying the same goods, we feel that the intrinsic value of their enjoyment is the same." Gregory Vlastos, "Justice and Equality," in *Social Justice*, Richard B. Brandt, ed. (Englewood Cliffs, NJ: Prentice-Hall, 1962), pp. 50–1. And "We believe . . . that in some sense every citizen, indeed every human being . . . deserves equal consideration. . . . We know that most people in the past have not shared [this belief]. . . . But for us, it is simply there." Bernard Williams, "Philosophy as a Humanistic Discipline," *Philosophy* 75 (2000): 477–96/492.

4   "All humans have an equal basic moral status. They possess the same fundamental rights, and the comparable interests of each person should count the same in calculations that determine social policy. . . . These platitudes are virtually universally affirmed. A white supremacist or an admirer of Adolf Hitler who denies them is rightly regarded as beyond the pale of civilized dialogue." Richard J. Arneson, "What, If Anything, Renders All Humans Morally Equal?" in Dale Jamieson, ed., *Singer and His Critics* (Oxford: Blackwell, 1999), p. 103; "We cannot reject the egalitarian principle outright, because it is . . . immoral that [the government] should show more concern for the lives of some than of others." Dworkin, *Sovereign Virtue*, p. 130, and "a distribution of wealth that dooms some citizens to a less fulfilling life than others, no matter what choices they make, is unacceptable, and the neglect of equality in contemporary politics is therefore shameful." Ronald Dworkin, "Equality – An Exchange," *TLS*, Dec. 1 (2000), p. 16; "Some theories, like Nazism, deny that each person matters equally. But such theories do not merit serious consideration." Will Kymlicka, *Liberalism, Community, and Culture* (Oxford: Clarendon Press, 1989), p. 40; "Any political theory that aspires to moral decency must try to devise and justify a form of institutional life which answers to the real strength of impersonal values" and commits one to "egalitarian impartiality." Nagel, *Equality and Partiality*, p. 20.

5   Arneson, "What, If Anything," p. 126.

6   Brian Barry, "Equality," in Lawrence C. Becker and Charlotte B. Becker, eds., *Encyclopedia of Ethics* (New York: Garland, 1992), p. 324.

7   Isaiah Berlin, "Equality" in Henry Hardy, ed., *Concepts and Categories* (London: Hogarth Press, 1978), p. 102.

8   Dworkin, *Sovereign Virtue*, pp. 117–18.

9   Dworkin, *Sovereign Virtue*, p. 118.

10 Joel Feinberg, *Social Philosophy*, (Englewood Cliffs, NJ: Prentice-Hall, 1973), p. 94.

11 Kymlicka, *Contemporary Political Philosophy*, pp. 4–5.

12 Thomas Nagel, *Mortal Questions* (Cambridge: Cambridge University Press, 1979), p. 108.

13 Nagel, *Mortal Questions*, p. 112.

14 Nagel, *Equality and Partiality*, p. 5.

15 John Rawls, *A Theory of Justice* (Cambridge, MA: Harvard University Press, 1971), pp. 507, 509.

16 "The core of this tradition is an insistence that the forms of social life be rooted in the self-conscious value affirmations of autonomous individuals." Bruce A. Ackerman, *Social Justice and the Liberal State* (New Haven, CT: Yale University Press, 1980), p. 196; "The most important task for which autonomy has been harnessed in contemporary political philosophy is to argue for a certain ideal of the liberal state. . . . The root idea is that the

A Reasonable Alternative to Egalitarianism

state must recognize and acknowledge the autonomy of persons." Gerald Dworkin, "Autonomy," in *A Companion to Contemporary Political Philosophy*, p. 361; "The liberal individual is fully rational, where rationality embraces both autonomy and the capacity to choose among possible actions on the basis of one's conception of the good as determined by one's reflective preferences. . . . As an autonomous being, the liberal individual is aware of the reflective process by which her later selves emerge from her present self, so that her preferences are modified, not in a random or uncontrolled way, but in the light of her own experiences and understanding." David Gauthier, *Morals by Agreement* (Oxford: Clarendon Press, 1986), p. 346; "Acting autonomously is acting from principles that we would consent to as free and equal rational beings. . . . They are the principles that we would want everyone (including ourselves) to follow were we to take up together the appropriate general point of view. The original position defines this perspective." Rawls, *Theory of Justice*, p. 516; see also Rawls's *Political Liberalism* (New York: Columbia University Press, 1993), p. 72; "One common strand in liberal thought regards the promotion and protection of personal autonomy as the core of the liberal concern." Joseph Raz, *Morality of Freedom* (Oxford: Clarendon Press, 1986), p. 203; "The essence [of liberalism] is that individuals are self-creating, that no single good defines successful self-creation, and that taking responsibility for one's life and making of it what one can is itself part of the good life." Alan Ryan, "Liberalism," in *A Companion to Contemporary Political Philosophy*, p. 304.

17   "I am autonomous. I obey laws, but I have imposed them on, or found them in, my own uncoerced self. Freedom is obedience, but 'obedience to a law which we prescribe to ourselves'. . . . Heteronomy is dependence on outside factors, liability to be a plaything of the external world that I cannot myself fully control." Isaiah Berlin, "Two Concepts of Liberty" in *Four Essays on Liberty* (Oxford: Oxford University Press, 1969), p. 136; "Autonomy is a second-order capacity of persons to reflect critically upon their first-order preferences, desires, wishes, and so forth, and the capacity to accept or attempt to change these in the light of higher-order preferences." Gerald Dworkin, "Autonomy," p. 360; an autonomous individual is "one who can step back from his moral beliefs and his desires . . . and . . . test their validity by reference to an inbuilt standard, which is his own tendency to rational coherence and consistency in thinking." Stuart Hampshire, *Morality and Conflict* (Cambridge, MA: Harvard University Press, 1983), p. 56; an autonomous individual is "a subject with ends he has chosen, and his fundamental preference is for conditions that enable him to frame a mode of life that expresses his nature as a free and rational being as fully as circumstances permit." Rawls, *Theory of Justice*, p. 561.

18   Nagel, *Equality and Partiality*, p. 28.

19   See Note 4 above.

20   John Stuart Mill, *On Liberty* (Indianapolis, IN: Hackett, 1978 [1859]), p. 51.

21   In formulating this view, I drew on the rapidly growing recent work on what it means to say that something is or is not deserved. See, e.g., Joel Feinberg, "Justice and Personal Desert," in Carl J. Friedrich and John W. Chapman, eds., *Nomos VI: Justice*, (New York: Atherton, 1963); William Galston, *Justice and the Human Good* (Chicago: University of Chicago Press, 1980); John Kekes, *Against Liberalism* (Ithaca, NY: Cornell University Press, 1997), Ch. 6; David Miller, *Social Justice* (Oxford: Clarendon Press, 1976); Michael J. Sandel, *Liberalism and the Limits of Justice* (Cambridge: Cambridge University Press, 1982); and George Sher, *Desert* (Princeton, NJ: Princeton University Press, 1987).

22   "The idea of rewarding desert is impracticable." Rawls, *Theory of Justice*, p. 312. See also Friedrich A. Hayek, *The Constitution of Liberty* (Chicago: University of Chicago Press, 1960), Ch. 6.

DEMOCRACY AND ITS LIMITS

THE VALUE OF DEMOCRACY

CHAPTER ELEVEN

The Supposed Right to a Democratic Say

Richard J. Arneson

Democratic instrumentalism is the combination of two ideas. One is instrumentalism regarding political arrangements: the form of government that ought to be instituted and sustained in a political society is the one the consequences of whose operation would be better than those of any feasible alternative. The second idea is the claim that under modern conditions democratic political institutions would be best according to the instrumentalist norm and ought to be established.

"Democratic instrumentalism" is not a catchy political slogan apt for car-bumper stickers. To my knowledge people have never marched in solidarity under its banner. In fact it is a dreary political abstraction. Yet it has a lot going for it, morally, politically, and intellectually. This essay defends democratic instrumentalism.[1]

The democratic instrumentalist opposes the doctrine of the divine right of kings along with the idea that aristocrats are inherently more worthy than commoners and as such are uniquely entitled to rule. Striking a more controversial note, the democratic instrumentalist also opposes the suggestion that each adult person has a fundamental moral right to be admitted as a full member of some political society, entitled to run for office and vote (on a one-person-one-vote basis) in free elections that select the public officials in top government posts and directly or indirectly determine the content of the laws and policies that the government enforces on all members of the society. Call this the right to a democratic say.[2]

Here a moral right is an individual claim that others ought to honor. If one has a moral right, one is wronged if others do not honor it; a given right is constituted by specified duties that specified others are bound to fulfill. A fundamental moral right holds independently of social and political arrangements, cultural understandings, or people's opinions. It also holds, at least to some degree, independently of the consequences that would ensue if it were upheld or not upheld.[3] A fundamental moral right might be hedged with conditions. For example, one might hold that people have a fundamental moral right to a democratic say in political decision-making just in the case that mass literacy obtains and the society has a sufficiently developed and wealthy economy. The democratic instrumentalist denies not only the absolutist position that people have a right to a democratic say whatever the consequences, but also weaker nonabsolutist versions of the doctrine, and she likewise denies not only unconditional affirmations of the fundamental right to a democratic say, but also any conditional affirmations of such a right.

Any consequences caused by instituting and sustaining one or another political system are relevant to its assessment according to the instrumentalist or best results account. Some have speculated that the operation of political democracy might work to improve people's character on the average.[4] If so, a democratic political order might be preferable to a nondemocratic alternative all things considered even if the laws and public policies generated by the nondemocratic order would be superior to those democracy would produce.

The democratic instrumentalist might be an instrumentalist across the board who denies that anyone ever has any fundamental moral right as just specified. On this view all claims about moral rights, if valid at all, are valid in virtue of being instrumentally justified. In this essay I focus on a narrower instrumentalist position. The narrow instrumentalist does not assert that there are no fundamental moral rights but holds that if there are any such things, the fundamental right to a democratic say (or to the status of political equality) is not among them.

The Ideal of Democracy

Democracy is not all or nothing. A political order can be democratic or undemocratic to various degrees. Instrumentalism provides a standard for fixing the desirable degree of democracy for any given society. The optimal degree of democracy for a given society is that extent of democracy having which produces consequences morally better than those that having any other level of democracy in place would produce.

The instrumentalist issues a challenge to those who would affirm that democracy is intrinsically and not merely instrumentally just, which I am taking as equivalent to the claim that persons have a fundamental moral right to a democratic say. Anyone who makes such assertions owes us an account of how much democracy is deemed intrinsically just and an explanation of how and where and why the line is drawn between the extent of democracy that is a matter of moral right and the further extent of democracy which is left morally optional.

Consider the right to a democratic say as characterized above (paragraph 3). The features that constitute this right that can hold to varying degrees include the following:

1. A political order with majority voting but lacking freedom of speech is not truly democratic. Freedom of speech obtains in a society when laws effectively protect the freedom of willing speakers to address willing audiences on any matters of public concern. Freedom of speech can obtain to varying degrees.
2. Endorsing representative democracy, J. S. Mill asserts that "the ideally best form of government is that in which the sovereignty, or supreme controlling power in the last resort, is vested in the entire aggregate of the community."[5] This says nothing about elections. In the same publication Mill explains that "The meaning of representative government is, that the whole people, or some numerous portion

Richard J. Arneson

of them, exercise through deputies periodically elected by themselves the ultimate controlling power."[6] Having power over something in the last resort looks to be compatible with having power to determine how that thing goes only in the long run. In the short run, one might be powerless, while controlling the issue in the last resort. Here then is a dimension along which a government structure might be more or less democratic. The shorter the time lag between the time of the formation of a majority will on some issue and the time at which that majority will is put into effect, the more democratic the political process.

3.   Another dimension along which a political system can register as more or less democratic is the extent to which policies and laws are determined by majority rule as opposed to being fixed independently of that will. A society in which there is a bill of rights that constrains the policy choices the elected legislature may permissibly make, the bill of rights itself not being revocable or alterable by legislative decision, is less democratic than one in which the elected legislature is not so constrained. In the same way, if public policies and laws in some policy area are set by a king, and the elected legislative has the authority only to enact public policies and laws in the remaining policy domains, the political system is less democratic, the smaller the scope of the authority of the elected legislature. Also, the more it is the case that a public policy established by an impeccably democratic procedure is effectively implemented (provided the majority wills effective implementation), the more democratic the society, other things being equal.[7]

4.   A fourth dimension along which a political system can be variously democratic is equal opportunity for political influence. Equal opportunity for political influence obtains in a society when any two persons with equal political ambition and equal political talents have the same chances of influencing political outcomes.[8] The closer a society comes to achieving equality of political influence, the more democratic it is, in this respect. In the society that achieves this ideal, such factors as wealth, social status, social connections, sex, race, sexual orientation, and so on, do not *per se* affect the degree of political influence an individual commands.

5.   A fifth dimension is the degree to which a political order is deliberatively democratic. A society is more deliberatively democratic, the more it is the case that its laws and policies are picked by majority vote of an electorate all of whom have reflected carefully about where the common good (the requirements of social justice) lies and have voted conscientiously with the aim of advancing this common good as they see it. (It is not incoherent to postulate that people have a moral right to inhabit a society that is deliberatively democratic. This would be a right possessed by an individual that imposes on other members of the electorate the duty to conduct themselves so that the political process is deliberatively democratic.)

In Favor of Instrumentalism

Why deny that there is a fundamental moral right to a democratic say, or alternatively, that democracy is intrinsically just? That a choice of political system would produce better outcomes than any alternative is widely agreed to be a factor morally relevant to the judgment that one or another political system ought to be introduced. The controversial question is whether it is the only factor that matters. Roughly speaking, the opponent of instrumentalism holds that democracy is an intrinsically fair political procedure, and that its intrinsic fairness can outweigh some shortfall in production of good consequences.[9]

One consideration appears in J. S. Mill's *Considerations on Representative Government*. Mill in effect urges that the political franchise is a small bit of political power, power to control the lives of other persons, and one has no fundamental moral right to have power over other persons in any case. In particular circumstances it might be morally best, all things considered, for an individual to place herself in a position of power over others and exercise it and best for others to allow this power over their lives to be exercised. But a moral case for having and exercising power over others is never straightforwardly an individual moral right but instead is justified by a showing that this use of power in the given circumstances would fairly advance the interests of all persons affected by it.

Objection: Doesn't any moral right whatsoever give the rightholder power over other people? If I have a moral right of ownership of a cabin, that gives me the power to exclude others from its use. Looked at this way, the right to a democratic say is not problematic.

Response: I deny that any moral right whatever gives one power over others. Some rights do and some do not. Consider the claim that each person has a moral right to personal sovereignty, to do what she chooses so long as she does not thereby harm nonconsenting other people. This right against paternalistic interference gives each person power over her own life, not the lives of others. Moreover, moral rights that do involve power over others vary in the character and quality of such power. The power to set rules that other people will be coerced to obey by threat of serious penalty for noncompliance is a special power to direct the lives of others. The right to participate by voting in the legislative and executive processes of a democratic state is in a small way an instance of a right to exercise a special power to direct the lives of others. Other moral rights such as the right to free speech lack this character. So one can deny that anyone ever has a basic moral right to power to direct the lives of others without denying that anyone ever has a basic moral right of any sort.

If it is true across the board that any assumption of power by an individual is justified only by a showing that the assumption would fairly advance the interests of all people affected, this will also be true of the assumption of political power, and even the assumption of the tiny bit of political power that goes with the political franchise.

The Instrumentalist Case against Democracy

Further light on democratic instrumentalism is shed by considering the instrumentalist case against democratic political institutions. A convincing democratic instrumentalism must rebut this case.

One familiar claim is that members of society differ in ability and disposition to exercise sound political judgment, and that if (this is of course a big if) a reliable

Richard J. Arneson

selection process can be found to pick out those specially qualified to rule, they should be the rulers. But it is worth noting that a case against democracy can be made without relying on such claims about unequal qualifications to rule.

Suppose that we are considering a democratic political order that would be instituted in a complex modern society with a large adult population. With a large population, the democratic franchise confers only a tiny bit of political power. Think of a national election in a society with hundreds of millions of voters. The chance that any given individual voter would be decisive in casting her vote one way or the other is extremely small. Even if one's vote influences the votes of others, the chances that how one votes might affect the outcome of the election are still extremely small. One's vote will not change who is elected or what party controls the legislature. One's vote does affect the outcome in a small way – the total vote count would have been different if Smith had voted for candidate X rather than candidate Y. But this effect is trivial.

Although one's vote is, in terms of efficacy, inconsequential, the responsibility to vote well is nonetheless a heavy responsibility. I assume the voter does not discharge her duty as a citizen by voting her self-interest (though deciding how to vote on this basis would still be dauntingly complex). The voter is expected to discover and support policies that are best according to appropriate moral standards. One should seek by one's vote to support policies that compared to alternatives on offer do most to advance the common good or the cause of justice. What these policies are is exceedingly difficult to discern. Having a sound understanding of fundamental moral principles is itself a mountain of a task, but gaining such understanding does not suffice to determine how one's vote should be cast. One needs also to know the relevant empirical facts that bear on the issues up for review. To become genuinely well informed and able to vote with sound understanding even on a rather simple matter such as a local sewage and water policy issue would require an enormous investment of time and other resources by each voter. To become a well-informed voter able and disposed to vote wisely on the entire range of issues presented in a single national election would be an enormous task, draining resources that could be well used in other areas of one's life. And for what? As mentioned already, one's vote is a drop in the bucket, inconsequential.

In fact the responsibilities of voting do not weigh heavily on citizens in democracies. We voters routinely wave them aside without much concern. And in fact given the tremendous investment of resources that one would have to make to vote wisely in each election and the tremendous inconsequence of one's vote however carefully considered it might be, it is implausible to suppose that all things considered there is a serious moral obligation to vote wisely.

In voting models that presume self-interested motivation on the part of voters, a stable result is rational voter ignorance: in self-interested terms, becoming well-informed is a bad bet.[10] But rational voter ignorance is prescribed also if the background assumption is that one is morally required to vote for the common good as best one discerns it and that voters are not purely self-interested but are motivated to some degree to vote according to the common good.

There are some tricks one can play to economize on information-gathering and reduce the cost of moral and political deliberation preparatory to responsible exercise of the right to vote, but they do not in my judgment seriously alleviate the problem. One can choose a political party that reflects one's normative outlook and trust the party to pick out policies that effectively pursue these norms in current circumstances. But what party can be trusted? Anyway, the decision to pick a party is itself exceedingly complex, and a morally responsible voter would have to keep checking his initial decision to support a particular party in kaleidoscopic continually changing political circumstances. One might look to political pundits for guidance, but the same problems recur at the level of deciding which authorities to accept. This decision is itself very complex and needs more or less continuously to be reviewed and reconsidered.

The upshot of this discussion is that for any morally responsible agent who is a voter in a complex modern society with large population, the costs and benefits of voting in a fully informed and fully reflective manner are such that remaining ignorant and refraining from full reflection are at least morally permissible and very probably morally required. Given limited personal resources, for almost any voter, other moral demands crowd out the demand to vote well. But then one can hardly expect democracy under these circumstances to function well. Even morally disposed and conscientious citizens will not vote well. It would be a fluke if citizens who are not moral and conscientious voted well, so one should expect bad voting and poor control of politics by voters in political systems in which majority rule is important.

The moral permission/requirement to vote without becoming well informed and deliberating carefully holds only given certain conditions. If large numbers of voters abstained from exercising their right to vote, at some point the efficacy of the votes left in the hands of remaining voters would be large enough to trigger requirements to use the vote well. But this is an unlikely scenario. In the conditions that Jean-Jacques Rousseau may have assumed as background conditions for his argument for political democracy, namely a society with a small population and a simple homogeneous mode of life, the problem just discussed does not arise.[11] But these conditions will not hold in the settings in which we advocate political democracy today; nor should we strive to change the world so that the conditions do obtain.

The argument from rational voter ignorance does not show that, all things considered, democracy is a bad political system that should not be established and sustained. One expects democracy to work poorly and to be a poor tool for generating just laws and social policies, but perhaps all feasible alternatives to democracy would expectedly perform even worse.

But the inherent structural weakness of democracy as a device for securing good policy casts a dark shadow on the claim that there is a strong moral presumption in favor of political democracy independent of the expected consequences of its operation.

This shadow falls on doctrines that hold that democracy is a uniquely fair procedure for determining the substance of the laws and policies that government enforces on the members of society. Democracy as I have just characterized it is a system of governance that places morally conscientious individuals in a bind: the ideal of democracy is that policies should be chosen by the majority vote of citizens choosing in free elections with full information after careful adequate deliberation directed toward determining where the common good lies. If people do less than this, there is no particular reason to think that policies will be guided by a defensible conception of the common good. But the information gathering and fact sifting and empirical theory understanding and deliberating on moral principles and applying of

Richard J. Arneson

carefully selected moral principles to the facts at hand that are required if voting is to fulfill the ideal of democracy are in almost all circumstances more than one is morally obligated or even morally permitted to do (given the press of other moral concerns). How can this political procedure be fair at all, let alone uniquely fair?

Notice that the doubts about political democracy raised so far in this section do not rely on any claims about the unequal practical reasoning ability and conscientiousness and political expertise capacity of citizens. The problem arises even if all citizens are equally competent and known to be so.

One could meet the concerns about rational voter ignorance without adopting anything resembling elitist minority rule. For example, one might pick at random a small group of citizens and assign them the responsibility to become enlightened on the issues of the day and to participate in majority vote that directly or indirectly determines what laws shall be established and what persons shall become top government officials. Periodically a new random draw is made from the set of citizens and a new group of people is assigned the responsibility of voting. Call this system *random subset democracy.*

Suppose that under some circumstances assigning people important responsibilities induces them to rise to the task, to put forth extra conscientious effort. The hat makes the man, as the saying goes. Then under the right circumstances a permanent assignment of political power to randomly selected citizens might be expected to lead to better political outcomes than maintaining random subset democracy. At this point one has an argument for a nondemocratic political order that does not rely on the claim that some people are more able than others to exercise political power wisely.

Democratic instrumentalism becomes plausible by successful rebuttal of the claims that rational voter ignorance and unequal distribution of political wisdom across citizens can be parlayed into arguments for nondemocratic political order.

Democracy and Mutual Respect

The idea that democracy is intrinsically just is supported by claims to the effect that failure to accord every member of society who possesses rational agency capacity the opportunity to participate on equal terms with the other members in the making of the laws enforced on all is failure to respect each person as a rational agent. A closely related claim is that each person rationally must safeguard for herself a level of self-respect and self-esteem needed for effective agency. A condition for maintaining this necessary self-respect is that one is respected by others, that one's status as a rational agent is supported not undermined, and being denied the right to a democratic say is being denied this elemental and necessary respect from others. Democracy is intrinsically just *inter alia* because it is a necessary condition of mutual self-respect which no rational agent can abjure.

This is obviously a crude capsule version of an argument that cries out for detailed elaboration. But I hope that the simple objection I raise would apply to any elaboration of it.

Many of us spend much of our lives working in decidedly undemocratic hierarchical organizations. We work in large, top-down, bureaucratic organizations to fulfill plans set by top officials. These organizations include government agencies, business firms, and nonprofit organizations. The relation of subordinates to bosses in these hierarchies is in a way unlike the relation of citizens to the state, in that we have some voluntary control as to whether to submit to the authority of an enterprise hierarchy and less voluntary control as to whether or not to allow the state to impose its will on us. But this contrast is not stark. In any realistic sense, one often has no reasonable employment option except to subordinate oneself to an enterprise hierarchy, and often the costs for the individual of shifting from association with one particular enterprise are large. On the other side, the individual has options to exit from any particular state jurisdiction.

No doubt bureaucratic enterprises often mistreat those who labor for them, especially those low on the chain of command. But I find it hard to take seriously the idea that failure to accord the right to a democratic say to the members of such enterprises is *per se* disrespectful mistreatment or treatment that is incompatible with conditions of mutual respect and promotion of the self-respect of all.

This issue is hard to address in the absence of a developed theory of humane bureaucracy. It surely matters whether or not democratic organization of the enterprise would better advance legitimate enterprise goals, balanced against the costs and gains that accrue to other legitimate interests affected by this advancement, compared to nondemocratic modes of organization. If not, the maintenance of a nondemocratic mode of organization that is vindicated by a morally sensitive cost and benefit assessment is not inherently disrespectful or insulting to those denied a democratic say in decisions about how to run the enterprise. Also, in a humane bureaucracy relations between persons at different layers of the organizational hierarchy are regulated by rules designed both to advance the fulfillment of enterprise goals and to protect those lower in the hierarchy from arbitrary tyrannical supervision and also from overzealous supervision that imposes excessive costs on subordinates in the course of advancing enterprise goals. More generally, the rules and policies of the humane bureaucracy ensure proper attribution of credit for achievement and fair sharing of the benefits and burdens of the cooperative project.

It is important to anyone who is a subordinate in such an enterprise that it should be dedicated to serving morally valuable goals and reasonably well organized to achieve success in this pursuit. Obeying orders that are arbitrary and capricious, not reasonably aimed at furthering the morally acceptable enterprise goals, is dispiriting and ultimately degrading. But obeying rules and commands and policies set by other persons without regulation by any democratic process is not *per se* inimical to self-respect or mutual respect.

So my broad suspicion is that if democracy at the society-wide level is intrinsically just and morally mandated, so should be democracy at the enterprise level. But the inference is better run in the other direction: democracy at the enterprise level is not a requirement of justice, nor is it morally mandatory as necessary for necessary self-respect at the society-wide level.

I admit that there are morally important differences between undemocracy in bureaucratic organizations and undemocracy at the level for the nation-state. So one might hold that basic requirements of mutual respect for persons mandate democracy as intrinsically just only at the level of the state. One salient difference that one might exploit to make this argument would be the gross difference in voluntariness of submission. To some degree one has the option whether to submit oneself to the

Richard J. Arneson

undemocratic authority of an employing enterprise, but every citizen must submit to widespread state coercion that affects their lives deeply and continuously. The state massively coerces the citizen and seriously crimps her personal sovereignty and this imposition is compatible with mutual self-respect among all citizens only if the political order is democratic. So one might hold.

I doubt that that the fact that the state massively coerces those subject to its jurisdiction under conditions that do not allow for significant individual voluntary consent to this coercive imposition generates a moral requirement of democracy as a condition of mutual respect. Coercion *per se* is not morally momentous. If one is coerced for no good reason, that is a terrible infringement of one's right to autonomy. But being coerced to comply with demands that one is anyway morally bound to fulfill is not a serious infringement, at least if the coercion is proportionate to the gravity of the requirement (it is not acceptable to threaten the death penalty even to serve the good cause of inducing people to refrain from jaywalking). If the state's criminal justice system coerces me not to murder my wife, this coercion does not seriously infringe my autonomy if I have no desire to murder her, and although it does seriously infringe my autonomy if I do harbor murderous aims, in this unfortunate scenario the drop in my autonomy is not to be regretted.

The same is true across the board. When a number of persons engage in a mutually advantageous cooperative venture according to rules, and thus restrict their liberty in ways necessary to yield public goods for all, those who have submitted to these restrictions have a right to a similar acquiescence on the part of those who have benefited form their submission.[12] If the goods provided to all are sufficiently important, and the rules provide for fair sharing of the benefits and burdens of cooperation, coercion necessary to sustain the scheme and ensure that all who benefit contribute their fair share to the project can be morally acceptable, in my view. This can be true in virtue of the good substance of the cooperative scheme and independently of how it came to be or how it is currently administered. This all holds true if the scheme is provision of public goods including the rule of law and good order by a state that claims a monopoly of the use of force on its territory. Mutual respect in such a scheme is sustained by morally defensible substance. The process of deciding on the terms of the scheme and deciding how to administer it matters morally because it affects the degree to which the substantive outcomes of the scheme are fair and right. But those affected by the scheme, including those coerced to contribute their fair share to it, do not have a basic right to be treated by any particular sort of process or procedure, democratic or otherwise.

Rights, Disagreement, and Democracy

Consider this instrumentalist position: the primary proper job of the state is to safeguard people's important moral rights (other than the disputed right to a democratic say), and so if it can be shown that some nondemocratic political order would in given circumstances do better than any democratic alternative to safeguard these moral rights, the nondemocratic order ought to be instituted. Appealing to the moral imperative of respecting moral rights, one might defend constitutional features such as judicial review that limit the extent to which a political order qualifies as democratic.

Jeremy Waldron has argued that the assumptions (1) that people have important moral rights, which can be violated by policies established by majority rule, and (2) that claims about what moral rights people have are genuine assertions that can be objectively true or false do not give any traction to one who argues for curtailing majority rule in order to protect people's important moral rights.[13] First, any form of governance can give rise to violations of people's moral rights, so the possibility of rights violation does not automatically tell in favor of any particular form of governance. Second, one of the central background facts that create the need for authoritative policy making with coercive enforcement that governments provide is that rights are controversial. People disagree about the content of the moral rights of individuals. Part of the point of having a government is to provide a practical resolution of such disagreement so that the disagreements do not erode social order. The moral disagreements remain, but where convergence in people's actions on one specification of rights is needed, some governmental decision-making generates the needed specification. You can grant that there are rights and that questions about what moral rights people have admit of correct answers, but that does nothing to eliminate the need for authoritative governmental specification on these matters in the absence of uncontroversially known right answers to questions of moral right. This appeal to rights, their real existence, their centrality in moral life, their objective status does nothing at all to overturn the natural and reasonable presumption that when people disagree as to what rights should be proclaimed, guaranteed, and enforced by the state, the morally appropriate method of decision to settle governmental rights policy is a democratic process in which all members of society have the opportunity to participate on equal terms and with an equal vote. According to Waldron, the objective reality of moral rights and the evil of their violation have no bearing on the case for democratic majority rule.

Many of the pieces fit together in Waldron's argument are correct, but he neglects to mention big pieces of the puzzle, and by ignoring them he reaches a wrong conclusion.

Disagreement among people as to what moral rights people have can be roughly divided into three categories: (1) there is disagreement among people in cases about which reasonable, well-informed, competent judges would not disagree, (2) there is disagreement among people where reasonable, well-informed, competent judges would find themselves in stable disagreement, in our present epistemic condition, and (3) there is disagreement among people where reasonable, well-informed, competent judges would disagree, because some reasonable, well-informed, competent judges are here making a demonstrable mistake (perhaps a subtle mistake on a difficult question).

If there is a case for curtailing or limiting or even abolishing democratic political rule with respect to a particular range of issues, in particular circumstances, in a particular country, the case emerges from considering disagreement of types 1 and 3. Such claims as these would be relevant. Many citizens who exercise the vote in democracies are not reasonable, competent, well-informed judges of the moral issues at stake, so they sometimes vote in ways that issue in government laws and policies that enforce or allow serious violations of people's moral rights the nature and existence of which are beyond the pale of reasonable disagreement. Many citizens who exercise the vote in democracies are morally lax in that they allow themselves to vote for policies that suit their interests and prejudices even when their own practical

Richard J. Arneson

reasoning rightly signals to them that what they are voting for is clearly morally wrong. Many citizens who exercise the vote in democracies are less competent, well-informed, and reasonable judges than the minority of citizens who are well above average in these respects, so that when faced with difficult and subtle policy issues involving complex determinations of moral right, the bulk of citizens predictably goes wrong and votes for rights-denying policies when the morally more competent citizens get it right and do not vote for rights-denying policies. These claims do not by themselves make even a prima facie case for limiting or abolishing democracy in particular settings, but they are germane. Waldron has his eye only on type 2 disagreement, but that is not the type that leads sensible people to be ambivalent about the moral propriety of majority rule and open to limitations on it in the name of protecting moral rights.

Of course the possibility of rights violations perpetrated through majority rule does not raise doubts about the moral propriety of majority rule governance unless one has some sensible view that minority rule or curtailments on majority rule might do better. If one conceives of moral disagreement about rights as always and everywhere reasonable disagreement among reasonable people on difficult, perhaps intractably difficult and unsolvable moral questions, the possibility of tyranny of the majority will be hard to discern.

But alongside reasonable disagreement among reasonable people thinking reasonably on the particular occasion about questions of rights, there is also disagreement that is manifestly and blatantly unreasonable and disagreement that is unreasonable (would not persist if all parties reasoned correctly and exercised practical reasoning excellently) though not manifestly or blatantly so. If we grant the possibility of moral knowledge, we should also grant the possibility of moral expertise – superior developed practical reasoning ability. If there is moral expertise, it is dogmatic to insist that it must be spread evenly across the population of a modern society. Is there moral expertise? Although this is a large question and this essay cannot work through it, my hunch is that there is a deep tension in any position that combines affirmation of moral knowledge and denial of moral expertise. Denial of moral expertise presses one toward moral skepticism.

It's a long way from acknowledgement that there are moral experts to the claim that authoritarian rule by people selected by some process as moral experts would be a good idea in any particular society. The democratic instrumentalist holds that this argumentative traverse cannot be successfully completed.

Nonetheless the democratic instrumentalist position has a certain affinity with the position that possession of moral expertise by a group of people in a society can justify their claim that their authoritarian rule is morally legitimate. The democratic instrumentalist objects to the argument that the moral experts should be the political rulers on practical and empirical grounds, not on grounds of high principle. There is no reliable way to select moral experts to be political rulers. Even if there were a theoretically valid selection procedure, any attempt to put it into effect would be fraught with difficulty, and likely fail. Rule by moral experts might provoke extra-constitutional measures by groups excluded from the political process that would result in bad consequences. Rule by moral experts might generate a popular culture of alienation from public life or in other ways degrade public culture, and good public policies might prove unable to eliminate these bad effects.

Political Liberalism

Philosophers sometimes associate the right to a democratic say with themes of political liberalism. In modern societies that do not engage in suppression of freedom of speech, people will not converge over time on any single conception of the good or theory of moral right. Instead they will tend to fan out in their beliefs, embracing diverse mutually conflicting doctrines. This tendency to pluralism is not merely a result of the fact that some people are inept and irrational in forming their evaluative and nonevaluative beliefs. In a modern society reasonable people will over the long haul continue to disagree about fundamental ethical and moral issues.

The project of political liberalism aims to develop a conception of justice suitable for a modern society marked by stable pluralism of belief. The key idea is that the society should be regulated by principles acceptable to all reasonable persons from their divergent perspectives. When society is effectively regulated according to such principles, all members of society can affirm the basic arrangements despite their across-the-board disagreements about how to live and what we owe each other. The flip side of this thought is that it is wrong to impose on people in the name of principles they could reasonably reject. John Rawls formulates what he calls a "liberal principle of legitimacy:" "our exercise of political power is fully proper only when it is exercised in accordance with a constitution the essentials of which all citizens as free and equal may reasonable be expected to endorse in the light of principles and ideals acceptable to their common human reason." He adds that basic questions of social justice as they arise in the course of politics should be settled according to principles and ideals acceptable to all.

The liberal principle of legitimacy might seem immediately to rule out of court nondemocratic political constitutions. Perhaps in a homogeneous community, for example, a community of religious believers sharing a common faith, all might find acceptable a rule of succession that confers political power on the person singled out by a council of elders as wisest and holiest. Criteria for elite rule might be found acceptable to all. But in a diverse society, any proposed movement away from the symmetry of one-person-one-vote will be controversial, and will be rejected by some reasonable persons.

If there is some sound argument from the legitimacy principle to the right to democracy, and if the legitimacy principle itself is compelling, then we have an argument for the right to a democratic say that is independent of claims about the good or bad consequences of instituting and maintaining a democratic regime. Any such argument bears careful examination. It clearly threatens democratic instrumentalism. But I shall argue that the threat from this quarter is inert.

Rather than engage with the details of this argument, I want to voice a broad objection. In any context in which it is plausible to claim that restricting political power to an elite group would produce better justice results than retaining democracy, the norm of political equality that dictates majority rule and one-person-one-vote as the basic political charter will itself be controversial, reasonably rejectable from normative standpoints that give great weight in choosing political arrangements to the consequences of putting any proposed set of arrangements in place. So the idea that democratic arrangements are uniquely uncontroversial and hence singled out as uniquely acceptable by the filter of the liberal legitimacy norm looks to be

Richard J. Arneson

off-base from the outset. If any and every nondemocratic constitution is similarly rejectable, then one of two conclusions must follow. Either the liberal legitimacy rule sets the bar of acceptability so high that no constitution and policy could clear the bar and all are ruled out as unacceptable, or this result must be taken as an initial problem for higher-order deliberation. If the "no constitution is morally legitimate" outcome is also unacceptable to reasonable persons, then further refining of the liberal legitimacy norm is needed, so that a standard that grades proposals for degrees of unacceptability and that singles out some proposal as least unobjectionable even when no proposal is fully unobjectionable is identified and affirmed. Neither the conclusion that no constitution is legitimate nor the conclusion that the legitimacy norm needs to be relaxed to avoid this result yields an endorsement of democracy as uniquely just in the face of pluralism of belief.

The Ideal of Democratic Equality

Ruminating on the unique opportunity for honor and glory that the English soldiers had, facing a larger French force in the great battle of Agincourt, Shakespeare's King Henry V is moved to grand speech: "We few, we happy few, we band of brothers: / For he today that sheds his blood with me / Shall be my brother."[14] What is being spoken of here is a promised island of meritocratic solidarity in a sea of ascriptive feudal hierarchy. But a democratic version of the sentiment readily comes to mind, and has a clear appeal. One can imagine a Walt Whitman-inspired Shakespeare writing, "We many, we happy many, we band of brothers and sisters." The appeal is to an ideal of democratic equality, meant to hold across a political society.

The society of democratic equality is one in which people relate to each other as equals.[15] Encounters between persons are not rigidly structured by expectations and conventions tied to hierarchical status relations of race, class, gender, or even accomplishment, occupation, or celebrity. Each person is addressed as mr. or ms. – ranks and titles ascribed at birth are abolished. In this society a continuous successful effort is made to ensure that everyone regards everyone as fundamentally equal in status and worth. Differences in native talents, developed skills, earned merit, virtues and vices, and so on are recognized, but not too much is made of them. Also, a great many kinds of excellence are prized, and one is always aware that people who manifestly score low on many dimensions of excellence may score high along other dimensions of excellence that are for the present or from a particular vantage point not visible. The individual who appears to be a dunce or buffoon may be a fine preacher or clever engineer; the bum on the street may be a poet. Anyway, excellence in achievement is not the basis of mutual respect and concern, which are reciprocally accorded to all compatriots, regarded as brothers and sisters. Sustaining a culture of democratic equality requires constant vigilance to prevent distinctions, honors, and fashionable status from congealing into new forms of caste hierarchy or their equivalent.

The ideal of political equality and the associated right to a democratic say are both major constituents of a culture of democratic equality and important, very likely indispensable means to the establishment and maintenance of other elements of such a culture. If democratic equality is valuable, so is political equality.

The democratic instrumentalist need not be committed to denying the value of democratic equality. She can embrace it as an element of a valuable way of life. She can also accept the claim that political democracy is an important element of democratic equality and the further empirical claim that political democracy is an important, perhaps indispensable means to other elements of the democratic equality package. A best results standard for determining what political arrangements ought to be instituted can allow that bringing about the good of democratic equality can figure among the results that affect the all things considered instrumental assessment of possible political arrangements.

But from the fact that democratic equality is good it does not follow that people have a moral right to political democracy any more than it follows from the fact that honey is good that people have a moral right to beehives or to pots of honey. According to instrumentalism, the political rights that people morally ought to have are those having which would be productive of best consequences. In this essay the standards for assessing consequences are left as a topic for another occasion. I don't rule out the possibilities that a culture of democratic equality is a formidably good state of affairs and that political equality promotes this culture. These normative claims might be part of the case for democratic instrumentalism, but they could just as well be accepted by an instrumentalist who at the end of the day decides that the best results standard singles out some form of nondemocratic politics as morally mandatory.

Acknowledging the goodness of a culture of democratic equality allows the instrumentalist to avoid the perhaps unpalatable position that there is nothing to regret if an instrumentalist assessment establishes that a nondemocratic political order in given circumstances would produce better outcomes than a democratic order, so democracy should not be sustained. If instituting a nondemocratic political order reduces the good of democratic equality, it is regrettable that we ought to opt for an undemocratic regime even though it is best all things considered.

In passing I note that it is an open question, to what extent what is attractive in the vague but compelling ideal of democratic equality might be achieved in a nondemocratic political order. A nondemocratic political order that we could imagine emerging as best by the best results standard would not be authoritarian or despotic. It would be a liberal society with free speech guarantees and a freewheeling ongoing public dialogue on the issues of the day. Procedures for contesting political decisions that some citizens view as wrongheaded would be in place. The stated and actual goals of politics would be to achieve an inclusive common good, not the advancement of some elite class. Checks and balances, both political and cultural, would have to be working to guard against the tendency of bias and prejudice in the ruling elite to solidify into unjust class privilege. A popular culture of cap-in-hand submissiveness and deference in the face of political authority would be unhelpful and counterproductive in this regard; instead what would be needed is a culture of democratic assertiveness.

It is hard to get a grip on the question, could a nondemocratic political order sustain a culture of democratic equality, because the latter ideal is vague and elusive. As Samuel Scheffler observes, relations of unequal power, authority, and status are ubiquitous in modern democratic societies.[16] What sorts of unequal relationship are compatible with the democratic culture ideal? One partial response is to distinguish

Richard J. Arneson

limited-purpose deference from across-the-board kowtowing.[17] One defers to the medical authority of one's doctor but does not reasonably regard her as a higher sort of being, obeys one's boss (sometimes, as appropriate) but does not regard him as an aristocrat or king, and so on. But this is still vague and metaphorical. Moreover, a difficulty lurks. If we respond that people should be deferential to officials just where deference is called for, cede to experts of various types just the right measure of authority, conform to the will of their boss just to the degree that doing so best advances legitimate enterprise goals balanced against competing values, and so on, then we are dangerously close to saying that democratic equality says that people should behave as they ought to behave and develop and display the attitudes they ought to develop and display. Democratic equality so construed would be an unobjectionable but unhelpful directive.

I do not intend by the remarks in the last paragraph to register an opinion that the democratic equality ideal collapses under scrutiny and fails to identify significant good. What we should rather say is that further articulation and analysis of this ideal would be desirable. Perhaps it will turn out to be not one ideal but several, of varying worth and significance.

Conclusion

These scrappy remarks aim to establish that democratic instrumentalism is a promising approach to the questions, "what justifies a democratic political order?" and "what morally determines how democratic a political order ought to be?" This approach merits further scrutiny.

Notes

1　This essay draws on Richard Arneson, "Democratic Rights at National and Workplace Levels," in David Copp, Jean Hampton, and John E. Roemer, eds., *The Idea of Democracy* (Cambridge: Cambridge University Press, 1993), pp. 118–48; Arneson, "Defending the Purely Instrumental Account of Democracy," *Journal of Political Philosophy* 11 (2003): 122–32; and Arneson, "Democracy Is Not Intrinsically Just," in Keith Dowding, Robert E. Goodin, and Carole Pateman, eds., *Democracy and Justice* (Cambridge: Cambridge University Press, 2004), pp. 40–58.

2　Among those who endorse the idea that a democratic political order for a modern society is intrinsically and not merely instrumentally just are John Rawls, *A Theory of Justice*, 2nd edn. (Cambridge, MA: Harvard University Press, 1999); Joshua Cohen, "For a Democratic Society," in Samuel Freeman, ed., *The Cambridge Companion to Rawls* (Cambridge: Cambridge University Press, 1993), pp. 86–138; Jeremy Waldron, *Law and Disagreement* (Oxford: Oxford University Press, 1999); Thomas Christiano, *The Rule of the Many* (Boulder, CO: Westview Press, 1996); Christiano, "Knowledge and Power in the Justification of Democracy," *Australasian Journal of Philosophy* 79 (2001): 197–215; David Estlund, "Beyond Fairness and Deliberation: The Epistemic Dimension of Democratic Authority," in James Bohman and William Rehg, eds., *Deliberative Democracy: Essays in Reason and Politics* (Cambridge, MA: MIT Press, 1997), pp. 173–204.

3　On the nature of rights, see Judith Jarvis Thomson, *The Realm of Rights* (Cambridge, MA: Harvard University Press, 1990).

4   See J. S. Mill, *Considerations on Representative Government.*

5   Mill, *Considerations on Representative Government*, Ch. 3.

6   Mill, *Considerations on Representative Government*, Ch. 5.

7   The parenthetical phrase allows that majority will might favor the enactment of a law but not its effective implementation. For example, the majority might will that a law against gambling be on the books but not enforced. In such a case, the majority is getting its way. But if a majority is able to bring it about that a law or policy is formally established but not that it is effectively implemented, for example, because the police force or some other bureaucratic agency is able to exert its will against majority will, to that degree the society fails to be fully democratic.

8   This is a rough formulation. For one thing, in determining whether two individuals have equal prospects of being politically influential, one must abstract from the actual distribution of political attitudes and opinions in the society. Two persons with equal political ambition and equal political talent, one pursuing a conservative political aims in a society whose members have conservative attitudes and opinions, one pursuing radical communist political aims in the same society, may well have very different prospects of being politically influential. The ideal of equality of opportunity for political influence is formulated by John Rawls in *Political Liberalism* (New York: Columbia University Press, 1996).

9   One could of course reject instrumentalism without holding that principles of procedural fairness entail a moral right to a democratic say.

10 Mancur Olson, *The Logic of Collective Action: Public Goods and the Theory of Groups* (Cambridge, MA: Harvard University Press, 1971).

11 Jean-Jacques Rousseau, *The Social Contract.*

12 The words of this sentence are taken from Rawls, *Theory of Justice*, p. 96.

13 Jeremy Waldron, "The Core of the Case Against Judicial Review," *Yale Law Journal* 115 (2006): 1346–1406; Jeremy Waldron, "A Right-Based Critique of Constitutional Rights," *Oxford Journal of Legal Studies* 13 (1) (1993): 18–51.

14 William Shakespeare, *King Henry V*, 4.3.60–2.

15 A seminal articulation of the idea is in Michael Walzer, *Spheres of Justice: A Defense of Pluralism and Equality* (New York: Basic Books, 1983). See also David Miller's essay in the collection he co-edited with Michael Walzer, *Pluralism, Justice, and Equality* (Oxford: Oxford University Press, 1995). See also Elizabeth Anderson, "What Is the Point of Equality?", *Ethics* 109 (1999): 287–337; also Samuel Scheffler, "What Is Egalitarianism?", *Philosophy and Public Affairs* 31 (1) (2003): 5–39; also Scheffler, "Choice, Circumstance, and the Valuer of Equality", *Philosophy, Politics, and Economics* 4 (2005): 5–28.

16 Scheffler, "Choice, Circumstance, and the Value of Equality," p. 17. It should be noted that Scheffler is not here voicing skepticism about the ideal of democratic equality (equality of democratic status), which he embraces.

17 Another partial response is that to treat another person as an equal is to respond to her on the basis of one's perceptions of her particular traits relevant to action in the circumstances rather than to perceptions of her general traits, her membership in various classifications of people. But as stated this proposal suffers from the defect noted above in the text. In many situations responding to people on the basis of their general traits is perfectly appropriate: if you know I am a pedophile, that is probably all you need to know, to know that I am not to be entrusted with unsupervised responsibility to care for your young child; if you know I am a drunkard, that should disqualify my application to be the regular school bus driver. What counts as a particular versus a general trait is not especially clear, and not much hangs on the distinction. These points do not gainsay the fact that sometimes responding to people merely on the basis of stereotypes, e.g., being saddened that one's daughter is marrying a man of another race, is morally vicious.

Democracy: Instrumental vs. Non-Instrumental Value

Elizabeth Anderson

What is democracy? Does it have only instrumental value? One common picture of democracy identifies it with certain governing practices, and claims that it has only instrumental value. On this view, the purpose of government, like that of the market, is to satisfy individual preferences. Individual preferences are assumed to be formed exogenously to democratic processes. Democratic mechanisms of accountability are instituted to ensure that government tries to satisfy these preferences. The main such mechanism is voting, a device for choosing public officials and policies by aggregating individual preferences into a collective decision. Voting is the primary way in which citizens participate in democracy. Its value, like the value of other democratic governing practices, is plainly instrumental.

In this essay, I shall not deny that voting has instrumental value. If voting were not a means to reaching collective decisions responsive to the desires of the electorate, or if it led to results that systematically undermined the interests of the electorate, it would be worthless. But it does not follow that voting has *only* instrumental value. In our consumer culture, we take it for granted that shopping is an activity many people enjoy, beyond its instrumental value in enabling people to acquire goods they desire. Even if a computer could be perfectly programmed with a consumer's tastes so that it automatically ordered online exactly what the consumer prefers, many consumers would prefer to personally survey their options and choose for themselves. For these consumers, shopping has noninstrumental as well as instrumental value. *Yet its noninstrumental value is conditional on its instrumental value.* Although some people can content themselves with pure window-shopping for goods beyond their reach, most would stay home if shopping malls contained only goods that they could not acquire by shopping.

I shall argue the same about democratic participation. It would make no sense if it didn't achieve the ends for which it is instituted. Yet in virtue of its instrumental value, it acquires a noninstrumental value too – if not, for many citizens, as an activity people *enjoy*, then as something they rightly value as a constitutive part of a way of life that they value noninstrumentally. Even if a dictatorship could give them what they wanted, as the government of Singapore claims it does for its subjects, democratic citizens would prefer to govern themselves.

I shall also argue that the democratic way of life can be justified as a matter of justice. Each member of a state is entitled to have equal standing to make claims on others regarding the protection of their interests, and to participate in decisions concerning the shared background conditions of their interactions and the adoption of collective goals. The democratic way of life realizes the universal and equal standing of the members of society, and is therefore justified as morally right.

To appreciate these noninstrumental values of democracy, we need to alter our understanding of democracy. I join a tradition of democratic thinking advanced by John Stuart Mill and John Dewey. Both held that democracy is more than a set of governing practices. It is a culture or way of life of a community defined by equality of membership, reciprocal cooperation, and mutual respect and sympathy and located in civic society. On Mill's view, democratic participation is a way of life that unites two higher pleasures – sympathy and autonomy. On Dewey's view, it is the exercise of practical intelligence in discovering and implementing collective solutions to shared problems, which is the basic function of community life. On both of their views, voting is just one mode of democratic self-expression among many others that constitute a democratic way of life.

I'll also be arguing for a change in the way we think about instrumental vs. noninstrumental justification. Here, I join John Dewey, who offered a trenchant critique of traditional ways of understanding noninstrumental or "intrinsic" values. As my shopping example illustrates, "intrinsic" values cannot always be identified prior to and independently of instrumental values. Among reflective persons, judgments of intrinsic and instrumental value interact bi-directionally. This contrasts with the standard philosophical view, according to which we fix on the intrinsic values first, and then identify the instrumental values as whatever brings about the intrinsic values.

Democracy as a Way of Life

I shall begin by broadening our conception of democracy. Democracy can be understood on three levels: as a membership organization, a mode of government, and a culture. As a membership organization, democracy involves universal and equal citizenship of all the permanent members of a society who live under the jurisdiction of a state. As a mode of government, democracy is government by discussion among equals. As a culture, democracy consists in the freewheeling cooperative interaction of citizens from all walks of life on terms of equality in civil society. These three levels work together. In particular, democracy as a mode of government cannot be fully achieved apart from a democratic culture. At the same time, the point of a democratic culture is not simply to make democratic government work; rather, democratic government is a manifestation of democratic culture; its point is to serve the democratic community, to realize its promise of universal and equal standing.

Consider first democracy as a membership organization. A constitutive principle of democracy is that all who are permanently subject to the laws of a government should be entitled a say in its operations, either directly, in participatory democracy,

Elizabeth Anderson

or indirectly, through the election of representatives. This entails that all the permanent members of a society should be entitled to the status of *citizens*, not subjects, with rights to vote upon reaching adulthood, and all of the other rights – to permanent residence, freedom of speech, to petition government, run for political office, sit on juries, etc. – that are required for having a say.

Exceptions to the general rule of universal citizenship may be tolerable at the margins, with respect to small numbers of legal permanent residents who may work in a country without acquiring citizenship. But even here, a democratic society's interest in universal citizenship is substantial (Brubaker 1989: 162). The democratic ideal supports the major push that occurred in the 1990s to move permanent U.S. residents to citizenship, and the relaxation of standards for foreign permanent guest workers to gain citizenship in several European countries. What democracy cannot allow for long without compromising itself is a large permanent population of metics, of people designated as outsiders, subject to laws although they have no rights to participate in shaping them (Walzer 1983).

This is intolerable because democracy as a membership organization requires equality as well as inclusion. Pressure toward universal inclusion follows from the demands of equality. Equality is understood here as a relation among persons, whereby each adult actively recognizes everyone else's equal authority to make claims concerning the rules under which all shall live and cooperate, and this recognition is common knowledge among all. As the standard democratic slogan goes, everyone counts for one and no one for more than one. This is not merely a voting aggregation rule ("one man, one vote") but a more general principle for organizing social interaction in a democratic society.

Consider next democracy as a mode of government. We are accustomed to thinking of democracy as a set of governing institutions, involving such things as a universal franchise, periodic elections, representative public officials accountable to the people, decisions by majority vote, transparent government, a free press, and the rule of law. What is the point of this set of governing institutions? Democratic theory is split between two broad views: majority rule (aggregation of given preferences), and deliberative democracy. Following the second view, Walter Bagehot (2001 [1872]: 89) famously defined democracy as "government by discussion." It contrasts both with government by custom and government by the decree of a ruling class. I would add to Bagehot's definition that democracy is government by discussion *among equals*. In a democracy, there is but one class of citizens; no citizen is second-class, and no permanent member of society is excluded from access to citizenship.

Deliberative democrats have several reasons for resisting the "majority rule" formula for democracy. First, within a conception of democracy as majority rule, individual rights tend to be construed as constraints on democracy rather than constitutive features of it. "Majority rule" suggests that the majority is entitled to get whatever it wants. If the majority prefers to silence, marginalize, or subordinate various minority groups, majority rule supports this outcome. Against this, many have decried the "tyranny of the majority" as a threat to individual rights. On this construal, individual rights impose *constraints* on democracy.

From the standpoint of deliberative democracy, this way of counter-posing individual rights to democratic forms is deeply confused. Many individual rights are *constitutive* of democracy (Ely 1980: 87–104). Democracy requires that citizens from different walks of life *talk* to one another about matters of common interest, to determine what issues warrant collective action, what kinds of action might make sense, and who is most trusted to hold political office. This entails that numerous rights, including the rights to vote, and freedom of speech, association, and movement, are part of the structural features of democracy rather than constraints upon it. The same point applies to various rights that help secure the equality of citizens, such as rights against establishment of religion, the prohibition of religious tests for holding public office, and the prohibition of racial segregation in public institutions and civil society. It applies as well to the U.S. Constitutional limitation on criminal charges of treason to making war against one's country or aiding its enemies – a limitation designed to secure room for the "loyal opposition" of minorities who are out of power. A majority that silences or segregates minorities, limits their rights to participate because they have the "wrong" religion, or threatens dissenters with treason charges, is tyrannically *un*democratic.

A second reason deliberative democrats reject "majority rule" as a definition of democracy is that the latter takes individual preferences as unqualified inputs into collective decisions. But not every preference is entitled to collective satisfaction, even if it is held by a majority of citizens. As we have seen, some preferences, such as to stamp minority groups with badges of inferiority, or to mark them as outsiders, are ruled out by the requirements of democracy itself. More generally, democratic discussion is a critical way for the public to come to an understanding of what its aims are as a public – to decide *which* concerns are properly matters of public interest, entitled to lay a claim on collective resources and cooperation to secure their fulfillment. Democratic dialogue does not take preferences as given, but transforms them, not just in the sense of changing individuals' minds about what each wants, but of changing *our* mind of what *we* want when we act collectively as citizens.

A third reason deliberative democrats reject "majority rule" as a definition of democracy is that it fails to make central a role for intelligence and learning in democratic decision-making. If democracy is just giving the majority what it wants, why not just let the public decide issues directly by popular referendum? Deliberative democrats reply that to make intelligent decisions and learn from their mistakes, decision-makers must be able to think and deliberate *together*. This requires that legislative bodies be relatively small, investigate issues jointly, and reason together on the basis of common knowledge. They must have feedback mechanisms, tied to mechanisms for accountability, that inform them of the consequences of their decisions and provide them with the means and incentives to revise their decisions in light of knowledge of their effects. While the representative vs. direct democracy distinction is orthogonal to the deliberative vs. preference aggregation distinction, deliberative democrats, because they stress the centrality of deliberation to democratic processes, have an edge in explaining why representative institutions are preferable.

Deliberative democrats have sometimes been thought to go too far in assuming that the aim of democracy is to construct and promote a common good, which is the object of overwhelming consensus. If that were consistently possible, then we would hardly need voting rules such as the majority rule at all. Decision-making

Elizabeth Anderson

could proceed by consensus. Those who are experienced with decision-making by consensus understand its weaknesses. Often, decisions must be made before a true consensus has been reached. The need to make a decision puts overwhelming pressure on dissenters to conform. That process isn't democratic. It is essential to the democratic process to leave room for legitimate dissent.

Because democratic decisions must often be made in the absence of consensus, and must preserve room for legitimate dissent, voting is a necessary moment in the extended process of democratic decision-making. But even when dissenters lose, their role is not thereby cancelled. Deliberative democrats who follow Dewey (1927) stress the provisional and experimental character of voting. Voting does not make a final decision, but rather represents the citizens' or the state's legitimate decision of what to try next until something better comes along. Citizens' collective deliberation and feedback on public decision-making is continuous and does not stop just because a law has been enacted. The rise of the regulatory state has entailed that administrative agencies issue thousands of rules pursuant to general laws. Critical to the democratic process is participatory citizen feedback on proposed regulations prior to their enactment (Richardson 2002). This is a form of citizen input into regulatory deliberation. Once a regulation is adopted, citizens provide feedback to one another and to public officeholders on the effects of the regulation as they see it. This provides further deliberative input into the regulatory process, sometimes leading to revision or withdrawal of regulations. If the effects of policies are bad enough as judged by affected citizens, they will demand reform and elect those whom they view as better able to make them.

On the view of democracy I propose, voting and deliberation represent alternating moments in a continuous process of provisional decision-making, the aim of which is simultaneously to learn about what works and to decide upon criteria of what counts as working from the perspective of citizens acting and thinking collectively. Decisions are provisional and continuously subject to revision in light of feedback from citizens about their consequences. Feedback gets its bite through mechanisms of accountability, including not just periodic elections but public protest, petitions to representatives, citizen participation in regulatory deliberation, and participation in public opinion polling, among many other mechanisms, not least scrutiny of public problems, policies, and officeholders by a skeptical press. Citizens communicate not just with their representatives and other public officeholders, but with one another, so that they may come to an understanding of what they demand *as a public*, and not just as isolated individuals.

None of this would work if democracy were nothing more than a set of governing institutions. Dewey urged us to "to get rid of the habit of thinking of democracy as something institutional and external and to acquire the habit of treating it as a way of personal life," for only so could genuine democracy be realized (Dewey 1981: 228). Democratic institutions amount to little unless citizens enact, in their day-to-day interactions, a spirit of tolerant discussion and cooperation. This leads to the third aspect of democracy, which is cultural. As a culture or way of life, democracy consists in "free gatherings of neighbors on the street corner to discuss back and forth what is read in uncensored news of the day," and "personal day-by-day working together with others." It is the belief that even when needs and ends or consequences are different for each individual, the habit of amicable cooperation – which may include, as in sport, rivalry and competition – is itself a priceless addition to life. To take as far as possible every conflict which arises – and they are bound to arise – out of the atmosphere and medium of force, of violence as a means of settlement into that of discussion and of intelligence is to treat those who disagree – even profoundly – with us as those from whom we may learn, and in so far, as friends. (Dewey 1981: 227–8)

As the citizens of ex-communist countries of Eastern Europe are aware, democracy requires not just the installation of democratic governing institutions but the flourishing of civil society. Civil society, the locus of democratic culture, is a sphere of life intermediate between the private sphere of family and friends, and the sphere of the state. It consists in the domains where citizens freely interact and cooperate, spontaneously in public streets and parks, and in more organized fashion in firms and non-profit associations of all kinds. These are the primary locations where citizens from different walks of life communicate with each other, in ways that shape their sense of what their proper goals are *as a public*. This is where citizens' preferences are transformed through discussion and become matters of public and even shared interest, not simply isolated private preferences. This is where matters of private concern can *become* matters of public concern, when citizens pool information about their problems and discover that some problems they thought were personal are shared by others in the same predicament, and caused by factors subject to collective control (Dewey 1927).

The construction of a democratic culture in civil society requires several elements. One – foremost in the minds of those who seek to construct civil society in Eastern Europe – is to promote the spontaneous self-organization of citizens into numerous associations not directed by the state. Most of these associations, including private firms, clubs, and fraternal associations, do not have direct political aims. Yet they contribute to a democratic culture by providing experience in citizen self-organization and self-governance on a small scale, settings in which informal discussions contribute to the formation of public opinion, and sites of feedback on government decisions (Estlund 2005; Rosenblum 1998; Skocpol 2003).

My own work on democracy stresses another requirement of a democratic culture: associations where citizens from different walks of life can learn to interact and cooperate on terms of equality (1995, 2004). This requires that the dominant associations of civil society, notably the workplace, be *integrated* along whatever social divisions – racial, ethnic, religious, sexual – mark significant systematic inequalities among citizens. Successful integration requires not just contact, but willing and active cooperation. In such cooperative associations, citizens learn to treat one another as equals: as eligible for inclusion in collective projects, entitled to an equal voice, whose concerns merit equal attention and response.

The Values of a Democratic Way of Life

What good is leading a democratic way of life – living in a democratic culture, based on universal and equal membership of all permanent residents of a state, constituted

Elizabeth Anderson

in part by political participation? Here I want to stress the plurality of goods realized in living up to democratic ideals, postponing consideration of whether these goods are "intrinsic" or "instrumental." First, democracy embodies relations of mutual respect and equality, which are required as a matter of right. Second, democracy helps avoid some of the evils of undemocratic ways of life. It helps secure individuals against abuse, neglect, subordination, and pariah status. It also protects against the corruption of character of those who occupy privileged positions in society. Third, democratic ways of life realize the shared goods of sympathy and autonomy. Fourth, democracy is a mode of collective learning.

My list of the goods of a democratic way of life focuses on goods *specific* to or *inherent in* that way of life. This approach contrasts with another way one might argue for democracy: one could first lay out the goods that any government is supposed to provide for its people, and then argue that democracy is best able to secure them. Any minimally decent government needs to provide basic external and internal security for its members; to lay out common rules of interaction and cooperation; and to either directly supply or secure the conditions for other institutions to supply public goods such as the infrastructure of transportation and communication, and public health measures. If we start off with a fixed list of such goods, as in theories of the minimal state, it could be argued that democracy is not necessary to secure them. Singapore has been cited as a counterexample to that claim. Against this, Amartya Sen has argued on empirical grounds that democracies are *more likely* to provide the goods needed for their members to flourish. For example, Sen argues that no mass famine has ever happened in a democracy (Sen 1999). There is much to be said for Sen's view. But I shall set this argumentative strategy aside, along with more generic strategies that argue that democracy will better satisfy most citizens' preferences than alternative modes of government, in order to focus on goods that are more tightly connected to democratic ways of life.

Turning to the first item on my list, the core value of democracy is equality of social relations. By equality I do not mean that everyone enjoys equal esteem or reputation, or equally good jobs or income, nor that everyone is equal in virtue or merit. Democratic equality rather denotes a kind of standing in civil society to make claims on others, that they respect one's rights, pay due regard to one's interests, and include one as a full participant in civil society, including those that inform democratic governance. Democracy regards each citizen as "a self-originating source of claims" (Rawls 1980: 543). They make claims in their own right, not merely as functionaries in a social order designed for other ends, such as the greater glory of God or the state. Everyone *counts*, and everyone counts *equally*.

This is a claim of right. Call the "good" that which properly *appeals* to us or attracts us; and the "right" that which may be *exacted* from us, as an authoritative demand (Dewey and Tufts 1981: 216). I claim as a matter of right that everyone subject to a common set of coercive rules and policies is entitled to equal consideration in their construction. I shall not offer an elaborate argument for this claim. Instead, I point to the experience in which it is rooted: namely, the experience of being called to account by another whose interests we are neglecting or would otherwise neglect (Darwall 2004). This experience is a deep, constitutive part of growing up in society. Granting its purported authority with respect to some persons, there is no case for denying it to anyone. The failure of all arguments of the form "the purported authority of claims originating from people of type x is invalid" where x refers to any of the supposed grounds of antidemocratic subordination (race, ethnicity, class, caste, sex, religion, ignoble birth, etc.), vindicates the democratic standard of right.

The experience of the authority of another's claims is the feeling known as respect. We express this feeling in action by heeding other's claims – taking them seriously in deliberation, weighing them equally with the symmetrical claims we make on others. Democracy is a way of life whereby we collectively heed our mutual claims on one another in constructing rules and goals for those parts of our lives that we live in common with our fellow citizens. It thereby embodies relations of mutual respect, which are required as a matter of right. This is the first distinctive value of democracy.

Having distinguished the right from the good, we may wonder whether a democratic way of life is also *good*, or whether it is merely something exacted from us reluctantly. What is the good of democratic equality? Consider what life is like for those in undemocratic societies, who are deemed not to count at all, or only as subordinates or functionaries. Nonpersons, pariahs, untouchables, and outlaws enjoy no protection against the cruelty and abuse of others. Subordinates suffer under the humiliating contempt of superiors. Mere functionaries are thrown away when no longer useful. These evils are avoided by effective standing as an equal. Thus, John Stuart Mill argued that even if women were properly subordinate to their husbands, they would still need political rights to ensure against men's abuse of their domestic authority. "Men, as well as women . . . need political rights . . . in order that they may not be misgoverned" (Mill 1975: 192).

Mill also argued that the character of those who enjoy superior rank in undemocratic societies is corrupted by their power over others (Mill 1975). Where lords are free to exploit their tenants, slaveowners to whip their slaves, husbands to rape their wives, Hindus to riot against Muslims, those on top become cruel, despotic, and depraved. Even milder forms of inequality, institutionalized through norms that exclude and silence those of lower rank, propagate ignorance and negligence on the part of the powerful. Democratic equality protects the advantaged from the vices of arrogance, malice, and stupidity.

A democratic way of life is not merely good for each member of society, considered individually. It is also a *shared* good, realized by all of us together. Call a good "shared" by the members of a group if a condition of its goodness is that it be good, and commonly known to be good, for everyone else in the group (Taylor 1985). Equality of social relations, as realized in a democratic community, is a shared good. Democratic citizens feel this whenever they decry the subordination or exclusion of their fellow citizens. It is felt as an assault not just on their fellow citizens, but on them – even if they are, through that subordination, granted a superior status. To be placed high through the degradation of fellow citizens – as whites were placed high through the subordination of blacks in the U.S. – is, from a democratic point of view, to be deprived of the good of equal standing, and hence to be in an important sense degraded. As John Stuart Mill claimed,

There ought to be no pariahs in a full-grown and civilized nation. . . . Everyone is degraded, whether aware of it or not, when other people, without consulting him, take upon themselves unlimited power to regulate his destiny. (Mill 1862: 173)

Elizabeth Anderson

True democrats despise titles of nobility and badges of higher-caste status that may be offered to or imposed on them as not simply unjust but degrading, in depriving them of the equal standing they need to live in democratic community with their fellow citizens. To be held high is to be excluded from camaraderie and candid relations with others. To be a democrat is to locate one's sense of dignity in equal social relations with others, and one's good in living in a community of mutual respect and sympathy with them.

The democratic way of life in a community of equals has characteristic forms of activity: meeting together and talking freely about common problems, forging collective plans to solve these problems, observing what life in accordance with these plans is like and revising the plans accordingly, all with equal regard to the interests of all members of the community. These activities exercise three powers: sympathy, autonomy, and intelligence.

Sympathy or solidarity – what Mill called the "feeling of unity with others" – is expressed in a person's never conceiving of himself "otherwise than as a member of a body" whose governing principle is that of a "society between equals," which "can only exist on the understanding that the interests of all are to be regarded equally" and "consulted" (Mill 1957: 40). Mill thought such mutually sympathetic societies of equals existed in many forms, including marriage and workers' cooperatives. But its broadest form is democratic government.

To insist on the importance of sympathy among citizens is not to deny that partisan rivalry and competition among interest groups is part and parcel of democratic life. Recalling Dewey's remarks above, democratic sympathy requires recognition of rivals as loyal opponents from whom one may learn. (Partisan rivals are often loath to publicly admit this, even while "stealing issues" from one another.) It also requires that one cast one's justifications for public policies in terms of the public interest, and not just in terms of narrow partisan or factional interests. Finally, it requires a search for mutually acceptable cooperative solutions to problems, instead of conquest and repression.

Autonomy in democratic participation is expressed in citizens' setting shared principles, goals, and representatives for themselves. What counts as a legitimate matter of public interest is not given to citizens. It is something they decide for themselves, through discussion, voting, and petitioning. The process of coming to a shared understanding of problems of public interest and determination to solve these problems collectively (either directly, or through representatives) was what Dewey (1927: 283) called the public coming to recognize itself as a public. For members of a community to recognize themselves as constituting a public is for them to become a collective agent in determining their own affairs – for citizens to act together to determine the collective conditions and goals of their cooperative life. This is to exercise autonomy collectively (Anderson 2002).

Finally, democratic activity is an exercise of intelligence, in the sense of learning better ways to live our collective lives. Citizens from all walks of life learn from one another in sympathetic discussion about their problems and prospective solutions to them. More heads are generally better than fewer, in that they bring to bear a wider diversity of experiences and knowledge to the identification and solution of collective problems, and ensure that everyone's interests are voiced. Citizens also learn from discussing problems with the solutions they have already implemented.

Democracy: Instrumental vs. Non-Instrumental Value

Here I endorse an "epistemic" conception of democracy without claiming that the outcome of voting constitutively determines the right answer. The true epistemic virtues of democracy are not found in the static outcomes of voting but rather in the dynamic processes of discussion and feedback to government on policies already implemented. Dewey (1927) saw democracy as the collective implementation of experimental intelligence in determining how to live. Voting does not decide what answer is right. It rather selects a preferred hypothesis to be tried – that these officeholders will lead the country in a better direction, that these policies will solve our problems. These hypotheses are then tested by living in accordance with them, seeing what happens, and pooling information about disparate citizens' favorable and unfavorable responses to them. The feedback mechanisms of democratic participation – voting, petitioning, discussion in public media – deliver judgments that either support the current leadership or demand change in what the public hypothesizes is a better direction. By these means, citizens roughly steer the ship of state, but not toward a destination determined outside of the democratic way of life itself. Rather, we figure out on the way what paths seem more promising, much as hikers exploring new territories without a map take the trails that interest them at the time.

Intrinsic and Instrumental Values of Democracy

Does my list of the values of democracy show it to be only instrumentally valuable? On a standard instrumentalist model, we first establish intrinsically valuable states of affairs to be attained, where the value of these states is independent of the processes that bring them about, and then justify actions and institutions as causally efficacious in bringing about these independently identified states. Some aspects of my account of the value of democracy appear to fit this model. Thus, I argued that democracy helps avoid the oppression and neglect of those who would otherwise lack a voice in governance, and corruption of the character of those who would otherwise have arbitrary power over those without voice.

Notice, however, that in characterizing democracy as a mode of collective autonomy, I reject the idea that we can comprehensively identify, independent of democratic processes, the proper goals that democracy should seek. There are *some* such goals, such as security and social order. But these can be attained by a libertarian minimal state. The goals of a democratic state range more widely, but not, in a liberal state, over anything whatever. (Recall the liberal state's abstention from religious impositions.) Rather, democracy is a mode of collective governance whereby citizens work out together what goals they shall share. This is specifically to *reject* the idea that democracy is a generic preference satisfaction mechanism (Anderson 2002). In democracies, some outcomes, even if *individually* preferred by a majority, enjoy no public standing.

Suppose we adopted an expanded instrumentalist model, according to which some of the intrinsically valuable states of affairs include causal processes, and not just outcomes. On such an expanded view, some worlds can be better than others because their end states were achieved in a particular way. To justify democracy on the expanded model is to claim not just that democratic processes bring about better states than nondemocratic processes, but that the world is a better place for containing acts that

Elizabeth Anderson

instantiate democratic processes. I do not think this model captures the value of democratic processes, however. We do not vote in order to have more acts of voting in the world. The world is not better for containing more such acts than fewer.

On the instrumentalist model, whether standard or expanded, states of affairs are assumed to have "intrinsic" value, and everything else is *extrinsically* valuable as an instrument to bringing about the intrinsically valuable states of affairs. Here, "intrinsic" value denotes the point at which justification comes to an end. This is the point where we have identified something that is valuable, independent of the value of anything else. Value is essentially normative for action and feeling: it prescribes an "ought" to agents to bring about and/or care about what is valuable. So, to say that something is intrinsically valuable means we have reason to bring about and/or care about it, independently of any reason we may have to care about anything else.

There are models of politics that posit intrinsically valuable states of the world, which it is the point of politics to realize. On Plato's (1961) view, the point of politics is to achieve a harmonious ordering of social classes, so as to produce a harmonious internal ordering of individual souls, in which the virtue of justice consists. A world of virtuous souls is an intrinsically valuable world, and politics is justified for bringing this world about. Contemporary "teleological" egalitarians adopt a similar model, in holding that the world is better for containing a more equal distribution of goods (Parfit 2000).

I reject models of political justification of this sort, because they bring justification to an end at the wrong place. The proper point of politics is to serve *people*. The proper form of political justification, then, recognizes that states of affairs are to be pursued *for the sake of people, in recognition of the authority of people to set their own ends*. This entails that the states of affairs properly sought in politics do *not* figure in political justification as intrinsic values. They are only extrinsically valuable. We properly care about states of affairs in the political realm, only because we care about people. People, not states of the world, are what has intrinsic value in politics. Instrumentalist models of political justification neglect this point. Thus, even when my list of the values of democracy appears to be instrumentalist, it is not, because the outcomes democratic processes are supposed to bring about are themselves not intrinsically valuable, but good only for the sake of people, who are the original sources of value.

The proper form of political justification starts from the premiss that people are intrinsically valuable, in the sense that they are self-originating sources of claims, and have equal authority to make claims. Recall my three-level account of democracy: as a membership organization, a form of culture or way of life, and a mode of governance. Each of these three levels is founded on recognition of the value of people as equal and self-originating sources of claims. As a membership organization, democracy recognizes the universal and equal standing of all permanent residents within the territorial jurisdiction of the state to make claims as citizens. As a culture or way of life, the locus of which is civil society, democracy realizes this equality in habits of mutual consultation and cooperation that express respect and sympathy for all fellow citizens. As a mode of governance, institutions and practices such as "one person, one vote," recognition of a loyal opposition, a free press, protests and petitions, aim to realize equal consideration of citizens' claims and thereby establish citizens as equals in relation to each other. Hence, my justification of democracy as grounded in considerations of right or justice, tracks the proper form of political justification.

I hasten to distance myself from a particular way of understanding political justification that might look similar to what I have proposed. On that model, political justification is an *a priori* affair, a matter of principle rather than pragmatism. This follows from the supposition that, in rejecting an instrumentalist justification of democracy, one commits oneself to *a priori* arguments that abstract from consideration of the consequences of democratic practices.

I ally myself with John Dewey in rejecting the premisses behind this model. There *is* a deep principle of equal moral standing underlying the justification of democracy. However, like all moral claims, this one is not derived from pure *a priori* argument, but rooted in our *experiences* of the authority of others to make claims on us, which are rooted in our experiences of respect for them. (That these experiences are veridical – i.e., ought to be heeded – and that their proper ground is not based on arbitrary characteristics such as ancestry, requires critical reflection on these experiences as well as on the consequences of heeding them.)

Furthermore, the supposedly sharp distinction between principled and pragmatic justification is itself questionable. I agree with Dewey and Mill that practical principles are subject to empirical testing through experiments in living. We test our principles by living in accordance with them, and seeing whether doing so solves the problems we were trying to solve, and delivers other consequences that we find acceptable. There is no *a priori* deduction of the value of periodic elections, transparent government, a free press, and so forth. If these processes led to social disorder and misery, as conservative critics of democracy supposed, they would be bad. Nor can we simply examine the concept of equal standing of citizens so as to logically deduce what concrete social norms of democratic interaction in civil society actually realize this elusive ideal. Rather, such insights can only be won through the hard work of testing rival democratic conceptions in practice and seeing how they work. This requires systematic reform not just of external institutional rules, as of voting, but of our habits and affects. A century and a half after abolishing slavery, Americans are still mired in disdain and antipathy for the descendents of slaves, and many of us are still searching for a shared way out.

To insist on the importance of evaluating practical principles in light of their consequences is *not* to revert to "merely" instrumentalist justification. Recall: consequences are not good in themselves; their value depends on the value of people, for the sake of which we seek them. Moreover, for purposes of political justification, that the consequences are autonomously willed by citizens as a collective goal is not an accidental feature of most goals of a democratic state, but critical to legitimating the use of state coercion to bring them about. Hence, the justification of political goals does not rest outside of democratic processes. Which goals are legitimately pursued by the state is itself determined within democratic processes, and justified in part because those processes embody a form of collective autonomy.

I have been focusing on a large object of evaluation: democracy as a membership organization and as a way of life, including a mode of governance. I have argued that the justification for democracy, so understood, is not merely instrumental, but is based on a conception of persons as self-originating sources of claims, as worthy

Elizabeth Anderson

of respect and sympathy. Justification takes the consequences of democratic organization and practices into account. But those consequences are not intrinsically valuable. They are rather justified in terms of democratic processes, which express the autonomy and equal standing of citizens.

Most debates over the value of democracy have focused more narrowly on democratic processes or activities in a narrow sense: those activities of citizens that directly impact governance, such as voting, participating in town meetings, and petitioning representatives. Perhaps *these* are only "instrumentally" justified, in the sense that their value is limited to their production of independently justified states of affairs? Again, not if "independently justified" means justified independently of the democratic character of the processes that bring them about.

Suppose we narrow our target of evaluation further, by setting aside considerations of justice and legitimacy, and just look at the good or appealing value of democratic activities. Should we say then that their goodness is wholly dependent on the value (appeal) of their consequences? Since I reject the idea that political practices can be justified apart from consideration of their consequences, I do agree that the value of democratic practices does depend on their consequences. If democratic elections regularly resulted in policies catastrophic to the electors – and worse than what alternative systems of governance would deliver – they would not be justified.

But this is not enough to show that their goodness is *wholly* derivative of the goodness of their consequences. The proper test of the noninstrumental goodness of an activity is not whether we'd still prefer to do it, even if it didn't result in desirable consequences. It is rather whether we'd still prefer to engage in it, even if the same consequences could be brought about by other (passive) means.

I alluded to this test in the introduction to this paper, when I discussed the value of shopping. Even if a computer perfectly predicted all of one's wants, shopped on one's behalf, and arranged for the goods to be delivered to one's home without any intervention on one's own part, one may still prefer to shop oneself. The activity itself is valued: imagining oneself wearing various clothes and jewelry, actually trying on the props, is an enjoyable form of adult play, as well as an expression of autonomy in forming one's preferences.

I follow Mill and Dewey in holding that participating in democratic ways of life, including democratic governance, satisfies the same test of noninstrumental appealing value. Even if a dictator delivered the same consequences as the people would want, were they to choose democratically, citizens would still prefer to achieve those consequences through democratic activities.

Why should this be so? Recall that democratic activities express sympathy for fellow citizens, exercise our collective autonomy, and manifest a form of collective learning. Mill argued that sympathetic and autonomous activities, as expressions of higher faculties, are higher pleasures: those experienced with them would not give them up even for any amount of lower pleasures (those that gratify the motives we share with animals) (Mill 1957: 12). Even if a dictator could arrange our affairs to our liking, we would still prefer to be autonomous – to manage our collective affairs for ourselves, according to our own collective judgment. And even if a dictator could deliver happiness to all, we'd still prefer to do this ourselves, as a way of expressing mutual sympathy and respect for our fellow citizens.

Dewey made the same case for the value of learning. Activity is not valuable just for the states of the world it achieves. The value of life is in the active living of it, not some goal external to activity (Dewey 1976a: 193–9). Learning is integral to human living. We are always learning about what is good by confronting problems, testing solutions, seeing what works, incorporating discoveries about what works into our practices. We are constantly remaking our practices in light of reflection on living in accordance with them. This does not describe a mere phase of life, but the whole of practical intelligence in action. Learning is not just for the sake of knowing; those who take this attitude are forever postponing gratification in the learning process, until it is "complete." But learning is never complete, because circumstance are always changing, requiring the continuous modification of our practices. To desire to skip ahead to the "final results" is to desire to skip human life itself. Democracy as a way of life is the collective exercise of practical intelligence or learning, applied to the problems of living together as equals. It makes no more sense to skip ahead to "the end" than it does to exit the life of a democratic community itself.

Dewey (1976b) argued that the sharp contrast between "instrumental" and "intrinsic" valuation, as applied to activities and states of the world, is false. They represent transitory and alternating moments in an ongoing process of living, not fixed points of justification and evaluative dependence. What is immediately valued at one moment is reassessed in light of its consequences, which may either reinforce or undermine the original immediate valuation. Valuations of the consequences themselves may change, once we understand what it takes to achieve them. What is valued as a means at one moment is valued in itself at another. The same point applies to the values of a democratic way of life, of which participation in governance is a constitutive part. Once we see democracy as a way of life of a community of equals, and not just as a mode of governance, it is hard to conclude otherwise. The good of a way of community life is in the active living of it with others, not in some state of the world external to it.

References

Anderson, Elizabeth. 1995. "The Democratic University: The Role of Justice in the Production of Knowledge," *Social Philosophy and Policy* 12: 186–219.

Anderson, Elizabeth. 2002. "Consumer Sovereignty vs. Citizens' Sovereignty: Some Errors in Neoclassical Welfare Economics," in Herlinde Pauer-Studer and Herta Nagl-Docekal, eds., *Freiheit, Gleichheit und Autonomie* (Vienna and Munich: Verlag Oldenbourg).

Anderson, Elizabeth. 2004. "Racial Integration as a Compelling Interest," *Constitutional Commentary* 21: 101–27.

Bagehot, Walter. 2001 [1872]. *Physics and Politics* (Kitchener, ON: Batoche Books).

Brubaker, William Rogers. 1989. "Membership Without Citizenship" in William Rogers Brubaker, ed., *Immigration and the Politics of Citizenship in Europe and North America* (Lanham, MD: University Press of America).

Darwall, Stephen. 2004. "Respect and the Second-Person Standpoint," *Proceedings and Addresses of the American Philosophical Association* 78: 43–60.

Dewey, John. 1927. *The Public and Its Problems* (New York: H. Holt and Company).

Dewey, John. 1976a. *Human Nature and Conduct*, in J. A. Boydston, ed., *The Middle Works of John Dewey, 1899–1924*, Vol. 14 (Carbondale, IL: Southern Illinois University Press).

Dewey, John. 1976b. "Valuation and Experimental Knowledge," in J. A. Boydston, ed., *The Middle Works of John Dewey, 1899–1924*, Vol. 13 (Carbondale, IL: Southern Illinois University Press).

Dewey, John. 1981. "Creative Democracy: The Task Before Us," in J. A. Boydston, ed., *The Later Works of John Dewey, 1925–1953*, Vol. 14 (Carbondale, IL: Southern Illinois University Press).

Dewey, John, and James Tufts. 1981. *Ethics,* rev. edn., in J. A. Boydston, ed., *The Later Works of John Dewey*, 1925–1953, Vol. 7 (Carbondale, IL: Southern Illinois University Press).

Ely, John Hart. 1980. *Democracy and Distrust* (Cambridge, MA: Harvard University Press).

Estlund, Cynthia. 2005. *Working Together: How Workplace Bonds Strengthen a Diverse Democracy* (Oxford: Oxford University Press).

Mill, John Stuart. 1862. *Considerations on Representative Government* (New York: Harper & Brothers).

Mill, John Stuart. 1975. "Subjection of Women," in *Three Essays* (Oxford: Oxford University Press).

Mill, John Stuart. 1957. *Utilitarianism* (Indianapolis, IN: Bobbs-Merrill).

Parfit, Derek. 2000. "Equality or Priority?" in Matthew Clayton and Andrew Williams, eds., *The Ideal of Equality* (New York: St. Martin's Press).

Plato. 1961. "Republic," in *The Collected Dialogues of Plato*, ed. Edith Hamilton and Huntington Cairnes, trans. Paul Shorey (Princeton, NJ: Princeton University Press).

Rawls, John. 1980. "Kantian Constructivism in Moral Theory," Dewey Lectures, *Journal of Philosophy* 77: 515–72.

Richardson, Henry. 2002. *Democratic Autonomy* (Oxford: Oxford University Press).

Rosenblum, Nancy. 1998. *Membership and Morals* (Princeton, NJ: Princeton University Press).

Sen, Amartya. 1999. "Democracy as a Universal Value," *Journal of Democracy* 10: 3–17.

Skocpol, Theda. 2003. *Diminished Democracy* (Norman, OK: University of Oklahoma Press).

Taylor, Charles. 1985. "The Diversity of Goods," in *Philosophy and the Human Sciences* (Cambridge: Cambridge University Press).

Walzer, Michael. 1983. *Spheres of Justice* (New York: Basic Books).

DEMOCRACY AND ITS LIMITS

DELIBERATIVE DEMOCRACY

Deliberative Democracy

Russell Hardin

For more than a century, roughly from John Stuart Mill (1977 [1861]) to Carole Pateman (1970), democratic theory as pragmatically applied to large modern societies was often about participatory democracy. It was often hortatory in saying people should participate, at a minimum by voting intelligently. More recently that focus has been displaced by or redefined as concern with deliberation. As was true for participation, deliberation is not a well-defined or universally understood term, because it is apparently so attractive a term that it covers a multitude of considerations and practices, depending on the author of the moment.

Early in this development there has been a deeply skeptical vision of the practical impossibility or desirability of either participation or deliberation in any meaningful or substantial sense (Schumpeter 1950 [1942]; Downs 1957; Converse 2006 [1964]; Stimson 2004).[1] If our concern with democracy is pragmatic as opposed to idealistic, there can be little doubt that the skeptics have the better arguments, not least because they actually have data on voters' knowledge and political beliefs. The data are merciless and brutal.[2] The typical voter is politically ignorant and often misguided.

Consider two striking and demoralizing facts. First, since polling began in the 1930s, about a fifth of U.S. voters call themselves conservatives and vote accordingly but take liberal stands on major issues (Stimson 2004). If these voters corrected their own self-assessments and voted for liberal candidates, the Democratic Party would massively dominate American politics. Second, even those who participate often do so with corrupted knowledge and understanding of the issues that motivate them. Here is one easily assessed example. The internet is acclaimed for its potential to enhance political participation. There are more than 12 million blogs currently active, many of them concerning political issues. About 400,000 of these address environmental issues. The scientific consensus on rates of species extinctions are currently a maximum between 74 and 150 species going extinct every day. A survey of thirty sites reveals that they claim from one to several thousand every day (Ashlin and Ladle

2006). Presumably the average blogger spends a lot of time and effort on publishing claims over the web. But their effort is often trivially bad. They and their readers are commonly eco-illiterate even in this instance in which it is not hard to discover scientific views. In both these examples, even energetic participation may be generally harmful both to the participators and to the general public.

Alexis de Tocqueville (1966 [1835 and 1840]: 159–61) holds that small nations are the cradle of political liberty from the participation of citizens; growing large means a loss in participation and hence of freedom. And, indeed, there is no historical example of a large republic. But there are compensating advantages of large scale in the economy, the arts, and invention, and in a reduced threat of military conquest. Because in the large United States, there are fewer opportunities to rise above the many to have power, the ambition for power gives place to love of well-being, a more vulgar but less dangerous passion.

Tocqueville (1966 [1835 and 1840]: 57, 96) says that when citizens are all more or less equal, they will find it difficult to defend their freedoms against power. The argument is roughly that of the logic of collective action. With equality of benefit from seeking liberty for all, no one has a strong enough interest alone to fight for it. With great asymmetry of wealth and power, there will be some individuals who have sufficient interest in defending their liberty that they will do so. Against the claim that small societies are the cradle of liberty, however, Tocqueville may overestimate the costs of defending one's liberty. One might argue that large liberal nations with strong court systems are especially good at securing individual liberties, in large part by making the justice system responsive even to those without great fortunes, at least in so far as defending their constitutional liberties is at issue. Next to virtue, Tocqueville says, nothing is so beautiful as rights, which are the conception of virtue applied to politics (Tocqueville 1966 [1835 and 1840]: 237–8). As a French observer writing on the U.S., this view is perhaps too easy. These two nations have led the way on constitutionalizing enumerated rights.

Participatory Democracy

It is perhaps heresy to say such a thing, but it is possible that most citizens will be better off if their participation in politics is very limited, as in fact it is for the typical person in all large-scale representative democracies. For the vast majority of citizens in a populous representative democracy to do much more than vote in regular elections might well have negative consequences for the stability and coherence of government. As an individual you might in any case suppose more often than not that your own social ideals or your interests will be best furthered by well-organized groups and by actual politicians rather than by the participation of the mass of people who happen to share your interests and ideals. Most citizens cannot spend the time to master the issues well enough to take meaningful stands on any but occasional major issues, such as whether to go to war or to continue with a war, or whether to introduce major social legislation to address a failing economy or inequalities in their society. Madison (2001 [1787]: 329) told his fellow citizens that they should have no active role in politics beyond voting in elections. Between elections they should acquiesce in the policies of their governors.

Russell Hardin

The reason democracy might work well at all in a society as large and diverse as classical Athens is that it maps the distribution of knowledge (as in Austrian economic theory). For example, the knowledge that "Athens" had was the usual distributed knowledge of a productive and varied society with many functions to be filled (agricultural and market production, political and military leadership, etc.). No one person or even significant institution could oversee or master all of this knowledge, even in the small society of Athens. A reason for democracy's sometime failure, from going to war for example, may be that it is less good than monarchy in looking after the collective interest of the whole society, which is commonly (but not always) the interest of the monarch (this is an argument of Thomas Hobbes 1994 [1651]: Ch. 19, p. 120).[3] Hence, even if we wish to defend democracy, participatory democracy, or deliberative democracy, we should make the Austrian theory of knowledge a centerpiece of our argument. Mill (1977 [1861]: 399–400) seems to agree with this theory when he says a central administration cannot know enough to govern well. Similarly, Tocqueville (1966 [1835 and 1840]: 91) assumes a version of this theory in his claim that central administrative power cannot know enough to do its job; it excels at preventing, not doing.[4] As he notes, people may hold a firm belief without investigating it. Most people either will believe without knowing why or will not know what to believe. Few will achieve conviction born of knowledge, but such belief may not inspire the ardor and devotion that dogmatic beliefs inspire (1966 [1835 and 1840]: 187, 187n). As a consequence, people who lack time and means to study issues, can be misled easily (198).

A society of 150 or even several hundred people might be a face-to-face society, in which all can participate with all in governance of the society (see further, Laslett 1956). It is at least technically possible that Athens, with perhaps 6,000 citizens in its heyday, solved the problem of making politics work almost as though it were in a face-to-face society. But in increasing the scale from several thousand to several million or even several hundreds of million citizens, it is inconceivable that we can make the society work as though it were face-to-face. This is the fundamental problem of the application of virtually all ideal theories to large-scale contemporary democracies. Hence, democracy in, say, the U.S. does not have the appeals of democracy in Athens. Indeed, on any commonsense definition of it, participatory democracy may be neither desirable nor even possible in the U.S. if it is supposed to go much beyond voting and maybe a bit of time spent in study groups or reading political blogs.

Social Capital and Participatory Democracy

Alexis de Tocqueville (1966 [1835 and 1840]: 243) supposes that participation includes activity in associations, perhaps especially those that have no political object (513). Political activity in associations spills over into civil society, and this is a great advantage of democracy. But activity in non-political associations spills over into politics through the educational or training effect of activities in associations, activities whose mastery may be useful in manifold ways, political and private. They create a special form of human capital.[5] Civil associations therefore pave the way for political ones and vice versa (521). The result is enlightenment born of experience (304), participation in legislation, not merely from reading or study. A standard criticism of at least U.S. democracy in our time is that civil society is crumbling and therefore democracy is threatened with decline (Putnam 2000). We supposedly participate less in various non-political groups and therefore also less in politics. This thesis still is in need of demonstration. At best it is a broad but weak correlation, not a causally demonstrated fact. In recent decades in the U.S., citizens have mobilized over civil rights and the war in Vietnam, but even in such major crises, the number of those who are active is small. The feminist movement may have engaged more people than either of these movements, possibly because there were often significant personal benefits from participating.

Note a peculiarity of the civil society thesis. We live locally. Tocqueville's observations of civic life in the U.S. are almost all also local. He says it is hard to get people to be interested in general politics, easier to interest them in local issues that directly affect their own property (Tocqueville 1966 [1835 and 1840]: 511). It is not clear that what he recounts is relevant to national politics today unless, perhaps, it affects elections to national legislative bodies. Local politics is in decline in many places where professional managers run many public projects. Our more grievous problem, however, is that national politics seems to be in decline. This problem seems to be a matter of the logic and institutionalization of political power more than a matter of the popular stance toward government. Politicians have become a class apart. If participation in local associations affects national politics, we need an account of how that works.

Here is Tocqueville's (1966 [1835 and 1840]: 520) limited account. He says that the more we join in associations, the more we develop a capacity to pursue great aims in common. This seems to imply that we develop both human and social capital. Such capital might be of use and even of great value in varied contexts. With some training through your membership in associations, you may find it easy to affect how you or family members are treated by government agencies, such as schools. You might also locally develop the capacity to affect politics at higher levels, although there seems to be relatively little activity of citizens taking part in national politics.

Ideal Theory

Anyone who reads contemporary theories of democracy must often be led to wonder where the world of democratic practice fits in the theory. In his *Considerations on Representative Government*, John Stuart Mill (1977 [1861]) spends his last few chapters trolling through problems of how to make democratic government work on the ground in various contexts. He gets lost and loses his readers in a morass of minute points, but one can at least say he stays relevant to our experience because it is actual experience that drives his concern. Bernard Manin (1997) fits democratic practice over the millennia to the theories it might ground or reflect. He relates changing conceptions of democracy to changing social conditions, especially to the increasing scale of the societies to be governed.

Much of contemporary democratic theory, however, is argued at the level of almost abstract theory, as a definitionalist or ideal exercise. Some theorists might be committed to ideal theory independently of its relevance to actual practice. For example, one might hold that the practice in some nation should not be a guide to us in

Russell Hardin

creating democratic institutions elsewhere. This complaint might generally be apt. But the practice in many nations that have struggled to create democratic institutions might suggest real limits on what can be done – or real possibilities for what we might do. Hence, actual conditions set the context for democratic theory. The only theory that can be compelling for us must be pragmatic, not ideal. David Estlund (2007) holds that there is no need to show or argue the practical importance of the theory. Not even for its possibility? Can our theory require that every child in Lake Woebegon be above average?

Note that hostility to a democratic political philosophy that is utopian does not turn on such facts as that voters are woefully ignorant (see further, Estlund 2007: Ch. 1). The deep problem with voter ignorance is that it is entirely rational and moral (Hardin 2006a). It would be wrong for most voters to invest substantially in mastering politics and public policy. Most voters should not waste the time to become far more knowledgeable unless they have reasons other than their own effect as voters on the outcomes. Fear of normative standards that just happen unlikely ever to be met is not the issue here. The issue is also not whether adequate knowledge could be had, but whether it *should* be. There are far more valuable things, including morally praiseworthy things, most people can do with their time than master knowledge of politics and political possibilities. One might read Schumpeter's (1950 [1942]: 262) account of voter ignorance as critical or even accusatory. But it can be better read as justificatory. He is explaining from the voters' own interests why they know so little about politics. And his explanation justifies their ignorance.

Incidentally, this rejection of ideal theory applies as well to moral as to political theory.[6] For example, the moral rules deduced from Kant's Kingdom of Ends (fully rational beings) are irrelevant for us and our world because there is good reason to suppose that they should not apply in the real world of far less morally committed or rational beings. Indeed, to apply some of them in the real world would be heinous and immoral, and yet Kantian theory is commonly supposed to require that we follow these rules. A utilitarianism that assumes that utility is interpersonally comparable over very fine distinctions in utility, as critics of utilitarianism often assume, is similarly irrelevant to our lives and is little more than a game that some philosophers play.

Deliberative Democracy

Much of the literature on deliberative democracy is about how it should work. Too little is about how it is actually used in real societies.[7] Deliberative democracy might be possible if defined in certain ways, but then it is unlikely to be of any real interest. For example, at a public meeting on these issues, when I said there is very little real deliberation in American politics, I was rebuked with the claim that there is deliberation everywhere, for example in the U.S. Congress. I noted that there had been little deliberation in Congress in recent years or even decades, that speeches in the Congress are more about re-election than about designing good policies, and my respondent retorted that there is deliberation among the (un-elected) staff members of congressional committees.[8]

A major argument for deliberation is that it helps us discover truths. For example, Manin (1997: 185) somewhat vaguely says that debate discovers truth; hence the best way to make laws is through a body that can debate, such as a legislature or a parliament. This is vague because it does not specify the kind of truth that the legislative body can discover. There are three distinctively different issues for the truths that might be sought in politics. First, deliberation cannot lead us to find any truths that do not exist, such as the normative "truth" of what is the best way to live or to organize government. Values and ends are not decidable. Reason will not determine them. They may finally be agreeable, and a substantial majority may adopt or support the same values or ends. But this is a contingent, not a necessary, fact. The only discovery at issue here is not that of intellectual debate but that of a poll of everyone to find out what their diverse interests might be.

Second, deliberation can lead us to a better grasp of better means to achieve a goal by discovering causal facts. But deliberation over means is apt to be especially productive of good insights if the deliberators are experts of relevant kinds. The average run of the population cannot compete with expertise on such matters, nor for that matter can elected officials. The broad population is actually asked to perform the task of discovering truth in one very important realm: trial by jury. The history of the rise of trial by jury undercuts some of the normative acclaim for it. In the days of circuit-riding judges in ancient England, the judges had no resources for establishing the truth of any accusation, so they turned to the peers of the accused to ask them whether the accused was likely to have committed the crime at issue (Green 1985). Pity the poor person in a village who was widely disliked, an offense that must often have become capital.

Third, deliberation can help us discover the seriousness of our disagreements over ends. In its early history, parliamentary government was supposed to yield virtually unanimous agreement over policies because there was supposed to be such agreement, and indeed votes were virtually unanimous (Kishlanski 1977). Homogeneity arguably made direct democracy possible in ancient republics (Manin 1997: 186)[9] but the growth of states eventually fractured homogeneity. And the hope for unanimity in modern legislatures or polities is long dead. When students today are told that there was a time when parliamentary bodies voted with near unanimity on major issues they are incredulous.

A best state of affairs

Perhaps the biggest single disagreement between contemporary rational choice theorists and Aristotle (and other Greeks) is Aristotle's insufficiently argued assumption that there is a best form for society. James Buchanan and many others are withering in their scorn for such a view (see especially Brennan and Buchanan 1985). Perhaps the main result of any effort at participatory democracy will be to re-discover the lack of coherence of popular views and interests and therefore the lack of a best state of affairs to which we can aspire politically.

Joseph Schumpeter (1950 [1942]) says there is no public interest in the sense of an interest that overrides individual interests. He does not rule out the possibility that we might all agree on some interest or policy, but in that case the public interest is merely an aggregation of the individual interests. Brian Barry's example of a public interest is that Americans would universally agree that turning the bombers of the Strategic Air Command against American cities would be bad. An easy posi-

Russell Hardin

tive good is the driving convention, and the variety of conventions – about two dozen – mentioned by Hume (2000 [1739–40]: Book 3). Brennan and Buchanan distinguish the difference between truth-seeking and value-seeking. Only in choosing means to accomplish a political goal is truth-seeking at issue for them. For deciding on the goal, truth-seeking is not at issue. Some deliberative democrats seem to suppose that the conclusions of deliberation constitute the truth about rightness or justice. This might be an odd move from facts to values. This move is philosophically legitimate only if we make agreement the criterion of the right, as some theorists of deliberative democracy do (see further, Christiano 2004, p. 267).

Political debate is about both truth and values or ends. It is about the best means (commonly a social scientific or military issue, and therefore an issue of the facts of the matter) and about ends, although it would be wrong to speak of the best ends (unless one is not yet in the world of modern political and moral philosophy). In characterizing Hannah Arendt's views, David Estlund (2007: 21) says, "truth is not an appropriate category, since politics must not begin with conclusions." Because facts often matter in normative political debate, debate over the truth of one or another fact is not a matter of beginning with conclusions, nor does it even guarantee reaching conclusions, at least not conclusions that most or all would accept (social science is often very hard). Arendt here seems simply not to note the clear distinction between truth (causal claims) about means and truth (value claims) about ends.

The Platonic and Aristotelian assumption (not always consistently held) that there is a best way to organize a society seems absurd in our world. A best way to organize a society of radical Muslims and liberal secularists? Utterly hopeless. But Austrian and other economic knowledge arguments continue to work for economic productivity even in our societies. Economic production is relatively distributed and much of it is local.

Means and expertise

Knowledge has several distinct roles in governance. Sometimes we need to have expert knowledge. Sometimes knowledge is very important for selecting a point of coordination. Sometimes knowledge is local in some compelling sense. Austrian economic and social theory is grounded in the value or usefulness of local knowledge that cannot be aggregated. To some extent, democratic participation draws on or at least in principle takes account of such knowledge. Coordination knowledge very is important in making policies, especially if the policies are supposedly beneficial to the whole group or society.

Although putting local or coordination knowledge to work might be difficult at times, the use of expertise may be the most fraught issue in democratic practice. Are legislators eventually experts as well as representatives of particular communities? If we defer to experts, as we regularly do in medical care, civil engineering, and many other specialized undertakings, then we *de facto* make them authoritative over some issue. A move from expertise to authority is a move from truth to values and is clearly illegitimate philosophically, with perhaps a major exception. Democratic theory probably requires a legal system with courts.

Democratically elected office holders, as discussed further below, are *de facto* a professional class. Their training is not via educational institutions but via trial by fire. They have specialized skills that can be used to benefit citizens but that can also be used for self-aggrandizement. Without the occasional Dan Rostenkowski, we cannot expect tax or other complicated legislation to be well crafted or to be made appealing to enough legislators to get it passed. But when a Rostenkowski is enormously sophisticated at handling such issues, he may turn his mind to benefiting himself through corrupt actions. Yet, while in office and before exposure, he is an authoritative figure, because what he says on tax policy has a great chance of becoming the policy. And citizens would think it right, more or less, for him to have such authority as devolved upon him over the years through standard congressional practices of selecting a leadership. His expertise brings him authority.

Conflicting interests

To this day, commentators still refer to *the* public good as though there were a relatively far-reaching consensus on many political issues.[10] In fact, however, even to speak of political issues is usually to evoke a sense of conflict. For example, increase in national income is generally thought to be a good. But that depends on how the increase happens. If poverty increases while overall wealth increases, many would think the change not a good.[11] For another example, almost everyone favors welfare programs to some degree to prevent grim poverty, especially for children. But Europeans increasingly worry that generous welfare programs are a major factor in the separatist isolation and growing hostility of immigrant groups who, with welfare supports, avoid integration into the national economy, polity, and society (Buruma 2006). For virtually every conceivable object of general improvement, one can imagine tradeoffs that would make it not a unanimously approved change. There is almost in principle no chance of consensus on major social issues.

For political deliberators who are open to discovery, coming to recognize the depth of real disagreements and conflicts of interest is a major result of deliberation, perhaps the major result. This seems to be the point of Manin's (1997: 186–7) claim that it is the collective and diverse character of the representative organ, and not belief in any supposed virtues of debate, that explains the role of discussion in a legislature. As he says, the very idea of representative government is virtually always linked with the idea of diversity, meaning difference of views and hence likely conflict. The founders of representative democracy did not confuse parliament with a learned society (190). For theorists of deliberative democracy, the fact that there is legislative debate is thought to justify legislative results. It apparently does not matter that today the staffs of un-elected bureaucrats draft most laws of any significance (191). Or that a disconcerting fraction of major pieces of legislation are crafted for their value in enabling the re-election of legislators (see, e.g., Dahlberg and Johansson 2002).

Audience Democracy

Bernard Manin (1997) argues that representative democracy has been transformed into "audience democracy" in recent times. The main phenomenon is that socioeconomic status no longer determines voting patterns (218). Voters choose a person, not a platform or party. And they campaign by television. We therefore see not a change in

Russell Hardin

representative democracy but a change in the nature of those who are elected. They are media experts, as remarkably analyzed by the great playwright Arthur Miller (2001). We still meet the minimum vision of democracy that, at the very least, we can turn incumbents out of office – although this claim is severely undercut by deliberate gerrymandering of legislative electoral districts to protect incumbents of both major U.S. parties. (This change contributes to the rise of corporatist democracy, as discussed below.)

The end results of these developments are that politicians have the initiative in setting the terms of debate and that the electorate is reduced to being an audience. Candidates are the performers whom they watch (Manin 1997: 222–3). This change results in part from a change of issues: left-right economic policy is no longer a big divider because the view that the economy should mostly run itself has become widely accepted by members of both main parties in the U.S. and often of the multiple parties in Europe, so that the issue space of relevance to voters is increasingly fractured and largely incoherent (see further, Hardin 2006b, Chapter 8).[12]

Similarly, as C. E. Lindblom (1977) persuasively argues, business does so much of what government needs that it is perverse to think of it as a mere interest group, on a par with doctors, farmers, environmentalists, or lawyers. It is a partner, indeed a more than equal partner in many respects. On many fundamentally important issues, it is even a partner to labor and its unions because its success or failure means success or failure for workers, as workers in dying or shrinking industries learn all too painfully. Union and corporation leaders join together in lobbying government on many issues of joint concern. While that relationship was at its height, however, corporations used their power to slowly destroy unions and eventually even to destroy workers' jobs. Nevertheless, most of us are economically dependent on large corporations and we do not generally oppose them politically. The economy dominated by large corporations is one of the things Tocqueville thinks are done well outside the control or sponsorship of government.

Unfortunately these changes elevate the problem of the cost of information for knowing how to vote one's interests, because parties no longer symbolize or stand for specific interests (Manin 1997: 228) and business interests do not even define a party. Party democracy in an earlier era made it possible to vote prospectively because parties could be identified with important interests. That is much harder in the age of audience democracy, when elected office-holders are in a performance role as individuals rather than as representatives of a party, and when government officials are virtually a class apart so that they have more interests in common with each other than with groups in their constituencies. The result of all of these changes is to heighten the problem that voters have in learning enough to vote in their interests. These developments undercut the possibilities of meaningful participation and deliberation. The rise of theories of deliberative democracy therefore comes when their applicability has diminished to almost nothing. Their core idea is too late for us.

Corporate Democracy

Tocqueville (1966 [1835 and 1840]: 242–3), echoing Adam Smith, remarks on the bustle and activity of a free country. Despite all of the bustle, there seems to be declining participation or declining payoffs for participation in politics and public-spirited activities in general despite the prevalence of major issues for democratic decision. In, for example, Sweden over the past several decades such major issues have included whether to maintain the welfare state substantially, to be open to substantial migration, to continue to rely on nuclear energy, and to move fully into the European Union. In the United States during the same period, wars loom distressingly very large. But policies on racial division, taxation, and welfare have also had major effects on the society. Many of the changes in these areas have come more from political leaders than from popular politics, although substantial protests probably played real roles in desegregation and the withdrawal from Vietnam.

Many major policies adopted during those decades were not subject to extensive popular democratic participation but were determined by administrations elected for other reasons.[13] The policies were then undemocratically imposed from above. The change in the Swedish driving convention from driving on the left to driving on the right in September 1967 was autocratically carried out by the national government after the change was overwhelmingly rejected in an advisory, non-binding 1955 referendum by a vote of 82.9 percent to 15.5 percent.[14] The administration of George W. Bush has introduced some of the most far-reaching policy changes of the postwar era, and yet few of those changes have been supported by popular mandates. Even if one supposes that extensive democratic participation is good or is likely to have good results, one must grant that it commonly has only very limited effectiveness in determining policy.

The story of these changes is not one of popular use of social capital nor is it plausible that such capital could have substantially affected the adoptions of the relevant policies. Popular participation in elections and the social capital that helped to mobilize voters around the relevant issues presumably did play substantial roles in the nature of the parties that ran these two nations during the 1930s. But it would be stretching to say that social capital had any articulate effect on the nature of the policies that were adopted then. In the U.S., for example, Franklin Roosevelt was empowered basically to do what he could to bring prosperity back, and in the early 1940s he was empowered to run the war as he saw fit. Extensive application of social capital to influence the major policies of these two periods would not have been beneficial for any but perhaps very special interests. In 1937, five years into Roosevelt's administration, the economy reached its lowest point, and yet he was re-elected handily in 1940.

This assessment of the effects of extensive political participation suggests that such participation might not merely be unlikely but also be destructive. It would be costly at the level of the individual citizen in the following sense. A typical citizen in a very large representative democracy can have only vanishingly small effect on political outcomes (Downs 1957; Schumpeter 1950 [1942]). If this is true, then typical citizens have little incentive to vote. But if this is true, then it cannot be worth very much to these citizens to invest in learning enough about policies to vote intelligently in their own interests or according to their own ideals (Hardin 2002). Indeed, one can reasonably say that it is good that many people invest their time in other, more rewarding activities rather than in mastering public policy issues. Hortatory claims that citizens should participate fully in politics are hence wrong on two counts. Such participation would commonly be disruptive without offsetting benefit and it

Russell Hardin

would take citizens away from doing more valuable things for which they have greater competence (see Downs 1957: 260ff., on rational abstention).

Unfortunately, these trends augur ill for democracy as representative. Instead, we increasingly have what can be called corporate democracy, with the government separating itself ever further from the people and making the governors the officers of our corporation. These officers make policy more or less independently of popular will because much of the time there is no easily specified popular will. On some issues large parts of the populace can be mobilized to take part at the least through electing officials whose views they think are in line with their own. For example, so-called moral issues of abortion and gay marriage and issues such as immigration that might entail some conflict of interest can provoke voters to act.

As John C. Calhoun (1992 [1853]) argues, the members of the government become a separate class by virtue of holding their offices. They even share an interest in defending all members of this class against the larger society despite the fact that they are divided into supposedly conflicting parties. In the U.S., for example, they collude in gerrymandering their electoral districts to secure their re-election at an astonishing high rate. Anthony Downs (1957: 112) contends "that the desire to obtain and keep power per se plays a larger role in the practical operation of democratic politics than the desire to implement ideological doctrines or serve particular social groups."

It would be wrong to argue that we should construct government to be corporate in this sense. But it is also wrong to ignore the powerful forces that push us toward such a form of "democratic" government. The second President Bush openly declared that he would run the government as a committee of like-minded bulldogs who would push their own program. He asserted to Congress that he would sign hundreds of pieces of legislation but would regularly append a commentary – a signing statement – saying to what extent he would or would not actually be bound by them. But the drift into corporate democracy is largely unintended. We the citizens who are not members of the governing class enjoy the fruits of private life. In that life, as Tocqueville (1966 [1835 and 1840]: 244–5) insists, it is not the things done by public administration that are great in a democracy but those things done without its help and beyond its sphere.[15] Democracy may bring no great creations but it will help to bring great prosperity and well-being, which may distract us from government as we focus on our individual and familial prosperity.

Normative Claims for Democracy

Tocqueville (1966 [1835 and 1840]: 235) says that in aristocracy men do evil without intent; in democracies they bring about good without intent. Oddly, beginning with the rise of corporate democracy in recent decades, the politically quiet mass of citizens have helped to bring about what they would think bad without intending to. They have helped their government to hive itself off from the larger society. Possibly not even the politicians who are class beneficiaries of this development recognize it and they might even insist on calling themselves servants of the people. Some service.

Manin (1997: 189) says that what turns a proposition into a public decision is not discussion but consent. But for citizens consent has come to have even less forceful meaning than what Madison insisted is the role of the citizen apart from voting in elections: acquiescence. In his time, many may have known that they merely acquiesced. After all, in explaining the workings of the proposed new constitution, drafted in 1787, Madison forcefully told them that was all that was wanted from them. Many people in our time are insulted by the claim that they merely acquiesce. Consent does not make a political action or decision good or right (Hardin 1990). Moreover, although "consent seems an appropriate basis for legitimate authority in morally permissible or even admirable associations, it is not the basis of political authority" (Christiano 2004: 283).

Typically, you and I are bound by democratic decisions. This is not a normative but only a positive claim. A competent democratic state can generally enforce its decisions. Unfortunately, this means that a corrupted democracy can do so as well, as can a competent autocracy. The implication of audience and corporate democracies is that they can broadly fail to achieve normatively compelling outcomes. Hence we cannot make a straight normative claim in defense of such democracy. Tocqueville supposes, with Smith, that our self-seeking will benefit the larger society without our intending to serve the good of the society. In Smith, my profit-seeking will provide desired goods to others. "The natural effort of every individual to better his own condition, when suffered to exert itself with freedom and security, is so powerful a principle, that it is alone, and without any assistance, not only capable of carrying on the society to wealth and prosperity, but of surmounting a hundred impertinent obstructions with which the folly of human laws too often encumbers its operations; though the effect of these obstructions is always more or less either to encroach upon freedom, or to diminish its security" (Smith 1976 [1776] Book 4, Ch. 5, p. 540).

Therefore, it is the interest of each to work for the good of all (Tocqueville (1966 [1835 and 1840]: 525; this is also the view of Downs 1957: 28–9). Because he is implicitly a welfarist, Tocqueville concludes that the doctrine of self interest properly understood is *the best moral theory* for our time (1966 [1835 and 1840]: 527). This, however, is presumably not a support for democracy, because, again, he supposes that what is truly great in a democratic society is what the citizens themselves achieve independently of what government does.

Downs (1957: 19) asserts that there is only one normative element in democracy. That is the principle: one person, one vote. In truth, of course, democracies have often violated this principle, sometimes by giving some individuals more than one vote and sometimes by depriving many citizens of any vote at all. Mill (1977 [1861]: 473–9) favored giving more than one vote to the educated elite; he refers to universal but unequal suffrage, and even then only of those who are literate. Many democrats argue that the great merit of democracy is its capacity to throw the rascals out. But even that capacity has been grievously weakened in many cases. Elected tyrants win large majorities to amend their constitutions to allow them to continue "serving" indefinitely despite constitutionally prescribed term limits. American legislators have gerrymandered themselves into extremely secure voting districts. In the supposedly decisive election of 2006, the U.S. House of Representatives saw less than one incumbent in twenty lose their seats. We can turn them out primarily when they attempt to move on to higher office. With their control of party lists, European parties commonly guarantee the selection of party leaders for enduring incumbency even when those leaders have done very badly in office.

Russell Hardin

Concluding Remarks

Democracy in any traditionally strong sense does not and very likely cannot work in our context. Mill (1977 [1861]: 467) supposes that fully representative democracy is the only true democracy in a complex society.[16] Almost everyone seems to agree. But Mill's defenses of this view are not convincing. He says that only through participation can one ensure one's own rights (404). One might wonder how this is to work. For example, even where they had the vote, black Americans in the 1950s were hardly able to secure their own rights. Mill also sweepingly says that the best government is participatory. Madison (2001 [1787]: 329) forcefully disagrees if participation is supposed to go very far beyond voting. In *Federalist* 63 he says that the newly drafted U.S. constitution markedly differed from classical democracies in that it provided for "*the total exclusion of the people in their collective capacity* from any share" in the proceedings of government. And Mill says that participation in all things is useful. For millions of people attempts at participation must commonly have produced frustration and even harm, not benefits. All of Mill's claims add up to commend representative government (412). Strangely, however, he concludes that among the foremost benefits of participation is education (467–8). The great educational lesson many people learn is that their participation does not count in any significant political result. A bit of numerical logic would be enough to teach this lesson, although that particular bit of numerical logic seems very difficult to master. Of course, participatory government in a small state need not be representative, so Mill here is addressing his kind of society, of many millions of citizens.

The claim that democracy is good for the reason that it enhances personal autonomy or character independently of its effects on the public business is attributed to Mill. But the argument that democracy is good because it contributes to our personal development is odd even in Mill's (1977 [1861]: 400) own discussion of it. He disqualifies the claim in his account of the need for causal efficacy if our actions are to have meaning:

> A person must have a very unusual taste for intellectual exercise in and for itself, who will put himself to the trouble of thought when it is to have no outward effect, or qualify himself for functions which he has no chance of being allowed to exercise. The only sufficient incitement to mental exertion, in any but a few minds in a generation, is the prospect of some practical use to be made of its results.

The test of real and vigorous thinking, the thinking which ascertains truths instead of dreaming dreams, is successful application to practice (Mill 1977 [1861]: Ch. 3, paras. 2 and 17). With these claims, Mill gives full force to the Schumpeter–Downs argument that most citizens do not even have adequate reason to know enough to vote intelligently, because he recognizes that "all cannot, in a community exceeding a single small town, participate personally in any but some very minor portions of the public business," so that they have insufficient incitement to mental exertion over politics (Ch. 3, final para.; see also Pateman 1970: 28–35).

Furthermore, such a democracy has within it the tendency toward corporate democracy and the end of extensive representation. It need not lead to disaster to have some degree of democracy, as an attempt to introduce it in Burundi did and as another attempt perhaps will in Iraq if ever it is put into place there. But we should be glad if the sum of all private undertakings far surpasses anything the government might have done, as Tocqueville (1966 [1835 and 1840]: 95) supposed nearly two centuries ago in the fresh bloom of a democratic society heady with expectations.

It would be wrong to say we should therefore junk representative democracy and try something else. Historically we have tried many other forms of government and they have not been better than democracy with all its flaws. Perhaps corporate democracy will fall into bad hands and we will suffer badly from it. But in advanced societies, there may be scant possibility that anyone can gain full control of government against both the class of citizens and Calhoun's class of our governors. Moreover, the countervailing power of business may constrain – as well as enable – any government that wishes to prosper. Classical liberals might well be glad that business performs this political service for us because it is a service that citizens cannot perform for themselves, and it is a service that democratic (or any other) government cannot perform for us.

Notes

1 Subsequent contributions are voluminous. See Converse (1975, 1990, 2000); Delli Carpini and Keeter (1996); Friedman (1998); Kull and Destler (1999); Somin (1998); Stimson (2004). There are also many arguments against the thesis of voter ignorance and also many arguments that such ignorance does not actually matter.

2 For recent accountings, see special issue of *Critical Review* 18 (1–2) (2006).

3 Tocqueville (1966 [1835 and 1840]: 228–30) has a similar view. He says that democracy is inferior in the conduct of foreign affairs (228). In foreign policy, aristocracy's interest is typically the same as the nation's (229). An aristocracy has very stable views; a monarch can vacillate or die; an aristocracy is too small to be swept by passions; an aristocratic body is a firm and enlightened man who never dies (230).

4 This claim recalls a bit of standard French humor: Bureaucrats have almost no power. The only power they have is the power to deny any reasonable request. At the time he wrote, Tocqueville (1966 [1835 and 1840]: 125) claimed that there were 138,000 government bureaucrats in France but only 12,000 in the U.S.

5 Many people acquire such capital through their professional activities (Hardin 1999).

6 Estlund (2007) rhetorically asks whether utopian moral theory might similarly be criticized for its impossibility.

7 But see Gutmann and Thompson (1996).

8 The exchange was reminiscent of the claims of the Kingston trio that their next number would be in French. And for those who speak French, the introduction continued, it is in Louisiana creole French; and for those who speak Louisiana creole French, it is in Louisiana creole French as spoken in northwestern Louisiana. Eventually the field of play could be narrowed down to a relevant realm for the claims.

9 Mill (1977 [1861]: 548–9) continues to hold this view into the modern era when homogeneity is not possible in any large nation. He says that boundaries of governments should coincide with boundaries of nationalities.

10 Mill (1977 [1861]: 447) often refers to the general interest and seems to suppose that it is a broad category.

11 Rawls (1999 [1971]) and Okun (1975) suppose that there is a substantial tradeoff between overall production and equality.

12 Some evidence for this claim is the nearly universal praise for Milton Friedman after his death in November 2006. He was once a pariah to liberals, but today many of his views have become widely accepted and he is seen as having trumped John Maynard Keynes in policy circles.

13 The argument of this section draws on Hardin (2004).

14 See "Rules of the Road" at www.answers.com/topic/rules-of-the-road.

15 Mill (1977 [1861]: 396–7) perhaps disagrees a bit with this claim. He says that government must enable the people to do well. Tocqueville seems to think that it is sufficient for government to leave us largely alone.

16 Mill does not add the disclaimer of applying his view only to a complex society. But he is clearly concerned with the England of his own time, and that was a very complex society with numerous groups often in conflict with each other.

References

Ashlin, Alison, and Richard J. Ladle. 2006. "Environmental Science Adrift in the Blogosphere," *Science* 312 (April 14): 201. This brief article is enhanced at www.sciencemag.org/cgi/content/full/312/5771/201/DC1 (active as of November 25, 2006).

Brennan, Geoffrey, and James M. Buchanan. 1985. *The Reason of Rules: Constitutional Political Economy* (Cambridge: Cambridge University Press).

Buruma, Ian. 2006. *Murder in Amsterdam: The Death of Theo van Gogh and the Limits of Tolerance* (New York: Penguin).

Calhoun, John C. [1853] 1992. *A Disquisition on Government.* In *Union and Liberty: The Political Philosophy of John C. Calhoun*, ed. Ross M. Lence (Indianapolis, IN: Liberty Fund), pp. 3–78.

Christiano, Thomas. 2004. "The Authority of Democracy," *Journal of Political Philosophy* 12 (3): 266–90.

Condorcet, Jean Antoine. [1795] 1999. "Essay on the Application of Mathematics to the Theory of Decision-Making," in Condorcet, *Selected Writings* (Indianapolis, IN: Hackett), pp. 33–70.

Converse, Philip E. 2006 [1964]. "The Nature of Belief Systems in Mass Publics," *Critical Review* 18 (1–2): 1–75.

Converse, Philip E. 1975. "Public Opinion and Voting Behavior," in Fred I. Greenstein and Nelson W. Polsby, eds., *Handbook of Political Science.* Reading, MA: Addison-Wesley, Vol. 4.

Converse, Philip E. 1990. "Popular Representation and the Distribution of Information," in John A. Ferejohn and James Kuklinski, eds., *Information and Democratic Processes.* Urbana, IL: University of Illinois Press.

Converse, Philip E. 2000. "Assessing the Capacity of Mass Electorates," *Annual Review of Political Science* 3: 331–53.

Dahlberg, Matz, and Eva Johansson. 2002. "On the Vote-Purchasing Behavior of Incumbent Governments." *American Political Science Review* 96 (March): 27–40.

Delli Carpini, Michael X., and Scott Keeter. 1996. *What Americans Know about Politics and Why It Matters* (New Haven, CT: Yale University Press).

Downs, Anthony, *An Economic Theory of Democracy* (New York: Harper and Row, 1957).

Estlund, David. "*Democratic Authority: A Philosophical Framework*" (Princeton, NJ: Princeton University Press, 2007).

Friedman, Jeffrey. 1998. "Public Ignorance and Democratic Theory," *Critical Review* 12 (4): 397–411.

Green, Thomas Andrew, *Verdict According to Conscience: Perspectives on the English Criminal Trial Jury, 1200–1800* (Chicago: University of Chicago Press, 1985).

Gutmann, Amy, and Dennis Thompson. 1996. *Democracy and Disagreement* (Cambridge, MA: Harvard University Press).

Hardin, Russell. 1990. "Contractarianism: Wistful Thinking," *Constitutional Political Economy* 1: 35–52.

Hardin, Russell. 1999. "Social Capital," in James Alt, Margaret Levi, and Elinor Ostrom, eds., *Competition and Cooperation: Conversations with Nobelists about Economics and Political Science* (New York: Russell Sage Foundation), pp. 170–89.

Hardin, Russell. 2002. "The Street-Level Epistemology of Democratic Participation," *Journal of Political Philosophy* 10 (2): 212–29.

Hardin, Russell. 2004. "Transition to Corporate Democracy?" in *Building a Trustworthy State in Post-Socialist Transition*, ed. Janos Kornai and Susan Rose-Ackerman (New York: Palgrave Macmillan), pp. 175–97.

Hardin, Russell. 2006a. "Ignorant Democracy," *Critical Review* 18 (1–2): 179–95.

Hardin, Russell. 2006b. *Trust* (London: Polity Press).

Hobbes, Thomas. [1651] 1994. *Leviathan*, ed. Edwin Curley (Indianapolis, IN: Hackett).

Hume, David. [1739–40] 2000. *A Treatise of Human Nature* (Oxford: Oxford University Press), ed. David Fate Norton and Mary J. Norton.

Kull, Steven, and I. M. Destler. 1999. *Misreading the Public: The Myth of a New Isolationism* (Washington, DC: Brookings Institution Press).

Kishlanski, Mark. 1977. "The Emergence of Adversary Politics in the Long Parliament," *Journal of Modern History* 49 (4): 240.

Laslett, Peter. 1956. "The Face to Face Society," in Peter Laslett, ed., *Philosophy, Politics and Society*, 1st ser. (Oxford, Blackwell), pp. 157–84.

Lindblom, Charles E. 1977. *Politics and Markets: The World's Political-Economic Systems* (New York: Basic Books).

Madison, James. 2001 [1787]. "Federalist 63," in Alexander Hamilton, John Jay, and James Madison, *The Federalist*, ed. George W. Carey and James McClellan (Indianapolis, IN.: Liberty Fund), pp. 325–32.

Manin, Bernard. 1997. *The Principles of Representative Government* (Cambridge: Cambridge University Press).

Mill, John Stuart. 1977 [1861]. *Considerations on Representative Government*, in Mill, *Essays on Politics and Society*, Vol. 19 of *Collected Works of John Stuart Mill* (Toronto: University of Toronto Press), ed. J. M. Robson, pp. 371–577.

Miller, Arthur. 2001. *On Politics and the Art of Acting* (New York: Viking).

Okun, Arthur M. 1975. *Equality and Efficiency: The Big Tradeoff* (Washington, DC: Brookings Institution).

Pateman, Carole. 1970. *Participation and Democratic Theory* (Cambridge: Cambridge University Press).

Putnam, Robert D. 2000. *Bowling Alone: The Collapse and Revival of American Community* (New York: Simon and Schuster).

Rawls, John. 1999 [1971]. *A Theory of Justice* (Cambridge, MA: Harvard University Press).

Schumpeter, Joseph A. 1950 [1942]. *Capitalism, Socialism and Democracy*, 3rd edn (New York: Harper).

Smith, Adam. 1976 [1776]. *An Inquiry into the Nature and Causes of the Wealth of Nations*, ed. R. H. Campbell, A. S. Skinner, and W. B. Todd (Oxford: Oxford University Press).

Somin, Ilya. 1998. "Voter Ignorance and the Democratic Ideal" *Critical Review* 12 (4): 413–58.

Stimson, James A. 2004. *Tides of Consent: How Public Opinion Shapes American Politics* (Cambridge: Cambridge University Press).

Tocqueville, Alexis de. 1966 [1835 and 1840]. *Democracy in America*, trans. George Lawrence (New York: Harper and Row).

Reflections on Deliberative Democracy

Joshua Cohen[1]

1. Introduction

For more than two decades, egalitarian-democrats have sought to describe a "post-socialist" political project. The socialist project, including its social democratic variant, comprised a set of political values and an institutional and political strategy for advancing those values. The values were egalitarian and participatory. The institutional models and the political strategy focused on the state.

Contemporary debate among egalitarian-democrats begins in the conviction that this approach is misguided, and moves along two paths.

The first, growing out of appreciation of the state's limits as an economic manager is sometimes called "asset-egalitarianism." The idea is to shift the distribution of income by changing the distribution of income-generating assets. It is an important idea, particularly with pressures from globalization on income security, but not my topic here.[2]

A second – and this will provide my focus – is more political. Building on what I will describe as "radical-democratic" ideas, it seeks to construct models of political decision in which "local" players can be involved more directly in regulation and in collective problem solving, with a center that coordinates local efforts, rather than dictating the terms of those efforts. Thus, local – or, more exactly, lower level actors (nation-states or national peak organizations of various kinds; regions, provinces or sub-national associations within these, and so on down to whatever neighborhood is relevant to the problem at hand) – are given autonomy to experiment with their own solutions to broadly defined problems of public policy. In return they furnish higher-level units with rich information about the goals as well as the progress they are making towards achieving them. The periodic pooling of results reveals the defects of parochial solutions, and allows the elaboration of standards for comparing local achievements, exposing poor performers to criticism, and making good ones (temporary) models for emulation.

This "radical-democratic" project builds on two distinct strands of thought.[3]

With Rousseau, radical democrats are committed to broader *participation* in public decision-making – though not, as Rousseau supposed, through regular meetings of a legislative assembly open to all citizens.[4] According to this first strand, citizens should have greater direct roles in public choices or, in a less demanding formulation, participate in politics on the basis of substantive political judgments and be assured that officials will be responsive and accountable to their concerns and judgments. Though more participatory democrats disagree on the precise locus of expanded participation, they all are troubled when democratic participation is largely confined to a choice between parties competing for control of government, and particularly when that choice is not founded on clearly articulated substantive programmatic-political differences between and among parties and pursued with the expectation that the parties will be held accountable to their announced programs. The underlying participatory idea is that citizens in a democracy are to engage with the substance of law and policy, and not simply delegate responsibility for such substantive engagement to representatives.

Along with participation, radical democrats emphasize *deliberation*. Instead of a politics of power and interest, radical democrats favor a deliberative democracy in which citizens address public problems by reasoning together about how best to solve them – in which, at the limit, no force is at work, as Jürgen Habermas said, "except that of the better argument."[5] According to the deliberative interpretation, democracy is a political arrangement that ties the exercise of collective power to reason-giving among those subject to collective decisions. Once more, we see substantial differences among different formulations of the deliberative-democratic ideal. Some see deliberative democracy as a matter of forming a public opinion through dispersed and open public discussion and translating such opinion into legitimate law; others as a way to ensure that elections – or legislative debates, or perhaps discussions within courts or agencies – are themselves infused with information and reasoning; others as a way to bring reasoning by citizens directly to bear on addressing regulatory issues. But in all cases, the large aim of a deliberative democracy is to shift from bargaining, interest aggregation, and power to the common reason of equal citizens – democracy's public reason – as a guiding force in democratic life.[6]

In this essay, I will explore these two distinct strands of the radical-democratic project – participatory and deliberative – though I will focus on the deliberative because that is the topic here. My central point is that participation and deliberation are both important, but different and important for different reasons. Moreover, it is hard to achieve both, but the project of advancing both is coherent, attractive, and worth our attention. I begin by presenting an idea of deliberative democracy. Second, I will sketch three attractions of deliberative democracy. Third, I discuss four lines of skeptical argument. Fourth, I sketch three tensions between deliberation and participation. Fifth, I consider two political and institutional strategies for blunting those tensions. I conclude by mentioning two large challenges.

2. Deliberation

Carl Schmitt said that deliberation belongs to the world of the parliament, where legislators reason together about how to address public problems. It does not belong

Joshua Cohen

to the world of mass democracy, where ethno-culturally homogeneous peoples find leaders who pick the people's friends and enemies. According to Schmitt, "The development of modern mass democracy has made argumentative public discussion an empty formality."[7] Rejecting Schmitt's view, as well as its more benign contemporary progeny, deliberative democrats explore possibilities of combining deliberation with mass democracy. And not just explore: we are hopeful about the possibilities of fostering a more deliberative democracy.

Deliberation, generically understood, is about weighing the reasons relevant to a decision with a view to making a decision on the basis of that weighing. So an individual can make decisions deliberatively; a jury has a responsibility to deliberate; and a committee of oligarchs can deliberate: deliberation, in short, is not intrinsically democratic. The "democracy" in "deliberative democracy" is not pleonastic.

Democracy is a way of making collective decisions that connects decisions to the interests and judgments of those whose conduct is to be regulated by the decisions. The essential idea is that those governed by the decisions are treated as equals by the processes of making the decisions. Democracy, as Tocqueville emphasized, is also a kind of society – a society of equals – but I will be confining myself as a general matter to the more specifically political understanding of democracy. Of course, even if we think of democracy politically, as a way to make binding collective decisions, constructing a more deliberative democracy is not a narrowly political project: deliberative democracy requires attention to encouraging deliberative capacities, which is, *inter alia*, a matter of education, information, and organization.[8] I will return briefly to this point near the end.

Deliberative democracy, then, combines these two elements, neither reducible to the other. It is about making collective decisions and exercising power in ways that trace in some way to the reasoning of the equals who are subject to the decisions: not only to their preferences, interests, and choices, but also to their reasoning. Essentially, the point of deliberative democracy is to subject the exercise of power to reason's discipline, to what Habermas famously described as "the force of the better argument," not the advantage of the better situated. Deliberative democracy does not aim to do away with power, an idea that makes no sense; nor simply to subject power to the discipline – such as it is – of talking, because talking is not the same as reasoning (consider verbal assaults, insults, racial slurs, lies, blowing smoke, exchanging pleasantries, exploring common experiences); nor is it simply to reason together, because reasoning together may be without effect on the exercise of power.

Moreover, the notion of reason's discipline is not nearly definite enough. Plato's philosopher-guardians subject power to reason's discipline – that, at any rate, is what they say they are doing. But deliberative democracy is a kind of democracy, so the reasoning must be in some recognizable way the reasoning of the equal persons who are subject to the decisions. And not just the process of reasoning, but the content of the reasons themselves must have a connection to the democratic conception of people as equals. Deliberative democracy is about reasoning together among equals, and that means not simply advancing considerations that one judges to be reasons, but also finding considerations that others can reasonably be expected to acknowledge as reasons. That's why deliberation focuses, as a constitutive matter, on considerations of the common good, and also why – or so I have argued elsewhere – basic personal liberties are essential elements of a deliberative democracy. Deliberative democracy is not majoritarian, and these substantive conditions – the common good and personal liberties – are essential to democratic deliberation, under conditions of reasonable pluralism. In short, the ideal of deliberative democracy is to discipline collective power through the common reason of a democratic public: through democracy's public reason.[9]

To be sure, discussion, even when it is founded on reasons, may not – and often does not – issue in consensus. No account of deliberative democracy has ever suggested otherwise. All complex practical problems – from trade and security to organizing schools and transportation, providing clean water and public safety, allocating health care and ensuring fair compensation – implicate a range of distinct values, and reasonable people disagree about the precise content of and weights to be assigned to those values. In any allocative decision, for example, there are likely to be people who think that the worst-off person should have priority, others who think there should be equal chances, others who think the person who benefits most should get the good. In allocating medical resources, some will think that priority goes to the worst off; others, to those who would benefit most; others will think we should assist the largest number of people; others may hold that we should ensure that all people have fair chances at receiving help, regardless of the urgency of their situation and of expected benefits from treatment. So no matter how deliberative the democracy gets, collective decisions will always be made through voting, under some form of majority rule. Indeed, deliberation may work best when participants do not (as in a jury setting) feel the pressure to adjust their views for the sake of consensus – as if attention to reasons ensured convergence, and disagreement revealed bias or incapacity or some other failure.[10]

There may be some temptation to think that the prospect of majority rule defeats deliberation: because collective decision-making concludes with a vote, participants – anticipating that final stage of resolution – will not have any incentive to deliberate in earlier stages, so will focus instead on counting heads rather than on weighing reasons: aggregation at the end of the day, then aggregation all day. But that temptation should be resisted. Even if everyone knows that, at the end of the day, heads may be counted, they may still accept the idea of arriving at a collective judgment based on considerations that others acknowledge as reasons. They may, for example, believe that reason-giving is an important expression of respect, or that it is the right way to acknowledge the collective nature of the decision. If they do, they will be willing to deliberate in the stages leading up to the vote, even when they know a vote is coming.

Deliberative democracy, thus understood, is a distinctive interpretation of democracy: democracy, no matter how fair, no matter how informed, no matter how participatory, is not deliberative unless reasoning is central to the process of collective decision-making. Nor is democracy deliberative simply because the process and its results are reasonable: capable of being given a rational defense, even a rational defense that would be recognized as such on reflection by those subject to the decisions. The concern for reasonableness must play a role in the process. Thus the contrast between deliberative and aggregative democracy. In an aggregative democracy, citizens aim to advance their individual and group interests. If the process is fair, the results may

Joshua Cohen

well be reasonable. But unless the reasonableness is aimed at by participants in the process, we do not have deliberation.

Of course, it might be argued that reasonable results must be aimed at to be achieved, and that democracy must therefore be deliberative to be reasonable. So, for, example, if we have a hypothetical test for the rightness of decisions, where the hypothetical process involves reasoning under idealized conditions about what is best to do, then it might be said that the actual process must look something like the hypothetical to provide a basis for confidence in the rightness of results.[11] Still, it is best to see this connection between reasonableness and deliberation as a broadly empirical claim, and to keep deliberation as a way of deciding – a way that comprises both the nature of the process and the content of the reasons – distinct from reasonableness as a property of decisions.

Aggregative and deliberative democracy do not exhaust the space of interpretations of democracy. Consider a community of politically principled citizens, each of whom endorses a conception of justice. The conceptions they endorse differ, but each person accepts some conception as setting bounds on acceptable policy and decent institutions. Assume further that they do not see much point in arguing about what justice requires, though they discuss issues with an eye to generating information, and each conscientiously uses his or her own conception in reaching political decisions. No one in this political community thinks that politics is simply about advancing interests, much less a Schmittian struggle between friends and enemies. But reasoning together plays a very restricted role in public political life: the members accept that they owe one another an exercise of conscientious judgment, but not that they owe a justification by references to reasons that others might reasonably be expected to accept. I will not develop this distinction further here I mention it to underscore that the case for deliberative democracy needs to be made not simply in contrast with accounts of democracy that focus on interests and power but also in contrast with views that assume a conscientious exercise of moral-political judgment by individual citizens, although not deliberation.

This emphasis on subjecting power to reason's discipline is a thread that runs through much of the literature on deliberative democracy.[12] Thus, Amy Gutmann and Dennis Thompson say that "deliberative democracy's basic requirement is 'reason-giving'."[13] Jon Elster also emphasizes that deliberation is about argument, in fact arguments addressed to people committed to rationality and impartiality.[14] John Dryzek says that a "defining feature of deliberative democracy is that individuals participating in democratic processes are amenable to changing their minds and their preferences as a result of the reflection induced by deliberation."[15] Elsewhere he emphasizes "communication that encourages reflection upon preferences without coercion."[16] But Dryzek's characterizations of deliberative democracy are not literally *defining*: they follow from the more fundamental characteristics of deliberative democracy. The *point* of deliberative democracy is not for people to reflect on their preferences, but to decide, in light of reasons, what to do. Deciding what to do in light of reasons requires, of course, a willingness to change your mind, since you might begin the deliberative task with a view about what to do that is not supported by good reasons. But the crucial point is that Dryzek emphasizes that deliberation is basically about reasoning – about rational argument – and that other kinds of communication need to be "held to rational standards."[17]

Reflections on Deliberative Democracy

3. Reasons for Deliberative Democracy

Why is deliberative democracy a good thing? It is of course hard to deny that the exercise of collective power should be supported by appropriate reasons. But deliberative democracy is not simply the undisputed idea that the exercise of power should be rationally defensible, thus non-arbitrary. The question is why it is important to discipline the exercise of power by actually reasoning together. I will mention three considerations.

The first is about promoting justice. Thus suppose we think that requirements of justice are fixed by idealized reasoning under conditions of full information and equal standing. One argument for deliberative democracy is that actual deliberation is needed if collective decisions are to meet the standards of political right that would be accepted under idealized conditions of information and equality. So if justice is fixed by impartial reasoning in hypothetical conditions in which agents aim to justify principles to others, then, arguably, we will only achieve justice if we make collective decisions using reasoning of a similar kind. We cannot trust the achievement of justice to the pursuit of individual and group interests, even under fair conditions.

A second line of argument is that reason-giving is a distinctive form of communication, and that it may have desirable consequences, apart from promoting justice. Thus, the requirement that I defend my proposals with reasons that are capable of being acknowledged as such by others, will – whatever my own preferences – impose some desirable constraint on the proposals I can advance and defend. Of course if every proposal can be rationalized in an acceptable way, then the requirement of defending proposals with acceptable reasons will not have much effect: but I am skeptical about this claim. Moreover, the need to give reasons acceptable to others might produce desirable consequences if reason-giving itself changes preferences, or at least saliences. So while I start preferring most what is best for me or my group, the practice of defending proposals with reasons may change my preferences, dampening the tension between my beliefs about what is right or politically legitimate and my preferences: not because that is the point of deliberation, but because that is its effect. In addition, deliberation may improve results by eliciting information: though there are certainly truth-telling equilibria for strategic actors, I assume that the informational effects of deliberation depend in part on a commitment to truthfulness or sincerity in communication, which may itself be reinforced through deliberation, although it is hard to construct from nothing. But that is true about the entire account of deliberation: though deliberation may reinforce a prior commitment to argue on terms that others can acknowledge as reasons, some such prior commitment must be in place if the enterprise of mutual reason-giving is to get off the ground and be sustained.

A third case for deliberative democracy, not about consequences, is that the deliberative view expresses the idea that relations among people within a pluralistic, democratic order are relations of equals. It requires that we offer considerations that others, despite fundamental differences of outlook, can reasonably be expected to accept, not simply that we count their interests, while keeping our fingers crossed that those interests are outweighed. The idea of collective authorization is reflected not only in the processes of decision-making, but also – as I said earlier – in the form and the content of democracy's public reason.

252   **Joshua Cohen**

This point about the attractions of the deliberative interpretation of collective decisions can be stated in terms of an idea of self-government. In a deliberative democracy, laws and policies result from processes in which citizens defend solutions to common problems on the basis of what are generally acknowledged as relevant reasons. To be sure, citizens will, as I mentioned earlier, interpret the content of those considerations differently, and assign them different weights. The reasons relevant to particular domains are complex and often competing, and there often will be no clear, principled basis for ranking them: reasonable people may reasonably disagree on how they should be weighted, even after all the reasons have been aired. Nevertheless, they may accept the results of the deliberative process in part by virtue of the process having given due consideration to reasons that all reasonably accept.

When citizens take these political values seriously, political decisions are not simply a product of power and interest; even citizens whose views do not win out can see that the decisions are supported by good reasons. As a result, members can – despite disagreement – all regard their conduct as guided, in general terms, by their own reason. Establishing such political deliberation would realize an ideal of self-government or political autonomy under conditions of reasonable pluralism. It may be as close as we can get to the Rousseauean ideal of giving the law to ourselves.

4. Skepticism About Deliberation

I want now to consider four objections that have been raised against the deliberative conception of democracy. The interest of exploring the tensions between deliberation and participation will be greater if some of these concerns can be dispelled.

1. The first is about inequality. It begins with the observation that reasoning is an acquired capacity, and not equally distributed among all. So collective decision-making through reason-giving may not *neutralize* power, but may instead create a "logocracy," in which political power is effectively shifted to the rhetorically gifted (or at least to the verbally uninhibited), which may well compound existing social inequalities, and deliver political power to the educated, or economically advantaged, or men, or those possessed of cultural capital and argumentative confidence.[18]

While the concern is important and understandable, the evidence, such as it is, suggests that this objection exaggerates the feared effect, in part by "depoliticizing" it – more precisely, by underestimating the capacity to recognize and alleviate it, should it arise. Democracy, to borrow a phrase from Jane Mansbridge, is always a work in process, and much can be done to address this concern. Thus Archon Fung finds that citizen participation in Chicago policing efforts is greater in poorer neighborhoods (not a very large surprise, given crime rates in different neighborhoods), and that the city, cognizant of obvious concerns about cultural and class bias, invested resources in training participants in policing and schooling efforts.[19] Studying the case of participatory budgeting in Porto Alegre, Abers and Baiocchi find high rates of involvement by poorer, less-educated citizens, and substantial rates of participation by women and Afro-Brazilians.[20] The thread running through these and related cases is that participation is not exogenously given. Deliberative bodies can undertake affirmative measures to address participatory biases. In particular, they can help to train participants in the issues decided by the body and in how to frame arguments about the relevant policies.

Now it might be argued that in the favorable cases just noted, the deliberative bodies aim to solve relatively concrete problems – to improve policy in relatively well-defined areas (say, pertaining to the provision of local public goods) – not to have an open-ended public debate. Inequalities of argumentative skills on broader matters may resist remedy.[21] But evidence from deliberative polling suggests otherwise: deliberative capacities seem reasonably widely shared, even when issues are more abstract and less locally focused. Critics of deliberation, it seems, were too quick to conclude that deliberative decision-making empowers the verbally agile.

2. A second objection is about effectiveness. Thus it might be said that a deliberative process does not mitigate the effects of power on outcomes of collective decisions. In addressing this issue, we face a large methodological problem. As a general matter, and putting aside the issue of deliberative democracy, it is hard to make an empirically compelling case that process changes produce outcome changes, because changes in process and in result may well both be produced by some third factor: as, for example, when a party with a redistributive project empowers the less advantaged and promotes a shift in economic resources as well, thus suggesting (incorrectly) that the change in process produced the change in result.

A few studies, though not of deliberative democracy, have forcefully addressed these problems of spuriousness. Ansolabehere, Gerber, and Snyder have shown that court-ordered reapportionment in the 1960s shifted public goods spending in the states in the direction of previously underrepresented districts: a special case because reapportionment was a court-ordered exogenous shock.[22] Similarly, Chattopadhyay and Duflo have made the case that reserved seats for women on Indian village councils have led to shifts in public goods spending, with greater spending on goods that are preferred by women when the head of the village council is a woman.[23] Here the problem of spuriousness is solved by randomness in the process that determines which village councils will be headed by women. We have no comparably compelling case that increased deliberativeness leads to changes in the content of the decisions.

Still, we have some suggestive evidence. Thus, participatory budgeting in Porto Alegre and in village councils in Kerala appear to have produced substantial shifts in the allocation of public resources to the poor: in Porto Alegre, for example, there is now full coverage of water and sewers, and a threefold increase in school attendance.[24] Similarly, Lucio Baccaro has argued that internal democratic reform in Italian unions produced large shifts in union policy in directions more favorable to the interests of outsiders (pensions, employment, and regional development issues). To be sure, the results in these cases may come not from deliberation, but from broader participation or the dominance of a left party. But deliberation seems to be part of the story, both because deliberation shifts preferences and because it shifts collective decisions by making some proposals harder to defend: namely, proposals that cannot be defended in public on the basis of acceptable reasons. (Baccaro makes a good case that deliberation made the difference.)[25]

3. A third concern is about deliberative pathologies. A social-psychological variant of this concern says that group discussion imposes normative pressure on group members: a variance-reducing pressure not to be less extreme than the group median, and a mean-shifting pressure not to be less extreme than the group mean. A cognitive

Joshua Cohen

story claims that group discussion in a relative homogeneous group is dominated by arguments embraced by the majority, so that when people update on a relatively homogeneous argument pool, they consolidate. In either case, it is bad for outsiders.[26]

These are very serious concerns, but at least in principle, the remedies seem straight-forward, whatever the likelihood of their adoption. If deliberation under conditions of homogeneity drives polarization, then it is important to ensure that deliberative settings in some way reflect the wider diversity: in some deliberative settings, the competitive quality of the decision – when the issue at stake is the allocation of scarce resources – engenders such expression. In other settings, ensuring diversity of opinion may be a matter of institutional principle or the responsibility of a moderator. In settings of group discussion, this might mean ensuring that some time is devoted to expressing beliefs or judgments that are assumed not to be shared by others in the group: ensuring that this happens seems to be well within the reach of moderators or participants themselves.

Putting it more generally, the point is that studies of deliberative pathologies need to be treated with some care. Those pathologies may emerge from group decision-making conducted without efforts to avoid the pathological results. So such studies may often be interpretable as sources of cautionary notes and recommendations for improvement rather than as undermining the case for deliberation. That said, it is also true that the more fragile deliberation is, the more structure that needs to be in place to move from discussion to good deliberation, the less confidence we can reside in the project of building a more deliberative democracy. A naïve version of the deliberative ideal supposes that people are waiting to deliberate, and need only to get competitive polit-ical structures out of the way. Deliberation may be a more fragile accomplishment.

4. The final objection is about naïveté concerning power.[27] Because constraints on what counts as a reason are not well defined, the advantaged will find some way to defend self-serving proposals with considerations that are arguably reasons. For example, they may make appeals to ideas of the common advantage, but press a conception of the common advantage that assigns great weight to a deeply unequal *status quo*. Or if they fail in this, the advantaged will simply refuse to accept the discipline of deliberation.

If this objection is right, then proposals for deliberative democracy that are inattentive to background relations of power will waste the time of those who can least afford its loss: those now subordinate in power. The time and energy they spend in argument, laboring under the illusion that sweet reason will constrain the power that suppresses them, could have been spent in self-organization, instrumental efforts to increase their own power, or like efforts to impose costs on opponents.

The complaint that deliberative democracy is touchingly naïve about power betrays vertiginously boundless confusion.

First, the importance of background differences in power is not a criticism of the deliberative ideal *per se*, but a concern about its application. Deliberative democracy is a normative model of collective decision-making, not a universal political strategy. And commitment to the normative ideal does not require commitment to the belief that collective decision-making through mutual reason-giving is always possible. So it may indeed be the case that some rough background balance of power is required before parties will listen to reason. But observing that does not importantly lessen the attraction of the deliberative ideal; it simply states a condition of its reasonable pursuit.

Thus, in Habermas's account of the ideal speech situation, or in my own account of an ideal deliberative procedure, inequalities in power are stipulated away for the sake of presenting an idealized model of deliberation.[28] These idealizations are intended to characterize the nature of reasoned collective decision-making and in turn to provide models for actual arrangements of collective decision-making. But actual arrangements must provide some basis for confidence that joint reasoning will actually prevail in shaping the exercise of collective power, and gross inequalities of power surely undermine any such confidence. So discussion that expresses the deliberative ideal must, for example, operate against a background of free expression and association, thus providing minimal conditions for the availability of relevant information. Equally, if parties are not somehow constrained to accept the consequences of deliberation, if "exit options" are not foreclosed, it seems implausible that they will accept the discipline of joint reasoning, and in particular reasoning informed by the democratic idea of persons as equals. Firms retaining a more or less costless ability to move investment elsewhere are not, for example, likely to accept the discipline of reasoned deliberation about labor standards, with workers as their deliberative equals.

Saying "If you don't listen to reason, you will pay a high price" is not a joke: it is sometimes necessary to resort to destabilization, threats, and open conflict as answers to people who won't reason in good faith. A sucker may be born every minute, but deliberative democracy is not a recommendation that we all join the club. But if the willingness to reason does depend on the background distribution of power, doesn't that defeat the point of deliberative democracy by reducing deliberation to bargaining under a balance of power? Not at all. Once people do listen to reason, the results may reflect not only the balance of power that defeated their previous imperviousness, but their attentiveness to reasons that can be shared. If I need to drink some espresso to concentrate hard enough to prove a theorem, it does not reduce theorem-proving to a caffeine high. So similarly, paying attention to power and threats to exercise it doesn't reduce deliberation to bargaining. To suppose otherwise is like thinking that if you need to trust your math teacher in order to learn how to do a proof then there is nothing more to proof than trust. It confuses conditions that make an activity possible with that activity itself.

5. Some Tensions Between Participation and Deliberation

I started by noting two strands in the radical democratic tradition: participatory and deliberative. But I have not said much at all about political participation: deliberative democracy is about political reasoning, not the breadth and depth of participation. To be very brief: participation is particularly important in connection with achieving fair political equality, because shifting the basis of political contestation from organized money to organized people is a promising alternative to the influence conferred by wealth. Similarly, expanding and deepening citizen participation may be the most promising strategy for challenging political inequalities associated with traditional social and political hierarchies. Moreover, it may be important in encouraging a sense of political responsibility.

Joshua Cohen

But participation is one thing, and deliberation is another, and they may pull in different directions. Consider three sources of tension.[29]

1. Improving the quality of deliberation may come at a cost to public participation. Suppose, for example, that legislators, regulators, and judges were to embrace a deliberative form of decision-making. Instead of seeking to advance the interests of their constituents or single-mindedly maximizing their prospects of re-election, for example, legislators would engage in reasonable discussion and argument about policies. Judges would, in turn, reinforce the legislators by requiring explicit attention to reasons in legislative and administrative decision-making. But doing so might require insulation from public pressures.

2. Expanding participation – either the numbers of people, or the range of issues under direct popular control – may diminish the quality of deliberation. Initiatives and referenda, for example, allow voters to exercise more direct and precisely targeted influence over legislation, policy questions, and even elected officials. But far from improving deliberation, such measures – in part because they ultimately focus on a yes/no decision on a well-defined proposition – may discourage reasoned discussion in creating legislation. And even bringing people together to discuss specific laws and policies may – with a homogeneous collection of people, or a lack of commitment to addressing a common problem – diminish deliberation, as discussion dissolves into posturing, recrimination, and manipulation.[30]

3. More fundamentally, social complexity and scale limit the extent to which modern polities can be both deliberative and participatory. Deliberation depends on participants with sufficient knowledge and interest about the substantive issues under consideration. But on any issue, the number of individuals with such knowledge and interest is bound to be relatively small, and so the quality of deliberation will decline with the scope of participation. Of course, knowledge and interest are not fixed, and deliberation may improve both. Still, time and resource constraints make it undesirable for any particular area of public governance to be both fully deliberative and inclusively participatory.

6. And So?

These three tensions notwithstanding, public decision-making in liberal democracies could become both more participatory and deliberative. The challenge is to devise practical projects that can incorporate both. Radical democrats have two broad strategies for achieving that aim. which I will sketch in very broad strokes.

The first aims to join deliberation with mass democracy by promoting citizen deliberation on political matters in what Habermas calls the "informal public sphere," constituted by networks of associations in civil society.[31] Because such informal discussion does not aim at a practical decision but – insofar as it has an aim – at informed opinion, it can pursue an unencumbered discussion about political values and public goals. Moreover, these dispersed discussions – one element of a political society's process of collective decision-making – are potentially very broadly participatory, for they take place through structures of numerous, open secondary associations and social movements. For this mix of mass democracy and deliberation, the essential ingredients, apart from ensuring basic liberties, are a diverse and independent media, vibrant, independent civil associations, and political parties that operate independently from concentrated wealth and help to focus public debate. All of this arguably helps to foster deliberative capacities – a point I mentioned earlier, and promised to return to. The marriage of open communication in the informal public sphere with a translation – through elections and legislative debate – of opinion formed there into law provides, on this view, the best hope for achieving a greater mix of participation and deliberation under conditions of mass democracy and a rule of law.

Much of the attractiveness of this view, then, hinges first upon the deliberativeness of discourse in the public sphere and then upon the strength of the links between such deliberation and the decisions of legislative bodies and administrative agencies. But because dispersed, informal public deliberation and public policy are only loosely linked, a more participatory and deliberative informal public sphere may have little impact on decisions by formal institutions. Citizen participation in the informal public sphere, then, may be of limited political relevance, and the marriage of reason with mass democracy may proceed in splendid isolation from the exercise of power. To be clear: I am not here objecting to this first approach, only pointing to a concern and a possible limitation.

A second radical-democratic approach builds on the distinctive practical competence that citizens possess as users of public services, subjects of public policy and regulation, or as residents with contextual knowledge of their circumstances. The idea is to draw on these competencies by bringing ordinary citizens into relatively focused deliberations over public issues. Typically, such strategies create opportunities for limited numbers of citizens to deliberate with one another or with officials to improve the quality of some public decision, perhaps by injecting local knowledge, new perspectives, and excluded interests, or by enhancing public accountability.

One approach randomly selects small groups of citizens to deliberate on general political issues such as laws and public policies. Citizen juries in the United States and planning cells in Germany, for example, empanel small groups (12–40) of randomly selected citizens to discuss issues such as agriculture, health policy, and local development concerns.[32] Fishkin and his colleagues have sponsored larger gatherings of 300–500 citizens – with randomization – to deliberate upon such issues as the adoption of the Euro in Denmark, public utility regulation in Texas, and U.S. foreign assistance.[33] On an ambitious *analytical* interpretation, post-deliberation polls provide insight into what *the people* think about a policy issue. Political impact is another matter. As with citizens juries and planning cells, their political impact – to the extent that they have impact – comes from their capacity to serve in an advisory role, and to alter public opinion or change the minds of public officials.

Another strategy convenes groups of citizens to deliberate and develop solutions to particular problems of public concern. Such participatory-deliberative arrangements – characteristic in different ways of associative democracy and directly-deliberative polyarchy – differ from political juries in two main ways. Whereas political juries usually consider *general* issues such as economic, health care, or crime policy, these deliberations aim to address more specific problems such as the management of an ecosystem, the operation of a public school or school district, crime in a neighborhood, or a city's allocation of resources across projects and neighborhoods. Whereas political juries recruit impartial and disinterested citizens by randomly selecting them,

Joshua Cohen

participatory-deliberative arrangements recruit participants with strong interests in the problems under deliberation.

Because of the specificity of these arrangements, citizens may well enjoy advantages in knowledge and experience over officials. In Chicago, for example, residents deliberate regularly with police officers in each neighborhood to set priorities on addressing issues of public safety, using their background knowledge as a basis for deliberation. And in Porto Alegre citizens meet regularly at the neighborhood level to agree upon priorities for public investment (for example, street paving, sanitation, and housing); the capital portion of the city's budget is produced by aggregating the priorities that emerge from those deliberations.

Participatory-deliberative arrangements – in areas such as education, social services, ecosystems, community development, and health services – show promising contributions to political equality by increasing popular engagement in political decision-making. As I mentioned earlier, in Chicago's community policing program, for example, participation rates in low-income neighborhoods are much higher than those in wealthy neighborhoods. Similarly, poor people are substantially overrepresented in both the budgeting institutions of Porto Alegre and local development and planning initiatives in Kerala, India. Directly-democratic arrangements that address problems of particular urgency to disadvantaged citizens can invert the usual participation bias in favor of wealth, education, and high status. They can also, however, create large potential political inequalities. If systematic and enduring differences – in deliberative capabilities, disposable resources, or demographic factors – separate those who participate from those who do not, decisions generated by participatory-deliberative arrangements will likely serve the interests of participants at the expense of others.

The proliferation of directly-deliberative institutions fosters democratic self-government by subjecting the policies and actions of agencies such as these to a rule of common reason. But these contributions to self-government are, however, limited by the scope of these institutions. Most participatory-deliberative governance efforts aim to address local concerns and do not extend to broader issues of policy and public priorities. Moreover, there is the danger of administrative "capture": that by entering the circuit of regulatory problem solving with its pragmatic concern about the effectiveness of policy, participating citizens and groups lose their capacity for independent action and their sense of the importance of open-ended reflection and morally motivated criticism and innovation.[34] They may become dependent on the state and its official recognition for power and resources, and their political horizon may come to be undesirably confined by attention to policy constraints. If this is right, then the alleged limitation of informal, society-wide deliberation – the fact that its impact is so indirect – is really its virtue. The precondition of the unconstrained discussion on which public deliberation depends requires distance between civil society's associative life and the state's decision-making routines.

Final Reflections

So achieving both participation and deliberation is complicated. But because of their more direct bearing on the exercise of power, participatory-deliberative arrangements have a particular promise as a strategy for achieving the ends of radical democracy. Two large challenges, however, lie on that path.

The first concerns the relationship between conventional institutions of political representation and participatory-deliberative arrangements.[35] Participatory-deliberative arrangements make it possible to address practical problems that seem recalcitrant to treatment by conventional political institutions. But those arrangements are not a wholesale replacement of conventional political institutions: they have limited scope and limited numbers of direct participants. To the extent that they are successful, however, participatory-deliberative arrangements and conventional political representation can be transformed and linked so that each strengthens the other. If such arrangements became a common form of local and administrative problem solving, the role of legislatures and public agencies would shift from directly solving a range of social problems to supporting the efforts of many participatory deliberations, maintaining their democratic integrity, and ensuring their coordination. Conversely, those who participated directly in these new deliberative arrangements would form a highly informed, mobilized, and active base that would enhance the mandate and legitimacy of elected representatives and other officials.

The second challenge is to extend the scope of radical democracy. Can participatory deliberation help democratize large-scale decisions about public priorities – war and peace, health insurance, public pensions, and the distribution of wealth? One way to address these larger questions is to connect the disciplined, practical, participatory deliberations about solving particular problems – say, efforts to reduce asthma rates in a low-income community, or efforts to provide decent medical care in New Orleans or Los Angeles – to the wider public sphere of debate and opinion formation – about the costs of health care, access to it, and the importance of health relative to other basic goods. Participants in direct deliberations are informed by the dispersed discussions in the informal public sphere, and those more focused deliberations in turn invest public discussion with a practicality it might otherwise lack. The ambitious hope is that citizens who participate in constructing solutions to concrete problems in local public life may in turn engage more deeply in informal deliberation in the wider public sphere and in formal political institutions as well.

In the end, then, radical democracy – understood as an effort to combine the values of both participation and deliberation – has promise to be a distinctive form of democracy, in which the informal public sphere and conventional democratic institutions are reshaped by their connections with participatory-deliberative arrangements for solving problems. Whether it will deliver on that promise remains, of course, a very open question.

Notes

1 I presented earlier versions of this essay at the University of Southern California Law School and at a Princeton University conference on deliberative democracy. I am grateful to the audiences on both occasions for their comments and criticisms.

2 For representative ideas, see John Roemer, *Equal Shares: Making Market Socialism Work* (New York and London: Verso, 1996); Samuel Bowles and Herbert Gintis, *Recasting Egalitarianism: New Rules for Communities, States and Markets* (New York and London: Verso, 1999); Stuart White, *The Civic Minimum* (Oxford: Oxford University Press, 2003);

Bruce Ackerman and Anne Alstott, *The Stakeholder Society* (New Haven, CT: Yale University Press, 2000); Richard Freeman, *The New Inequality* (Boston, MA: Beacon Press, 1998).

3 I have written elsewhere on this radical-democratic project: with Joel Rogers (on associative democracy), Chuck Sabel (on deliberative polyarchy), and Archon Fung (on participation and deliberation). In writing this essay, I have drawn freely on this joint work, and am very grateful to my co-authors for the collaborations that produced it. See Joshua Cohen and Joel Rogers, *Associations and Democracy* (London: Verso, 1995); Joshua Cohen and Charles Sabel, "Directly-Deliberative Polyarchy," *European Law Journal* 3 (4) (Dec. 1997): 313–42; Joshua Cohen and Joel Rogers, "Power and Reason," in Archon Fung and Erik Olin Wright, eds., *Deepening Democracy: Institutional Innovations in Empowered Participatory Governance* (New York and London: Verso, 2003); Joshua Cohen and Charles Sabel, "Global Democracy?," *New York University Journal of International Law and Policy* 37 (4) (2006): 763–97; Joshua Cohen and Archon Fung, "Radical Democracy," *Swiss Journal of Political Science* 10 (4) (2004).

4 Rousseau himself explored other forms of democratic participation, particularly in his *Constitution of Poland*, where considerations of size precluded direct citizen participation in law-making.

5 Jürgen Habermas, *Legitimation Crisis*, trans. Thomas McCarthy (Boston, MA: Beacon Press, 1973), p. 108. In this passage, Habermas is not describing an idealized democracy, but a hypothetical situation suited to the justification of norms.

6 We now have many statements of the deliberative conception. For my own, which I draw on here, see Joshua Cohen, "Deliberation and Democratic Legitimacy," Alan Hamlin and Phillip Petit, eds., *The Good Polity* (Oxford: Blackwell, 1989); "Procedure and Substance in Deliberative Democracy," in Seyla Benhabib, ed., *Democracy and Difference: Changing Boundaries of the Political* (Princeton, NJ: Princeton University Press, 1996); "Democracy and Liberty," in Jon Elster, ed., *Deliberative Democracy* (Cambridge: Cambridge University Press, 1998); and "Privacy, Pluralism, and Democracy," in Joseph Keim Campbell, Michael O'Rourke, and David Shier, eds., *Law and Social Justice* (Cambridge, MA: MIT Press, 2005).

7 Carl Schmitt, *The Crisis of Parliamentary Democracy*, trans. Ellen Kennedy (Cambridge, MA: MIT Press, 1985), p. 6.

8 In *Is Democracy Possible Here?* (Cambridge, MA: Harvard University Press, 2006), Ronald Dworkin emphasizes the importance of education in a well-functioning, deliberative democracy, and asserts that "the most daunting but also most urgent requirement is to make a Contemporary Politics course part of ever high school curriculum" (148). The idea of such a course is sensible enough, but it hardly seems the most urgent issue about the reform of our educational system, for the purposes of fostering the partnership in argument that is so central to democracy.

9 As Rawls observes, an idea of public reason is one of the "essential elements of deliberative democracy." See "The Idea of Public Reason Revisited," in *Law of Peoples* (Cambridge, MA: Harvard University Press, 1999), p. 139.

10 On problems with deliberation under a unanimity rule, see David Austen-Smith and Timothy Feddersen, "Deliberation, Preference Uncertainty, and Voting Rules," *American Political Science Review* 100 (2006): 209–18.

11 See, for example, Jürgen Habermas, *Between Facts and Norms*, trans. William Rehg (Cambridge, MA: MIT Press, 1996), pp. 296, 304.

12 The emphasis on deliberation as reason-giving is not captured in models of deliberation as cheap talk signaling, where the point is to convey some piece of private information, and success depends on beliefs about the trustworthiness of the speaker (see Austen-Smith and Feddersen, "Deliberation, Preference Uncertainty, and Voting Rules"). For an interesting effort to model deliberation as reasoning – arguing from premises to conclusions,

where individuals can check the quality of the reasoning themselves – see Catherine Hafer and Dimitri Landa, "Deliberation as Self-Discovery and Institutions for Political Speech," *Journal of Theoretical Politics* 19 (3) (2007).

13 Amy Gutmann and Dennis Thompson, *Why Deliberative Democracy?* (Princeton, NJ: Princeton University Press, 2004), p. 3.

14 "Introduction," *Deliberative Democracy* (Cambridge: Cambridge University Press, 1998), p. 8.

15 *Deliberative Democracy and Beyond* (Oxford: Oxford University Press, 2004), p. 31.

16 *Deliberative Democracy and Beyond*, p. 8.

17 *Deliberative Democracy and Beyond*, p. 167; and, in general, Ch. 3.

18 I believe that Lynn Sanders was the first to raise this objection, in "Against Deliberation," *Political Theory* (1997): 347–76.

19 Archon Fung, *Empowered Participation: Reinventing Urban Democracy* (Princeton, NJ: Princeton University Press, 2004), Ch. 4.

20 See Rebecca Abers, "Reflections on What Makes Empowered Participatory Governance Happen," in Fung and Wright, *Deepening Democracy*, p. 206, and more generally her *Inventing Local Democracy* (Boulder, CO: Lynne Rienner, 2000); Gianpaolo Baiocchi, *Militants and Citizens: The Politics of Participatory Democracy in Porto Alegre* (Stanford, CA: Stanford University Press, 2005).

21 In his critique of deliberative democracy, Posner is less hostile to locally focused discussion about the provision of public goods, perhaps for reasons of the kind noted in the text. See *Law, Pragmatism, and Democracy* (Cambridge, MA: Harvard University Press, 2003).

22 Stephen Ansolabehere, Alan Gerber, James M. Snyder, "Equal Votes, Equal Money: Court-Ordered Redistricting and the Distribution of Public Expenditure in the American States," *American Political Science Review* (Aug. 2002).

23 Esther Duflo, "Women as Policy Makers: Evidence from a Randomized Policy Experiment in India," *Econometrica* 72 (5) (2004): 1409–43.

24 Gianpaolo Baiocchi, The Citizens of Porto Alegre, *Boston Review* 31 (2) (Mar. –Apr. 2006).

25 Lucio Baccaro, "The Construction of Democratic Corporatism in Italy," *Politics and Society* 30 (2) (Jun. 2002): 327–57.

26 Cass Sunstein, "Group Judgments: Statistical Means, Deliberation, and Information Markets," *NYU Law Review* 80 (Jun. 2005): 962–1049; and Tali Mendelberg's very instructive discussion of deliberation and small-group decision-making, in "The Deliberative Citizen: Theory and Evidence," in Michael X. Delli Carpini, Leonie Huddy, and Robert Shapiro, eds., *Political Decision-Making, Deliberation, and Participation: Research in Micropolitics*, vol. 6 (Greenwich, CT: JAI Press, 2002), pp. 151–93.

27 See Cohen and Rogers, "Power and Reason."

28 See Cohen, "Deliberation and Democratic Legitimacy," and Habermas, *Between Facts and Norms*, Ch. 7.

29 Diana Mutz explores a different tension between deliberation and participation in her important book, *Hearing the Other Side Deliberative Versus Participatory Democracy* (Cambridge: Cambridge University Press, 2006). Mutz argues that deliberation among the diverse encourages greater toleration, but dampens participation because of a desire to avoid conflict with the people to whom one talks. Participation in turn is animated by a sense of passion that is dampened by deliberation. I am not sure that Mutz's results extend outside participation in highly competitive political settings. But the challenge she raises is deep and needs to be addressed.

30 See, for example, Derek Bell, "The Referendum: Democracy's Barrier to Racial Equality," *Washington Law Review* 54 (1) (1978): 1–29; Yannis Papadopolous, "A Framework for Analysis of Functions and Dysfunctions of Direct Democracy: Top-Down and Bottom-Up Perspectives," *Politics and Society* 23 (1995): 421–48.

Joshua Cohen

31 Habermas, *Between Facts and Norms*, Ch. 8; John Rawls, *Political Liberalism* (New York: Columbia University Press, 1996), pp. 14, 382–3.

32 Julia Abelson, Pierre-Gerlier Forest, John Eyles, Patricia Smith, Elisabeth Martin, and François-Pierre Gauvin, "Deliberations about Deliberative Methods: Issues in the Design and Evaluation of Public Participation Processes" in *Social Science and Medicine* 57 (2003): 239–51; Ned Crosby, "Citizens' Juries: One Solution for Difficult Environmental Questions," in O. Renn, T. Webler, and P. Wiedelmann eds., *Fairness and Competence in Citizen Participation: Evaluating Models for Environmental Discourse* (Boston, MA: Kluwer Academic Press, 1995), pp. 157–74; G. Smith and C. Wales, "The Theory and Practice of Citizens' Juries," *Policy and Politics* 27 (3) (1999): 295–308; John Gastil, *By Popular Demand* (Los Angeles and Berkeley: University of California Press, 2000).

33 For a sketch of polls and implications, see Bruce Ackerman and James Fishkin, *Deliberation Day* (New Haven, CT: Yale University Press, 2005), esp. Ch. 3.

34 See Lucio Baccaro and Konstantinos Papadakis, "The Downside of Deliberative Public Administration" (unpublished).

35 For discussion of the issues sketched here, see Cohen and Sabel, "Directly-Deliberative Polyarchy," Cohen and Sabel, "Global Democracy?," and Cohen and Sabel, "Sovereignty and Solidarity in the EU," in Jonathan Zeitlin and David Trubek, eds., *Governing Work and Welfare in a New Economy: European and American Experiments* (Oxford: Oxford University Press, 2003), pp. 345–75.

DEMOCRACY AND ITS LIMITS

CONSTITUTIONALISM

Constitutionalism – A Skeptical View

Jeremy Waldron

1. Introduction

In this chapter, I will cast a skeptical eye over the political theory associated with the term "constitutionalism." I know that "constitutionalism" is a term of approbation; we are all supposed to be constitutionalists now. But it may be worth sounding a critical note or two. Apart from anything else, even supporters of constitutionalism should worry that, without an occasional live critic to contend with, their faith may become a dead dogma rather than a living truth, a superstition or prejudice clinging accident-ally to a form of words that once conveyed something interesting and controversial.[1]

2. The Weakest Meaning of "Constitutionalism"

The potential for "constitutionalism" to degenerate into an empty slogan is exacerbated by the fact that the word is sometimes used in a way that conveys no theoretical content at all. Often the term seems to means little more than the thoughtful or systematic study of constitutions and various constitutional provisions. There is nothing wrong with this use of "constitutionalism." People can use words however they like, and the *Oxford English Dictionary* seems to accept this usage. The first meaning suggested for "constitutionalism" is "a constitutional system of government."[2] It is not an unreasonable usage. "Constitutionalism" is a grandiose word: why not use its seven or eight syllables to make the study of constitutions, constitutional law, and constitutional systems of government sound important?

3. Constitutionalism as a Theory

Still, the last two syllables – the "-ism" – should at least alert us to an *additional* meaning that does denote a theory or set of theoretical claims. Constitutionalism is like liberal*ism* or social*ism* or scient*ism*. It is perhaps worth asking what that theory is and, whether the claims it comprises are true or valid.

I mentioned a moment ago the dictionary definition of the term. The second meaning proposed for the term by the *Oxford English Dictionary* refers to an attitude or disposition – "[a]dherence to constitutional principles."[3] A constitutionalist, in this sense, is one who takes constitutions very seriously and who is not disposed to allow deviations from them even when other important values are involved. "Constitutionalism" therefore refers to the sort of ideology that makes this attitude seem sensible. Constitutionalism, the theory, includes at the very least the claim that a society's constitution matters, that it is not just decoration, that it has an importance that justifies making sacrifices of other important values for its for its sake.

4. Particular and General Constitutionalism

Such a view might have two aspects: (i) it may be the view that the principles of a particular constitution are important; or (ii) it may be the general view that constitutions *as such* are important.

For example, under heading (i), we might think that English constitutionalism attributes great importance to parliamentary sovereignty whereas American constitutionalism includes great affection for federal structures and for the separation of powers.[4]

Under heading (ii), by contrast, we would try and look at what various constitutionalisms have in common, even when they chauvinistically celebrate differently-shaped arrangements. Roger Scruton's definition of the term in his *Dictionary of Political Thought* is helpful as an example of (ii): he defines "constitutionalism" as the advocacy of constitutional government, i.e. of "government channeled through and limited by a constitution."[5] On this view, a constitutionalist is one who thinks it important for government to be organized through and restrained by a set of constitutional rules; such a person will be opposed to various forms of absolutism, because that involves repudiating the idea of rules limiting government at the highest level.[6] We might say that despite the differences between (say) Australian and American constitutionalism, constitutionalists in both countries celebrate and advocate forms of political structuring that limit the power of government in various ways. Some of these forms are similar (like federalism); some of them are different (like the more extensive provision for judicial review of legislation in the United States). But the idea of using formally articulated structure to restrain government is held in common by the two sets of constitutionalists, and it may be contrasted, on the one hand, with the view that governments are best restrained by an unarticulated ethos of moderation and, on the other hand, by the absolutist conviction that it may not be appropriate to try to limit government at all.

5. Explicit and Implicit Constitutions

But maybe these are false contrasts. Perhaps we ought to say that every stable system of government has a constitution, if by a constitution we mean a set of fundamental

Jeremy Waldron

rules establishing the way governmental powers are exercised, who exercises them, what their jurisdiction is, how laws are made and changed, and so on. On this account, even a dictatorship or an absolute monarchy has a constitution; its constitution may differ from that of a system of parliamentary sovereignty or from a republican system of checks and balances; but it is still a constitution.[7] If government were imaginable without a constitution, it would be as the adventitious persistence of traditional ways of doing things without any consciousness of them as rules; but even then some would say that these ways of doing things can be identified and spoken about as constitutional norms at least by outsiders, even if it doesn't occur to participants to think about them in these terms. When Alexander Hamilton remarked at the very beginning of *The Federalist Papers* that

> it seems to have been reserved to the people of this country, by their conduct and example, to decide the important question, whether societies of men are really capable or not of establishing good government from reflection and choice, or whether they are forever destined to depend for their political constitutions on accident and force.[8]

he seemed to be assuming that countries whose systems of government are not established by reflection and choice do still have constitutions.

But even if that is right, I think constitutionalism – the general ideology – means something a little bit more specific than this. It is often associated specifically with the sort of thing that Hamilton thought distinguished the United States from other systems of government, i.e., the importance of conscious reflection and choice upon the forms, structures and arrangements for government.

6. Constitutionalism and Written Constitutions

Is constitutionalism the celebration of *written* constitutions? It is often said that the main advantage of putting one's constitution into writing is that it establishes its authority as higher law, making it enforceable by the judiciary. This is what Justice Marshall said in *Marbury v. Madison*:

> [A]ll those who have framed written constitutions contemplate them as forming the fundamental and paramount law of the nation, and consequently the theory of every such government must be, that an act of the legislature repugnant to the constitution is void. This theory is essentially attached to a written constitution. . . .[9]

On its face, however, this is an implausible argument. The written-ness of a constitution is compatible with its being (treated as) ordinary legislation, like the New Zealand Constitution Act of 1986. Or it is compatible with it being treated merely as a piece of paper, with little legal effect, like the Soviet Constitution of 1936. On the other hand, judicial review on constitutional grounds can be thought legitimate even where the relevant provision of higher law is unwritten.[10]

A more plausible account of written-ness is that it allows the constitution to have a more palpable presence in the polity. Hannah Arendt said that, in America, it was important that the Constitution be "a tangible worldly entity," "an endurable objective thing, which, to be sure, one could approach from many different angles and upon which one could impose many different interpretations, . . . but which never-theless was never a subjective state of mind, like the will."[11]

This may be particularly important when constitutional arrangements are being considered and debated. A set of implicit rules is very hard to reflect upon in any coherent way among a large number of people. Deliberation can seem futile unless it is focused on a text that serves as a focal point for debate – a written text, by which issues are separated, and on which amendments may be registered.[12]

I do not want to quarrel with this aspect of constitutionalism. It is highly desirable for attention to be given explicitly to the constitutional arrangements of a society: they are too important to be left to "accident or force" as Hamilton put it. I would enter three caveats however.

First, what is important is not just that there should be some form of conscious and explicit reflection on constitutional arrangements, but that this should be the work of *the people whose society is to be governed by these arrangements*. I will talk more about this in section 11.

Second, the textual quality of a written constitution may have drawbacks, par-ticularly in the context of legalism and judicial review. With a written constitution as their battlefield, lawyers, and judges are likely to be heavily distracted in their discussions by side-arguments about interpretive theory. Alternatively, the written formulations of a Bill of Rights encourage rigid textual formalism; the words of each provision take on a life of their own, becoming a sort of obsessive catch-phrase for expressing in a way that makes it difficult to focus on what is really at stake. (For example, in assessing American social and economic legislation in the early years of the twentieth century, was it really worth spending so much energy discussing whether "due process" can be substantive?) I suspect that these disadvantages of textuality are probably outweighed by the earlier points about facilitating deliberation. But they are drawbacks nonetheless. And there is a danger that the balance will slip the other way. The case that I have made for a written text is that it helps concentrate the minds of those who are deliberating upon and choosing constitutional arrangements. But for many constitutionalists, reflection and choice is a matter of history, often quite distant history – a matter for "the Framers" not for current politics. From this perspective, the value of the written text is the way the venerable calligraphy of the eighteenth century endues the rules it embodies with an aura of ancestral authority and immutability. And that seems to me to count against written-ness. For I am not accepting – this is my third caveat – that the value of a written text consists in the effectiveness of the constraints that it embodies. Whether it is actually the point of a constitution to *constrain* government, as opposed to *empower* it, is something that needs to be discussed.

7. Constitutionalism and Constraint

This brings us to the more substantive aspect of constitutionalism. Unlike, say, the Rule of Law, constitutionalism is not just a normative theory about the *form* of governance.[13] It is about controlling, limiting, and restraining the power of the state. Numerous books on constitutionalism make this clear in their titles. Scott Gordon's book on the subject is called *Controlling the State: Constitutionalism from Ancient*

Athens to Today and András Sajó entitles his book *Limiting Government: A Introduction to Constitutionalism.*[14] In a foreword to Sajó's book, Stephen Holmes writes that "[c]onstitutions are giant restraining orders motivated by a passion for avoidance. They are inevitably propelled by the desire to escape specific dangerous and unpleasant political outcomes."[15] The theme is a perennial one. "In all its successive phases," according to C. H. McIlwain, "constitutionalism has one essential quality: it is a legal limitation on government."[16]

There are some more nuanced views. Cass Sunstein insists that limited government is just one of many principles associated with constitutionalism.[17] But this goes against the general trend. For most writers, constitutionalism equals constraint. They accept McIlwain's characterization or that of Carl Friedrich, who spoke of constitutionalism as "effective regularized restraint" on government.[18]

Constitutionalism seems to assume that the power of the state needs to be restrained or limited or controlled, lest it get out of hand. It is part of what Judith Shklar called "the liberalism of fear."[19] The idea is that the concentration of power leads to its abuse and this is why the power-dispersing, the power-slowing, the power-checking elements of constitutional structure are important.

How seriously should we take the language of constraint? Especially in the American law review literature, there is a tendency just to repeat well-worn formulations and slogans, and to pay little attention to the detailed formulation of one's position. For consider the terms that are used for this connection between constitutions and various forms of constraint. The most commonly used phrase is "limited government," but there is also talk of a connection between constitutionalism and "restraints" upon power and of constitutionalism as a doctrine of "control" (as in Scott Gordon's title "Controlling the State"). Now, considered analytically these phrases – "limited government," "restrained government," and "controlled government" – are not synonymous. They mean different things and they have different connotations in the theory of politics.

Let us begin with "control." The idea of controlling the state is not necessarily a negative or constraining idea. If I control a vehicle, I determine not only where it does not go, but also where it does go. And if government is controlled, one might think that the important question is who is in the driving seat. Often constitutional structure has this aspect of control: we subordinate the courts to the legislature and the executive to the courts, so that the sort of control envisaged in legislation is conveyed to those responsible for executing the law.

Someone may respond that what I have just said is about *intra*-governmental control, whereas those who talk of controlling the state have in mind control of the whole entity, of the legislature as well as the courts and the executive. But even at this level, we need not take the view that control is equivalent to constraint. We may say instead that it is important for the government as a whole to be controlled *by the people* and, again, we may understand this control as not something purely negative, but as a matter of articulate response to the people's will. If the people want their government to ameliorate poverty, for example, it is the task of the constitution to provide institutions that can be controlled by this desire.

Restraint, on the other hand, is definitely a negative idea: it is the idea of preventing the government from doing certain things. A "restraint" view proceeds on the basis that we can identify certain abuses that we want to avoid and we specifically prohibit them, building these prohibitions into the very document that constitutes governmental authority. Such prohibitions often take the form of rights – a right not to be tortured, a right to be free from interference with religious belief, and so on. The idea is that whatever the government affirmatively does, it must not do *these* things. In some cases, the prohibition is absolute – as in most constitutions it is in the case of torture. In other cases, the prohibition works as a specification of the conditions under which things may be done which might otherwise be oppressive: no detention without trial, no trial without the assistance of counsel, and so on. Much of the popularity of modern constitutionalism is due to the fact that it connects with human rights in this way. But it is interesting that few constitutionalists are willing to rest their theory on this basis alone. Not content with restraints on power, constitutionalists often say that the function of constitutions is also to limit affirmatively the sort of thing that governments can do.

"Limited government," then, refers not just to the avoidance of particular abuses, but to a broader sense of what is and what is not the government's proper function.[20] No doubt, there is some continuity between the two ideas. One might say, as a matter of restraint, that the government may not interfere with religious freedom. Or one might say as a matter of limits that it is not the government's function to establish any form of public worship. For other cases, however, the overlap between restrain and limit is deceptive. One might say, as the U.S. Constitution says, that the government is restrained from passing "any . . . law impairing the obligation of contracts."[21] But it would be a further step – quite a drastic step – to say that it is not the function of the government to interfere in the market economy.

If, however, one treats limited government as the core principle of constitutionalism, then one is in a position to move more directly to the idea that many of the aspirations of government – particularly democratic government – are *per se* illegitimate. Those who set up a democracy may be hoping for government intervention to ameliorate poverty, promote public health, and protect the environment. They know they are likely to face opposition from opponents who claim that this is none of the government's business. But now it seems that these opponents can take on the mantle of constitutionalism, and add to their case against intervention that the interventionists do not take the constitutional dimension of governance seriously enough. Constitutionalism, as a result, gets associated with something like the political theory of traditional minimal-state liberalism, and commentators begin to talk of "laissez-faire constitutionalism," not just as one extreme form of constitutionalist ideology, but as something to which all constitutions should aspire.[22]

Am I being too pedantic in this exploration of the differences between control, limitation, and restraint? Surely all that is meant, when these terms are used loosely as synonyms of one another, is that a constitution consists of rules which regulate the actions and practices they apply to. We might accept this as an abstract point, but if we refused to go beyond this in our analysis of constitutionalism, I think we would drain the concept of much of its distinctive character as a theory. No doubt many constitutionalists would be happier with a situation in which no one looked too closely at the content of their position, so that they were free to capitalize on a certain looseness in the rhetoric and use the equivocations that the language of control, restraint, and limit makes possible to leverage the good-hearted moderation of the person who believes that the government shouldn't be allowed to do just

Jeremy Waldron

anything into acceptance of the doctrine that it is unwise to allow the government to do too much. But it is not our task in the study of constitutionalism to assist them in that practice.

8. Empowerment and Authority

What do constitutions do that constitutionalists downplay? First and foremost they empower: they establish institutions that allow people to cooperate and coordinate to pursue projects that they cannot achieve on their own. To take a simple but obvious example: we need an agency to act decisively in large-scale natural emergencies for which individual or voluntary efforts will be inadequate; a constitution provides the institutional auspices under which that agency can be created and empowered. The need may be for people to act in concert in large numbers (perhaps hundreds of thousands, even millions), and they cannot do that without the sort of articulated power that institutions provide. Constitutions also invest institutions like this with public authority. By that I mean, they not only provide the institutions with powers of coercion, they also ensure that they can act credibly in the name of the whole society and they see to it that this amounts to more than just a label but to a substantial source of their actual legitimacy. Governmental institutions have to have standing in the community as a focus of loyalty and as a point of reference or orientation for the millions of others in the society who are figuring out how their concerns and actions and resources are to be related to the concerns, actions, and resources that the institution commands. All sorts of institutions need to be established in this spirit. A constitution has to set up courts to resolve disputes in the name of the whole society; it has to establish a legislature as an agency which in the name of the whole society will keep its standing rules under review; and it has to establish armed organizations to keep the peace in a society and to defend its interests, again in the name of the whole society. The manner in which the constitution performs that task, the mode of operation it establishes for these institutions, and the way it relates them to one another, are all crucial components to the establishment of authority in this sense.

What I have just said is platitudinous and some readers will think that constitutionalists can be forgiven for brushing past these obvious points and cutting straight to the question of how the institutions set up in these ways and for these purposes are to be limited or controlled. They may accept that constitutions are necessary to constitute the power of the state. But their constitution*alism* is something extra. In Sajó's words, "[c]onstitutions are about power, a constitution impregnated with the ideas of constitutionalism is about limited power."[23] But even putting the matter like that still leads to a distortion in our thinking. It indicates that the establishing of political power does not need the sort of attention that constitutionalism devotes to the subset of provisions concerned with restraint and limitation.

Besides actually establishing centers of public power, constitutions lay down procedures for their operation, often quite formalistic procedures limiting not so much what can be done but *how* it is done. A constitutionalized politics is an articulate politics that moves deliberately and deliberatively from stage to stage and forum to forum, taking seriously the integrity of each part of (say) the law-making process or of other processes of political decision. I have in mind processes like bicameral legislation, the requirement of executive consent, and the articulate relation between legislature on the one hand, and the courts and agents of the executive who administer, interpret and enforce the laws. From a constitutionalist perspective, there is a tendency to think simplistically of devices like these: they are conceived just as *brakes* upon the law-making process, points of possible resistance against oppressive legislation. Equally there is a tendency to think of the formal separation of powers between (say) legislature, executive, and judiciary simply as ways of diluting power and making it harder for it to be exercised. Everything is seen through the lens of constraint.

But such devices need not be seen in this light: articulate process can be seen as a way of structuring deliberation; bicameral arrangements can be seen as ways of empowering different voices in the community; and the separation of powers can be seen as a way of taking seriously the integrity of what comes into existence as the result of a genuine legislative exercise.[24] That the legislature may not control what happens to an Act once it passes into the hands of the courts is not just a method for preventing oppression (by ensuring that the legislators themselves are subject to the force of what they have enacted),[25] it is also a way of marking something about what has been done in the legislature. By virtue of the legislature's solemn decision, what has been produced comes to have the special status of *law*; it is not just another governmental measure. And its handling after it leaves the legislature is the tribute paid to that fact through institutional articulation.

In general, we need to understand the importance of the way in which a constitution provides *housing* for the political activity of a society, establishing an in-between of furniture and formality so that public deliberation becomes a structured enterprise, allowing the views of one person to be brought articulately into relation with the views of others and facilitating the formation of well-thought-through, responsible, and politically effective opinions. This is not primarily a matter of constraint;[26] it is a matter of what a constitution affirmatively makes possible out of what would otherwise be the loose and lurching politics of the street.[27]

9. Democracy: Constraint or Empowerment?

Many of the points I have made apply most vividly to democracy, and the skeptical notes that I am sounding about constitutionalism as an ideology are democratic notes.

When a constitutionalist thinks of democracy, his first thought is: How can we prevent democracy from degenerating into tyranny of the majority? What devices are available to restrain the tyrannical excesses to which democracies are endemically liable? But of course there are prior questions that need to be attended to as well. How is a democracy to be constituted? What is to be the system of representation? What are the different requirements of democracy for different kinds of political office (the election of a head of the executive, for example, versus the election of a legislator)? How is the integrity of the electoral process to be guaranteed? And above all, dominating all of these questions: How is the central principle of *political equality*, which is the foundation of democracy, to be upheld and enforced?

I think there is an important contrast here between the constitution of power in democratic and non-democratic societies. In *non*-democratic systems of government,

Jeremy Waldron

it is usually the task of the constitution to formalize the authority of those to whom, as it were, power comes naturally or who, as it happens, have been vested historically with power over a given society. The constitution of a democracy, by contrast, involves empowering *those who would otherwise be powerless*, the ordinary people who in most polities are the subjects not the agents of power. The man whom Colonel Rainborough referred to as "the poorest he that is in England" is the hardest man to empower, because if things are left to themselves he will have no political power at all.[28] If his empowerment is achieved, it is the achievement of a democratic constitution that goes out of its way to ensure that he has as much formal political authority as "the greatest he."

Also, it is not enough to *give* the people equal political power; one has to *maintain* them in that status because this equality is endemically liable to subversion from all sorts of directions. When one is dealing with millions of people, the maintenance of political equality requires considerable attention. It is something a political system has to work at, keeping not only its formal representative and electoral arrangements under constant review, but also paying attention to the surrounding phenomena of politics, such as the influence of wealth and other forms of social and economic power, to ensure that the political equality definitive of democracy remains a reality for the members of the society and not just decoration.

But if, on the other hand, we preoccupy ourselves – as constitutionalists do – with checking, restraining, limiting political power in the hands of those to whom it is formally assigned, then there is a danger that this constant necessary attention to equality will fall by the wayside. Constitutionalism is a doctrine about where attention is properly directed so far as a society's basic legal and political arrangements are concerned: by being directed constantly towards constraint, attention is distracted from those constitutional arrangements in a democracy whose function it is to keep faith with the enfranchisement of ordinary people.

10. Constitutionalism versus Democracy

If anything, matters are in even worse shape than this. The problem is not just that constitutionalism neglects the task of empowerment; constitutionalism takes democracy and the power that is assigned to ordinary people through elective and representative procedures as its natural enemy. One would think that a theory of politics devoted to imposing constraints upon the abuse of power would have in its sights all forms of tyranny, all forms of oppression. But again and again in the constitutionalist literature, one reads that it is the tyranny *of the majority* that constitutionalism is concerned to check, not tyranny in general.

So, for example, we hear scholars talking of "constitutionalism's fundamental commitment to protect certain decisions from current majoritarian impulses"[29] and describing constitutionalism as "at base, protection against the consequences of majoritarian power."[30] It is possible, I suppose, that this emphasis on *majoritarian* oppression (as opposed to other forms of oppression) and the dangers of *democracy* (as opposed to the dangers of oligarchy) is borne of a sense that we can take for granted the ascendancy of democracy, and that it is only its abuses that we need to worry about. But then that returns us to the concerns of the previous section.

I don't want to be painting too Manichean a picture from either perspective – democracy as constitutionalism's natural enemy, or constitutionalism as the constant object of a democrat's fear and suspicion. One way in which the opposition may be blurred is through the *redefinition* of "democracy" to associate it more closely with the constitutionalist ideal. Ronald Dworkin has taken this approach. He maintains that true democracy does not exist unless the members of a political community treat one another as their equals in a sense that goes far beyond formal political equality: they must also evince equal concern for one another and equal respect for one another's autonomy. Without this, he says, any version of democracy that requires "deference to temporary majorities on matters of individual right is . . . brutal and alien, and . . . nations with firm democratic traditions now reject it as fake."[31] So he concludes that a true democracy will contain in its ruling structures provisions that ensure this more extensive form of equal concern and respect, even at the cost of disempowering a majority. How far we should take this is a matter of debate.[32]

11. Popular Sovereignty

One area where we find that constitutionalists *are* prepared to emphasize democratic ideas has to do with the authorship of a constitution. I said earlier that constitutionalists think it important for there to be conscious reflection upon the design of a society's constitution. But that puts the matter too passively. Constitutionalists believe it is important for *the members of a society* to pay attention to the constitutional design of their polity: the constitutional scheme needs the imprimatur of popular legitimacy. Though it is widely believed that constitutional design is a science, in which right answers are well known to experts, still it is thought important that the lessons of this science be seen to be freely adopted by the citizens of the polity that is to be bound by them. In this way, the limitations that a constitution imposes on the ordinary operation of the democratic process have some sort of legitimacy that can withstand competition with the legitimacy of the measures adopted by a current majority.[33] So, for example, the U.S. Supreme Court in *Marbury v. Madison* began from the premiss that "the people have an original right to establish, for their future government, such principles as, in their opinion, shall most conduce to their own happiness" and argued that a judicial power to strike down unconstitutional legislation was necessary to give effect to the "original and supreme will" of the people.[34]

If constitutionalism is committed to popular sovereignty, what becomes of what I have described as its inherent suspicion of democracy? The two elements are not inconsistent. Popular sovereignty and democracy share obvious common commitments, but the idea that the people have the right to establish their own form of government is in theory compatible with their establishment of a non-democratic constitution or a heavily compromised form of democracy.[35] Nevertheless tensions do inevitably surface in this model.

One difficulty is that even if the constitutional restrictions on majority will represent a popular commitment at the constitution-making stage, most such restrictions are phrased very vaguely in constitutional documents, leaving open major choices for the society about rights and constitutional structure. The sense that these choices are constitutional in character leads, on the constitutionalist model, to a conviction

Jeremy Waldron

that at all costs they must not be made by a current majority. But then if they are to be made at all (in the ordinary life of a polity) they must be made by a non-majoritarian branch of government, such as the judiciary, and this can lead to difficulties which we will explore in section 12.

The other difficulty has to do with the perceived distance in time between the decisions of the popular sovereign and the popular majority which it is supposed to be presently constraining. Larry Alexander has argued that constitutionalism represents the power of past majorities over present and future majorities.[36] But obviously there is a legitimacy problem depending on how distant in the past the constraining majority is perceived to be. We may revere the framers of the constitution, but ancestor-worship by itself is a poor competitor to the sort of legitimacy that a measure enacted by a current democratic majority can claim. If we want to present the constraint on the current majority as a precommitment of the sovereign people themselves, then we must find a way to connect the people who made that precommitment six generations ago to the people who now seem to be subject to its constraint.[37] Maybe we can say that if the people have not bothered to amend the constitution, then that signifies their present consent. But this is almost always an unconvincing argument, resting everything as it does on a tenuous and contestable extrapolation from mere acquiescence to oppose a measure that has the real imprimatur of the people granted through a democratic process working actually and explicitly right now.

In confronting this difficulty, modern constitutionalists characteristically veer between an argument that tries, however unconvincingly, to rescue the popular-sovereignty credentials of the constitutional norm and a case that by-passes popular sovereignty altogether and argues simply for the moral necessity of the constraint. But the difficulty with the latter case is that it ignores the significance of moral disagreement. Members of the majority which enacted the constitutionally problematic measure presumably deny that the constitutional norm embodies an objective moral truth. Their best moral judgment is that the norm is wrong or outdated; that is why they voted for the present measure. They may be wrong about that, but then the constitutionalist's position begs the question of how these rival claims of right and wrong are to be adjudicated in a constitutional context.

As a last-ditch effort, the constitutionalist may try to claim that the current majority's decision represents nothing more than the ascendancy of its *preferences*; it is not a *moral* position that can be opposed to the moral principle embodied in the constraint. But this too is unconvincing. There is no reason for saying that popular majorities are incapable of thinking in principled terms; time and again representative institutions prove this constitutionalist prejudice wrong when they produce principled deliberations that, in their moral character, rival anything that can be seen in the non-elective branches of government.[38]

12. Judicial Review of Legislation

This brings us, finally, to the question of judicial power in a constitutional system. If a constitution is not to be merely a set of paper rules, there must be some way in which the force of its provisions is brought to bear on current political activity. Various methods are possible. One is to nurture an ethos of respect for the constitution among members of the polity, particularly active players in the political system, so that a sense of constitutional obligation becomes a shared point of reference in all their decisions. Another is to design institutions so that the way in which they accommodate the dynamics of power and ambition yields constitutional outcomes by a sort of invisible hand, even when few or none of the participants takes constitutional obligation seriously for its own sake.[39]

Few modern constitutionalists are satisfied with options like these. They tend to be interested in formal mechanisms of enforcement, among the most popular of which is the use of judicial power in the constitutional system to patrol breaches of constitutional constraints by other branches of government. If constitutional rules are seen as constitutional law, then it seems appropriate to entrust their enforcement to courts in the way that the enforcement of other legal rules is entrusted. And if, as constitutionalists believe, the point of the most important provisions of a modern constitution is to restrain or limit the exercise of legislative authority, then it makes sense to see these not just as law, but as higher law, enforceable by the courts against ordinary statutes. Support for judicial review, therefore, seems to be part and parcel of what is meant by modern constitutionalism.

Elsewhere, I have criticized the practice of strong judicial review as undemocratic.[40] That critique of course is question-begging in the present context, since most constitutionalists think that *being undemocratic* is part of the point of constitutional arrangements. But there are a couple of further difficulties.

Treating judicial authority as the main basis for constitutional enforcement leaves the constitutionality of judicial power itself effectively unchecked. Connected with this is the danger that judicial review might too easily become a form of constitutional law-making by the judiciary. Many of the provisions found in modern constitutions are left deliberately vague or abstract, usually as the cost of securing the sort of popular acceptance of them that would justify their imposition as constitutional constraints. As a result, major features of the country's political arrangements, the limits on government, or the restraints imposed on governmental power are left undefined. (American experience has shown that these issues are not always marginal or borderline issues; often they are major watershed issues about the shape and nature of the polity and of individual and minority rights.) This can lead to the following difficulty. When a legislative measure is challenged in court for violating one of these provisions, it is likely that the court will try to settle the constitutional issue by pinning down the meaning of the provision in question more precisely. From the court's point of view, this may seem no more than fulfilling its duty to interpret the provisions it is required to apply. But from a point of view that pays attention to the sources of constitutional change, it will seem as though a major decision about the shape and character of the society's constitution is now being made by a body that has no greater right than the elective branches to take on the mantle of popular sovereignty.

Some constitutionalists may be happy to say that the courts are entitled to speak for the popular sovereign when the people cannot actually assemble in a constitutional convention to settle some point of uncertainty or dispute. Others are simply resigned to the prospect, reckoning that any other method of settling disputed points

Jeremy Waldron

would have the effect of disempowering the courts even in cases where judicial review does not run into this difficulty and the effect of empowering the very majorities that constitutional provisions are supposed to disable.

Still, unless the commitment to popular sovereignty is nothing but lip service, one cannot avoid the thought that the current deliberations and decisions of the elective branches of government on matters constitutional have at least as much claim to be identified with popular sovereignty as the deliberation and decisions of unelected judges. Probably it is a mistake for *any* branch of government to assume the mantle of popular sovereign.[41] But if there is a major unresolved issue in the constitution and if the matter needs to be settled right now, one would think that whoever finds themselves stuck with the decision ought to be as sensitive as possible to the views of all elements in the polity, and not just insist that their one branch – let alone the least representative branch – be the one to take the decision.

One way or another, we are left with the conclusion that any commitment to popular sovereignty on the part of modern constitutionalists is rather thin. Constitutionalists will use the language of popular sovereignty when it is useful to legitimatize the constraints that they propose to place upon current political majorities. But they will retreat quickly from the logic of popular sovereignty, as soon as it threatens the authority of non-populist institutions like courts, which they take to have been entrusted with the task of restraining and limiting the popular will.

14. Concluding Remark

I have tried in this chapter to present a picture of constitutions differing somewhat from the picture usually put forward in the name of constitutionalism. Constitutions are not just about retraining and limiting power; they are about the empowerment of ordinary people in a democracy and allowing them to control the sources of law and harness the apparatus of government to their aspirations. That is the democratic view of constitutions, but it is not the constitutionalist view. Accordingly, I have emphasized the opposition between constitutionalism and democracy and, through constitutionalism's embrace of the idea of limited government, the ideological antipathy between constitutionalism and many of democracy's characteristic aims.

Of course, it is always possible to present an alternative to constitutionalism as an alternative form of constitutionalism: scholars talk of "popular constitutionalism" or "democratic constitutionalism."[42] I have nothing against such usages, though I have tried to sharpen the issues that I have been discussing by avoiding them. No doubt this has led to some exaggeration. No doubt a more moderate constitutionalism can be envisaged. (And no doubt all sorts of equivocations are imaginable by which the issues discussed in this chapter can be fudged.) But I think it is worth setting out a stark version of the antipathy between constitutionalism and democratic or popular self-government, if only because that will help us to measure more clearly the extent to which a new and mature theory of constitutional law takes proper account of the constitutional burden of ensuring that the people are not disenfranchised by the very document that is supposed to give them their power.

Notes

1   I have adapted these formulations from John Stuart Mill, *On Liberty*, ed. Currin V. Shields (Indianapolis, IN: Bobbs-Merrill, 1956), p. 43.

2   *Oxford English Dictionary* online, entry for "Constitutionalism" (visited Feb. 19, 2007).

3   *Oxford English Dictionary* online. The instances given are "1871 Daily Tel. 2 Nov., They persuaded the King that Constitutionalism was his natural role" and "1889 Times 19 Feb. 9/2 The frigid and negative constitutionalism of M. Carnot."

4   A. V. Dicey, *Introduction to the Study of the Law of the Constitution*, 8th edn. of 1915 (Indianapolis, IN: Liberty Classics, 1982), p. 386, uses "constitutionalism" in this sense when he writes that "the aim of Australian statesmen has been to combine . . . ideas borrowed from the federal and republican constitutionalism of the United States, . . . with ideas derived from the Unitarian and monarchical constitutionalism of England."

5   Roger Scruton, *A Dictionary of Political Thought* (London: Macmillan 1982), p. 94.

6   The best-known version of absolutism is that of Thomas Hobbes in *Leviathan*, ed. Richard Tuck (Cambridge: Cambridge University Press, 1996), Chs. 18 and 26.

7   But compare the response of Paul J. Magnarella, "The Comparative Constitutional Law Enterprise," *Willamette Law Review* 30 (1994): 510. "By definition, every state, even one with a dictatorship, has a constitution – a set of legal norms and procedures that structure its legal and governmental systems. . . . In the absence of the ruling elite's commitment to limited governmental powers under the rule of law, a state may have a constitution without constitutionalism. In such a case, comparativists would label its constitution 'nominal,' rather than 'normative'."

8   Alexander Hamilton, John Jay, and James Madison, *The Federalist*, ed. George W. Carey and James McLellan (Indianapolis, IN: Liberty Fund, 2001), p. 1.

9   *Marbury v. Madison* 5 U.S. 137 (1803), at 177.

10 This was the stance of the High Court of Australia in *Australian Capital Television Pty. Limited v. Commonwealth of Australia* 177 CLR 106 (1992), striking down a federal election law deemed incompatible with the unwritten commitment of the common law to freedom of expression.

11 Hannah Arendt, *On Revolution* (Harmondsworth: Penguin Books, 1973), p. 157.

12 I have argued this point for textual law generally in Jeremy Waldron, *Law and Disagreement* (Oxford: Clarendon Press, 1999), pp. 69–87.

13 Cf. Lon L. Fuller, *The Morality of Law*, rev. edn. (New Haven, CT: Yale University Press, 1969), p. 96.

14 Scott Gordon, *Controlling the State: Constitutionalism from Ancient Athens to Today* (Cambridge: Harvard University Press, 1999) and András Sajó, *Limiting Government: An Introduction to Constitutionalism* (Budapest: Central European Press, 1999).

15 Sajó, *Limiting Government*, p. x.

16 C. H. McIlwain, *Constitutionalism Ancient and Modern* (Ithaca, NY: Cornell University Press, 1940), p. 24 (quoted by Gordon, *Controlling the State*, p. 5).

17 Cass R. Sunstein, "Constitutionalism after the New Deal," *Harvard Law Review* 101 (1987): 421, esp. 434–36.

18 Carl J. Friedrich, *Constitutional Government and Democracy: Theory and Practice in Europe and America*, 4th edn. (Waltham, MA: Blaisdell Pub. Co., 1968), pp. 35–6.

19 Judith N. Shklar, "The Liberalism of Fear," in a collection of her essays, *Political Thought and Political Thinkers*, ed. Stanley Hoffman (Chicago: University of Chicago Press, 1998), p. 3.

20 Notice, though, that sometimes a particular agency of government is limited, not to limit government as such, but effectively to empower some other agency of government with

the task that the first one is constrained from pursuing. This happens particularly in the way central government is limited in a federal system. I am grateful to Rick Hills for this point.

21   United States Constitution, Article I, 10.

22   Cf. Linda Bosniak, "Constitutional Citizenship through the Prism of Alienage," *Ohio State Law Journal* 63 (2002): 1285, esp. p. 1287. See also Douglas Sturm, "A Prospective View of the Bill of Rights: Toward a New Constitutionalism," *Journal of Law and Religion* 13 (1996–8): 27, esp. pp. 29–30: "[C]onstitutionalism, a tradition of political theory and practice with which the idea of human rights is often associated, has the connotation of limited government. At one extreme, constitutionalism is linked with the concept of a laissez-faire state. . . ."

23   Sajó, *Limiting Government*, p. 2.

24   Cf. Dicey's account of separation of powers in his attempt to reconcile parliamentary sovereignty and the rule of law: Dicey, *Introduction to the Study of the Law of the Constitution*, pp. 268–73.

25   Cf. John Locke, *Two Treatises of Government*, ed. Peter Laslett (Cambridge: Cambridge University Press, 1988), pp. 329–30 and F. A. Hayek, *The Constitution of Liberty* (Chicago: University of Chicago Press, 1960), pp. 154–5.

26   For an excellent account of how constraint on political participation may have, in the long run, an affirmatively empowering and structuring effect, see Samuel Issacharoff, "Fragile Democracies," *Harvard Law Review* 120 (2007): 1405–67.

27   The themes I have mentioned here are particularly prominent in the constitutional theory of Hannah Arendt; see Jeremy Waldron, "Arendt's Constitutional Politics," in *The Cambridge Companion to Hannah Arendt*, ed. Dana Villa (Cambridge: Cambridge University Press, 2001).

28   I am thinking of Colonel Rainborough's exclamation in 1647 at Putney: "[T]ruly I think that the poorest he that is in England has a life to lead as the greatest he; and therefore truly, sir, I think it's clear that every man that is to live under a government ought first by his own consent to put himself under that government" ("The Debates at the General Council of the Army, Putney, 29 October 1647," in *The English Levellers*, ed. Andrew Sharp, Cambridge: Cambridge University Press, 1998, p. 103).

29   Robert A. Schapiro, "Polyphonic Federalism: State Constitutions in the Federal Courts," *California Law Review* 87 (1999): 1415, at p. 1438.

30   Sandra Schultz Newman and Daniel Mark Isaacs, "Historical Overview of the Judicial Selection Process in the United States: Is the Electoral System in Pennsylvania Unjustified?" *Villanova Law Review* 49 (2004): 1 at p. 16.

31   Ronald Dworkin, *Freedom's Law: The Moral Reading of the American Constitution* (Cambridge, MA: Harvard University Press, 1996), p. 71.

32   I have criticized Dworkin's position in Waldron, *Law and Disagreement*, Ch. 13.

33   Cf. Bruce Ackerman, *We the People: 1. Foundations* (Cambridge, MA: Harvard University Press, 1991)

34   *Marbury v. Madison* 5 U.S. 137 (1803), at 176.

35   See Locke, *Two Treatises of Government*, pp. 329–30, 354–6, and Thomas Hobbes, *De Cive: The English Version*, ed. Howard Warrender (Oxford: Clarendon Press, 1983), pp. 37, 131ff.

36   Larry Alexander, "Constitutional Rules, Constitutional Standards, and Constitutional Settlement: Marbury v. Madison and the Case for Judicial Supremacy," *Constitutional Commentary* 20 (2003): 369, esp. p. 373, defines "constitutionalism" as "constraint of present majoritarian bodies by past majorities."

37   See Waldron, *Law and Disagreement*, pp. 255–81 for a critique of this idea.

38 See the comparison of judicial argument and parliamentary argument about abortion in Jeremy Waldron, "Legislating with Integrity," *Fordham Law Review* 72 (2003): 373, esp. pp. 390–1.

39 This was Madison's approach to separation of powers in Hamilton, Jay, and Madison, *The Federalist*, p. 268 (#51): "Ambition must be made to counteract ambition. The interest of the man must be connected with the constitutional rights of the place."

40 See most recently Jeremy Waldron, "The Core of the Case Against Judicial Review," *Yale Law Journal* 115 (2006): 1346.

41 I develop this argument further in Jeremy Waldron, "Judicial Power and Popular Sovereignty," in *Marbury versus Madison: Documents and Commentary*, ed. Mark Graber and Michael Perhac (Washington, DC: CQ Press, 2002), p. 181. The argument is based on principles enunciated by Emmanuel Joseph Sièyes, *What Is the Third Estate?* (1788), trans. M. Blondel (New York: Frederick A. Prager, 1964).

42 See, e.g., Larry D. Kramer, *The People Themselves: Popular Constitutionalism and Judicial Review* (New York: Oxford University Press, 2004) and Frank I. Michelman, "What (if Anything) Is Progressive-Liberal Democratic Constitutionalism?" *Widener Law Symposium* 4 (1999): 181. See also Mark Tushnet, *Taking the Constitution Away from the Courts* (Princeton, NJ: Princeton University Press, 2000).

CHAPTER SIXTEEN

Constitutionalism

Larry Alexander

What are constitutions, what functions do they perform, and are they on balance desirable? These are large questions, to be sure, and space does not permit me more than a quite superficial stab at answering them. Nevertheless, I hope to provide at least a useful framework within which more complete answers can be elaborated. I take up these three questions in turn.

I. What Are Constitutions?

Consider the following stylized account of how a constitution might arise and the various philosophical problems that it entails (Alexander 1998; Grey 1979; Kay 1998). At step 1, Jane begins with her own views about principles of justice and other aspects of political morality, about principles of wise governance, and about the institutional arrangements best suited to realizing these various principles. If Jane could impose these principles and institutions by herself, Jane would do so (unless they included principles, such as democratic side constraints, that prohibited their unilateral imposition). Because Jane does not have such power, however, Jane needs the assistance of others, others who will not share all of Jane's views about political morality, wise governance, and institutional arrangements.

At step 2, then, Jane seeks wide agreement on rules of governmental behavior and rules defining governmental institutions that realize Jane's own personal principles and views to a greater extent than any alternative set of such rules on which Jane can obtain wide agreement. In other words, under Jane's own principles, it is preferable that they not be fully realized than that anarchy prevail (because of lack of wide agreement), but that they be realized as fully as possible consistent with wide agreement. Others who hold different principles and views will reason similarly, which will result in agreement on rules of governmental behavior and rules defining institutions that no one believes are optimal but that most believe are good enough

– that is, superior to anarchy. (Obviously, not just any set of rules will be superior to anarchy according to everyone's principles of political morality and wise governance; the rules must be the best that can be widely agreed upon and above everyone's anarchy threshold of acceptability.)

Understanding how this agreement at step 2 can be achieved is worth pondering. For understanding this is the key to understanding how constitutions can change without formal amendment, how revolutions can be domesticated, how separate systems of authoritative rules can exist side by side in the same community (and why this happens less frequently than might be expected), and other mysteries of constitutionalism and of law more generally.

I shall begin with the simplest version of the story (Alexander and Sherwin 2001). Members of the community disagree about or are uncertain about how their common moral principles are to be applied concretely. They perceive the moral need for authoritative settlement of those disagreements and uncertainties. Jane prefers the rule "Let Jane decide." John prefers the rule "Let John decide." And so on for each member of the community.

Jane's second best rule is "Let Sarah decide." But although it is also Sarah's preferred rule, it must compete with John's second best rule, "Let Jim decide," which is, or course, supported by Jim and John.

But now suppose that everyone's third-, second-, or first-choice rule is "Let the majority decide." If everyone understands that other first- and second-choice rules will not command agreement – and if everyone believes that "Let the majority decide" is morally superior to the alternative of no authoritative decision-maker – then everyone has a strategic reason for accepting "Let the majority decide" as the foundational authoritative rule. I say "strategic" to emphasize that perhaps everyone will view the rule, not as the best rule for settling moral controversies, but as the best rule that they can get others to accept. (In an important sense, of course, because the purpose of authoritative rules is to settle moral controversies, by being the best rule everyone can accept and the only rule that will actually perform the settlement function, this suboptimal rule becomes, for everyone, the optimal rule.)

Now as we complicate the story and move from the one basic rule, "Let the majority decide," to a complex set of rules regarding rights, procedures, and institutions, including perhaps supermajority institutions with the power to promulgate, repeal, and amend those rules, it becomes more and more likely that the resulting set of rules that must be agreed upon is far from anyone's ideal set of such rules. Some of the rules may be some members' first or second choices, but others will be further down on their list, and some may even be morally repugnant. Still, all have good reason to agree to the entire set, including the rules that they find morally repugnant, if that is the best set of rules to which they can get the others to agree, and if that set of rules is morally preferable to the absence of authoritative settlement. And again, because authoritative settlement requires agreement on authoritative rules, the morally best rules on which agreement can be obtained are in some sense the morally best rules. Rules that cannot command agreement cannot perform their moral function of settling what should be done and are thus undesirable, no matter how good those rules would be if they did command agreement.

Here is the picture thus far. Our mythical community has reached agreement about certain foundational rules, rules that set up some institution (or person) as the basic

Larry Alexander

rule promulgator and decision-maker, that prescribe certain rights and procedures and set up certain additional institutions, and that set up a supermajoritarian institution for expanding or changing these basic rules. The members agree to this complex package of rules, but not necessarily because it is anyone's ideal, and not necessarily because there are no rules in the package that anyone finds morally repugnant as opposed to suboptimal. Rather, they agree to the package because it is from everyone's point of view both morally superior to the absence of authoritative settlement and also the morally best such package to which they can get others to agree. And because it meets those conditions, the package is in an important sense everyone's morally ideal package of rules.

The rules widely accepted at step 2 may be entrenched to various degrees. That is, it may be widely accepted that these rules may not be altered ever, may not be altered for a certain length of time, and/or may not be altered except by extraordinary procedures. The members of the community may believe that they have the best rules they can ever have, and that there is far more danger of loss of political wisdom or will or loss of moral concern than there is danger that wide agreement on better rules will be thwarted.

At the moment of agreement on the entrenched rules at step 2, the rules will mean what those who have agreed to them mean by them. In other words, those who have agreed to the rules will have not merely agreed to certain symbols or sounds, but to particular meanings of those symbols and sounds. Their agreement can be memorialized only in symbolic form, however, which means that the symbols they have agreed upon and what they mean by those symbols can come apart. Therefore, at step 2 they might agree not only on the rules of governmental behavior and institutions, but also on rules about who is to decide at later times what they meant by those rules.

It might be useful, then, to distinguish a constitution as a collection of agreed-upon symbols from a metaconstitution (or preconstitutional rules), with the latter consisting of agreed-upon norms – metarules – about which particular set of symbols is the constitution, who is to interpret those symbols, and whose semantic intentions shall count as the authoritative meaning of the symbols. The constitution and the metaconstitution are inseparable at the moment of agreement in step 2, but they can come apart at any time thereafter. Thus, although the community may at some later time lack the earlier substantive agreement regarding the content of the rules that they had at step 2 – for example, they might now disagree about what freedom of speech should cover or about whether separation of powers is a good idea – they can still have wide agreement on the metaconstitution. And that agreement might still be sufficient under our principles of political morality to favor the constitution over anarchy.

This discussion of the metaconstitution and its relation to the symbolic constitution illustrates various ways that a constitution might change at step 3. First, the symbolic constitution might change without a change in the metaconstitution. Constitutional amendment in pursuance of the (original meaning of the) amending rules laid down in the symbolic constitution changes the original constitution organically.

Second, a constitutional revolution might occur in which agreement on the first metaconstitution is replaced by agreement on another metaconstitution that in turn picks out a different symbolic constitution. The community may draft a brand new constitution, widely agree on what it means and that it is more desirable than the current constitution, and also agree that it, and not the current constitution, shall now be authoritative for them. (Arguably, the United States Constitution itself was the product of such a constitutional revolution.)

Third, the symbolic constitution might remain the same, but the metaconstitution might change. Thus, the original metaconstitutional agreement might be supplanted at step 3 by a new metaconstitutional agreement, one that deems some parts of the symbolic constitution to be nonauthoritative, that substitutes a new understanding of the symbols for their original meaning, or that "ratifies" otherwise improper interpretations of the symbolic constitution.

Just as it is understandable how people of differing moral and political views could nonetheless agree to entrench a set of constitutional rules and metaconstitutional rules, so it is understandable how they might come to agree on new rules and metarules and hence effect a constitutional revolution. Because it is only the agreement that these rules and metarules shall be supremely authoritative that makes them so, any subsequent agreement can supplant the original agreement to this effect. Of course, some who might have gone along with the original agreement and its constitution may not go along with the later one. For them, the new constitution will not be authoritative even if it is obliging. At least, it will not be so if their political-moral beliefs favor anarchy or resistance to the new constitution. But that will be the case for any dissenters from a constitutional agreement as long as their acceptance of the constitution is not necessary to achieve the degree of effectiveness required to sustain the others' acceptance of the constitution.

Why should Jane at step 4 accept as authoritative a constitution or constitutional provision – whether in the original constitution of step 2 or a supplanting constitution of step 3 – if she does not view the constitution or the relevant provision thereof to be morally and prudentially ideal? The reason is the same one she had at steps 1 and 2: an effective set of relatively good entrenched rules, even if nonideal, may be ranked by Jane's own ideal political morality as better than either anarchy or any other set of entrenched rules that has a chance of gaining wide agreement.

Finally, there is the question of why anyone should ever accept any rule or metarule as authoritative – that is, as providing her with a content-independent reason for action. What I have argued thus far is that Jane can have content-*dependent* reasons – reasons derived from her political morality – to establish and entrench rules that others recognize as authoritative. But why should *Jane* recognize those rules as authoritative? Why should Jane not depart from them whenever her political morality marks disobedience as the preferable course? Of course, if her political morality supports these rules as the best Jane can get agreement upon, then her political morality will never dictate disobedience if that would undermine agreement. *But it might well dictate secret disobedience.*

This is the central dilemma of rule-following. Following a rule because it is a rule is what is meant by attributing practical authority to the rule. But if practical authority is impossible, claims of practical authority will be false, and hence rules *qua* rules will be undermined, which by hypothesis is morally nonoptimal. So it appears, paradoxically, that it is morally optimal to make claims on behalf of rules that one might know to be false. And what goes for rules generally applies equally to the entrenched rules of constitutional law.

Larry Alexander

Let us now look more closely at various aspects of this "just so" story of adopting a constitution. First, the story assumes distinctions between, on the one hand, the constitution and the metaconstitutional rules and, on the other hand, the constitution and ordinary law. But how are these distinctions to be drawn?

Take the distinction between the constitution and the metaconstitution. Recall that at step 2, Jane and her community accepted a particular set of rules for making and changing valid laws (settlements of what they, as a society, should do), along with rules regarding how that first set of rules may amended, how it should interpreted, by whom, and with what degree of entrenchment if the interpretation is later thought to be wrong. Now suppose the rules for making and changing valid law (and perhaps the rules for amending these rules) are written, but the other rules (regarding the how, the who, and the effect of constitutional interpretation) are not. (This describes the United States Constitution on most understandings.) Are only the written rules "the constitution," with the unwritten rules being meta- or preconstitutional? All of these rules, written and unwritten, rest on acceptance. Moreover, the written rules could have been unwritten, and the unwritten rules could have been written.

Consider now the distinction between the constitution and ordinary law. Presumably, the constitution contains the rules governing how ordinary law is made and changed. But ordinary law may itself prescribe how other law is made and changed. (Consider legislation setting forth the rules governing the enactment and repeal of administrative regulations, or state legislation governing law-making by municipalities and counties.) Moreover, much of law consists of rules specifying how legal obligations can be created, modified, or expunged – the rules governing "private ordering." At which level in the hierarchy do the rules governing the making of other rules become "constitutional"?

One might be tempted to distinguish constitutions from ordinary law by subject matter. Constitutions, one might suppose, contain broad general rules establishing the basic procedures for governance and perhaps some individual rights and other limitations on governmental action. Ordinary laws, on the other hand, deal with more mundane matters or with temporary matters. But, of course, the preceding is not true of most existing constitutions as we understand them. The United States Constitution contains, in addition to the basic structural and empowering rules for the national government, and the magisterial rights in the Bill of Rights, several quite specific rules, many of which were responses to historical problems that have long since disappeared. And what is true of the United States Constitution is even more characteristic of other constitutions (Finer et al. 1995). The constitutions of France, Germany, and Russia, particularly the latter two, are chock-full of very specific rules addressing very limited problems or rooted in very time and place-bound traditions and concerns. On the other hand, much ordinary law establishes basic structures (for example, the Cabinet departments and administrative agencies) and basic individual rights (for example, those found in the 1964 Civil Rights Act and the 1965 Voting Rights Act).

What about "writtenness"? Does not the fact that constitutions are written distinguish them from metaconstitutional rules although not from ordinary statutory law?

I would submit that "writtenness" is neither necessary nor sufficient for constitutions, nor does it distinguish them from metaconstitutional rules. The latter might all be memorialized in writing. What would then distinguish them from "the constitution" might be only the fact that the authority of the metaconstitutional rules rests directly on the fact of acceptance, whereas the "constitution's" authority would derive from the authority of the metaconstitutional rules and would rest on acceptance one step removed. One could dissent from the constitutional rules but accept them as authoritative, whereas that would not be possible with metaconstitutional rules. Of course, because the whole edifice rests on acceptance – and because acceptance of metaconstitutional rules is rational even if they are not ideal from anyone's perspective, but only ideal in the sense that they are the best rules that everyone can accept – the line between "the constitution" and "the metaconstitution" appears impossible to draw as a theoretical matter.

Perhaps then we should just say that when the authority of written rules rests on unwritten metaconstitutional rules, the written rules can be deemed "the constitution." Although "writtenness" would then distinguish constitutions from metaconstitutions, it would still not distinguish constitutions from other written laws.

Moreover, just as "writtenness" is not sufficient for identifying constitutions, neither is it necessary. Although it would be impractical in any society over a certain size, or in any legal system intended to last for many years, there is no logical impossibility in having all laws, including the constitution, be unwritten. Memorializing rules in writing is enormously useful, of course, because it averts controversies over just what rules were posited. It would be a mistake, however, to view "writtenness" as a necessary attribute of law or of constitutions.

Perhaps the most promising way of distinguishing constitutions from metaconstitutional rules and from ordinary law is by reference to degrees of entrenchment. One might argue that constitutions are rules that are more entrenched against change than ordinary laws. Thus, in the United States, the Constitution may be changed only by the supermajority requirements set forth in Article V – and the rule giving "equal suffrage" to the states in the Senate may not be changed at all – whereas ordinary legislation and its repeal is accomplished by majority votes in Congress.

The relative entrenchment story is, however, a more complicated one. Consider, first, that the existence of the Constitution of the United States itself depends on the public's acceptance now and from moment to moment of the authority of the document drafted in Philadelphia in 1787 and ratified according to the terms it set forth. That acceptance – the metaconstitution – is never entrenched, nor could it be. Even the most entrenched part of the Constitution – the "equal suffrage" rule – is authoritative only because it is accepted as such at any given time. (This point reflects the paradox of authoritative rules: We accept them as means of settling disagreements about what should be done; but because, to effect such settlements, they must be determinate and thus must diverge in a range of cases from what is morally optimal, we have reason to depart from what we have reason to accept, and these competing reasons cannot be weighed or balanced because they are aspects of the same reason and operate at different levels.)

In saying that even the most entrenched rules rest on moment to moment acceptance, I am not overlooking the possibility that at their inception, these rules were agreed to by the entire community. There are three points to make about such constitutional agreements. First, it is difficult to think of an existing constitutional regime that was founded on universal agreement. The Constitution of the United States surely was not. Not only were many of those subject to it disenfranchised, but also many of those who could vote on its ratification opposed it.

Larry Alexander

Second, for the same reason that a promise to commit a wrong is not morally binding, an agreement to be bound by a rule is not morally binding when the rule is later assessed to be morally iniquitous.

Third, however many founders agreed to the constitutional rules, and whatever force such an agreement might have for *their* being bound, the successor generations are not bound by virtue of an original agreement of the founders. The founders' rules are authoritative for successor generations only through the successors' acceptance of that authority. Of course, that does not mean that if they do not accept the rules, it is wrong for those who do accept them to impose those rules on the dissenters. Once the level of acceptance declines sufficiently, however, the rules will become ineffective in settling community disagreements over what to do, which means that those who accepted the rules will now themselves have no reason to do so. The community will need to coordinate around a new set of rules in order to settle controversies.

The point here is that even the most entrenched rule – a rule like the "equal suffrage" rule that cannot be amended – ultimately rests on acceptance of its entrenchment. On the other hand, even the least entrenched rule – say, one that can at any time be overturned by a majority – must be entrenched for some period of time for it to be effective as a rule. Consider a rule that can be reconsidered over and over at any time, and that is alternately enacted and repealed with retroactive effect again and again within a single day. Such a rule is, during its various enactments, too unentrenched to perform its function.

That example is, in terms of entrenchment, the polar opposite of the totally entrenched "equal suffrage" rule. But between the two are rules that are entrenched to varying degrees. For example, we typically distinguish the provisions in the United States Constitution that can be repealed only through the supermajoritarian processes of Article V from ordinary statutes passed by Congress, which can be repealed by subsequent ordinary statutes. The latter we deem to be ordinary law, whereas the former we deem to be constitutional law. And it is true that constitutional provisions are more entrenched than ordinary statutes. But notice that to enact or repeal a statute, the statute must receive a majority vote in the two houses of Congress and then be signed by the President. If the President refuses to sign, the statute or repeal requires a two-thirds vote of both houses. Surely, then, the status quo of "ordinary" law of the United States is entrenched a good deal more than it would be if laws were passed and repealed solely by majority vote in a unicameral legislature or in a plebiscite.

In addition to the two house and presidential concurrence requirements of the United States Constitution, there are various additional rules in the United States and in other countries that entrench ordinary laws to varying degrees. There are usually numerous procedural rules about when and how issues may be raised that both entrench the status quo somewhat and avoid problems of cycling that Arrow's Theorem would otherwise predict for simple majoritarianism and unentrenched rules. And as John McGinnis and Michael Rappaport illustrate in their exhaustive study of the topic, the United States Constitution has a number of rules that entrench ordinary laws against change, such as the two-thirds vote in the Senate required to approve a treaty or to convict a federal official in an impeachment trial (McGinnis and Rappaport 2002).

Thus, although constitutions might be distinguished by the degree to which their rules are entrenched, ordinary, nonconstitutional laws are always entrenched to some extent. And in constitutions such as that of the United States, many ordinary laws are highly entrenched due to the bicameralism and presidential concurrence requirements and to specific supermajority rules in the Constitution itself.

Many readers may believe that I have omitted the most obvious way to distinguish constitutions from ordinary law, which is not by relative degrees of entrenchment but is instead by location in the *hierarchy of legal validity*. On this view, ordinary laws are legally valid if they are consistent with the constitution. The constitution's legal validity, however, does not depend on its consistency with any higher law but rests on acceptance.

Moreover, on this view, ordinary laws may be *more* entrenched than the constitution. Thus, the constitution may provide that it can be amended by majority vote. A constitutional provision may, however, authorize entrenchment of ordinary laws, so that the legislature can enact statutes that may only be repealed by supermajorities. Therefore, according to this view, degree of entrenchment cannot be the criterion that distinguishes constitutions from ordinary laws.

Now I wish to concede that a constitution could provide for the entrenchment of statutes passed by majorities. And the constitution itself might be amendable by a bare majority. Such a state of affairs is possible, though it would obviously be a quite fragile arrangement. If a majority wished to repeal a statute that has been entrenched against majority repeal, it would surely be tempted to amend the constitution to allow it to do so, given that it could amend the constitution by majority vote. Indeed, it could amend the constitution, repeal the statute, and then change the constitution back again to re-allow statutory entrenchments. Of course, it might exercise enormous self-restraint and refuse to take this course of action. But there are obvious reasons why entrenchments are usually not authorized by non-entrenched provisions.

Having conceded the possibility that a "constitution" might be less entrenched than "nonconstitutional law," why not distinguish constitutions from ordinary law in terms of what validates what? The problem with using location in the hierarchy of legal validity relations to mark off constitutions is this: What we normally regard as unitary constitutions are themselves made up of parts that are located at different points in the legal validity hierarchy.

Consider the United States Constitution. Arguably, it is Article VII thereof, which describes the ratification requirements for the Constitution itself, that is the most fundamental provision in the Constitution, the provision that validates all others. This provision was what was accepted as the "rule of recognition," so that even those who voted against ratification would accept the Constitution if it were ratified according to Article VII's terms (Green 2004).

If Article VII stands at the top of the validity hierarchy, Article V, the amendment provision, is one step below it. And that means that those amendments made in pursuance of Article V are two steps below Article VII. If, therefore, location in the validity hierarchy were the criterion that distinguished constitutions from ordinary law, and not relative entrenchment, the Fourteenth Amendment would be ordinary law, not part of the constitution rightly so called. Indeed, so would Articles I through VI.

I suggest that location in the validity hierarchy is not a descriptively cogent method for identifying what we normally call constitutions. I concede, however, that it is possible for what we normally call constitutions to be less entrenched than what we normally might call ordinary law. I believe that degree of entrenchment will normally mark off what we think of as constitutions better than validity relations, but the two criteria will more frequently than not go together. And, of course, the entire edifice rests on acceptance.

II. What Functions Do Constitutions Perform?

If constitutions are laws that are more entrenched than ordinary laws – remembering that entrenchment is often a matter of degree, and that even the most entrenched laws ultimately rest on moment to moment acceptance – what functions do constitutions perform? Theoretically, a constitution could entrench a complete legal code, with no mechanisms for changing that code other than through constitutional amendment or revolution. In modern societies, however, such a static legal system would be highly dysfunctional. Therefore, realistically, at a minimum, constitutions entrench the rules governing the making and changing of ordinary (nonconstitutional) law. Those rules might do no more than establish a simple, unicameral parliamentary democracy. Even such a simple constitutional system would probably have rules regarding how the parliament is selected, who the eligible voters are, and so on, though it is possible that these rules might not be entrenched and could be altered by parliament itself in its ordinary law-making capacity. If the constitutional entrenchments are not absolute, then the constitution will normally contain entrenched rules about how the constitution can itself be altered.

Most constitutions go beyond entrenching a simple parliamentary democracy and procedures for constitutional amendment. They may entrench rules setting up more complex law-making procedures – for example, the bicameral and presidential concurrence requirements of the United States Constitution. They may entrench rules establishing executive and judicial departments and specifying their powers, procedures, and membership criteria. They may entrench federal systems of divided and limited law-making powers. And, of course, they may entrench certain rights held by individuals against the government or against other individuals.

Why entrench rules against repeal or amendment by current majorities? After all, no matter how wise and virtuous, constitutional founders know that they are fallible both morally and prudentially. What would motivate them to entrench rules that may well turn out to be suboptimal or even mischievous?

There are several reasons that might justify entrenchment. One is a reason that lies behind all attempts to guide behavior through posited, determinate rules, namely, settlement of controversies over what should be done. Such controversies produce moral and prudential costs in terms of decision-making time and expense, failure to coordinate decisions, and the inability to make optimal use of expertise. Determinate rules simplify decision-making, make coordination possible, and, if posited by authorities selected for their expertise or their ability to utilize expertise, are more likely to be morally and prudentially optimal or near optimal than random decisions.

Determinate rules produce these settlement benefits to a greater extent the more they are entrenched against repeal. If such rules are subject to repeal at any moment upon a slight shift in majority sentiment, they are less reliable for coordination purposes, and more resources will be spent in attempting to repeal them (and fighting off such attempts). So although there is a danger in entrenching rules – the rules may be imprudent or iniquitous – there are settlement benefits derived from entrenchments.

Moreover, there are particular classes of rules that founders might think are particularly apt for entrenchment. Some rule-entrenchments protect against predictable legislative shortsightedness. For example, the "contracts clause" of the United States Constitution in Article I, section 10, which forbids the states from impairing the obligations of contracts, was entrenched because in economic downturns, debtors, who greatly outnumber creditors, find it in their interest to have legislatures pass laws relieving them of their debts. Such laws benefit the current debtors, but because they make extension of credit risky, they raise the interest rates future debtors must pay and are ultimately economically disastrous. Legislative majorities cannot be counted on to protect future generations of debtors, who, of course, cannot currently vote.

The scenario that lies behind the contracts clause is a typical example of the type that is of interest to public choice theorists regarding when legislative majorities will predictably be untrustworthy and where an entrenched rule will be of benefit. Other examples in this vein are entrenched rules that are, in John Ely's words, "representation-reinforcing" (Ely 1980). Thus, rules that define who is eligible to vote for the legislature might be entrenched so that a momentary majority cannot freeze out those who favor the opposition by disenfranchising them. Similarly, rules that guarantee free speech might be entrenched to prevent momentary majorities from silencing their critics.

Another class of rules that might seem quite appropriate for entrenchment are those Adrian Vermeule calls "veil of ignorance rules," "eligibility rules," and "recusal rules," all of which find expression in provisions of the United States Constitution (Vermeule 2001). Veil-of-ignorance rules are rules, such as those requiring that laws be general and prospective, that prevent the predictable legislative abuses that occur when legislators are aware of the particular people whom their laws benefit and burden. Eligibility rules and recusal rules prevent predictable conflicts of interest from occurring. All of these types of rules are entrenched, when they are, because the dangers that self-interest will impair governmental judgment outweigh whatever dangers attend entrenchment itself.

Of course, the rules whose entrenchments in constitutions are often most controversial are those establishing certain rights. One source of controversy is over whether such constitutional rights should be restricted to rights against government action – rights that government not infringe various liberties, that government not take or excessively regulate property, or that government not discriminate along various axes, such as on the basis of race, sex, religion, or nationality – or whether constitutional rights should include claim rights *to* certain governmental actions, such as rights to employment or to a certain level of income, health care, and the like, or should include rights against private parties and institutions in addition to rights against the government. Negative rights protecting liberty and property have the advantage of being easier to enforce judicially than affirmative claim rights to employment, health care, and income, particularly because they are frequently viewed as less sensitive to context, though this does not in itself make the latter unsuitable for constitutional entrenchment (Sunstein 2001). The pre-legal (moral) existence of negative rights is also less controversial than the existence of affirmative ones.

Larry Alexander

The more important controversy regarding the constitutionalization of rights is whether there is sufficient justification for entrenching rights against democratic revision. On one view, rights are particularly apt for constitutional entrenchment because they represent limits on what majorities are entitled to do, and because majorities cannot be trusted to uphold rights when rights thwart their ambitions. On the opposing view, rights should be left to majority determination because the content of rights is frequently controversial, and no past determination of that content should constrain the current majority's view of it. This controversy is more fully elaborated and evaluated in the final section.

III. Are Constitutions Desirable?

Constitutions entrench rules so that they cannot be overturned by mere legislative majorities. For that reason, constitutionalism and judicial review – the practice giving courts the authority to overturn majoritarian decisions found by them to be inconsistent with constitutionally entrenched rules – have been attacked as antidemocratic and therefore morally illegitimate. Is such an attack warranted?

At the outset it will be useful to distinguish between attacking constitutionally entrenched rules because they cannot be *overturned* by current majorities and attacking those rules because they are *interpreted* by nondemocratic bodies. The former attack is on the very idea of constitutional entrenchment. The latter is on the practice of judicial review. One can have a constitution of entrenched rules but leave the interpretation of those rules to democratic decision-making, and many countries do just that.

Nonetheless, the two attacks are closely related in this sense. If the constitutional rules are quite determinate, so that a democratic majority will likely interpret them no differently from how a court would, that majority is still being bound by a decision made, not by the current majority, but by the constitutional founders. Judicial review does not change matters. The "despotism" is that of the founders. On the other hand, if the constitutional rules are indeterminate standards, judicial review essentially becomes rule by the courts or judicial despotism. Only the combination of an indeterminate set of constitutional standards "interpreted" by current majorities leaves those current majorities untethered. In other words, only if we are free to decide what to do based entirely on what the current majority deems best have we satisfied the pure democrat. Determinate constitutional rules legislatively interpreted are no less antidemocratic than indeterminate rules judicially interpreted.

Jeremy Waldron is well known for his defense of the supremacy of decisions made by democratic legislatures over the enforcement of written constitutional guarantees by judges (Waldron 1999; Waldron 1998). In other words, Waldron is firmly on the side of majoritarian decision-making and against judicial review. Because we live in what Waldron calls the circumstances of politics – we each hold different judgments regarding what we as a group ought to do, and what we as a group ought to allow individuals to do; and we each prefer that we adopt a single policy on these matters, even if it is not the one we favor, than that we each act on our own but differing judgments about what ought to be done – therefore, argues Waldron, we need a mechanism for collectively deciding upon such a single policy, and democratic legislation is the morally superior of the possible mechanisms. Moreover, for Waldron, a bill of rights, judicially enforced, that is supposed to trump any democratically made decisions inconsistent with it, is a morally inferior mechanism to democratic decision-making, even with respect to protecting individual rights. For if we disagree, as we do and will, about what those rights are, how they are to be elaborated, and what weight they possess vis-à-vis other values, then we will need to reach a decision about these contested matters. And democratic decision-making is morally superior to nondemocratic judicial review when the contested matters are individual rights and their contours, just as it is with respect to other policy disputes. In other words, the circumstances of politics apply to questions of individual rights as much as to other issues, and democratic decision-making is morally mandated for all contested matters.

That is Waldron's position painted with a very broad brush. But the argument from the circumstances of politics to the moral superiority of democratic-majoritarian decision-making is, I find, elusive. I shall examine what I believe are the three possible arguments that Waldron might make. In the end, I conclude that none of the three can get Waldron what he wants, namely, a knockdown moral case against constitutionalism and judicial review.

What are the three arguments that might be advanced to support the moral superiority of democratic decision-making over constitutionalism with judicial review? One argument is epistemic. The decisions enacted by democratic majorities might be more likely morally correct than those enforced by judges in the name of rights endorsed at some point in the past. Present democratic majorities might be better informed than past majorities and their judicial agents, both because they can draw upon the wisdom of both the past and the present, and because they are better able to assess the interests of all who will be affected by their decisions. And, *pace* Condorcet, whom Waldron cites on this point, the more who support a decision as the morally correct one, the more likely the decision is to be correct, at least given the assumption that individuals are each more likely to decide correctly than incorrectly. (Condorcet's application to choices that are not binary is, however, much less optimistic. See Estlund 2005.)

The epistemic argument for the superiority of democratic decision-making over constitutionalism with judicial review is not rejectable on analytic grounds, but it is hostage to the facts. And the facts about democratic decision-making do not establish its epistemic superiority across the board on those issues within its purview. Majorities are better informed on some moral matters than on others. They are more likely to deliberate thoughtfully on some matters than on others. The same goes for constitutional framers and for judges. The proof of the pudding here is whether unconstrained majoritarianism produces morally better legislation than the impure majoritarianism of, say, the American legal system, with its mix of bicameralism, executive veto, federalism, and, of course, constitutional rights, the constitutional amendment procedure, and judicial review. Conceivably, unconstrained majoritarianism might be epistemically superior at some times and places. But I doubt that it can be shown to be for all times and places. In the end, with respect to the epistemic argument, I conclude that even though the more who oppose me on some moral issue, the more I should be aware of my own fallibility, in the end, numbers do not guarantee moral correctness, and he who swims against the moral current is not always wrong to do so. Although Waldron does not dispute this point, I believe that this point ultimately

Larry Alexander

undermines any epistemic argument for democracy. For the same epistemic reasons we exclude infants, the insane, and perhaps felons from the franchise, we might also establish bicameralism, the veto, and judicially enforced constitutional rights. We know we are subject to political weakness of will and other forms of cognitive and moral distortion. We know about public choice predicaments and rent-seeking costs. And particularly if the constitutionally entrenched rules were adopted by a supermajority after full deliberation, we may have more confidence in the decisions of long-dead constitutional founders than in present-day bare majorities.

The epistemic argument turns as well on whether the constitutional founders entrenched structures and rights through determinate rules or through indeterminate standards. There are in reality three principal possibilities to consider.

First, the constitutional founders may have attempted to settle what our rights require and entrenched that settlement through constitutional *rules* implementing those rights. Because the rights would be entrenched in the form of rules, they would clearly warrant judicial interpretation and enforcement. Such a constitutional entrenchment through rules has clear settlement advantages. Moreover, it has some epistemic advantages – the "constitutional moment" of the founding may have produced unusually widespread and thoughtful deliberation – and some democratic warrant, particularly if ratified by a supermajority. Those advantages pass through to the courts that apply the constitutionally entrenched rules.

Second, the constitutional founders may have entrenched rights in the form of standards, and the courts, in interpreting and implementing those standards, might translate them into rather determinate doctrinal rules (Schauer 2005). In this scenario, because the courts are both resolving controversial evaluative matters and then "legislating" – coming up with implementing rules – in a way that trumps the legislature itself, the courts are on weaker ground than in the first scenario. If they are appointed rather than elected, the courts have no democratic warrant, not even from a ratifying supermajority, as the founders delegated the rights questions rather than resolved them. As for the epistemic case, the courts may or may not have an epistemic advantage over the legislature, depending on whether you believe Ronald Dworkin or believe Waldron (Dworkin [1985] argues famously that because courts are "forums of principle," they *do* have an epistemic advantage over legislatures in ascertaining our moral rights.)

Third, the constitution may either entrench rights in the form of standards or be silent regarding rights, and the content and implementation of moral rights is not left to courts but is left entirely to contemporary democratic bodies acting in their ordinary legislative modes. Those bodies will, of course, have democratic warrant for their decisions about rights. And they may have some epistemic advantages over courts – for example, they are unconstrained by the adjudicative form – and over the constitutional founders (they have more history to draw upon and live in the circumstances to which their legislation will apply). These are Waldron's points. But these bodies will also have epistemic disadvantages vis-à-vis courts (Dworkin's point) and vis-à-vis the founders (they are less behind a morally useful veil of ignorance, they are quite likely to be less deliberative, and they will face various distorting pressures from perhaps rights-insensitive majorities or minorities).

In assessing which of these three alternatives is preferable, one not only has to weigh the epistemic and democratic advantages and disadvantages, but one also has to determine how desirable or undesirable is the entrenchment through rules of the resolutions of controversial moral questions. Entrenchment through rules has the ordinary advantages of settlement – predictability, coordination, and decision-making efficiency. And it has the ordinary disadvantages of settlement as well – the settling rules will be blunt (over and underinclusive) even if ideal as rules; and given human fallibility, they will almost surely *not* be ideal. What degree of entrenchment do our resolutions of moral questions call for? Not absolute entrenchment for sure. Entrenchment that only supermajorities can overturn? Entrenchment that only super-majorities or courts overruling judicial precedents can overturn? Or no entrenchment whatsoever?

As stated, the epistemic argument is hostage to the facts. For some, epistemic considerations should be dispositive (Alexander 2002; Alexander 1998; Arneson 2004). They believe that whatever decision-making form produces the morally best decisions should be chosen, democratic or not. Democracy is only a means to an end, and if another means is instrumentally better, so much the worse for democracy.

The second argument in favor of democratic decision-making is a straightforward moral one. Where A believes morality dictates policy X, and B and C believes it dictates policy Y, B and C have a moral right to have policy Y prevail *even if* (from the God's-eye point of view) *policy X is morally correct and policy Y is morally flawed.* Assuming both X and Y affect the lives of those who oppose them, the moral right of B and C to have incorrect policy Y prevail is then a moral right to commit moral wrongs against others. The right to democratic decision-making is, on this argument, a right to do wrong.

Now I believe there indeed are some rights to act immorally. But this argument goes far beyond that limited set of rights and applies to all moral wrongs so long as the democratic majority votes to permit or compel them. But such a right to do wrong is untenable.

To see this, imagine that for A, the circumstances of politics do not exist because A can enforce his will against B and C. (He is endowed with superior strength and technology.) And suppose A believes – we shall assume correctly – that what B and C propose is profoundly unjust. On the argument under consideration, A must let B and C have their way, despite the fact that what they propose is morally wrong and that A can prevent the immoral outcome. But such a moral must is quite implausible. Numbers do not, any more than might, make right.

Consider as an illustration a variation of the situation described in Walter Van Tilburg's *The Ox Bow Incident* (1940). A large posse has captured some suspected killers and cattle rustlers. Most of the posse wants, on moral grounds, to hang them on the spot rather than turn them over to the lawful authorities and lawful processes. A few on the posse dissent, however, and argue vigorously for the latter course. After lengthy discussion, the posse votes, and immediate hanging wins by a large margin. The dissenters, however, appalled at the decision, discuss whether they should employ the element of surprise, pull their guns on the majority, and force it to hand over the suspects to the dissenters, who would see that the suspects received full due process. Waldron can be read as arguing that the dissenters would be acting morally wrongly in following their own rather than the majority's moral view of the matter. I, on the other hand, like others (Arneson), cannot see why the majority's decision should be given more moral weight than its epistemic credentials warrant.

Larry Alexander

Nor does the notion of "respect" morally dictate that A accede to B and C's immoral proposal. A's moral theory may hold that B and C must be respected as persons, or some such thing; but it would be a strange moral theory that contains a notion of respect that made the moral theory "self-effacing" (Alexander and Kress 1997).

Waldron sometimes appears to be making a moral argument on behalf of democratic decision-making. But if suspension of the circumstances of politics does not leave A with a moral obligation to accede to the immoral B and C, it is difficult to see how placing A in the circumstances of politics creates a moral obligation to do so. The circumstances of politics do bear on what A is morally obligated to do, as I shall show. But they do not do so in the way this argument claims.

Waldron does not deal at length with control of the franchise. But such control affects the moral argument for democratic decision-making. Suppose B, C, and D vote to exclude E from the franchise. (E is uneducated, and B, C, and D enact a franchise restriction excluding the uneducated.) A believes – correctly, we shall assume – that such an exclusion is unjust, and votes against the exclusion, along with E. Because the two of them are outvoted, E is excluded. Now B, C, and D vote for another measure (X) that A believes – again, correctly – is unjust. Is A bound by such an unjust measure passed by a democratic majority that has unjustly excluded some from the franchise? If unjust measures are morally obligating if democratically enacted, does that apply to democratically enacted limitations of the franchise? (Christiano 2000). (Remember, E did vote on his own exclusion; he just lost.) Again, it is difficult to see how one can distinguish the two types of unjust but democratically enacted measures. But it is also difficult to believe that democratically enacted but unjust measures are morally obligatory when the democratic franchise has been unjustly restricted.

(Waldron also does not discuss Arrovian problems in defining the output of democratic majorities. Those problems are usually avoided by various rules controlling the agenda or privileging the status quo ante, rules that violate Arrovian conditions. With those rules, we do not have pure majoritarianism; without them, we would have trouble, because of cycling, etc. identifying the relevant democratically endorsed positions.)

I think it is a mistake to posit democratic decision-making as a deontological side-constraint on governance. The case for democracy that I favor is the Winston Churchill one – it's better than the competitors. And if it's better as a general matter, it might be better still if it is representative rather than direct, if it has separated powers, and if it is limited by rights that are judicially enforced.

In short, I reject a moral right to democratic decision-making, except as an infelicitous way of claiming democracy's superiority on consequentialist grounds, including a consequentialism of rights protection. The alleged moral right to democracy surely does not follow from any plausible egalitarianism. It does not follow from equality of welfare (or the opportunity therefor), nor from equality of resources, both of which might be better secured in a benign despotism. Nor does it follow from equality of respect; for what is up for respect here is not other people's welfare, but other people's *judgments* about what everyone's moral rights and duties are. Those judgments may be wrong, in which case respecting them may entail allowing those whose judgments they are to impose immoral constraints and duties on other people. Respect for persons does not extend to respecting their violations of others' rights, and respect cannot be demanded for erroneous moral judgments in the form of acceding to them. There is no right to violate others' rights so long as enough people agree with you.

The third argument Waldron might make against constitutional entrenchment *does* take the circumstances of politics seriously. It is described at the beginning of section I and is what I shall call a strategic moral argument. Suppose that A believes that moral theory T is correct. Were A all-powerful, A would impose T, even over the objection of everyone else. But A is not all-powerful.

The question then is what is the moral imperative that A faces given the circumstances of politics? More particularly, is that moral imperative to opt for majoritarian decision-making?

I believe that the answer goes something like this. A wants an outcome that is as close as he can get to the outcome dictated by correct moral theory T. He therefore wants that system of government that is (1) most likely to produce results closest to what T dictates and (2) most likely to be agreed upon by a sufficient number of people to eliminate the circumstances of politics problem. If either A and B or A and C are sufficiently powerful to impose their will, and B's moral views are closer to T than C's, A will join with B in whatever form of government they can agree to. Moreover, if C morally prefers the likely outcomes of the A-B system to anarchy, C will have a moral reason to accept the authority of that system. The system might turn out to be majoritarian democracy, *but it might turn out to be something else.* What each of us has a moral reason to accept is that form of government that is most likely to get it right from our point of view among those forms that we can get enough others to accept. Because the moral costs of anarchy are usually assessed to be quite high from most people's moral standpoints, many governmental arrangements would be accepted over anarchy. Majoritarian democracy may be one of them. But so might constitutionalism and judicial review.

References

Books

Alexander, L., and E. Sherwin. 2001. *The Rule of Rules* (Durham, NC: Duke University Press).
Dworkin, R. M. 1985. *A Matter of Principle* (Cambridge, MA: Harvard University Press).
Ely, J. H. 1980. *Democracy and Distrust* (Cambridge, MA: Harvard University Press).
Finer, S. E., V. Bognadorand, B. Rudden. 1995. *Comparing Constitutions* (Oxford: Clarendon Press).
Sunstein, C. R. 2001. *Designing Democracy* (Oxford: Oxford University Press).
Van Tilburg, W. 1940. *The Ox Bow Incident* (New York: Random House).
Waldron, J. 1999. *Law and Disagreement* (Oxford: Clarendon Press).

Articles in Books

Alexander, L. A. 1998. "Introduction," in L. A. Alexander (ed.), *Constitutionalism: Philosophical Foundations* (Cambridge: Cambridge University Press), pp. 1–15.
Arneson, R. J. 2004. "Democracy Is Not Intrinsically Just," in K. Dowding, R. E. Goodin, and C. Pateman (eds.), *Justice and Democracy* (Cambridge: Cambridge University Press), pp. 40–58.

Grey, T. C. 1979. "Constitutionalism: An Analytic Framework," in J. R. Pennock and J. W. Chapman (eds.), *Constitutionalism* (New York: New York University Press), pp. 189–209.

Kay, R. S. 1998. "American Constitutionalism," in L. A. Alexander (ed.), *Constitutionalism: Philosophical Foundations* (Cambridge: Cambridge University Press), pp. 16–63.

Waldron, J. 1998. "Precommitment and Disagreement," in L. A. Alexander (ed.), *Constitutionalism: Philosophical Foundations* (Cambridge: Cambridge University Press), pp. 271–99.

Articles in Journals

Alexander, L. A. 2003. "Constitutional Rules, Constitutional Standards, and Constitutional Settlement: *Marbury v. Madison* and the Case for Judicial Supremacy," *Law and Philosophy* 20: 369–78.

Alexander, L. A. 2002. "Is Judicial Review Democratic?: A Comment on Harel," *Law and Philosophy* 22: 277–83.

Alexander, L. A. 1998. "Are Procedural Rights Derivative Substantive Rights?," *Law and Philosophy* 17: 19–42.

Alexander, L. A., and K. Kress. 1997. "Replies to Our Critics," *Iowa Law Review* 82: 923–41.

Christiano, T. 2000. "Waldron on Law and Disagreement," *Law and Philosophy* 19: 513–43.

Estlund, D. 2005. Book review, *Ethics* 115: 609–14.

Green, M. 2004. "Legal Revolutions: Six Mistakes About Discontinuity in the Legal Order," *North Carolina Law Review* 83: 331–409.

McGinnis, J. O., and M. B. Rappaport. 2002. "Our Supermajoritarian Constitution," *Texas Law Review* 80: 703–806.

Schauer, F. 2005. "The Tyranny of Choice and the Rulification of Standards," *Journal of Contemporary Legal Issues* 14: 803–14.

Vermeule, A. 2001. "Veil of Ignorance Rules in Constitutional Law," *Yale Law Journal* 111: 399–442.

PERSONS, IDENTITY AND DIFFERENCE

INDIVIDUALISM AND COMMUNITY

Individualism and the Claims of Community

Richard Dagger

In the last two decades of the twentieth century, the so-called liberal-communitarian debate occupied much of the attention of political philosophers. The debate lingers on in the new century, but it seems increasingly clear that the "communitarians" have abandoned the field, either by forswearing communitarianism or by taking up related causes, such as multiculturalism. But that is not to say that communitarianism has been utterly vanquished or that there is nothing of value in the positions communitarians advanced in the course of the debate. If nothing else, their arguments should help us to see that individualism can be taken too far and the claims of community taken too lightly. So, at least, I shall try to demonstrate in this essay.

What I shall *not* try to demonstrate is that political philosophers must choose between the claims of the individual and those of the community. There are times, certainly, when those claims seem to pull in opposite directions. The individual's right to own and operate a business sometimes comes into conflict with community standards of decency or health, for example; or the community's need to guard against terrorism may conflict with the individual's freedom of association and expression. Cases such as these require decisions that are seldom clear-cut and often painful. Yet they should not obscure the fundamental point, which is that communities cannot exist without individual members and individuals cannot exist, much less thrive, without community. Where persons are concerned, in other words, there are no individuals, no individuality, and no individualism without community of some sort.

Communities take various forms and directions, however, just as individuals do, and some of them are more likely to stifle individuality than to foster it. If individualism can be pressed too far, so too can the claims of community. The challenge is to bring the claims of the individual and community into balance. To meet this challenge is to find and support forms of community that promote not simply individuality, but the kind of public-spirited individuality that recognizes how much it owes to others and strives to discharge this debt.

I. Liberals versus Communitarians?

As often happens with academic disputes, the liberal–communitarian debate has been a murky affair, with the opposing positions vaguely defined and the participants frequently talking past one another. To some, in fact, the entire debate appears either to have been "misconceived" or marked by "cross-purposes and just plain confusion. . . ." (Caney 1992; Taylor 1995: 181). One point, however, seems clear. Deep as its roots in older controversies may go, the liberal–communitarian debate of recent years began with the publication of four books in the early 1980s: Alasdair MacIntyre's *After Virtue* (1981), Michael Sandel's *Liberalism and the Limits of Justice* (1982), Michael Walzer's *Spheres of Justice* (1983), and Charles Taylor's *Philosophical Papers* (1985).[1]

Each of these books expressed, in its own way, dissatisfaction with the aims and ambitions of liberalism, especially in the form of liberal theories of justice and rights. The main target was John Rawls's *A Theory of Justice* (1971), but Robert Nozick's *Anarchy, State, and Utopia* (1974), Ronald Dworkin's *Taking Rights Seriously* (1977), and Bruce Ackerman's *Social Justice in the Liberal State* (1980) also came in for criticism. A typical complaint was that the theories Rawls and the others have advanced are too abstract and universalistic. In opposing them, Walzer proposed a "radically particularist" approach that attends to "history, culture, and membership" by asking not what "rational individuals . . . under universalizing conditions of such-and-such a sort" would choose, but what would "individuals like us choose, who are situated as we are, who share a culture and are determined to go on sharing it?" (1983: xiv, 5). In this way Walzer called attention to the importance of community, which he and others took to be suffering from both philosophical and political neglect.

Nor did Walzer and the others who came to be known as communitarians believe that philosophical or theoretical indifference had merely coincided with the erosion of community that they saw in the world around them. In various ways Walzer, MacIntyre, Sandel, and Taylor, among others, all charged that the liberal emphasis on distributive justice and individual rights works to divide the citizens of the modern state against one another, fostering isolation, alienation, and apathy rather than commitment to a common civic enterprise. Liberals responded to these complaints, of course, and the debate was on.

Those enlisted on the communitarian side of the debate have pressed four major objections against their "liberal" or "individualist" opponents. The first, already noted in Walzer, is that abstract reason will not bear the weight philosophers have placed on it in their attempts to ground justice and morality. This "Enlightenment project" (MacIntyre 1981) is doomed by its failure to recognize that reasoning about these matters cannot proceed apart from shared traditions and practices, each with its own set of roles, responsibilities, and virtues. Second, the liberal emphasis on individual rights and justice comes at the expense of civic duty and the common good. In Sandel's words, "justice finds its limits in those forms of community that engage the identity as well as the interests of the participants"; "to some I owe more than justice requires or even permits . . . in virtue of those more or less enduring attachments and commitments which taken together partly define the person I am" (1982: 182, 179). Contemporary liberals are blind to these enduring, unchosen attachments and commitments, according to the third charge, because they too often rely on an atomistic

Richard Dagger

conception of the self – an "unencumbered self," in Sandel's terms – that is supposedly prior to its ends and attachments. Such a conception is both false and pernicious, for individual selves are largely constituted by the communities that nurture and sustain them. When Rawls and other "deontological liberals" teach individuals to think of themselves as somehow prior to and apart from these communities, they are engaged, quite literally, in a *self*-defeating enterprise. The fourth objection, then, is that these abstract and universalistic theories of justice and rights have contributed to the withdrawal into private life and the intransigent insistence on one's rights against others that threaten modern societies. In such conditions there is little sense of a common good or even a common ground on which citizens can meet. In MacIntyre's words, the conflict between the advocates of incommensurable moral positions has so riven modern societies that politics now "is civil war carried on by other means ..." (1981: 253). The best we can do in these circumstances is to agree to disagree while we try to fashion "local forms of community within which civility and the intellectual and moral life can be sustained through the new dark ages which are already upon us" (MacIntyre 1981: 263).

The communitarians have not pressed all of these objections with equal force, nor have they all understood themselves to be criticizing liberalism from the outside. Taylor (1995), for instance, has argued that reasonable liberals and communitarians share a commitment to "holist individualism" – a view to which I shall return in section II of this essay. Other theorists with communitarian leanings continue to regard themselves as liberals (Galston 1991; Spragens 1995, 1999). From their point of view, the fundamental worry is that some prominent liberals are so preoccupied with the rights and liberties of abstract individuals that they put the survival of liberal societies at risk. Whether this worry is well founded is a question that the "liberal" side of the debate has raised in response to the "communitarians."

Here we may distinguish three interlocking responses. The first is that the communitarians' criticisms are misplaced because they have misunderstood what the liberals have been trying to do. In particular, the communitarians have misunderstood the abstractness of the theories they criticize. Thus Rawls maintains (1993: Lecture I) that his "political" conception of the self as prior to its ends is not a metaphysical claim about the nature of the self, as Sandel believes, but simply a way of representing the parties who are to choose principles of justice from behind the "veil of ignorance." Nor does this conception of the individual as a self capable of choosing the ends it shall pursue require liberals to deny that individual identity is in many ways the product of unchosen attachments and social circumstances. "What is central to the liberal view," according to Will Kymlicka, "is not that we can *perceive* a self prior to its ends, but that we understand ourselves to be prior to our ends, *in the sense that no end or goal is exempt from possible re-examination...*" (1989a: 52, emphasis in original). To say that the self is prior to its ends is thus to say that no particular self is completely defined or exhausted by its current ends. If I were somehow to compile a comprehensive catalogue of my ends, commitments, and attachments, that catalogue would no doubt provide a broad and deep account of who I am: of *myself*. It also would include some ends and attachments, such as those involving family and country, that were at least partly fixed at birth. Yet it could not capture everything about my *self*, for it would not include my (self's) ability to add new items to that catalogue while amending and discarding others. There is a conceptual sense, then, in which the self is prior to its ends even though some of its ends and attachments necessarily precede it temporally.[2] Sandel and other communitarians are no doubt right as a matter of philosophical anthropology. We are the persons we are largely because of family, tribe, sect, nation, and other formative forces. To the extent that liberals have argued as if we were isolated atoms, altogether free from such influences, they are guilty of the charge of misconceiving the self. But that is not a misconception that liberals must adopt, nor is it one that necessarily attaches to those who claim that the self is prior to its end.

The second "liberal" response has centered on the meaning and value of community. In this case the response has taken both a defensive and offensive form. Defensively, liberals have denied that they are either hostile or indifferent to community. Joel Feinberg, for example, has insisted that

> there is nothing in the liberal's ideology that *need* blind him to the social nature of human beings and the importance to all of us of community memberships. . . . [H]e can, indeed he must, concede what is plain fact, that most of what we fulfill when we fulfill ourselves are dispositions implanted by our communities, and most of what we exercise when we exercise our autonomy is what our communities created in us in the first place. (Feinberg 1988: 89, emphasis in original)

The liberals have also taken the offensive by charging that communitarians neither make clear what they mean by "community" nor have sufficient faith in people's ability to form and sustain communities. As Kymlicka says,

> Liberals believe that people naturally form and join social relations in which they come to understand and pursue the good. . . . It is communitarians who seem to think that individuals will drift into anomic and detached isolation without the state actively bringing them together to collectively evaluate and pursue the good. (Kymlicka 1989b: 904)

The third "liberal" response, finally, is to point to the dangers of the appeal to community norms. Communities have their virtues, but they have their vices, too – smugness, intolerance, and various forms of oppression and exploitation among them. The fact that communitarians do not themselves embrace these vices simply reveals the perversity of their criticism: they "want us to live in Salem, but not to believe in witches" (Gutmann 1992: 133). If liberals rely on abstractions and universal considerations in their theories of justice and rights, that is because they must do so to rise above, and critically assess, local prejudices that communitarians must accept so long as their standard is simply the good of community as such.

Communitarian rejoinders indicate their sensitivity to this last point. Without abandoning his criticism of "rights-oriented liberalism," Sandel has come to identify himself with "republicanism" (1996, 2000), observing that the "term 'communitarian' is misleading . . . insofar as it implies that rights should rest on the values and preferences that prevail in any given community at any given time" (2005: 212–13). For his part, MacIntyre has denied that he is or ever was a communitarian.[3] Others continue to embrace the communitarian label, but their rejoinders to "liberal" criticisms stress their desire to strike a balance between individual rights and civic responsibilities in order to "move closer to the *ideal* of community life" – a life in which "we

Richard Dagger

learn the value of integrating what we seek individually with the needs and aspirations of other people" (Tam 1998: 220, emphasis added; also Etzioni 1996; Selznick 2002).

If this, however, is what communitarians truly want – a life in which people freely pursue their individual ends while remaining responsible members of the community – then it seems that the debate rested in large part on a false dichotomy between liberal individualism and situated selves embedded in community. Once that dichotomy is rejected, the debate turns out to be an intramural affair among people who all value toleration and individual freedom – that is, a debate reflecting "internal tensions within liberalism" (Feinberg 1988: 82). To be sure, a strict communitarian might continue to insist that liberal individualism truly is opposed to community, but taking such an anti-individualistic stance simply allows liberals to present themselves as champions of freedom and their opponents as collectivists of a vague but dangerous sort (Bird 1999: 204–11).

That is not to say, however, that the liberal-communitarian debate has been fruitless. On the contrary, MacIntyre, Sandel, Taylor, Walzer, and others on the communitarian side have performed at least two valuable services, first by directing more attention to the value of community and, second, by raising reasonable concerns about the implications of individualism. Testimony to the value of these services is evident in the recent efforts of liberal philosophers to address problems of belonging, identity, and community in their own work (e.g., Kymlicka 1989a, 1995; Dworkin 1986, 1992; Gewirth 1996; Mason 2000; Kukathas 2003).[4] Liberals have rightly denied that liberalism is necessarily hostile to community, in other words, but they also do well to recognize that community and community-like considerations require not only philosophical attention but political care.

II. Individualism

One indication of this sensitivity to considerations of community may be found in the indices of Rawls's works. No entry for "community" appears in the index to *A Theory of Justice* (1971), but one does in both *Political Liberalism* (1993) and *Justice as Fairness: A Restatement* (2001). In the last book, to be sure, the brief entry reads "Community vs. Democratic Society," followed by a reference to the more extensive entry for "Political Society." Nor does Rawls embrace community as an ideal either in that book or in *Political Liberalism*. On the contrary, he takes pains to distinguish community from both "association" and his own ideal of a "democratic" or "well-ordered" political society (1993: 40–3; 2001: 3–4, 198–200).[5] That he saw the need to draw these distinctions in his later works, however, suggests that the communitarians' efforts were not without effect.

What Rawls had no need to do in his later work was to abandon or defend the atomistic, abstract individualism that communitarians have often associated with liberalism. There is abstraction aplenty in *A Theory of Justice*, but the abstract individuals in the Rawlsian "original position" who agree to principles of justice behind the "veil of ignorance" are not, as we have seen, reflections of Rawls's belief that human beings are essentially "unencumbered" selves. When Rawls portrays these individuals as "mutually disinterested," moreover, he does so to prevent envy and partiality from infecting the principles of justice that the parties to the social contract choose, not because he takes people to be self-contained atoms. He says, in fact, that "it is only in active cooperation with others that one's powers reach fruition. Only in a social union is the individual complete" (Rawls 1971: 525, n. 4). Rawls may well be an individualist, but he clearly is not one of the atomistic kind.

Nor is Rawls an exception to the liberal rule in this regard. If liberals are all individualists, the differences among them illustrate the variety of forms that individualism can take. Indeed, Colin Bird has distinguished six ways of construing the claim, supposedly characteristic of liberalism, that "the individual is prior to society" (Bird 1999: 47–72). For present purposes, though, the important point is that individualism may take forms that are more and less congenial to the claims of community. Alexis de Tocqueville and John Stuart Mill provide an illuminating contrast here, for both feared the stifling effects of "the tyranny of the majority" on the individual's freedom to think and act in unconventional ways. Mill celebrated *individuality*, however, while Tocqueville deplored *individualism*, which he defined as "a calm and considered feeling which disposes each citizen to isolate himself from the mass of his fellows and withdraw into the circle of family and friends . . . , [leaving] the greater society to look after itself" (1969: 506). If what we mean by "individualism" is something like the recognition and promotion of individuality, then we should regard it as a vital contribution to a healthy community – at least (as Mill and every other advocate of individuality must acknowledge) if it is not carried too far. But individualism in Tocqueville's sense of the word is always a threat to community. Communities and polities require care, and "citizens" who isolate themselves from the mass of their fellows will not freely and happily provide it.

There are, then, good and bad forms of individualism, and there are liberals who advocate each kind, if inadvertently so in the case of the bad forms. The bad forms are those that do not give community (or community-like considerations) its due, typically because they rest on a conception of the individual that is not true to the facts of human life. Much as we may like to think of ourselves as autonomous, self-determining, or independent individuals, the fact is that we are, in MacIntyre's phrase (1999), "dependent rational animals." We are not born of our own efforts, nor can we live entirely by them. As the ancient riddle of the Sphinx teaches, the period of our lives in which we walk upright, and perhaps set our own path, falls between infancy and the infirmities of old age – two periods during which we are highly dependent on others. Even in the fullness of life, whatever independence we enjoy is largely owing to the efforts of parents, teachers, and others who enabled us to become, and help us to remain, "independent practical reasoners" (MacIntyre 1999: 96). That is true, moreover, of the most able-bodied and sharp-minded of us. If we suffer from some serious disability, our dependence on others is even more extensive. When individualism begins and ends with a conception of the individual as a fit and rational adult, it simply fails to recognize these facts of life.

This failure has important implications for the ethics of individualism. One of these is the failure, in ethical theory as in public policy and daily life, to value care and care-givers properly. As a number of feminists have observed, such neglect is likely to occur when "the individual" is assumed to be a fit and rational adult *male*; for it is women who do most of the care-giving (Noddings 1984; Friedman 1993: Part II; Held 2000; Tronto 2001). Another implication of this false individualism is the neglect – again, in both theory and practice – of disabled individuals (Kittay 1999; Wellman

Richard Dagger

2005). And another, as the communitarians have insisted, is a failure to acknowledge what we owe, as individuals, to the communities, societies, traditions, or practices that enable us to achieve whatever measure of independence or autonomy we come to enjoy. As Taylor points out, we cannot even aspire to autonomy or self-development until we learn to conceive of ourselves as individuals with the potential for "developed freedom"; yet "this self-understanding is not something we can sustain on our own, but ... is always partly defined in conversation with others or through the common understanding which underlies the practices of our society" (Taylor 1985: 209).

Rawls, I have claimed, is not a proponent of this misguided form of individualism, nor are most of those in the liberal tradition. But Thomas Hobbes is, and so are those followers of his now called "contractarians." So, too, are today's libertarians and "philosophical anarchists."[6] Hobbes provides perhaps the most colorful statement of this extreme individualism in *De Cive*, where he invites us to "return again to the state of nature, and consider men as if but even now sprung out of the earth, and suddenly, like mushrooms, come to full maturity, without all kind of engagement to each other" (Hobees 1978: 205).[7] In Hobbes's case, of course, atomistic individualism leads to the conclusion that we must vest all authority in an all-powerful sovereign, and in that respect he differs markedly from most extreme individualists, whose suspicion of political authority typically leads them to call for strict limits to the powers of government.

Some of these individualists – perhaps because they find their inspiration in Kant or Locke rather than Hobbes – go so far as to deny the legitimacy or authority of the state. Among these are libertarian anarchists, who would abolish government if they could (e.g., Rothbard 1973), and the more circumspect group of philosophical anarchists. Anarchists of the latter sort hold that the state is illegitimate, but they deny that there is "a strong moral imperative to oppose or eliminate states; rather, they typically take state illegitimacy simply to remove any strong moral presumption in favor of obedience to, compliance with, or support for our own or other existing states" (Simmons 2001: 104). Some philosophical anarchists – most notably Robert Paul Wolff – maintain that states necessarily lack moral legitimacy. As they see it, the state's claim to the authority to issue binding laws is contrary to the individual's primary moral duty of autonomy, which requires "submission to laws which one has made for oneself" (Wolff 1998: 14). Others agree with John Simmons (1979: 194–201; 2001), who argues in *a posteriori* fashion that the repeated failure of attempts to establish the moral legitimacy of the state is what warrants the philosophical anarchists' conclusion. Either way, the philosophical anarchist obeys the law not because it is *the law*, but because he or she finds independent moral reasons for obedience.

What makes these anarchists important for present purposes is not their anarchism so much as the way they arrive at it. After all, Peter Kropotkin (1972) and other anarcho-communists value community so highly that they think its promotion requires the abolition of the state. The problem with the libertarian and philosophical anarchists is their atomistic or voluntaristic individualism. In Wolff's case, autonomy is not only a moral duty but something that the individual must protect against anyone who claims to have authority over her. How we come to develop autonomy, and what we owe to those who enable us to exercise it, is not Wolff's concern.[8] For Simmons, the fact that we are "born into political communities" is much the same as "being 'dropped into' a cooperative scheme" that we have not consented to join (1979: 137–8).

The tendency in both kinds of philosophical anarchism is thus to envision the individual as a fit and rational adult who is set apart from a community or cooperative scheme that is trying to impose its will on her.

Philosophical anarchists may respond that they are not hostile to community or even to government, which performs useful services, in their view, despite its lack of moral legitimacy. These anarchists may even desire the formation of communities, at least if a community is understood to be a group of individuals who share interests or values and who are free to enter or leave the group when they choose. What they do not want is to identify communities with states. Communities do not claim the authority to issue binding commands, as states do, nor do they impose these commands on individuals who have not truly consented to become members. Community is compatible with the individual's autonomy, in short, but the state is not.

This response seems plausible, but a closer look at philosophical anarchism exposes three significant problems. One is that it is too optimistic or cavalier where the preservation of community is concerned – a point I shall return to in section IV. The second is that the emphasis on the individual's autonomy, or the need for the individual to consent to being under an obligation, has a corrosive effect on the state's perceived authority – an effect that the philosophical anarchists both do and do not want to achieve. That is, they want us to obey the law, at least most of the time, on the grounds that the law often forbids us to do what we have independent reasons for not doing – committing murder and assault, for example – and because people develop reasonable expectations about how to conduct their lives based on traffic regulations and other laws. Yet they also want us to recognize that the law as such has no authority over us. This is tantamount to pointing out that the emperor has no clothes without expecting the people so informed to mock or scorn him. Whether the skepticism they want us to adopt is compatible in the long run with general obedience to the law is, in other words, doubtful. Simmons argues that the likely outcome is a properly chastened and "less statelike" state (Simmons 2001: 118), but it looks to others as if the widespread adoption of philosophical anarchism must weaken the state more drastically than these anarchists themselves desire. As one critic remarks, a "democratic state can only be vitiated by popular doubts about its right to exist, and a weakened state is to that extent less able to do what only it can do, for example, protect the weak and meek against the strong and loud" (Edmundson 1998: 1).[9]

Let us grant, however, that the philosophical anarchists can accomplish the trick of undermining the state's perceived authority without rendering it ineffective. Even so, the third problem remains. Assuming that the adoption of philosophical anarchism would not produce rampant disobedience, it would still have the effect of diminishing the state and denigrating public service. The spread of this attitude among people who are supposedly self-governing poses two dangers. On the one hand, if everyone becomes a philosophical anarchist, there will be no one left to make the decisions and run the government. On the other (and more likely) hand, if too many stand on the side lines, government either will become so weak as to lose its ability to perform the useful functions that even the philosophical anarchists want it to perform, or it will fall into the hands of those who are all too eager to claim authority and wield power over the rest of us. Philosophical anarchism, in sum, fosters Tocquevillean individualism by encouraging people to leave "the greater society to look after itself." The result, as Tocqueville warned, is likely to be despotism, whether of a soft or hard form. In either case, the result will not be one that pleases philosophical anarchists, liberals in general, or individualists of any kind.

The threatened result, however, does support the claim that there are bad forms of individualism. Furthermore, the example of philosophical anarchism shows that communitarians have not been completely wrong to charge that liberalism is susceptible to atomistic or excessively voluntaristic individualism. Most liberals do not adhere to this kind of individualism, as I have said, but the philosophical anarchists do. So do those libertarians who conceive of rights as "side-constraints" (Nozick 1974), or inviolable barriers that shield people from – rather than relate them to – one another. And so do those "contractarians" who hold that the way to justify not only political authority but morality as a whole is to demonstrate how they can be derived from the choices of rational, self-interested individuals (e.g., Gauthier 1986). But it is wrong to attribute atomistic or excessively voluntaristic individualism to Rawls and those who are now called "contractualists."

Contractualists differ from contractarians because they begin with a commitment to morality, understood roughly as impartiality, and then try to determine the principles of morality or justice that individuals would choose were they not only rational but *reasonable* – that is, willing to live together under terms that all can accept as free and equal persons. As Rawls says, in phrases that reverberate throughout his later works, the "most fundamental idea in this [i.e., Rawls's] conception of justice is the idea of society as a fair system of cooperation over time from one generation to the next" (Rawls 2001: 5). The contractualist individual is not, then, someone who stands apart from society, or thinks of herself as "dropped into" a cooperative scheme without her consent. She may be in the society without consent, but that is probably because she was born into it, seeing herself not only as a part of it now, but over time and across generations. She is willing to do her part, moreover, and asks only the assurance that the society will be cooperative and fair. She is an individual, of course, with interests of her own, but she is an individual embedded in, if not a community, then a political society that she hopes to see well ordered.

Contractualism thus affords an example of liberal theory that promises to promote individuality while respecting the claims of community, or of something resembling community. It is thus compatible, at least, with "holist" or "holistic" individualism, which Taylor defines as "a trend of thought that is fully aware of the (ontological) social embedding of human agents but, at the same time, prizes liberty and individual differences very highly" (Taylor 1995: 185).[10] It is the kind of individualism, in other words, that is both true to the facts of human life and committed to the value of individuality. Whether liberalism of the Rawlsian or contractualist variety – or, indeed, any brand of liberalism that subscribes to this good form of individualism – is *sufficiently* appreciative of the value of community is the question to which we must now turn. To answer this question, we shall have to look more closely at the concept of community.

III. Community

In *Liberalism and the Limits of Justice* Sandel distinguished between "weak" and "strong" conceptions of community.[11] Liberal views of community have been weak, he asserted, because they are either "instrumental" – "where individuals regard social arrangements as a necessary burden and cooperate only for the sake of pursuing their final ends" – or "sentimental" – as in Rawls's vision of a situation in which "the participants have certain 'shared final ends' and regard the scheme of cooperation as a good in itself" (Sandel 1982: 148; quoting Rawls 1971: 522). Against these weak conceptions, Sandel proposed what he took to be a truer conception of community:

> On this strong view, to say the members of a society are bound by a sense of community is not simply to say that a great many of them profess communitarian sentiments and pursue communitarian aims, but rather that they conceive their identity – the subject and not just the object of their feelings and aspirations – as defined to some extent by the community of which they are a part. For them, community describes not just what they *have* as fellow citizens, but also what they *are*, not a relationship they choose (as in a voluntary association) but an attachment they discover, not merely an attribute but a constituent of their identity. In contrast to the instrumental and sentimental conceptions of community, we might describe this strong view as the constitutive conception. (Sandel 1982: 150; emphasis in original)

According to Sandel, then, liberals cannot be sufficiently appreciative of community, for they are blind to the way in which communities constitute our identities. But is he right? As the arguments of the preceding section of this essay indicate, I think that Sandel is right about some liberals – philosophical anarchists, libertarians, and contractarians in particular – but wrong about most of them. There is nothing to prevent liberals from rejecting atomism in favor of a holist ontology, or account of social life, and they may do so without committing themselves to a collectivist position in ethics or politics (Taylor 1995). Moreover, those who embrace this holist individualism will readily agree with Sandel that our identity is "defined *to some extent* by the community of which [we] are a part" (1982: 150; emphasis added). They will deny, however, that this agreement is enough to make them communitarians who proceed from a constitutive conception of community.

There are at least three reasons to find Sandel's constitutive conception of community unsatisfactory, including one already touched on in this essay. That is, Sandel's constitutive conception seems to be too strong. If this conception takes a community to be an association that shapes the identity of its members, then it apparently approves of a situation in which the individual's sense of identity with the community is so powerful and deep that he or she will be unable to think at all critically about its practices and traditions. The sense of identity could be so powerful, in fact, that people who cannot conceive of themselves as individuals in any way apart from the community may be consigned to a life of community-sanctioned oppression and exploitation. Individualism can be taken too far, as I have argued, but so too can identification with one's community. That is why it is important to stress three words when Sandel says that identity is "defined *to some extent* by the community of which they are a part." No doubt it is, and a good thing, too, as the sense of identity or belonging contributes to a secure sense of self – up to a point. That point is passed, however, when one's identity is defined almost entirely by one's community; for then there is little room left for a sense of self, let alone individuality.

The second problem with the constitutive conception of community is the suggestion that one and only one community constitutes the individual's identity. Such

Richard Dagger

a view of community is implausible, at least in the modern world, for only in exceptional circumstances will *a* community substantially constitute anyone's identity. Chandran Kukathas goes too far in the opposite direction, I think, when he says that the "truth about the nature of community is that *all* communities are in fact 'partial associations' (2003: 169; emphasis in original). We can certainly conceive of a community so isolated and all-encompassing as to form the sole constituent of its members' identities – as I have done in the preceding paragraph – and I see no reason to doubt that such a community may exist or take shape somewhere in the world. Nevertheless, Kukathas is right to insist that an all-encompassing community would be much different from the communities that we ordinarily encounter. The communities with which we are familiar are indeed "partial associations" that may constitute some part of a person's identity, but not the whole of it. When one community pulls a person in one direction and a second tugs him or her in another, furthermore, the person caught in this conflict will have to rise above both commitments and act as a self in some sense prior to its ends and attachments. Sandel admits as much in *Democracy's Discontent* when he observes that we "multiply-situated selves" and "multiply-encumbered citizens" must "negotiate our way among the sometimes overlapping, sometimes conflicting obligations that claim us, and . . . live with the tension to which multiple loyalties give rise" (1996: 350).

Sandel's constitutive conception of community is both too strong, then, and implausible. It also rests on a distinction that is misleadingly tidy. When Sandel distinguishes among instrumental, sentimental, and constitutive conceptions of community, he suggests that we cannot or should not conceive of community in two or more of these ways at once. Yet there is ample reason to believe that we can and even should think of community in both instrumental and constitutive terms. People who are born and raised in a small town, for example, may see themselves as bound up with their community, but that firm sense of identity need not prevent them from asking whether the community is treating them fairly or providing them with opportunities they want to pursue. To conceive of community, in other words, is not to choose between a thoroughly instrumental vision within which everyone's sole concern is "What's in it for me?" and a thoroughly constitutive vision within which everyone's constant preoccupation is "doing what's best for the group." There is a middle ground between these two visions, and it is likely to provide a more solid foundation for a healthy community than either a strictly instrumental or a strictly constitutive conception.

Nor is there any reason to think that liberals of a holist inclination cannot be comfortable in this middle ground, where instrumental reasons, sentiment, and a sense of identity all contribute to community. To put the point another way, liberals *can* be sufficiently appreciative of community. How far that appreciation should extend, however, is a question that requires a clearer definition of "community" – a term that I have thus far used, in keeping with common practice, rather loosely. Statements such as Sandel's "the members of a society are bound by a sense of community . . ." illustrate the difficulty here. On the one hand, a society seems to be a (kind of) community, for it makes sense to say that its members can be bound by a sense of community; on the other hand, a society cannot be a community itself, for we often speak of the many communities within a society. Moreover, it seems clear that some societies – and some associations and polities – are more like communities than others. There are communities, then, and there are community-like entities. But what *is* a community?

The one point on which everyone who wrestles with this question agrees is that a group forms a community, rather than a mere aggregation, when its members share values or interests. Whether those common interests or values are sufficient to make a community of a group is a disputed point. For my part, I am always happy to find that others share my admiration for the novels of Jane Austen or my devotion to the St. Louis Cardinals baseball team, but I think it stretches the concept too far to say that we Janeites or Cardinals fans form a community. The people who work in a coal mine and the people who own it will share an interest in the mine's prosperity, but that is hardly to say that they form a community – especially when the "owners" are shareholders who never set eyes on the mine or its miners. Members of a community must be more closely associated than that. But they cannot be too closely associated, for then they form a *unit* – as in Feinberg's example of a "well-married couple" (Feinberg 1988: 104) – rather than a community.

Defining "community" thus presents a quantitative problem in that having too little or too much in common may preclude a group from being a community. There is a qualitative problem, too, as the connotations of "community" seem to be generally positive. Indeed, some people hold that community – or at least "true" or "genuine" community – is by definition a good thing. William Galston, for instance, states that

> *every community represents a cooperative endeavor in pursuit of shared purposes.* Each term of this proposition offers a key ingredient of community. "Cooperation" presupposes mutual benefit, rather than the exploitation of some members by others through force or fraud; "endeavor" implies that the good must be created, rather than passively received or consumed; and "shared purposes" define a common good the community seeks to bring into being and to sustain, not merely private individual advantage. (Galston 1992: 59, emphasis in original)

There are advantages to defining "community" in this way, especially as it would block the complaint that Sandel's strong conception allows for people to accept their oppression or exploitation as part of what it means to be a member of the community. There are also disadvantages, however. One is that this definition would disqualify some identity-constituting groups or entities that Sandel and others believe have a claim to our allegiance. In *Democracy's Discontent*, for instance, Sandel suggests that Robert E. Lee was right, on the eve of the Civil War, to identify with "'my native state and share the miseries of my people'" (1996: 15). As a slave-holding society, however, Lee's native state of Virginia could not count as a community under Galston's definition no matter how powerful its identity-constituting force was.

Nor is it clear that we would gain anything by declaring communities good as a matter of definition. With a neutral definition, we leave open the possibility that *this* community may be good and desirable while *that* one is to be deplored and dissolved; with a positive definition, we will find it necessary to distinguish the true and genuine from false or illusory "communities." We might, following Andrew Mason (2000: 20–38), distinguish "moralized" from "ordinary" concepts of community, thereby dispelling the confusion that often arises when one person takes X to be an example of a bad

Richard Dagger

community and another denies that X is a community at all. Helpful as that distinction might be, it would still leave us with the question of whether an entity is a community in the moral or only in the ordinary sense, if either; and complete or ready agreement on that question is unlikely. An "ordinary" community, furthermore, will constitute its members' identities to some extent, leaving us to determine what, if anything, we owe to a community that may be oppressive and exploitative.

"Community," in short, is a troublesome term for both quantitative and qualitative reasons. Nor do I see any way to escape these troubles. We must choose, it seems, among four possibilities: a definition of community that (1) is restrictive rather than expansive in what it will count as a community and aims at neutrality by denying that community is necessarily good; or that (2) is restrictive but positive in that it takes community to be necessarily good; or that (3) is expansive but aims at neutrality; or that (4) is expansive and positive. My own view is that we should take the first option and define "community" as narrowly and neutrally as possible. Doing so will resist the conceptual inflation that threatens to rob the term of its value. It will also help us to appreciate both the value of the communitarians' worries about the corrosive effects of liberal individualism and the limitations of the focus on community.

IV. From Community to Republic

For a suitably narrow and neutral definition, we may turn to Michael Taylor's *Community, Anarchy and Liberty*. According to Taylor, "community is characterized by shared values and beliefs, direct and many-sided relations, and the practice of reciprocity . . ." (Taylor 1982: 32). The last two conditions especially make this a narrow definition, for in

> a large and changing mass of people, few relations between individuals can be direct or many-sided, and reciprocity cannot flourish on a wide scale, since its continuation for any length of time requires *some* actual reciprocation, which in turn requires stable relations with known individuals. (Taylor 1982: 32, emphasis in original)

The definition is narrow, then, but not absolutely precise, as each of the three criteria "can be satisfied in varying degrees, so that a collection of individuals may be *more or less* of a community" (ibid.: 32, emphasis added). Even so, the definition is precise enough to rule out many things that are now often called communities – such as the "academic community" and the "global community" – and to raise doubts about the "political community," among others.

Whether it is wise or desirable to rule out or raise doubts about many so-called communities is, as I have said, a controversial and troublesome matter. I doubt, however, that we will lose anything other than the halo that so often surrounds the use of "community" if we speak instead of academic or global *society*, for example, or simply of *academics* and *academic principles*, or of *people* who have *human rights*. In any case, Taylor's restrictive definition clearly identifies the central or core meaning of "community" as the small, face-to-face society, the kind of place in which the person at the cash register is not merely a clerk but someone you know to be, say, a neighbor, parent, member of the church choir, and holder of political views quite different from yours. This restrictive definition also has the virtue of helping, in two ways, to clarify the communitarian side of the liberal–communitarian debate.

First, the restrictive definition helps to explain why some political philosophers worry about the loss of community. This worry strikes some liberals as both misplaced and paradoxical, as I noted in section I, quoting Kymlicka:

> Liberals believe that people naturally form and join social relations in which they come to understand and pursue the good. . . . It is communitarians who seem to think that individuals will drift into anomic and detached isolation without the state actively bringing them together to collectively evaluate and pursue the good. (Kymlicka 1989b: 904)

There is reason to wonder, though, whether it is the communitarians' worry or Kymlicka's optimism that is misplaced. Kymlicka may well be right to think that "people naturally form and join social relations" and that they do not need the state to bring them together. Still, there is a difference between "social relations" and the bonds of community, a difference that is especially clear if we take community to involve shared values and beliefs, direct and many-sided relations, and reciprocity. If it is community in this restrictive sense that contributes most effectively to a secure sense of the self – more effectively, at least, than mere social relations – then there is reason to believe not only that community may be lost, but that its loss will be of dire consequence. In our increasingly urban, commercial, and cosmopolitan world, moreover, neither the person at the cash register – now working for Wal-Mart – nor the "neighbor" down the street is likely to be someone with whom we have direct and many-sided relations. In these circumstances, the possibility "that individuals will drift into anomic and detached isolation" is not to be dismissed out of hand.

The restrictive definition of "community" helps to clarify the communitarian side of the debate in a second way, too, but this time in a way that is more congenial to the critics than the advocates of communitarianism. That is because communitarians have not adhered to a narrow or restrictive definition of "community." On Sandel's "strong view," for example, "the members of a *society* are bound by a sense of *community*" when "they conceive their identity . . . as defined to some extent by the *community* of which they are part" (1982: 150, emphasis added). In "The Procedural Republic and the Unencumbered Self" he writes of "those loyalties and convictions whose moral force consists partly in the fact that living by them is inseparable from understanding ourselves as the particular persons we are – as members of this *family* or *community* or *nation* or *people*, as *bearers of that history*, as *citizens* of this republic" (Sandel 2005: 167, emphasis added). Furthermore, those loyalties are undercut by "the liberal vision" that is "parasitic on a notion of community it officially rejects . . ." (ibid.: 168–9). The sense of community thus seems to be something desirable in associations ranging from families to nations, peoples, and historical traditions. It is easy to see why Sandel and others draw so heavily on the sense of community, for it is something that grounds individuals who might be anomic, anonymous, and rootless without it. It is also a rich source of what has come to be known as "social capital" (Putnam 2000). To draw this heavily on it, however, is to load more onto community than it can properly bear. It is to take what is true of communities

Richard Dagger

in the restrictive sense and to assume that it applies to all sorts of community-like entities. To do this is not only to draw too heavily on community but to denigrate other forms of association and attachment.

Consider, in this light, the so-called political community. As I said earlier, Taylor's restrictive definition raises doubts about the existence of political communities. It is possible, of course, that a polity may be small and stable enough for its members to share beliefs and values, engage in direct and many-sided relations, and experience reciprocity with one another. Most modern polities, political societies, or political associations, however, will be much too large and fluid to count as communities on Taylor's definition. In addition, there is a sense in which a community has little or no need of politics, taking "politics" to refer to the conscious and deliberate effort to guide a group's affairs. Especially when they are removed from exogenous influences, communities may operate on the basis of custom generation after generation, with little awareness of the possibility of conducting their affairs in any way but the traditional. Political associations may be communities, in short, but they need not be; and communities may be political associations, but they need not be.

These doubts about "political community" bear on communitarianism in two ways. First, communitarians have regarded as communities groups or associations, including political societies, that very likely help to constitute the identity of individuals, but are not truly communities. Second, communitarians have a special interest in politics and political bodies that takes them well beyond the realm of community as such. Neither citizenship nor the rule of law need be a feature of a community, for example, yet none of the philosophical communitarians has evinced any interest in abandoning either citizenship or the rule of law. On the contrary, they believe that citizenship is in need of revival and the rule of law in need of protection. In Sandel's words, we should worry that "the *civic* or formative aspect of our politics has largely given way to the liberalism that conceives persons as free and independent selves, unencumbered by moral or *civic* ties they have not chosen" (Sandel 1996: 6, emphasis added).

It is noteworthy, though, that this statement is to be found in *Democracy's Discontent*, a book in which Sandel advances a *republican* rather than communitarian position. The appeal is to *civic* concerns, not to community as such. That, in my view, is as it should be. Community has its claims, but so does the *republic* or the *commonwealth*. The sense of community is valuable, but so are the bonds of *civic friendship*, which work through "the constitution, a doctrine of individual rights, and the public standards of acceptable civic behavior" (Schwarzenbach 1996: 122). Civic friendship may be found in a community, but it need not be. It may also be found in a liberal society that respects individuality but demonstrates that respect in large part through the care and understanding of citizens for their fellow citizens (ibid.: 122; Spragens 1999: Ch. 7). It is a *community-like consideration*, but it is not the sense of community as such.

Community has its claims, and it would be unwise to neglect them. The polity has claims, too, and it would be unwise to neglect them – or to conflate them with those of community. Neither the polity nor community is threatened by liberalism or individualism, however, but only by those atomistic, voluntaristic forms of individualism that would dissolve the bonds of community and lead the individual to retreat from the common civic enterprise of public life.

Individualism and the Claims of Community   317

Acknowledgments

This essay was largely written while I was a Faculty Fellow of the Center for Ethics and Public Affairs at Tulane University. I owe a deep debt of gratitude to the Center not only for the fellowship, but for sustaining me and the other 2005–06 fellows in the aftermath of Hurricane Katrina. I am also indebted to George Klosko, Jonathan Quong, and audiences at Vanderbilt University and Washington University in St. Louis for valuable comments on earlier drafts of this essay – more valuable, I fear, than they will find reflected in this final draft.

Notes

1 For a brief attempt to trace the historical roots of the debate, see Dagger (2004), on which I draw in this section. Avineri and De-Shalit (1992) collects many of the key writings in the debate, and Hampton (1998: 170–91), provides a lucid short survey. The standard full-length account is Mulhall and Swift (1992, 2nd edn. 1996), and Bell (1993) puts the debate into the form of a dialogue between a communitarian and a liberal.

2 For elaboration of this point, see Dagger (1999: esp. 184–95).

3 See Bell (1993: 4 and n. 14), on the reluctance of MacIntyre, Walzer, Taylor, and Sandel to admit to being communitarians. See also MacIntyre (1998: 243–50, and esp. 1994: 302): "Contemporary communitarians, from whom I have strongly disassociated myself whenever I have had an opportunity to do so, advance their proposals as a contribution to the politics of the nation-state."

4 R. A. Duff has even grounded a powerful theory of criminal punishment on "a liberal-communitarian idea(l) of political society . . ." (2001: xviii).

5 In *Restatement*, Rawls says that his theory of justice as fairness "does indeed abandon the ideal of political community if by that ideal is meant a political society united on one (partially or fully) comprehensive religious, philosophical, or moral doctrine" (2001: 198–9; also 1993: 201). But he goes on to say that "a political society is a community if we now mean by a community a society, including a political society, the members of which – in this case citizens – share certain final ends to which they give very high priority, so much so that in stating before themselves the kind of person they want to be they count their having these ends as essential" (2001: 199–200). As the context makes clear, a "well-ordered society" may be considered a community in the latter sense if its citizens share "the end of supporting just institutions and giving one another justice accordingly, not to mention the other ends they must also share and realize through their political cooperation" (199).

6 I take it that most, if not all, contractarians, libertarians, and philosophical anarchists are also liberals, broadly construed, but Samuel Freeman (2002) argues that libertarians – as distinct from such 'classical liberals' as Milton Friedman and Friedrich Hayek – fall outside the liberal fold. In any case, I believe (with Bird 1999: 29) that one need not be a liberal to be an individualist.

7 Hampton (1999: 42) quotes this passage from Ch. 8, §1 of *De Cive*. For a less colorful translation, see Hobbes (1998: 102).

8 As I argue elsewhere (Dagger 1997: 66–8), Wolff overlooks the social dimension of autonomy.

9 See also the exchange between Thomas Senor and Simmons in *Philosophy and Public Affairs* (1987).

10 See also Pettit (1993: 217–24, 284–6) and Ryan (1993: esp. 98–105).

11 Parts of this section draw on Dagger (1997: 48–59).

Richard Dagger

References

Ackerman, Bruce. 1980. *Social Justice in the Liberal State* (New Haven, CT: Yale University Press).

Avineri, Shlomo, and Avner De-Shalit, eds. 1992. *Communitarianism and Individualism* (Oxford: Oxford University Press).

Bell, Daniel. 1993. *Communitarianism and Its Critics* (Oxford: Oxford University Press).

Bird, Colin. 1999. *The Myth of Liberal Individualism* (Cambridge: Cambridge University Press).

Caney, Simon. 1992. "Liberalism and Communitarianism: A Misconceived Debate," *Political Studies* 40.

Dagger, Richard. 1997. *Civic Virtues: Rights, Citizenship, and Republican Liberalism* (New York: Oxford University Press).

Dagger, Richard. 1999. "The Sandelian Republic and the Encumbered Self," *The Review of Politics* 61: 181–217.

Dagger, Richard. 2004. "Communitarianism and Republicanism," in Gerald Gaus and Chandran Kukathas, eds., *Handbook of Political Theory* (London: Sage Publications).

Duff, R. A. 2001. *Punishment, Communication, and Community* (Oxford: Oxford University Press).

Dworkin, Ronald. 1977. *Taking Rights Seriously* (Cambridge, MA: Harvard University Press).

Dworkin, Ronald. 1986. *Law's Empire* (Cambridge, MA: Harvard University Press).

Dworkin, Ronald. 1992. "Liberal Community," in S. Avineri and A. De-Shalit, eds., *Communitarianism and Individualism* (Oxford: Oxford University Press).

Edmundson, William. 1998. *Three Anarchical Fallacies: An Essay on Political Authority* (Cambridge: Cambridge University Press).

Etzioni, Amitai. 1996. *The New Golden Rule: Community and Morality in a Democratic Society* (New York: Basic Books).

Feinberg, Joel. 1988. "Autonomy and Community," in Feinberg, *Harmless Wrongdoing: The Moral Limits of the Criminal Law*, vol. 4 (New York: Oxford University Press).

Freeman, Samuel. 2002. "Illiberal Libertarians: Why Libertarianism Is Not a Liberal View," *Philosophy and Public Affairs* 30: 105–51.

Friedman, Marilyn. 1993. *What Are Friends For?* (Ithaca, NY: Cornell University Press).

Galston, William. 1991. *Liberal Purposes: Goods, Virtues, and Diversity in the Liberal State* (Cambridge: Cambridge University Press).

Galston, William. 1992. "In Pursuit of Shared Purposes," *The Responsive Community* 2 (3): 58–61.

Gauthier, David. 1986. *Morals by Agreement* (Oxford: Oxford University Press).

Gewirth, Alan. 1996. *The Community of Rights* (Chicago: University of Chicago Press).

Gutmann, Amy. 1992. "Communitarian Critics of Liberalism," in S. Avineri and A. De-Shalit, eds., *Communitarianism and Individualism* (Oxford: Oxford University Press).

Hampton, Jean. 1998. *Political Philosophy* (Boulder, CO: Westview Press).

Held, Virginia. 2000. "Rights and the Presumption of Care," in Marilyn Friedman, Larry May, Kate Parsons, and Jennifer Stiff, eds., *Rights and Reasons: Essays in Honor of Carl Wellman* (Dordrecht, The Netherlands: Kluwer Academic Publishers), pp. 65–70.

Hobbes, Thomas. (1978 [1642]). *The Citizen [De Cive]*, in *Man and Citizen: De Homine and De Cive*, ed. Bernard Gert (Gloucester, MA: Peter Smith).

Hobbes, Thomas. 1998. *On the Citizen*, ed. Richard Tuck and Michael Silverthorne (Cambridge: Cambridge University Press).

Kittay, Eva Feder. 1999. *Love's Labor: Essays on Women, Equality, and Dependency* (New York: Routledge).

Kropotkin, Peter. 1972 [1902]. *Mutual Aid, A Factor in Evolution* (New York: New York University Press).

Kukathas, Chandran. 2003. *The Liberal Archipelago: A Theory of Diversity and Freedom* (Oxford: Oxford University Press).

Kymlicka, Will. 1989a. *Liberalism, Community, and Culture* (Oxford: Oxford University Press).

Kymlicka, Will. 1989b. "Liberal Individualism and Liberal Neutrality," *Ethics* 99: 883–905.

Kymlicka, Will. 1995. *Multiculturalism and Citizenship* (Oxford: Oxford University Press).

MacIntyre, Alasdair. 1981 (2nd edn. 1984). *After Virtue* (Notre Dame, IN: University of Notre Dame Press).

MacIntyre, Alasdair. 1994. "A Partial Response to My Critics," in *After MacIntyre: Critical Perspectives on the Work of Alasdair MacIntyre* (Notre Dame, IN: University of Notre Dame Press).

MacIntyre, Alasdair. 1998. *The MacIntyre Reader*, ed. Kelvin Knight (Notre Dame, IN: University of Notre Dame Press).

MacIntyre, Alasdair. 1999. *Dependent Rational Animals: Why Human Beings Need the Virtues* (Chicago: Open Court Publishing).

Mason, Andrew. 2000. *Community, Solidarity, and Belonging: Levels of Community and Their Normative Significance* (Cambridge: Cambridge University Press).

Mulhall, Stephen, and Adam Swift. 1992 (rev. edn. 1996). *Liberals and Communitarians* (Oxford: Blackwell Books).

Noddings, Nel. 1984. *Caring: A Feminine Approach to Ethics and Moral Education* (Berkeley and Los Angeles: University of California Press).

Nozick, Robert. 1974. *Anarchy, State, and Utopia* (New York: Basic Books).

Pettit, Philip. 1993. *The Common Mind* (Oxford: Oxford University Press).

Putnam, Robert. 2000. *Bowling Alone: The Collapse and Revival of American Democracy* (New York: Simon & Schuster).

Rawls, John. 1971 (rev. edn. 1999). *A Theory of Justice* (Cambridge, MA: Harvard University Press).

Rawls, John. 1993 (expanded edn. 1996). *Political Liberalism* (New York: Columbia University Press).

Rawls, John. 2001. *Justice as Fairness: A Restatement* (Cambridge, MA: Harvard University Press).

Rothbard, Murray. 1973. *For a New Liberty* (New York: Macmillan).

Ryan, Alan. 1993. "The Liberal Community," in *NOMOS XXXV: Democratic Community*, ed. John Chapman and Ian Shapiro (New York: New York University Press).

Sandel, Michael. 1982 (2nd edn. 1998). *Liberalism and the Limits of Justice* Cambridge: Cambridge University Press).

Sandel, Michael. 1996. *Democracy's Discontent: America in Search of a Public Philosophy* (Cambridge, MA: Harvard University Press).

Sandel, Michael. 2000. "What Money Can't Buy: The Moral Limits of Markets," in Grethe Peterson, ed., *The Tanner Lectures on Human Values*, vol. 21 (Salt Lake City: University of Utah Press).

Sandel, Michael. 2005. *Public Philosophy: Essays on Morality in Politics* (Cambridge, MA: Harvard University Press).

Schwarzenbach, Sibyl. 1996. "On Civic Friendship," *Ethics* 107: 97–128.

Selznick, Philip. 2002. *The Communitarian Persuasion* (Washington, DC: Woodrow Wilson Center Press).

Senor, Thomas. 1987. "What If There Are No Political Obligations? A Reply to A. J. Simmons," *Philosophy and Public Affairs* 16 (2) (Spring): 260–8, 269–79.

Simmons, A. John. 1979. *Moral Principles and Political Obligations* (Princeton, NJ: Princeton University Press).

Simmons, A. John. 1987. "The Anarchist Position: A Reply to Klosko and Senor," *Philosophy and Public Affairs* 16: 270–5.

Simmons, A. John. 2001. "Philosophical Anarchism," in Simmons, *Justification and Legitimacy: Essays on Rights and Obligations* (Cambridge: Cambridge University Press).

Spragens, Thomas. 1995. "Communitarian Liberalism," in Amitai Etzioni, ed., *New Communitarian Thinking: Persons, Virtues, Institutions, and Communities* (Charlottesville, VA: University of Virginia Press.)

Spragens, Thomas. 1999. *Civic Liberalism: Reflections on Our Democratic Ideals* (Lanham, MD: Rowman and Littlefield).

Tam, Henry. 1998. *Communitarianism: A New Agenda for Politics and Citizenship* (New York: New York University Press).

Taylor, Charles. 1985. *Philosophy and the Human Sciences: Philosophical Papers*, vol. 2 (Cambridge: Cambridge University Press).

Taylor, Charles. 1995. "Cross-Purposes: The Liberal-Communitarian Debate," in Taylor, *Philosophical Arguments* (Cambridge, MA: Harvard University Press).

Taylor, Michael. 1982. *Community, Anarchy and Liberty* (Cambridge: Cambridge University Press).

Tocqueville, Alexis de. 1969 [1840]. *Democracy in America*, trans. George Lawrence, ed. J. P. Mayer (Garden City, NY: Doubleday).

Tronto, Joan. 2001. "Who Cares? Public and Private Caring and the Rethinking of Citizenship," in *Women and Welfare: Theory and Practice in the United States and Europe* (New Brunswick, NJ: Rutgers University Press).

Walzer, Michael. 1983. *Spheres of Justice: A Defense of Pluralism and Equality* (New York: Basic Books).

Wellman, Christopher Heath, ed. 2005. "Symposium on Disability," *Ethics* 116 (Oct.): 5–213.

Wolff, Robert Paul. 1998 [1970]. *In Defense of Anarchism*, 3rd edn. (Berkeley and Los Angeles: University of California Press).

Liberalism, Communitarianism, and the Politics of Identity

*Margaret Moore**

1. Introduction

This paper explores some basic criticisms and concerns raised by both communitarians and proponents of multiculturalism/identity politics against liberal political theory. This paper argues that the challenges posed (first by communitarians and then, in a different form, by multiculturalists) cannot be resolved at the abstract level, as they were originally posed in the liberal–communitarian debate. They are more fruitfully explored at a contextual level, by considering precisely what types of claims can legitimately be included in a liberal theory of justice, and what types can't be. Throughout this section I argue that, if we take seriously the possibility that interpreting equality as equal treatment might, in the context of deep differences in material and social position, and in culture and identity, have unfair results, then what multiculturalism demands is that liberals attend to, rather than abstract from, difference.

In order to proceed, it is necessary to clarify my use of the various terms and labels. This paper will, following Buchanan, identify liberalism with a liberal political thesis about the proper scope and limits of the state, viz., the thesis that the state is to enforce basic civil and political rights, rather than a more encompassing conception of the self, society or human nature.[1] Communitarianism is a fairly amorphous critical tradition, claiming roots, variously, in Aristotle and Hegel, but there are a number of central criticisms of liberalism that unite it.[2] This paper does not attempt to review the entire liberal–communitarian debate, nor its central points of contention. Rather, it focuses on two related arguments or criticisms that communitarians made against liberals in the original debate, viz., the Individualistic Self criticism; and the Structural Injustice objection. The politics of identity/recognition/multiculturalism is also a fairly loose "tradition" – with multiculturalists tending to focus on particular *political* policies and practices, whereas theorists who self-identify as interested in the politics of identity tend to be more concerned with cultural critique.[3] Indeed, as Homi Bhabha has argued, sometimes it seems that "multiculturalism is a portmanteau term for anything from minority discourse to postcolonial critique."[4] I will not attempt to trace the relationship between these different theories or identify any core arguments, but simply focus on two arguments that have been made. For the benefit of the reader, I will refer to this tradition as involving the politics of identity, encompassing theorists as different as Will Kymlicka's liberal multiculturalism and Iris Young's argument in *Justice and the Politics of Difference*.

My strategy in this paper is to outline briefly two criticisms made by communitarians against liberalism; and the liberal rejoinder to these. This helps to set the stage for a comparison with the politics of identity/recognition/multiculturalism. I examine how these arguments have been re-deployed in a more recent debate about the politics of identity and/or multiculturalism. I will argue that two of the challenges mirror similar concerns raised by communitarians, and that this debate has been more fruitful, to the extent that it has engaged in a more precise, contextually specific analysis.

2. Liberalism and Communitarianism: An Abstract Debate

In the 1980s and early 1990s, one of the central debates within contemporary political theory was the so-called liberal–communitarian debate. The crucial issues in the liberal–communitarian debate were never particularly clear, partly because there are different liberal theorists and different theorists under the communitarian banner, and partly because some of the claims were not clearly presented. In the "first wave" of communitarian criticism – put most forcefully in the work of Alasdair MacIntyre, Charles Taylor, and Michael Sandel, and, to a lesser extent, Michael Walzer[5] – the main criticisms seemed to focus on the excessively individualistic nature of liberalism. Communitarians argued that liberalism devalued, neglected, or undermined community, which is an important ingredient in a good life; that it failed to account for the importance of unchosen obligations and commitments; that it presupposed a defective, excessively individualistic, and/or abstract conception of the self; and, further, that this rendered the theory non-neutral between conceptions of the good.[6]

Taking these criticisms separately, it seems that one of the most often-repeated criticisms made by communitarians is that liberalism presupposes an "abstract self." One element of this "abstract self" criticism, developed by Sandel, is discussed entirely in terms of Rawls's metaphor of the original position, which it is presumed stands in for all liberal theory. Rawls's original position metaphor, Sandel argues, tends to conceive of all values, commitments and conceptions of the good as ultimately objects of choice – and insofar as something is an object of choice, the person or chooser must be conceived of as distinct from and prior to it. But this – Sandel alleges – is internally incoherent, for Rawls's difference principle cannot be justified on such grounds.[7]

Another criticism – developed more clearly by Charles Taylor in his essay on "Atomism" – is that this (the liberal view of the self) fails to consider properly the social environment that provides meaningful choices, and supports the development of the exercise of autonomy. He identifies liberals as endorsing the ideal of personal autonomy – i.e, the ideal of a self-choosing and self-forming being, which includes the capacity to assess what is of value – as fundamental to liberalism.[8] He argues that this developed capacity for autonomy requires a social environment of a certain kind:

the free individual of the West is only what he is by virtue of the whole society and civilization which brought him to be and which nourishes him. . . . [S]ince the free individual can only maintain his identity within a society/culture of a certain kind, he has to be concerned about the shape of this society/culture as a whole.[9]

It is clear that this criticism of the abstract liberal self applies to Nozick's theory, but it is not clear that it applies to more sociologically sophisticated liberal thinkers, like J. S. Mill's "On Individuality" or indeed a whole range of theorists who accept the liberal political thesis.

Related to the above criticism about the excessively abstract nature of the liberal person was a second criticism: that there are biases associated with liberalism. On this view, liberalism is non-neutral in a pernicious sense: it is biased against particular (communal) ways of life and communities. The conception of the person underlying liberal rules of justice, it was alleged,[10] was of an autonomous chooser: this explained, in Sandel's terms, "the priority of the right over the good," viz., the fact that liberal rules were decisive in the political sphere and so were legitimate arbiters of rival conceptions of the good (held by distinct individuals).[11] This, according to Sandel, seems to negate the possibility of basing the society or community on a shared conception of the good.[12] He identifies parallels between the liberal conception of the person, which is abstract, and devoid of a conception of the good (at least for the purposes of arriving at a conception of justice); the liberal conception of the state, which eschews controversial substantive moral conceptions; and the deficiencies of the current American state, which involves a politics of the right rather than a politics of the common good. Sandel identifies a "gradual shift, in our practices and institutions, from a public philosophy of common purposes to one of fair procedures, from a politics of good to a politics of right, from the national republic to the procedural republic."[13] Communitarian arguments – arguments based on a common good – were excluded from liberal political theory, which tended to be focused on identifying a politics of the right; and this exclusion is manifest in Rawls's own procedure in *A Theory of Justice*, whereby the selves in the original position must reason behind a veil of ignorance, and included in the veil are conceptions of the good (not just conceptions of what one personally finds good, but also of the common good).

Although these criticisms formed a fairly coherent line of attack, focusing on the individualistic nature of liberalism, they tended to be stated in very abstract terms, and the criticisms were either not clearly deployed against *particular* liberal theorists[14] or they were deployed against one particular theorist but then assumed to apply to the whole liberal tradition.[15]

This lack of clarity encouraged liberals to defend basic liberal values by arguing that they were fully compatible with moderate communitarianism; that liberalism was not self-interestedly egoistic, incapable of embracing community, unable to account for unchosen obligations, and so on.[16] Both Raz and Kymlicka, for example, claimed that it is wrong to conceive of liberalism as fundamentally individualistic or abstract; and they proved their point by justifying liberal political principles in terms of a conception of a valuable life, which includes other (substantive) values. Raz argued that his liberal theory escapes the charge of being individualistic because collective goods and communal values are constitutive of his objective conception of the good life.[17] The Sandelian version of the "abstract self" criticism was easily addressed in

Margaret Moore

the following way: liberalism does not presuppose an "empty" self; indeed, it is entirely consistent with the view that the self is often embedded in a range of social practices. The Taylor argument about the social conditions of individual autonomy was generally viewed as a fair argument against libertarian liberals, like Nozick, but that the social conditions criticism was not applicable to many more sociologically sensitive versions of liberalism. Indeed, Kymlicka claimed that

> liberalism couldn't be based on ... [abstract individualism]. ... If abstract individualism [was] ... the fundamental premise [of liberalism], there'd be no reason to ... suppose that people are being made worse off by being denied the social conditions necessary to freely and rationally question their commitments.[18]

Kymlicka then went on to argue that liberals presuppose only that the conception of the good, or ends of life, are revisable and change over time (within a life). This, he claimed is sufficient to justify liberal rights to protect the pursuit of people's liberty.

Allen Buchanan offered a more specific rejoinder to the non-neutrality objection, aimed at criticisms that took the form that liberalism is biased against, or hostile to, communities. He detailed various ways in which specific liberal rights – e.g., freedom of expression, freedom of association, freedom of religion – help to protect communities, and so presuppose the value of communities. The real threat to communities, he argued, comes from totalitarian states; and these rights help to provide a bulwark against the totalitarian impetus of the modern state.[19] He argued in the conclusion of his essay for "a fruitful convergence of what is best in liberalism and communitarianism, not a victory of the one over the other."[20]

Although many now regard the liberal–communitarian debate as "sterile" in the sense that the particular points of contention seemed to evaporate on closer examination, it did contribute to the articulation of more sophisticated versions of liberalism, and more sophisticated defenses of liberal political principles.[21] However, the debate was not very helpful, ultimately because it was insufficiently contextual, and so the issues between them, stated abstractly, tended to evaporate upon closer examination.

3. Multiculturalism/Identity Politics: Non-Neutrality and Structural Injustice

A decade later, an important challenge to liberalism has come from proponents of what is variously called the politics of identity, the politics of recognition or the politics of multiculturalism. Theorists in the politics of identity/recognition/multiculturalism "tradition" are also difficult to define, because there are many different versions, but the central plank in this challenge is the view that the presence of deep cultural diversity within modern liberal democratic states poses a significant challenge to traditional liberalism, or indeed any sort of liberal theory. As with the liberal–communitarian debate, there are many liberals who believe that an adequate liberal political theory can incorporate the legitimate claims of identity/multicultural politics into their theory (although, of course, even these liberals disagree on what constitutes a legitimate claim).[22] Interestingly, many of the criticisms raised by proponents of identity/

multicultural politics are similar to, or possibly, more sophisticated or more precise versions of, the criticisms raised during the "first wave" of the liberal-communitarian debate by so-called communitarians. In this paper, I argue that there are real issues at stake, but these are more fruitfully explored in relation to particular demands and strategies of accommodation.

Just as communitarian theorists argued that liberalism was based on an individualistic and abstract conception of the person – and that it was therefore not neutral among conceptions of the good (because biased against more communitarian conceptions) – so proponents of identity politics argue that the liberal model of equal citizenship and political inclusion fails to accommodate fully or authentically people who locate themselves in the social landscape differently. It was also non-neutral or biased, although here the bias was not against particular (communal) ways of life but against certain categories of person.

Second-wave feminism, the Black Civil Rights Movement in the U.S., gay and lesbian liberation, and, to a lesser extent, ethnic and national group claims to recognition, are based on arguments about injustices done to particular social groups. Many of these social movements begin from an analysis of oppression, and especially the idea that membership in certain social groups renders people particularly vulnerable to certain forms of oppression: marginalization, exploitation, cultural imperialism (stereotyping), powerlessness, and group-targeted violence.[23] These five "faces" of oppression tend to mark those whose identities have been historically neglected, suppressed or interpreted by dominant social groups, e.g., Blacks, women, gays and lesbians, Chicanos, Asians, indigenous peoples, and disabled people.

In this paper, I focus on the claim made by some proponents of identity politics that liberal models of inclusion are insufficient.[24] There are two aspects to this criticism: one dimension is the claim, which mirrors to a significant extent the earlier "abstract self" criticism of the communitarian theorists, that liberalism is based on an excessively individualistic and/or abstract self and so cannot properly or fully include people who have a different identity. It can incorporate rights and individual interests, but claims that take the form that "such-and-such shouldn't be allowed because it violates my religious or ethnic or national identity" or that "such-and-such is required as an expression of respect for my identity" – is not the sort of claim that can be accommodated within a liberal political order. Liberalism regards legitimate political demands as rooted in interests: fundamental interests, such as the interest in autonomy, are accorded the protection of liberal rights, but other sorts of interests have to be subject to the give-and-take of democratic politic. Liberal justice is insufficient, critics suggest, because it cannot address the legitimate justice-based demands that arise from group-based identity claims.[25] The second aspect of the criticism concerns the related issue of how liberal rules and rights tend to presuppose a certain type of person, and so are non-neutral for certain people in society, particularly the bearers of historically denigrated identities. Iris Young, for example, has argued that normalizing standards tend to disadvantage members of historically excluded groups, and that the liberal commitment to impartiality tends to mask the particularist standards that lurk behind the impartialist ideal.[26] This latter criticism – which we can label the Structural Injustice objection – is importantly related to the first type of criticism, because it presupposes that identity claims represent legitimate political demands in the first place.

There are two common liberal responses to these types of criticism, neither of which is very satisfactory; and, while they may seem opposed, they often appear together in the sense that many theorists adopt them as dual strategies. The first strategy – which I will call "identity denial" – argues that any claim that is based on identity or the accommodation of a particular identity is problematic, not just for liberal politics, but problematic in itself, and should not be considered. Waldron argues that identity claims should not legitimately enter political discourse, because they pose an "incompossibility problem" – the problem that respecting different people's identities in the same state may not be compossible (possible together) because respecting A's identity requires a policy or proposal that is inconsistent with respecting B's identity.[27] If identity claims conflict in the way that Waldron suggests that they will, then it will not be possible to set up a constitutional or legal regime that respects everyone's identity, since different identities give conflicting answers to the same set of questions. This is troubling because of two characteristic features of identity claims, as opposed to claims about interest: (1) the attachment to identity renders the claim relatively non-negotiable; and (2) identity claims, by their nature, are subjective and difficult to verify. The first feature refers to the idea that the language of identity renders the claims non-negotiable in a way that is detrimental to the give-and-take of democratic politics. The idea here is that the significance of the claim is enhanced by its attachment to the person's very identity. The second feature of identity claims is the relative lack of evidentiary standards related to identity. In this context, Waldron suggests that liberals, socialist, egalitarians and others are right to be concerned about the elasticity of the concept – which he identifies as related to its subjective character – and worry about whether we can organise a framework of laws and rights to live under which respects everyone's identity. "The viability of the liberal enterprise," he writes,[28] "depends on claims of this sort being fairly limited." He suggests that, under standard liberal theory, there are only a small number of interests that require the special non-negotiable treatment that is usually associated with rights; and that it is the potential proliferation of identity claims, and their unverifiable nature, which poses a challenge to the liberal order.

A second type of response is the suggestion that these sorts of identity claims, insofar as they represent claims to fair treatment, are fully dealt with in the liberal polity. Actually, this response is often part of the first strategy, which is hostile to formulations in terms of particular identities, but still wants to claim that liberal rules of justice in fact are based on the fact of pluralism, and can accommodate many different forms of life and conceptions of the good, subject only to rules of justice. On this view, the liberal political thesis should not be seen as dependent on a deeper, highly individualistic philosophy of the self: on the contrary, the rights that the thesis endorses – rights to freedom of religion, thought, association and expression – can accommodate a wide range of different forms of life and conceptions of the good, and protect people so that they can form communities free from state coercion and other forms of interference. Indeed, a key feature in Rawls's argument is the assumption of reasonable pluralism. The fact that people have different conceptions of the good, different aims, identities and interests, is a key justificatory plank in Rawls's argument for liberal principles and rights; these political rules and rights are justified precisely because they are important in protecting people's diverse aims and interests.

At this point, it seems that the argument between liberals and identity politics proponents has reached the same sort of impasse that the liberal–communitarian debate reached, with liberals denying that they do have the metaphysical commitments and hence structural biases that communitarians and identity politics theorists allege. But – in fact – much of this debate has occurred at a more concrete level, and it is at this level that it is possible to see precisely the kinds of accommodations that liberalism can make towards recognition of particular identities, and the limitations of its forms of accommodation. Indeed, my central argument in this chapter is that the only way this debate makes any sense is if we leave the abstract level and consider precisely what types of claims can legitimately be included in a liberal theory of justice, and what types can't be.

Although there are different criticisms leveled by proponents of a politics of identity, I want to focus on the two arguments outlined above. The first demonstrates the reasons why identity is politically important and should not be ignored, and this debate is related to the first criticism concerning the abstract and individualistic nature of the liberal self. The second argument, which is strongly related to the first, presses on the possibility that conceiving of equality as equal treatment, in the context of deep differences in material and social position, and cultural differences, can be unfair. In certain cases, this can impose unfair burdens on certain categories of people in societies. This structural injustice objection to liberalism presupposes the validity of identity claims, since it conceives of ignoring or denying forms of identity as *unjust*.

4. Liberal Individuals and Their Identities

Identity claims are directly relevant to the criticism that liberalism is excessively individualistic and abstract. This is because identity claims are claims to consideration precisely on the basis of (typically) collective forms of identity, and in terms of concrete interests, aims, and attachments.

There are three reasons why we might think that identity claims should be treated seriously, and so ought to be an object of accommodation in a liberal state.[29] We can call these (1) the integrity reason; (2) the ethical commitment reason; and (3) the ascriptive reason.

When someone claims that something is central to his/her identity, it suggests an integral relationship to the self. One's identity is linked, causally, with one's sense of self, or one's integrity as a person. It is the basis on which one's other (non-identity) interests, values, and preferences are based. This suggests that we should think very carefully about enforcing rules and policies that violate people's identities, or require people to act contrary to what they regard as central to their sense of self. At the very least, the state should have very good reasons for policies that force people to act in way that they experience as a violation of their very identity.

Second, and following from the integrity notion, one's identity is strongly linked with the moral core of the person. It is generally accepted that there is a strong relationship between one's sense of self and one's essential ethical commitments. It is often thought to be unreasonable for the state to demand that the person conform to rules an policies that are directly counter to his/her strongest moral beliefs, or, at least, that it shouldn't do so for trivial or even utilitarian reasons.

Margaret Moore

Finally, the ascriptive aspect of many identities is relevant to the burdens that the state can legitimately place on members of particular identity groups. There are at least two reasons for describing identities as non-voluntary: one is that they are hard-wired or biologically based; the second is whether they are ratified by others, regardless of whether or not the person identifies with them. One argument that has been raised by gay men and women about the unequal treatment that they experience at the hands of the state is that their identities are biologically based: these are not *mere* preferences, but are hard wired, as it were. Unequal treatment of the two different sexual orientations is therefore profoundly unfair. Others focus on the idea that identities have to be ratified by others: there is a limit to the identities that are genuinely available to one; and some identities are difficult to escape. This is not simply the point that the identities that one comes to have are partly the product of involuntary socialization and education by others – I think all identities may be described this way – but in the much deeper sense that identities depend, to a large extent, on how others see one and identify one. Both types of non-voluntariness are morally relevant since it may be thought that the state has a responsibility not to impose onerous burdens on the bearers of particular (unchosen) identities.

It is interesting that the appeal to identity is at one remove from a direct appeal to the beliefs that a person has, which is typically the object of liberal pluralism. The claim to accommodation of an identity is unlike a claim based on a particular conception of the good in the sense that an identity claim by its very nature appeals to a generalizable interest in having an identity of a certain kind and the implications of this. To see this, consider the difference between saying, for example, "X is required by my religion" and "X is required by my religious identity." The former refers to the reasons for the belief. It explains the person's belief structure, the motivational and possibly justificatory reasons for his/her actions, but one that, in the context of religious diversity, is not helpful to resolving disagreements about the policies or practices of the society. The reference to identity, by contrast, appeals to a generalizable interest, which everyone can understand, in having an identity of a certain kind, in having deep moral commitments and a sense of self. It appeals, that is, to the underlying integrity, moral commitment, and sense-of-self arguments. The appeal to identity, rather than the values directly implicit in the identity itself, makes sense especially in the context of diversity. It is not an argument that one would make when appealing to someone within one's identity group, an interlocutor who already accepts one's religion or the importance of one's cultural practices. But it is an argument that one would make to outsiders, who may not be convinced by the truth of the religion, or the superiority of the practice, but can at least understand that it is important to you, and that it bears on your very sense of self.[30]

These three considerations – the integrity, moral commitment and ascriptive reasons – do not bear on all identities, and are not perfectly aligned. Some religious identities may be reasonably voluntary, especially in the case of a convert, but tend to rank quite high on the dimension of importance to the person and relationship to the core ethical commitments of the self. A racial or gender identity may be more ascriptive, but may not be as closely bound up with the normative commitments of the self. They are, however rooted in some biological facts about the person, and so may be experienced by the person as central to his or her sense of self. Although these considerations do not map neatly on each other, and none independently represents a necessary condition for the possession of an identity, they are the kinds of reasons we have for thinking that identity-related claims should be taken seriously. They help explain the normative force of particular identity claims.

If we accept the above argument for why identity claims represent a legitimate type of claim in a liberal-democratic polity, and why a full theory of social justice should be attentive to such concerns (which doesn't mean that it should accommodate automatically each and every claim), then we have gone some way to accepting the argument of identity politics proponents. It implies that we do not accept the dismissive strategy adopted by Barry and Waldron, viz., the argument that these sorts of claims are simply not acceptable, even as claims, in a liberal order.

Of course, ultimately, the central question is whether a liberal order is fair to diverse types of identities, and this can only be resolved by examining precisely how, and the extent to which, the liberal order has the resources to accommodate diverse identity claims and practices.

5. Liberal Rules and Structural Injustices: Rules-and-Exemptions

This brings us to the second, most compelling criticism of liberalism, which is that particularist forms of identity are not properly or fully accommodated in the liberal state, or that the liberal state has structural biases against the bearers of particular kinds of identities. This second criticism can be called the Structural Injustice objection to liberalism (SIO). It is important to consider this criticism, because it bears on the second element of the liberal response to the identity/multicultural challenge, viz., that liberalism is capable of accommodating and responding to all sorts of diversity (including, implicitly, diversity of identities). Indeed, we might accept the first view – that identity claims represent an important claim to justice which should be accommodated – but still think that liberalism has the conceptual resources to fully accommodate and address these sorts of claims. This, then, is the most important argument that both the communitarians and the identity politics proponents have made.

In order to deal with the Structural Injustice Objection, it is necessary to consider the concrete ways in which the neutral liberal state might be thought to be biased against the bearers of particular identities. In that context, it is necessary to think of the type of accommodations that are consistent with liberalism, which a liberal state could, and often does, make.

Many of the claims put forward by multicultural groups are attempts to ensure that state policies do not unfairly disadvantage certain groups: they are arguments for acceptance of particular practices, not simply in the sense that the practice is de-criminalized, and so open to the individual in the private sphere, but in the deeper sense that the practices and policies of the state do not unfairly disadvantage members of the identity group. Muslim girls in France and Quebec have challenged rules denying them the right to wear headscarves in schools, Sikhs in Canada have argued that motorcycle helmet laws and the code of appropriate dress in the Royal Canadian Mounted Police – where the uniform includes a hat that is not compatible with a turban – discriminates against them. Orthodox Jews in the United States military have sought the right to wear the yarmulke. Gays and lesbians in many countries have argued that the definition of the family in law and in state policies has served to exclude them and to deny them the benefits accorded to heterosexual married couples.

In all these cases, the basic claim is to be treated fairly, to ensure that a particular cultural practice or way of life is included in the larger society. In many cases, the claim for a form of accommodation is not only a claim about fairness, but also a claim in which accommodation can take the form of exemption to a rule.[31] In all the above cases, the offending practice is forced on an unwilling subject, and the person argues that the practice violates her religious, sexual orientation, gender, or cultural/national identity. Many of these legal cases are this kind, and involve an exemption from a state-wide rule or practice. In most of the cases above, the argument advanced by the identity group is an argument for toleration. It is an argument for toleration of a particular religiously associated form of dress, or exemptions (for *halel* and *kosher* meats) from animal cruelty laws to allow or permit a certain religiously orientated practice. In each case, the state-wide law created burdens for the minority. Further, in none of these cases was Waldron's concern about incompossibility a potential problem: these demands do not require that the rule be scrapped in favor of a new (state-wide) rule, as a condition of *my* identity, but only that the practice or dress or ritual be tolerated by the majority society.

It is hard to see what is particularly *illiberal* about accommodating this type of identity claim. First, there is a long-standing issue in liberal theory surrounding conscientious objection, which takes precisely the exemption-from- rule form, and which has a long history of accommodation within liberal states. In the case of conscientious objection (to war), the state admits exemptions for a whole category of people (typically, those who can demonstrate either membership in a pacifist religious group, such as the Quakers, or people who can demonstrate a long-standing moral commitment to pacifism).[32]

Moreover, the exemptions asked for do not reify the cultural practices in question. The exemption only applies if the person in question is actually a practicing member of a particular religious group. Consider, for example, the demand that Sikhs should be granted an exemption from certain rules regarding headgear to permit them to wear a turban. The exemption, it is true, is granted to people on the basis of a religion, and it may be thought that the exemption is over-inclusive in the sense that there may be "beneficiaries" of this exemption who do not care much about their religion. However, if the claim to accommodation is a claim for an exemption from a state-wide rule (on the basis of an identity claim), there is no problem connected to including people who should not be granted an exemption. Exemptions, by their very nature, do not require the person to take them up: if the person cares little for his or her religion, he or she will not need the exemption in the first place. The exemption for Sikhs is only necessary if the person actually does wear a turban. A non-practicing Sikh, who does not conform to Sikh dress codes, would have no need of such an exemption.

Now, at this point, the Structural Injustice Objection can be reformulated as follows: although it is true that blatantly unfair applications of rules can be dealt with by exemptions, this isn't fully adequate. It fails to address the issue that there is still a rule or standard, which is presented as normalizing, and which define certain categories of people as deviant. This can be called the Structural Injustice Objection 2 (SIO2).

It is hard to know how to respond to this formulation of the objection, since it seems to have a wide application (far beyond specifically liberal rules) to any laws or rules in modern large-scale bureaucratic societies that take a general form. In many cases, there are very good reasons for general rules and so it does not seem a good idea (nor possible in a modern bureaucratic society) to avoid all general rules. [33] In the case of motorcycle helmet legislation, for example, the general justificatory argument is in terms of a safety requirement. This safety concern still applies to Sikhs, but it is deemed overridden by the religious requirements. Moreover, many of the proposals on offer within the multicultural/identity literature are "guilty" of this objection. Consider, for example, Iris Young's own proposals for a deliberative forum in which different groups are included and their input is important in shaping the rules under which people live. This is not mere hopeful thinking, since Young makes some concrete institutional proposals for how this might be realized, such as a veto over areas that are of particular concern to particular groups.[34] Much can be said both for and against this proposal, but what is interesting here is that it raises the same structural problems as the rule-and-exemption proposal. It carves out a particular area of jurisdictional authority, a particular area of interest for groups, and doesn't permit outside interference in that area. It is therefore subject to the normalizing standard objection (SIO2), and for precisely the same reason, viz., elsewhere jurisdictional authority takes a general form, and people can see themselves as collective authors of the rules under which they live and the conditions of their existence, except in cases where an argument can be made that this rule shouldn't apply.

In conclusion, it seems that liberalism is capable of responding to the first and most coherent version of the Structural Injustice objection, and it is capable of doing so because liberalism is a theory that takes equality seriously. The "equality" principle implicit in most justifications of liberalism is admittedly an abstract principle, but it is not purely formal: it embodies a particular substantive value – namely, equal treatment by the state. If equality is interpreted as equal treatment, then, where equal treatment has profoundly and demonstrably unfair results, there is a strong argument for remedying this. However, interestingly, this only makes sense if one takes seriously the possibility that interpreting equality as requiring equal treatment might, in the context of deep differences in material and social position, and cultural and identity diversity, have unfair results; and this is a claim that many liberals can, and do accept. One way to view that challenge is that it has forced liberals to focus on the need to attend to, rather than abstract from, such difference; and the need to contextualize the specific requirements of liberalism. Rules and exemptions do not represent a systematic way to ensure such a contextualization of the equality requirement,[35] but they do suggest the need to examine the specific ways in which liberal rules and principles are institutionalized in concrete settings.

6. Liberal Toleration and Structural Injustice: Equality as Recognition

In the previous section, I argued that multicultural and identity politics claims that take the form of demanding an exemption from a general rule do not pose a fun-

Margaret Moore

damental challenge to liberalism, but are fully in accord with a certain interpretation of equality, which is a fundamental principle of liberal theory. However, other demands pose a deeper challenge to liberal theory, at least insofar as they suggest the insufficiency of the traditional liberal model of toleration, and the supposed neutrality of the state on decisions that are essentially moral.

The argument by gay and lesbian activist groups for a change in the definition of the family to include gay and lesbian marriages is, I think, entirely consistent with the liberal commitment to equal treatment of all citizens, and public neutrality on moral questions. Gays and lesbians in many countries have argued, I think compellingly, that the definition of the family in law and state policies has served to exclude them and to deny them the benefits (both financial and symbolic) accorded to heterosexual married couples.

In many ways, this is similar to the structural injustice objection, since it points out a deep inequality in the structure of the laws and policies of (supposedly) liberal states and the liberal principles regarding equal treatment of citizens and public neutrality on questions of the good life ought to apply. For this reason, liberals should have no difficulty accommodating this particular identity-related claim.

However, it is interesting to note, first, that in this case the remedy to the injustice that they face (change in marriage laws) is somewhat different from the ones discussed in the above section. Gays and lesbians do not seek simply *toleration* of their practices and ways of life by the wider society but full recognition and acceptance in the rules and practices of the society. They do not seek merely exemptions from state-wide rules, but, rather, to alter the rules of the over-arching society and thereby claim equal status for their way of life.

It is useful to compare the old liberal model of toleration literature with this new demand for recognition.[36] The standard liberal toleration doctrine, which developed in the seventeenth century, as a means to reconcile divergent religions, assumed moral pluralism – not social and cultural pluralism.[37] In the case of classical regimes of toleration, toleration revolved around the privatization of diverse (religious) identities: people would privately view certain religious views as profoundly worrying, even heretical, but they would tolerate them. The term "toleration" in this sense does not mean celebrating their practices or beliefs or in any way affirming them: indeed, it has a certain "grit–your teeth" component when faced with objectionable beliefs and practices, which nevertheless have to be tolerated in the sense that the state cannot justifiably interfere in these beliefs and practices. Privatization of religious beliefs was necessary for mutual coexistence, while at the same time it did not require the tolerant person to acknowledge the value or validity of the offending or immoral practice (so in that sense wasn't based on a deeper skepticism).

Clearly, classical toleration is insufficient from the standpoint of gays and lesbians, who do not seek decriminalization (and therefore privatization) of homosexuality, but its affirmation as a valid way of life. In that sense, the demand for a change to the unfair marriage laws does not represent a mechanism to accommodate pluralism: it involves precisely the rejection of the religious person's views of the sanctity of heterosexual marriage, and establishing laws, not on the basis of mutual accommodation, but on the basis of equality. Similarly, the U.S. Clinton Administration's doctrine regarding homosexuality in the military – the famous "don't ask, don't tell" policy was, like classical liberal toleration, focused on the privatization of diverse identities and orientations. It was also similarly inadequate in dealing with the deep structural biases of the military's policies in the first place.

Interestingly, however, this case does not affirm Waldron's argument about the relationship between identity claims, which have a strongly subjective element, and incompossibility (the problem that it might not be possible to create general rules that respect or affirm different sorts of identities). At first glance, it might seem to raise issues of incompossibility, insofar as these identity claims require a change in the marriage law, and this might conflict with a more conservative religious person's identity claim, which links their religious identity with the view that marriage is a union of a man and a woman. In fact, however, the gay and lesbian claim, like the multicultural claims examined above, is a claim for equality, for the removal of a structural injustice, not a claim that is appropriately conceived as a method to achieve stability in the context of moral pluralism.[38]

This suggests that the original roots of liberal toleration, which developed in the context of religious diversity, as a means to avoid conflict and violence, may result in a different prescriptive proposal than claims rooted in the principle of equal treatment by the state of various different identities. The original model suggested privatization of all identities, and was mainly defended in terms of the need to *regulate* diverse views. By contrast, the new politics of recognition, based as it is on a substantive reading of the equality principle, suggests equal treatment of all citizens and identities by the state. This tradition implies that equality as a norm has a significant substantive content, which cannot always be reconciled with different moral conceptions. Liberal rules can be neutral among individuals in the sense that their justificatory argument is not based on a particular conception of the good[39] – as liberals have argued in their defense of justificatory neutrality – but it requires a fundamental commitment to individual equality, and in practice this will conflict with some moral conceptions.

It is also consistent with a fairly typical liberal view concerning a division of labor between individuals and social institutions. On this view, political and social institutions are required to embody impartial concern, and equality among the interests of individuals, whereas individuals can be partial towards themselves and their families, and act in ways that do not embody impartiality, as long as they don't harm others or violate their rights.[40]

7. Structural Injustice and Jurisdictional Authority

There are cases where the claim on the part of identity groups to equal treatment poses a serious challenge to the neutral liberal state. These are cases where there is limited public space over which identity groups contest; where such groups demand a change in state policy or structure; and where state retreat from the contested area is not possible (as it was in the case of religious diversity); and where fairness is difficult to achieve.

In this section, I will discuss two types of cases: demands for linguistic fairness on the part of minority language groups; and demands for self-determination by minority nationalists. In both types of cases – as in the gay and lesbian family case – the group in question is making a basic demand for fair treatment or neutral treatment or equal treatment. Typically, they are advancing their claim in a context where the background or baseline is unfair. Minority language groups, for example, often operate in states where the minority language is relegated to the private sphere, and some other (usually, majority) language is the language of the state's courts, bureaucracy, education system, and so on. Minority language groups are not making a claim for special treatment, but for equality.[41]

Traditional liberal theory, which is concerned to regulate conceptions of the good and justify rules and practices in a way that is neutral between conceptions of the good, does not address this sort of fairness issue. This is because liberals (and democrats) have often operated with convenient simplifying assumptions: they have been concerned to justify and argue for the rule of law, the practice of distributive justice, democratic governance, and respect for human rights, but have failed to consider the domain of the rule of law, democracy or distributive justice. They have considered what rights we (ought to) have, but not which language the rights have been written in, or what language(s) should the business of the courts or the legislature be conducted in.

While the basic claim is one of fairness, it is clear that the reproduction of language requires a public sphere, so that state decisions on language teaching in public schools and language requirements in the state legislature and bureaucracy are crucial to the success or demise of particular languages. Privatization is not an option, because the modern, bureaucratic state cannot escape some decisions on these issues.[42] Moreover, it is not clear what precisely fairness requires in the case of diverse linguistic identities. One problem stems from the very reason why privatization is not possible: the state is deeply implicated in linguistic accommodation decisions; and this is so for reasons that run deep into the functional imperatives of the modern state.[43]

As Gellner has argued, since the rise of the modern bureaucratic state, with mass literacy and increasingly standardized modes of interaction, the state is inextricably linked with the reproduction of values and cultures.[44] It is not possible to have a modern state and give equal recognition to all the languages spoken in diverse cosmopolitan cities. Signs, education, public debate has to be in one or two or three languages – there is clearly an upper limit here – but there is certainly a need for some common language(s), in which different people meet and discuss their commonalities and recognize each other as fellow citizens.

I am not suggesting there that we deny the legitimacy of identity claims in the public sphere, as Waldron and Barry propose. There is a difficult, but fundamental, question of how the state should treat its diverse people fairly and with equal respect. Policies of absolutely equal treatment – multilingualism – are not possible in the modern state. Privatization is also not a possibility, and is not, in any case, fair. Unfortunately, it is not clear what a liberal state, which seeks to treat its diverse identities fairly, or at least seeks to balance identity related interests with other legitimate interests of a more functional kind, would do. It is not clear whether fair treatment of linguistic identities, for example, requires a policy of official bilingualism, for example, or whether it is a fairer model to opt for a norm and exemption approach.[45] Alan Patten has offered reasons for thinking that official bilingualism is the fairer model, but much would seem to depend (as he says) on the context one is operating with, such as: how many linguistic groups there are, and how accommodation affects people's non-identity related interests in communication and their interests in having a functioning modern state.[46]

Minority nationalists, too, make a claim to structural injustice, similar to the claims made by various cultural groups, gays and lesbians, and minority language groups. Minority nationalists have argued that the liberal state is not in fact neutral among various national identities, for the state in fact is crucial to the reproduction of particular national groups on the territory. More precisely, minority nationalists have argued that political borders – or, more precisely, where political borders are drawn – can privilege some groups and not others. They do not mean here simply economic or material "privilege" but are also referring to the fair treatment of certain kinds of identities. Indeed, in the case of national identities, where a crucial component of being a national group is having a political identity as a member of a potentially collectively self-governing group, the state structure is crucial to whether this aspiration is realized. In most cases, national groups have the capacity to be democratically self-governing; to dispense justice and create a common, public life in which people can participate. Related to this, they are generally sufficiently territorially concentrated that the exercise of self-government is possible, and is only denied by a state order, in which they are a minority, and which typically permits some other (e.g., majority) group to be collectively self-governing. The state cannot be disconnected from this issue: whether the minority national identity is recognized or denied, the group's aspirations fulfilled or unfulfilled, is inextricably bound up with the institutional structure of the state and majority willingness or unwillingness to countenance changes to the state structure. It is the state, typically controlled by the majority national community, which either functions to facilitate this political self-government through devolved power, or some other institutional expression of this aspiration, or serves to deny it. Indeed, in the current political order, where the state is inextricably linked with the reproduction of identities, fairness to national groups is often assumed to require either a fair multinational state, in which the minority national group realizes some sort of collective self-government (short of secession), or secession from the state to become its own state.

Liberals – or at least liberal multiculturalists and liberal nationalists – have gone some way towards addressing the minority nationalist version of the structural injustice objection. Their particular form of accommodation typically involves three inter-connected arguments. The first involves accepting borders as in some sense consistent with liberal theory. The second consists of a more complex argument to the effect that minorities may require group-differentiated rights – and included here is a right to political autonomy or jurisdictional authority – to equalize their condition vis-à-vis majority groups.

The first claim concerns whether political boundaries are defensible in the first place, on liberal theory. This is contested: on the one hand, boundaries represent a significant embarrassment to the universality and moral worth of persons, which undergirds most liberal theory, insofar as it is clear that people's life chances, opportunities, well-being, and exercise of autonomy – and indeed the protection of their rights – depends on where they are born. As Joe Carens has argued, people born on one side of the Rio Grande are born into the modern equivalent of the nobility, while people born a few miles on the other side of the border are born into the modern equivalent of serfdom.[47] On this view, boundaries are not themselves justified on liberal grounds; however, liberal theory can proceed, pragmatically, as it were, to assume their existence as a baseline from which theory proceeds, since political cosmopolitanism is not likely in the foreseeable future.

There is, however, another liberal argument, argued for suggestively by John Rawls in *Law of Peoples*, that differentiated political authorities are necessary protection for liberty, insofar as centralized power is more susceptible to abuse, and inefficiency, and dispersed power is more consonant with effective, and yet restrained government. Rawls writes:

> These principles [of global justice] ... will not affirm a world state. Here I follow Kant's lead in *Perpetual Peace* (1795) in thinking that a world government – by which I mean a unified political regime with the legal powers normally exercised by central governments – would either be a global despotism or else would rule over a fragile empire torn by frequent civil strife as various regions and peoples tried to gain their political freedom and autonomy.[48]

Having established that political boundaries are either justified or are a baseline from which (non-ideal normative) reasoning should proceed, the next, and indeed crucial, element in the argument is the claim that minority nationalists need some jurisdictional authority, some political self-government, to equalize their condition vis-à-vis the majority national group on the territory. This argument proceeds in several steps. First, as Will Kymlicka, the most famous exponent of this position, has argued, liberal rules are justified in terms of their role in facilitating personal autonomy; and culture is an important background condition for the exercise of autonomy. A central move in this argument is the claim that culture provides the context from which individuals' choices about how to live one's life can be made. According to Kymlicka, "individual choice is dependent on the presence of a societal culture, defined by language and history."[49] Culture provides the options from which the individual chooses, and infuses them with meaning, so that self-forming autonomous beings have some conception of value with which to guide their choices. The next step in the argument is the claim that, since a rich and flourishing culture is an essential condition of the exercise of autonomy, liberals have good reason to adopt measures that would protect culture. At this point, the argument has only shown that the existence of a (or some) flourishing cultural structure is necessary to the exercise of autonomy, but not a particular culture. However, he then makes the empirical point that "most people have a very strong bond to their own culture."[50] Kymlicka then points to the equality principle to justify jurisdictional authority for minority groups: it is unfair for majorities to have the protection of their culture which comes from being a majority in the state, for this places an unfair burden on minorities, who find that they have to bear the costs for maintaining their culture. This supports his conclusion that minority national (or societal) cultures should be supported as a context in which personal autonomy is exercised.[51] This takes a number of forms,[52] but the one of interest to minority nationalists is political autonomy, or jurisdictional authority, which is explored (in Kymlicka's work) within the state context, although it seems that this type of argument would justify secession from the state if this is necessary to ensure that the group has the jurisdictional authority to protect its own culture.

This kind of argument – indeed, the minority nationalist claim to structural injustice – does raise incompossibility issues, insofar as it is not possible to make a decision that fully satisfies the identity-related demands of diverse groups. Moreover, in this sort of case, unlike in the case of rule-and-exemption, the claim is to a change in the basic laws, policies or structure of the state; and this raises the potential for including or applying to people who are not members of the identity group in question. This raises the possibility of imposition on people who do not share the identity. Interestingly, however, the problem does not seem intrinsically connected to identity claims, as such, as Waldron and Barry both claimed. The problem arises because states are territorial, not personal: indeed, in the context of a multinational state like Canada, Waldron's proposal (of making identity claims inadmissible) simply represents *de facto* support for the Canadian national identity and a denial of the legitimacy of minority (e.g., Quebec) national identities. The liberal multicultural response is at least an attempt to equalize, as far as possible, the unfairness attached to the policies and structure of the contemporary territorial state.

8. Conclusion

In this paper, I have assessed two related criticisms of liberal political theory, which have been deployed by both communitarians and proponents of multiculturalism or identity politics. These are (1) the criticism that the liberal self is excessively abstract and individualistic; and (2) that there are biases associated with liberalism, viz., that liberalism is either non-neutral or biased against particular (communal) ways of life and communities (communitarianism) or against certain categories of people (politics of identity).

One theme of this paper has been to note the similarities between the criticisms of communitarians and multiculturalists. The central argument, however, is that these sorts of criticisms can only be considered and assessed by examining precisely *how* liberal rules are supposed to be unfair, and whether liberalism has the resources to accommodate these concerns and address these sorts of unfairness.

As long as liberal theorists are prepared to accept the possibility that conceiving of equality as equal treatment might be unfair in contexts of deep division of individual and social position, and cultural difference, they will then accept the need for a contextual assessment of the operation of the rules of justice or principles of liberalism in the society. Liberalism is fundamentally committed to equal treatment, and this principle does not in itself preclude more contextual assessment of rules and policies in the interests of equality. Indeed, in examining these various claims, I have argued that the liberal commitment to equality – the commitment to equal respect which underlies human rights and rules of justice – supports granting exemptions in the case of demonstrated burdens and changing rules and policies when these discriminate against individuals in society.

This paper argues that forms of accommodation that take a rule-and-exemption form are the easiest to implement and the least problematic, but that general changes in the rules and structure of society to address unfairness can be justified. I have argued that these are sometimes problematic. First, they can conflict with the regulatory dimension of liberal justice (as when people's moral conceptions conflict with

Margaret Moore

the equality principle) and, second, there might be no way to equalize fully the position of all people in a large, bureaucratic and law-governed society. Nevertheless, since the main criticisms are in terms of equality and since liberalism is fundamentally a theory that takes equality seriously, it is capable of being extended in directions that address the claims of structural injustice raised by theorists and activists in the multicultural/politics of identity camp.

The central argument in this paper is that these issues cannot be resolved at the abstract level, in the way in which they were originally debated in the "first wave" of the liberal–communitarian debate. This is because they are fruitfully explored in terms of rival conceptions of the legitimacy of certain types of arguments and claims in the public sphere, and this requires an analysis of what precisely is being claimed, in order to know whether it can be incorporated within a defensible liberal theory. At a general level, then, this essay is a plea for a much more contextual and precise discussion of these issues. More specifically, this essay argues, with regard to identity politics, that liberals can incorporate some features of identity politics and identity claims, especially claims that take a rule-and-exemption form, but that are limits to this; and that the debate must be addressed in more concrete terms about specific proposals, claims and rights.

Notes

* The author would like to thank Mira Bachvarova for helpful comments on an earlier version of this essay, and permission to incorporate some shared work in this paper.
1 Allen Buchanan, "Assessing the Communitarian Critique of Liberalism", *Ethics* 99 (Jul. 1989): 852–82, esp. 853.
2 Allen Buchanan identifies five fundamental criticisms of liberalism, which he associates with communitarianism in his article "Assessing the Communitarian Critique." Will Kymlicka focuses on two central criticisms, one of which is the complicated criticism that he labels "the social thesis." See Will Kymlicka, *Contemporary Political Philosophy, an Introduction*, 2nd edn (Oxford: Oxford University Press, 2002), pp. 208–83.
3 Iris Marion Young, William Connolly, Judith Butler, and Bonnie Honig are interested in "difference" theory and what I call here the politics of identity.
4 Homi Bhabha, "Cultures in Between," in David Bennett, ed., *Multicultural States: Rethinking Difference and Identity* (London: Routledge, 1998), p. 31.
5 Alasdair MacIntyre, *After Virtue; A Study in Moral Theory* (London: Duckworth, 1981); Alasdair MacIntyre, *Whose Justice? Which Rationality?* (Notre Dame, IN: Notre Dame University Press, 1988); Michael Sandel, "The Procedural Republic and the Unencumbered Self," inShlomo Avineri and Avner de-Shalit, eds., *Communitarianism and Individualism* (Oxford: Oxford University Press, 1992), Michael Sandel, *Liberalism and the Limits of Justice* (Cambridge: Cambridge University Press, 1982); Charles Taylor, *Philosophy and the Human Sciences: Philosophical Papers, vol. ii* (Cambridge: Cambridge University Press, 1985); Michael Walzer, *Spheres of Justice: A Defense of Pluralism and Equality* (Oxford: Blackwell, 1983).
6 This list is mainly drawn from Allen Buchanan, "Assessing the Communitarian Critique."
7 The difference principle is Rawls's central principle of redistributive justice, which justifies inequalities only if they are to the advantage of the worst-off. Sandel's point here is that this principle is essentially a principle of sharing, and seems to presuppose some conception of the community in which such redistribution would take place.

8 Taylor identifies personal autonomy with the capacity for "conceiving alternatives and arriving at a definition of what they really want, as well as discerning what commands their adherence or their allegiance." Charles Taylor, "Atomism," in Avineri and de-Shalit, *Communitariansim and Individualism*, p. 43.

9 Taylor, "Atomism," pp. 45–7.

10 Sandel, *Liberalism and the Limits of Justice*, pp. 55–9; Charles Taylor, *Hegel and Modern Society* (Cambridge: Cambridge University Press, 1979), pp. 75–8.

11 Buchanan argued, persuasively, that this could be explained solely by the fact of pluralism. He writes: "Rawls' contract approach only assumes that these are individuals or groups with different conceptions of the good. This does not seem to be an excessively restrictive assumption for a theory of justice to make. At the very least it is hard to see how a theory that did not make this assumption would be relevant to our undeniably pluralistic world" (Buchanan, "Assessing the Communitarian Critique," p. 864).

12 See Sandel, "The Procedural Republic and the Unencumbered Self," pp. 81–96.

13 See Sandel, "The Procedural Republic and the Unencumbered Self', pp. 26–7.

14 See Taylor's critique of liberalism in "Atomism."

15 See Sandel's critique of Rawls in *Liberalism and the Limits of Justice*.

16 See Will Kymlicka, *Liberalism, Community and Culture* (Oxford: Oxford University Press, 1989); Buchanan, "Assessing the Communitarian Critique," pp. 852–82.

17 Joseph Raz, *The Morality of Freedom* (Oxford: Clarendon Press, 1986), p. 216.

18 Kymlicka, *Liberalism, Community and Culture*, p. 18.

19 Buchanan, "Assessing the Communitarian Critique," pp. 862–4.

20 Buchanan, "Assessing the Communitarian Critique," p. 882.

21 Often this is within a tradition that emphasises well-being, rather than just individual autonomy. See James Griffin, *Well-Being: Its Meaning, Measurement and Moral Importance* (Oxford: Oxford University Press, 1986); Martha Nussbaum, *Women and Human Development: The Capabilities Approach* (Cambridge: Cambridge University Press, 2000); Amartya Sen, *Rationality and Freedom* (Cambridge, MA: Harvard University Press, 2002).

22 Liberal multiculturalists – or multicultural liberals – such as Joseph Raz, Will Kymlicka, Jacob Levy, and indeed myself in a recent book – tend to go further than other liberals in incorporating such concerns into the theory, whereas many liberal theorists tend to think that these concerns are not legitimate. See Kymlicka, *Multicultural Citizenship* (Oxford: Clarendon Press, 1995); Jacob Levy, *Multiculturalism of Fear* (Oxford: Oxford University Press, 2000); Joseph Raz, "Multiculturalism: A Liberal Perspective", *Dissent* (Winter 1994): 67–79; Margaret Moore, *Ethics of Nationalism* (Oxford: Oxford University Press, 2001).

23 See Iris Marion Young, *Justice and the Politics of Difference* (Princeton, NJ: Princeton University Press, 1993), pp. 39–65.

24 There is an enormous debate around the metaphysical tension between identity and difference, and particularly the problem of essentialism in the face of the fluidity and hybridity of identities. See Elizabeth Spelman, *Inessential Woman: Problems of Exclusion in Feminist Thought* (Boston, MA: Beacon Press, 1988); Jane Roland Martin, "Methodological Essentialism, False Difference, and Other Dangerous Traps," *Signs* 19: 630–57. See, however, Gayatri Spivak, *The Post-Colonial Critic: Interviews, Strategies, Dialogues* (New York: Routledge, 1990) for an argument that identity claims should be regarded politically and strategically, but that they need not imply a deeper unity.

25 Young, *Justice and the Politics of Difference*.

26 Sometimes this is presented as necessarily implicated in the quest to arrive at universal standards. She writes: "Moral reason that seeks impartiality tries to reduce the plurality of moral subjects and situations to a unity by demanding that moral judgment be detached, dispassionate, and universal. But . . . such an urge to totalization necessarily fails.

Reducing differences to unity means bringing them under a universal category, which requires expelling those aspects of the different things that do not fit into the category. Difference thus becomes a hierarchical opposition between what lies inside and what lies outside the category, valuing more what lies inside than what lies outside" (Young, *Justice and the Politics of Difference*, p. 103).

27 Jeremy Waldron, "Cultural Identity and Civic Responsibility," in Will Kymlicka and Wayne Norman, eds., *Citizenship in Diverse Societies* (Oxford: Oxford University Press, 2000), pp. 155–74.

28 Waldron, "Cultural Identity and Civic Responsibility,", p. 159.

29 The discussion here draws on a similar discussion in my article, "Identity Politics and Identity Claims: A Limited Defence," in Igor Primoratz and Aleksandar Pavkovic, eds., *Identity and Self-determination* (London: Ashgate, 2006).

30 The argument in terms of respect for one's identity contains within it an implicit recognition that other people also have identities, which are important to them. The way the argument is formulated suggests that one could not argue for the imposition of *shariah*, for example, as a requirement of respect for my religious identity. It might be a requirement of my religion, properly understood. But an argument in terms of religious identity refers to the importance of having an identity, and insofar as that is a generalizable interests, it recognizes that other people, too, have identities, possibly of different kinds, and it would be wrong to require things of them that would violate their deeply held commitments and identities.

31 However, as I will show below, the gay and lesbian argument against the definition of the family in many liberal states does not take this form.

32 Amy Gutmann talks about this case at length. Historically, exemptions were accorded to members of pacifist religious groups only – such as the Quakers – but the relevant moral distinction – between conscientious and nonconscientious objection – does not map neatly on the religion–nonreligious distinction. For this reason, there is now a move to include nonreligious but still demonstrable and moral commitments to nonviolence as possible cases of conscientious objection. See Amy Gutmann, *Identity in Democracy* (Princeton, NJ: Princeton University Press, 2003), pp. 180–2.

33 Indeed, it is not clear that it is generally desirable to seek to avoid general formulations of laws and rules, since this formulation may be helpful in avoiding nepotism and elite interests, and less general formulations may have the negative consequences of exacerbating fragmentation and division.

34 Young, *Justice and the Politics of Difference*, pp. 184–8.

35 Deliberative democratic theory does try to offer a more systematic way in which different voices are included in the formulation of policies. Also, many theories of justice – most notably, Rawls's theory – does have a systematic requirement consider how rules and principles get operationalized. This is one way to interpret his methodological commitment to reflective equilibrium.

36 See here Anna Elisabetta Galeotti, *Toleration as Recognition* (Cambridge: Cambridge University Press, 2002).

37 For a debate that the requirements of liberal toleration are quite different from modern demands for recognition, see John Horton and Susan Mendus, eds., *Aspects of Toleration* (London: Methuen, 1985); Steven Smith, "Toleration and Liberal Commitments," in Jeremy Waldron and Melissa Williams, eds., *NOMOS XLVIII: Toleration and Its Limits* (New York: New York University Press, 2008), pp. 243–81; Bernard.Williams, "Tolerating the Intolerable," in Susan Mendus,ed., *The Politics of Toleration in Modern Life* (Durham, NC: Duke University Press, 2000).

38 Moreover, I argue in "Identity Claims and Identity Politics," it is wrong to interpret the conservative religious person as making a claim about identity. The conservative

Christian cannot legitimately claim that her very identity requires a heterosexist inter-pretation of the family: rather, such a view of the family is an important element of her religious belief. Her basic argument here is that gay marriage or, indeed, a gay way of life, is wrong. The gay person, by contrast, *is* making an identity claim, which, like the others, is centrally about toleration of his/her community's practices: he/she is accepting that there are different versions of the family and asking only that her type of family also be included *as a family*.

39 For an excellent discussion of justificatory neutrality, see Brian Barry, *Culture & Equality: An Egalitarian Critique of Multiculturalism* (Cambridge, MA: Harvard University Press, 2001).

40 See Thomas Nagel, *The View from Nowhere* (New York: Oxford University Press, 1986). This leaves it unclear whether the division of labor represents a fundamental division, where there are actually different standards or different moralities, or whether there is only one fundamental moral standard, but that the division of labor represents the most efficient way to promote the ends of morality. See here Samuel Scheffler, *Boundaries and Allegiances, Problems of Justice and Responsibility in Liberal Thought* (Oxford: Oxford University Press, 2001), pp. 82–96 for an excellent discussion of split-level morality.

41 For this reason, it is wrong to claim, as Waldron does, that the claim is for the protec-tion of identity-related interests, in the same way as other types of interests (which are then treated as rights). The basic claim is to equality. He is right to point to the difficulty of meeting these various sorts of claims, however.

42 This is different from Kymlicka's recent emphasis on the relationship between nation building by the dominant state and minority nationalist mobilization behind self-determination projects. I think this is a valid empirical point, and one that puts the burden on the majority-dominated state, but it is wrong to think that nationalist conflict can be avoided simply by avoiding coercive forms of nation-building. There are certain structural imperatives in the modern state, which may have a side-effect of creating unfair-ness. Moreover, simple minority status, in itself, does not – contra Young's analysis in *Justice and the Politics of Difference* – seem to warrant the charge of "oppression."

43 The argument about the functional imperatives of the modern state is drawn from my book *Ethics of Nationalism* (Oxford: Oxford University Press, 2001), Ch. 5.

44 Ernest Gellner, *Nations and Nationalism* (Ithaca, NY: Cornell University Press, 1983), pp. 17–40.

45 Alan Patten, "Liberal Neutrality and Language Politics," *Philosophy & Public Affairs* 31 (4) (Autumn 2003): 356–86.

46 Patten, "Liberal Neutrality and Language Politics," pp. 379–86.

47 Joe Carens, "Aliens and Citizens: The Case for Open Borders," *Review of Politics* 49 (3) (1987): 251–73.

48 John Rawls, *Law of Peoples with "the Idea of Public Reason Revisited"* (Cambridge, MA: Harvard University Press, 1999), p. 36.

49 Kymlicka, *Multicultural Citizenship*, pp. 85–6.

50 Kymlicka, *Multicultural Citizenship*, p. 8.

51 Of course, this argument only justifies group-differentiated rights that provide external protections – that is, rights which are designed to defend groups from external threats to their existence. It does not justify internal restrictions, which are limitations on rights that groups impose on their members to maintain group identity (see Kymlicka, *Multicultural Citizenship*, pp. 34–48).

52 Kymlicka, *Multicultural Citizenship*, pp. 34–48. Polyethnic rights, self-governments rights and special representation rights are all designed to equalize the position of majority and minority groups.

Margaret Moore

PERSONS, IDENTITY AND DIFFERENCE

IDENTITY AND THE POLITICS OF DIFFERENCE

Relational Liberalism and Demands for Equality, Recognition, and Group Rights

Anthony Simon Laden

Political philosophy, despite occasional protestations of purity to the contrary, generally develops in reaction to and conversation with actual political events and developments. This is one of the truths behind Hegel's remark that "the owl of Minerva begins its flight only with the onset of the dusk,"[1] and it is captured somewhat less poetically in R. G. Collingwood's claim that "the history of political theory is not the history of different answers to one and the same question, but the history of a problem more or less constantly changing, whose solution was changing with it."[2]

During the end of the twentieth century, perhaps no area of political philosophy was more explicitly tied to particular political movements and developments than that variously described as articulating a politics of identity, difference or recognition. Philosophers like Catharine MacKinnon, Iris Young, and James Tully all begin their philosophizing less in the dominant theories of their day and more in the demands of various social movements.[3] Because of this close tie between identity politics and its philosophy, the debates surrounding this area of political philosophy raise not only substantive questions about standard topics like justice, equality, citizenship, or rights, but also more methodological questions about the relationship between philosophy and politics. To understand how these debates have developed and how they might move forward, it is important to place them in their political context, to connect them to the political and social movements that inspire them, and to understand why partisans of those movements felt there was a need to articulate and develop philosophical positions in connection with them.

I will suggest that much of the philosophy that has been developed to support identity politics arises as an attempt to respond to various deflationary interpretations of the political demands of social movements by established political institutions and agents. That is, the philosophy of identity politics is born out of the failure of political and social institutions to hear and respond adequately to the demands of social movements. It is thus motivated by the thought that this failure is rooted in some deep feature of the political system in place, probably in its legitimating and structuring philosophical ground. The move to philosophy is meant to shift that ground so that the political demands of social movements can be properly heard. The resulting philosophy has generated a rich set of criticisms of liberal theory and practice, but it has also, more often than not, merely pushed the failure to be heard to the level of theory. In this sense, though the move to philosophy has been philosophically fruitful, it has not yet provided a solution to the problem of misunderstanding that inspired it. One reason for this is that just as political institutions have not adequately heard the demands of various social movements, many mainstream political philosophers have failed to grasp the challenges raised by the philosophy of the politics of identity, difference and recognition. This deeper failure has moved some philosophers to even more foundational criticisms.[4]

In this paper, however, I suggest a different path. I argue that the way forward requires some philosophical excavation from the liberal side of things. Within the basic building blocks of liberal theory lie some of the ingredients for constructing a philosophical common ground between liberal institutions and the demands of social movements. It is, very roughly, the ground of democracy. The result is not a neat philosophical victory for either side, but rather some philosophical moves that might advance the work for which the philosophy of identity politics arose: making possible the articulation of the demands of social movements in a language that neither distorts them nor dooms them to misunderstanding. Opening up such a possibility is the work of philosophy. But philosophy reaches its limits at the boundaries of conceptual clarity and possibility, and thus making use of the possibilities suggested below will require ongoing politics.

I begin with the demands for equality made by the women's and civil rights movements, and the philosophical criticisms of liberal theories of equality that followed. One form the misunderstanding of these claims has taken is their treatment as demands for the recognition of difference. Thus, the discussion of equality leads conceptually if not historically to the demands for recognition of ethnic, cultural and linguistic difference, and the resultant discussions of multiculturalism, and the place of identity in politics. These demands have often been misheard as demands for special group rights, and so I am led, finally, to nationalist demands for self-determination and the debate over the existence and place of group rights. These three types of struggle have thus generated philosophical debate over the nature of equality, identity, and rights. In the last part of the paper, I offer a democratic interpretation of these three concepts as fundamentally relational and intersubjective, and argue that so understood they provide the necessary common ground for productive political deliberation.

1. Demands for Equality

In the United States in the latter half of the twentieth century, strong social movements demanded equality for women and nonwhites. At the beginning of these movements, women and nonwhites were unequal to white men in at least two broadly different ways. First, they were excluded from a variety of social, political, and economic opportunities and activities open to white men. Since such exclusion involves the separation

Anthony S. Laden

of people into distinct categories (on the basis of race or sex) and the differential treatment of each category, such exclusion is a matter of discrimination. Second, they were systematically subordinated to white men in the sense that white men exercised the power and authority over major political, economic and social decisions in a manner that meant that beyond their mere exclusion, women and nonwhites were systematically disadvantaged, controlled and confined to particular areas of life. Such control can but need not function through discrimination and exclusion. Since it is fundamentally a matter of hierarchical relationships of power, such inequality is fundamentally a question of oppression.

It is arguable that both social movements' demands for equality were demands for the end of oppression. However, they were taken up and responded to as demands for the end of discrimination. In some sense, this should not be surprising. Ending discrimination involves widening the boundaries of inclusion, but not fundamentally altering the terrain within those boundaries. That is, ending discrimination against women can be accomplished by treating women the same as men, by ignoring the mere difference in sex but nevertheless keeping in place all the other social factors that go into the criteria for the distribution of rights, privileges and opportunities. It is thus relatively easy to accomplish politically, legally, and socially.

It is also easy to justify in terms of the kind of liberal theory that serves as an intellectual support for U.S. law and politics. Discrimination on the basis of sex or race is only justified on such a theory if distinctions in race and sex are not "arbitrary from a moral point of view."[5] There are any number of ways to justify the claim that sex, and especially race, are arbitrary from a moral point of view, and arguably one effect of the social movements for women's and civil rights were to make it plain to a wide swath of the American public that this was the case, that those demanding inclusion were essentially no different from those already included.

Within the conceptual and political framework that saw the end to discrimination as meeting the demands of these social movements, however, the movements' continued demands for equality were met with confusion and often hostility – "What more do these people want?" And it was this response that was arguably the inspiration for feminist and other radical discussions of equality in terms of oppression. The work of philosophers like Catharine MacKinnon and Iris Young in the 1980s and 1990s made a two-step argument. First, the demands of the social movements that inspired them were in fact demands for an end to oppression and not merely discrimination. Second, there was some deep block to the social and political structures grasping this fact. Catharine MacKinnon, for instance, argues that the interpretation of sex equality in terms of nondiscrimination is not capable of addressing the oppression of women, most of which it leaves unchecked. But she goes on to argue that the problem here is not one of brute political obstinacy but the philosophical theory of what equality is at the heart of liberal theory, a theory that defines equality in terms of treating similar cases similarly, and which she labels the "difference approach."[6] Furthermore, she argues that liberals are prone to adopt the difference approach because of an even deeper theoretical commitment to a particular norm of objectivity. It is this commitment, she claims, that prevents them from seeing arguments about the oppression of women as raising legitimate political claims.[7]

Similarly, Iris Young, in her *Justice and the Politics of Difference*, provides a rich picture of what she calls the "five faces of oppression" and how the nature of oppression is such that it cannot be captured merely in terms of an unequal distribution of rights and goods. But she goes on to argue that liberalism is unable to fully appreciate the harm of oppression because it relies on an individualistic "distributive paradigm." In other words, demands for the end to oppression have been misheard by the liberal state and society because of the nature of its underlying philosophy, which rests on what Young calls an "individualist conception of society."[8]

Thus, both MacKinnon and Young, as well as many others who have worked along roughly the same paths, trace the political failure of the social movements that inspire them in part to philosophical sources and join the struggle at that level. It is worth noting several consequences of this general move. First, it has been philosophically productive, as it has widened philosophical debates about equality to include questions of oppression, hierarchy, and domination and subordination. This can be seen in part by looking at the transformation in mainstream political philosophy from the rather limited "equality of what" debates in the 1980s and 1990s which focused on the index for measuring distributive inequality to the broader debates among republicans, liberals, feminists, and critical race theorists that consider the issues raised by MacKinnon, Young, and others, and more explicitly theorize the relationships between freedom, equality, and politics.[9] At a deeper level, their critiques have also provoked important philosophical reconsiderations of the nature of objectivity and individualism. Second, it has been fruitful in providing a philosophical vocabulary and precision for clearly articulating the demands of oppressed groups, and thus helped to inspire the current philosophical vibrancy (if not always the wider acceptance) of such once completely marginalized areas of the field as feminism and critical race theory. But third, their deepest philosophical criticisms of mainstream theories have met with a great deal of resistance and incomprehension. Whereas many liberal theorists might now acknowledge that oppression is a distinct form of inequality from discrimination, they are much less likely to give up on norms of objectivity or a fundamental individualism, and to the extent that they have interpreted MacKinnon or Young as claiming that the political demands for the end to oppression rest on the rejection of objectivity or individualism, this has actually provided them with a kind of philosophical cover for not taking seriously the more radical political demands being made by these philosophers and the social movements that inspire them. Thus, in an important sense, the move to philosophy as a way of addressing incomprehension has so far proved ineffective. And this may in part account for the fourth consequence: these philosophical interventions have not made much political difference.[10] At least in the U.S., mainstream political debates over such policies as affirmative action, abortion, pornography, or parental leave are still very much couched in the language of discrimination and the distribution of individual rights and privileges.

Because the philosophical challenges to liberalism have been met more with resistance and incomprehension than accommodation and dialogue, liberals have often been moved to re-classify the continued demands for an end to the oppression of women and nonwhites in the U.S. and elsewhere as demands for the recognition of difference rather than the end of oppression. That is, from within the mainstream framework that assesses political systems in terms of how they distribute rights, opportunities, and goods, if a group of people faces no discrimination and thus to that extent has equality of basic rights and opportunities but nevertheless continues to

Anthony S. Laden

demand something else, those demands can only possibly be demands for some set of special privileges, either in the form of special rights or special forms of recognition of difference. Thus, the demands for equality that characterize the women's movement and the civil rights movement get folded into the demands made by other social movements to which I now turn.[11]

2. Demands for Recognition

The social movements that are most easily connected with the demands for recognition are those which advocate on behalf of national, cultural, and linguistic minorities for various forms of what has come to be called multicultural accommodation. Demands for recognition, like demands for equality, can be seen as a demand for a form of inclusion that goes beyond nondiscrimination, and this is no doubt one of the reasons why demands for sex and racial equality are so often conflated with demands for recognition. As I claimed above, a policy of nondiscrimination is consistent with the maintenance of unequal criteria for the distribution of goods, rights, and opportunities. In the case of failures of recognition, the problem arises because these criteria are culturally specific and serve to place demands on minority groups that are not placed on the majority. As a result, the price of inclusion for such groups is a form of assimilation. What social movements that demand recognition demand, then, is that those for whom they advocate be included in the social and political life of the society without having to give up some aspect of their identity such as their cultural practices or language. Thus, as with the movements for civil and women's rights, these movements demand not only that the circle of inclusion be widened to include those for whom they advocate, but that the terrain within the circle be altered so that it accommodates them on even terms.

In practice, the demands of such movements have often come in the form of demands for particular exemptions to general laws or government subsidies to particular groups or their representative organizations. Sikhs have demanded exemptions to helmet requirements and uniform codes that interfere with the wearing of turbans. Observant Muslims and Jews have demanded exemptions from animal cruelty laws in order to prepare meat according to religious requirements, and from school dress codes to allow for religious clothing such as headscarves and yarmulkes. Other religious groups have demanded exemptions from certain educational requirements where these conflict with their community practices or religious beliefs. Cultural groups have demanded permission to engage in a variety of otherwise prohibited practices that they claim are important to their way of life, from female genital cutting to ritual animal sacrifice to the use of hallucinogenic drugs. Finally, some groups have requested government support for cultural institutions and festivals or official government recognition of particular holidays or events.

Because these demands are all particular in the sense that they seek differential treatment for members of a given minority, they have often been met with hostility and rejection by those who claim to be upholding liberal norms of equality and neutrality. From the perspective of many liberal thinkers, the differential accommodation of various cultural groups looks structurally indistinguishable from any number of overtly discriminatory regimes from the Ottoman Empire to the Jim Crow

Southern U.S. to apartheid South Africa. From this liberal perspective, demands for particular recognition can only be demands for differential rights, opportunities, or claims to goods, and such demands fly in the face of even liberal commitments to equality.

It is, then, arguably this kind of conflation between demands for inclusionary recognition and explicitly racist regimes that has inspired philosophical articulations of the demand for recognition. And it should thus not be surprising that the philosophical work in this domain has grown out of a series of diagnoses of the source of the misunderstanding. Three interrelated diagnoses have been offered and used as a basis for re-articulating the demands for recognition.

First, some philosophers have argued that the problem lies in the standard liberal method for accommodating difference, a strategy that grew out of attempts to accommodate doctrinal differences among European Christians in the sixteenth and seventeenth centuries. That strategy basically involved a de-politicization of religious identities. That is, liberals argued that the way for people of different faiths to nevertheless live together in harmony as fellow citizens was to see one's faith as a nonpolitical or private matter, a question of individual conscience, and as such, not one that should affect one's political status. As this strategy of privatization is generalized, the result is to treat any and all differences within a population via liberty of conscience and freedom of assembly.[12] One's religious beliefs, one's cultural affiliations, even one's native language all become matters of individual connection, perhaps varying in importance along a spectrum that runs from mere tastes to matters of conscience. The liberal state thus allows people to behave and think as they wish outside of the political realm, and to congregate with whomever they choose, but expects all citizens to leave such beliefs and connections behind as they don the role of citizen. It considers that citizens have been treated fairly if they all have the same basic rights of belief, assembly, and exit.

Advocates of a politics of recognition claim that this framework of de-politicization prevents liberals from understanding what demands for recognition demand. That is, those who demand recognition are essentially demanding that some aspect of their identity that differentiates them from the majority be recognized as politically relevant.[13] Since the liberal theoretical framework assigns all particular identities to a sphere outside of (though admittedly protected by) politics, it has no space to grasp what is being demanded. Those who argue for a politics of recognition go beyond diagnosing the failure of communication here, and urge that the liberal framework is ultimately mistaken. The problem, they suggest, is that the liberal is left imagining citizens as stripped-down mere rights bearers, and thus not only fails to adequately describe the importance of particular minority identities but also fails to capture accurately what is involved in being a citizen, even for members of the majority culture. This further line of criticism can then lead advocates of the politics of recognition towards support for various forms of nationalism and communitarianism, but it need not. Republicans, for instance, also reject the characterization of citizens as essentially mere rights-bearers and instead argue that citizens should be seen as engaged in the collective activity of self-government.

The second diagnosis also points to the relatively thin characterization of citizens in liberal theory, though draws a somewhat different conclusion. What draws liberal theory to this thin characterization, this second line of argument goes, is the mistaken

Anthony S. Laden

conflation of similarity with equality. Although this point echoes in some way MacKinnon's argument in that it draws attention to and criticizes a link between similarity and equality, it draws a slightly different lesson. Here, the worry is not so much that a focus on similarity blinds us to inequality when it takes the form of oppression, but rather that the connection between equality and similarity leads liberal theory and liberal states to search out a common core of humanity which can serve as the basis of equality. This not only has the consequence of driving liberals to adopt thin descriptions of citizenship, but also of seeing deep differences between people as something to be erased and overcome rather than fairly negotiated. The result is that liberal theory has embraced what James Tully calls an "empire of uniformity."[14] Against this background, demands for recognition of difference can't be squared with equal treatment and can only come across as calls for special privileges or separatism and thus threats to political unity, stability, and equality.[15]

From this diagnosis, advocates of a politics of recognition have argued for a different conception of equality, one that turns not on some common human similarity but on an equal ability to participate in dialogue about the conditions under which we live. The equality a state concerned with treating its citizens fairly should thus guarantee above all is the equal ability of each citizen to speak, be heard and taken seriously in turn.[16]

Finally, a third line of diagnosis follows on the first by drawing two further consequences from the liberal strategy of de-politicization of identity. First, this strategy obscures an important distinction between the choices we make, and the background against which we make those choices. If certain features of our identity, such as our cultural background, our religion or our language, form the background against which we make other choices, then to treat them as matters of individual conscience fundamentally mistakes the role they play in our lives and thus their political significance. Second, the liberal strategy of de-politicization of identity makes the importance of this distinction for matters of equality particularly hard to see as it pushes into the background the wider cultural and social background against which all citizens, majority and minority, make choices. It thus obscures from view an unfair advantage that members of a majority culture may have: the secure entrenchment and support of the background culture against which they can make meaningful choices. Seen this way, demands for recognition and cultural protection are not demands for special privileges in the sense of demands for something over and above what citizens of the majority culture receive, but demands for a kind of compensatory subsidy to ensure that all citizens have equally secure backgrounds against which to make the choices that the liberal state aims to protect. Champions of this diagnosis also point out that the fact that the culture of the majority enjoys the entrenched and thus invisible status that it does is not merely the result of the blind workings of numerical advantage, but is often the result of quite conscious efforts on the part of even liberal states to engage in nation-building in support of the dominant culture and at the expense of minority groups.[17]

Liberal responses to these philosophical moves have, in general, been no more friendly or accommodating than those that have met the philosophical interventions of radical feminists and critical race theorists. And once again, these responses can be seen as the reassertion of a deep commitment to a kind of individualism and the claim that the source of the philosophical criticisms raised on behalf of those demanding recognition must be an ultimately muddle-headed rejection of that individualism. Thus, for instance, appeals to the political importance of cultural identity are taken to require a belief in some organic unity called a culture or a nation or a people, of which its members are mere appendages.[18] Moreover, demands for recognition are thought to require a deference to the current characteristics of particular cultures, and thus a kind of essentialism about cultural identity which unfortunately identifies all members of a culture with the particular ideology of the dominant members of that culture.[19] Failing to see the ways in which many demands for recognition are not only particular demands, but are made against particular context, and thus failing to appreciate that the context in which these demands are made may make a difference, defenders of abstract universal liberal theory often assume that all these demands must be making a fundamentally similar demand, and since that can not be a demand for individual rights of conscience and assembly or any of the other standard liberal individual rights, they must be arguing for the protection of a new species of rights: group rights. As a result, a final move often made to rebuff demands for recognition is to fold them into demands for the self-determination of particular groups and thus the demand for so-called group rights, a subject to which I now turn.[20]

3. Demands for Self-Determination

In order to distinguish demands for self-determination from demands for recognition, it helps to distinguish between two types of rights claims. Membership rights are rights that individuals have in virtue of their membership in a particular group. They are thus not held by all members of a given society, but are nonetheless individual rights. The rights of Quakers to avoid military service, or of Sikh members of the Royal Canadian Mounted Police to wear turbans instead of the traditional wide-brimmed hat are membership rights. As a non-Quaker and non-Sikh, I do not have such rights, and thus if I join the RCMP, I cannot avoid wearing the uniform even if I have a set of deeply held reasons for not wanting to wear wide-brimmed hats. Some demands for recognition come in the form of demands for membership rights. Contrast these with group rights, which are rights that belong to entire groups. Group rights are most often demanded by nationalist and anti-colonial movements that demand rights of self-determination and secession from the wider societies or empires in which they find themselves. If I claim that the Quebecois have a right to secede from Canada and form their own state, I am claiming that they collectively possess a group right. It does not follow from the possession of this right that any individual Quebecoise can decide to leave the Canadian federation and start her own state. Of course, just how to interpret claims to group rights is a matter of some controversy, to which I will return below.[21]

Demands for self-determination by colonized peoples have, of course, historically met with combinations of brute force and racist arguments about the people in question's capacities for self-government. But even liberals who shy away from either of these moves have been generally wary of such demands by minority nations, such as the Quebecois, the Catalans, or various Aboriginal peoples. Sometimes these demands are rejected for reasons similar to those used to reject demands for equality and recognition: in the absence of discrimination, and given various membership rights, there

Anthony S. Laden

is no room left for legitimate complaint. But in addition, three kinds of considerations are given that pertain specifically to demands for self-determination. First, concerns are expressed for the protection of the equality and individual rights of people within the minority nation, whether internal minorities (e.g. non-Francophones in Quebec), otherwise at risk sub-populations (e.g. women in aboriginal or religious nations), or just individual dissidents who do not endorse the nationalist project in its current form.[22] Second, concern is expressed over how the group goes about exercising its collective right. Those who demand rights of self-determination may hold positions of authority that give them the ability to make these demands, but not in ways that legitimately allow them to speak for the entire group. Third, even if it is accepted that particular groups possess some rights of self-determination, these are claimed not to extend to matters of seccession. The Quebecois, on this line of argument, have the rights of a province to elect their own government, and make demands within the existing structure of the Canadian federation for various subsidies, regulations, and powers, and even for changes to that structure, but they do not have the right to exit completely that structure unilaterally.

Once again, unsympathetic political responses have led to attempts at further philosophical articulation. Two issues have been at the forefront of these debates. The first turns on questions of essentialism. The idea here is that part of the resistance to the recognition of demands for group self-determination is the assumption that such demands rest on a kind of essentialism about cultures, whereby cultures or peoples or nations are said to have particular essential features that distinguish them from other groups, and it is in the service of protecting these essential features that they need rights to self-determination. Cultural essentialism is then blamed for the failure of proponents of group rights to be sensitive to internal divisions and debates within a group. Defenders of demands for self-determination have thus argued that these demands, and the presence of group rights need not rest on problematic assumptions of cultural essentialism.[23] One path for doing this is to draw similarities between group and corporate rights. Various well-constituted organizations have rights within various legal systems that belong to the organization as a whole rather than to individual members. Thus, such rights are group rather than membership rights, but the recognition of such rights is not generally thought of as requiring an essentialist view of the organization. Thus, for instance, within a professional sports league, teams have various rights to trade players, draft players entering the league, and appeal decisions of referees and league officials. These are rights held by teams, not players, unlike, say the rights of members of a given team to wear its uniform on the field during league games. But no one thinks that the intelligibility of these rights turns on claims about the essential nature and characteristics of particular teams.

The second issue turns on the nature and usefulness of group rights, and here it helps to separate out two issues. First, some liberals have denied that groups, as opposed to well-constituted organizations, like teams and corporations, can have rights. Second, even if the ontological status of such rights is not disputed, many liberals claim that they add nothing of value to individuals, and thus deserve no protection.

Debates over the ontological status of group rights generally turn on questions about the nature of rights more generally, since the foundations of a theory of rights is generally thought to determine such questions as which rights are "real" and who can be said to have them.[24] Here defenders of group rights and the liberals who deny the possibility of such rights often come to loggerheads over liberalism's individualism.[25] Liberalism is arguably defined by its prioritizing of individual rights claims over claims of general social welfare, and it is thought by both liberal theorists and their critics that the basis for this priority is an individualist ontology that claims that society is built up from essentially separate individuals, and that there is nothing in a society that is not ultimately reducible to its constituent individuals, their interests, desires, plans, projects, goods, etc. Starting from an individualist ontology, it can seem obvious why the features of individuals, like their being agents, having interests, being naturally free or endowed by their Creator, should be the source of their having rights.[26] The question then becomes whether this framework can be extended beyond individual human beings, and especially to rather loosely defined collectivities like peoples, cultures, or nations. Some defenders of group rights have thus challenged this individualist ontology, arguing that there is no reason to assume that we should begin our account of rights from isolated individuals and thus no reason to assume that groups are more problematic bearers of rights than individuals.[27]

A somewhat different issue turns not on the possible existence of group rights, but on the need for them in a liberal society. The claim here is that there is no harm to individuals that can be caused by the denial of group but not individual rights, and that, moreover, much harm can come to individuals if the exercise of group rights comes at the expense of individual rights.[28] Thus, even if the category of group rights does not rest on a conceptual confusion, their protection in a liberal state would be a mistake. Once again, defenders of demands for self-determination have tried in part to answer this charge on a philosophical level, though here their work dovetails with issues covered in the discussion of demands for recognition. The harm most often cited by denials of group rights are harms to the possibility of maintaining certain particular identities as members of the group in question. Thus, for instance, if a given native tribe is unable to collectively protect its land-holdings, or to manage certain fisheries that are central to its way of life, then it is possible for these collective resources to slip away through a series of individual rights-respecting transactions. Individual tribal land-owners sell their land to people outside the tribe. Non-tribal fisherman fish the land in accordance with government, but not tribal regulations, with the result that the fishery is depleted. As a result, members of the tribe in question can no longer maintain their identities: the tribe winds up with no land, or no traditional fishing grounds.[29] Of course, whether these harms to individuals count as politically relevant depends on our view of the political importance of such identities. If identities are essentially nonpolitical matters, then even if I have a right to engage in the practices that my identities demand, I don't have a right to the protection of the proper space for those practices. If I am a user of Crest toothpaste, though I have a right not to be prevented from buying and using Crest, and not to be forced to buy Colgate, I have no right to force the maker of Crest to continue manufacturing it. If my identity as a Navajo or Quebecois or Catalan is basically like my identity as a Crest-user, then the demise of those cultures may harm me but not in any way that a liberal government need heed. On the other hand, if identities are politically relevant, then it may be the case that the demise of a culture robs me of something of political value even in the absence of the denial of individual rights. Thus the question of the value of group rights ultimately turns on the political relevance of particular identities.

Anthony S. Laden

4. Shifting the Grounds of Liberalism

The demands for equality, recognition, and self-determination have thus inspired philosophical challenges to the basic liberal conceptions of equality, identity and rights. In each case, philosophers inspired by those demands have argued that liberals' individualist conceptions of these ideas prevent them from grasping the basic justice of the demands of various social movements, and have urged alternative social ontologies and conceptual frameworks in which such demands can be adequately heard. Of course, not all liberals have been hostile to the demands of these social movements, and in some cases, liberals have gone a long way towards trying to fit concerns with oppression, the political relevance of particular identities and group rights into liberal theories while holding onto an individualist ontology.[30] In this final section of the paper, I sketch out reasons for thinking that liberalism does not and ought not rest on an individualist ontology to begin with, and how shifting our understanding of the basis of liberal theory provides a more accommodating conceptual framework in which the social movements' demands can be properly heard.[31]

The basic thrust of my argument is that the core elements of liberal theory are better understood as taking as their subject matter not the aggregation of individuals and their actions, but rather the nature of the relationships between and among people, and as such, the concepts of rights, identity and equality can be interpreted in ways that allow the various claims of identity politics to be properly heard. The difference between taking the subject matter of a theory to be individual agents and their individual actions on the one hand, and the relationships between people on the other is both deep and hard to fully grasp. I will not be able to give a full account of the details of this difference here nor argue for its general theoretical importance.[32] The basic idea, however, should be clear enough. It is the difference between asking questions like, which individual actions are permitted, and how much stuff does each person get on the one hand, and asking whether the relationships among people are characterized by hierarchy or reciprocity, violence and coercion, or the deliberative give and take of reasons. Rather than unpacking the general distinction here any further, I instead argue why several key liberal commitments to the priority of rights, the diversity of identity, and equality show that liberalism is, at its heart, a relational theory.

Two features of rights prove particularly difficult for theorists of rights to explain. First, at least some rights come with correlative duties. If I have what is often called a claim right to something then this implies that others (perhaps all others) have a duty to not interfere with (and possibly aid me in my pursuit of) my having it. But if I treat rights as basically issuing permissions to individuals, as basically governing the actions of individuals, it can be hard to see why they should also generate duties for others. The looseness of the connection between some rights and others' duties has formed the basis of arguments against extending the terrain of rights beyond some core liberal rights like those to liberty of conscience or even for abandoning over-reliance on rights-talk entirely.[33] But I think the problem ultimately stems from trying to treat rights as the possessions of individuals and certain relevantly similar agents. Within such a framework, there is always a gap to be bridged between the rights possessed by one person and the duties that places on others.

Second, rights stand in an uncomfortable relation to the good. One of the obvious values of individual rights, especially for liberals, is that the guarantee of such rights prevents certain types of actions from being taken in the name of various goods such as overall social welfare. One standard criticism of a utilitarianism that either recognizes no rights or justifies them in terms of their value in maximizing the good, is that it can not rule out and may even serve to advocate the horrific treatment of some individuals if that will bring about greater total good. But if rights are to act as side constraints or trumps on our individual or collective pursuit of the good, then we are left wondering about their ultimate justification.[34] One standard individualist argument is that rights protect various individual goods, such as the good of being in control of your own life or pursuing what you take to be good regardless of prevailing opinion on the matter. But if this is right, then it is hard to see why rights should be given the kind of absolute priority they are given in liberal theory. After all, if the point of protecting an individual's rights is ultimately as a means to or a constituent of promoting his good (even his good as he see it), then it does look like there will be cases where we more fully advance the good (even his good as he sees it) by violating rather than protecting his rights.[35]

But both of these problems dissolve if we think about rights as structuring relationships. That is, rather than thinking about morality as governing what we do, and what we do to one another, think of it as governing the structure of our relationships. Then, rights enter the picture not as a necessary add-on that prevents some pursuits of the good from getting out of hand, but rather as part of the description of what our relationships to one another can and ought to be. Enshrining rights into law is important not so much for contributing to the good of society via the provision of a basic level of security, as John Stuart Mill argued, but as a kind of public announcement that democratic citizens make to one another that they are taking certain kinds of social calculations off the table.[36] The point of such public announcements, on such a view, is that they constitute part of the reciprocal relationship among free and equal people that is the hallmark of democratic citizenship. So, on this view, the basis of various rights lies not in the inherent qualities of individuals, but in a view about the moral value of certain kinds of relationships. And their justification need not ultimately come down to questions about promoting some ultimate good; it can rest directly on the kinds of relationships they create.

If we think of rights this way, then it is also easier to see the relationship between rights and duties. They are, on this view, really just flip sides of the same coin. They both describe aspects (and arguably the same aspects) of various relationships. Both now become intersubjective terms. At the same time, we can see the intelligibility of articulating and guaranteeing certain rights without identifying those who bear the correlative duties. Part of the point of establishing a set of social and economic rights that might serve to institutionalize an egalitarian liberal theory of distributive justice (such as Rawls's difference principle) would be not only to publicly recognize that each citizen has a set of non-negotiable ends that merit reciprocal respect (this being the point of rights of conscience, assembly, etc.), but also to recognize that each merits status as a fully contributing member of the social and economic life of the society, and, as Rawls puts the point, the poor are not merely the objects of our charity and compassion.[37] And part of the effect of establishing such rights even in the absence of an institutionalized scheme of correlative duties would be to recognize the nature of certain kinds of demands. When those who fare poorly in a given economy make claims on the broader public, do we recognize those claims as asserting

Anthony S. Laden

rights or merely asking for kindness? The difference here is important even if we have not decided ahead of time who is responsible for answering their claims.

But now note that by shifting the ground of rights to a relational view, we are also in a position to think differently about the demand for group rights. The basis of rights claims lies in an ideal of reciprocal relationships between free and equal persons. To establish the need for certain rights, one needs to show how they support such relationships or how they might overcome their current absence. At least some of the arguments for group rights, and a great deal of those for membership rights, turn on or can be reformulated without damage to turn on, precisely this sort of consideration.[38] My point here is not that all group rights claims will or even should find a home within a liberal theory, but rather that the discussion over the need for particular group rights can continue at the right level. That group rights are intelligible does not make them automatically advisable, so advocates of self-determination must make their case. But that case can not be ruled out ahead of time by philosophical reflection about the nature of "real" rights that dismisses the possibility that loosely bound groups like peoples and nations could be the bearers of rights.

Turn then to the place of identity in a relational liberalism. If liberalism is, ultimately, about how we relate to one anther, what place do the sorts of identity that animate demands for recognition play? A great deal, it turns out. To see why, note two things about those demands. First, recognition is itself intersubjective. The demand for recognition is, after all, a demand that others whose recognition matters to you, relate to you in a particular way, and so it involves not only the demand that they act a certain way, but that you relate to one another in a certain way. As recognition theorists from Rousseau and Hegel to Charles Taylor and Axel Honneth have insisted, recognition is a two-way street. Furthermore, when the demand for recognition is a demand that one be recognized as a bearer of a certain identity, that identity is also always relational. That is, to say that I have a given identity is not merely to make a claim about my individual characteristics, but more importantly, is to say something about how I relate to others. It may highlight the nature of my relationships to those who share the identity, whether the mere fact that we form a cohesive group or that we relate to one another in particular ways. It may also highlight the relationship we bear to the wider society, both in the sense of demanding that that relationship change from one where we are excluded and despised to one where we are treated as full equals and respected in our difference, and in the sense of insisting on the ways in which we stand apart at least in some things.[39]

The recognition that advocates of multiculturalism, the politics of recognition and membership rights thus all demand fits into the framework of a relational liberalism. In fact, it might be argued that the essential features of liberalism all derive their point from establishing a kind of regime of reciprocal recognition among diverse but equal citizens. Part, but not all, of that regime is constructed from rights. Other parts are constructed from guarantees of social and economic fairness, democratic procedures and deliberation, and the rule of law. Seen in this way, however, the demands for recognition can clearly be seen as challenges to particular liberal practices, but not to its underlying foundations.

Finally, turn to the question of equality. Philosophers like Iris Young draw a contrast between distributive conceptions of justice and relational conceptions of justice that focus on the elimination of institutionalized relations of domination and oppression.[40] The distributive conception takes equality to describe particular allocations of goods to individuals. If every individual has roughly the same goods in her basket, then there is equality. The relational view, in contrast, conceives of equality as the absence of domination, of hierarchical relations. If liberal theories are fundamentally relational, however, then we should expect them to have relational conceptions of equality at their core. I have already claimed that the relationship liberalism describes among citizens casts them as free and equal, and that suggests one link between its conception of equality and nondomination. Clearly, our ability to relate to one another as equals is hindered by relations of domination and hierarchy between us in a much more direct way than the mere difference in the quantity of goods in our respective baskets.[41]

To see how this relational conception of equality finds its articulation in the details of liberal theory, I note several features of Rawls's theory as an example.[42] First, most of the egalitarian work in justice as fairness takes place in the parts of the two principles that are lexically prior to the difference principle: in the guarantee of equal basic liberties and the guarantee of fair equality of opportunity. Both of these guarantees can be seen as ensuring that even the sorts of inequalities in private holdings of primary goods that the difference principle allows can not serve to establish hierarchical relations among citizens. That they are meant to play this role is further emphasized when Rawls names the interpretation of the two principles that he favors "democratic equality." It is the kind of equality that befits democratic citizens, people engaged in a collective project of self-government through their relationships to one another as free and equal. Second, the ultimate basis for this conception of equality lying at the heart of his conception of justice is that it would meet with agreement from citizens. Here it is important to note that the agreement in question is not merely that of the stripped-down parties in the original position, but real citizens on whose continued reflective endorsement considerations of stability turn. From this point, the third point follows: the fundamental equality in Rawls's conception of justice is political equality: the equal ability to participate in and influence the course of democratic deliberation. That is a form of equality that is clearly hampered by the kinds of inequality that the women's and civil rights movements aimed to make visible and eradicate.

As with the demands for group rights and recognition, the demands for equality find a hearing within a relational liberalism: they turn out to be couched in very recognizably liberal language, even if many liberals have failed to recognize this fact! That an argument or demand is couched in the appropriate language to be heard and taken seriously does not, of course, mean that it ought to be accepted. It does mean that if it is to be rejected, it must be met head on. Neither liberals nor their feminist and critical race theoretical critics can end the political discussion through philosophical considerations alone. The demands these movements make for equality understood as the absence of oppression are demands liberals are theoretically committed to taking seriously. But there is still a gap between taking an argument seriously and accepting its conclusions. Whether any democratic citizens should grant various demands for equality, recognition and group self-determination is, however, not something for philosophy alone to answer.[43]

The philosophers associated with social movements making these demands in the late twentieth century were, I have argued, largely moved to philosophy by the failure

Anthony S. Laden

of these movements to get a proper hearing. They were not trying to replace politics with philosophy. If liberal philosophers can meet them on the sort of common ground I have sketched here, then perhaps we will be able to conclude, when dusk falls on the twenty-first century, that these efforts were not only philosophically fruitful, but successful on their own terms.

Notes

1 G. W. F. Hegel, *Elements of the Philosophy of Right*, trans. H. B. Nisbet, ed. Allen Wood (Cambridge: Cambridge University Press, 1991), p. 23 (Preface).

2 R. G. Collingwood, *An Autobiography* (Oxford: Oxford University Press, 1939), p. 62.

3 See, for instance, Catharine MacKinnon, *Feminism Unmodified* (Cambridge, MA: Harvard University Press, 1987), and *Women's Lives, Men's Laws* (Cambridge, MA: Harvard University Press, 2005), James Tully, *Strange Multiplicity* (Cambridge: Cambridge University Press, 1995), Iris Marion Young, *Justice and the Politics of Difference* (Princeton, NJ: Princeton University Press, 1990), and *Inclusion and Democracy* (Oxford: Oxford University Press, 2000).

4 Catharine MacKinnon, for instance, has criticized liberalism's reliance on norms of objectivity.

5 John Rawls, *A Theory of Justice* (Cambridge, MA: Harvard University Press, 1971, rev. edn., 1999), pp. 72–5, rev. edn., pp. 63–5. I do not mean to suggest here that Rawls's theory in its entirety spells out, much less serves as, the intellectual underpinning of U.S. law and politics. Rawls is actually quite critical of much of those underpinnings. But his use of arguments to eliminate distributive effects that are based on distinctions that are arbitrary from a moral point of view are in line with that tradition (interestingly enough, they play much less, if any, role in Rawls's later articulations of the argument for his theory of justice. See his *Justice as Fairness: A Restatement* (Cambridge, MA: Harvard University Press, 2000).

6 C. A. MacKinnon, "Towards a New Theory of Equality," in *Women's Lives, Men's Laws*, pp. 44–57.

7 For discussion of this criticism, see Sally Haslanger, "On Being Objective and Being Objectified," in Charlotte Witt and Louise Antony, eds., *A Mind of One's Own* (Boulder, CO: Westview Press, 1993): 85–125, and Anthony Simon Laden, "Radical Liberals, Reasonable Feminists: Reason, Objectivity and Power in the work of MacKinnon and Rawls," *Journal of Political Philosophy* 11 (2) (Jun. 2003): 133–52.

8 Young, *Justice and the Politics of Difference*, p. 36, but see pp. 15–38 generally.

9 Key articles in the equality of what debate include: Amartya Sen, "Equality of What?," repr. in his *Choice, Welfare and Measurement* (Cambridge, MA: MIT Press, 1982): pp. 353–69; Ronald Dworkin, "What Is Equality? Part 2: Equality of Resources," *Philosophy and Public Affairs* 10 (4) (Autumn 1981): 283–345; G. A. Cohen, "On the Currency of Egalitarian Justice," *Ethics* 99 (4) (Jul. 1989): 906–44. For an example of the kind of broader reflection on politics in part inspired by the work discussed here, see Philip Pettit, *Republicanism: A Theory of Freedom and Government* (Oxford: Oxford University Press, 1999).

10 Of course, this may be more the consequence of the general fact that philosophical developments of any sort rarely have any tangible political impact, or of a more local but general conservative backlash, than a consequence of the particular philosophical moves discussed above.

11 For critical discussions of this move, see Charles Mills, "Multiculturalism as/and/or Anti-Racism" and Iris Marion Young, "Structural Injustice and the Politics of Difference,"

both in *Multiculturalism and Political Theory*, David Owen and Anthony Simon Laden, eds. (Cambridge: Cambridge University Press, 2007).

12 See, for instance, Chandran Kukathas, "Are There Any Cultural Rights?" *Political Theory* 20: 1 (1992): 105–39.

13 For three related versions of this argument, see Charles Taylor, "Multiculturalism and the Politics of Recognition," in Amy Gutman, ed., *Multiculturalism* (Princeton, NJ: Princeton University Press, 1992); Tully, *Strange Multiplicity*; Axel Honneth, *The Struggle for Recognition* (Cambridge, MA: MIT Press, 1995). For some further connections between the demand for recognition and the demand for equality, see my *Reasonably Radical: Deliberative Liberalism and the Politics of Identity* (Ithaca, NY: Cornell University Press, 2001) and "Reasonable Deliberation, Constructive Power and the Struggle for Recognition," in Bert van den Brink and David Owen, eds., *Recognition and Power* (New York: Cambridge University Press, 2007), pp. 270–89.

14 Tully, *Strange Multiplicity*, pp. 58–98. See also: Chantal Mouffe, *The Democratic Paradox* (London: Verso, 2000), pp. 17–36; Bonnie Honig, *Political Theory and the Displacement of Politics* (Ithaca, NY: Cornell University Press, 1993).

15 See, for instance, Brian Barry, *Culture and Equality* (Cambridge, MA: Harvard University Press, 2000), and Arthur Schlesinger, *The Disuniting of America* (New York: W. W. Norton, 1998).

16 This language follows that of Tully most closely, but others have made similar moves.

17 Will Kymlicka, "The New Debate over Minority Rights" in his *Politics in the Vernacular* (Oxford: Oxford University Press, 2001), and David Owen, "Culture, Equality and Polemic" *Economy and Society* 32 (2) (2003): 325–40.

18 See Kukathas, "Are There Any Cultural Rights?" and Barry, *Culture and Equality*.

19 See, for instance, Susan Okin, "Is Multiculturalism Bad for Women?," in Joshua Cohen, Matthew Howard, and Martha Nussbaum, eds., *Is Multiculturalism Bad for Women?* (Princeton, NJ: Princeton University Press, 1999); Ayelet Shachar, "Feminism and Multiculturalism: Mapping the Terrain," in Owen and Laden, *Multiulturalism*, pp. 115–48; Amartya Sen, *Identity and Violence*, (New York: W. W. Norton, 2006); Anthony Kwame Appiah, *The Ethics of Identity* (Princeton, NJ: Princeton University Press, 2005). Shachar's article doesn't so much voice this concern as discuss the debates that it has generated. Though both Sen and Appiah do raise this worry, and are thus more skeptical of demands for recognition than philosophers like Taylor and Tully, their skepticism does not lead them to complete rejections of the political importance of identity.

20 This conflation is critically discussed in Kymlicka, "The New Debate over Minority Rights."

21 For discussions of the difference between membership and group rights, see David Miller, "Group Rights, Human Rights, and Citizenship" *European Journal of Philosophy* 10 (2) (2002): 178–95. Miller there distinguishes between category rights and group rights, and then between group rights that are exercised by members of the groups, and those exercised by the group as a whole. See also Peter Jones, "Human Rights, Group Rights and People's Rights," *Human Rights* Quarterly 21 (1) (1999): 80–107, where he distinguishes between collective and corporate conceptions of group rights.

22 For a discussion of some of these issues, see Daniel Weinstock, "Liberalism, Multiculturalism and the Problem of Internal Minorities" and Ayelet Shachar, "Feminism and Multiculturalism," in Owen and Laden, *Multiculturalism*.

23 See Andrew Mason, "Multiculturalism and the Critique of Essentialism," in Owen and Laden, *Multiculturalism*.

24 See, for example, Carl Wellman, *Real Rights* (Oxford: Oxford University Press, 1995).

25 Young, *Justice and the Politics of Difference*.

26 Alan Gewirth argues for an agent-based theory of rights in "The Basis and Content of Human Rights," in J. Ronald Pennock and John W. Chapman, eds., *Human Rights* (New York: New York University Press, 1980). Joseph Raz defends an interest-based theory of

Anthony S. Laden

rights in "On the Nature of Rights," *Mind* 93 (1984): 194–214. John Locke argued for rights claims on the basis of a natural law of freedom in his *Second Treatise of Government*, and Thomas Jefferson for rights as the endowment of a Creator in *The Declaration of Independence*.

27 Iris Young, *Justice and the Politics of Difference*, p. 37, and *Inclusion and Democracy*, pp. 81–121.

28 Kukathas, "Are There Any Cultural Rights?"

29 Tully, *Strange Multiplicity*; Will Kymlicka, *Liberalism, Community and Culture*, (Oxford: Oxford University Press, 1989); and Charles Taylor, "Shared and Divergent Values," in his *Reconciling the Solitudes* (Montreal: McGill-Queen's University Press, 1993), pp. 155–87.

30 Will Kymlicka's work is the best-known example of this strategy.

31 Much of what follows draws on arguments I have made at greater length in my *Reasonably Radical*.

32 I have, however, done so, elsewhere. See my "Taking the Distinction Between Persons Seriously," *Journal of Moral Philosophy* 1 (3) (2004): 277–92, and "Evaluating Social Reasons: Hobbes vs. Hegel," *Journal of Philosophy* 102 (7) (Jul. 2005): 327–56.

33 See, for instance, Onora O'Neill, "Women's Rights: Whose Obligations?" in her *Bounds of Justice* (Cambridge: Cambridge University Press, 2000), and Maurice Cranston, "Are There Any Human Rights?" *Daedalus* (1983): 1–17. For one response to these criticisms, see Amartya Sen, "Elements of a Theory of Human Rights," *Philosophy and Public Affairs* 32 (4) (2004): 315–56.

34 This worry is raised by T. M. Scanlon in his "Rights, Goals and Fairness," *Erkenntnis* 2 (1) (1977): 81–94. Scanlon goes on there to offer an individualist theory of rights that attempts to answer this worry. In later work, however, Scanlon has urged a more relational approach to moral philosophy that he calls contractualism. See, for instance, *What We Owe to Each Other* (Cambridge, MA: Harvard University Press, 1998).

35 This is related to the so-called paradox of deontology. My response here shares much with and is indebted to the work of Tamar Shapiro. See Shapiro, "Three Conceptions of Action in Moral Theory," *Noûs* 35 (1) (2001): 93–117.

36 Mill's argument is to be found in Ch. V of *Utilitarianism*. The alternative argument is made by John Rawls, *Theory of Justice*, p. 161.

37 Rawls, *Justice as Fairness*, p. 139.

38 See Miller, "Group Rights, Human Rights, and Citizenship."

39 One important way that liberals imagine recognition that is often overlooked by advocates of a politcs of identity is in the form of the respect we show each other by leaving one another alone and not demanding of each other justification for some of our actions and choices. I am grateful to Sam Fleischacker for reminding me of this point.

40 Young, *Justice and the Politics of Difference*, p. 15.

41 Laden, *Reasonably Radical*, Ch. 6.

42 These are all discussed in more detail in my "John Rawls: *A Theory of Justice*," in John Shand, ed., *Central Works of Philosophy, vol 5: Quine and After* (London: Acumen, 2006), pp. 64–85.

43 I do not mean to deny here that philosophical work such as that above cannot help shape our understanding of how to go about engaging politically. One recent move in this direction which I think is philosophically in line with the arguments offered here advocates what some call a politics of "civic engagement." See David Owen and Russell Bentley, "Ethical Loyalties, Civic Virtue and the Circumstances of Politics" *Philosophical Explorations* 4 (3) (2001): 223–39; Bert van den Brink, "Imagining Civic Relations in the Moment of their Breakdown: A Crisis of Civic Integrity in the Netherlands," in Owen and Laden, *Multiculturalism*; Danielle Allen, *Talking to Strangers* (Chicago: University of Chicago Press, 2005); and Young, *Inclusion and Democracy*.

Structural Injustice and the Politics of Difference[1]

Iris M. Young

As a social movement tendency in the 1980s, the politics of difference involved the claims of feminist, anti-racist, and gay liberation activists that the structural inequalities of gender, race, and sexuality were not well perceived or combated by the dominant paradigm of equality and inclusion. In this dominant paradigm, the promotion of justice and equality requires nondiscrimination: the application of the same principles of evaluation and distribution to all persons regardless of their particular social positions or backgrounds. In this ideal, which many understood as the liberal paradigm, social justice means ignoring gender, racial, or sexual differences among people. Social movements asserting a politics of difference, and the theorists following them, argued that this difference-blind ideal was part of the problem. Equating equality with equal treatment ignores deep material differences in social position, division of labor, socialized capacities, normalizing standards and ways of living that continue to disadvantage members of historically excluded groups. Commitment to substantial equality thus requires attending to rather than ignoring such differences.

In the context of ethnic politics and resurgent nationalism, another version of a politics of difference gained currency in the 1990s, which focused on differences of nationality, ethnicity, and religion. Like the anti-racist and feminist politics of difference, this version challenges the notion that liberal equality requires the application of the same principles to all in the same way. It emphasizes the value of cultural distinctness to individuals and argues that public accommodation to and support of such cultural difference is compatible with liberal institutions.

In this essay I first distinguish the arguments of these two versions of a politics of difference, which I call the structural inequality model and the societal culture model, respectively. The first term is my own coinage, and I take some of my own writing on the politics of difference as paradigmatic of this approach. The second term I take from Will Kymlicka, whose theory of multicultural citizenship I take as paradigmatic of the second approach. Their differences bear noting because some political and theoretical treatments of a politics of difference or multiculturalism tend to merge the two or pass from premises more typical of the first to conclusions more typical of the second. I discuss some of the similarities and differences between the two approaches and locate several political theorists in these terms.

The structural inequality and societal culture approaches to a politics of difference share some commitments, and their arguments are compatible in many contexts. Both models raise important issues and proponents of each offer good arguments for public and private practices to pay attention to group difference for the sake of justice. I will argue, however, that the ascendancy of the society cultural approach over the structural inequality approach among political theorists – which has counterparts in trends in general public discourse – improperly narrows the scope of issues of justice. Racism as a form of structural injustice, for example, I will argue, tends to disappear from view, leaving only ethnic difference. Whereas the structural inequality approach to a politics of difference challenges liberal conceptualizations of the relation of public and private, I will suggest, the societal culture approach reinstates it in ways that both obscure some of the mechanisms for producing injustice and limit the imagination for remedy. The societal cultural approach also tends to reconfigure conflict concerning group differences from struggles about opportunities for achieving well-being to concerns about tolerance and its limits. This reconfiguration sometimes operates to reinscribe a logic of normal and deviant that the structural inequality approach criticizes.

I. The Structural Inequality Approach

Structural social groups are relationally constituted through interactions that make categorical distinctions among people in a hierarchy of status or privilege. Major structural axes in modern societies include: the social division of labor; relative power to decide institutions' actions, or to change the incentives faced by large numbers of people; the establishment and enforcement of hegemonic norms.[2] The production and reproduction of what Charles Tilly calls "durable inequality" involves processes where people produce and maintain advantages for themselves and disadvantages for others, in terms of access to resources, power, autonomy, honor, or receiving service and deference, by means of the application of rules and customs that assume such categorical distinctions.[3] In Tilly's model, economic differences often brought under the rubric of class difference – in income, property ownership and control, occupational privilege, and the ability to pass these on to one's children – intersect with and usually work through these other categorical differences.

The presence of categorical relations of relative privilege and relative disadvantage does not imply that all members of a subordinated category are badly off or that all members of a privileged category are well off. Nor does it mean that there are no persons that slip out of or over the categories. Some African-American men or white women, for example, occupy positions of considerable privilege. Inequality of structured social groups does mean that persons categorized in the subordinate positions generally face greater obstacles in the pursuit of their ambitions and interests, or have a narrower range of opportunities offered to them for developing capacities and exercising autonomy over the conditions of their action. Such structural inequality counts as group based injustice, then, because it violates a principle of substantive equality of opportunity.[4]

A first step in resisting structural inequality consists in challenging formal rules that require or allow institutions or individuals explicitly to confine some categories of persons to disadvantaged or subordinate positions. A commitment to principles of the equal moral worth of individuals, and therefore that all deserve opportunities for achieving well-being, however, stands on shifting sands wherever it exists today. The structural inequality approach to a politics of difference argues that public and private institutional policies and practices that interpret equality as requiring being blind to group differences are not likely to undermine persistent structural inequalities and can tend to reinforce them. Even in the absence of formally discriminatory laws and rules, adherence to normal rules and practices of occupational assignment, body esthetic, struggle over power, and the like, will tend to reproduce given categorical inequalities unless institutions take explicit action to counteract such tendencies. Thus to remove unjust inequality it is necessary explicitly to recognize group difference and either compensate for disadvantage, revalue some attributes, positions, or actions, or take special steps to meet the needs of and empower members of disadvantaged groups.

Now I will explicate three examples of categorical structural inequality, along with correlative arguments for why attending to rather than being blind to group difference is an appropriate response to this inequality: the structural position of people with disabilities, institutional racism, and gender inequality.

A. Difference Blindness and Disability

In his recent book attacking all versions of a politics of difference, Brian Barry devotes considerable space to defending a standard principle of merit in the allocation of positions. Merit involves equality of opportunity in the following sense: it rejects a system that awards positions explicitly according to class, race, gender, family background, and so on. Under a merit principle, all who wish should have the opportunity to compete for the desirable positions, and those most qualified should win the competition. Positions of authority or expertise should be occupied by those persons who demonstrate excellence in particular skills and who best exhibit the demeanor expected of people in those positions. Everyone else is a loser in respect to those positions, and they suffer no injustice on that account.[5]

In this merit system, according to Barry, it is natural that people with disabilities will usually turn out to be losers.

> Surely it is to be expected in the nature of the case that, across the group (disabled) as a whole, its members will be less qualified than average, even if the amount of money spent on their education is the average or more than the average.[6]

Barry's is a common opinion. In our scheme of social cooperation, certain skills and abilities can and should be expected of average workers, and it is "in the nature of the case" that most people with disabilities do not meet these expectations. Thus they do not merit the jobs and income attendant on meeting them. These people's deficiencies are not their fault, of course. So a decent society will support their needs in spite of their inability to contribute significantly to social production.

One of the objectives of the disability rights movement has been to challenge this bit of liberal common sense. Most people who have not thought about the issues

Iris M. Young

very much tend to regard being "disabled" as an attribute of persons: some people simply lack the functionings that enable normal people to live independently, compete in job markets, have a satisfying social life, and so on. Many in the disability rights movement, however, conceptualize the problem that people with disabilities face rather differently. The problem is not the attributes individual persons have or do not have. The problem, rather, is the *lack of fit* between the attributes of certain persons and structures, practices, norms, and esthetic standards dominant in the society. The built environment is biased to support the capacities of people who can walk, climb, see, and hear within what are thought of as a "normal range" of performance, and presents significant obstacles for people whose capacities are outside that range. Both interactive and technical ways of assessing the intelligence, skill, and adaptability of people in schools and workplaces assume ways of evaluating aptitude and achievement that unfairly exclude or disadvantage many people with disabilities. The physical layout and equipment in workplaces and the organization of work process too often make it impossible for a person with a disability to use the skills they have. Hegemonic standards of charm, beauty, grace, wit, or attentiveness position some people with disabilities as monstrous or abject.

These and other aspects of the division of labor and hegemonic norms constitute structural injustice for people with disabilities. Many people with disabilities unfairly suffer limitation on their opportunities for developing capacities, earning a living through satisfying work, having a rewarding social life, and living and autonomous adults. A difference blind liberalism can offer only very limited remedy for this injustice. It is no response to the person who moves in a wheelchair who tries to go to a courtroom accessible only by stairs that the state treats all citizens in the same way. It is no response to the blind engineer that this company uses the same computer equipment for all employees. The opportunities of people with disabilities can be made equal only if others specifically notice their differences, cease regarding them as unwanted deviance from accepted norms and unacceptable costs to efficient operations, and take affirmative measures to accommodate the specific capacities of individuals so that they can function at their best and with dignity.

The 1990 Americans with Disabilities Act recognized this in principle when it requires that employers, landlords and public services make "reasonable accommodation" to the needs of people with disabilities. It codified a politics of difference. Unfortunately, the only enforcement power the ADA contains is permission to litigate infraction. Coupled with the cost saving and fear of denying interests of most people who think of themselves as able-bodied, the ADA's limitations conspire to reproduce these injustices to people with disabilities as a group.

The example of people with disabilities represents a clear case where difference-blind treatment or policy is more likely to perpetuate than correct injustice. It is also a clear case where relevant social differences are constituted by the relation of some persons to hegemonic cultural norms and dominant definitions of efficiency, rather than by internal processes of mutual identification such as religion.

I have begun with the example of injustice towards people with disabilities because I wish to suggest that it is paradigmatic of the structural inequality approach to a politics of difference in general. It represents a clear case where difference-blind treatment or policy is more likely to perpetuate than correct injustice. The systematic disadvantage at which facially neutral standards puts many people in this case, however, does not derive from internal cultural attributes that constitute a group, people with disabilities. It may be plausible to speak of a Deaf culture, to the extent that many Deaf people speak a unique and common language and sometimes live together in Dear communities. In a wider sense, however, there is no community or culture of people with disabilities. Instead, this category designates a structural group constituted from the outside by the deviation of its members from normalized institutional assumptions about the exhibition of skill, definition of tasks in a division of labor, ideals of beauty, built environment standards, comportments of sociability, and so on. Although justice for people with disabilities certainly involves more public recognition of their distinctive and diverse experiences and perspectives on social life, justice in this case does not consist in the recognition of a group culture or way of life. Instead, the remedy for injustice to people with disabilities consists in challenging the norms and rules of the institutions that most condition the life options and the attainment of well-being of these persons structurally positioned as deviant.

Issues of justice raised by many group-based conflicts and social differences, I suggest, follow this paradigm. They concern the way individuals with structurally similar physical attributes, socialized capacities, cultural repertoires, sexual orientations, family and neighborhood resources, and so on, are positioned in the social division of labor, relations of decision-making power, and hegemonic norms of achievement, beauty, respectability, and the like. The structural inequality approach to a politics of difference focuses on these issues of inclusion and exclusion, and the availability or limitation of substantive opportunities for developing capacities and achieving well-being.

B. Racial Inequality

Clearly this essay's purpose is not to give an account of the structural inequalities of institutional racism. In this context, I want to make only a few points about racial inequality and the politics of difference. One of the main worries that motivates these reflections on recent political theory of difference is that the ascendance of what I will shortly describe as the societal culture model of a politics of difference seems to obscure racism as a distinct and virulent form of structural injustice. It operates with a model of groups internally constituted by cultural identification, who understand each other as culturally distinct and side by side. Consequently "race" seems to be reconstituted as ethnicity in the societal cultural mode. Thus here I want only to point out some salient features of racism as a structural process, one often built on but not reducible to cultural difference. Although I will focus on racialized processes of structural inequality in the United States, I think that racial inequality structures many societies in the world. I characterize racism as structural processes that normalize body esthetic, determine that physical, dirty, or servile work is most appropriate for members of racialized groups, produces and reproduces segregation of members of racialized groups, and renders deviant the comportments and habits of these segregated persons in relation to dominant norms of respectability.

What distinguishes "race" from ethnicity or nation, conceptually? The former naturalizes or "epidermalizes" the attributes of difference. Racism attaches significance to bodily characteristics – skin color, hair type, facial features, and constructs hierarchies of standard or ideal body types against which others appear inferior, stigmatized, deviant, or abject. In Western structures of anti-Black racism this hierarchy appears both as dichotomous and scaler.[7]

Processes of racialization stigmatize or devalue bodies, body types, or items closely attached to bodies such as clothing; this stigmatization and stereotyping appear in public images and in the way some people react to others. Racialization concerns, moreover, understandings of the proper work of some and its hierarchal status in relation to others. The stigma of blackness in America, for example, has its origins in the division of labor, namely slavery.[8] The slave does hard labor under domination, from which owners' accumulate profits; or the slave does servile labor to attend the needs and elevate the status of the rule group. While chattel slavery was abolished a century and a half ago, racialized positions in the social division of labor remain. The least desirable work, the work with the lowest pay, least autonomy, and lowest status, is the hard physical work, the dirty work, and the servant work. In the United States these are racialized forms of work, that is, work thought to belong to black and brown people primarily, and these increasingly are also foreigners. A similar process of racialization has occurred in Europe, where persons of Turkish, North African, South Asian, and Middle Eastern origin, in addition to persons of Southern African origin, are positioned as other and tend to be restricted to lower status positions in the social division of labor.

Segregation is a third common structure of racial inequality. Although racialized segregation may build on or exploit perceived ethnic difference, urban processes of clustering and processes of segregation are different.[9] Even when not produced by legally enforced spatial exclusion, racial segregation is a process of residentially concentrating members of bodily stigmatized groups that operates to accrue material goods as well as status for dominant groups – more space, lower prices, neighborhood effects of affluence, and so on.

With segregation, the stigma of racialized bodies and denigrated labor marks space itself and the people who grow up and live in neighborhoods. People who live together in segregated neighborhoods, moreover, tend to develop group specific idiom, styles of comportment, interests, and artistic forms. These also are liable to be devalued and stigmatized by dominant norms. People who wish to appear respectable and professional, for example, had better shed the habits of walking, laughing, and talking in slang they have learned on the home block.

These structural relations of bodily affect, meanings and interests in the social division of labor, segregation, and normalization of dominant culture habitus, operate to limit the opportunities of many to learn and use satisfying skills in socially recognized setting, to accumulate income or wealth, or to attain to positions of power and prestige. A politics of difference argues that such liabilities to disadvantage cannot be overcome by race-blind principles of formal equality in employment, political party competition, and so on. Where racialized structural inequality influences so many institutions and potentially stigmatizes and impoverishes so many people, a society that aims to redress such injustice must *notice* the processes of racial differentiation before it can correct them. Even when overt discriminatory practices are illegal and widely condemned, racialized structures are produced and reproduced in some of the most everyday interactions in civil society and workplace. Projects to redress racial injustice must notice these as well.

C. Gender Inequality

At least as these appear in the literature of political theory, the structural inequality model and the societal culture model of the politics of difference position women's issues differently. As I will discuss below, some proponents of a societal culture model implicitly invoke gender justice under norms of equal treatment. In the structural inequality model, by contrast, feminist politics are a species of the politics of difference. Let me explain how.

In the last quarter-century there have been many changes in gendered norms of behavior and comportment expected of men and women, with a great deal more freedom of choice in taste and self-presentation available to members of both sexes than in the past. Many women nevertheless suffer adverse consequences when they deviate from a normalized, implicitly male, body that does not menstruate, is not pregnant, does not breastfeed. In these respects at least, the female body retains a monstrous aspect in the societal imagination.[10]

People too often react to public evidence of these female specific conditions with aversion, ridicule, or denial. Public institutions which claim to include women equally too often fail to accommodate to the needs of menstruating, pregnant, and breastfeeding women. This sometimes discourages them from participation in these institutions. Sometimes the costs to women of being positioned as deviant in relation to normal bodies are small inconveniences, like remembering to carry tampons in anticipation that the women's room at work will not supply them. Sometimes, however, women suffer serious discomfort, threats to their health, harassment, job loss, or forego benefits by withdrawing in order to avoid these consequences.[11] Including women as equals in schools, workplaces, and other institutions entails accommodating to our bodily specificity to the extent that we can both be women and excel in or enjoy the activities of those institutions.

The social differences produced by a gender division of labor, however, are more fundamental for gendered structural inequalities to which institutions and practices aiming at justice toward women should attend. Although there have been huge changes in attitudes about the capacities of men and women, and most formal barriers to women's pursuit of occupations and activities have been removed, in at least one respect change has been slow and minor. A structured social division of labor remains in which women do most of the unpaid care work in the family, and most people of both sexes assume that primary responsibility for care of children, other family members, and housecleaning falls primarily to women.

As Susan Okin theorized it more than fifteen years go, this gender division of labor accounts in large measure for injustice to women, whether or not they themselves are wives or mothers. The socialization of girls continues to be oriented toward caring and helping. Occupational sex segregation continues to crowd women in a relatively few job categories, keeping wages low. Heterosexual couples find it rational to depend on a man's paycheck for their primary income. Thus women and their children are vulnerable to poverty in case they raise their children alone.[12]

Most employers institutionalize an assumption that occupants of a good job – one that earns enough to support a family at a decent level of well-being and with a decent pension, vacation time, and job security – can devote himself or herself primarily to that job. Workers whose family responsibility impinge on or conflict with employer

Iris M. Young

expectations are deviants, and they are likely to be sanctioned for trying to combine real work and family responsibility.

Feminism construed as a politics of difference thus argues that real equality and freedom for women entail attending to both embodied, socialized, and institutional sex and gender differences in order to ensure that women – as well as men who find themselves positioned like many women in the division of labor or in comportment and taste – do not bear unfair costs of institutional assumptions about what women and men are or ought to be doing, who they feel comfortable working with or voting for, and so on. For women to have equal opportunities with men to attain positions of high status, power, or income, it is not enough that they prove that their strength, leadership capacities, or intelligence are as good as men's. This is easy. It is more difficult to overcome the costs and disadvantages deriving from application of supposedly difference-blind norms of productivity, respectability, or authoritatativeness that in fact carry structural biases against many women.

To summarize, the structural inequality approach to a politics of difference considers the problems of injustice to which it responds as arising from processes of the division of labor, social segregation, and a lack of fit between hegemonic norms and interpreted bodies. Under such circumstances of structural inequality, truly equalizing opportunities requires attending to such structural normalizing differences.

II. Societal Culture Approach

Although the structural inequality approach to a politics of difference continues to be expressed, the societal culture approach has come to dominate political theory literature that argues for attending to group difference in politics and policy. I take the term "societal culture" from Will Kymlicka, who pioneered this approach. In *Multicultural Citizenship*, Kymlicka himself distinguishes his approach toward the politics of difference from one concerned with the situation of disadvantaged social groups. "The marginalization of women, gays and lesbians, and the disabled," he says, "cuts across ethnic and national lines – it is found in minority cultures and homogeneous nation-states as well as national minorities and ethnic groups – and it must be fought in all these places."[13]

Kymlicka argues that it is important to distinguish these sorts of issues of a politics of difference from those that involve difference in "societal culture." This term refers for him only to differences of nation and ethnicity. A "societal culture," says Kymlicka, is

> synonymous with "a nation" or "a people" – that is, as an intergenerational community, more or less institutionally complete, occupying a given territory or homeland, sharing a distinct language and history. A state is multicultural if its members either belong to different nations (a multi-nation state), or have migrated from different nations (a polyethnic state), and if this fact is an important aspect of personal identity and political life.[14]

On the societal culture model, the question of the politics of difference is this: given that a political society consists of two or more societal cultures, what does justice require in the way of their mutual accommodation to one another's practices and forms of cultural expression, and to what extent can and should a liberal society give public recognition to these cultural diversities?

The problem to which the arguments of the societal culture model offer the solution is also one of inequality. The assumed starting point of the societal culture model is a state or polity in which a majority culture dominates, and by political means can limit the ability of one or more cultural minorities to live out their forms of expression; or more benignly, the sheer ubiquity of the dominant culture threatens to swamp the minority culture to the extent that its survival may be endangered. Under these circumstances of inequality or unfreedom, members of embattled cultural groups frequently demand special rights of territorial governance, language rights in public institutions, support for cultural expression and preservation, and so on.

The societal culture approach explicitly rejects political principles and practices which assume that a single polity must coincide with a single common culture. Freedom and affirmation of cultural difference is compatible with liberalism and a single state constitution that arranges political cooperation among diverse cultural groups. For Kymlicka, issues of a politics of difference concern: freedom of expression and practice, territorial autonomy and self-government for historic nations, public support for culture preservation, arguments for exempting members of some groups from certain regulations on cultural grounds; measures to ensure representation of minority cultures in major political institutions of the state; defense against members of minority cultures having to bear unfair costs due to their desire to remain committed to and maintain their culture. The main reason that individuals' commitments to cultural membership should be recognized and supported in political life, on this model, is that the forms of expression, practices, and community relationship of the societal culture provide individuals with the context for their options and decisions.[15] Kymlicka considers the question of whether liberal polities ought to go so far as to tolerate practices that a culture regards as important, but which a wider societal judgment finds violate standards of liberal accommodation and individual human rights. He argues that such practices should not be tolerated.

I have dwelt on Kymlicka's text because he more explicitly than others distinguishes societal culture approach from what I am calling the structural inequality approach. With one exception, the issues and arguments he advances in *Multicultural Citizenship*, and which he elaborates in more recent writings, moreover, cover the range of issues debated in the huge literature about issues of politics and difference under the societal culture model in the last decade. Writers disagree on the limits of toleration, the rights of national minorities, the claims of immigrants and ethnic minorities, the extent to which states and majority cultures are obliged by justice to support cultural preservation, and similar issues.[16] To the issues Kymlicka treats, other voices in these debates have added another: the extent to which religious difference should be accommodated and affirmed in a multicultural liberal polity.[17] While writers take varying positions on this question as well, it is clear that religion has gained more attention as a specific form of cultural membership that provides a context for the choices of many people who claim specific rights on that account. Thus I include religious difference in the societal culture model as it is has evolved.

Since both of these theoretical approaches are versions of a politics of difference, it should not be surprising that they share some features. I find two major similarities

Iris M. Young

in the analyses and arguments of the structural inequality approach and the societal culture approach. Both worry about the domination some groups are able to exercise over public meaning and control over resources. Second, both challenge difference-blind public principle. They question the position that equal citizenship in a common polity entails a common commitment to a common public interest, a single national culture, and single set of rules that applies to everyone in the same way. They both argue that commitment to justice sometimes requires noticing social or cultural differences and sometimes treating people differently.

While they are logically distinct, each approach is important and their arguments are often compatible in given political contexts. The societal culture approach is important because it offers vision and principle to respond to dominative nationalist impulses. We can live together in common political institutions and still maintain institutions by which we distinguish ourselves as peoples or cultures with distinct practices and traditions. Acting on such a vision can and should reduce ethnic and nationalist violence. The structural inequality approach is important because it highlights the depth and systematicity of inequality, and shows that inequality before the law is not sufficient to remedy this inequality. It calls attention to relations and processes of exploitation, marginalization, normalization that keep many people in subordinate positions.

My project in this essay, then, is not to argue that political actors and theorists ought to accept one of these approaches and reject the other. I wish, rather, to argue that it is important to notice the difference between them, a difference sometimes ignored in recent literature. A major difference that I will discuss in the meaning of the term "culture" as it arises in each. I will argue, further, that the ascendancy of the societal culture approach in political theory is problematic for several reasons. Emphasizing the societal cultural approach tends to obscure structural inequalities such as racism. Because the societal culture approach usually brings issues of difference under a liberal paradigm, moreover, it tends to narrow the issues of justice at stake in a politics of difference to those concerning freedom and autonomy, paying relatively little attention to issues of equal opportunity. As under a liberal paradigm, finally, the societal culture approach often reconfigures questions of attention to social group difference in terms of toleration and its limits. This framing of the issues introduces a normalizing discourse of the sort that the structural inequality model exposes and criticizes. Before I proceed with these arguments, however, I will indicate which of various political theorists take one or both approach, as I perceive them.

III. Who's Who in the Politics of Difference?

In *Culture and Equality*, Brian Barry includes a huge array of political theorists in the single demonized category of those who depart from the straight and narrow of difference-blind liberal equality and wander into hopeless thickets of cultural recognition. In so doing he often merges the arguments of those I categories under the structural inequality approach with those I put under a societal culture approach. I have already referred to some of these writers, but at this point I may be useful to locate some key contributors to this literature in terms of the two approaches I have laid out. This will hardly be a comprehensive review of the literature, but serves simply as a way that readers might apply the distinction among types of theories that I have drawn.

Most of my own writing on justice, democracy and difference has emphasized the structural inequality approach. Both *Justice and the Politics of Difference* and *Inclusion and Democracy* critically assess the tendency of both public and private institutions in contemporary liberal democratic societies to reproduce sexual, racial and class inequality by applying standards and rules in the same way to all. Each book, however, contains elements that relate more to a societal culture approach. *Justice and the Politics of Difference* refers to claims of indigenous people, and speaks approvingly of movements of structurally oppressed groups to resist stigma by constructing positive group affinities. In one chapter of *Inclusion and Democracy* I argue for a relational notion of self-determination to contrast with more rigid standard notions of national sovereignty; here I intend to make a move in the societal cultural approach to a politics of difference. Thus the dominant orientation of my writing about politics of difference has operated with the structural inequality approach, but as a body the work straddles the distinction. One motivation for this paper, indeed, is to sort these distinctions out for myself.

Amy Gutmann's recent book, *Identity and Democracy*, straddles the distinction with the opposite balance. Most of her chapters concern how liberal polities ought to respond to the presence of ethnic and religious differences in these societies. In a chapter about what she labels "ascriptive identity," however, Gutmann treats issues of stigma, exclusion and discrimination more typical of those whom I have said are positioned in relations of structural inequality, such as women, people who transgress heterosexual norms, African Americans and members of other racialized groups. Whereas recognizing and accommodating cultural and religious difference within the limits of liberal rights is the proper response to ethnic and religious political conflict, according to Gutmann, this argument does not apply to ascriptive groups. Gutmann's arguments in this chapter coincide to a large extent with those belonging to what I call a structural inequality approach. A major difference, however, concerns the implied theory of the basis of inequality. Gutmann's category of ascriptive groups obscures the social process of constituting work, normalizing behaviors, and defending positions of power that produce or allow individual discrimination.

To the extent that Nancy Fraser argues for a politics of difference, she interprets it largely in terms of the structural inequality approach. In a recent statement of her distinction between redistribution and recognition, Fraser distinguishes two forms of what she calls recognition politics: one that seeks "participatory parity" and the other that seeks affirmation of group specificity.[18] This difference which for her is within approaches to a politics of recognition is analogous in certain ways to the distinction I am drawing between a structural inequality and societal culture approach to a politics of difference. Except for Charles Taylor, Fraser gives little attention to writers I associate with the societal culture approach, and she favors the approach she calls participatory parity as a response to structural inequalities of gender, race, and sexuality.

By insisting on a categorical distinction between what she calls "redistribution" and "recognition," however, I think that Fraser's theory obscures the operations of such structural inequalities. In the first place, some of the major sources of structural inequality, such as the social division of labor, the definition of tasks and qualifications for them within a given occupation, decision-making power over public and

Iris M. Young

private investment, are more fundamental than issues of distribution and redistribution. In the recent essay, however, Fraser says that she aims to include all these within the category of redistribution. If all these issues are included, however, then "redistribution" is a misleading name for the issues of justice at stake.

More importantly, perhaps, I think that it is both too polarizing and too simplifying to construct a dichotomy between economy and culture as mutually exclusive categories, and then admit that some structural inequality combines both. I think that it is more useful to have several categories referring to social processes that limit opportunities or access to resources (such as exploitation, marginalization, domination, normalization, or stigmatization), and then to consider the account needed for various structurally positioned groups.[19]

I find that few other political theorists writing about a politics of difference adopt a structural inequality approach. Melissa Williams assumes the issue as structural inequality in her arguments for special attention to voice and representation for historically marginalized groups.[20] Anne Phillips' arguments about group conscious policies of political representation and policies promoting other opportunities also adopt a structural inequality approach.[21]

In my observation, most recent political theorizing challenging a difference-blind liberalism takes the societal culture approach. They define the kinds of groups whose difference is a course of political conflict requiring adjudication largely in terms of national, ethnic or religious groups. In addition to Kymlicka, prominent contributors to the societal culture approach to a politics of difference include Charles Taylor, Yael Tamir, James Tully, Chandran Kukathas, Joseph Carens, Rainer Bauboeck, Jacob Levy, Ayalet Shachar, Bhikhu Parekh, Jeffrey Spinner-Halev, Duncan Ivason, and Seyla Benhabib. This is a very partial list in an ever-enlarging field of discussion. There are many differences in specific issues treated and specific positions taken among these writers, and the debates among them are rich with theoretical nuance. In the next section I will discuss some difference among them in the extent to which they conceptualize culture as unified or differentiated. I will analyze the issues that occupy them and arguments they make further in the concluding section, where I raise some critical questions about how the societal culture approach has evolved.

IV. The Meaning of Culture

Brian Barry cites the definition of culture I offer in *Justice and the Politics of Difference*, and notes that it is rather different from that offered by Kymlicka in *Multicultural Citizenship*. Noticing the differing meanings does not prevent Barry from merging the two accounts and criticizing both – as well as that of others, including Nancy Fraser, James Tully, and Bhikhu Parekh – for "politicizing" culture. As in this case, some of the confusion between the two versions of a politics of difference that I distinguish here can be attributed to sliding between usages and meanings of culture. The structural inequality approach to a politics of difference and the societal cultural approach use the term "culture" in different ways.

The definition of the term culture that I offer in the work Barry cites is the following: culture includes "the symbols, images, meanings, habitual comportments, stories and so on, through which people express their experience and communicate with one another."[22] Considering how debates about the politics of difference have played out, if I were to rewrite my version of the structural inequality approach, I would not give the term culture so prominent a place as it has in that book, and would substitute several more specific terms, such as normalization, habit, and practice.[23] I nevertheless stand by the intent of the definition as identifying an aspect of processes that produce and reproduce structural inequality.

In this usage, culture refers to an aspect of all action insofar as it is communicative action. Culture simply refers to specific meanings that people use and understand when they interact – from simple gestures such as bowing, to the formalities surrounding and content of the public speech of one head of state to another, to the implicit norms involving tone of voice, mode of standing, and sentence structure that signal "authoritative" in a modern western society. In this usage, people understand, partly understand, misunderstand or do not at all understand meanings conveyed by speech, bodily comportments, or symbols. To the extent that some people do not understand or misunderstand, this may well be due to their having a cultural repertoire derived from a different place or group. On this meaning of culture, however, there is no reason to refer to *a* culture as a single substantial entity, with coherent bounded limits that unify it and distinguish it entirely from other similarly substantial cultures outside it. The definition of culture as the meanings of communicative action is entirely compatible with, indeed even requires, an understanding of culture as fluid, changing, and without fixed borders distinguishing inside and outside.

Understood in this sense, culture is a pervasive aspect of processes that produce and reproduce structural injustice. The feelings of aversion or pity some sighted or walking people feel in the presence of blind people or people who move in wheelchairs are part of our culture, in that their expressions are learned, understood, and to a certain extent shared. Gender differences involve many widely understood meanings, symbols, bodily habits, styles of speaking, tastes, and so on. Racial stereotypes are one aspect of the production and reproduction of racial inequality. None of the structures that disadvantage people with disabilities, women, or racially marked groups can be reduced to culture. The organization of the division of labor, for example, involves a project to extract benefits for themselves by persons or sectors that control that organization. While the physical layout of buildings or cities which constitute an aspect of the structures that position racially disadvantaged groups or people with disabilities have some cultural determinants, they are not reducible to culture. A social theory needs concepts such as resources, power, the organization of cooperative and competitive relations, in addition to culture, in order to give an account of structural processes. Because structures are produced and reproduced by actions and actions usually involve communication, however, it is usually impossible to distinguish factors of power, resource use, organizational networks, the manipulation of incentives, and so on, from cultural meanings.

Structural inequalities associated with class, moreover, are just as much cultural on this understanding as are those of race, gender, and disability. Pierre Bourdieu, for example, describes how the privileges of being middle and upper class are constituted and reproduced not simply by having access to or command over material resources, but simultaneously by internalizing tastes and bodily comportment typical of those in that class position.[24] Again, in my view, such an account does not

Iris M. Young

reduce the material manifestations of affluence or organizational power to culture, but says that cultural meanings are usually an aspect of them.

According to the structural inequality approach to a politics of difference, then, political projects to reduce structural injustice must often have a cultural aspect: creating affirmative expression for denigrated groups, becoming self-conscious about and reforming some bodily habits of interaction, and so on. As I will discuss shortly, not the state but civil society is the primary site of efforts to change habits, meanings and forms of expression with a view to undermining injustice.

The societal culture approach to a politics of difference, by contrast, understands *a* culture as a substantive, coherent, bounded entity. As I quoted above, Kymlicka defines societal culture as "an intergenerational community, more or less institutionally complete, occupying a given territory or homeland, sharing a distinct language and history."[25] Understood as a substantive, a societal culture refers to the entirety of shared understandings and way of life of a community or people who take themselves as distinct from other communities or peoples. As Kymlicka rightly notes, this is a meaning of culture with wide currency.

This is the meaning of culture that has come to predominate in debates about a politics of difference, one referring to nation, ethnic group, or religion primarily. Debates about politics and culture, so understood, tend to come under the paradigm of liberal pluralism. Modern societies contain a plurality of distinct cultures – systems of beliefs and practices that are to a certain extent incommensurate. The political problem is what it means to give adherents of each due respect and at the same time enforce principles of justice over all of them. For all their differences, the theories of Joseph Carens, Ayalete Shachar, Chandran Kukathas, Jacob Levy, Susan Okin, Amy Gutmann, operate along with Kymlicka within this general liberal pluralist paradigm.

Because the societal culture approach defines group difference as difference in comprehensive culture, it has a tendency to essentialize cultures or regard them as self-identical within. What makes a group a group is that all its members share attributes – speaking the same language, say, or adhering to a specific set of historic traditions. Because the concept of societal culture defines a group in terms of a shared community of insiders distinguished from outsiders, it can appear to freeze the notion of culture the group has. This tendency appears not only among theorists of societal culture, but also in nationalist and ethnic politics. Leaders define their cultural or religious groups in static and essentialist terms that they construct as other than and incompatible with neighboring cultures.

Critics of a politics of difference typically raise the specter of essentialism and cultural conflict as reasons to recommit us to difference blind formalism. Despite the dangers of considering cultures as too unified and bounded that attend this approach, the theorists operating within it nearly always condemn essentialism and fundamentalism and offer a vision where cultural difference is not rigid or closed. These theories generally aim to develop principles of open interaction and cooperation as an answer to the problems of alleged incommensurability and conflict of commitments in actual politics. Writers such as Charles Taylor, James Tully, Bhikhu Parekh, and Joseph Carens offer varying accounts of politics as intercultural dialogue.[26] More recently, Seyla Benhab adds to these an account of the relation of individuals to the cultures to which they think of themselves belonging as involving a narrative of self in relation to others.[27] This narrative interpretation of societal culture allows for change, influence, and individual variation at the same time that it can retain a notion of cultural distinctness.

I have distinguished the meanings of culture I find typical of the structural inequality and societal culture models of a politics of difference, because I think commentaries and criticisms of these currents too often conflate them. There are important differences between saying, on the one hand, women aspiring to be corporate executives in the United States are sometimes disadvantaged by evaluative norms that privilege "cultural" attributes associated with masculine comportment, and on the other hand, saying that Japanese and American "cultures" each have differences in their norms of masculinity. The second of these usages is more totalizing than the first. It might be a good idea to excise the general term "culture" entirely from our theoretical vocabularies and use more specific terms. In any case, the usages are compatible, but different, and conclusions drawn about the second should not be applied to the first.

V. Worries about the Ascendancy of the Societal Culture Model

Although the societal culture approach has a different logic than the structural inequality approach, I have argued that each is important and that their arguments are often compatible in a particular political context. There are reasons nevertheless, I suggest, to find disturbing the trend among political theorists to operate largely within the societal culture model. Approaching issues of political conflict and social group difference primarily within the societal culture model inappropriately narrows the issues of justice at stake. Because most writers using the societal culture approach position the politics of difference under a liberal paradigm, furthermore, it tends to operate with too state-centered a conception of political action and tends toward the very sort of normalization that the structural inequality approach criticizes.

As I discussed above, the main kinds of claims that national, ethnic, and religious groups make on which theorists of the societal culture model reflect center around issues of freedom: the freedom of individuals to pursue life plan within a cultural context that gives substance to their sense of self; the freedom of members of ethnic or religious groups to express their commitments in public, to associate with like-minded others, under circumstances of respect from others; the ability of groups to establish and perpetuate their own institutions of self-government and cultural preservation. While not all claims of national, ethnic, or religious groups on this order should be supported all the time, they deserve to be taken seriously as claims of justice.

To the extent that the societal culture model comes to be identified with political issues involving group difference, however, some issues of justice recede from view. As I have argued in my account of the structural inequality approach, these issues include the following. Interactive norms constitute the bodies of some people as abject. The organization of the social division of labor privileges some and disadvantages others in ways that tend unfairly to limit opportunities of many people for developing capacities and achieving a decent level of material well-being. Institutional decision-making power is concentrated in the hands of dominant structural groups. Dominant standards of moral, intellectual, and occupational evaluation assume norms biased against members of subordinated groups. These sorts of processes often operate together to circumscribe many people in categorically defined positions of disadvantage that are reproduced over generations, but none of them is well conceptualized under paradigms of liberty or freedom of expression and association. Taking national, ethnic, and religious groups as the main sorts of groups at issue, the societal culture model gives little attention to the oppression of being positioned as disabled, the normalizations produced by class hegemony, or racialist inequality. Let me dwell on the case of theorizing racism.

I think that the societal cultural model of a politics of difference does not have a conceptual place for racial difference. Race is, of course, a social construct, not some kind of natural division among human beings. Racialized social processes are usually built upon perceived differences in societal culture – language, cosmological beliefs, religion, and so on; many perceptions of cultural difference and even violent conflicts between groups who constitute themselves as differing peoples, however, historically have not and today do not count as racialized. Historically, racism has often entailed comprehensive ideologies of the physiognomic, moral intellectual, and esthetic hierarchy of peoples. While today such comprehensive racialist doctrines are less common, as I summarized above, racialized social structures pervade many societies. The signs of this are stereotyped and despised bodies, as well as items associated with bodies, such as clothing, the assignment of menial, dirty, or servile work with members of groups so stereotyped, the structural marginalization of group members from high-status positions, and tendencies toward spatial segregation. Much of what some people in European societies tell themselves is conflict arising from cultural or religious difference involves, in my opinion, racism in at least some of these ways.

The societal culture approach tends to obscure the way that many group-based political claims and conflicts in contemporary multicultural societies involve both issues of cultural freedom *and* issues of structural inequality such as racism. Where there are problems of a lack of recognition of or accommodation to national, cultural, religious or linguistic groups in liberal democratic societies today (as well as others), these are often played out through dominant discourses that stereotype members of minority groups, find them technically inept or morally inferior, spatially segregate them and limit their opportunities to develop skills and compete for high-status positions.[28]

Issues of justice for Latinos in the United States, for example, concern not only cultural accommodation and acceptance, but also exposure and criticism of institutional racism. Many believe that the two are deeply intertwined. Demands for and implementation of policies that mandate English only in public institutions such as courts and schools both limit the freedom of some Latinos to express themselves freely, stigmatize them, and often limit their ability to develop marketable skills. The position of many Latinos is racialized, moreover, in that their brown skin and facial features categorize them together as a group in the eyes of many Anglos, in spite of the fact that they or their parents hail from different parts of Latin America and experience differences of language and tradition among themselves. Within the dominant structures, "Hispanics" occupy particular positions in the social division of labor, and the benefits that employers derive from this positioning are significant enough to limit the opportunities of members of this racialized group to move into other occupational positions.[29]

Everywhere that indigenous people make claims to freedom of cultural expression and political self-determination, to take another example, they do so in the context of racialized structural inequality. Indians in North America, Aboriginals in Australia, indigenous in Latin America, are all victims of historically racist policies of murder, removal, spatial concentration, theft of their land and resources, and limitation of their opportunities to make a living. Structures of racialized inequality run deep in these societies and discrimination against, and stereotyping of, indigenous people persist.

The claims to cultural freedom and autonomy of many groups, moreover, often stand in for or derive added resonance from grievances deriving from structural relations of privilege and disadvantage. The claims of many Muslims that they should be free to wear headscarves or make their prayer calls in the European cities where they live should not be divorced from the marginalized status of the majority of members of these groups in labor markets and political institutions.

Bringing such conflicts squarely under a liberal paradigm, as do most formulations of the societal culture approach, suppresses these structural issues of exploitation, marginalization, and normalization as they underlie some of these debates about accommodation to cultural difference. In most political contexts, claims for cultural recognition are not asserted nor are they disputed purely for their own sake. They are part of demands for political inclusion or economic opportunity, under circumstances where these are systematically limited for many members of groups defined as different from the dominant norms.

The liberal paradigm under which the societal culture model operates narrows the account of politics and difference in another significant way. It presumes that political struggle is about state policy primarily, and thus fails to find non-state institutions as locations of injustice and sites of struggle for redress.

The societal culture model generally assumes a simple model of political community as consisting of what is public – which coincides with what is under the administrative regulation of the state, and what is private, which is everything else. Under this liberal model, the main questions are: What shall the state permit, support, or require, and what shall it discourage or forbid? Most of the issues and debates about politics and cultural difference in recent political theoretical literature concern state policy in that way. Shall the state allow or even support cultural autonomy? Should the state allow exemptions from some of its regulations for the sake of respecting cultural or religious difference? Can granting special language rights be compatible with shared political community? Can religious expression be allowed in state-sponsored institutions? Are special rights of group representation in political bodies of the state compatible with a principle of equal political rights? Framing questions of the politics of difference largely in terms of what the state should or should not do ignores civil society as an arena of action, institutional decision-making, policy, and struggle which is very important to causing injustice and making change to remedy it.[30]

The assumption that politics concerns only what the state allows, requires or forbids, moreover, can generate serious misunderstanding about positions taken by proponents of a politics of difference, particularly within the structural inequality model. Brian Barry is once again a case in point. He quotes disapprovingly my claim in *Justice and the Politics of Difference* that "no social practices or activities should be excluded as improper subjects for public discussion, expression and collective choice,"

Iris M. Young

and then cites Robert Fullinwider's interpretation of this statement to the effect that I advocate political intervention and modification into "private choices."[31]

The specter that Barry and Fullinwider fear is limitation of individual liberty backed by state sanction. Apparently they envision no object of public discussion and collective choice other than state policies and laws. Certainly these are important objects of public discussion and choice in a democracy. A political theory concerned with the production and reproduction of structural inequalities even when laws guarantee formally equal rights, however, must shine its light on other corners as well. Movements of African Americans, people with disabilities, feminists, gay men and lesbians, indigenous people, as well as many ethnic movements, realize that societal discrimination, processes of segregation, and marginalization enacted through social networks and private institutions must be confronted in their non-state institutional sites. While law can provide a framework for equality, and some remedy for egregious violations of rights and respect, the state and law cannot and should not reach into every capillary of everyday life. A politics of difference seeking to undermine structural inequalities thus recommends that churches, universities, production and marketing enterprises, clubs and associations all examine their policies, practices, and priorities to discover ways they contribute to unjust structures and recommends changing them when they do. Such a position is not tantamount to calling the culture Gestapo to police every joke or bathroom design. Many of the social changes brought about by these movements in the last thirty years have involved actions on the part of many people that were voluntary, in the sense that they were neither required nor encouraged by state policy. Indeed, state policy as often follows on action within civil society directed at undermining structural inequality as leads it.[32]

Seyla Benhabib distinguishes such a "dual track" approach to politics, which she associates with critical theory, and argues that liberal political theory typically ignores non-state dimensions of politics.

> In deliberative democracy, as distinguished from politic liberalism, the *official* public sphere of representative institutions, which includes the legislature, executive and public bureaucracies, the judiciary and political parties, is not the only site of political contestation and of opinion and will formation. Deliberative democracy focuses on social movements, and on the civil, cultural, religious, artistic, and political associations of the *unofficial* public sphere, as well.[33]

Barry and others who consider issues of difference under a liberal paradigm, ignores this unofficial public sphere of contestation and action, and thus "attempts to solve multicultural conflicts through a juridical calculus of liberal rights."[34] A conception of justice able to criticize relations of domination and limitation of opportunity suffered by gender, racialized, ethnic, or religious groups must consider relations within private activities and civil society and their interaction with state institutions.[35]

Bringing issues of the politics of difference under a liberal paradigm, finally, tends to recast them in terms of questions of toleration. In this logic, a tendency to pose issues of the politics of difference in terms of societal culture and applying to them liberal theory tends to reinforce each other. The question of difference in a liberal society is what sorts of differences in beliefs and practices can we allow, tolerate, and what not. The primary social group differences visible in that question are religious and ethno-cultural differences. Structured differences in access to spaces, opportunities for the development of capacities, or interactive styles are irrelevant to this question.

Framing issues of difference in terms of toleration, however, often introduces a normalizing logic into debates about multiculturalism. The logic of the questions and arguments, that is, tends to presume a point of view of a normal, majority culture debating among themselves just how far they can go in accommodation to and affirmation of a culture marked as deviant. As such debates are theorized, they seem not to include the point of view of those persons whose beliefs or practices are at issue. The idea of toleration, moreover, implies a limit beyond which some practices are intolerable. From the point of view of persons whose activities are the subject of such debates, however, it is often demeaning to be positioned as deviants in this way, even when some actions or practices are contested among themselves.

A funny thing often happens to gender issues when the societal culture model of difference politics frames its debates under this logic of toleration. In many writings on multiculturalism, gender issues serve as tests to the limits of toleration. Can we tolerate rules of a national minority that refuse to recognize the women who marry outside the group as members? Can we allow communities and families to expect or pressure women to cover their heads in public? Surely we cannot permit arranged marriages of teenage women or genital cutting under any circumstances?

In calling attention to the role that gender issues often play in liberal debates about accommodation to cultural and religious groups, I do not aim to take positions on these particular questions. I bring this up as an instance of a construction of normal and deviant that often appears in these debates, and which positions gender issues quite differently from the way the structural inequality model constructs them. On the structural inequality model, you will recall, feminism is a politics of difference. Because the social division of labor, gendered socialization, and norms of power and authoritativeness operate to limit the real opportunities of many women, a commitment to equality for women entails noticing some of these differences in policy and practice, in order to undermine their disadvantaging consequences.

When women's issues appear in the multicultural tolerance debates, however, they are invoked with a resonance of equality as sameness. The limit beyond which toleration should go, it is suggested, is one that denies that women should have the same rights as men. In these debates the position claimed by the normalizing "we" is a feminist position, suggesting that gender inequality is not a serious issue for the dominant cultures in Western liberal societies. These assumptions mask the gendered inequalities that persist in many institutions and practices.[36]

The purpose of this essay has been to clarify differences in approaches to political and theoretical debates about whether and to what extent justice calls for paying attention to rather than ignoring social group differences. I have argued that a societal cultural approach to a politics of difference has more occupied political theorists in recent years than a structural inequality approach. This trend is lamentable, I have suggested, because it tends to narrow the groups of concern to ethnic, national, and religious groups, and to limit the issues of justice at stake to those concerned with freedom and autonomy more than equal opportunity to develop capacities and live a life of well-being. Its reliance on a liberal paradigm, moreover, tends to limit

Iris M. Young

politics to state policy and to reintroduce normalizing discourses into what began as denormalizing movements. My objective in making these distinctions and arguments has not been to reject the societal culture model, but to encourage political theorists to recommit their attention to group differences generated from structures of power and the division of labor, as they continue also to reflect on conflicts over national or religious difference.

Notes

1   Editors' note: This essay was completed in draft form at the time of Prof. Young's death. She intended to revise the piece further, although a version of these same ideas was produced for a *Multiculturalism and Political Theory*, ed. Anthony Laden and David Owen (Cambridge: Cambridge University Press, 2007). With the permission of Prof. Young's literary executor, David Alexander, we are including this essay in the form we received it. In our judgment, this is a polished and valuable essay that raises important issues about the politics of difference and social identities; we therefore present it here with the caveat that its author would likely have made further changes to it had she been given the chance. We have made minor typographical changes and completed the bibliographical citations without notation; any other changes are duly indicated in notes.

2   I have elaborated a notion of structural group difference and structural inequality in several previous writings. See *Inclusion and Democracy* (Oxford: Oxford University Press, 2000), pp. 92–102; "Equality of Whom? Social Groups and Judgments of Injustice," *Journal of Political Philosophy* 9 (Mar. 2001): 1–18; I elaborate these three axes of structural inequality – division of labor, decision-making power, and fit with hegemonic norms – in two recent papers. See "Lived Body vs. Gender: Reflections on Social Structure and Subjectivity," *Ratio* 15 (4) (Dec. 2002): 410–28 and "Taking the Basic Structure Seriously," *Perspectives on Politics* 4 (2006): 91–7; see also my essay "Gender as Seriality: Thinking about Women as a Social Collective," in Iris Marion Young, *Intersecting Voices: Dilemmas of Gender, Political Philosophy, and Policy* (Princeton, NJ: Princeton University Press, 1997).

3   Charles Tilly, *Durable Inequality* (Berkeley, CA: University of California Press, 1999).

4   Substantive equality of opportunity means more than not being formally prevented from pursuing projects or competing for goods. It means be able, both because of the skills and dispositions one has developed, and because of the relations one has with others, to enact a plan for oneself among a range of reasonable options. For one theory of substantive equality of opportunity, see John Roemer, *Equality of Opportunity* (Cambridge, MA: Harvard University Press, 1999).

5   I have argued that so-called merit standards often normalize attributes, comportments, or attainments associated with social groups, and thus often do not serve the impartial purpose they claim. See my *Justice and the Politics of Difference* (Princeton, NJ: Princeton University Press, 1990), Ch. 7; Brian Barry rebuts this critique in *Cultural and Equality* (Cambridge: Polity Press, 2001), pp. 90–102; For a good reply to Barry on these points from the point of view of a structural inequality approach to a politics of difference, see Paul Kelly, "Defending Some Dodos: Equality and/or Liberty?," in Paul Kelly, ed., *Multiculturalism Reconsidered* (Cambridge: Polity Press, 2002), pp. 62–80; see also Clare Chambers, "All Must Have Prizes: The Liberal Case of Interference in Cultural Practices," in the same volume, pp. 151–73.

6   Barry, *Cultural and Equality*, p. 95.

7   See Lewis Gordon, *Bad Faith and Anti-Black Racism* (Atlantic Highlands, NJ: Humanities Press, 1995).

8   See Glen Loury, *Anatomy of Racial Inequality* (Cambridge, MA: Harvard University Press, 2002).

9   See Iris Marion Young, *Inclusion and Democracy*, Ch. 6.

10 See Christine Battersby, *The Phenomenal Woman: Feminist Metaphysics and the Patterns of Identity* (New York: Routledge, 1998).

11 In another place I discuss some of the stigma and disadvantage that comes to women because institutions often fail to accommodate menstruation. See "Menstrual Meditations," in *On Female Body Experience: "Throwing Like a Girl" and Other Essays* (New York: Oxford University Press, 2005).

12 Susan Okin, *Justice, Gender and the Family* (New York: Basic Books, 1989).

13 Kymlicka, *Multicultural Citizenship*, p. 19; cf. Kymlicka, *Liberalism, Community and Culture* (Oxford: Oxford University Press, 1989).

14 Kymlicka, *Multicultural Citizenship*, p. 18.

15 On culture as a context of self formation and choice, see Charles Taylor, *Multiculturalism and the "Politics of Recognition"* (Princeton, NJ: Princeton University Press, 1992) and Yael Tamir, *Liberal Nationalism* (Princeton, NJ: Princeton University Press, 1993).

16 In addition to writings already cited: Jacob Levy, *The Multiculturalism of Fear* (Oxford: Oxford University Press, 2000); Bhikhu Parekh, *Rethinking Multiculturalism* (Cambridge, MA: Harvard University Press, 2000); Joseph Carens, *Culture, Citizenship, and Community: A Contextual Exploration of Justice as Evenhandedness* (Oxford: Oxford University Press, 2000).

17 See especially Jeff Spinner-Halev, *Surviving Diversity: Religion and Democratic Citizenship* (Baltimore, MD: Johns Hopkins University Press, 2000).

18 "Social Justice in the Age of Identity Politics," in Nancy Fraser and Axel Honneth, *Redistriubution or Recognition? A Political-Philosophical Exchange* (London: Verso, 2003): 7–109.

19 See Iris Marion Young, "Unruly Categories: A Critique of Nancy Fraser's Dual Systems Theory," *New Left Review* I/222 (Mar.–Apr. 1997): 147–60.

20 See Melissa S. Williams, *Voice, Trust, and Equality* (Princeton, NJ: Princeton University Press, 1997).

21 Anne Phillips, "The Politics of Presence," in Ricardo Blaug and John J. Schwarzmantel, eds., *Democracy: A Reader* (New York: Columbia University Press, 2001): 161–4.

22 Young, *Justice and the Politics of Difference*, p. 23.

23 I take some steps in this direction in "Taking the Basic Structure Seriously."

24 Pierre Bourdieu, *Distinction: A Social Critique of the Judgement of Taste* (Cambridge, MA: Harvard University Press, 1984).

25 Kymlicka, *Multicultural Citizenship*, p. 18.

26 Prof. Young indicated that she intended to expand on this observation in further revisions of her paper (Eds.).

27 Seyla Benhabib, *The Claims of Culture: Equality and Diversity in the Global Era* (Princeton, NJ: Princeton University Press, 2002).

28 See my *Inclusion and Democracy*, pp. 102–7.

29 See Iris Marion Young, "Structure, Difference, and Hispanic/Latino Claims of Justice," in Jorge J. E. Gracia and Pablo de Greiff, *Hispanics/Latinos in the United States: Ethnicity, Race and Rights* (New York: Routledge, 2000), pp. 147–66.

30 In Ch. 5 of *Inclusion and Democracy* I further discuss the virtues and limitations of action in civil society for remedying injustice.

31 Barry, *Culture and Equality*.

32 Brian Barry also blanches at the assertion I make in *Justice and the Politics of Difference* that the remedy for normalizing social processes is "cultural revolution." In this phrase, which I borrowed from Julia Kristeva, "culture" carries the first of the two meanings I

discussed in the previous section. It refers to modes of comportment, gestures, speech styles and other modes of communication and how people understand these. "Revolution" may be an overly dramatic term. Eliminating ways that women, people with disabilities, or poor people are sometimes denigrated, however, among other things requires changing some symbolic meanings and interactive habits of some people. In her reaction to the phrase "cultural revolution" Amy Gutmann also manifests an assumption that state and law are the primary motors of social change to undermine injustice.

33 Benhabib, *The Claims of Culture*, p. 21.
34 Benhabib, *The Claims of Culture*, p. 21.
35 See also Benhabib, *The Claims of Culture*, pp. 118–21.
36 Prof. Young indicated in her draft text that she intended to expand on this point (Eds.).

GLOBAL JUSTICE

COSMOPOLITANISM

Cosmopolitanism and Justice

Simon Caney[1]

[T]hese Gentleman have formed a plan of Geographical morality, by which the duties of men in public and in private situations are not to be governed by their relations to the Great Governor of the Universe, or by their relations to men, but by climates, degrees of longitude and latitude, parallels not of life but of latitudes. As if, when you have crossed the equinoctial line all the virtues die.... This Geographical morality we do protest against. (Edmund Burke, "Speech on Opening of Impeachment" (of Warren Hastings), February 16, 1788, in Burke 1788 [1999]: 221)

> I am
> a Jew. Hath not a Jew eyes? hath not a Jew
> hands, organs, dimensions, senses, affections, passions?
> fed with the same food, hurt with the
> same weapons, subject to the same diseases,
> healed by the same means, warmed and cooled
> by the same winter and summer, as a Christian
> is? If you prick us, do we not bleed? if you
> tickle us, do we not laugh? if you poison us,
> do we not die?
> (Shylock, *The Merchant of Venice*, Act 3, Scene 1, lines 56–65)

The world is characterized by extensive global poverty and marked inequalities. In addition to this, the Earth's climate is undergoing profound changes and the rising sea-levels – increased temperatures and increase in unpredictable weather events will have dramatic effects on the basic interests of many. These phenomena prompt the question of whether there are global principles of distributive justice. It has traditionally been assumed that principles of distributive justice apply, if they apply at all, within a state. Debates about distributive justice have often taken it for granted that the scope of distributive justice is set by the borders of the state (or the nation) and the focus has been more on what distributive principle is appropriate as well as on what should be distributed. The concept of international justice, in this context, referred not to any principles of distributive justice but to principles of non-intervention and just war theory (Rawls 1999a: 331–3). In recent years, however, a number of political philosophers have defended a "cosmopolitan" account of distributive justice. They have, that is, argued that there are global principles of distributive justice, which include all individuals within their scope. In this chapter I shall provide an analysis of some leading cosmopolitan perspectives on distributive justice and also provide some support for what I take to be a compelling version of it.

I: Three Conceptions of Cosmopolitanism

§1.

It is necessary to start with a further clarification and elaboration of the concept of cosmopolitanism. Cosmopolitanism affirms that persons are "citizens of the world." Such ideas have an ancient lineage. It is said of Diogenes the Cynic that when he was "[a]sked where he came from, he said, 'I am a citizen of the world'" (Diogenes Laërtius 1931: 65). For Diogenes the Cynic, "[t]he only true commonwealth was, he said, that which is as wide as the universe" (ibid.: 75). These ideas were taken further by Stoic thinkers such as Cicero, Seneca, Plutarch, Epictetus, and the Roman emperor Marcus Aurelius. All of the latter affirmed the ideal of being a citizen of the world. Persons, on this view, are not simply citizens of their city-state – rather their country is the whole world (indeed the cosmos).

Cosmopolitan ideals were also commonly invoked during the Enlightenment and political philosophers of very different hues identified themselves as cosmopolitans. Both Jeremy Bentham and Immanuel Kant, for example, adopted a cosmopolitan perspective. Thus Bentham begins his essay on the "Objects of International Law" by asking what a citizen of the world would want: "If a citizen of the world had to prepare an universal international code, what would he propose to himself as his object? It would be the common and equal utility of all nations" (1843 [1786–9]: 537). Furthermore, Immanuel Kant invokes the cosmopolitan ideal and affirms some (minimal) principles of "cosmopolitan right" in his essay on "Perpetual Peace" (1989 [1795]: 105–8).

§2.

My focus is, however, on contemporary cosmopolitan theories which, though they share a commitment to the concept of world citizenship, provide different interpretations of this ideal to that offered by either ancient or Enlightenment cosmopolitan thinkers. Focusing now wholly on contemporary cosmopolitanism, it is important to draw attention to three distinct kinds of cosmopolitanism – what I shall term juridical cosmopolitanism, ethical cosmopolitanism, and political cosmopolitanism.

Juridical cosmopolitanism is a claim about the scope and nature of distributive justice. It maintains that there are global principles of distributive justice that include all persons in their scope. Put slightly differently, what I have termed juridical cosmopolitanism (and what others like Samuel Scheffler call "cosmopolitanism about

Simon Caney

justice" (Scheffler 2001: esp. 111)) avers that the scope of some principles of distributive justice should include all persons within their remit. We are all citizens of the world in the sense that we should all be included within a common scheme of distributive justice. This view stands opposed to those who maintain that distributive justice applies only among members of the same nation or state. This kind of cosmopolitanism is affirmed by a variety of different thinkers. In *Political Theory and International Relations* (1999) Charles Beitz draws on Rawls's theory of justice and argues that there should be a global difference principle. Furthermore, Henry Shue argues in *Basic Rights* (1996) that there is a human right to subsistence which entails negative duties on others not to deprive them and positive duties to provide such subsistence if it be necessary. To give a third example, Thomas Pogge's more recent *World Poverty and Human Rights* (2008) provides an argument for the existence of global principles of distributive justice.

Consider now a second kind of cosmopolitanism – what I have termed ethical cosmopolitanism. Whereas juridical cosmopolitanism is a claim (or set of claims) about the right, ethical cosmopolitanism is a claim (or set of claims) about the good. Ethical cosmopolitanism holds that persons are citizens of the world in the sense that to flourish one need not conform to the traditional ways of life of one's community. Flourishing may include (and, on some construals, should include) drawing on aspects of other cultures. A fine example of this is Jeremy Waldron's important essay on "Minority Cultures and The Cosmopolitan Alternative." In this Waldron celebrates the ideal of someone who draws on ideas and beliefs from a variety of different countries (Waldron 1992). Scheffler refers to a similar view and terms it "cosmopolitanism about culture" (Scheffler 2001: esp. 111). Although the kind of cosmopolitanism at stake undoubtedly raises questions about culture I think that this title is rather misleading. It is worth distinguishing between two different aspects of any culture – those aspects which concern what makes life fulfilling (the views about the good life that are embedded in the culture) and those aspects which concern the functioning of the political system (what political scientists term "political culture"). Now Waldron and Scheffler's concerns are about the first kind (they are interested in the tenability of a cosmopolitan ideal of the good life) but, as the concept of "political culture" attests, not all cultural questions are concerned with the good life.

Consider now finally what is often called political cosmopolitanism.[2] This holds that there should be supra-state political institutions. So this kind of cosmopolitanism maintains that persons are citizens of the world in the sense that there should be political institutions that encompass all. One version of political cosmopolitanism holds, for example, that there should be a system of multilevel governance, in which there are supra-state institutions, state-like institutions, and sub-state political structures (Pogge 2008: Ch. 7; cf. also Caney 2005a: Ch. 5, 2006).

§3.

With these three kinds of cosmopolitanism in hand, we should now note that each of them comes in a mild or a radical form.[3] The mild version of juridical cosmopolitanism, for example, holds (i) that there are some universal principles of distributive justice which include all within their scope but it also (ii) allows that there might be some national-level or state-level principles of distributive justice. The radical form of juridical cosmopolitanism, by contrast holds affirms (i) but denies (ii). The same distinction might be applied to political cosmopolitanism. The mild version (i) holds that there should be some global political institutions and (ii) allows that there might be some national-level or state-level political institutions. Again the radical version – encapsulated in the view that there should be a world state – affirms (i) but denies (ii). Finally, to complete the survey we can apply the same distinction to ethical cosmopolitanism. The mild version holds (i) that the "cosmopolitan" conception of the good is a fulfilling conception of the good and (ii) allows that more "local" conceptions of the good might also be fulfilling conception of the good. The radical version, by contrast, affirms (i) and denies (ii).

Some have argued that mild juridical cosmopolitanism is not a helpful category on the grounds that on this definition pretty much everyone is a cosmopolitan (Miller 2002: 975). I believe that this is mistaken. In the first place, we should note that the cosmopolitan claims not simply that there are global principles of distributive justice (which is compatible with states having duties of distributive justice to other states): it requires that they apply principles of distributive justice to all *individuals*. Given this, applying a mild cosmopolitanism would require a radical transformation in the way that powerful states act in the world and may (depending on what global principles are affirmed) require considerable changes to the power and role of international institutions. It also bears noting that this approach would be denied by very many different schools of thought. It stands opposed to almost all "realist" thinking (perhaps the dominant approach among international relations scholars). It would be rejected by those who adhere to the ideal of a society of states. In addition to this it is incompatible with Michael Walzer's account of the scope of justice (1983) and John Rawls's treatment in *The Law of Peoples* (1999b). Mild cosmopolitanism is also denied by Thomas Nagel (2005). So the idea that mild cosmopolitanism is a commonplace is, regrettably, not the case. Perhaps the most important point is this, however. Whether the mild view is banal and overly inclusive depends on (a) its content and (b) its moral weight. If, for example, a mild cosmopolitanism affirms an ultra minimal content then it is more open to the charge that it is saying something that pretty much anyone can accept, whereas one that affirms, say, fairly egalitarian principles would not. Similarly, a mild cosmopolitan who affirms cosmopolitan principles that are very easily overridden is, again, failing to provide a distinctive viewpoint. Mild cosmopolitanism is only an uninteresting view if it is committed to rather weak and anodyne principles that no one disputes. It can take this form but there is no reason why it should.

II: Two Kinds of Juridical Cosmopolitanism

Let us turn now to juridical cosmopolitanism. A number of different kinds of cosmopolitanism have been proposed. It is worth distinguishing, in particular, between two approaches to cosmopolitan distributive justice.

First, some argue that principles of distributive justice apply to persons who belong to a common "scheme", where I use the word "scheme" as a catch-all phrase to refer to some kind of systematic interaction and interdependence. Proponents of this approach then argue that there is a global scheme and hence, there are global principles of

Simon Caney

distributive justice that include all persons in their jurisdiction. On this approach, one may have humanitarian duties to non-members but one does not have duties of distributive justice to them. Put otherwise: this view maintains that the scope of principles of distributive justice is defined in terms of who belong to which schemes. Let us term this the "interdependence-based" conception. Sophisticated versions of this kind of argument have been advanced by Charles Beitz (1999) and Thomas Pogge (1989, 2008) and we shall turn to their arguments shortly.

Prior to doing so we should introduce a second kind of approach. This second kind holds that principles of distributive justice should apply globally irrespective of whether a global scheme exists. It simply holds that all persons, qua human beings, should be included within the scope of justice. It is motivated by a commitment to the dignity of persons and the sentiments eloquently expressed by Shylock in the quotation at the start of this chapter. Let us term this the "humanity-based" conception.[4] On this account, one might have a natural duty of justice to aid others, regardless of whether they are in one's scheme or not (Buchanan 1990, 2004: cf. also Caney 2005a, 2007). One has obligations of justice to others because they are fellow human beings – with human needs and failings, and human capacities for, and interests, in autonomy and well-being – and facts about interdependence do not, in themselves, determine the scope of distributive justice. One early statement of this view comes from David Richards. He reasoned that all persons, in virtue of their humanity, should be included in a global original position (Richards 1982).[5] Of course, consequentialist theories also fit into this mold. Since they maintain that utility should be maximized they attribute no fundamental moral importance to national or state boundaries (Singer 2002).[6]

The two kinds of cosmopolitanism differ, then, in the concepts of "moral personality" that they employ.[7] Whereas the second maintains that persons have entitlements simply qua human persons and in virtue of their humanity, the first maintains that persons have entitlements qua members of a socioeconomic scheme. Since they differ in their account of moral personality they will sometimes differ in their account of the scope of distributive justice. If there is a truly global "scheme" (however that term is defined) then they will converge, but if there is not then their conclusions about the scope of distributive justice will diverge.

III: Beitz on Cosmopolitan Justice

With these two accounts in mind, let us consider two eminent versions of the first approach. The first major attempt to argue in this way was developed by Charles Beitz in *Political Theory and International Relations* (1999) – originally published in 1979. Beitz sought to argue that Rawls's theory of justice should lead us to embrace a global difference principle. Beitz thus accepts, like Rawls, that principles of distributive justice apply to what Rawls terms the "basic structure" (Rawls 1999a: 6–10). He then argues, however, that such is the extent of global interaction and interdependence that there is in fact a global basic structure. Drawing on a large empirical literature, Beitz claims that Rawls's assumption that societies were self-contained is false. The extent of trade and communication and the growth of transnational regimes and institutions is such that we can now say that we are living in a global basic structure. In the light of this, Rawls's approach should commit us to adopting a global original position, and, given Rawls's argument, it would follow that there should be a global difference principle (1999: 143–53).

Beitz's argument raises several questions. The first concerns the extent of interdependence at the global level. As Beitz points out, it would be implausible to think that a tiny bit of trade is sufficient to make the difference principle applicable. As he notes, it would be implausible to think that one country selling some apples to another country in exchange for some pears suffices to establish that there should be a transnational difference principle (Beitz 1999: 165). Beitz infers from this that a global difference principle is applicable only if the volume and intensity of interdependence reaches a certain level. He suggests that there is "a threshold of interdependence above which distributive requirements like a global difference principle are valid, but below which significantly weaker principles hold" (1999: 165, 165–7). This raises two further questions. First, what degree of global integration must exist for a global difference principle to come into play? This is not simply a practical problem but a philosophical one. We lack any criteria as to where to draw the line and it is not clear how we would go about deriving such criteria. But we need such a criterion if Beitz's derivation of a global difference principle is to succeed. Second, what principle applies at the sub-threshold level of integration? How would we ascertain such a principle? Again we appear to lack any method for deriving that principle or principles. Beitz's account of the relationship between the level of economic integration and the content of global distributive justice is inherently problematic for it cannot tell us when a global difference principle or any other principle is appropriate.

Second, and even more fundamentally, one might ask why principles of distributive justice should apply to the members of a basic structure.[8] Why does the scope of distributive justice depend in this way on whether there is a global or non-global basic structure? Beitz's answer is an orthodox Rawlsian one. The basic structure matters because of its impact on people's lives. It affects the extent to which people can realize their interests (Rawls 1999a: 7; Beitz 1999: 166, 201). However, to say this is to ascribe importance as to whether people can enjoy their interests. It is to be concerned with realizing certain outcomes. Now if this is the case then we have a moral reason to assist in the furtherance of these interests *whether or not we are in the same scheme as them*. If we ascribe importance to whether persons can engage in the activities in which they have an interest then this should surely bear not simply on how the basic structure is organized but also on the behavior of those who are external to it but who may be able to have a considerable effect on those interests (Caney 2007: 283).[9]

IV: Pogge on Cosmopolitan Justice

Given these problems let us turn to a second interdependence-based account of cosmopolitanism – that advanced by Thomas Pogge. Pogge has developed his arguments in many articles and in the last part of *Realizing Rawls* (1989: Part III). His most systematic exposition of his arguments is, however, in his book justly influential book *World Poverty and Human Rights* (first published in 2002 and then published in an

Simon Caney

expanded version in 2008). In the latter Pogge makes the following three claims. *First*, he maintains (very plausibly) that agents have a negative duty of justice not to participate in unjust social practices or institutions. Pogge sometimes presents this as a negative duty not to harm others. This requires an analysis of "harm". This leads us to the second component of Pogge's argument. *Second*, Pogge argues that we should think of harm as follows. Harm is defined in terms of (i) those impacts on human rights that (ii) are produced by social institutions. Furthermore, Pogge's focus is on (iii) the duty of those who create and uphold these social institutions. Finally, Pogge maintains than an institution is harmful only if its malign effects on human rights are (iv) "foreseeable", (v) "reasonably avoidable" and (vi) the creators/upholders of the institutions know that these institutions can be designed to avoid these malign effects.[10] Now, if we put Pogge's claim that there is a negative duty not to harm with this account of harm we reach the conclusion that agents are under a negative duty of justice not to create or uphold institutions which foreseeably and avoidably result in a "human rights deficit" (2008: 26).

Pogge's *third* step is an empirical one. He argues that we are living in a "global institutional order" (2008: 15). Global practices and rules have an enormous effect on people's lives and the security of their rights. Many, of course, resist such a claim, arguing that human rights abuses stem from "local" variables – such as corrupt elites and despotic rulers. However, Pogge makes a good case for thinking that global rules often encourage such unjust forms of governance. He persuasively argues, for example, that the assumption that the government of a country is entitled to take out loans ("the international borrowing privilege") and that it is entitled to sell the resources within its jurisdiction ("the international resource privilege") fuel unjust regimes (2008: 118–21).

Now if we combine these three tenets, then we reach the conclusion that agents have a negative duty of justice not to uphold a global order which foreseeably and avoidably fails to secure human rights. Agents have a duty to eradicate global poverty – not because they have a positive duty of justice to aid the needy – but because there is a negative duty of justice not to impose such unjust rules on the rest of the world.

Pogge's work is rich and rewarding and merits more analysis than I can give it here. The negative duty of justice that he postulates is a compelling one. In addition to this his analysis of the ways in which international practices contribute to poverty is persuasive. Furthermore, since we often ascribe greater moral importance to honoring negative duties than to positive duties, Pogge's use of negative duties of justice gives it an important motivational advantage over other arguments.

One potential problem with Pogge's account concerns how much global poverty it can address. Though Pogge has made a good case for thinking that affluent states and international rules play a major role in causing global poverty, there are other relevant causal variables – including (a) the nature and policies of states in developing countries and (b) geographical factors. To start with (a): as Pogge would recognize, some global poverty stems, in part, from corrupt or misconceived policies adopted by states in developing countries and their corruption or incompetence is not wholly explicable by global variables. So local actors must bear some responsibility. Turning now to (b), Jeffrey Sachs and Paul Collier have both argued that geographical factors play a causal role in the production of global poverty (Collier 2007: Ch. 4; Sachs 2005: 57–9; Sachs 2008: 212–17; Gallup et al. 1999). Two causal factors, in particular, are emphasized. First, both argue that whether a country is land-locked or not makes a significant contribution to whether it is impoverished or not (Collier 2007, Chapter 4; Gallup et al. 1999, esp. p. 184). Second, Sachs has argued that malaria contributes to economic underdevelopment and so those who live in malaria-prone areas are disadvantaged by that fact (Sachs 2005: 196–9; Sachs 2008: 216–17; Gallup and Sachs 2001: 85–96).

This has the upshot that even if affluent states honor their negative duty of justice there are like to be some, perhaps many, living in grinding and degrading poverty (Caney 2007: 291ff.) – people impoverished because of government corruption or incompetence or because of an inhospitable climate or their geographical location. Pogge's theory cannot, therefore, eradicate global poverty. To do that it needs to be supplemented by positive duties. Furthermore, it is not clear why Pogge eschews positive duties of justice and whether he can consistently do so. To see whether he can we need to know what rationale he has for adhering to his negative duty of justice not to impose an order on others. If, for example, the argument is that persons have vital needs which would be unmet if people imposed an unjust order on them the obvious response is that if we attribute fundamental significance to people having their needs met then we should also accept some positive duties of justice (Buchanan 2004: 89–92).

V: Cosmopolitanism and Humanity

§1.

Let us turn now to a second kind of juridical cosmopolitanism – what I termed earlier a "humanity-centered" conception. Why adopt this approach? The best argument in favor of this humanity-centered conception of cosmopolitan justice starts from the observation that there is a strong conviction that persons should not fare worse in life because of morally arbitrary characteristics such as their ethnicity or their religion or their regional identity. Distributive justice, we hold, should be blind to such features of persons. This is evident in our understanding of equality of opportunity. Here we hold that certain factors – someone's class or ethnicity – should not bear on their opportunities. Now humanity-centered cosmopolitanism adopts the same intuition and concludes that persons should not also face worse opportunities because of their nationality or their citizenship. To do so would also be to penalize people for morally arbitrary reasons.

Thus far this argument is in agreement with those cosmopolitans who hold that principles of distributive justice only apply within economic schemes. Pogge, for example, has famously argued that national boundaries are morally arbitrary. In an oft-quoted passage he writes that "[n]ationality is just one further deep contingency (like genetic endowment, race, gender, and social class)" (1989: 247). In a similar spirit Darrel Moellendorf writes that "[s]ince one's place of birth is morally arbitrary, it should not affect one's life prospects or one's access to opportunities" (2002: 55). On this humanity-based cosmopolitans and interdependence-based cosmopolitans are agreed.

However, humanity-centered cosmopolitanism then argues that the reasoning that both types of cosmopolitanism employ to criticize the moral relevance of national boundaries also shows that the boundaries of economic schemes are also morally arbitrary. If one's "place of birth is morally arbitrary" (Moellendorf) then surely one's birth into one institutional scheme rather than another is also arbitrary and thus should also not "affect one's life prospects" (Moellendorf). To ascribe differential entitlements to people because of their membership of different schemes is to penalize some for morally arbitrary reasons. Isn't one's membership of a scheme "just one further deep contingency" (Pogge)?

This argument might be presented in a different way. Theories of justice comprise, at least, two components – an entitlement-bearer component (that specifies who is entitled to what) and a duty-bearer component (that specifies who is duty-bound to do what). Let us focus first on the entitlement-bearer component. Judged from an entitlement-bearer perspective, it is hard to see why membership of a "scheme" has any fundamental moral relevance. Compare two people – one in scheme A and one in scheme B. Suppose then that they are equally talented, equally needy, equally industrious, and so on. Judged from the entitlement-bearer perspective there is no reason why one should receive more or less than their counterpart. "Membership of a scheme" is a morally irrelevant factor (Barry 1989: 239). No one is entitled to more because of it for it does not correlate with any normal distributive criterion.

§2.

We gain a better understanding of this argument if we consider a recent criticism of it developed by David Miller. Miller argues that arguments to the effect that nationality is "moral arbitrary" rely on an ambiguity between two distinct notions of moral arbitrariness (Miller 2007: 32–3). On the one hand, moral arbitrariness is used as a premiss. Under this reading a feature is said to be morally arbitrary if it is one "for which people cannot be held morally responsible" (ibid.: 32). Let us call this version 1. Miller then says that sometimes referring to a property as morally arbitrary is to "signal the conclusion of the argument as opposed to its premise" (ibid.: 32). Calling a property morally arbitrary is to say that persons should not treat people differently on the basis of this property (ibid.: 32). Let us call this version 2. Miller's claim is that one cannot simply affirm version 2: we need an argument for it. But he also claims that version 1 does not support version 2.

He adds that it would if one introduced a new premiss (premiss 2 below) and reasoned as follows:

Argument A:
premiss 1: a person's nationality is a property for which she cannot be held morally responsible (version 1 arbitrariness)
premiss 2: if a property is one for which a person is nor morally responsible then it is wrong to treat them differently because of this property (new premiss)
Therefore:
Conclusion: it is wrong to treat persons differently because of their nationality (version 2 arbitrariness). (Miller 2007: 33)

However, as Miller points out, premiss 2 in this argument is obviously false. Consider someone who is in need. This is a property for which (let us stipulate) someone cannot be held morally responsible but at the same time it is not true that it is wrong to treat them differently to an able-bodied person because of this property (2007: 33). We ought to treat people differentially here. Premiss 2 is therefore incorrect. And the claim that that people are not morally responsible for their nationality does not show that it is a morally arbitrary fact about them.

I believe that this argument is unsuccessful for three reasons. First, and crucially, the cosmopolitans Miller has in mind do not, contra Miller, affirm Miller's second conception of moral arbitrariness. They do not hold that it is wrong to treat people differently because of morally irrelevant differences. What they hold is that it is wrong that people face worse opportunities because of morally irrelevant differences (what we might call version 3). So the (radical) cosmopolitan claim is that it is wrong that people face worse opportunities because of their nationality. That X is a member of one nation should not inform what entitlements they receive. Cosmopolitans are thus not seeking to establish the Conclusion as it is described in Argument A above.

This is crucial and if we bear this in mind we can see that the arbitrariness-inspired reasoning for cosmopolitanism sidesteps Miller's objection. For rather than offering Argument A, they will offer Argument B below, which reformulates the Conclusion and premiss 2 of Argument A in light of the point I have just made above. This argument reads as follows:

> *Argument B*:
> premiss 1: a person's nationality is a property for which she cannot be held morally responsible (version 1 arbitrariness)
> premiss 2*: if a property is one for which a person is nor morally responsible then it is wrong that they possess different entitlements because of this property (new premiss)
> Therefore:
> Conclusion*: it is wrong that persons possess different entitlements because of their nationality (version 3 arbitrariness)

Now if a humanity-centered cosmopolitan makes this argument, they can easily accommodate Miller's point about need. They can agree that neediness is (with the possible exception of some self-imposed harms) a property for which persons cannot be held responsible. However, and this is the crucial point, they can also agree with Miller's claim that the state should treat people differently because of this morally arbitrary property. Premiss 2* does not deny this. In fact premiss 2* emphatically affirms this point, calling for differential treatment so that no one is worse off because of morally arbitrary factors. Thus Argument B provides a valid argument that moves from the fact that people are not responsible for their nationality to the conclusion that nationality should not affect what opportunities they face in life.

This is sufficient to undermine Miller's argument. However, a second point is also worth noting. Miller's critique of cosmopolitan invocations of the morally arbitrary nature of nationality assumes that cosmopolitans must affirm his version 1 conception of moral arbitrariness. It is therefore worth noting that this is not the case. A cosmopolitan might eschew version 1 and affirm instead a fourth notion of moral arbitrariness where this fourth conception holds that a property is morally arbitrary if it does not track any morally relevant properties.[11] Employing this conception of "moral arbitrariness", someone may hold that nationality is morally arbitrary – not on the grounds that it is a property for which a person is not morally responsible (version 1) – but on the grounds that a person's nationality does not correspond to any morally relevant characteristics. There are a number of credible criteria that one might claim should inform who is entitled to what. The fact that someone is *needy* or that they are *talented* or *industrious* or that they are *performing an important task* are all quite reasonable possible grounds for distributing resources to them. (I am not endorsing any of these, just saying that they are at least plausible possible grounds.) But membership of a nation does not track any of these. To claim that I am entitled to some more because I have performed an unpleasant task (I have cleaned the sewers, say) or because I have worked very hard or because I am in great need are all reasonable candidates as entitlement-generating properties. To say I am entitled to more because I am Swedish, by contrast, is not. We lack a reason to think either that nationality is an entitlement-generating property or that it tracks some entitlement-generating property.[12] Let us call this Argument C.

Note that this argument is more ecumenical than Argument B. It does not rely on "luck egalitarian" sentiments such that no should be penalized because of properties for which they are not morally responsible. It can allow that people may be rewarded for properties (like talent) for which they are not morally responsible. Thus, unlike Argument A, it is compatible with a desert-based theory of justice (e.g., one that holds that people should be rewarded according to their talents). It just argues that nationality is morally arbitrary on the grounds that it does not map on to any standard or defensible distributive criteria.

In short, then, cosmopolitans can give two separate arbitrariness-inspired arguments for cosmopolitan justice, neither of which rest on the ambiguity that Miller identifies. It might be helpful to close the discussion here by reflecting on class or ethnicity because they illustrate the case for cosmopolitan justice. It is widely held that class and ethnicity are morally arbitrary and therefore should not inform people's entitlements. My claim is that a person's nationality should be thought of in an analogous fashion. The reasoning underlying the irrelevance of both class and ethnicity, on the one hand, and nationality, on the other, might be either (i) that these are properties which people are not morally responsible for possessing (à la Argument B) or (ii) that these properties do not track any morally relevant distributive criteria (à la Argument C). Whichever version we adopt, the point is that the examples of ethnicity and class illustrate a case where we all (including Miller) would see them as morally arbitrary and hence as factors which should not affect people's entitlements. Once we see that nationality is directly analogous to these two other categories we can make further sense of the moral arbitrariness of nationality.

§3.

Miller's argument is intended to undermine both interdependence-based and humanity-based cosmopolitanism. Let us now turn to a challenge to humanity-centered approach. Many, for example, think that it has highly counterintuitive implications. Moellendorf, for example, challenges this kind of approach on the grounds that it entails the conclusion that we owe obligations of justice to "intelligent beings with whom we have no intercourse but only an awareness of their existence – say, intelligent beings on the second planet orbiting some distant star" (2002: 31).

I do not think, however, that this is a persuasive argument. Consider four points in reply. First, it is worth noting that by referring to some "distant star" and to "intelligent beings" Moellendorf's argument runs together two issues – whether there are obligations of justice to nonhumans (are these intelligent beings aliens?) and whether there are obligations of justice to persons outside of our institutional framework. Reference to those on another planet thus unnecessarily muddies the water. Second, the fact (if it is a fact) that it is counterintuitive to hold that there are duties of distributive justice to persons on other planets can be explained by other considerations. In the first place, (i) we might very naturally think that it is not possible to help people on a "distant star," and if this is the case then (assuming that "ought implies can") we would conclude that we lack duties of distributive justice to those living on this other planet. In the second place, (ii) we might also think that even if it is it is possible to aid those on a distant star it would be unduly onerous. It is natural to think, for example, that to transport food supplies, medicines, or technology to people on a distant star would be very expensive. The thought that we lack obligations of distributive justice to those on a distant planet can thus be explained by (i) and (ii). Put otherwise: the claim that

(A) "we lack duties of distributive justice to persons on a distant planet"

does not then entail that

(B) "we lack duties of distributive justice to all who live outside of our 'scheme'."

There are reasons which explain (A) which do not entail (B).

Given these first two points, a better way to test the intuition that Moellendorf is advancing would be to consider the following example. Imagine a situation with the following four features. First, there are persons who live outside of our scheme and with whom we have no link. They live on an island and neither we nor anyone else in our scheme have any diplomatic or trade links with them. We also have no impact on their environment. It is not the case, for example, that we are emitting greenhouse gases which lead to dangerous climate change or that we are destroying the ozone layer. Imagine too that we are not preventing them coming to us. The waters between us and them are perilous and they are unable to traverse them but this inability on their part stems wholly from natural obstacles. In short we have absolutely no contact with them at all. Second, let us suppose that they are badly off. Third, suppose that we know of their existence (we can see what they do across the channel that divides us by looking through telescopes). Fourth, and finally, suppose that we can in fact help them and at a reasonable cost. We are both extremely wealthy and we have the know-how to eradicate their poverty.

This, I think, is a better example to use than the distant planet example. It makes it clear that those involved are human beings. Furthermore, by making clear that those outside the scheme can help and can do so at a reasonable cost, it overcomes the limitations of the distant planet example. It makes us focus on what is at stake here – should someone's membership or not of our scheme settle whether they are included within the scope of distributive justice or not? Once we reflect on this situation and we bear in mind the moral arbitrariness of being on one side of the channel as opposed to the other it does not seem counterintuitive to hold that those in the wealthy scheme have duties of distributive justice to alleviate the poverty

Simon Caney

across the channel.[13] None of the orthodox distributive criteria – such as distribution according to need or to desert – could give us reason to exclude them from the scope of justice. The difference between the needy on the mainland and the needy on the island is simply their different physical location and this is hardly a morally significant property.

§4.

Two further points bear noting about the humanity-centered approach. First, although it holds that the *scope* of principles of distributive justice is not determined by whether a global scheme exists or not it need not deny that the extent to which there is global interdependence does have moral relevance. Indeed it can recognize that facts about global interdependence have moral relevance in three distinct ways. The extent of global integration affects (i) the *content* of distributive justice and the magnitude of people's entitlements, (ii) the type of *duty* of justice that people are under, and (iii) the *moral weight* of the duty of justice that people are under.[14] Let us examine each in turn, starting with (i). Consider needy people who live in a remote section of Indonesia and suppose that while Indonesia is within a global scheme, there are, at time t1, only rather minimal trade and transport links with the rest of the world. Suppose now that the intensity of trade between the rest of the world and Indonesia increases such that at time t2 it is much easier to further the interests of these impoverished Indonesians. Now in virtue of this increased contact one might say that the disadvantaged have an entitlement to more assistance than they could claim under t1. At t1, members of the rest of the world may not, for example, have been able to provide the necessary medication for certain diseases but now at t2 they can do so at a reasonable cost. As a consequence, it seems reasonable to say that the needy people are now entitled to the necessary medication whereas before they were not. The extent of global interdependence can then affect the nature of people's entitlements. Consider now (ii). The point to be made here is that humanity-based cosmopolitans can argue that whether there is global interdependence affects the type of duty that persons are under. They will say that without a global scheme of interdependence there are positive duties of justice to bring about a fair world. They can also add though (drawing on Pogge) that if there is global interdependence then there is a negative duty of justice not to be part of an unjust global order (Pogge 2008). Affirming a humanity-based approach does not preclude one from affirming Pogge's powerful claim about the existence of negative duties not to collaborate with an unjust set of practices and institutions. Let us turn now to (iii). This third point follows on from the last point but it makes the additional, plausible, point that we tend to ascribe greater moral weight, all things considered, to negative duties than to positive duties. So, with this in mind, a humanity-based cosmopolitan can also accept that the degree to which there is global integration affects the moral weight of our responsibilities to others. For if it is the case that we have negative duties of justice to those within our scheme and if it is true that negative duties enjoy priority then it follows that where global interdependence exists then persons are under weightier global responsibilities than they would be without such interdependence. In these three ways, then, a humanity-based cosmopolitanism can accept that the nature of global interdependence is morally relevant.

Second, it is also worth recording that the humanity-centered brand of cosmopolitanism can recognize that the extent or not of interdependence is morally relevant in a further way. For example, it can hold the view that inequalities within states have certain distinctive worrying effects – for example, they lead to lack of trust and poor health all round (Marmot 2004; Wilkinson 2005). To hold that egalitarian principles should apply globally independently of whether there is a global scheme is compatible with holding that there might be some considerations in favor of equality that may apply only within the state.

VI: Three Challenges to Cosmopolitan Justice

Having sought to motivate support for an egalitarian liberal brand of cosmopolitanism, one grounded in particular on the dignity of persons, I shall conclude the analysis by considering three objections often leveled against egalitarian cosmopolitan ideals of distributive justice.[15]

§1.

One argument that has been developed by Miller and Rawls starts from a commitment to self-governing political communities. It then holds that if a society is self-determining it, rather than outsiders, should be treated as accountable for the standard of living of its members. So if one society selects policies that prove to be successful and a second one selects policies that are far less successful then it is wrong to redistribute from the former to the latter (Miller 1995: 108; Miller 2007: 68–75; Rawls 1999b: 117–18). Global egalitarianism is thus untenable. It requires redistribution where none is justified.

Several comments should be made about this often-invoked argument. The first concerns its target. Miller and Rawls employ this argument to reject global egalitarianism. At the same time they also embrace some minimal rights (Miller 2007: Ch. 7; Rawls 1999b: 65) and so presumably hold that when political communities take truly calamitous decisions their members should be spared bearing the consequences of their polity's actions. So the argument is thought to undermine some distributive ideals (egalitarian ones) but not others (minimal ones). The problem here is that while one can see the force of this argument against a strictly egalitarian view many "egalitarian" cosmopolitans call for something else like a global difference principle. And it is unclear here why Miller and Rawls's argument should give us reason to abandon a global difference principle (as Rawls thinks it would (1999b: 117)). A proponent of a global difference principle can reason as follows: we should design a global set of institutions and rules so that, given the predictable choices of individuals, firms and states that operate within this framework, this global set of institutions and rules will promote the condition of the global least advantaged. Within this fair framework, agents (including states) should take some responsibility for their decisions but the global framework is structured so as to maximize the position of the least advantaged.

A second distinct weakness in Miller and Rawls's argument is that it is unfair to individuals. Why should a member of a developing country be economically

Simon Caney

disadvantaged because of a decision that an elite in that country made and with which they disagreed (Caney 2005a: 130)? Of course, as we have just seen, Miller and Rawls may rightly reply that they both affirm a threshold below which people should not fall. So the extent to which individuals will suffer the consequence of others' evil or incompetence is limited. However, how satisfactory this is depends partly on how low that threshold is. Suppose someone defends a very minimal set of human rights, then this second challenge has considerable force. Why should someone live at just above subsistence level and another live in glorious comfort when the differences in their quality of life stem from the decisions of their respective governments *and when neither has had any input into them*? On the other hand, if the threshold level is rather high, then allowing differential outcomes is less troubling. Miller and Rawls's argument thus faces a dilemma: either they affirm a very minimal set of rights (in which case their argument is very unfair to minority individuals who suffer because of bad decisions taken by others) or they affirm a maximal set of rights (in which case, their position becomes much less distinguishable from egalitarian cosmopolitanism).

§2.

Consider now a second challenge. It is widely recognized that persons have special obligations to some (e.g., family members). Some build on this, arguing that persons also have special obligations of justice to fellow nationals and/or fellow citizens (Miller 1995: Ch. 3, 2007: 34–43). They then fault radical cosmopolitanism on the grounds that it fails to recognize this. The complaint then is that radical cosmopolitanism flies in the face of people's intuitions about special duties.

Again a number of options are available to the defender of radical cosmopolitanism. First, some might challenge the nationalist claim that there are special obligations of justice to fellow nationals. Such a critic might (I think should) affirm the claim that persons have special duties to family members and to friends. But she might challenge either the claim that we have special duties to fellow nationals or the claim that any such duties are duties of distributive justice. It is not immediately apparent that an individual has special duties of distributive justice to others just because they happen to share their nationality. A second response would be to adopt a more conciliatory approach and argue that there are duties to fellow nationals but insist that these should operate within the parameters set down by cosmopolitan ideals of justice.[16] This adopts a mild form of cosmopolitanism.

There is, however, a third response which both seeks to accommodate the objection's core claim (unlike the first response) but which also affirms a radical cosmopolitanism (unlike the second response). This third view starts from the observation made earlier that theories of distributive justice comprise both claims about persons' entitlements and claims about persons' obligations. Now if one is persuaded by the arguments adduced in section III–V one will hold that person's entitlements should be specified by a cosmopolitan theory of justice. However, one can affirm this and yet hold that persons' duties of justice should be informed by one's membership of a state. On this view, persons might (as citizens of a state) have a special duty to protect the cosmopolitan rights of their citizens, as well as a general duty not to violate and to protect the cosmopolitan rights of all.[17] Such an approach combines a cosmopolitan account of persons' entitlements with a (partially) statist account of persons' responsibilities.[18] In this way radical cosmopolitans can accommodate the intuition driving the argument from special duties.

§3.

Consider now a third challenge. Recently some have argued that some or all principles of distributive justice apply only within coercive frameworks and they infer from this that these principles apply only within the state. Thomas Nagel, for example, has claimed that no principles of distributive justice apply outside of coercive frameworks and he affirms only humanitarian duties to aid the global needy (2005). More moderately, Michael Blake has argued that some principles of distributive justice (those securing the conditions of autonomy for all) apply outside of coercive frameworks but that other principles of distributive justice (in particular, egalitarian ones) apply only within the kind of coercive system characterized by the modern state (2001).

Why should coercion matter so much? The fullest answer to this is given by Blake and so I shall concentrate on his analysis. Indeed Nagel, rather engagingly, concedes that

> [t]he cosmopolitan conception has considerable moral appeal, because it seems highly arbitrary that the average individual born into a poor society should have radically lower life prospects than the average individual born into a rich one, just as arbitrary as the corresponding difference between rich and poor in a rich but unjust society. (2005: 126).[19]

Consider then Blake's argument. He maintains that autonomy is valuable and, as such, coercion can be permissible only if it is justified to those subject to it. He further maintains that a commitment to justification leads to a commitment to equality. This, however, justifies equality within the state but it does not justify global egalitarianism because the international system, he contends, is not coercive (Blake 2001).

One obvious line of criticism protests that the international order is in fact coercive. Border restrictions are, for example, an obvious instance of this (Arneson 2005: 150; Tan 2004: 176–7: cf. 173; Abizadeh 2007: 348ff.). Blake, however, has anticipated this line of criticism (2001: 265, 280). His reply is that the kind of coercion practiced by the state is different in kind to other types of coercion, including the coercion involved in preventing people from migrating. His considered view is that there are various different forms of coercion and "each distinct form of coercion requires a distinct form of justification" (2001: 280, fn. 30). But then this second position is also problematic.[20] In the first place it is not clear what form of justification would follow from other kinds of coercion such as "international" coercion. In the second place, we have been given no reason to think that these other kinds of justification would not justify equality. Why should we assume that the kind of justification that is required by state-like coercion leads to equality? In short, then, either Blake claims that states coerce only their own citizens (version 1), or, he allows that other kinds of coercion exist (such as states coercing foreigners or the international system coercing all within its reach) but insists that they do not lead to the forms of justification that require equality (version 2). Neither version is palatable. The first is false but the second is mysterious and unsubstantiated.

Simon Caney

A second problem with Blake's claim concerns his assertion that there is a link between the necessity of justification, on the one hand, and equality, on the other. Two points can be made here. First, if coercive policies are enacted for a good reason then it is not clear why there is need for any kind of egalitarian remuneration. If autonomy is justifiably restricted (say to prevent harm or force) then that rationale alone gives us reason enough to justify coercion. No further financial payment is due to those who have been coerced (Arneson 2005: 137–8, 145–6). Second, Blake's argument is arguably culpable of a category mistake. Consider coercion again. The exercise of coercion, one can agree, does have normative significance. It requires that coercive actors justify their actions. But – and this is the crucial point – this can be done without leading to any commitment to equality. One might, for example, hold that the exercise of coercion is justified if (i) it respects people's human rights, (ii) the decision-making process is procedurally fair and gives everyone subject to the laws a fair opportunity to participate in the process, and (iii) the decision-makers give the reasons for their policies. This seems – to me at least – a legitimate and fair way to treat those subject to coercion. And if this is correct, it shows that there is no necessary link between the claim that "those who are coerced by the state are owed a justification," on the one hand, and the claim that "those who are coerced by the state should receive equal entitlements," on the other. Put bluntly: the fact of coercion calls for a *legitimate* decision-making process not *egalitarian distributive justice.*[21]

VII: Concluding Remarks

Cosmopolitanism's commitment to the equal moral standing of all persons (Pogge 2008: 175) and its emphasis on the arbitrariness of national and state borders make it an appealing view. Given the extent of globalization it is natural to focus on interdependence-based versions of cosmopolitanism. In this chapter, I hope, though, to have brought out the appeal of a humanity-based cosmopolitanism. The latter gives expression to a political morality that is based on respecting persons – not qua members of one's nation nor qua members of one's economic scheme – but as fellow human beings.

Notes

1 This paper was completed while I held a Leverhulme Research Fellowship. I am very grateful to the Leverhulme Trust for its support.
2 Others use other terms. Beitz calls it "institutional cosmopolitanism" (Beitz 1994: 124–5) and Pogge terms it "legal cosmopolitanism" (Pogge 2008: 175).
3 The distinction between "mild" and "radical" cosmopolitanism follows a similar distinction made by Samuel Scheffler between "moderate" and "extreme" cosmopolitanism (Scheffler 2001: 115ff.).
4 For the distinction between these two types of cosmopolitanism see Caney (2003: 295–8, 2005a: 111–15, 2007: 278ff.). The distinction is similar to, but distinct from, Andrea Sangiovanni's distinction between "relational" and "nonrelational" approaches (2007: 5–8). Sangiovanni defines a relational approach as follows: "Those who hold that principles of distributive justice have a relational basis hold that the practice-mediated relations in which

individuals stand condition the content, scope, and justification of those principles" (2007: 5). Nonrelational approaches deny this and see facts about the existence of practices as merely issues of how antecedently defined principles should be "applied" (2007: 6). As we shall see, what I term the humanity-centered approach allows that the "content" of principles (and the "justification" of that content to those principles) may be informed by the existence or otherwise of practices. Facts about social practices are thus not simply a matter of how antecedently "principles are applied" (2007: 6).

5 See also Beitz (1983: esp. 595).

6 I have also sought to defend such an approach: Caney (2001, 2005a, 2007).

7 The concept of "moral personality" comes from Rawls (1999a: 442–6).

8 There are (at least) two kinds of issue that this question raises. First, there is the question of whether principles of distributive justice include in their scope people who do not belong to their basic structure. Its focus is on which people are included within the scope of distributive justice. Second, there is the question of whether principles of distributive justice apply to people's personal conduct or whether they apply only to the basic institutions that comprise the basic structure. Its focus is not on who is included within the scope of distributive justice but on whether it should inform people's personal life (their choice of career, salary level, how they spend their money). For a seminal contribution to the latter, see Cohen (2000). My focus here is on the first question. Note that to say that the two issues are distinct is not to say that there is no connection between the two. See note 9 below.

9 The argument that I give in this paragraph is similar in spirit to Cohen's (2000: 136–40). In both cases, the critique claims that the reason given for focusing on the basic structure (its effects on people's lives) does not yield the intended conclusion. For further discussion of this point see Caney (2007: 283 fn. 14).

10 These six features of harm come from Pogge (2008: 26).

11 The notion of "tracking" comes from Robert Nozick's *Philosophical Explanations* (1981: 317–26) though I employ it in a different way.

12 This point is made by Friedrich Hayek in an interesting discussion in *The Constitution of Liberty* (1960). Hayek repudiates "the contention that membership in a particular community or nation entitles the individual to a particular material standard that is determined by the general wealth of the group to which he belongs" (1960: 100). As he writes, "[t]here is clearly no merit in being born into a particular community, and no argument of justice can be based on the accident of a particular individual's being born in one place rather than another" (1960: 100).

13 For the opposite view see Robert Nozick's example with ten Robinson Crusoes on ten islands in *Anarchy, State and Utopia* (1974: 185). Nozick does, though, have an excellent sustained interrogation of the assumption that distributive justice arises only where there is social cooperation (1974: 185–9). For a response in line with the view defended in the text see Fabre (2007: 152).

14 The relationship between global integration and these three issues is rarely discussed. For an exception see the interesting discussion by Jon Mandle of the links between the extent of global integration, on the one hand, and the "content" of distributive justice and the "strength" of the duties of distributive justice, on the other (2006: esp. 618–21).

15 What follows, obviously, cannot claim to be exhaustive. Other arguments are examined in Caney (2005a: Ch. 5).

16 See Pogge (2008: Ch. 5) and Tan (2004: Part III). On the more general question of the compatibility of global egalitarianism with special duties, see Abizadeh and Gilabert (2008).

17 For the distinction between special and general rights and duties, see H. L. A. Hart (1985).

18 Note that the original proponent of this kind of reconciliation was David Miller in *On Nationality*. He argued there that membership of a *nation* generates obligations to uphold

Simon Caney

the human rights of one's fellow nationals (1995: 75–7). I am sympathetic to this reconciliatory strategy, but, unlike Miller, do not think that the special responsibilities arise from membership of a nation. Rather they arise from membership of a state or other political organizations.

19 For criticism of Nagel's account, see Cohen and Sabel (2006) and Julius (2006).

20 For further analysis, see (2008) and also Abizadeh (2007: 349–51).

21 Another way of making the same point is to say that the exercise of coercion raises the kind of questions concerning the nature of liberal legitimacy that Rawls examines in *Political Liberalism* (1993) and it is quite separate from the questions concerning the nature of distributive justice that Rawls examines in *A Theory of Justice* (1999a).

References

Abizadeh, Arash. 2007. "Cooperation, Pervasive Impact, and Coercion: On the Scope (not Site) of Distributive Justice", *Philosophy and Public Affairs* 35 (4): 318–58.

Abizadeh, Arash and Gilabert, Pablo. 2008. "Is There a Genuine Tension between Cosmopolitan Egalitarianism and Special Responsibilities?," *Philosophical Studies* 138 (3): 349–65.

Arneson, Richard. 2005. "Do Patriotic Ties Limit Global Justice Duties?", *Journal of Ethics* 9 (1–2): 127–50.

Barry, Brian. 1989. *Theories of Justice: A Treatise on Social Justice*, Vol. 1 (London: Harvester Wheatsheaf).

Beitz, Charles. 1983. "Cosmopolitan Ideals and National Sentiment," *Journal of Philosophy* 80 (10): 591–600.

Beitz, Charles. 1994. "Cosmopolitan Liberalism and the States System," in Chris Brown, ed., *Political Restructuring in Europe: Ethical Perspectives* (London: Routledge), pp. 123–36.

Beitz, Charles. 1999. *Political Theory and International Relations* (Princeton, NJ: Princeton University Press), with a new afterword by the author.

Bentham, Jeremy. 1843 [1786–9]. "Objects of International Law," *Essay I* of *Principles of International Law,* in *The Works of Jeremy Bentham*, Vol. 2 (Edinburgh: William Tait), ed. John Bowring, pp. 537–40.

Blake, Michael. 2001. "Distributive Justice, State Coercion, and Autonomy," *Philosophy and Public Affairs* 30 (3): 257–96.

Buchanan, Allen. 1990. "Justice as Reciprocity versus Subject-Centred Justice," *Philosophy and Public Affairs* 19 (3): 227–52.

Buchanan, Allen. 2004. *Justice, Legitimacy, and Self-Determination: Moral Foundations for International Law* (Oxford: Oxford University Press).

Burke, Edmund. 1788 [1999]. "Speech on Opening of Impeachment," in *Empire and Community: Edmund Burke's Writings and Speeches on International Relations* (Oxford: Westview), ed. David P. Fidler and Jennifer M. Welsh, pp. 203–34.

Caney, Simon. 2001. "Cosmopolitan Justice and Equalizing Opportunities," *Metaphilosophy* 32 (1/2): 113–34.

Caney, Simon. 2003. "Entitlements, Obligations, and Distributive Justice: The Global Level," in Daniel A. Bell and Avner de-Shalit, eds., *Forms of Justice: Critical Perspectives on David Miller's Political Philosophy* (Lanham, MD: Rowman and Littlefield), pp. 287–313.

Caney, Simon. 2005a. *Justice Beyond Borders: A Global Political Theory* (Oxford: Oxford University Press).

Caney, Simon. 2005b. "Global Interdependence and Distributive Justice," *Review of International Studies* 31 (2): 389–99.

Caney, Simon. 2006. "Cosmopolitan Justice and Institutional Design: An Egalitarian Liberal Conception of Global Governance," *Social Theory and Practice* 32 (4): 725–56.

Caney, Simon. 2007. "Global Poverty and Human Rights: the Case for Positive Duties," in Thomas Pogge, ed., *Freedom from Poverty as a Human Right: Who Owes What to the Very Poor?* (Oxford: Oxford University Press), pp. 275–302.

Caney, Simon. 2008. "Global Distributive Justice and the State," *Political Studies* (forthcoming).

Canovan, Margaret. 1996. *Nationhood and Political Theory* (Cheltenham, Glos: Edward Elgar).

Cohen, G. A. 2000. *If You're an Egalitarian, How Come You're so Rich?* (Cambridge, MA: Harvard University Press).

Cohen, Joshua, and Charles Sabel. 2006. "Extra Rempublicam Nulla Justitia?," *Philosophy and Public Affairs* 34 (2): 147–75.

Collier, Paul. 2007. *The Bottom Billion: Why the Poorest Countries Are Failing and What Can Be Done about It* (Oxford: Oxford University Press).

Fabre, Cécile. 2007. "Global Distributive Justice: An Egalitarian Perspective," *Canadian Journal of Philosophy*, suppl. vol. 31: 139–64.

Freeman, Samuel. 2007. *Justice and the Social Contract: Essays on Rawlsian Political Philosophy* (New York: Oxford University Press).

Gallup, John Luke, Jeffrey D. Sachs and Andrew Mellinger. 1999. "Geography and Economic Development," *International Regional Science Review* 22 (2): 179–232.

Gallop, John Luke, and Jeffrey D. Sachs (2001) "The Economic Burden of Malaria," *The American Journal of Tropical Medicine & Hygiene* 64 (1–2): 85–96.

Hart, H. L. A. 1985. "Are There Any Natural Rights?," in Jeremy Waldron, ed., *Theories of Rights* (Oxford: Oxford University Press), pp. 77–90.

Hayek, F. A. 1960. *The Constitution of Liberty* (London: Routledge and Kegan Paul).

Julius, A. J. 2006. "Nagel's Atlas," *Philosophy and Public Affairs* 34 (2): 176–92.

Kant, Immanuel. 1989 [1795]. "Perpetual Peace: A Philosophical Sketch," in *Kant's Political Writings* (Cambridge: Cambridge University Press), ed. with an intro. and notes by Hans Reiss, trans. H. B. Nisbet, pp. 93–130.

Laërtius, Diogenes. 1931: (orig. pubn. date unknown) "Diogenes," in *Lives of Eminent Philosophers*, Vol. II (Cambridge, MA: Harvard University Press), with English translation by R. D. Hicks, pp. 22–85.

Mandle, Jon. 2006. "Coercion, Legitimacy, and Equality," *Social Theory and Practice* 32 (4): 617–25.

Marmot, Michael. 2004. *Status Syndrome: How Your Social Standing Directly Affects Your Health* (London: Bloomsbury).

Miller, David. 1995. *On Nationality* (Oxford: Clarendon Press).

Miller, David. 2002. "Caney's 'International Distributive Justice': A Response," *Political Studies* 50 (5): 974–7.

Miller, David. 2007. *National Responsibility and Global Justice* (Oxford: Oxford University Press).

Moellendorf, Darrel. 2002. *Cosmopolitan Justice* (Boulder, CO: Westview Press).

Nagel, Thomas. 2005. "The Problem of Global Justice," *Philosophy and Public Affairs* 33 (2): 113–47.

Nozick, Robert. 1974. *Anarchy, State, and Utopia* (New York: Blackwell).

Nozick, Robert. 1981. *Philosophical Explanations* (Oxford: Clarendon Press).

Pogge, Thomas. 1989. *Realizing Rawls* (Ithaca, NY and London: Cornell University Press).

Pogge, Thomas. 2008. *World Poverty and Human Rights: Cosmopolitan Responsibilities and Reforms*, 2nd edn. (Cambridge: Polity Press).

Rawls, John. 1993. *Political Liberalism* (New York: Columbia University Press).

Rawls, John. 1999a. *A Theory of Justice*, rev. edn. (Oxford: Oxford University Press).

Rawls, John. 1999b. *The Law of Peoples with "The Idea of Public Reason Revisited"* (Cambridge, MA: Harvard University Press).

Richards, David A. J. 1982. "International Distributive Justice," in J. Roland Pennock and John W. Chapman, eds., *Ethics, Economics, and the Law: NOMOS XXIV* (New York and London: New York University Press), pp. 275–99.

Simon Caney

Sachs, Jeffrey D. 2005. *The End of Poverty: How We can Make it Happen in Our Lifetime* (London: Penguin).

Sachs, Jeffrey D. 2008. *Common Wealth: Economics for a Crowded Planet* (Penguin: New York).

Sangiovanni, Andrea. 2007. "Global Justice, Reciprocity, and the State," *Philosophy and Public Affairs* 35 (1): 3–39.

Scheffler, Samuel. 2001. *Boundaries and Allegiances: Problems of Justice and Responsibility in Liberal Thought* (Oxford: Oxford University Press).

Shue, Henry. 1996. *Basic Rights: Subsistence, Affluence, and U.S. Foreign Policy*, 2nd edn. with new afterword (Princeton, NJ: Princeton University Press).

Singer, Peter. 2002. *One World: The Ethics of Globalization* (New Haven, CT and London: Yale University Press).

Tan, Kok-Chor. 2004. *Justice Without Borders: Cosmopolitanism, Nationalism, and Patriotism* (Cambridge: Cambridge University Press).

Waldron, Jeremy. 1992. "Minority Cultures and The Cosmopolitan Alternative," *University of Michigan Journal of Law Reform* 25 (3–4): 751–92.

Walzer, Michael. 1983. *Spheres of Justice: A Defence of Pluralism and Equality* (Oxford: Blackwell).

Wilkinson, Richard G. 2005. *The Impact of Inequality: How to Make Sick Societies Healthier* (London and New York: Routledge).

Distributive Justice at Home and Abroad[1]

Jon Mandle

The last decade or so has seen a dramatic increase in philosophical work on issues of global justice. One of the main questions has been whether principles of domestic justice appropriately apply at the global level. More specifically, do the arguments that support liberal egalitarian principles of distributive justice domestically entail similar or identical principles globally? Leaving aside skeptics who simply deny that any normative standards apply internationally, three families of answers to this question have emerged. Some say yes – the same egalitarian distributive principles apply at both the domestic and global levels because they both follow from a commitment to treating individuals as entitled to equal concern and respect. Treating individuals unequally on the basis of nationality or citizenship would be like treating them unequally on the basis of skin color or any other morally irrelevant property.[2] Others, however, say that egalitarian principles only hold when individuals are in certain types of relationships with one another. Typically these are thought to be relationships that are institutionally mediated. Many who hold this position also assert that the recent process of globalization – principally, economic integration – has generated the necessary relationships or institutions on a global level, hence, egalitarian principles now apply.[3] But others deny that economic relations alone are sufficient to establish the relevant type of relationship that would trigger egalitarian demands.[4] I'll be defending a version of this last position.

Before doing so, however, I want to emphasize that defenders of all three positions can recognize that the current global order, characterized by widespread and extreme poverty, is unjust.[5] For some (roughly, the global egalitarians in the first two groups), this situation is unjust because justice demands an egalitarian distribution of wealth on a global scale, and the current distribution dramatically violates that requirement. For others (roughly those, like myself, in the third group), it is unjust because extreme poverty makes it impossible for many people to function at a minimally adequate level. According to this account, global inequality is evidence of the opportunities available to relieve this extreme poverty. But inequality would not in itself be objectionable if everyone had resources that allowed them to function at a minimally decent level. I will be taking this latter position, but it is important to emphasize that given the current state of the world, there is likely to be considerable practical overlap between these three positions.

On my view, the duty of justice that each of us has toward everyone else has two parts. It requires, first, that we respect basic human rights, and second, that nobody be subordinated to the arbitrary choices of another person. The focus of this paper will be on the nonsubordination requirement, but let me first make a comment about the human rights requirement. Following the work of Henry Shue, I believe that human rights generate both so-called negative and positive duties.[6] For example, in addition to having a duty owed to everyone not to murder them, we also have a duty owed to everyone to help them avoid being murdered. Perhaps a violation of the former would be a more serious injustice than a violation of the latter – perhaps, that is, in the event of a conflict, the former negative duty should receive greater weight than the latter positive duty. But this doesn't mean that we can simply ignore the latter, or that it might not outweigh some other negative duties (for example, the duty not to lie). When human lives are at stake, even a positive duty can have great weight. If we accept that there is a human right to a share of resources necessary for a decent level of human functioning, this obviously implies that we all have a duty not to deprive people of those resources. But it also implies that there is a duty to assist them in securing such necessities. And given the extent of severe poverty in the world today, we citizens of wealthy countries are violating the positive duties – and arguably some negative duties, as well[7] – that we owe toward those in extreme poverty.

But even if a focus on securing basic human rights generates duties of considerable urgency, it does not by itself generate a commitment to egalitarian principles of distributive justice. Once basic human rights, including a necessary share of resources, have been secured, distributive inequalities above that level do not (in general) violate human rights. Nor, I claim, does the nonsubordination requirement generate a *general* principle of egalitarian distribution. So, it's somewhat unclear how my commitment to human rights and nonsubordination will generate *any* egalitarian principles of distributive justice at all. I will try to answer that question later, but first I want to develop a criticism of an influential argument for global egalitarianism that, as we will see, is based on a kind of luck egalitarianism.

Consider Kok-Chor Tan's version of global egalitarianism which holds that "a just global distributive scheme would be one which meets [Rawls's] second principle of justice – equality of opportunity and the regulation of global equality by the difference principle."[8] Tan holds that "the idea of equal respect and concern applies globally to all individuals and not just to citizens within bounded groups."[9] If a commitment to equal concern and respect generates Rawls's egalitarian principles domestically, he argues, it also requires them on a global scale. However, Tan recognizes that "an account of global justice that does not allow sufficient space for the special ties and commitments that people reasonably find valuable is one which people may reasonably reject."[10] These special ties and commitments have independent worth and are not to be valued simply based on the instrumental contribution that they make toward achieving the goal of distributive justice. On the contrary, Tan holds, "theories of justice begin from the assumption that personal and partial pursuits are what give meaning and worth to individual lives, and that the aim of principles of justice is not to rule out these partial commitments and pursuits as such, but to define the social context within which individuals may freely and fairly pursue their own projects."[11] I agree, and this is a fundamental point about liberal conceptions of justice: they are uncompromising but not all-controlling.[12] Therefore, Tan restricts the application of the egalitarian principles to institutional design rather than to the regulation of "individuals' day-to-day interaction with each other as such."[13] The model here, of course, is Rawls's focus on the basic structure of society, now extended by Tan (and others) to the global institutional order.

But Rawls's focus on the basic structure has been criticized by G. A. Cohen and Liam Murphy, among others. Cohen argues that "justice cannot be a matter only of the state-legislated structure in which people act but is also a matter of the acts they choose within that structure, the personal choices of their daily lives."[14] Cohen identifies the following as his "root belief": "there is injustice in distribution when inequality of goods reflects not such things as differences in the arduousness of different people's labors, or people's different preferences and choices with respect to income and leisure, but myriad forms of lucky and unlucky circumstance."[15] If justice aims at distributing benefits and burdens in a way that is isolated from such lucky or unlucky circumstances, there is certainly good reason to be concerned about the design of basic social institutions. But there is no good reason to be concerned *exclusively* with institutional design. After all, the "ethos" of a society and the choices made by individuals will also affect the pattern of distribution of goods. Or, as Liam Murphy asks,

> if equality or well-being is the underlying concern that produces a theory of justice, why would people not be directly concerned about these things? If people have a duty to promote just institutions, why do they lack a duty to promote whatever it is that just institutions are *for*?[16]

If we have a duty to promote institutions that eliminate the influence of brute luck, why don't we have a duty to eliminate such influence directly?

Now on an extreme interpretation of Cohen's approach, it would be wrong for individuals ever to act in such a way that resulted in an inequality unchosen by the people subjected to it. As it happens, Cohen rejects this extreme form of moral rigorism – or *justice* rigorism. He allows that "each person has a right to pursue her own self-interest to some reasonable extent."[17] In other words, Cohen grants that individuals have a self-interested prerogative that *sometimes* allows them to overrule the demands of distributive justice. David Estlund argues that these prerogatives should properly be much wider than Cohen suggests: "Given Cohen's acceptance of a prerogative that limits the claims of justice, allowing some room for the pursuit of self-interest, he ought to recognize a range of related prerogatives."[18] But such prerogatives are less a modification of the account of justice and more a recognition that other values can sometimes be more important. As Estlund explains, these prerogatives are "permissible deviation[s] in individual deliberation from what social justice would require considered alone."[19] That is, prerogatives are generated by competing values that sometimes override what distributive justice itself would require. An analogous position is available to a global egalitarian. She could, for example, recognize *national* prerogatives, which would provide scope for countries to pursue their own narrow interests even when doing so generates inequalities among individuals globally that would be contrary to what distributive justice would require considered alone. But any such prerogatives would require that we abandon our understanding of justice as uncompromising but not all-controlling. If justice is a matter of promoting a certain pattern of equal distribution,[20] then the only way to avoid making it all-controlling is to compromise it when it competes with other values that might also affect the pattern of distribution.

Consider an example in the domestic context. Suppose I own and run a pizza shop. I've invested everything in it, and I'm doing pretty well. I'm squarely in the middle quintile in income in my society. You, too, are in the middle quintile, working as an accountant. But you're ready for a career change. You decide to open a sushi bar, and you do so down the street from my pizza shop. Your restaurant does great business, lures away my customers, and soon I'm forced to shut down. I fall into the lowest quintile, while you make it into the top. Assume that although my level of well-being plunges, thanks to various forms of social provision, I still have access to adequate food and shelter and healthcare – and the same for my family members and dependents – so that we're all above the level at which our basic functioning would be in jeopardy. In fact, suppose our society has arranged its institutions so that citizens in the lowest quintile – like me, now – are at least as well-off as the citizens in the lowest quintile would be if we had any other set of institutions.

Your actions resulted in a dramatic lowering of my level of well-being (as well as my "access to advantage"[21]). You created a new and significant inequality, unrelated to how hard I worked or any changes in my preferences or anything that I agreed to. From my point of view, it was simply bad luck that you opened your restaurant where you did. And yet, I want to insist, you committed no injustice against me. It's not clear to me whether Cohen would say that your conduct falls within a personal prerogative. Perhaps he would say that that depends on your intentions in opening the business and perhaps what you do with the money that you make. But even if he thinks that your conduct would fall within a personal prerogative, that wouldn't show that it is just. Rather, it would show that it is permissible despite being contrary to what distributive justice would require if considered alone. In contrast to Cohen's analysis, I believe that in cases like this[22] not only is your conduct just (not unjust), your motives are irrelevant. Of course, other virtues besides justice may be at stake, and your motives may be relevant to those virtues. Perhaps you were inconsiderate or even malicious. But as far as distributive justice is concerned, you have done no wrong, regardless of your motives or the effects of your actions on my welfare or even the effects of your actions on the general welfare.

This is not to say that the only issue of justice is whether your conduct is legal (a view that Cohen sometimes attributes to his opponents). Perhaps there are no laws concerning slander, and you scared customers away from my restaurant by falsely claiming that my pizza was making people sick. Or worse, suppose you engage in this slander, knowing that there are laws against it but that courts will not admit testimony from plaintiffs of my race against defendants of your race. Justice is not merely a matter of conformity with law, since laws can be inadequate or unjust. Your conduct *might* be unjust even if in conformity with the law. But in examples like these, the injustice is not that you have violated the norms of distributive justice.

Tan defends his institutional focus against Cohen's criticisms by arguing:

if we are concerned about equality because of a direct concern with mitigating the effects of contingencies on people's life chances, there is no immediate reason why such a concern must take us beyond the basic structure. The belief of institutional (luck) egalitarians is that an appropriately ordered basic structure will come close to annulling the effects of chance and brute luck on people's lives *without* intruding on people's liberties to pursue their ends.[23]

But we have just seen a case in which a concern with mitigating the effects of contingencies would take us beyond the basic structure. Although institutions can (and should) mitigate some of the most damaging effects of bad luck, they cannot come anywhere close to "annulling the effects of chance and brute luck." Tan offers two replies to this criticism. The first is that the outcome of "a business venture . . . is not the kind of luck that luck egalitarians need to nullify, even though how things actually do turn out in this venture is to some degree affected by luck."[24] Perhaps it is a matter of "option luck" (for which we hold individuals responsible) rather than "brute luck" (for which we compensate individuals). However, if the impulse to egalitarianism is to compensate individuals for outcomes that they have not chosen or are not responsible for, it is hard to see why I shouldn't be entitled to compensation from you when you drive me out of business. I didn't form any agreement with you and if not for your conduct, I would have been much better off. It may be true that there are actions that would have protected me against this outcome. But the test of option luck cannot be that individuals could have taken steps that would have led to a different outcome since this would expand option luck to encompass virtually all outcomes. Being struck by a meteorite is brute luck, not option luck, even if I could have moved to a different spot just before it struck, to take Ronald Dworkin's example.[25]

Tan's other "more important" reply is that the institutional focus is necessary in order to make space for individual choice and pursuit of diverse ends.

> As long as the effects of luck can be sufficiently (even if not completely) mitigated by institutional means, any attempt at countering the effects of luck in personal conduct by interfering with personal pursuits within the rules of just institutions will be overly broad. The residual inequalities of luck on personal life is acceptable given the greater costs of attempting to eliminate these inequalities.[26]

I agree with Tan that a comprehensive application of egalitarian demands to personal conduct is overly broad. But as we saw with Cohen's personal prerogatives, Tan's argument here is not that personal conduct is just even when it generates inequalities that are not chosen (by those affected by it). Rather, his argument is that enforcing justice in such cases would be too costly in terms of other competing values such as personal autonomy. Ultimately, Tan shares something like Cohen's "root belief" regarding the nature of justice. As he says, "The aim of distributive justice is to counter the effects of unchosen inequality of circumstances on persons. . . ."[27] But once again, virtually any action that affects others risks generating an inequality that is not chosen by those affected by it. If distributive justice is a matter of eliminating these effects, it threatens to be all-encompassing. Both Cohen and Tan resist this implication – Cohen by granting personal prerogatives and Tan with his institutional focus, which is, in effect, simply a very large personal prerogative. But they can only avoid

Jon Mandle

making distributive justice all-encompassing by compromising it when it competes with other values (such as personal autonomy).

In order to restore our understanding of justice as uncompromising but not all-controlling, we should begin again with the two components I asserted at the beginning of the paper: respect for basic human rights (including a right to a share of resources necessary for adequate functioning) and nonsubordination. Distributive inequality does not violate basic human rights as long as the rights are secured at an adequate threshold level for all. Nor does distributive inequality necessarily subordinate the will of one person to another. As Tim Scanlon observes, "It does not seem that in general we are under even a 'prima facie' duty to promote the equal welfare of all."[28] On the other hand, when individuals share political and legal structures, the nonsubordination requirement puts constraints on the permissible designs of those structures. Individuals have a duty to ensure that basic institutional structures are just. They do not have a duty to ensure that any particular pattern of distribution is achieved. So on my view, there is no mystery as to why opening your restaurant would involve no injustice toward me. You have no direct egalitarian duty of distributive justice toward me, although you do have a duty to ensure that the basic structure that we share is just, and assuming it to be just, you have a duty to comply with its requirements. If these duties are satisfied, then there is no injustice because although your actions have a negative effect on my well-being, not chosen by me, they do not subordinate my will to yours.

This view may look suspiciously libertarian. There may appear to be a close similarity between my restaurant example and Nozick's rejection of patterned principles of distributive justice and his famous discussion of Wilt Chamberlain.[29] But there is a crucial difference, and my position is not libertarian. After all, in my example, I specified that your conduct takes place within a basic structure in which members of the lowest quintile do at least as well as the members of the lowest quintile would under any other institutional arrangement. I defend an egalitarian standard, such as the difference principle, for evaluating the basic structure.[30] But what grounds are there for restricting the egalitarian focus to the basic structure and not evaluating individual conduct according to that same standard? For that matter, why should egalitarian principles apply at all if, as I've said, inequality does not in general violate the nonsubordination requirement?

The answer can be developed from an element of Kant's political philosophy.[31] Suppose that you and I were in a state of nature – that is, outside of any political or legal structures. Each of us cultivates our crops in isolation from each other, and we are able to satisfy our basic needs. Justice does not require distributive equality in such a situation. The fact that you've produced more than I have, whether this is due to hard work or to brute luck, does not by itself subordinate my will to yours. As long as our basic rights are secure, there is not yet any injustice in view. Of course, in this condition our basic rights are not very secure for a variety of reasons, and this creates pressure to enter political society. But I want to focus elsewhere, and from here on, I will assume basic human rights are not at issue.

There is a kind of proto-property in this condition. In the simplest case, if I steal the rice that you have grown, I have committed an injustice against you. I have deprived you of the means that you are entitled to use in pursuing your ends and have appropriated those means to my ends. I have, in effect, subordinated your will

– or part of it, anyway – to mine. We can also imagine, in this condition, simple trading. I may exchange some of my beans for some of the rice that you have produced. Assuming, in the classic formulation, that there is no force or fraud, there is no injustice because there is no subordination. But simple cases like this, on which the libertarian edifice is constructed, are misleading because they do not take us far enough. If we interact with one another more than only occasionally, we will be able to sustain this system of proto-property only for a short time and only if we are very lucky. Or more precisely, only if we are very lucky will we be able to avoid committing injustice toward each other.

To see why, consider first Locke's argument for entering political society from a state of nature much like the one I've described. Now in the ideal, individuals would be in

> a *State of perfect Freedom* to order their Actions, and dispose of the their Possessions, and Persons as they think fit, within the bounds of the Law of Nature, without asking leave, or depending upon the Will of any other Man.[32]

In the ideal, we would exist in a state of justice. Unfortunately, human nature being what it is, sooner or later someone will be inclined to violate the law of nature and to act unjustly.[33] I may be tempted to steal your rice, for example. In order for the law of nature not to be in vain, Locke argues, it must be enforced, and if anyone has the power to enforce it, then everyone has that power.[34] But again, human nature being what it is, "it is unreasonable for Men to be Judges in their own Cases, [since] Self-love will make Men partial to themselves and their Friends."[35] Hence, Locke concludes: "*Civil Government* is the proper Remedy for the Inconveniences of the State of Nature, which must certainly be Great, where Men may be Judges in their own Case."[36] So, for Locke, it is *possible* for us to interact in the state of nature without violating the nonsubordination requirement. However, owing to the deficiencies of human nature – our tendency to violate the law of nature and our inability to enforce it impartially – this is very unlikely. As a result, it makes sense to set up a state with the power to enforce the law of nature impartially. For Locke, entering political society does not fundamentally change the structure of property rights that existed in the state of nature. What is gained is the effective and impartial enforcement of those pre-existing rights.

For Kant, however, the structure of property rights in the state of nature really is inadequate – he calls it "provisional"[37] – and not only because of human failings and the lack of impartial enforcement. A political structure is necessary "however well disposed and law-abiding human beings might be."[38] The important issue is not the human tendency to violate natural property rights but rather their indeterminacy. Suppose that the beans that I deliver to you in exchange for your rice are not of the quality that you expected, but are no different from any others that I produce. Or suppose that you claim two un-owned plots of land, intending to rotate your crops over time. You plant seeds on one plot and allow the other to go fallow. Seeing that the second plot has not yet been worked, I plant it and claim it for my own. Or suppose that I allow you to use my trap to hunt, while I use your fishing pole. You use the trap properly, but it is destroyed by a wild animal. I keep your fishing pole as compensation, but you demand it back, claiming that you did no wrong. In cases like these, the main problem is not that I have violated your property rights or that

Jon Mandle

we lack adequate enforcement. The problem is deeper. There are indefinitely many property regimes that would seem to be consistent with the nonsubordination requirement. According to some of these, my actions would be just while according to others they would be unjust. The specification of additional details in these cases would not help resolve these indeterminacies, nor would further reflection on basic human rights and the nonsubordination condition. We need a political regime not only to apply and enforce property rights impartially, but also to make the rights determinate in the first place.[39]

So, for Kant it is possible that in the state of nature we will successfully trade beans for rice. But if we do so, it is only because we are simply lucky that our understandings of our property rights have not brought us into conflict. And we can't count on sustaining that luck. Although there are many schemes of property rights that would be consistent with the nonsubordination requirement, there is no way to *select* one without subordinating the will of one person to another. No individual has the authority to impose any particular scheme on anyone else. It is precisely because of the diversity of potentially permissible schemes and the lack of a legitimate mechanism for selecting one of them that there is no way to avoid injustice in the state of nature. As Kant explains,

> It is true that the state of nature need not, just because it is natural, be a state of *injustice*, of dealing with one another only in terms of the degree of force each has. But it would still be a state *devoid of justice*, in which when rights are *in dispute*, there would be no judge competent to render a verdict having rightful force.[40]

In such a condition, *any* resolution would be unjust because any imposition of a particular scheme would subordinate the will of one person to that of another.

In order to avoid the injustice of subordinating the will of one person to that of another in the selection of an economic scheme and system of private property, we need a just political structure. We need, that is, a political mechanism that itself respects the nonsubordination requirement. And here we first see the transformation of the nonsubordination requirement into a demand for equality – in this case, political equality. A political mechanism selects laws that will be coercively imposed on a society, so if individuals are not treated as equals in this process, the choices of others will be coercively imposed on them, and this is precisely what the nonsubordination requirement prohibits.

Now the political equality that is required to satisfy the nonsubordination requirement is not the same as distributive equality, and it may seem as though the nonsubordination requirement only entails the former.[41] The thought would be that once a just political mechanism is in place, it can select any of the economic schemes that we have already seen are compatible with the nonsubordination requirement. And there is a sense in which that is correct. Any choice that a just political mechanism makes from this range of permissible economic schemes would be *legitimate*. But this does not mean that all of these choices would be equally *just*. Different members of the society, we assume, have different preferences concerning which of the permissible schemes would be best. Now consider the issue from the perspective of a participant in the political process – a legislator, for example. On what grounds should the legislator vote for one scheme over another? If she votes for one scheme because she believes that her own interests would best be served under that scheme, her vote would be violating the nonsubordination requirement. She would be saying that she can elevate her own interests over the interests of others in the design of the basic scheme of rights that will be imposed on everyone. Voting on the interests of any narrow constituency would be objectionable for the same reason. To respect the nonsubordination requirement in selecting an economic scheme, a conscientious legislator must vote on the basis of principles that can be justified to all reasonable citizens, not only to some.

It is a nontrivial task to determine which principles can be justified to all reasonable citizens. One way to model this choice is to consider it from Rawls's original position. This heuristic device has the virtue of displaying the transition from the nonsubordination condition to the egalitarian principles of distributive justice. I think a strong case can be made that the parties would choose Rawls's principles of justice – an equal scheme of basic liberties (including ensuring the fair value of the political liberties), as well as fair equality of opportunity and the difference principle – but my argument does not depend on the details of these principles. The point is that we will get some kind of egalitarian constraint on the design of the basic economic institutions. Anything else would subordinate the will of one to that of others in the selection and imposition of a scheme and therefore would be unjust. A scheme that is less egalitarian than the principles require may still be *legitimate* if it is selected by a just political procedure. And this may be sufficient to avoid the problem of injustice in the state of nature that we discussed. But if the selection of the scheme is based on principles that cannot be justified to all, then there is still a violation of the nonsubordination requirement and therefore the selection of that scheme, even if legitimate, is unjust.

So, I've argued that from the state of nature it is a requirement of justice that individuals make a collective decision concerning the scheme of property rights that they will enforce against one another. We need a political mechanism to do this, and the nonsubordination requirement must apply to this process as well as to the scheme chosen. This is more demanding than it might seem, for the nonsubordination requirement in effect becomes a standard of reciprocity that applies to the design of the political structure as well as to the justifications that are offered within that process. An equal right to vote, for example, is insufficient by itself. If a numerical majority selects a scheme on the basis of their narrow self-interest, a minority may properly complain that their wills are being subordinated to those of the majority in the selection process. Fundamental political decisions must not be merely an expression of the private interests of the majority. They must not simply reflect the will of all, as Rousseau would put it. Political actors must aim to provide justifications that all reasonable citizens can accept. They must aim at identifying the general will.[42] By reflecting on the choice from the original position, we can consider which principles should apply to the scheme of property rights in order to meet this justificatory burden. Whatever the details – and again, I leave them aside – it seems clear that it will involve some kind of egalitarian commitment. The collective decision regarding economic schemes must treat all individuals as free and equal.

On the view that I have been defending, a scheme of property rights is not purely conventional, since it must respect basic human rights and the nonsubordination requirement. However, property rights are essentially indeterminate and incomplete outside

Jon Mandle

of a legitimate political and legal system that can specify them, apply them to particular cases, and enforce those judgments.[43] Kant's insight was that justice itself requires that we enter into a legitimate political structure in order to avoid injustice in our property claims. When it comes to the selection of a scheme of property rights through a just political mechanism, the nonsubordination requirement entails an egalitarian standard. However, distributive justice is not a matter of achieving any particular pattern of distribution. As Rawls puts it, "If it is asked in the abstract whether one distribution of a given stock of things to definite individuals with known desires and preferences is better than another, then there is simply no answer to this question."[44] Instead, distributive justice, as opposed to allocative justice, is a matter of pure procedural justice.[45] Once a just scheme of property rights and economic institutions is in place, "the distribution that results will be just (or at least not unjust) whatever it is."[46] A large inequality in the resulting allocation of goods may be unjust if it came about through a violation of just procedures, or if it undermines the fair value of the political liberties, or if it undermines fair equality of opportunity, or if it generates excusable envy that undermines self-respect. Beyond this, a large inequality may be *evidence* that the basic structure does not satisfy the difference principle if it seems likely that the least advantaged would do better under a different economic regime. But even if this is so, the injustice lies not directly with the shares that different people receive but with the background institutional arrangement. The institutional scheme, not the specific allocation of goods, is subject to an egalitarian requirement because it is in the selection of the scheme that the nonsubordination requirement might be violated.

Up to this point, I've been talking about the global egalitarians in the first group that I identified at the beginning of this paper. Now I want to say something very briefly about those in the second group who predicate their egalitarianism on the emergence of global institutions. Near the beginning of *A Theory of Justice*, when Rawls introduces the idea of the basic structure, he writes: "The basic structure is the primary subject of justice because its effects are so profound and present from the start."[47] Cohen cites this passage to make the case for applying an egalitarian standard not only to the basic structure but to individual actions as well.[48] After all, as we have seen, individual actions can dramatically affect the distributive shares of others. In an era of globalization, international institutions can also have profound effects on the well-being of individuals around the world. Not surprisingly, Darrel Moellendorf cites this same passage from Rawls when he argues that because

the global economy has a substantial impact on the moral interests of persons in virtually every corner of the world . . . duties of justice exist between persons globally and not merely between compatriots The effects of global economic institutions and principles on the life prospects of persons are, in Rawls's words, "profound from the start."[49]

But I have been arguing that having profound effects on others is insufficient to establish that there are egalitarian demands of distributive justice.[50] Economic schemes must satisfy an egalitarian standard because that is the only way for them to satisfy the nonsubordination requirement. But assuming such a scheme to be in place, an individual action does not violate this requirement even when its effect on the allocation of goods is profound.

Justice does not require that the distribution of goods conform to any particular pattern, either domestically or globally. Distributive inequality *as such* does not offend justice, either domestically or globally. Of course, as I said earlier, human rights do apply globally, and given the extreme poverty in the world today, inequality points to our unfulfilled obligation to provide assistance in securing them. The nonsubordination condition also puts constraints on permissible global interactions that are arguably violated by current practice.[51] For example, although all members of the World Trade Organization have nominally equal standing, so-called "green-room" negotiations often exclude all but the most powerful states, and "close to 70 percent of the total developing-country membership of the WTO . . . was handicapped" by lack of adequate staffing. Among developing countries, "the vast majority have only weak or no representation."[52] And the International Monetary Fund, which one *defender* of globalization has described as "a secretive and arrogant organization," does not have even a formal policy of one country, one vote.[53] These policies and practices arguably subordinate the choices of the members of one state to those of another. But again, none of this entails an egalitarian principle of global distributive justice.

Let me conclude by considering two objections. First, it might be acknowledged that global inequality as such does not violate the nonsubordination condition and so is not unjust. However, with increased international trade, there are more and more opportunities for conflicts among different systems of property and private law. If there is a dispute among parties to an international contract, under which system should it be adjudicated? Just as in the state of nature the imposition of one party's judgment (even if reasonable in itself) on another would violate the nonsubordination requirement and be unjust, it might be argued that we need a global system of property that will carry egalitarian demands with it.

This argument is not successful because there are crucial differences between individuals in the state of nature, where there are no legitimate political structures, and individuals who are subject to different legitimate systems of property.[54] International contracts can raise difficulties, but these are issues of jurisdiction which can usually be resolved through a large body of case law, bi- or multilateral treaties, or, perhaps most simply, by having the contract itself specify the applicable system for dispute resolution. None of these mechanisms is available to parties in the state of nature, where *no* system of private law is available, and therefore there is no nonarbitrary mechanism for the specification of rights, or for their application to particular cases, or for the enforcement of such judgments.

Whether or not it is a requirement of justice that we establish a global system of property, perhaps it will be said that we already have one, carrying with it egalitarian demands. Nothing I've said rules out the possibility of creating such a global scheme, but it does not yet exist. We do not have a global political mechanism that can specify the content of property rights, a global judiciary that can apply them to particular cases, or a global enforcement mechanism. The WTO has made some controversial moves in this direction with respect to intellectual property.[55] But we are far from the point that we could properly say that there is a single global system of property and private law, and there are essentially no prospects for such a system in the short or even medium term. The European Union is perhaps another matter, and it may very well be the case that it is sufficient to generate egalitarian distributive demands across the borders of its member states. The specifics of this case continue

Jon Mandle

to evolve, and I remain agnostic on this point. Still the very uncertainty about this case reveals just how far we are from a single system of property and private law on a global scale.

Globalization has increased our influence on one another across borders. We now have new opportunities to enter into cooperative projects to pursue our various goals. There are also new opportunities for injustice, when we fail to respect the basic human rights of others or subordinate and exploit them. But justice does not require that we promote a pattern of equal distribution of goods on a global scale any more than it requires that we do so in our ordinary, day-to-day activities. Rather, it requires that we use egalitarian standards when we design our basic institutions, including both our political institutions and the structure of our property rights. The strong temptation is to think that egalitarian demands on the design of the basic structure arise from the independent value of an equal allocation of goods. But this gets things close to backwards. As Arthur Ripstein argues, it is a mistake to assume "that morality is complete without institutions, so that institutions should be designed so as to approximate a result that can be specified without reference to them."[56] Justice requires that we enter a political structure guided by the ideals of freedom and equality in order to make our rights complete and determinate. Such structures fundamentally change our relations with one another because they give each of us a scheme of determinate rights compatible with a like scheme for others. In order to avoid unjust subordination, we must assess those schemes that we coercively impose on ourselves according to an egalitarian standard. If we had a global political structure that had the ability to specify rights, apply them, and enforce them, then it too would be subject to an egalitarian standard of evaluation. But a global political order is not required by justice, and in its absence there is no occasion for egalitarian demands of distributive justice on a global scale.

Notes

1 Versions of this paper were presented at the XXIII World Congress of Philosophy of Law and Social Philosophy in Krakow, Poland, August 2007, and at the University of Tennessee, in November 2007. Thanks to both audiences, and to Kristen Hessler, George Klosko, and Arthur Ripstein for valuable discussion and suggestions.

2 See, for example, David Richards, "International Distributive Justice" in J. Roland Pennock and John Chapman, eds., *Ethics, Economics, and the Law: NOMOS XXIV* (New York: New York University, 1982); Kok-Chor Tan, *Justice Without Borders: Cosmopolitanism, Nationalism and Patriotism* (Cambridge: Cambridge University Press, 2004), and Simon Caney, *Justice Beyond Borders: A Global Political Theory* (New York: Oxford University Press, 2005).

3 See, for example, Charles Beitz, *Political Theory and International Relations*, with a new afterword (Princeton, NJ: Princeton University Press, 1999); and Darrel Moellendorf, *Cosmopolitan Justice* (Boulder, CO: Westview Press, 2002).

4 See, for example, John Rawls, *The Law of Peoples* (Cambridge, MA: Harvard University Press, 1999); Michael Blake, "Distributive Justice, State Coercion, and Autonomy," *Philosophy and Public Affairs* 30 (3) (Summer 2001); and Jon Mandle, *Global Justice* (Cambridge: Polity Press, 2006).

5 See, for example, the data cited in Mandle, *Global Justice*, Ch. 5.

6   Henry Shue, *Basic Rights: Subsistence, Affluence, and U.S. Foreign Policy*, 2nd edn. (Princeton, NJ: Princeton University Press, 1996). Cf. Mandle, *Global Justice*, Ch. 4.

7   See Thomas Pogge, *World Poverty and Human Rights* (Cambridge: Polity Press, 2002).

8   Tan, *Justice Without Borders*, pp. 60–1.

9   Tan, *Justice Without Borders*, p. 6.

10 Tan, *Justice Without Borders*, p. 135. See also his "Justice and Personal Pursuits," *Journal of Philosophy* 101 (7) (Jul. 2004).

11 Tan, *Justice Without Borders*, p. 157.

12 This phrase is used by David Estlund, "Liberalism, Equality, and Fraternity in Cohen's Critique of Rawls," *The Journal of Political Philosophy* 6 (1) (1998), p. 107, who cites Rawls's claim that although justice is "given precedence," that does "not make it all controlling." (John Rawls, *A Theory of Justice*, rev. edn. (Cambridge, MA: Harvard University Press, 1999), p. 495).

13 Tan, *Justice Without Borders*, p. 157.

14 G. A. Cohen, *If You're an Egalitarian, How Come You're So Rich?* (Cambridge, MA: Harvard University Press, 2000), p. 122.

15 Cohen, *If You're an Egalitarian . . .* , p. 130.

16 Liam Murphy, "Institutions and the Demands of Justice," *Philosophy and Public Affairs* 27 (4) (Fall 1998): 280. It is not obvious that Cohen would endorse this position. See Thomas Pogge, "On the Site of Distributive Justice: Reflections on Cohen and Murphy," *Philosophy and Public Affairs* 29 (2) (Spring 2000), esp. 154–63.

17 Cohen, *If You're an Egalitarian . . .* , p. 206, n. 24. Cf. G. A. Cohen, "Incentives, Inequality, and Community," in Grethe Peterson, ed., *The Tanner Lectures on Human Values*, vol. 13 (Salt Lake City: University of Utah Press, 1992), pp. 302–3.

18 Estlund, "Liberalism, Equality, and Fraternity in Cohen's Critique of Rawls," p. 102. For other valuable discussions of Cohen's position, see Andrew Williams, "Incentives, Inequality, and Publicity," *Philosophy and Public Affairs* 27 (3) (Summer 1998); Paul Smith, "Incentives and Justice: G. A. Cohen's Egalitarian Critique of Rawls," *Social Theory and Practice* 24 (2) (Summer 1998); Joshua Cohen, "Taking People as They Are?" *Philosophy and Public Affairs* 30 (4) (Fall 2001); Samuel Scheffler, "Is the Basic Structure Basic?" in Christine Sypnowich, ed., *The Egalitarian Conscience: Essays in Honour of G. A. Cohen* (Oxford: Oxford University Press, 2006).

19 Estlund, "Liberalism, Equality, and Fraternity in Cohen's Critique of Rawls," p. 102.

20 In general, I will now use "inequality" as shorthand for any distribution contrary to whatever pattern is taken to be required by the principles of distributive justice, including, for example, the goal of eliminating the influence of luck or unchosen circumstances. The precise metric is unimportant to my argument.

21 G. A. Cohen, "On the Currency of Egalitarian Justice," *Ethics* 99 (4) (Jul. 1989).

22 Cases, that is, in which: 1. the basic structure is just; 2. the conduct is legally permissible; 3. the basic institutional design is not at stake; 4. basic human rights violations are not at stake; and 5. no person's private will is subordinated to another's.

23 Tan, "Justice and Personal Pursuits," p. 356. In this article, Tan does not endorse luck egalitarianism, but elsewhere he does. See, for example, note 27 below.

24 Tan, "Justice and Personal Pursuits," p. 357.

25 Ronald Dworkin, *Sovereign Virtue* (Cambridge, MA: Harvard University Press, 2000), p. 73.

26 Tan, "Justice and Personal Pursuits," pp. 358–9, note excluded.

27 Tan, *Justice Without Borders*, p. 70.

28 T. M. Scanlon, "The Diversity of Objections to Inequality" repr. in *The Difficulty of Tolerance* (Cambridge: Cambridge University Press, 2003), p. 206.

29 Robert Nozick, *Anarchy, State, and Utopia* (New York: Basic Books, 1974), pp. 149–64.

30 There are other important differences between my position and standard libertarian views. For example, libertarians often assume that there are no positive duties in the state of nature. But I have already asserted that human rights generate both negative and positive duties. See note 6 above.

31 My aim is not to offer an interpretation of Kant, but to pursue and develop a line of argument that he suggests. I'm indebted to a series of articles by Arthur Ripstein that bring out this position. See esp. "Authority and Coercion," *Philosophy and Public Affairs* (1) (Winter 2004); "Private Order and Public Justice: Kant and Rawls," *Virginia Law Review* 92 (2006); and "Kant and the Circumstances of Justice" in Elisabeth Ellis, ed., *Kant's Political Theory: Interpretations and Applications* (University Park, PA: Penn State Press, forthcoming).

32 John Locke, *Two Treatises of Government*, ed. Peter Laslett (Cambridge: Cambridge University Press, 1960), second treatise, sec. 4, p. 269.

33 Or, more precisely, someone will *accuse* someone else of violating the law of nature. The structure of the problem is the same whether there was an actual violation or not.

34 Locke, *Two Treatises of Government*, second treatise, sec. 7, pp. 271–2.

35 Locke, *Two Treatises of Government*, second treatise, sec. 13, p. 275.

36 Locke, *Two Treatises of Government*, second treatise, sec. 14, p. 276.

37 All citations to works by Kant will be to the translations included in *Practical Philosophy*, ed. Mary Gregor (Cambridge: Cambridge University Press, 1996), as follows: *The Metaphysics of Morals*, sec. 9 and 15, pp. 409, 416 [Ak. 6: 256, 264].

38 Kant, *The Metaphysics of Morals*, sec. 44, p. 456 [Ak. 6: 312].

39 Kant himself recommends resolutions to some analogous problems in the state of nature, despite his claim that "The indeterminacy, with respect to quantity as well as quality, of the external object that can be acquired makes this problem (of the sole, original external acquisition) the hardest of all to solve." (*The Metaphysics of Morals*, sec.15, p. 418 [Ak. 6: 266]. For example, he asks, "in order to acquire land is it necessary to develop it (build on it, cultivate it, drain it, and so on)?" And he answers: "No.... When first acquisition is in question, developing land is nothing more than an external sign of taking possession, for which many other signs that cost less effort can be substituted" (*The Metaphysics of Morals*, sec. 15, p. 417 [Ak. 6: 265]). Signs, however, are conventional, and are subject to dispute in the absence of an authoritative determination. He also suggests that when an object is loaned, the borrower is responsible if the object is lost or damaged (regardless of negligence). But this seems to be largely an appeal to convention as well: "For it is not a matter of course that the owner, in addition to granting the borrower the use of his thing ... has also issued the borrower a *guarantee* against any damage that could arise from his having let it out of his custody" (*The Metaphysics of Morals*, sec. 38, p. 444 [Ak. 6: 298–9]).

40 Kant, *The Metaphysics of Morals*, sec. 44, p. 456 [Ak. 6: 312].

41 Kant himself apparently thought this. See, for example, "On the Common Saying: That May Be Correct in Theory but Not in Practice," p. 292 [Ak. 8: 291–2]. On the other hand, he did hold that a legitimate state must "maintain those members of the society who are unable to maintain themselves. For reasons of state the government is therefore authorized to constrain the wealthy to provide the means of sustenance to those who are unable to provide for even their most necessary natural needs" (*The Metaphysics of Morals*, sec. 49, p. 468 [Ak. 6: 326]); cf. "On the Common Saying ...," p. 298 [Ak. 8: 298–9].

42 For Rousseau, the general will is the basis of the demand for the equality among citizens: "the fundamental pact, rather than destroying natural equality, on the contrary substitutes a moral and legitimate equality for whatever physical inequality nature may have placed between men, and that while they may be unequal in force or in genius, they all become equal by convention and by right." Rousseau, *The Social Contract and Other Later*

Political Writings, ed. Victor Gourevitch (Cambridge: Cambridge University Press, 1997), Bk. I, Ch. 9, para. 8, p. 56.

43 Ripstein, "Authority and Coercion," p. 32.

44 Rawls, *A Theory of Justice*, p. 76.

45 Rawls, *A Theory of Justice*, p. 77.

46 Rawls, *A Theory of Justice*, p. 267.

47 Rawls, *A Theory of Justice*, p. 7.

48 Cohen, *If You're and Egalitarian . . .* , pp. 138–9.

49 Moellendorf, *Cosmopolitan Justice*, pp. 37–8.

50 See Ripstein, "Private Order and Public Justice," p. 1437.

51 Thus, the view I am defending is a form of what Joshua Cohen and Charles Sabel call "weak statism" in "Extra Rempublicam Nulla Justitia?" *Philosophy and Public Affairs* 34 (2) (Spring 2006), p. 150.

52 Constantine Michalopoulos, *Developing Countries in the WTO* (London: Palgrave, 2001), pp. 159–60. On exclusive negotiations at the WTO, see Kent Jones, *Who's Afraid of the WTO?* (New York: Oxford, 2004), p. 26.

53 Martin Wolf, *Why Globalization Works* (New Haven, CT: Yale University Press, 2004), p. 289.

54 Compare Kant, "Toward Perpetual Peace," p. 327 [Ak. 8: 355–6]: "what holds in accordance with natural right for human beings in a lawless condition, 'they ought to leave this condition,' cannot hold for states in accordance with the right of nations (since, as states, they already have a rightful constitution internally and hence have outgrown the constraint of others to bring them under a more extended law-governed constitution in accordance with their concepts of right)." Instead, he argues, reason requires a "*pacific league*" that "does not look to acquiring any power of a state but only to preserving and securing the *freedom* of a state itself and of other states in league with it, but without there being any need for them to subject themselves to public laws and coercion under them (as people in a state of nature must do)."

55 The Agreement on Trade-Related Aspects of Intellectual Property Rights (TRIPS) itself arguably violated the nonsubordination requirement in both its content and the process of its creation. It "was a major source of the North–South contention in the lead-up to the Uruguay Round [that created the WTO]." Eventually, "the EC and the United States successfully drafted an intellectual property agreement in the context of the Uruguay Round and imposed it on developing countries." John Barton, Judith Goldstein, Timothy Josling, and Richard Steinberg, *The Evolution of the Trade Regime: Politics, Law and Economics of the GATT and the WTO* (Princeton, NJ; Princeton University Press, 2006), p. 140. TRIPS is a rather anomalous part of the WTO, since "the main effect of the agreement is to protect rents in profitable activities. The thrust of the TRIPS is therefore very different from the notion of 'driving out' rents by the steady reduction of protection at the border." Barton, et al., *The Evolution of the Trade Regime*, p. 142. Even many defenders of the WTO are critical of TRIPS. See, for example, Jones, *Who's Afraid of the WTO?*, pp. 158–60, and Wolf, *Why Globalization Works*, pp. 216–17.

56 Ripstein, "Private Order and Public Justice," p. 1411, n. 47; cf. p. 1392.

GLOBAL JUSTICE

HUMAN RIGHTS

The Dark Side of Human Rights[1]

Onora O'Neill

In his *Reflections on the Revolution in France* Edmund Burke asks

> What is the use of discussing a man's abstract right to food or medicine? The question is upon the method of procuring and administering them. In that deliberation I shall always advise to call in the aid of the farmer and the physician rather than the professor of metaphysics.[2]

Burke's question is sharp. What is the point of having a right? More specifically what is the point of having an abstract right, unless you also have a way of securing whatever it is that you have a right to? Why should we prize natural or abstract rights if there is no way of ensuring their delivery? And if we need to secure their delivery, are not "the farmer and the physician" not merely of greater use than abstract or natural rights, but also of greater use than positive rights to claim food or medicine? For a hungry person, positive and justiciable rights to food are to be sure better than abstract rights that are not justiciable: but those who know how to grow, harvest, store, and cook food are more useful, and having the food is better still. When we are ill, positive and justiciable rights to healthcare are to be sure better than abstract rights that are not justiciable: but skilled doctors and nurses are more useful, and receiving their care is better still.

In a way it is surprising to find Burke discussing abstract rights to food or healthcare, for these presumed rights came to full prominence only in the late twentieth century. They are commonly called welfare rights, and contrasted with liberty rights. This, I think, is a misnomer. The salient feature of these rights is not that they contribute to the welfare of the recipient (although they are likely to do so), but that they are rights to goods or services. If there are to be rights to goods or services, those goods and services must be provided, and more specifically provided *by someone* – for example, by the farmer and the physician.

Most of the abstract rights against which Burke campaigned were the rights proclaimed in the *Declaration of the Rights of Man and of the Citizen* of 1789 (*Declaration of 1789*). They are what we now call liberty rights. The short list in Article 2 of the *Declaration* states succinctly "the natural rights of man, which must not be prevented . . . are freedom, property, security and resistance to oppression."[3] Needless to say, the right to property is not to be understood as a right to some amount of property, but as a right to security of tenure of property: it too is a liberty right, not a right to any goods or services.[4] Much of the *Declaration of 1789* is concerned with the rights to process needed to make liberty rights justiciable: rights to the rule of law, to habeas corpus, to what we would now call accountable public administration. The rights of the *Declaration of 1789* are rights against *all* others and *all* institutions. Liberty rights are universal – and so are the corresponding obligations. They are compromised if *any* others are exempt from those counterpart obligations. If anyone may infringe my rights to freedom, property and security, or to resist oppression, I have only incomplete and blemished rights of these sorts.

On closer consideration, matters have turned out to be rather more complicated. The institutions for securing and enforcing liberty rights require an allocation of certain obligations to specified others rather than to all others. First-order obligations to respect liberty rights must be universal, but second-order obligations to ensure that everyone respects liberty rights must be allocated. There is no effective rule of law without law enforcement, and law enforcement needs law enforcers who are assigned specific tasks; there is no effective accountability of public administration without institutions that allocate the tasks and responsibilities and hold specified office-holders to account. Nevertheless, the asymmetry between abstract liberty rights and abstract rights to goods and services is convincing: we can know who violates a liberty right without any allocation of obligations, but we cannot tell who violates a right to goods or services unless obligations have been allocated.

This well-known point has not impeded the rise and rise of an international human rights culture that is replete with claims about abstract rights to goods and services, now seen as universal human rights, but often muddled or vague, or both, about the allocation of the obligations without which these rights not merely cannot be met, but remain undefined. The cornucopia of universal human rights includes both liberty rights[5] and rights to goods and services, and specifically rights to food and rights to healthcare. The right to food is proclaimed in Article 11 of the 1966 *International Covenant on Economic, Social and Cultural Rights* (*CESCR*), which asserts "the right of everyone to an adequate standard of living for himself and his family, including adequate food, clothing and housing, and to the continuous improvement of living conditions"[6] (the *continuous improvement* is a nice touch!). Article 11 of *CESCR* has been adopted as a guiding principle of the Food and Agriculture Organization (FAO), which has made its mission "food security for all".[7] The right to health (to *health*, not just to *healthcare*: another nice touch!) is proclaimed in Article 12 of the *CESCR*, which recognizes "the right of everyone to the enjoyment of the highest attainable standard of physical and mental health."[8] Article 12 has been adopted as the guiding principle of the World Health Organization (WHO).[9]

There is an interesting difference between Articles 11 and 12 of *CESCR*. The right to food is viewed as a right to *adequate food*, not to the *best attainable food*; the right to health is viewed as a right to the *highest attainable standard . . . of health*,

Onora O'Neill

and not as a *right to adequate health*. One can see why the drafters of the *Covenant* may have shrunk from proclaiming a *right to adequate health*, but in qualifying this right as a *right to the highest attainable standard of health* many questions were begged. Is this right only a right to the standard of health that a person can attain with locally available and affordable treatment – however meagre that may be? Or is it a right to the highest standard available globally – however expensive that may be? The first is disappointingly minimal, and the latter barely coherent (how can everyone have a right to the best?). And what is required of the farmer, the physician and others who actually have to provide food and healthcare? Uncertainties of this sort are unavoidable unless the obligations that correspond to rights to goods and services are well specified.

Norms, aspirations and cynicism

Does any of this matter? Perhaps we should view the Declarations and Covenants that promulgate human rights as setting out noble aspirations, which are helpful to articulate and bear in mind when establishing institutions, programs, policies and activities that allocate obligations. In effect, we would concede that the rhetoric of universal human rights to goods or services was deceptive, but defend it as a noble lie that helps to mobilize support for establishing justiciable rights of great importance. There is something to be said for this view of human rights Declarations and Covenants as ideological documents that can help mobilize energy for action that makes a difference, but many would see this as cynical.

In any case, this interpretation of human rights claims would be wholly at odds with ordinary understandings of rights. Both liberty rights and rights to goods and services are standardly seen as *claim rights* or *entitlements* that are valid against those with the counterpart obligations. Rights are seen as one side of a normative relationship between right-holders and obligation-bearers. We normally regard supposed claims or entitlements that nobody is obliged to respect or honor as null and void, indeed undefined. An understanding of the normative arguments that link rights to obligations underlies daily and professional discussion both of supposedly *universal* human rights, and of the *special* rights created by specific voluntary actions and transactions (treaty, contract, promise, marriage, etc.). There cannot be a claim to rights that are rights against nobody, or nobody in particular: universal rights will be rights against all comers; special rights will be rights against specifiable others.

Only if we jettison the entire normative understanding of rights in favor of a merely aspirational view, can we break the normative link between rights and their counterpart obligations. If we take rights seriously and see them as normative rather than aspirational, we must take obligations seriously. If on the other hand we opt for a merely aspirational view, the costs are high. For then we would also have to accept that where human rights are unmet there is no breach of obligation, nobody at fault, nobody who can be held to account, nobody to blame and nobody who owes redress. We would in effect have to accept that human rights claims are not real claims.

Most advocates of human rights would be reluctant to jettison the thought that they are *prescriptive* or *normative* in favor of seeing them as merely *aspirational*.[10] We generally view human rights claims as setting out requirements from the standpoint of recipients, who are *entitled to* or *have a claim to* action or forbearance by others with corresponding obligations. From a normative or prescriptive view, the point of human rights claims would be eroded if nobody were required to act or forbear to meet these claims. A normative view of rights claims has to take obligations seriously, since they are the counterparts to rights; it must view them as articulating the normative requirements that fall either on all or on specified obligation-bearers. Few proponents of human rights would countenance the thought that there are human rights that nobody is obliged to respect. (The converse thought is unproblematic: there can be obligations even where no claimants are defined; such "imperfect" obligations are generally seen as moral obligations, but not as obligations of justice with counterpart rights.)

The claim that rights must have well-specified counterpart obligations is not equivalent to the commonplace piety that rights and responsibilities go together, which asserts only that right-holders are also obligation-bearers. This is often, but not always, true. Many agents – citizens, workers, students, teachers, employees – are both right-holders and obligation-bearers. But some right-holders – infants, the severely disabled, the senile – cannot carry obligations, so have no responsibilities. By contrast, the claim that rights must have counterpart obligations asserts the exceptionless logical point that where anyone is to have a right there must be identifiable others (either all others or specified others) with accurately corresponding obligations. From a normative view of rights, obligations and claimable rights are two perspectives on a single normative pattern: without the obligations there are no rights. So while obligations will drop out of sight if we read human rights "claims" merely as aspirations rather than requirements, so too will rights, as they are usually understood. Unsurprisingly, aspirational readings of human rights documents are not popular. However, such readings at least offer an exit strategy if we conclude that claiming rights without specifying counterpart obligations is an unacceptable deception, and find that we can't develop an adequate normative account of obligations and rights.

Clearly it would be preferable to offer a serious account of the allocation of obligations that correspond to all human rights. But do Declarations and Covenants provide an account – or even a clue – to the allocation of the obligations that are the counterparts to rights to goods and services? This point was complicated at the birth of human rights by the unfortunately obscure drafting of the 1948 *UDHR*,[11] which gestures to the thought that certain obligations lie with states, then confusingly assigns them indifferently to nations, countries and peoples as well as states. Not all of these have the integrated capacities for action and decision-making needed for agency, and so for carrying obligations.[11] For present purposes I shall leave problems arising from this unfortunate drafting aside, and rely on the fact that in later documents, including *CESCR,* these ambiguities are apparently resolved in favor of assigning obligations to states party, that is to the signatory states.

This approach has apparent advantages – and stings in its tail. The first sting is that states that do not ratify a Covenant will not incur the obligations it specifies: not a welcome conclusion to advocates of universal human rights, since these states thereby escape obligations to respect, let alone enforce, the rights promulgated. The second sting is sharper. The obligations created by signing and ratifying Covenants are *special*, not *universal* obligations. So the rights that are their corollaries will also be *special* or *institutional rights*, not *universal human rights*. Once we take a normative view of rights and obligations, they must be properly matched. If human rights are independent of institutional structures, if they are not created by special transactions, so too are the corresponding obligations; conversely if obligations are the creatures of convention, so too are the rights.

These unwelcome implications of taking the human rights documents at face value might be avoided in several ways. One well-known thought is that so long as we confine ourselves to liberty rights there is no allocation problem, since these rights are only complete if *all* others are obliged to respect them. We can coherently see universal liberty rights as independent of institutions or transactions, and read the parts of instruments that deal with liberty rights as affirming rather than creating those rights (justifying such claims would be a further task). But the fact that liberty rights do not face an allocation problem (although enforcing them raises just that problem) offers small comfort to those who hope to show that rights to goods or services, for example to food or medicine, are universal human rights rather than the creatures of convention. A normative view of human rights cannot view rights to food and medicine as pre-institutional while denying that there are any pre-institutional counterpart obligations or obligation holders; it must take a congruent view of the counterpart obligations. But this suggests that such rights must be special, institutional rights rather than universal human rights. There is, of course, nothing wrong or problematic about conventional or institutional rights, but if Declarations and Covenants create rights to goods and services, claims that they are universal or human rights lack justification. Declarations and Covenants cannot show that some particular configuration of institutional rights and obligations is universally optimal or desirable, or even justifiable.

This dilemma might be fudged by allowing the idea of human rights to goods and services to drift between two interpretations. A view of rights to goods and services as independent of institutions and transactions could be cited as offering a basis for justifying some rather than other institutional arrangements. A view of rights to goods and services as the creatures of convention could fit with well-defined counterpart institutional obligations, but offers no claims about their justification other than the fact that (some) states have signed up to them. Equivocation is a desperate justificatory strategy. Yet this equivocation is disconcertingly common in discussions of human rights claims.

This dilemma within normative views of rights and obligations can be resolved in more than one way. We could conclude that liberty rights are fundamental and universal, and claim that they can be justified without reference to Covenants or institutions, but concede that rights to goods and services are special (institutional, positive) rights that can be justified only by appeal to specific transactions, such as signing and ratifying Covenants. We could try to justify a configuration of special rights and the institutional structures that secure them and their counterpart obligations. For example, we might argue that certain rights to goods and services and their counterpart obligations protect basic human needs or interests, or that they have utilitarian or economic justification. Or we could justify institutional structures that define and secure special rights and obligations more deeply by appealing to a theory of the good (moral realists) or a theory of duty (Kantians). The option that is closed is to claim that human rights and obligations are corollary normative claims, but that there are some universal rights without counterpart obligations. So there are plenty of possibilities – although each may raise its own difficulties. If none of these possibilities can be made to work, the default position would be to reject normative views of human rights and to see human rights claims as aspirational (noting that aspirations need justification too) and to treat the task of establishing institutions that allow for justiciable claims as a task to be guided in part by appealing to those aspirations. And then, it may seem, we in effect endorse a cynical reading of the human rights Declarations and Covenants.

State obligations

These are awkward problems, but I think that others may lie deeper. The deepest problem may be that the obligations assigned to states by some of the most significant Declarations and Covenants are *not* the corollaries of the human rights that the documents proclaim. The Covenants do not assign states straightforward obligations to respect liberty rights (after all, liberty rights have to be respected by all, not only by states), but rather second-order obligations to *secure* respect for them. Equally, they do not assign states obligations to meet rights to goods and services, but rather second-order obligations to *ensure* that they are met. For example, Article 2 of the *CESCR* proclaims that

> Each State Party to the present Covenant undertakes to take steps, individually and through international assistance and co-operation, especially economic and technical, to the maximum of its available resources, with a view to achieving progressively the full realisation of the rights recognized in the present Covenant by all appropriate means, including particularly the adoption of legislative measures.[12]

"Achieving progressively the full realisation of . . . rights . . . by all appropriate means" is evidently not merely a matter of respecting the rights recognized in *CESCR*. It is a matter of ensuring that others – both individuals and institutions – carry out the obligations that correspond to those rights. Later comments by the Office of the High Commissioner for Human Rights spell out some of the obligations that states are taken to assume if they ratify the two Covenants.[13]

An immediate and encouraging thought might be that if the obligations assigned to states by the international Declarations and Covenants are *not* the counterparts of the human rights proclaimed, but second-order obligations to ensure or secure respect for such rights, then this may resolve the allocation problem for rights to goods and services. States party to a Covenant are seen as acquiring special obligations by signing and ratifying the instrument. It would then be clear that those special, second-order obligations did not have counterpart rights, let alone counterpart universal human rights. They are second-order obligations to secure some configuration of first-order rights and obligations. This thought may be helpful: since obligations without counterpart rights are normatively coherent (unlike rights without counterpart obligations), we can take a normative view of the obligations assumed by states that sign and ratify the Covenants, and can see them as setting requirements. Human rights enter into the Covenants only indirectly as aspects of the content of second-order state obligations.

Onora O'Neill

But a second thought is far less congenial to those who would like to see human rights as normative. If the obligations that the Declarations and Covenants assign to states are *not* the counterparts of the human rights these instruments declare or recognize, then they also do not define the first-order obligations that are the counterparts of human rights. Rather the problem of giving a coherent normative instantiation of Declarations and Convenants is devolved to the states party, which may (or may not) set out to secure positive rights for their citizens. If the claims of the human rights documents have normative force they must be matched by obligations; if they are not matched by obligations, they are *at best* aspirational.

As I suggested earlier, it may not be wholly a misfortune if the supposed rights declared in the Declarations and Covenants are seen as aspirations. Legal commentators might be willing to say that there is still substance in there, in that the States party take on real obligations to realize these aspirations. Non-lawyers may habitually make the mistake of thinking that Declarations and Covenants claim that there are pre-institutional universal human rights, but their mistake is not necessary – although politically convenient – for progress toward the realization of the underlying aspirations, once states have signed up. This is a coherent position, but unlikely to be popular with those who seek to base ethical and political claims on appeals to human rights, which they see as normatively fundamental rather than as the creatures of the convention that are anchored in the Covenants that assign obligations to realize aspirations to states.

And there are further difficulties. If we read Declarations and Covenants as instruments by which states assume second-order obligations to define and allocate first-order obligations that correspond to certain human rights (now no longer seen as universal rights), why should all the obligations lie with states? A plausible answer would be that states, and only states, have the powers necessary to carry the relevant second-order obligations to define and allocate first-order obligations and rights to individuals and institutions. The story is told of a journalist who asked the bank robber Willie Sutton why he robbed banks and got the puzzled answer: "That's where the money is." Similarly we might reply to anyone who wonders why Declarations and Covenants assign obligations that are to secure human rights to states by pointing out that that's where the power is.

But the thought that it makes sense to assign all second-order obligations to define and allocate obligations to states because they, and only they, have the power to discharge these obligations is often less than comforting. Many states violate rather than respect human rights. Assigning second-order obligations to define and allocate first-order obligations and rights to agents who do not even reliably respect the first-order obligations that correspond to those rights may be rather like putting foxes in charge of hen houses. It is true enough that those who are to achieve progressively the full realization of human rights must have capacities to do so – but it does not follow that those with (a good range of) the necessary capacities can be trusted to do so. Some states – not only those we think of as rogue states – disregard or override many of the Covenant rights. Some sign and ratify the relevant international instruments, but make limited efforts to work toward their full realization.

Other states lack the power to carry the obligations to "achieve progressively the full realisation of the rights recognized" in Declarations and Covenants. Weak states – failed states, quasi states – cannot carry such demanding obligations. Although they may not always violate them, they cannot secure their inhabitants' liberty rights; still less can they ensure that their inhabitants have effective entitlements to goods and services. It is an empty gesture to assign the obligations needed for human rights to weak states, comparable to the empty gesture made by town councils in Britain in the 1980s that proclaimed their towns nuclear free zones. Indeed, even strong and willing states may find that they cannot "achieve progressively the full realisation of the rights recognized" in Declarations and Covenants. Strong states may have a monopoly of the legitimate use of force within their territories; but they seldom have a monopoly of the effective use of other forms of power. There are plenty of reasons for thinking carefully about the specific character of state power, and for questioning the assumption that powerful – let alone weak – states can carry the range of second-order obligations that they ostensibly take on in signing and ratifying human rights instruments.

Given these realities, it may be worth reconsidering whether all second-order obligations to secure human rights should lie with states. Perhaps some of them should lie with powerful nonstate actors, such as transnational corporations, powerful nongovernmental organizations, or major religious, cultural, and professional and educational bodies. The assumption that states and states alone should hold all the relevant obligations may reflect the extraordinary dominance of state power in the late twentieth century, rather than a timeless solution to the problem of allocating obligations to provide goods and services effectively. For present purposes, I shall leave these unsettling possibilities unexplored, but say a little more about some of the cultural and political costs that are linked to persistent confusion between normative and aspirational views of human rights.

Control and blame

If human rights are not pre-conventional, universal rights, but are grounded in the special obligations assumed by states, then there is – at the very least – an awkward gap between reality and rhetoric. The second-order obligations of states are discharged by imposing first-order obligations on others and enforcing them. The reality is that state agency and state power, and that of derivative institutions, is used to construct institutions that (partially) secure rights, and that to do this it is necessary to control the action of individuals and institutions systematically and in detail. If states party are to discharge the second-order obligations they assume in signing and ratifying human rights Covenants, they must not only ensure that liberty rights are respected by all, but must assign and enforce first-order obligations whose discharge will deliver rights to goods and services to all. Human beings, it is evident, will not merely be the intended *beneficiaries* of these obligations, but will carry the intended *burdens*.

The system of control that states must impose to ensure that these obligations are discharged is likely to be dauntingly complex. Yet, as Burke pointed out, what we really need if we are to have food and medicine is the active engagement of "the farmer and the physician." Can that active engagement be secured or improved by imposing detailed and complex obligations on those who are to carry the relevant first-order obligations? There is much to consider here, and I offer very brief comments under four headings: complexity, compliance, complaint and compensation.

Onora O'Neill

Complexity

Detailed control is needed to "achieve progressively the full realisation" of very complex sets of potentially conflicting rights, which must be mutually adjusted. It is no wonder that legislation in the age of human rights has become prolix and demanding. Those who frame it have to seek to ensure that individuals and institutions conform to a very large number of constraints in all activities, so have to set and enforce very detailed requirements.[14] It is now common in developed societies to find that legislation imposes highly complex procedures that bristle with duties to register, duties to obtain permission, duties to consult, rights to appeal, as well as proliferating requirements to record, to disclose, and to report. Such legislation is typically supplemented by copious regulation, relentless "guidance", prolix codes of good practice, and highly intrusive forms of accountability. These highly detailed forms of social control may be unavoidable in a public culture that aims to "achieve progressively the full realisation" of an extraordinarily complex set of rights, so has to impose complex demands and burdens on all activities and all areas of life.

The results are demanding for the state agencies that are supposed to set the requirements and police the system. They can be dementing for the institutions and individuals that are to carry the first-order obligations – not least for the farmer and the physician. Complex controls risk stifling active engagement. Those of whom too much that is extraneous to their basic tasks – growing food, caring for the sick – is required are likely to resent the proliferating and time-consuming requirements to obtain permissions, to consult third parties, to record, to disclose, to report, and to comply with the demands of inspectors or regulators. These requirements for control and accountability impose heavy human and financial costs, and are often damaging to the performance of primary tasks. Those who face these burdens on their attempts to perform demanding substantive tasks – the farmer and the physician – may comply and resent (and sometimes engage in defensive practices); they may protest and complain; or they may withdraw from activities that have been made too burdensome. The costs of complex control systems are paid in increasing wariness and weariness, skepticism and resentment, and ultimately in less active engagement by "the farmer and the physician," and by others who come to see themselves primarily as obligation-bearers rather than as right-holders.

Compliance

Individuals who are subject to hyper-complex legislation, regulation and control are offered two roles. As obligation-bearers their role is compliance; as right holders they are permitted and encouraged to seek redress and to complain when others fail to comply. The individuals and institutions on whom first-order obligations are imposed in the name of securing human rights are offered limited options: they can soldier loyally on in compliance with the obligations states impose; they can voice their discontent; they can exit from the tasks that have been made too burdensome by the excess complexity of legislation and regulation.[15] Loyal compliance becomes harder and more burdensome when the sheer number and complexity of requirements imposed damages the quality with which substantive tasks can be achieved. Voicing concern and objecting to these controls provides some, but limited relief.

Exit from the activities that have been made too burdensome may often be the most reasonable and the preferred option. For "the farmer and the physician," exit means giving up growing food and caring for the sick.

There may be ways of extending human rights that do not carry these costs, that use a "lighter touch", that achieve "better regulation".[16] But the jury is out on this matter. At present, and certainly in the U.K., the juggernaut of human rights demands, at every stage of legislation and of the regulatory process, tends to increase complexity even when the costs for "the farmer and the physician", and the damage to the services they provide, are high and well known.

Complaint

First-order obligation-bearers are also right-holders, and it may be that the burdens their obligations impose are recompensed by the rights they enjoy as a result of others discharging their obligations. However, the experience of right-holders is not symmetric with that of obligation-bearers. Individuals act as right-holders only when something has gone awry. In that situation they may complain, seek redress and compensation. The legislation and regulation of states that take human rights seriously often provide a range of remedies – for those with the time, energy, courage (or foolhardiness) to pursue them. When complaints work, redress may be achieved and, compensation may be secured. But often the experience of complainants is less than happy because the process of achieving redress is complex, exhausting and frustrating, and the remedies less than would satisfy and assuage a sense of injury. Since the role of complainant is too often one that exhausts, demoralizes, and undermines active engagement, many who are wronged do not choose this course of action. For "the farmer and the physician" and for many others the choice is mainly between loyalty and exit: giving voice is not generally a positive experience, since it requires complainants to see themselves as victims rather than as actively engaged.

Compensation and blame

The best outcome of the voice option is that, with luck and persistence, those who take on the role of victim or complainant achieve redress and compensation, or some opportunity for the dubious pleasures of casting blame. Compensation clearly has its positive side – although it may be hard to achieve, limited in amount and is not always worth the struggle through the complexities of process. Blaming by contrast is a readily available and cheap pleasure – even for complainants whose case is not upheld. Those who cast blame can appropriate, enjoy, and prolong their role and status as victims, can enjoy indignation and a feeling of superiority, even if they cannot quite identify or demonstrate the failings of others. If it proves impossible to identify a blameworthy culprit, they can at least blame the system, that is to say the institutional framework that is failing to achieve "progressively the full realisation of the rights recognized . . . by all appropriate means, including particularly the adoption of legislative measures"

There is a dark and tempting undercurrent of pleasure in blaming. Nobody has written about the psychology of blaming, or about its murky appeal and insidious

Onora O'Neill

psychological effects, more brilliantly and darkly than Nietzsche. Some of his comments are particularly apt to the realities of the farmer and the physician:

> Suffering people all have a horrible willingness and capacity for inventing pretexts for painful emotional feelings. They already enjoy their suspicions, they're brooding over bad actions and apparent damage. They ransack the entrails of their past and present, looking for dark and dubious stories, in which they are free to feast on an agonizing suspicion and to get intoxicated on their own poisonous anger. They rip open the oldest wounds, they bleed themselves to death from long-healed scars. They turn friends, wives, children, and anyone else who is closest to them into criminals. "I am suffering. Someone or other must be to blame for that".[17]

I do not wish to suggest that the human rights culture inevitably promotes this rancorous approach to life. But I do not think we should accept at face value the view that it is all about respect for persons and treating others as agents. Much of it is indeed about protecting the weak and vulnerable. But it is also about extending the power of states over nonstate actors and human individuals, about establishing systems of control and discipline that extend into the remotest corners of life, about running people's lives for them while leaving them with the consoling pleasures of blame. As Bernard Williams puts it, blame is "the characteristic reaction of the morality system" in which obligations and rights have become the sole ethical currency.[18]

We find it unsurprising that the ruling ideas of past eras have been superseded and modified, and we can hardly doubt that human rights are a central ruling idea of our age. Yet we do not find much current discussion of the likelihood that the idea of human rights may suffer the same fate. Public discourse is for the most part admiring, and often represents human rights as unquestionable truth and progress: we may question anything – except human rights. Indeed, unlike some earlier dominant ideologies, the human rights movement has acquired the beguiling feature of being an ideology not only of and for the ruling classes, but an ideology for – and increasingly of – the oppressed. This seems to me a good reason for thinking particularly carefully and critically about the internal structure of human rights claims, for trying to be less gestural about their basis and their limits, and for being more explicit about their costs as well as their benefits. The farmer and the physician, and others whose work and commitment are indispensable, are the key to securing a decent standard of life for all: their active enthusiasm and efforts are more valuable than their dour compliance with prescribed procedures, their resentful protest, let alone their refusal to contribute.

Notes

1 This is a revised version of the *Martin Wight Lecture* given at the London School of Economics on October 14, 2004. I am grateful for a number of helpful comments at and following the lecture, especially from Conor Gearty, Nick Rengger, and Chris Brown.

2 Edmund Burke, *Reflections on the Revolution in France*, ed. Conor Cruise O'Brien (London: Penguin Books, 1984), pp. 151–2.

3 *Declaration of the Rights of Man and of the Citizen*, 1789, www.magnacartaplus.org/ french-rights/ 1789.htm.

4 Note also Article 17 of the *Declaration* of 1789: "Property, being an inviolable and sacred right, no one may be deprived of it; unless public necessity, legally investigated, clearly requires it, and just and prior compensation has been paid."

5 Set out in the *UN International Covenant on Civil and Political Rights*, 1966 (*CCPR*). This Covenant also "recognizes" various rights that are not liberty rights. See www.magnacartaplus.org/uno-docs/covenant.htm.

6 *CESCR*, Art. 11. See www.unhchr.ch/html/menu3/b/a_cescr.htm.

7 See the FAO website at www.fao.org/UNFAO/about/index_en.html.

8 *CESCR*, Art. 12. The two Articles expand on rights proclaimed in Article 25 if the *Universal Declaration of Human Rights* of 1948 (UDHR), which runs 'Everyone has the right to a standard of living adequate for the health and well-being of himself and of his family, including food, clothing, housing and medical care and necessary social services, and the right to security in the event of unemployment, sickness, disability, widowhood, old age or other lack of livelihood in circumstances beyond his control'. For the text of the UDHR see www.bee-leaf.com/universaldeclarationhumanrights.html.

9 The WHO's objective, as set out in its Constitution, is "the attainment by all peoples of the highest possible level of health," defined expansively as "a state of complete physical, mental and social well-being and not merely the absence of disease or infirmity," www.who.int/about/en/.

10 See recently James Griffin, "Discrepancies between the Best Philosophical Account of Human Rights and the International Law of Human Rights," *Proceedings of the Aristotelian Society*, CI (2001): 1–28.

11 The text can be found at www.imcl/biz/docs/humanrights.pdf. For further comments on some confusions about obligations and agency in *UDHR*, see Onora O'Neill, "Agents of Justice," in Thomas W. Pogge, *Global Justice* (Oxford: Blackwell, 2001), pp. 188–203.

12 Article 2 *CESCR* at www.unhchr.ch/html/menu3/b/a_cescr.htm.

13 *The Nature of States Parties Obligations*, Art. 2, para. 1 of the Covenant, Fifth session, 1990, Office of the High Commissioner for Human Rights, *CESCR* General comment 3, www.unhchr.ch/tbs/doc.nsf/(symbol)/CESCR+General+comment+3.En?OpenDocument.

14 Michael Moran, *The British Regulatory State: High Modernism and Hyper-Innovation* (Oxford: Oxford University Press, 2003). Moran argues that the new regulatory state is neither liberal nor decentralizing, despite its commitment to human rights. Rather it is both interventionist and centralizing in ways that colonize hitherto relatively independent domains of civil society – including those of the farmer and the physician.

15 See Albert O. Hirschmann, *Exit, Voice and Loyalty: Responses to Decline in Firms, Organizations and States* (Cambridge, MA: Harvard University Press, 1970), for a classic analysis of these options.

16 The United Kingdom government established a *Better Regulation Task Force* in 1997. It promotes the "five principles of better regulation," which are said to be Proportionality, Accountability, Consistency, Transparency, and Targeting (consistency is a nice touch!). See the task force's website at www.brtf.gov.uk/.

17 Friedrich Nietzsche, *The Genealogy of Morals*, Pt. III, sec. 15. This translation, which draws on earlier received versions, can be found at *The Nietzsche Channel*'s website at www.geocities.com/thenietzschechannel/onthe3.htm#3e15.

18 Bernard Williams, *Ethics and the Limits of Philosophy* (London: Fontana, 1985), p. 177.

A Defense of Welfare Rights as Human Rights*

James W. Nickel

Human rights are now a settled part of international law and politics. By 2000 the main human rights treaties had been ratified by a large majority of the world's countries. As Ann Bayefsky writes, "Every UN member state is a party to one or more of the six major human rights treaties. 80% of states have ratified four or more" (Bayefsky 2001). This is not to say, of course, that most states fully comply with these treaties. Rights to economic benefits and services, variously known as "economic and social rights" or "welfare rights," are among the families of rights that are securely established in international law.

The American Declaration of the Rights of Man (Organization of American States 1948) and the Universal Declaration of Human Rights (United Nations 1948) asserted rights to an adequate standard of living, health services, and education. To make these rights part of international law, the United Nations created the International Covenant on Economic, Social, and Cultural Rights (hereinafter "Economic and Social Covenant," United Nations 1976). More than 140 countries have ratified this treaty. The Economic and Social Covenant's list of rights includes nondiscrimination in employment (Articles 2 and 3), freedom to work and opportunities to work (Article 4), fair pay and decent conditions of work (Article 7), the right to form trade unions and to strike (Article 8), social security (Article 9), the right to adequate food, clothing, and housing (Article 11), the right to basic health services (Article 12), and the right to education (Article 13).

Although economic and social rights are securely established within international law, the idea that they are fully justifiable human rights remains controversial among lawyers and political theorists. Economic and social rights are often alleged to be desirable goals but not really rights. This paper offers a defense of economic and social rights by constructing and applying a justificatory structure and by rebutting various objections to them.

I. The Vance Conception of Economic and Social Rights

Human rights are not ideals of the good life for humans; they are rather concerned with ensuring the conditions, negative and positive, of a minimally good life. If we apply this idea to economic and social rights it suggests that these standards should not be concerned with promoting the highest possible standards of living or with identifying the best or most just form of economic system. Rather they should attempt to address the worst problems and abuses in the economic area. Their focus should be on hunger, malnutrition, preventable disease, ignorance, and exclusion from productive opportunities.

Some philosophers have followed this line of thought to the conclusion that the main economic and social right is "subsistence." Henry Shue, John Rawls, and Brian Orend make subsistence the centerpiece of their concern for economic and social rights. Shue defines subsistence as "unpolluted air, unpolluted water, adequate food, adequate clothing, adequate shelter, and minimal preventive health care" (Shue 1996). Orend's definition is very similar: "Material subsistence means having secure access to those resources one requires to meet one's biological needs – notably a minimal level of nutritious food, clean water, fresh air, some clothing and shelter, and basic preventive health care" (Orend 2001). Rawls includes "subsistence" on his very short list of human rights, treating it along with security as part of the right to life. Rawls interprets "subsistence" as including "minimum economic security" or "having general all-purpose economic means" (Rawls 1999).

The idea of subsistence alone offers too minimal a conception of economic and social rights. It neglects education, gives an extremely minimal account of health services, and generally gives too little attention to people's ability to be active participants and contributors (see Sen 1999b: 27; Nussbaum 2001). It covers the requirements of having a life, but neglects important material conditions of being able to lead one's life.

If Shue, Rawls, and Orend err by making economic and social rights too minimal, international human rights documents make them excessively grandiose by including aspirations and ideals. They view economic and social rights as prescriptions for prosperity and an ample welfare state. For example, the European Social Charter, which set the pattern for other treaties in this area, includes a human right to vocational guidance, a human right to annual holidays with pay, and a human right to "protection of health" that aspires "to remove as far as possible the causes of ill-health" (Articles 9, 2, 11, and 26). I recognize, of course, that these are good things that political movements legitimately promote at the national level. As a resident of a rich country I would vote for them. But these standards go far beyond the conditions of a minimally good life. Further, it would not be plausible to castigate a country as a human rights violator because it fails to fund occupational guidance, to require employers to provide employees with holidays with pay, or to mount an anti-smoking campaign (smoking is surely one of the main causes of ill-health). The point is not merely that poorer countries should be excused from these requirements. It is that these formulations do not have a good fit with the idea of human rights as minimal standards even when we are thinking about rich countries.

I advocate a conception of economic and social rights that goes beyond subsistence to include healthcare and education. I call it the "Vance Conception" because

James W. Nickel

it conforms to the list advocated by former U.S. Secretary of State Cyrus Vance in his 1977 Law Day speech at the University of Georgia (Vance 1977). In that speech Vance set out a view of human rights that included "the right to the fulfillment of such vital needs as food, shelter, health care and education." Although this list is more expansive than subsistence alone, it adheres to the idea that economic and social rights, like other human rights, are concerned with the conditions of having a minimally good life. It thereby avoids the excesses of contemporary treaties on economic and social rights. This conception suggests that economic and social rights focus on survival, health, and education. It obligates governments to take actions and adopt and implement laws and policies that allow the following questions to be answered affirmatively:

1. *Subsistence* Do conditions allow all people to secure safe air, food, and water as well as environmentally appropriate shelter and clothing if they engage in work and self-help insofar as they can, practice mutual aid through organizations such as families, neighborhoods, and churches, and procure help from available government assistance programs? Do people enjoy access to productive opportunities that allow them to contribute to the well-being of themselves, their families, and their communities?
2. *Health* Do environmental conditions, public health measures, and available health services give people excellent chances of surviving childhood, achieving physical and mental competence, and living a normal lifespan?
3. *Education* Do available educational resources give people a good chance of learning the skills necessary for survival, health, functioning, citizenship, and productivity?

The Vance Conception of economic and social rights identifies three broad and interlocking rights whose fulfillment is needed for all people to have minimally good lives. The definition of the right to subsistence used in this conception is much like Shue's, except that health is moved to a separate category. Some health-related concerns remain within subsistence, however, since air, food, and water must be safe for intake, and shelter and clothing are required to be environmentally appropriate where that includes protections needed for health from cold, heat, and precipitation. Further, it includes access to economic opportunities and thus incorporates some aspects of the right to work (see Arneson 1990).

The Vance Conception views the right to health services in a broader way than Shue's "minimal preventive health care." It covers prevention through public health measures such as sanitation systems and inoculation programs. But it goes beyond these preventive measures to include emergency reparative services such as help in setting broken bones and dealing with infections. And it covers minimal services related to pregnancy and birth. These health services are costly, but they are necessary to many people's ability to have a minimally good life. Further, addressing major health problems promotes people's ability to pursue education and work in an energetic way.

The right to basic education focuses on literacy, numeracy, and preparation for social participation, citizenship, and economic activity. It helps orient economic and social rights towards action, choice, self-help, mutual aid, and social, political, and economic participation. The Universal Declaration emphasizes that basic education should be both free and compulsory. Families do not have the liberty to keep children uneducated and illiterate. But they do have regulated liberties to control the kind of upbringing and education their children receive (Article 26).

The Vance Conception is attractive because it views economic and social rights as minimal standards without limiting their requirements to subsistence and while expecting these standards to be exceeded in most countries. Keeping economic and social rights minimal also makes their realization a plausible aspiration for poorer countries and makes it more likely that economic and social rights can pass a reasonable test of feasibility.

Several of the articles of the Economic and Social Covenant conform to the Vance Conception. The treatment of food and of an adequate standard of living in Article 11 mostly fits. That article commits the countries ratifying the treaty to ensure everyone "an adequate standard of living for himself and his family, including adequate food, clothing and housing," and to "the continuous improvement of living conditions." The Vance Conception interprets "adequate standard of living" as requiring a level adequate for a minimally good life, not for an excellent life. It would reject the demand for "continuous improvement of living conditions" as a confusion of the desirable with the imperative.

There is also a fairly good fit with the statement of the right to education in the Economic and Social Covenant. Article 13 requires free and compulsory primary education for all children, that secondary education be generally available, and that higher education be equally accessible to those equally talented. The idea of giving priority to primary education is a good one. On the Vance Conception, higher education is not directly a matter of human rights. The European Convention's formulation is better, although arguably too vague: "No person shall be denied the right to education" (Protocol 1, Article 2). A still better formulation might describe a right of all persons to basic education, available free to all and compulsory for children, to achieve literacy, numeracy, and the knowledge and skills necessary for health, economic competence, citizenship, and social life.

Not all of the articles conform to the Vance Conception. For example, article 12 of the Economic and Social Covenant puts forward a right to health that recognizes "the right of everyone to the enjoyment of the highest attainable standard of physical and mental health." This article deviates from the idea of human rights as minimal standards in demanding optimization of health rather than setting a threshold.

II. Justifying Economic and Social Rights

Since economic and social rights remain controversial in some quarters, making a strong case for them will be useful. In sketching this case I will presuppose the Vance Conception of economic and social rights. We can begin by sketching a linkage argument that tries to show that the effective implementation of economic and social rights is necessary to the effective implementation of other human rights. After that I propose and use a justificatory framework to defend economic and social rights.

James W. Nickel

A. Linkage arguments

Henry Shue pioneered the use of linkage arguments to defend the right to subsistence. Linkage arguments justify a controversial right by showing that it is necessary to the effective implementation of another right that is already uncontroversial and accepted. Shue defended the right to subsistence by claiming that it was necessary to the effective implementation of any other right: "No one can fully . . . enjoy any right that is supposedly protected by society if he or she lacks the essentials for a reasonably healthy and active life . . ." (Shue 1996: 24–5). In his defense of a right to subsistence, Shue is not merely making the point, sometimes made by Marxists, that guarantees of security or political participation are not very valuable if one must constantly worry about where one's next meal is coming from. Instead, he is making the much stronger claim that a person who does not have an effectively implemented right to subsistence enjoys no rights at all. In Shue's view, a person does not really "enjoy" a right (or, alternatively, a right is not effectively implemented) unless there are social guarantees to protect the substance of the right against the most common threats.

It is important to guard against exaggerated claims about the impossibility of enjoying any other rights without enjoying subsistence rights. Shue's argument has an important limitation since the sacrifice of some people's subsistence rights might supply the means to implement rights to implement due process rights, say, for others. Shue's arguments therefore do not show that a society without subsistence rights for everyone cannot provide other effectively implemented rights to some people. At most they show that such a society cannot provide any other effectively implemented rights to *everyone*. Further, Shue's claim that implemented subsistence rights are needed for the successful implementation of any other rights suggests, contrary to fact, that property rights were not effectively implemented in nineteenth-century America since subsistence rights clearly were not implemented in the United States at that time.

But Shue's key idea can be stated in a more probabilistic form, one that says that without protections for subsistence, basic healthcare, and basic education, people in severe poverty will frequently be marginal right-holders. They will be unlikely to know what rights they have or what they can do to protect them, and their extreme need and vulnerability will make them hard to protect through social and political action. If you want people to be the kind of right-holders who can effectively exercise, benefit from, and protect their rights then you must ensure they enjoy basic economic and social rights.

B. Direct justifications

The justificatory framework I propose requires that a justified human right (1) fit the general idea of human rights, (2) be sufficiently important, (3) respond to recurrent threats, (4) require the modality of rights rather than some weaker norm, (5) impose burdens on the duty-bearers that are not wrongful or excessively heavy, and (6) be feasible in most of the world's countries today.

1. Do economic and social rights fit the general idea of human rights?

Economic and social claims are easily formulated as rights – norms with right-holders who have claims, powers, and immunities; addressees who have duties and liabilities; and scopes or objects specifying a liberty, protection, or benefit that the right-holder is to enjoy. Further, they can be implemented through legislation and adjudication (Fabre 2000).

It is sometimes objected, however, that we cannot identify the addressees of economic and social rights. Let's discuss this with reference to the right to food. People are often perplexed by the idea of an international right to adequate food because they are not sure what it means for them. Does it mean that they have an obligation to feed some fair share of the world's hungry? I propose a complex view of the addressees of human rights that holds that: (1) governments are the primary addressees of the human rights of their residents; (2) governments have negative duties to respect the rights of people from other countries; (3) individuals have negative responsibilities to respect the human rights of people at home and abroad; (4) individuals have responsibilities as voters and citizens to promote human rights in their own country; and (5) governments, international organizations, and individuals have back-up responsibilities for the fulfillment of human rights around the world. This view is easily applied to economic and social rights.

2. Are economic and social rights sufficiently important?

It is sometimes alleged that economic and social rights do not have the importance that civil and political rights have (Beetham 1995; Cranston 1973). If the objection is that some formulations of economic and social rights in international human rights documents are too expansive and go beyond what is necessary to a minimally good life, that point can be conceded and those formulations rejected. But if the objection is that core economic and social rights do not protect very important moral claims it is utterly implausible.

One way of showing the importance of basic economic and social rights has already been provided, namely, the linkage arguments given above. They show that effectively implementing other human rights for all is difficult or impossible in situations where many people's basic economic and social rights are unprotected and insecure.

Theoretical approaches to the justification of human rights typically require one to leave aside many plausible starting points and arguments in order to have an integrated and parsimonious theoretical structure. If human dignity, for example, is not one of the fundamental norms of the theory it is likely to disappear, never to be seen again. It will not do any work in justifying human rights, even if it is well suited to do so. Although normative theory is a valuable project within philosophy, its pursuit of theoretical simplicity may make human rights seem less justifiable than they actually are. When one pushes good ways of justifying human rights off the stage and puts a single favored ground in the limelight, the favored justification is likely to look thin and vulnerable. Alone under the spotlight, its weak spots are likely to be apparent and it may seem obvious that it cannot possibly justify the full range of human rights. Readers may think that if this is the best justification for human rights, those rights are really shaky.

James Griffin, for example, justifies human rights entirely by reference to the values of "personhood" (or autonomy) and "practicalities." He takes this to be the "best philosophical account of human rights":

What seems to me the best account of human rights is this. It is centered on the notion of agency. We human beings have the capacity to form pictures of what a good life would be and to try to realize these pictures. We value our status as agents especially highly, often more highly even than our happiness. Human rights can then be seen as protections of our agency – what one might call our personhood. (Griffin 2001a: 4; see also Tasioulas 2002)

Autonomy by itself doesn't seem likely to be able to generate economic and social rights, due process rights, or rights to nondiscrimination and equality before the law. To compensate, Griffin accordingly relies heavily on "practicalities" in allowing these rights. The result is to make the justification of rights other than liberties appear shaky and derivative. This could have been avoided by introducing some other fundamental values or norms, particularly a requirement of fair treatment when very important interests are at stake (more on this below). A fairness norm would be no more controversial than autonomy as a starting point for human rights, and it would allow due process rights to be as central and nonderivative as liberty rights.

If we think of an argument for a human right as providing a leg or support, writers who want to provide stable and widely appealing justifications for human rights have reason to prefer a many-legged approach. If a right has multiple justifications, the failure of one will be less likely to call the right's justification into doubt. Further, rights with multiple justifications have a better chance of transcending cultural and religious differences. Accordingly, I propose a pluralistic conception of the norms and interests underlying human rights. My starting point is a framework that suggests that people have secure, but abstract, moral claims on others in four areas:

- a secure claim to have a life;
- a secure claim to lead one's life;
- a secure claim against severely cruel or degrading treatment;
- a secure claim against severely unfair treatment.

These four abstract rights with associated duties are "secure" in the sense that they do not have to be earned through membership or good behavior (although claims to liberty can be justifiably suspended upon conviction of a crime). They are also "secure" in the sense that their availability to a person does not depend on that person's ability to generate utility or other good consequences.

These four principles ascribe abstract obligations to respect and protect to everyone – whether individuals, government officials, or corporate entities. Some of the duties involved are obviously positive; negative duties are not given a privileged position. Costs matter, but not whether those costs result from trying to fulfill a negative or a positive duty (Nickel 1987; Holmes and Sunstein 1999).

Each of the four claims is centered on a fundamental human interest. But the overall theory is deontological in the sense that it starts with abstract rights and associated duties. The basic interests serve to orient the rights and duties. A unifying idea for these four secure claims is that if perfectly realized they would make it possible for every person living today to have and lead a life that is decent or minimally good. This is a substantial but limited commitment to equality. Because these principles prescribe a secure floor of respect, protection, and provision for each person, they hold the prospect of grounding the universality of human rights. No person is to be denied respect, protection, or provision except on grounds of impossibility, unacceptably high costs to the basic interests of others, or as a reasonable punishment for a serious crime.

This theory of the supporting reasons for human rights is modest. It sets a low standard, namely a life that is decent or minimally good. As Shue emphasized, human rights offer a morality of the depths, not of the heights (Shue 1996: 18ff.). They are concerned with avoiding misery and ruinous injustice. Second, it recognizes that there are many sources of misery in human life that humans do not control such as natural disasters, diseases, and genetic misfortunes. Third, it recognizes that the specific human rights to be generated from these abstract rights will mainly address the standard threats in various areas to a decent or minimally good life. Perfect protection is not envisioned. Finally, it does not claim to offer a complete moral or political theory.

The secure claim to have a life

A central human interest is security against actions of others that lead to death, destruction of health, or incapacitation. The secure claim to life includes negative duties not to murder, use violence except in self-defense, or harm negligently or maliciously. It includes a claim to freedom and protection from murder, violence, and harm. There are positive duties to assist people when they need help in protecting themselves against threats of murder and violence (on the negative and positive dimensions of the right to life, see Rawls 1999: 65). In today's world these duties to protect and provide will mostly be discharged through the creation and funding of legal and political institutions at the local, national, and international levels.

Having a life, however, requires more than merely being free from violence and harm. One's body must be capable of most normal functions, and to maintain bodily capacities people must satisfy physical needs for food, water, sleep, and shelter. People can usually supply these things for themselves through work. But everyone goes through periods such as childhood, illness, unemployment, disability, and advanced old age when self-supply is impossible. People unable to survive on their own have claims upon others to assistance.

The secure claim to lead one's life

Normal adults are agents, and put great value on continuing to be agents. They evaluate, choose, deliberate, and plan. They recognize and solve practical problems. They make plans for the future and attempt to realize them. Evaluation, choice, and efforts at reform often extend to a person's own character.

The development, maintenance, and exercise of agency have physical, social, and political requirements. Requirements of survival and health are protected by economic and social rights. Social requirements are protected by rights to education and freedom of association. And the political requirements are protected by fundamental freedoms and rights of political participation. The claim to lead one's life yields claims to freedoms from slavery, servitude, and the use of one's life, time, or body without one's consent. It also yields claims to liberties in the most important areas of choice such as occupation, marriage, association, movement, and belief. And it yields claims to the liberties of a moral being – liberties to participate in social relations, to learn, think, discuss, decide, respond, act, and accept responsibility. As this suggests, specific freedoms are mainly selected as fundamental and therefore as protected under the liberty principle by showing their importance to the realization and use of agency. The claim to lead one's life is strongest in regard to actions that structure or set the direction for one's life, and involve matters that take up much of one's time such as work, marriage, and children. The secure claim to liberty is not just a claim to respect for or noninterference with one's liberty. It is also a claim to assistance in protecting one's liberty, and for the creation and maintenance of social conditions in which the capacity for agency can be developed and exercised.

A system of unqualified respect for liberty would licence other people to engage in violence and harm; such a system would set back one's fundamental interests more than it helped them. The solution is to build restrictions into the principle of liberty. Some of these follow, obviously, from the restrictions on violence already discussed. In deciding which liberties to include or exclude the appropriate questions are whether a particular liberty is essential to our status as persons and agents and whether the costs of respecting and protecting it are likely to be so high that it is not worth protecting.

Duties of assistance to others carve an exception into the claim to liberty. Within limits that prevent excessive burdens and severe unfairness, people can be called on to expend their time and resources in protecting and provisioning others and in supporting institutions that provide such assistance in systematic and efficient ways.

The secure claim against severely cruel or degrading treatment

A simple form of cruelty imposes severe pain on another person thoughtlessly or gleefully. This type of cruelty can degrade a person because it suggests that he has no feelings or that his suffering does not matter. More complicated forms of cruelty are calculated to degrade a person by suggesting, or bringing it about, that she is a creature that she and others will think base or low. Slavery is degrading because it treats the slave as if he lacks the agency needed to lead his own life. Rape is degrading because it treats a person as a mere sexual resource to be used without consent, or because in many cultures it destroys one's social standing as a virtuous and pure person. Degradation may deprive a person of the respect of self and others. A secure claim against severe cruelty forbids these sorts of actions and requires individual and collective efforts to protect people against them. The severity of cruelty depends on how degrading it can reasonably be taken to be, the degree of malicious intent, and the amount of harm that it is likely to cause.

The secure claim against severely unfair treatment

Humans are keenly attuned to unfairness, particularly when it takes the form of doing less than one's fair share in collective enterprises. Fairness and fair-mindedness are moral virtues, and some degree of fairness in dealing with others is a moral duty. Here, however, severe unfairness is an appropriate test because being subject to lesser forms of unfairness is probably compatible with having a minimally good life. For present purposes we are concerned with forms of unfairness so severe that they are matters of ruinous injustice. The severity of unfair treatment depends on the degree of unfairness, whether or not malicious intent is present, and the amount of harm or degradation that the unfairness is likely to cause. The claim against severely unfair treatment is a claim to freedom from such treatment and a claim to individual and collective efforts to protect people against it. For example, governments have a duty not to imprison innocent people and therefore a duty to provide the accused with fair trials.

All four principles protect aspects of human dignity

The Universal Declaration speaks of the "inherent dignity . . . of all members of the human family" and asserts that "All human beings are born free and equal in dignity and rights. They are endowed with reason and conscience." The four grounds of human rights that I have proposed provide an interpretation of these ideas. We respect a person's dignity when we protect her life and agency and when we prevent others from imposing treatment that is severely degrading or unfair (on dignity see Schachter 1983; Nussbaum 2001).

All four principles should be thought of as requirements of human dignity, of ways to recognize and respond to the value or worth that is found in life as a person. Accordingly, we can speak of dignity with reference to any particular feature of persons that has distinctive value (e.g., their ability to suffer, their lives, their agency, their consciousness and reflective capacities, their use of complicated languages and symbolic systems, their rationality, their individuality, their social awareness).

The secure claim to life plays a central role in justifying economic and social rights. Without safe food and water, life and health are endangered and serious illness and death are probable. The connection between the availability of food and basic healthcare and having a minimally good life is direct and obvious – something that is not always true with other human rights. Education also promotes the fundamental interest in life by teaching health-related knowledge and skills as well as ways of supporting one's life through work.

The secure claim to lead a life, to be able to develop and exercise one's agency, also supports the importance of basic economic and social rights. Developing and exercising agency requires a functioning mind and body as well as options and opportunities. The availability of food and basic healthcare promotes and protects physical and mental functioning. And the availability of basic education promotes knowledge of social, economic, and political options. In the contemporary world, lack of access to educational opportunities typically limits (both absolutely and comparatively) people's abilities to participate fully and effectively in the political and economic life of their country (see Hodgson 1998).

The secure claim against severely unfair treatment supports economic and social rights. It is severely and ruinously unfair to exclude some parts of the population (rural people, women, minorities) from access to education and economic opportunities. Basic economic and social rights protect against that kind of unfairness.

3. Recurrent threats?

Many have suggested that our formulations of constitutional and human rights arise from the experience of injustice (Shue 1996: 17, 32–3; Donnelly 2003 [1985]: 46, 92; Dershowitz 2004: 9). That experience may be direct (when one endures the injustice oneself) or indirect (when one learns of the injustice from those who endured it or from journalists or historians). The development of lists of rights to be protected through political action represents a kind of social learning. People gradually learn the most severe wrongs and injustices that human psychology and institutions produce and develop means of protecting themselves and their fellow citizens against those injustices.

The world's 200 or so countries now use similar sorts of political and legal institutions including centralized political power; a legal system including legislators, courts, and prisons; police and armed forces; large bureaucracies; media of mass communica-

James W. Nickel

tion; a monetary system; a mixture of public and private property; and tax systems (on the modern state, see Morris 1998). These institutions, used around the world, give countries shared problems and lead to the adoption of similar remedies for those problems. If all countries use the same basic institutions, and if these institutions pose some distinctive threats to values that most people share, then human rights will often float free of cultural differences.

Donnelly holds that human rights are needed in all countries because the modern state is now used everywhere and international human rights are socially learned remedies for its built-in dangers (Donnelly 2003 [1985]: 46, 92). The forms these threats take and how to deal with them are gradually learned, emerging "from the concrete experiences, especially the sufferings, of real human beings and their political struggles to defend or realize their dignity" (Donnelly 2003 [1985]: 58). Once the dangers and remedies have been learned, the lessons ought to be shared with all the users. Indeed, since the European colonial powers both developed and promoted the spread of the modern state, they have responsibilities to address its dangers. A recall of the product is not possible, but sharing the lessons about its dangers and remedies is. Donnelly describes the sorts of threats that make specific rights necessary as ones that are "widespread, systematic, and egregious" (Donnelly 2003 [1985]: 226).

It is a mistake, however, to put too much emphasis on the *modern* state. Contemporary political institutions evolved from earlier systems of government, law, and property, and it is implausible to suggest that none of the dangers of the modern state were present in the earlier versions. The dangers of the reckless and corrupt use of political power, of food scarcity due to systems of private agricultural property, and the dangers of unconstrained democracy have been known and discussed for more than 2,000 years

Inadequate access to subsistence, basic healthcare, and basic education is a major problem in many countries today. Countries that do not have political programs to ensure the availability of these goods to all parts of the population have high rates of hunger, disease, and illiteracy (Pogge 2002). People who recognize their responsibility to provide for themselves and their families may nevertheless find that limited abilities, harsh circumstances, or a combination of both make it impossible for them to gain sufficient access to subsistence. A drought may make it impossible to grow food, for example, or severe illness may make one unable to work, or the wages paid for working may be insufficient to cover basic needs. Further, action by individuals or families is often inadequate in the face of severe illness, infectious diseases, and matters of public health such as water and sewage systems.

4. Would some weaker norm be as effective?

Economic and social rights might be unnecessary if people participated in self-help, assistance to family members, and charitable giving to those in need. This proposal suggests that we can recognize that people have moral claims to assistance in regard to subsistence, healthcare, and education without having to view these claims as generating rights or as requiring political action.

A harmonious combination of self-help and voluntary mutual assistance is certainly to be encouraged, but such a mixture offers little prospect of providing adequately for all of the needy and incapacitated if it is viewed as a substitute for rather than as a supplement to politically implemented economic and social rights. First, some people are unable to help themselves because they are sick, disabled, very young, or very old. Second, some people lack families to assist them, and impoverished people often come from low-income families with limited abilities to assist their members. Third, the limits of charitable giving as sources of aid to the needy are obvious. There are often too few donors for the needs present. Further, coverage for the needy is likely to be spotty rather than comprehensive. This may be because no capable donor is within call or because the capable donors that are within call have used their discretion and given to other causes. This spottiness was noted by John Stuart Mill. He remarked that "Charity almost always does too much or too little: it lavishes its bounty in one place, and leaves people to starve in another" (Mill 1848, Book V, Chapter xi, section 13).

5. Are the burdens justifiable?

A familiar objection to economic and social rights is that they are too burdensome. Frequently the claim that economic and social rights are too burdensome uses other, less controversial human rights as a standard of comparison, and suggests that economic and social rights are substantially more burdensome or expensive than liberty rights, for example. Liberty rights such as freedom of communication, association, and movement require both respect and protection from governments. And people cannot be adequately protected in the enjoyment of liberties such as these unless they also have security and due process rights. The costs of liberty, as it were, include the costs of law and criminal justice. Once we see this, liberties start to look a lot more costly. To provide effective liberties to communicate, associate, and move it is not enough for a society to make a prohibition of interference with these activities part of its law and accepted morality. An effective system of provision for these liberties will require a legal scheme that defines personal and property rights and protects these rights against invasions while ensuring due process to those accused of crimes. Providing such legal protection in the form of legislatures, police, courts, and prisons is very expensive.

Further, we should not think of economic and social rights as simply giving everyone a free supply of the goods these rights protect. Guarantees of subsistence will be intolerably expensive and will undermine productivity if everyone simply receives a free supply. A viable system of economic and social rights will require most people to provide for themselves and their families through work as long as they are given the necessary opportunities, education, and infrastructure. Government-implemented economic and social rights provide guarantees of availability (or "secure access"), but it should not be necessary for governments to supply the requisite goods in more than a small fraction of cases. Basic healthcare and education may be exceptions to this since many believe that governments should provide free health services and education irrespective of ability to pay.

Countries that do not accept and implement economic and social rights still have to bear somehow the costs of providing for the needy. If government does not supply food, clothing, and shelter to those unable to provide for themselves, then families, friends, and communities will have to shoulder much of this burden. It is only in the past century that government-sponsored economic and social rights have taken over a substantial part of the burden of providing for the needy. The taxes associated with economic and social rights are partial replacements for other burdensome

James W. Nickel

duties, namely the duties of families and communities to provide adequate care for the unemployed, sick, disabled, and aged. Deciding whether to implement economic and social rights is not a matter of deciding whether to bear heavy burdens, but rather of deciding whether to continue with total reliance on systems of informal provision that provide insufficient assistance and whose costs fall very unevenly on families, friends, and communities.

Once we recognize that liberty rights also carry high costs, that intelligent systems of provision for economic and social rights need supply the requisite goods to people in only a small minority of cases, and that these systems are substitutes for other, more local ways of providing for the needy, the difference between the burdensomeness of liberty rights and the burdensomeness of economic and social rights ceases to seem so large.

Even if the burdens imposed by economic and social rights are not excessive, they might still be wrong to impose on individuals. Libertarians object to economic and social rights as requiring impermissible taxation. Without attempting here to provide a critique of libertarianism, I note that this view is vulnerable to an attack on two grounds. First, taxation is permissible when used to discharge the moral duties of taxpayers, as when it is used to support government-organized systems of humanitarian assistance that fulfill more effectively than charity duties of assistance that all individuals have (Beetham 1995: 53). Second, property rights are not so weighty that they can never be outweighed by the requirements of meeting other rights.

6. Feasibility

The final test of feasibility for an international human right is that most countries in the world today are able to implement the right in question. Feasibility is a challenging test for basic economic and social rights because some of the world's countries are too impoverished, troubled, and disorganized to respect and implement them effectively. This is particularly true in "low-income" countries (ones in the lowest quartile in terms of average individual income). These are countries such as Haiti, India, and Nigeria where the average income is less than U.S.$500 per year, the average lifespan is slightly under 60 years, childhood immunization is near 60 percent, and illiteracy rates are more than 40 percent.

The abilities and resources of the least capable countries are not an appropriate standard of feasibility. The legal duties of parents, for example, are not limited to the ones that even the least capable parents can satisfy. Instead, we set a higher standard that most but not all parents are able to satisfy. Analogously, the standard of feasibility for human rights should be one that most countries can satisfy. The appropriate question is whether countries in the top two quartiles and some of those in the third have the resources and capabilities to implement basic economic and social rights. Countries in the top quartile clearly can. They include countries such as Canada, Denmark, Greece, Japan, and Singapore. So can countries in the second quartile. They include countries such as Chile, Hungary, Mexico, and Poland. Average personal income in these countries is around U.S.$5000, the average lifespan is 73 years; infant immunization rates are around 95 percent, and illiteracy rates are less than 10 percent (World Bank Development Report 2003). Most of them already have programs to promote and protect basic economic and social rights, although the quality and efficiency of these programs is sometimes poor.

But what about countries in the third quartile? If some of them are able to implement basic economic and social rights, the feasibility test will be passed. These are countries such as Brazil, China, Columbia, Fiji, Jordan, and Turkey. The average personal income in these countries is U.S.$1350; the average lifespan is 69 years; childhood immunization rates are around 80 percent, and illiteracy is less than 20 percent. Many of these countries already have programs to reduce hunger, promote health, and provide education, but those programs are often underfunded and fail to cover all regions and parts of the population. But it seems likely that at least the top third of them are able to implement basic economic and social rights. Thus, if we use the Vance Conception of economic and social rights it seems that the feasibility test can be met.

If all of the appropriate justificatory tests can be met by economic and social rights, this means that these rights are justified for the whole world. Most countries can implement them and have no excuse on grounds of resources for not doing so as quickly as possible. In countries that are genuinely unable to implement them, these rights exist as justified international norms, but their governments and peoples are excused on grounds of inability for their failure to make them available. This does not render the rights irrelevant, however. They stand as norms to be realized as far and as soon as possible and whose lack of realization is an appropriate matter of regret. Further, those rights call upon secondary and back-up addressees to come forward and provide meaningful assistance.

The International Covenant on Economic and Social Rights only commits its signatories to progressive implementation of economic and social rights. Article 2.1 requires ratifying countries to "take steps, individually and through international assistance and co-operation . . . to the maximum of its available resources, with a view to achieving progressively the full realization of the rights recognized in the present Covenant." The Economic and Social Covenant treats the duties associated with economic and social rights as duties to try – to make a good-faith effort progressively over time to implement these rights for all of the population in all parts of the country. This allows countries to be in compliance with their legal duties even though subsistence, minimal healthcare, and basic education are not available to all of their people.

A better approach would have been to use the same commitment clause found in Article 2 of the Civil and Political Covenant, namely to "respect and to ensure to all individuals within its territory . . . the rights recognized in the present Covenant." A supplemental statement could have said that countries genuinely unable to implement economic and social rights are temporarily excused but have duties to implement these rights as soon and as far as they can. Beyond this, duties of richer countries to assist low-income countries in realizing basic economic and social rights should have been specified abstractly but explicitly (see Rawls 1999: 37).

Although the economic and social treaties call for progressive implementation, the committees administering these treaties have tried to deal with the deficiencies of this approach by introducing the supplemental ideas of making a good faith and measurable effort and of meeting minimum standards. The duties to try associated with the idea of progressive implementation allow countries that are doing little or nothing to implement economic and social rights to say that they are engaging in hopeful waiting, to say that they have done all that they can and that they are simply waiting for more resources to appear. This makes generally available a rationalization for

James W. Nickel

inaction. One possible response to this, of course, is to challenge the truthfulness of the claim about inability in light of expenditures on things that seem to have lower priority. Another approach is to require that countries be doing something, that they be taking measurable steps. Economic and social rights can be further strengthened by adding duties to satisfy without delay feasible minimal standards while making efforts to realize the right fully over a longer term. This is often described as a "minimum core." A right of this sort might be thought of as having two objects. One, the minimal object, is set at a level that almost all countries can meet and requires nearly immediate compliance. In regard to food, the minimum core might be a duty to prevent massive famines, while the outer core is secure access to adequate food for all. It sets a more demanding goal that provides a broader focus for the right and that is supported by a duty to try.

III. Implementing Economic and Social Rights

This section considers the objection that economic and social rights are deficient as rights because they cannot – or perhaps *should not* – be implemented by judges alone. It might be argued, for example, that judges can and should have the powers necessary to implement the right to freedom of religion or the right to a fair trial, but that they do not and should not have the powers necessary to implement the right to basic education. Judges, after all, cannot create or fund a school system – and in a democracy they should not try to.

When a country has accepted a right to freedom of religion by putting the right in its constitution or by ratifying an international human rights treaty, judges can proceed to implement it through judicial review. If the legislature passes a law forbidding the beliefs and practices of Jehovah's Witnesses, and a practitioner of that religion is convicted under that law, on appeal judges can nullify the conviction and declare the law unconstitutional or incompatible with the country's international obligations. Judges can make important and legitimate contributions to the implementation of freedom of religion.

Now suppose, in contrast, that a country has accepted a right to basic education by putting the right in its constitution or by ratifying an international human rights treaty. Perhaps the formulation of the right goes like this:

> Children have a right to education. Accordingly, the Legislature shall create and fund a system of free public schools open to all children and available in all parts of the country. Free public education shall be available for at least ten years of schooling.

Suppose further that the legislature ignores this instruction and neither creates nor funds schools. A group of parents who want free public education to be available file suit, asking the judge to order the legislature to perform its constitutional duties. A judge might issue such an order, but cannot enforce it by nullifying a law because there is no law to nullify.

Judges cannot do anything to implement the right until the legislature has created and funded a system of public schools. Beyond this, in a democracy it would be wrong for a judge to take over the role of legislator and say that if the legislature refused to fulfill its duty then the judiciary will design and implement a school system and appropriate the necessary funds. It is not a judge's proper role to take money from bridge construction or prisons and divert it to school funding.

The conclusion drawn from these contrasting examples might be that judicial implementation only works when judges can nullify laws or decisions, and accordingly that real rights are ones that are strictly negative, that forbid governments from suppressing any religion or infringing people's speech.

This argument cannot be sound because is it implies a false proposition, namely that due process rights are not real rights. To see this, consider an example exactly analogous to the one about the right to education. Suppose that a country has accepted a right to a fair trial by putting the right in its constitution or by ratifying an international human rights treaty. Perhaps the formulation of the right goes like this:

> In all criminal prosecutions, every accused person has the right to a fair and public trial, by an impartial jury. At trial, all accused persons have the right to the assistance of counsel, provided at public expense if necessary.

Suppose further that the legislature ignores this right and continues putting in jail without trial people that the police believe committed crimes. There are no criminal prosecutions, no legislative provision for them, and no system to provide free legal counsel. Accordingly, judges play no role in punishing criminals. Suppose now that a person who has been put in jail without prosecution or trial files suit, asking a judge to order the police to release him or bring him to trial. A judge might issue such an order, but cannot enforce it by nullifying a law because there is no law to nullify. Judges cannot do anything to implement the right until the legislature has created and funded a system of criminal prosecution and trial. The judges can order the police to stop imprisoning people without trial before a judge, but the police may scoff at this order, jesting that judges have very few weapons. Beyond this, in a democracy it would be wrong for a judge to take over the role of legislator and say that if the legislature refused to fulfill its duty then the judiciary will design and implement a criminal justice system and appropriate the necessary funds. It is not a judge's proper role to take money from bridge construction or schools and divert it to funding courts and lawyers.

Because of the prominent place of due process rights in historic bills of rights it is implausible to argue that due process rights are not real rights. Due process rights may seem to be negative rights, ones that merely require the government to refrain from certain actions. But in fact they are more like positive rights, ones that require their addressees to provide a service to the right-holders. I think that they are best classified as *conditionally positive*. They say that *if* the government plans to punish someone then it must give that person various procedural protections and legal services along with the opportunity to have a trial. The antecedent of this conditional is sure to be continuously satisfied because governments need to threaten and carry out punishments in order to govern, and thus governments will have duties to provide due process services in many cases. From a practical point of view due process rights impose duties to provide, just like the right to education. They require governments to provide expensive legal services that require large and expensive bureaucracies and infrastructures.

James W. Nickel

Claims about what judges can do to implement rights are relative to a background of institutions and practices. We think of judges as capable of implementing due process rights because we assume practices and laws giving judges significant power over criminal prosecutions. But take away that background and judges are no more able to implement rights to due process than they are able to implement the right to education when the legislature has never been willing to do anything about education. In almost all cases, the effective implementation of rights requires a joint effort by legislatures and courts.

To return to the example of the right to education, judges can play a significant role in implementing that right once a system of education has been created and funded. If some parents in a large region where no public schools have been provided file suit demanding that their children's right to education be fulfilled, a judge can order the Commissioner of Education to create a school in that region. Similarly, judges can deal with complaints of discriminatory exclusion of some students, or failures to provide ten years of instruction. The same is true for rights to subsistence and to basic healthcare. Once legislatively defined and funded, judges can implement these rights. With economic and social rights, however, it is probably more efficient to put implementation in the hands of specialized bureaucracies leaving judges the job of dealing with appeals from the decisions of those officials.

IV. The Widespread Acceptance of Economic and Social Rights

Economic and social rights conforming to the Vance Conception are very widely accepted. As noted earlier, about three-quarters of the world's countries have ratified the Economic and Social Covenant. Most capitalists, socialists, communitarians, authoritarians, and defenders of hierarchy accept the idea that governments have high-priority responsibilities to ensure that people can meet their basic needs. Radical libertarians are the only rejectionists.

I speculate that worldwide acceptance of economic and social rights, understood in accordance with the Vance Conception, already exists. Worldwide acceptance of a human right is the idea that in most countries a majority of people who have an opinion on the matter would endorse the right. We could test this speculation with opinion polls that asked questions pertaining to (1) universality; (2) high-priority; and (3) associated duties. Universality might be tested by asking people to indicate strong disagreement, disagreement, agreement, strong agreement, or lack of opinion concerning propositions such as:

- All people everywhere ought to enjoy opportunities to make a living through work.
- All those people who are genuinely unable to meet their basic needs through work or reliance on savings should be eligible to receive assistance from government-funded programs.

The idea that economic and social rights are mandatory or duty-generating might be tested by propositions such as:

- It is wrong for governments to fail to ensure that education is available to children when it is possible for them to do so.
- Governments have a duty to protect public health by ensuring that safe water is available.

Belief in the high priority of human rights could be tested by formulating propositions about specific rights, or families, of rights, as questions about importance. Questions about propositions such as these could be posed:

- It is very important that people enjoy protections against famines.
- It is imperative that children be ensured opportunities for education.

If it turns out that my speculation about the worldwide acceptance of economic and social rights is empirically correct, that would explain the political stability of such rights in democratic countries. The United States is not known for being strong on economic and social rights, but at least some of its programs to ensure them – in particular social security and public education – are politically untouchable. Politicians who put themselves in wholesale opposition to these programs would be voted out in the next election.

The politics of welfare rights may be more stable if the implementing programs also offer benefits or guarantees to the middle classes, thereby providing them with prudential reasons for political support. This makes the programs more expensive, but helps ensure that the quality of benefits will be adequate.

The Vance Conception of economic and social rights can help lead to a stable political balance because it accepts the most important demands of both the less and the more advantaged. It accepts the demand of the less advantaged that they be able to survive on terms that are at least decent, enjoy full citizenship and political participation, and have access to education and opportunities for economic participation. And it accepts the demand of the more advantaged that they not be subjected to a dictatorship of the proletariat; that they keep their political rights and economic liberties. Of course the Vance Conception provides a minimum, not a limit. Far more egalitarian arrangements are possible in countries having the necessary resources and popular support.

Note

* This essay is a revised and expanded version of "Poverty and Rights," *The Philosophical Quarterly* 55 (2005).

References

Aiken, W. and LaFolette, H., eds. 1996. *World Hunger and Morality* (Upper Saddle River, NJ: Prentice-Hall).
Alston, P. 1987. "Out of the Abyss: The Challenges Confronting the New UN Committee on Economic and Social Rights," *Human Rights Quarterly* 9: 332–81.

Arneson, R. 1990. "Is Work Special? Justice and the Distribution of Employment," *American Political Science Review* 84: 1127–47.

Bayefsky, A. 2001. *The UN Human Rights Treaty System: Universality at the Crossroads* (Ardsley, NY: Transnational).

Beetham, D. 1995. "What Future for Economic and Social Rights?" *Political Studies* XLIII: 41–60.

Bentham, Jeremy. 1970. "Anarchial Fallacies," in A. Melden, ed., *Human Rights* (Belmont, CA: Wadsworth), pp. 30–1.

Council of Europe. 1950. *European Convention for the Protection of Human Rights and Fundamental Freedoms.* Received enough ratifications to become operative in 1953.

Council of Europe. 1961. *European Social Charter.* Received enough ratifications to become operative in 1965.

Council of Europe. 1965. *European Social Charter.* Received enough ratifications to become operative in 1965.

Cranston, M. 1967. "Human Rights, Real and Supposed," in D. D. Raphael, ed., *Political Theory and the Rights of Man* (London: Macmillan).

Cranston, M. 1973. *What Are Human Rights?* London: Bodley Head.

Dershowitz, Alan. 2004. *Rights from Wrongs: The Origins of Human Rights in the Experience of Injustice* (New York: Basic Books).

Donnelly, J. 2003 [1985]. *Universal Human Rights in Theory and Practice*, 2nd edn. (Ithaca, NY and London: Cornell University Press).

Eide, A. 1989. "The Realisation of Social and Economic Rights and the Minimum Threshold Approach," *Human Rights Law Journal* 10: 35–51.

Fabre, C. 2000. *Social Rights Under the Constitution–Government and the Decent Life* (Oxford: Clarendon Press).

Gallup Organization. 2002. *Gallup Poll of the Islamic World.*

Gould, C. 2004. *Globalizing Democracy and Human Rights* (New York: Cambridge University Press).

Griffin, J. 1996. *Value Judgement: Improving Our Ethical Beliefs* (Oxford: Oxford University Press).

Griffin, J. 2001a. "Discrepancies Between the Best Philosophical Account of Human Rights and the International Law of Human Rights," *Proceedings of the Aristotelian Society.*

Griffin, J. 2001b. "First Steps in an Account of Human Rights," *European Journal of Philosophy* 9.3: 306–27.

Halstead, P. 2002. "Human Property Rights," *Convenyancer and Property Lawyer*: 153–73.

Henkin, L. 1994. "Economic Rights Under the United States Constitution," *Columbia Journal of Transnational Law* 32: 97–132.

Hodgson, D. 1998. *The Human Right to Education.* Aldershot, Hants: Ashgate Publishing.

Holmes, S., and C. Sunstein. 1999. *The Cost of Rights: Why Liberty Depends on Taxes* (New York: Norton).

Howard, R. 1987. "The Full-Belly Thesis: Should Economic Rights Take Priority over Civil and Political Rights?" *Human Rights Quarterly* 5: 467–90.

Mill, J. 1848. *Principles of Political Economy* (London: Longmans, Green and Co.).

Morris, C. 1998. *An Essay on the Modern State* (Cambridge: Cambridge University Press).

Morris, C. 2002. *An Essay on the Modern State* (Cambridge: Cambridge University Press).

Nickel, J. 1987. *Making Sense of Human Rights* (Berkeley and Los Angeles: University of California Press).

Nickel, J. 1993. "A Human Rights Approach to World Hunger," in Will Aiken and Hugh Lafollette, eds., *World Hunger and Morality*, 2nd edn (Englewood Cliffs, NJ: Prentice-Hall).

Nussbaum, M. 2001. *Women and Human Development: The Capabilities Approach* (Cambridge: Cambridge University Press).

O'Neill, O. 1988. "Hunger, Needs, and Rights," in S. Luper-Foy, ed., *Problems of International Justice* (Boulder, CO: Westview Press).

A Defense of Welfare Rights as Human Rights | 455

Organization of American States. 1948. *American Declaration of the Rights and Duties of Man*.

Orend, B. 2001. *Human Rights: Concept and Context* (Peterborough, ON: Broadview Press).

Peffer, R. 1978. "A Defense to Rights to Well-Being," *Philosophy and Public Affairs* 8 (1): 65–87.

Pew Research Center. 2003. *Global Attitudes Project*.

Pogge, T. 2002. *World Poverty and Human Rights* (Cambridge: Polity Press).

Rawls, J. 1999. *The Law of Peoples* (Cambridge, MA: Harvard University Press).

Schachter, O. 1983. "Human Dignity as a Normative Concept," *American Journal of International Law* 77 (4): 848–54.

Sen, A. 1981. *Poverty and Famines* (Oxford: Oxford University Press).

Sen, A. 1982. "Rights and Agency," *Philosophy and Public Affairs* 11: 3–39.

Sen, A. 1984. "Rights and Capabilities," in *Resources, Values and Development* (Cambridge: Cambridge University Press).

Sen, A. 1985. "Well-being, Agency, and Freedom," *Journal of Philosophy* 85: 477–502.

Sen, A. 1999a. *Commodities and Capabilities* (Oxford: Oxford University Press).

Sen, A. 1999b. *Development as Freedom* (Oxford: Oxford University Press).

Sen, A. 2004. "Elements of a Theory of Human Rights," *Philosophy and Public Affairs* 32: 315–56.

Shue, H. 1996. *Basic Rights*, 2nd edn (Princeton, NJ: Princeton University Press).

Tasioulas, John. 2002. "Human Rights, Universality and the Values of Personhood: Retracing Griffin's Steps," *European Journal of Philosophy* 10 (1): 79–100.

Vance, C. 1977. "Human Rights and Foreign Policy," *Georgia Journal of International and Comparative Law* 7: 223–9.

Index

Abers, Rebecca, 253
Abizadeh, Arash, 402
abortion, 187, 241, 348
absolutism, 198, 268
abstract self, 323–326, 328, 338
   see also persons
Abu Ghraib, 68
Ackerman, Bruce, 304
Adorno, Theodor, 61–62, 70
affirmative action, 348
After Virtue (MacIntyre), 304
agency: see persons
agent-relative vs. agent-neutral, 122–126,
      132, 156
aid, 17, 19, 141–142, 156, 158–159,
      173–175, 184, 389, 391, 393,
      398–399, 402, 409, 418, 439, 448,
      450
Alexander, Larry, 12, 13, 277
Alighieri, Dante, 17
American Civil Liberties Union, 92
anarchism, 94
   anarcho-communism, 309
   libertarian, 309
   philosophical, 309–312
Anarchy, State, and Utopia (Nozick), 7, 138,
      304
ancient Greece, 8, 10, 233
Anderson, Elizabeth, 11, 38, 221–222
animals, 133, 176, 231, 331, 349

Ansolabehere, Stephen, 254
apartheid: see South Africa
appropriation: see natural resources,
      property, property rights, proviso
Arendt, Hannah, 237, 269–270
aristocracy, 160–161, 197, 209–211, 221,
      241
Aristotle, 6, 8, 10, 17, 53–54, 101, 156,
      236–237, 322
armed organizations, 273, 330, 352, 379,
      446
Arneson, Richard, 11, 157, 180, 402–403
Arrow's Theorem, 289, 297
Ashlin, Alison, 231
atomism, 304–309, 311, 312, 317, 323–324
   see also identity, individualism
Aurelius, Marcus, 388
authoritarianism, 207, 210, 453
authority, 19, 84, 91, 93, 103, 133, 143,
      206, 211, 215, 219–220, 223–224,
      237–238, 242, 273 274, 279,
      284–287, 309–310, 332, 336, 347,
      353, 369, 380, 415
autonomy, 16, 52, 84, 95, 144, 157–158,
      171, 183–184, 205, 214, 219, 221,
      222, 224–225, 243, 253, 276, 306,
      308–310, 323–325, 336–337, 363,
      365, 367, 371, 378, 380, 391,
      402–403, 412–413, 442–443
   see also freedom, liberty, persons

Bagehot, Walter, 215
Baccaro, Lucio, 254
bailouts, 232
Baiocchi, Gianpaolo, 253
Barry, Brian, 180, 236, 330, 335, 338, 364,
        371, 373, 378–379, 395
Basic Rights (Shue), 389
basic structure, 17, 36, 63–65, 410,
        412–413, 417, 419
    global, 391–392
    see also institutions
Battle of Agincourt, 209
Bauboeck, Rainer, 373
Bayefsky, Ann, 437
Beitz, Charles, 389, 391–392
beneficence, 159
benevolence, 43, 55
Benhabib, Seyla, 373, 375, 379
Benn, S. I., 85
Bentham, Jeremy, 388
Bernlin, Isaiah, 180
Bhabha, Homi, 322–323
bias, 88, 162, 210, 250, 253, 324, 326, 328,
        330, 338
bills of rights, 199, 294, 452
    Bill of Rights (U.S.), 270, 287
    Declaration of the Rights of Man and of
        the Citizen (France), 426
Bird, Colin, 308
Blake, Michael, 402–403
blogging, 231–233
borders, 336–338, 387–388, 391, 394–395,
        402, 418–419
Bourdieu, Pierre, 374
Brazil, 253–254, 259, 449
Brennan, Geoffrey, 236–237
Brubaker, William Rogers, 215
Buchanan, Allen, 322, 325, 391, 394
Buchanan, James, 236–237
burdens of judgment, 68–69
Burke, Edmund, 62, 70, 387, 425–426,
        432
Buruma, Ian, 238
Burundi, 243
Bush, George Walker, 68, 240–241
Butler, Judith, 73–74

Calhoun, John C., 241, 244
Canada, 338, 352–353, 449

Caney, Simon, 18, 391–392, 401
capital punishment, 205, 236
    see also punishment
capitalism, 7–8, 44, 132, 272, 453
care, 308, 317
Carens, Joseph, 336, 373, 375
categorical imperative, 44
character, 100, 198, 219–222, 243, 444
    see also persons, virtue
Chattopadhyay, Raghabendra, 254
checks and balances, 210, 269
Chile, 449
China, 449
Christiano, Thomas, 237, 242
Churchill, Winston, 297
Cicero, 388
circumstances of justice, 4, 34–35, 42–43,
        50–51, 55
citizenship, 62–67, 70, 91, 184, 215, 217,
        233, 240, 248, 304–305, 308, 312,
        317, 345, 350–351, 356, 394, 401,
        408, 439, 454
    citizen of the world: *see* cosmopolitanism
    see also equality of citizenship,
        membership and inclusion, persons
civic friendship, 108, 112, 317, 350
civil liberties, 68, 257, 322
    see also freedom, liberty
civil rights movements, 15, 234, 326,
        346–347, 349, 358
    Civil Rights Act (1964), 287
    Voting Rights Act (1965), 287
    see also social movements
civil war: *see* war
class, 61, 209–210, 215, 220, 223, 253, 363,
        374, 377, 394, 397, 435
    see also hierarchy, social relations, social
        status
classical liberalism, 15, 94, 244
Clinton, William Jefferson, 333
coercion, 5, 16–17, 18, 83, 88–95, 103, 188,
        200, 205, 219, 224, 251, 273,
        327–328, 355, 402–403, 415, 419
cognitivism, 32
Cohen, G. A., 4, 41–46, 48, 54–58, 157,
        410–413, 417
Cohen, Joshua, 12, 37
Coles, Romand, 74
collective action problems, 24, 232

collective decision-making, 11–13, 16,
    213–218, 221–222, 224–226,
    247–259, 378–379, 416
collectivism, 312
Collier, Paul, 393–394
Collingwood, R. G., 345
Colombia, 449
common good, 3, 62, 123–126, 133, 159,
    199, 201, 202, 210, 214, 216, 218,
    233–234, 236, 238, 242, 249, 255,
    304, 306, 314, 317, 324, 411
communism, 218
communitarianism, 13–15, 156, 303–317,
    322–339, 350, 453
community, 214, 226, 251, 303–317,
    323–324, 336, 349, 366, 369, 375,
    378, 380, 389, 400
  moralized vs. ordinary, 314–315
  weak vs. strong, 311–312
  see also social environment
Community, Anarchy, and Liberty (Taylor),
    315
compassion, 9, 155, 159, 168–169, 184,
    356
competition, 33, 91, 191, 218, 221, 248,
    255, 364–367, 374, 377
compliance, 18, 51–52, 54, 86, 188–190,
    200, 328, 432–434
Condorcet, Marquis de, 294
Connolly, William, 73–74
consensus, 88, 92, 103, 114, 216–217, 238,
    250, 283, 358
  overlapping, 64–65, 92, 113
consent, 5, 85, 103, 105, 114, 137, 138,
    140–141, 143, 146–147, 200, 205,
    241–242, 444
Considerations on Representative
    Government (Mill), 200, 234
constitution, 370
  defined, 268–269
  explicit vs. implicit, 268–269
  written, 269–270, 287–288
constitutional essentials, 93–94, 208
constitutionalism, 2, 12–13, 267–279,
    283–298
  American, 268
  English, 268
  particular vs. general, 268
constructivism, 24, 37, 42, 49–50, 54, 57–58

contractarianism, 35, 50, 137, 208, 309,
    311, 312
  see also social contract
contracts, 10, 272, 292, 418, 427
contractualism, 103–105, 311
contribution, 43, 58, 356, 435, 438
Controlling the State (Gordon), 270–271
convergence, 88, 206, 250
cooperation, 11, 42, 45, 48, 64–65, 69, 71,
    141, 186, 205, 215–219, 221, 223,
    273, 309–311, 314, 364, 370,
    374–375, 419
cosmopolitanism, 2, 16–18, 336–337,
    388–403
  ethical, 388–390
  juridical, 388–403
    interdependence-based vs. humanity-
      based, 390–394, 396–397, 399–400,
      403
  political, 388–390
  radical vs. mild, 389–390, 396, 401
  see also distributive justice, global justice
crime and criminals, 8, 9, 15, 90, 157–158,
    165, 183–184, 205, 216, 220, 236, 253,
    258, 295, 443, 444, 448, 452–453
  see also decriminalization
Crisp, Roger, 168–169, 171
critical theory, 19, 322, 348, 351, 358, 379
culture, 13–16, 65, 214, 217–219, 223, 249,
    253, 304, 322, 324, 325, 329–332,
    335, 337, 346, 349–353, 362, 366,
    370–380, 389, 447
  cultural imperialism, 326
  see also multiculturalism, societal culture
Culture and Equality (Barry), 371

Dagger, Richard, 14
Dahlberg, Matz, 238
Darwall, Stephen, 219
De Cive (Hobbes), 309
de Tocqueville, Alexis, 232–234, 239–242,
    244, 249, 308, 310–311
de Vitoria, Francisco, 17
decriminalization, 330
deference, 211, 363
degrading treatment, 19, 73, 220–221, 356,
    380, 445–446
deliberation: see collective decision-making,
    democracy, public justification

democracy, 2, 4, 8, 10–12, 14–16, 18, 19,
        63, 93, 94, 156, 183, 197–211,
        213–226, 231–244, 247–260, 272,
        274–276, 279, 293, 296, 335, 346,
        357, 372, 379, 447, 451, 454
    accountability in, 215, 217, 242, 248, 258
    see also elections
    and judicial review, 278
    see also judiciary
    audience, 238–239, 242
    corporate, 239, 241–243
    deliberative, 11–12, 199, 201–202,
        215–218, 220–222, 231–239,
        248–260, 332, 346, 358, 379
    democratic society, 46, 65, 179, 184, 190,
        214–215, 217–223, 225, 235, 243,
        249, 307, 325, 326–327, 330–333,
        356, 377
    direct, 214, 216, 233, 236, 257, 260
    justification of, 10–11, 13, 214, 220,
        222–226
    see also instrumental value, intrinsic
        value
    laboratories of, 247
    radical, 247–248, 256–260
    random subset, 203
    social, 247
    see also participation, popular
        sovereignty, representation, voting
Democracy's Discontent (Sandel), 313–314,
        317
Denmark, 258, 449
dependence, 308–309
Derrida, Jacques, 74
desert, 10, 158, 171, 188–191, 397, 399
deserving, 157–158, 160–165, 168–169,
        174–175, 184, 186–188, 192
despotism, 210, 220, 225, 292, 297,
        310–311, 337, 393
    soft, 310–311
Dewey, John, 19, 41, 214, 217–219,
        221–222, 224–226
Dialectic of Enlightenment (Horkeimer and
        Adorno), 61
Dictionary of Political Thought (Scruton),
        268
difference, 14–16, 72–74, 179–182, 259,
        322, 326, 328, 345–350, 362–381,
        396

difference principle, 33, 37, 43–45, 55–58,
        323, 356, 358, 411, 413, 417
    global, 389, 391–392, 400, 409
differential rights: *see* identity politics,
        rights, special privileges
dignity, 19, 47, 63, 65, 69–71, 221, 365,
        391, 400, 442–447
Diogenes, 388
dirty hands, 90, 140–141
disability, 9, 16, 30, 142, 160, 172, 308,
        326, 364–366, 369, 374, 377, 379,
        396, 428
    Americans with Disabilities Act (1990), 365
discrimination, 15, 85, 162, 164, 347–350,
        352, 362, 364, 367, 372, 378–379,
        437, 453
dissidents, 216–217, 219, 223, 240, 255,
        286, 353
    see also minorities
distributive justice, 2, 6–8, 16–18, 42–44,
        56–57, 149, 165–166, 172–173, 250,
        258, 304, 335, 347–349, 355–358,
        387–392, 394–395, 397–403,
        408–419
    vs. allocative, 417
    see also justice, redistribution, social
        justice
diversity, 71, 74, 208, 238, 255, 257, 325,
        329–330, 332, 338, 357, 366, 370
divine right, 197
    see also religion
division of labor, 11, 16, 334, 362–363,
        365–369, 372, 374, 376–377,
        380–381
    see also sexual division of labor
domination, 4, 16, 62, 64–66, 72–73, 89, 94,
        221, 347–348, 351–352, 357–358,
        370–371, 373
Donnelly, Jack, 447
Downs, Anthony, 231, 240–243
drugs, 91, 93–94, 159, 349
Dryzek, John, 251
due process, 270, 441, 443, 445, 448,
        451–453
Duflo, Esther, 254
duties, 17, 53, 137, 140–143, 145, 149, 158,
        355–356, 387, 391, 395, 398–399,
        401–402, 413, 417, 433, 445
    civic, 201–203, 304, 306, 442

natural duty of justice, 391, 410
negative, 19, 121, 355, 389, 393–394,
    399, 409, 442–444
positive, 19, 355, 389, 393–394, 399, 409,
    443–444
to obey the law, 310
see also civic duties, obligations
Dworkin, Ronald, 157, 180, 276, 295, 304,
    412

economics, 165–167
Austrian economic theory, 233, 237
    see also political knowledge
economy, 8, 33, 43–45, 56, 198, 232,
    238–240, 247, 272, 292, 356–357,
    373, 392, 394–395, 403, 417
businesses, 239, 244
policy, 44, 91, 166–167, 239, 258, 270,
    292, 347
see also free market, globalization
Edmundson, William, 310
education, 19, 91, 95, 183–184, 234, 243,
    249, 250, 253–254, 258–259, 335,
    349, 364, 377, 437–441, 446–448,
    450–451, 453–454
egalitarianism, 4, 6, 8, 9, 18, 43, 46, 85,
    121, 137, 146, 148–149, 155–176,
    179–190, 247, 250, 297, 327, 356,
    358, 390, 400–403, 408–413,
    416–419, 454
asset, 247
instrumental vs. non-instrumental, 156
personal vs. impersonal, 156
telic vs. deontic, 156, 164
see also equality, inequality
elections, 11, 197–199, 201, 202, 215, 217,
    224–225, 232, 234–235, 238,
    240–242, 274, 454
gerrymandering, 239, 241–242
plebiscite, 289
see also voting
Elster, Jon, 251
Ely, John Hart, 216, 292
emotivism, 32, 86
Enlightenment, 3, 61–62, 70, 72, 114, 304,
    388
entitlement, 43, 44, 108, 130, 133, 395–397,
    399, 401–403, 413, 427
entrenchment, 285–298

environment, 231–232, 239, 272
global warming, 17, 387, 398
pollution, 94, 398
envy, 157, 307, 417
Epictetus, 388
epistemology, 41, 49
equality, 4, 5, 8, 9, 15–16, 33, 137, 140,
    149, 155, 159–160, 165–167,
    180–184, 215, 334, 338–339,
    345–353, 355, 357–358, 362, 369,
    379, 380, 400, 402–403, 415, 419
as comparability, 155–165, 168–170,
    174–176
as impartiality, 155–156
as universality, 155–156
ex ante vs. ex post, 161–163
of capabilities, 159–160, 165, 183–184,
    253, 259
of citizenship, 8, 10–11, 14, 46, 214–216,
    218–220, 224, 226, 232, 248–249,
    252, 274, 276, 326, 357–358, 371
democratic, 209–211, 249, 256
of concern, 9, 170, 179, 181–183, 186,
    188–190, 276, 408, 409
of consideration, 44, 47, 181, 218–219,
    221, 223, 351
of distribution, 8, 43, 223, 411, 413, 419
of income, 9, 159–160, 165–166, 219
of liberty and freedom, 7, 8, 46, 85, 144,
    159, 232, 358, 416
of life prospects, 8–9, 18, 148–149,
    162–165, 184, 394–395, 402, 412
of moral status and standing, 9, 84–84,
    214–215, 220–221, 223–225,
    250–251, 256, 336, 380, 403, 418
of need satisfaction, 159–161, 250, 396
of opportunity, 7, 8, 9, 15–16, 18, 44, 46,
    142, 149, 159–161, 164–165, 199,
    203, 297, 346, 358, 363, 365, 367,
    369, 371, 380, 394, 396, 409, 417
of power, 8, 12, 159, 210, 215, 253, 256,
    259, 274–275, 372, 378, 403
of resources, 9, 16, 149, 159, 179–180,
    259, 297
of rights, 378–379
of social goods, 8, 159, 232, 348, 358
of treatment, 15, 85, 156, 164, 180–183,
    322, 328–329, 332–338, 351, 362,
    368, 395–396, 408

equality (*continued*)
　of wealth, 1, 6–7, 8–9, 159, 165–166
　of welfare, 159–161, 297, 413
　of worth, 364
　see also egalitarianism, inequality
equity, 43, 156, 181, 347
error theory, 32
essentialism, 353, 375
essentially contested concept, 63
Estlund, Cynthia, 218
Estlund, David, 235, 237, 294, 410
ethics, 32, 49, 64
ethnicity, 16, 218, 220, 249, 326, 346,
　　362–363, 366–367, 369, 372–373,
　　375–376, 379–380, 394, 397
European Social Charter (1961, 1966), 438,
　　440
European Union, 240, 418
exemptions: *see* equality of treatment,
　　reform, special privileges
experiments in living, 224
exploitation, 47, 122, 306, 312, 315, 326,
　　371, 373, 378, 419
expressivism, 32
externalities, 9, 398

fact sensitivity, 4, 15, 23–38, 55–58
　see also principles
fairness, 7, 9, 63–65, 69, 71, 75, 114,
　　146–147, 155, 157–159, 161–165,
　　168–170, 172–176, 190, 200,
　　202–203, 205, 250–251, 252, 256,
　　311, 322, 324, 327–338, 350–351,
　　357, 376, 399–401, 403, 410, 417,
　　443, 445–446
　procedural vs. substantive, 161–165
fallibilism, 106
family, 9, 93, 166–167, 179, 234, 306, 308,
　　316, 331, 333, 364–365, 368–369,
　　380, 401, 411, 426, 448–449
　see also marriage
fascism, 70
feasibility, 4, 5, 11–12, 31, 160, 231, 257
federalism, 268, 294
Federalist Papers, The (Hamilton, Jay, and
　　Madison), 243, 269
Feinberg, Joel, 180, 306–307, 314
feminism, 15, 19, 234, 326, 347–349, 351,
　　358, 362, 368–369, 379–380
　see also identity politics, women

Feser, Edward, 147
Fiji, 449
Fishkin, James, 258
Foucault, Michel, 61–62, 70
France, 330
Frankfurt, Harry, 168
Fraser, Nancy, 372–373
free and equal: *see* persons
free markets, 8, 213, 272
　see also capitalism, economy
freedom, 1, 4, 5, 7, 14, 18, 28, 61–62, 72, 84,
　　144–146, 157, 160, 166, 171, 173,
　　232, 242, 307, 324, 348, 369–371,
　　376–378, 380, 410, 414, 419, 426
　developed, 309
　moral, 84–86, 127, 131, 144–145
　negative, 145
　of association and assembly, 216–217,
　　256, 303, 325, 327, 350, 352, 356,
　　377, 448
　of movement, 216, 402
　of religion, 216, 272, 325, 327, 330–331,
　　350, 451
　of speech and expression, 44, 198, 200,
　　208, 210, 215–216, 256, 272, 285,
　　292, 303, 327, 351, 370, 377
　of thought and conscience, 327, 352,
　　355–356, 444
　political, 19, 232, 237, 337, 416–417
　positive, 145
　practical, 43
　see also autonomy, civil liberties, liberty
Freeman, Samuel, 4
Friedrich, Carl, 271
Fullinwider, Robert, 379
Fung, Archon, 253

Gadamer, Hans-Georg, 69
Galston, William, 314
Gaus, Gerald, 5, 6, 109–111
Gellner, Ernest, 335
gender, 16, 209, 329, 331, 362, 364,
　　368–369, 372, 374, 379–380, 394
Gender Trouble (Butler), 73
George, Henry, 148
Gerber, Alan, 254
Germany, 258
GLBT, 15, 140, 241, 326, 329, 331,
　　333–334, 336, 362, 369, 372, 379
　see also marriage, sexual orientation

global justice, 2, 17, 19, 387–389, 393–394, 397–400, 408–409
   see also cosmopolitanism, distributive justice, justice
globalization, 74, 247, 403, 408, 417–419
good
   conception of, 6, 47–55, 64, 81–83, 88, 92–93, 99–108, 114, 122, 124, 133, 190, 208, 323–325, 327, 334, 335, 389–390
     see also pluralism
goods: *see* primary goods, property, public goods, social goods
Gordon, Scott, 270–271
Greece, 449
Green, Thomas Andrew, 236
Griffin, James, 442–443
Grotius, Hugo, 17
group rights: *see* rights
Grunebaum, James, 146
Gutmann, Amy, 251, 372, 375

Habermas, Jürgen, 19, 45, 248–249, 256, 257
Haiti, 449
Hamilton, Alexander, 269–270
happiness, 6, 25, 34–35, 70, 92–93, 145, 184, 225
Hardin, Russell, 11–12, 235, 239–240, 242
Hare, R. M., 45
harm, 19, 73, 104, 137, 179, 200, 232, 243, 334, 348, 354, 393, 403, 444–445
Harsanyi, John, 43–45
health and health care, 9, 19, 92–95, 159, 160, 166, 175, 182, 184, 219, 237, 250, 258–260, 292, 368, 399–400, 411, 425–427, 429, 432, 437–441, 446–450, 453–454
Hegel, G. W. F., 322, 345, 357
Heidegger, Martin, 61, 69
Henry V, 209
hierarchy, 4, 11, 16, 190, 203–204, 209, 220, 256, 347–348, 355, 358, 363, 377, 453
   see also class, social roles and positions, social status
Hobbes, Thomas, 6, 10, 105, 233, 309
Holmes, Stephen, 271
homogeneity, 16, 236, 249, 255, 257, 369
   see also social groups

Hong Kong, 134
Honneth, Axel, 357
honors, 6, 191, 363
Horkeimer, Max, 61–62
human nature, 4, 18, 24, 33, 42–43, 46, 49–55, 66, 70, 101–102, 322, 351, 414
   see also circumstances of justice, identity, persons
human rights: *see* rights
human rights deficit, 393
humanitarianism, 156, 159, 391, 402
Hume, David, 30, 43, 105, 237
Hungary, 449

ideal theory, 4–5, 233, 234–235, 252, 255–256
   see also non-ideal theory
identity, 14–16, 19, 46–47, 63–64, 71–75, 304–308, 312–313, 317, 322–339, 350–355, 357, 369, 394
   multiply-situated selves, 313
   unencumbered self, 305, 307, 316
   see also identity politics, persons
Identity and Democracy (Gutmann), 372
identity politics, 322–339, 345–346, 349–355, 362–381
   see also difference, social movements, societal culture, structural inequality
ideology, 61, 231, 233, 241, 268, 269, 272, 274, 352, 377
immigration, 17, 215, 238, 240–241, 367, 369
   see also freedom of movement
impartiality, 4, 45, 47, 81–82, 87–88, 93, 156, 179, 251, 307, 311, 326, 334, 414–415
   see also equality, neutrality
imperativism, 32
Inclusion and Democracy (Young), 372
income, 46, 56, 165–166, 238, 247, 259, 292, 363–364, 368–369, 410
India, 254, 259, 449
indigenous peoples, 15, 72–73, 326, 352–354, 370, 372, 378–379
individualism, 13–14, 47, 171, 303–317, 322–324, 326, 328, 338, 348, 351–353, 355–356
   holist, 305, 311–312, 375–376
   see also identity, moral individualism, persons, self-interest

inequality, 2, 16, 33, 37, 156–160, 163–170,
    172, 176, 218, 232, 253–256, 259,
    347–348, 351, 358, 387, 400, 408,
    411–413, 417, 418
  see also egalitarianism, equality, structural
    inequality
injustice, 2, 4–5, 15–16, 72, 75, 138, 140,
    142, 221, 297, 322, 326, 328,
    330–334, 336, 338–339, 362–381,
    393–394, 399, 402, 408–411,
    413–417, 419, 445–446
institutions, 1, 5, 10, 12, 13, 16, 18, 19, 34,
    43–46, 48, 51, 55, 56, 63, 156, 191,
    215–219, 222, 233, 235, 247, 251,
    259–260, 284–285, 287, 332, 334,
    336, 345–346, 362, 364, 366–367,
    368–372, 376–380, 389–390, 393,
    399, 408, 410, 412, 417, 419,
    426–427, 429–430, 433–434, 447
  see also basic structure, international
    institutions
instrumental value, 10–11, 13, 156, 172,
    213–214, 219, 222–226
instrumentalism, 197
  democratic, 197, 199–203, 222
interest groups, 12, 221, 232, 239–240,
    258
interests, 7, 11, 13, 14–16, 18–19, 24,
    46–47, 50–51, 89–90, 123–124, 137,
    140–141, 156, 171, 179, 181, 184,
    200, 213–214, 218, 221, 232,
    234–236, 238–241, 248–254, 259,
    326–329, 332, 334, 354, 363, 365,
    367, 387, 391–392, 399, 411, 429,
    443, 444
  see also preferences, self-interest
International Covenant on Economic, Social
    and Cultural Rights (1966, 1976),
    426–432, 437, 450
international institutions, 17, 389–391, 393,
    400, 408, 417–419
international law, 83, 437
international relations, 17, 72, 82–83, 390
intolerance: *see* discrimination, toleration
intrinsic value, 10–11, 156, 198–200, 214,
    219, 222–226
Iraq, 68, 244
is/ought, 23, 30, 37
Italy, 254
Ivason, Dunca, 373

Japan, 449
Johansson, Eva, 238
joint-ownership: *see* natural resources,
    property, rights
Jordan, 449
judiciary, 12, 232, 236, 237, 248, 277, 379,
    451–453
  judicial review, 13, 205, 269, 270, 276,
    277–279, 293–295, 298, 451
  juries, 236, 249–250, 258
just war, 17, 388
justice, 7, 8, 10, 13, 14, 16, 17–18, 24,
    31–38, 41–44, 46, 48–58, 61–66, 81,
    87, 93, 105–106, 108–109, 112, 114,
    137, 141–144, 157, 164, 171, 173,
    180, 201–204, 214, 223–224, 237,
    251–252, 322, 324, 327–328, 330,
    345, 355, 362–363, 365–366, 368,
    370–373, 376–377, 379, 380, 388–391,
    393–395, 397, 399, 401, 408–411,
    413–414, 417, 419, 428, 430, 441
  inter-generational, 311, 369, 377
  see also distributive justice, global justice,
    injustice, principles, social justice
Justice and the Politics of Difference
    (Young), 323, 347–348, 372, 373, 378
justice as fairness, 41–42, 52, 54, 58,
    108–109, 358, 389, 391–392
Justice as Fairness (Rawls), 307
justification, 5–6, 10–11, 27, 36, 41–45, 48,
    54, 57–58, 81–89, 91–95, 139, 140,
    171, 180–182, 185, 187, 222–224,
    226, 235, 324, 329, 332, 334, 337,
    356, 402–403, 408, 429, 437, 443,
    450
  holism of, 99, 112
  see also public justification

Kagan, Shelly, 128–129, 144
Kant, Immanuel, 17, 41–45, 47, 50, 54, 105,
    106, 156, 159, 173, 235, 309, 337,
    388, 413–416, 429
Kekes, John, 9–10
kingdom of ends, 235
Kishlanski, Mark, 136
Kropotkin, Peter, 309
Kukathas, Chandran, 313, 373, 375
Kymlicka, Will, 16, 180–181, 305, 306, 316,
    323–325, 337, 362, 369–370, 373,
    375

Laden, Anthony, 15–16
Ladle, Richard, 231
language, 334–335, 337, 346, 348–351, 366, 369–370, 375, 377–378
  see also identity politics
Larmore, Charles, 63–65
Laslett, Peter, 233
late-modern reasonableness, 61–75
law of nature, 84, 414
Law of Peoples, The (Rawls), 337, 390
laws: see legislation, rules
Lee, Robert E., 314
legal interpretation, 270, 285, 287, 293, 330–331
legalism, 270
legislation, 10, 12, 18, 43, 45, 81, 94, 232, 233, 238, 241, 248, 257, 274, 283–290, 293–294, 310, 433
legislatures, 12–13, 199, 216, 234–236, 237–238, 241–242, 248, 258, 260, 273, 289, 295, 335, 379, 451–453
  bicameral, 274, 289–291, 294–295
  reapportionment, 254
  unicameral, 289, 291
legitimacy
  appropriate bases, 8–9, 133, 397
  liberal principle of, 208
  of claims and demands, 322, 325–326, 328–330, 339, 347
  of institutions and laws, 13, 16, 17, 81, 94, 107–109, 113, 134, 207, 217, 242, 248, 273, 276–277, 309, 346, 415–418
  of power over others, 11, 13, 51, 84, 143–144, 217, 220–221, 222, 224, 252, 353, 403
  of principles, 4, 324
  of state action, 1, 5, 17, 89–92, 100, 102–103, 108, 110, 217, 224, 260, 272, 309, 432
  of the sovereign, 10, 242
leveling down, 9, 155, 160, 170–173
  see also equality, redistribution
Levy, Jacob, 373, 375
liberalism, 5–6, 13–17, 81, 83, 88, 90, 95, 113, 133, 140, 180, 222, 232, 257, 268, 322–339, 346–359, 362–363, 364–365, 370–373, 375–381, 400, 408, 410
  deontological, 305

justificatory, 107–111
minimal state, 219, 222, 272
  see also limited government
of fear, 271
political, 208–209, 379
  see also neutrality
Liberalism and the Limits of Justice (Sandel), 304, 311
liberation struggles: see identity politics, inequality, injustice, social movements
libertarianism, 7, 44, 90–92, 94, 121–135, 137–140, 143–149, 155–156, 222, 309, 312, 325, 413–414, 449, 453
  left-libertarianism, 8, 121, 124, 133, 137–138, 144, 146, 148–149
    equal opportunity left-libertarianism, 149
    equal share left-libertarianism, 148–149
  right-libertarianism, 7–8, 121, 133, 137–138, 147
  sufficientarian, 148
  see also classical liberalism
liberty, 12, 15, 34, 44, 46, 84, 132, 137–138, 141, 149, 173, 232, 250, 377, 379, 412, 448
  see also autonomy, civil liberties, freedom
limited altruism: see circumstances of justice
limited government, 95, 222, 268, 270–273
Limiting Government (Sajó), 271
limits of government, 81, 92, 95, 239, 309, 322
  see also legitimacy
Lindblom, C. E., 239
Locke, John, 6, 10, 84, 105, 130, 133, 148, 309, 414
  Lockean proviso, 133–134, 147–149
logocracy, 253–254
luck, 8, 43, 147, 155, 157–159, 165, 168–169, 174, 410–415
  option vs. brute, 158, 412
luck egalitarianism, 37–38, 44, 46, 56–58, 157–158, 397, 409, 412
  see also morally arbitrary

Machiavelli, Niccolò, 90
MacIntyre, Alasdair, 14, 304–307, 308, 323
Mack, Eric, 7, 8
MacKinnon, Catherine, 345, 347–348, 351
Madison, James, 10, 232, 242–243

Mandle, Jon, 18
Manin, Bernard, 234, 235–236, 238–239, 241
Mansbridge, Jane, 253
Marbury v. Madison (1803), 269, 276
marginalization, 16, 215, 326, 347, 369, 371, 373, 377–379
Markell, Patchen, 74
Marmot, Michael, 400
marriage, 15, 190, 220, 221, 241, 314, 331, 333–334, 380, 427, 444–445
Marshall, John, 269
Marx, Karl, 6
Marxism, 17, 441
Mason, Andrew, 314–315
maximin, 155, 159, 170
McGinnis, John, 289
McIlwain, C. H., 271
media, 12, 215, 217, 223–224, 257, 446–447
membership and inclusion, 187, 214–215, 218–219, 221, 223–224, 234, 304–307, 309, 312, 326, 347, 349–350, 352, 354, 362, 366, 370, 378, 395–396, 398, 400–401, 403, 443
  see also participation, social groups
merit, 6, 8, 209, 219, 364
metaethics, 24, 32, 35, 37, 42, 45, 56, 121
metaphysics, 41, 328
Mexico, 449
military service, 15, 144, 191, 330–331, 333–334, 352
Mill, John Stuart, 6, 10, 43, 65–66, 74, 85, 91, 198–200, 214, 220–221, 224–225, 231, 233, 234, 242–243, 308, 324, 356, 448
Miller, David, 390, 395–397, 400–401
minorities, 2, 15–16, 215–216, 331, 334–338, 349–353, 369–370, 377, 380, 401, 416
Moellendorf, Darrel, 394–395, 397–398, 417
monarchy, 10, 233
Moore, Margaret, 14–15
moral agency: *see* persons
moral claims, 64, 82–87, 89–90, 95, 138, 141, 147, 159, 174, 188, 214, 219–220, 224, 326, 425, 427–435
  persons as self-authenticating sources, 84–87, 219, 223–224
  see also duties, obligations, rights

moral demands, 82–84, 87–95, 202, 219, 326, 348–357
  see also duties, obligations, public justification
moral individualism, 8, 121–135
  see also individualism, prerogatives, separateness of persons
morality, 5, 7, 35, 47, 52–53, 57, 84–88, 90, 123, 124–126, 129–130, 135, 137–138, 141, 143, 160, 171, 179–185, 207, 235, 237, 308, 311, 333, 390, 419
  political, 103, 109, 113, 283, 285–286, 403
morally arbitrary, 8, 18, 159, 172, 224, 336, 347, 394–400, 402, 408
  see also luck
Multicultural Citizenship (Kymlicka), 369–370, 373
multiculturalism, 14, 303, 322–323, 325–326, 330, 332–339, 346, 357, 362–363, 369–370, 377, 379–380
  see also culture, identity politics, societal culture
Murphy, Liam, 410

Nagel, Thomas, 181, 390, 402
Narveson, Jan, 147
national interest, 91, 234, 250
nationalism, 184, 336–338, 346, 350, 352–353, 362, 370, 401
nationality, 61, 71, 292, 326, 331, 334–336, 349, 366, 369, 373, 375–377, 381, 394–397, 401, 403, 408
nation-state, 2, 10, 369, 389–390, 394, 402
  as a closed system, 17, 391
  see also borders
natural law, 6, 17–18, 84
natural resources, 133–134, 137–138, 142–149
  see also property, rights
need, 6, 9, 13, 18, 42–43, 46, 58, 141, 144, 159, 161, 168, 173, 189, 364–365, 368, 391, 393–397, 399, 402, 409, 413, 429
neutrality, 5, 13–15, 81–95, 102–106, 114, 323–326, 330, 333–336, 338, 349
  liberal moral neutrality, 5, 81, 83–84, 87–91, 95
  liberal political neutrality, 5, 81, 83, 88–95
  see also agent-relative vs. agent-neutral

New Zealand Constitution Act (1986), 269
Nickel, James, 19
Nietzsche, Friedrich, 53, 435
Nigeria, 449
non-coercion principle: *see* coercion, non-
   interference
non-cognitivism, 28
non-ideal theory, 235, 337
   see also ideal theory
non-interference
   with individuals, 7, 19, 109–111, 121–135,
      139–140, 144–145, 173, 186, 189,
      200, 327, 332–333, 349, 355
      see also paternalism
   with states, 17, 388
      see also sovereignty
normativity, 32, 36, 155, 170, 223, 242
norms, 123, 224, 254, 442–443, 447–450
   constitutional, 236, 269, 285
   hegemonic, 363, 365–367, 369, 371,
      373–374, 376–378
   identity-based, 16, 362–363, 365–369,
      372–376
   international, 17
Nozick, Robert, 7, 43, 92, 123, 130, 133,
      138, 147–148, 304, 324–325, 413

obligations
   of individuals, 2, 65–66, 75, 84, 87, 100,
      127, 141–142, 158, 168, 184, 187,
      189, 201, 203, 278, 286, 287, 297,
      391, 397–398, 401, 432–435, 442
   of officials and governments, 90, 105,
      168, 179, 182–184, 186, 188, 191,
      428–432, 442, 445
   of organizations, 432
   of unspecified agents, 426–428
   special obligations, 10, 323, 401–402,
      427–428
officials, 89–92, 213, 215–217, 222, 225,
      232, 234–242, 248–249, 257–258,
      260, 345, 371, 379, 415–416
Okin, Susan, 368, 375
oligarchy, 249
On Liberty (Mill), 65
O'Neill, Onora, 19
opportunity, 6, 16, 149, 165, 336, 346–350,
      363–367, 373, 376–378, 380, 394,
      396, 448, 454
   see also equality of opportunity

opportunity costs, 93
oppression, 5, 15–16, 73, 105, 221, 222,
      275, 306, 312, 315, 326, 347–348,
      351, 355, 358, 372, 377, 426, 435
Orend, Brian, 438
original position, 4, 32–34, 36, 43–46, 54,
      56, 84, 307, 323–324, 358, 416
   global, 391–392
Otsuka, Michael, 149
Ottoman Empire, 349
ought implies can, 30–31, 47, 51
overlapping consensus: *see* consensus

pacifism, 89, 331
Parekh, Bhikhu, 373, 375
Parfit, Derek, 46–47, 102, 223
participation, 10–12, 213–216, 219,
      221–222, 225–226, 231–234,
      236–237, 239–241, 243, 247–248,
      250–251, 253–260, 358, 368, 372,
      403
particularism, 304
Pateman, Carole, 231, 243
paternalism, 200
Patten, Alan, 335
perfectionism, 6, 10, 95, 99–114, 157
Perpetual Peace (Kant), 337, 388
personal identity, 46
persons
   as free and equal, 12, 34, 43–47, 49–52,
      54, 72, 83–88, 91, 93, 208, 356–358,
      416
   as moral agents, 42, 46–52, 54, 81,
      84–87, 89, 91, 140, 143, 160,
      171–172, 183–186
   as reasonable and rational, 12, 49–51, 54,
      65, 68, 72, 81, 83–84, 87–88, 93–94,
      208
   capacities of, 42, 46–47, 49–55, 62,
      183–184, 221, 234, 249, 253–254,
      258, 365–366, 368, 376, 380, 391
   conceptions of, 13–15, 47, 50, 235,
      323–324, 326, 350–351
   minimally decent functioning, 408–409,
      411, 413
   status as, 71, 391, 403
   see also identity
Peters, R. S., 85
Phillips, Anne, 373
Philosophical Papers (Taylor), 304

Plato, 6, 10, 17, 61, 223, 237, 249
pluralism, 51, 74, 327, 329, 333, 375
   moral, 9, 102–107, 113–114, 208, 334,
      410
   of principles, 9, 56, 157, 159–160, 168,
      173, 443
   political, 15, 252
   reasonable disagreement, 12–13, 24, 50,
      62, 64, 68, 93, 99–100, 103,
      105–111, 190, 205–209, 218, 236,
      238, 249–250, 253
Plutarch, 388
Pogge, Thomas, 389, 391, 392–395, 399
Poland, 449
political knowledge, 216, 219, 221, 225,
      231–233, 235–236, 239, 243, 251,
      257–258
Political Liberalism (Rawls), 63–65, 307
political parties, 12, 202, 231, 239–240, 242,
      248, 258, 367, 379
political power, 2, 3, 5, 6, 8, 11, 13, 46, 91,
      199–203, 208, 222, 232, 234, 241,
      248–249, 251–253, 255–256,
      258–260, 273–275, 278, 283, 353,
      363–364
   see also power, separation of powers
Political Theory and International Relations
      (Beitz), 389, 391
politicians: *see* officials
popular sovereignty, 198–199, 214, 216,
      276–279, 358
pornography, 348
post-colonialism, 19, 72, 74, 323, 352
post-modernism, 19, 62, 69
post-structuralism, 61
poverty, 2, 4, 93, 142, 166–168, 175, 184,
      238, 253–254, 259–260, 271,
      367–368, 387, 393–394, 399, 402,
      408–409, 418, 441
   see also income, subsistence, wealth
power, 62, 112–113, 138, 143–144,
      146–147, 200, 216, 232, 347, 364,
      369, 372, 374–375, 380–381, 390,
      414, 431–432, 435
   powerlessness, 199, 326
   see also political power
practical reason, 29, 41–42, 44, 48–49,
      51–52, 54–56, 61–62, 75, 86, 102,
      108–112, 185–186, 189, 236, 249,
      308

practices, 62, 71, 213–214, 223–226, 231,
      234–235, 309, 312, 322, 324–325,
      329–335, 349, 354, 357, 363–365,
      370–371, 374, 378–380, 393, 399,
      418
   see also traditions
pragmatism, 19
preferences, 67, 92–94, 213, 216, 218–219,
      222, 225, 249, 251–252, 254, 284,
      328, 329, 410–411, 415
prerogatives, 410–412
   against self-sacrifice, 122–135, 140–141
   national, 410–411
primary goods, 46–47
principles
   as evaluative standards, 1, 4–5, 15, 83,
      87–89, 91–94, 226
   constitutional, 268
   grounding of, 23–38, 41, 180–182, 323
   moral, 47–52, 56–57, 87, 95, 139, 284,
      311
   normative, 23–24, 32, 44, 49, 221
   objectivity of, 23, 32
   of conduct, 4, 43–45, 89, 224
   of justice, 4, 13, 31–37, 41–58, 61, 108,
      113–114, 283, 307–308, 311, 338,
      375, 388–390, 392, 399, 402
   pluralistic: *see* pluralism
   universal, 5, 13, 17, 61, 156
prioritarianism, 155, 159, 168–170,
      173–175, 250
prison, 91–92, 145, 173, 446, 448
privacy, 15, 140
Private Ownership (Grunebaum), 146
privilege, 16, 219–220, 253, 336, 351, 363,
      374, 376, 378
   see also class, identity politics, social
      status
procedures and processes, 94, 200, 203, 217,
      222–225, 241, 250–254, 259,
      284–285, 289, 324, 357, 373–374,
      377, 415–418, 433
   see also institutions, rules
promises, 10, 25–26, 182, 187, 427
property, 1, 7–8, 42, 94, 121, 124, 130–135,
      138, 141–143, 145–149, 187, 190,
      213–214, 234, 292, 358, 363,
      413–418, 426, 447
   property rights: *see* rights
property-owning democracy, 44

proviso: *see* Locke, Nozick

psychology, 4, 33, 167, 254
  see also human nature, persons

public choice, 292, 295

public goods, 7, 94, 205, 219–220, 254, 324, 358

public justification, 3, 11, 18, 42, 48–52, 56, 62–64, 82–89, 92, 94, 103, 107–114, 215–216, 221, 248–256, 332, 402–403, 416
  see also justification

public service, 310

publicity, 43, 49–52, 57

punishment, 10, 187, 188, 190, 444, 452
  see also capital punishment, crime, prison

Putnam, Robert, 234

Quebec, 330, 338, 352–354

Quine, W. V. O., 41

race and specific racial groups, 15–16, 19, 162, 199, 209, 216, 218, 220, 240, 243, 292, 326, 329, 346–352, 358, 362–364, 366–367, 371–372, 374, 377–379, 394, 408, 411

Rainborough, Thomas, 275

rankings: *see* hierarchy, preferences

Rappaport, Michael, 289

rational choice, 44–45, 52, 236, 323, 304, 311

rational ignorance, 110–111, 201–203, 235, 240–241, 243
  see also political knowledge

rational intuitionism, 32, 34, 50

rationality, 3, 31–32, 52, 72, 84, 86, 93, 101, 109–111, 122–124, 135, 156, 180, 183, 235, 251, 446

Rawls, John, 4, 6–7, 8, 15, 17, 32–37, 41–58, 63–65, 68–69, 84–85, 93, 100, 103, 105, 108–109, 111–113, 123, 155–156, 181, 208, 219, 304, 305, 307–309, 311–312, 323–324, 327, 337, 356, 358, 388–392, 400–401, 409–410, 416–417, 438, 444

Raz, Joseph, 16, 324–325

realism
  in international relations, 17, 390
  political, 90

Realizing Rawls (Pogge), 392

reason: *see* late-modern reasonableness, practical reason, public justification

reasonable disagreement: *see* pluralism

reason-giving: *see* public justification

reasons
  exclusionary, 113
  internal vs. external, 110–111

reciprocity, 55, 108–109, 111, 113, 209, 214, 309, 315–316, 355–357, 416

recognition, 15, 63–64, 71–75, 223, 322–323, 325–328, 332–336, 345–358, 366–367, 370–372, 377–378, 380

redistribution, 1, 7, 8, 9, 16, 91, 138, 156, 160, 164–167, 170, 247, 250, 254–255, 260, 372–373, 400, 410
  see also distributive justice, equality, inequality

Reflections on the Revolution (Burke), 425

reflective equilibrium, 57

reform, 1, 16, 217, 224, 240, 253–254, 333–338, 349

Reiman, Jeffrey, 89

Rejection of Consequentialism, The (Scheffler), 123

relativism, 45–46, 114

religion and specific religious groups, 15, 46, 50, 61–63, 68–69, 71, 92, 133, 208, 216, 218, 220, 222, 237, 272, 292, 326, 329–334, 349–350–353, 362, 365, 370, 372–373, 375–381, 394, 443, 451
  see also freedom of religion

rent-seeking, 295

representation, 14, 187, 198–199, 215–217, 232, 237–239, 241, 243–244, 248, 254, 260, 274, 370, 373, 378–379, 418

republicanism, 14, 232, 269, 306, 317, 348, 350

resident aliens: *see* immigration

respect, 12, 19, 25–26, 46, 51–52, 63, 65, 71, 85, 87, 203–205, 209, 219–221, 223, 225, 250, 278, 297–298, 326–327, 356, 366, 369, 375, 379, 403, 408, 444, 448
  see also recognition, self-respect

responsibility, 8–10, 18, 72, 74, 111, 143, 155–159, 164–165, 201–203, 256, 329, 357, 368–369, 393, 395–397, 399–402, 426, 428, 444, 453

revolution, 19, 62, 70, 284–286, 291
  see also social movements
rewards, 10
Richards, David, 391
Richardson, Henry, 217
rights, 5, 7, 11, 12, 14, 16, 108, 121–126,
        128–130, 133, 137–149, 171, 173,
        197, 200, 205–207, 215–216, 232,
        243, 284–285, 287, 294, 297, 304,
        306, 326–327, 334–335, 345,
        348–357, 372, 378–379, 400–401,
        425–435
  as side constraints, 122–123, 125, 140,
        215–216, 311, 356
  choice, 139, 200
  claims, 292, 427, 442
  constitutional, 232, 272, 292–295
  corporate, 353
  democratic, 197–211
  economic, 356, 437
  exit, 204, 310, 350
  group, 15, 346, 350, 352–358
  human, 2, 18–19, 47, 166–167, 272, 335,
        338, 370, 389, 393, 401, 403, 409,
        413, 416, 419, 425–435, 437–454
  interest-based, 2, 18, 139
  legal, 138, 443
  liberal and liberty, 378–379, 426–427,
        429–430, 432
    see also civil liberties, freedom
  membership, 352–353, 357
  natural, 7, 138
  negative, 19, 292, 452
  political, 216, 220, 322, 378, 442
  positive, 19, 292, 425, 429, 447, 452
  property, 1, 7–8, 94, 121, 124, 130–135,
        138–139, 145–149, 414–419, 426,
        441, 448
  to command, 310
  to do wrong, 296
  to life, 438, 444–445
  to work, 439
  welfare, 425, 437–454
Ripstein, Arthur, 419
Robespierre, Maximilien, 62
Rokeach, Milton, 92
Roosevelt, Franklin Denalo, 240
Rosen, Gideon, 55–56
Rosenblum, Nancy, 218
Ross, W. D., 43

Rostenkowski, Dan, 238
Rothbard, Murray, 147, 309
Rousseau, Jean-Jacques, 1, 10, 202, 248,
        253, 357, 416
rule of law, 5, 205, 215, 258, 270, 317, 335,
        357, 426
rule of recognition, 290
rules, 10, 35–37, 45, 132, 137, 181–182,
        186–192, 200, 204, 215, 217,
        219–220, 224, 269, 272, 284–295,
        326, 331–335, 338–339, 349,
        364–366, 372, 380, 400

Sachs, Jeffrey, 393–394
Sajó, András, 271, 273
Sandel, Michael, 13, 14, 304–307, 311–317,
        323–324
satisficing, 100
Scanlon, Thomas, 50, 171, 413
scarcity, 148, 159, 161, 167, 192, 202, 255
  moderate scarcity: *see* circumstances of
        justice
Scheffler, Samuel, 123–125, 127–129, 210,
        388–389
Schmitt, Carl, 248–249, 251
scholasticism, 6, 8, 17
Schumpeter, Joseph, 231, 235–236, 240,
        243
Schwartzenbach, Sibyl, 317
scientism, 268
scope of government: *see* legitimacy, limits
        of government
Scruton, Roger, 268
secession, 314, 336–337, 352–353
Second Treatise of Civil Government, The
        (Locke), 84
security, 1, 92, 137–138, 146, 149, 166,
        183–185, 187, 189–191, 219, 222,
        242, 250, 356, 426, 438, 441, 444,
        448
self-defense, 89, 444
self-determination, 15, 218–219, 253, 308,
        334, 336–337, 346, 350, 352–355,
        357–358, 370, 372, 376, 378, 400
self-development, 47, 309
  see also persons
self-interest, 11, 13, 61, 201, 206, 242, 255,
        257, 311, 324, 410, 416
self-ownership, 7–8, 121, 124, 128–135,
        137–149

self-respect, 46–47, 203–205, 417

Sen, Amartya, 156, 160, 219

Seneca, 388

separateness of persons, 7, 47, 121–125, 127, 142, 354

   see also non-interference, prerogatives

separation of powers, 241, 268, 274, 285, 297

sexes, 199, 218, 220, 253, 292, 347, 349, 362, 368–369, 372

   see also women

sexual division of labor, 16, 368–369

sexual orientation, 199, 329, 331, 334, 366, 372

   see also GLBT

Shachar, Ayalet, 373, 375

Shei, George, 91

Shklar, Judith, 271

Shue, Henry, 389, 409, 438–441, 444

Sidgwick, Henry, 43, 47, 55–57, 106

Simmons, A. John, 309

Singapore, 214, 219, 449

Singer, Peter, 391

Skocpol, Theda, 218

slavery, 8, 10, 34–36, 138, 141–144, 190, 220, 224, 367, 444–445

Smith, Adam, 239, 242

Snyder, James M., 254

social capacities, 362–363, 365–366

   see also persons

social capital, 233–234, 240, 316

social contract, 13, 95, 103, 187, 307–308

social environment, 8, 90, 134, 149, 323–325, 351, 365–366

   see also culture

social goods, 19, 47, 62, 168, 219, 348, 350, 354

social groups, 13–16, 220, 241, 250, 252, 326, 329–332, 336, 338, 348–349, 353, 363, 365–367, 369–373, 375–379, 409

   see also identity politics

social justice, 6, 199, 208, 330, 362, 410

   see also justice

Social Justice in the Liberal State (Ackerman), 304

social movements, 15–16, 17, 240, 257, 345–349, 352, 355, 358–359, 362, 365, 372, 379, 381, 435

   see also civil rights movements

social ontology, 63, 65–66, 69–74, 221, 353–358, 363

social relations, 16, 45, 49–51, 75, 172, 187–191, 215, 219–221, 252, 316, 355–358, 363, 375, 379, 419

social roles and positions, 16, 322, 328, 332, 362, 364, 367, 372, 374, 377, 408

social status, 199, 209–210, 238, 259, 362–363, 367, 369, 377

   see also hierarchy, recognition, social relations

socialism, 17, 44, 70, 247, 268, 327, 453

societal culture, 362–363, 366, 368–381

   see also culture, difference, identity politics, multiculturalism

sociology, 36, 324, 325

South Africa, 350

sovereignty, 372, 393

   see also non-interference

Soviet Constitution (1936), 269

special privileges, 327, 335, 346, 349, 351, 378

   see also rights

Spheres of Justice (Walzer), 304

Spinner-Halev, Jeffrey, 373

stability, 105, 108–109, 113, 166–167, 232, 315, 334, 351, 358, 454

starvation, 166–167, 219

state of nature, 50, 94, 95, 309, 413–416, 418

Steiner, Hillel, 148

stereotypes, 16, 326, 367, 377–378

Stimson, James, 231

stoics, 17, 388

structural inequality, 362–381

   see also difference, equality, identity politics, inequality

subjugation and subordination, 18, 89, 94, 114, 215–216, 219–220, 255, 347–352, 363–364, 370–371, 376–378, 409, 413–419

subsidies, 93, 353

subsistence, 167, 389, 401, 438, 441, 447, 450, 453

suffering, 28, 156, 159, 184, 435, 447

sufficiency, 168

Sunstein, Cass, 271

Sweden, 82, 240

sympathy, 24, 82, 214, 219–221, 223–225, 353

Taking Rights Seriously (Dworkin), 304
talents, 7, 8
Tamir, Yael, 373
Tan, Kok-chor, 402, 409–413
taxes, 1, 91–93, 184, 238, 240, 447–449
Taylor, Charles, 14, 65–69, 71, 220,
    304–307, 309, 311, 323–325, 357,
    372–373, 375
Taylor, Michael, 315–317
Temkin, Larry, 8–9
terrorism, 68, 141, 183, 303
textual formalism, 270
Theory of Justice, A (Rawls), 6–7, 34, 36,
    42, 52–54, 304, 307, 324, 417
Thompson, Dennis, 251
Thucydides, 17
Tilly, Charles, 363
toleration, 15, 75, 217, 306–307, 331,
    333–334, 363, 370–371, 379–380
torture, 68, 140, 173, 181, 272, 309, 312
totalitarianism, 325
trade, 17, 250, 391–392, 398–399, 414, 418
    see also economy, globalization
traditions, 14–15, 61, 71, 371, 375, 377, 389
Tufts, James, 219
Tully, James, 345, 351, 373, 375
Turkey, 449
tyranny, 175, 207, 216, 242, 274, 275, 337
    of the majority, 65, 215–216, 274–275, 356

unions, 90, 239, 254, 437
United Kingdom, 236, 434
United States, 19, 68, 93, 138, 175, 215,
    220, 224, 231–236, 239, 240–243,
    254, 258–260, 268, 269, 272, 324,
    333, 346–350, 366–367, 376–377
United States Constitution (1789), 216,
    242–243
Universal Declaration of Human Rights
    (1948), 428–432, 437, 440, 446
utilitarianism, 34–36, 43–48, 52, 55, 57, 67,
    123, 137, 140, 155–156, 159,
    170–171, 173, 180, 235, 328, 356,
    391, 429
utility, 45, 157, 159, 160, 162–163, 235,
    388

Vallentyne, Peter, 7, 8
value neutrality: *see* neutrality, pluralism
Vance, Cyrus, 439–440, 450, 453–454

veil of ignorance, 43–45, 50, 292, 295, 305,
    307, 324
Vermeule, Adrian, 292
Vietnam, 234, 240
violence, 4, 140, 187, 218, 326, 334, 355,
    371, 377–378, 380, 409, 444–445
virtue, 6, 8, 10, 191, 209, 219, 220, 223,
    232, 411, 445
    see also character
voluntarism, 309, 311, 317
voluntary
    voluntary agreements, 17, 188–191, 205,
        427
        see also contracts
    voluntary associations, 11, 218, 221,
        233–234, 257–259, 376
        see also freedom of association and
        assembly, social groups
    voluntary exchange, 7, 131–133, 139,
        142–144, 146
voting, 198–203, 206–208, 213–217,
    221–225, 231–233, 235–236,
    238–243, 250, 369, 416
    see also collective decision-making,
    elections

Waldron, Jeremy, 12–13, 206–207, 293–298,
    327, 330–331, 334, 335, 338, 389
Wall, Stephen, 6
Wal-Mart, 316
Walzer, Michael, 14, 215, 304–307, 323, 390
war, 82–83, 93, 175, 184, 232–233, 234,
    240, 260
    civil war, 314
wealth, 6, 19, 46, 56, 165–166, 168–169,
    191, 198, 199, 232, 238, 242, 253,
    256, 258–260, 367, 373, 398,
    408–409
    see also equality of wealth, redistribution
welfare state and welfare policies, 44, 94,
    238, 240, 438
well-being, 7–8, 9, 14, 28, 42, 55, 62,
    100–101, 121–122, 128, 135, 149,
    160–162, 166–168, 171–172, 175,
    184, 187–189, 192, 232, 241, 336,
    356, 363–364, 366, 368, 376, 380,
    391, 410, 411, 413, 417, 425, 439
well-ordered society, 52, 58, 108, 307, 311
White, Stephen, 3–4
Wilkinson, Richard G., 400

Williams, Bernard, 435
Williams, Melissa, 373
Wilson, Thomas Woodrow, 82
Wilt Chamberlain example, 413
Wittgenstein, Ludwig, 41, 69
Wolff, Robert Paul, 309
women, 8, 10, 15–16, 162, 190, 220,
    253–254, 326, 346–349, 353, 358,
    363, 368–369, 372, 374, 376, 380
  see also feminism, sexes

world government, 17, 337, 390, 418–419
  see also cosmopolitanism, international
    institutions
World Poverty and Human Rights (Pogge),
  389, 392–393

Young, Iris Marion, 16, 323, 326, 332, 345,
  347–348, 357–358

zero-sum, 15